Supervisory Management

THE ART OF INSPIRING, EMPOWERING, AND DEVELOPING PEOPLE

7e

Donald C. Mosley, Ph.D.
University of South Alabama

Paul H. Pietri, D.B.A.
University of South Alabama

Donald C. Mosley, Jr., Ph.D.
University of South Alabama

SOUTH-WESTERN
CENGAGE Learning

Australia • Brazil • Japan • Korea • Mexico • Singapore • Spain • United Kingdom • United States

SOUTH-WESTERN
CENGAGE Learning™

Supervisory Management: The Art of Inspiring, Empowering, and Developing People, Seventh Edition

Donald C. Mosley, Sr., Paul H. Pietri, and Donald C. Mosley, Jr.

VP/Editorial Director: Jack W. Calhoun

Publisher: Melissa Acuña

Acquisitions Editor: Michele Rhoades

Senior Developmental Editor: Mardell Glinski Schultz

Developmental Editor: Mike Guendelsberger

Senior Marketing Manager: Kimberly Kanakes

Content Project Manager: Elycia Arendt

Technology Project Editor: Kristen Meere

Manufacturing Coordinator: Doug Wilke

Compositor: International Typesetting and Composition

Project Management: Graphic World, Inc.

Printer: Quebecor World Versailles Versailles, KY

Art Director: Tippy McIntosh

Cover and Internal Design: John Walker Design

Cover Image: © Kenneth Noland/Licenses by VAGA, New York, NY; Tate Gallery, London/Art Resource, NY

Photography Manager: John Hill

Photo Researcher: Jan Seidel, Seidel Associates

For product information and technology assistance, contact us at **Cengage Learning, Customer & Sales Support, 1-800-354-9706**

For permission to use material from this text or product, submit all requests online at **www.cengage.com/permissions**
Further permissions questions can be emailed to **permissionrequest@cengage.com**

Library of Congress Control Number: 2006907654

ISBN 13: 978-0-324-42143-9
ISBN 10: 0-324-42143-5

South-Western Cengage Learning
5191 Natorp Boulevard
Mason, OH 45040
USA

Printed in China by China Translation & Printing Services Limited
2 3 4 5   10 09

The goal of **Supervisory Management, 7e** continues to be that of preparing students to be effective supervisors and leaders. As in the last edition the common thread throughout this text is that supervision is working *with* people to inspire, empower, and develop them so that they become better and more effective in their working roles. While coverage is provided of the management functions of planning, organizing, staffing, and controlling, the largest number of chapters are directly devoted to leading. These include a chapter on leadership itself, and also chapters on communication; motivation; managing change, group development and team building; meetings and facilitation skills; coaching for higher performance; and managing conflict, stress and time. These all are essential leadership tools.

As authors with strong real world consulting backgrounds, almost all of our research and consulting has involved thousands of team leaders and supervisors in many different types of organizations—profit and not-for-profit—including service, manufacturing, governmental and entrepreneurial firms. We have found some of the most exemplary, creative, and exciting practices of supervision and leadership in these environments. Many examples in this book, including interviews, examples, and cases, are taken from our interactions with leaders in real organizations. We pass these experiences on to you, continuing to appreciate Kurt Lewin's statement that "nothing is as practical as good theory."

This text closely follows the federal government's report of the Secretary's Commission on Achieving Necessary Skills (SCANS) requirements for work place competencies and a three-part foundation of skills and personal qualities needed for job performance. Out text strives to maintain a workplace context and a practical emphasis throughout.

The 7th edition reflects a number of changes to keep its skills focus timely, fast paced, and relevant to the action-oriented environments facing today's supervisors.

What's New in the Seventh Edition

- *Broader examples of supervisory/organizational settings.* In this edition, we have sought to provide balanced coverage of supervisory practices in the service, manufacturing, and not-for-profit sectors, in large, medium, and smaller entrepreneurial firms. For example, the Chapter 12 opening preview highlights the challenges and stresses faced by small business owners, while Chapter 13 focuses on leading and supervising in a 900+ hospital. A detailed example of a government municipality was provided in Chapter 2 to offer more diverse application of contingency and scenario planning. Students and present supervisors reading this book will appreciate that many more of the supervisory concepts presented apply to supervisors of all organizations.

- *Significant revisions and coverage of new topics.* The challenges which supervisors face in working in today's continuing diverse, technology driven, and changing organizational environment are emphasized throughout the book. All chapters have been updated and re-written to include a number of new and significantly revised topics, including differences in managing and leading, Myers-Briggs decision making styles, motivating the different generations of workers, emotional intelligence, effective tools in reaching consensus, elements of the Toyota Production System, active listening skills, role of employee assistance programs, benefits of employee mentoring, effects of harassment in the workplace, and supervisory ethics.

All chapters have been updated with new actual organizational examples and statistics.

- *Diversity coverage.* Throughout this book's chapters, emphasis is placed on the challenges supervisors and leaders face in managing a work force that is continuously more diverse. Such diversity is included throughout the text, ranging from supervisory challenges in communicating with the growing number of Hispanic workers whose English speaking skills are limited to issues dealing with a temporary work force. In addition to traditional coverage of diversity issues ranging from gender, ethnicity, and race, this edition is one of the first supervisory books to examine diversity issues posed by the different generations of workers—Traditionalists, Baby Boomers, Gen X, and Gen Y. Numerous examples and photos in each chapter reflect the diverse nature of the supervisor's work environment.

- *Continuing Emphasis on Ethics.* Ethics continues to be a key concept that is addressed throughout the book. It is a central topic in Chapter 3: Decision Making, Problem Solving, and Ethics.

Features of the Book

We continue to strive to make the book reader-friendly. To facilitate understanding and retention of the material presented, each chapter contains the following:

- *Learning Objectives.* Each chapter begins with a statement of Learning Objectives. Icons for identifying the learning objectives appear throughout the text material. The Chapter Review is also organized by the learning objectives.

- *Opening Preview Case.* A Preview Case sets the stage for each chapter by illustrating one or more major topics to be covered in the chapter. This piques students' interest in the chapter. Specifics from the opening case are often referred to within the chapter to reinforce key concepts discussed.

- *Key Terms and Phrases.* New terms and phrases are highlighted as each is introduced in a chapter. Marginal notes highlight definitions when they first appear in each chapter; at the end of each chapter is an alphabetical listing of all key terms.

- *Text Enhancing Exhibits/Photos.* Numerous exhibits and photos add insights into major concepts found in each chapter. They also give the text an inviting, reader-friendly appeal. Our goal is to inject these strategically so that they enhance, rather than fragment the chapter's continuity. Exhibits may be informational, such as Exhibit 1-10: "Changing Views of the Supervisor's Job; skills oriented, such as Exhibit 7-8: "How and When to Praise," and offer the student an assessment opportunity, as in Exhibit 6-13: "Rate Your Listening Habits."

- *Stop and Think.* Stop and Think questions appear several times within each chapter, allowing students to test their understanding of concepts as they learn new material. This feature also helps improve their study routines by serving as a simplified self-study guide. Some instructors report that they use Stop and Think questions as a basis for class discussion.

- *Chapter Review, and Questions for Review and Discussion.* Chapter Review and Questions for Review and Discussion encourage students to reflect upon what they have read in a way that will help them better understand and learn the material. Each Chapter Review highlights answers to the Learning Objectives identified at the beginning of each chapter.

- *Skill Builder Exercises*. Skill Builder Exercises appear at the end of each chapter; many relate to the SCANS requirements followed by many schools.

- *Cases*. Cases located at the end of each chapter can be used to synthesize the chapter concepts and stimulate the practice of supervision. A number of new cases are provided in this edition.

Instructional Resources

Instructor's Manual with Test Bank
0324543530

Prepared by Gayle Megginson Ross, the instructor's manual provides resources to increase the value of the text for both students and instructors. The manual provides an outline and lecture notes that include specific suggestions for using text content, PowerPoint, and videos. There are answers to the end-of-chapter questions and Skill Builders and case questions. The test bank, comprised of multiple-choice, true/false, and essay questions, is also included in this single volume manual. Accompanying the test bank is a chart that demonstrates how questions correspond with learning objectives for a true integrative approach. Electronic formats are available on the Instructor's Resource CD (0324543522).

Examview Testing Software

Accessible on the Instructor's Resource CD (0324543522), the test bank is available in electronic form to make test preparation a cinch. This testing software is easy to use and compatible with Microsoft Windows. Instructors can add or edit questions, instructions, answers, and select questions by previewing them on the screen, selecting them randomly, or by number. Instructors can also administer quizzes online.

Instructor's Resource CD
0324543522

Carry all of your resources on one disc! The Instructor's Resource CD-ROM includes key teaching materials, such as the Examview Testing Software and PowerPoint presentation. The instructor's manual and test bank (also available in print form) are available here in electronic format.

Supervisory Management DVD
0324543557

Videos compiled specifically to accompany SUPERVISORY MANAGEMENT use real-world companies such as PepsiCo and PF Chang's to illustrate the concepts outlined in the text. These videos give students an inside perspective on the situations and issues real corporations face. Also available on demand in VHS format.

Website
www.cengage.com/management/mosley

When you adopt the Seventh Edition of SUPERVISORY MANAGEMENT, you and your students will have access to a rich array of teaching and learning resources that you won't find anywhere else. The website will include the Instructor's Manual (on instructor website), Glossary and Key Terms.

Acknowledgements

Special acknowledgement in this 7th edition goes to our valued colleague, mentor, and co-author through the first six editions, Dr. Leon C. Megginson. Leon, at 86, having written 18 different books through 38 editions, is enjoying retirement. Don Sr. and Paul are fortunate to have been colleagues of Leon during his tenure at the University of South Alabama and have remained close associates during his stay at the University of Mobile, from which he retired several years ago. Much of our modest success as writers is credited to Leon, as we have collaborated with Leon on thirteen editions of two different books. Leon is truly a giant among management academicians, being a fellow of the Academy of Management. He has taught classes or given presentations in over 50 different countries, Leon's academic career involved teaching positions at Louisiana State University, the University of South Alabama and the University of Mobile.

We have missed Leon's direct collaboration on this edition, but his past participation as a valued co-author still contributes meaningfully to this seventh edition.

Rosemary Fittje was a unifying agent interfacing directly with the editors, putting much of our material into printed manuscript form. Her contributions, as in past editions, were critical to completing this project. Additional support was provided by Robin Hayes, a joy to work with. We appreciate the efforts of our publishing team at South-Western Cengage Learning, which is one of the best in the industry. From editors to sales reps, they have all been very supportive and responsive to our needs and concerns. Individuals whom we would like to especially thank include Senior Developmental Editor Mardell Glinski Schultz, Developmental Editor Mike Gluendelsberger, Senior Acquisitions Editor Joe Sabbatino, Acquisitions Editor Michele Rhoades and Content Project Manager Elycia Arendt.

DONALD C. MOSLEY Donald C. Mosley is professor Emeritus of Management at the University of South Alabama and also the founder and chairman of the Synergistic Consulting Group. Donald and the Synergistic Group have been pioneers in the area of partnering, having designed and developed a "partnering model" for the first formalized partnering workshop on large-scale construction projects in the public sector. The model has been adopted throughout the United States and used internationally as well. The Synergistic Group alone has conducted over 400 successful Partnering workshops in the United States, Canada, Puerto Rico and Guam.

In the 1960s, Donald helped a financially plagued chemical plant become the most profitable plant in the company's division. After joining Mississippi State University, Donald resigned as Chair of Management to spend a year as a visiting professor at the University of Otago in Dunedin, New Zealand, helping to develop one of the first MBA degree programs in New Zealand.

Donald was selected as the second Dean of the relatively new College of Business at the University of South Alabama in Mobile. After serving as Dean for a decade and helping the College become accredited by the American Assembly of Collegiate Schools of Business, he returned to teaching, research and consulting. In 1999 he received the University of South Alabama Alumni Association's Outstanding Professor award and is mentioned in *Who's Who Among America's Teachers*. He designed and developed a statewide leadership program for the Mississippi Economic Council, serving as Dean and lead instructor for twelve years.

Donald is proud that his son, Dr. Don Mosley, Jr., is now Assistant Professor of Management at the University of South Alabama and a new co-author of this seventh edition.

PAUL PIETRI Paul Pietri has an extensive background as a trainer/consultant to private and public sector organizations. He has designed, administered, and conducted training at the supervisory level for organizations in thirty-six states and Canada, the most recent being Toshiba USA of Wayne, NJ. Others include International Paper Company, Bowater Carolina, Shell, Dupont, and U.S. Departments of Agriculture, Labor, and Defense. Paul was chosen one of seven United States representatives selected by the Center of International Studies to participate in a São Paulo, Brazil conference designed to help Brazilian industry develop its first-line supervisors. He also helped design the curriculum for "Supervisory Communication" produced by Mississippi Public Television.

In the past five years, Paul has enjoyed teaching experiences in Germany and France. His most meaningful consulting experience was an extended involvement with a major U.S. manufacturer to help shift their culture. Over a six-year period, he logged 2000 training hours with all managers and supervisors in the 1,500 employee firm, helping them accept and learn the new skills of empowering, developing, coaching, and facilitating. His writings have reflected his training and design experiences and appeared in such journals as *Training, Organization Development Journal, Industrial Management, Journal of Business Communication, MSU Business Topics, Annual Handbook for Consultants*, and others. Paul is Professor of Management at the University of South Alabama, where he has received the Alumni Association's Outstanding Professor award.

DONALD C. MOSLEY JR. Don C. Mosley, Jr. is an Assistant Professor of Management in the Mitchell College of Business at the University of South Alabama. He received his Ph.D. in Business Administration from Mississippi State University. He earned a Bachelor of Arts degree from Millsaps College and a Master of Business Administration degree from the University of South Alabama.

Don has served as trainer/consultant to a variety of organizations in the private and public sectors. He has designed and implemented programs for organizations, such as Baykeeper, City of Fairhope, Corps of Engineers, Federal Emergency Management Agency, Johnstone, Adams Law Firm, Parsons Brinckerhoff, Thompson Engineering, USA Medical Center, as well as the Retirement Systems of Alabama tower project.

He teaches Management Theory and Practice and undergraduate and graduate Organizational Behavior. Mosley has published in such journals as *Educational and Psychological Measurement, Journal of Applied Social Psychology* and *Journal of Business Research*. His research interests include self-efficacy, staffing, work-family conflict, and emotional intelligence. Don is a member of the Academy of Management Association, Southern Management Association, Southwest Academy of Management, and Southwest Case Research Association.

Don thanks his wife, Emily, and daughters, Meredith and Caroline, for their encouragement and support during the revision process. He is quite proud to have been asked to join the Mosley, Sr. and Pietri author team for the seventh edition. It has always been a dream of his to work with his father on a textbook together, and at long last, the dream has been fulfilled.

BRIEF CONTENTS

CONTENTS

Supervisory Management
Roles and Challenges

Part **1**

Overview

1 Supervisory Management Roles and Challenges

© Dana White/Photo Edit

Many supervisors like Sharon Olds, featured in the chapter preview, face the common challenge of achieving results through the efforts of others.

Supervisors are linking pins who are members of, and link or lock together, independent groups within an organization.
—RENSIS LIKERT

Preview

Sharon Olds, Supervisor

With over $3 billion of outstanding leases and 2,500 employees throughout the United States, AutoFin is a major player in the auto leasing business. Sharon Olds is one of six remarketing supervisors in the company's Southeast Division, which has 300-plus employees (Exhibit 1-1).

As its primary function, the remarketing department contacts customers whose leases are nearing completion to persuade a customer to (1) extend the lease, (2) buy the car and finance it through AutoFin, or (3) buy the car outright. A fourth customer option—that of allowing the lease to expire and returning the car—is the least favorable for AutoFin, who will, at best, break even on this lease/sell transaction. Remarketing associates are goal-oriented, skilled communicators who must relate by telephone to people from all walks of life. Associate base pay is in the $20,000 range, but associates can earn as much as $35,000 to $50,000 through production incentives and overtime pay.

Sharon joined the company at age 25 as an associate trainee. She quickly became an excellent performer. Noting that most supervisors were either college graduates or had attended college, she took advantage of the company's tuition reimbursement plan and began working toward a degree in business at a local university. This initiative, coupled with her above-average job performance and excellent communication skills, caught management's attention. She was promoted to lead associate, a position in which she assumed a liaison position between her supervisor and four associates. In this position, she mentored new associates and resolved for her associate team a range of customer-related problems referred to her. Two years later, Sharon was offered and accepted her present supervisory position.

Sharon's supervisory effectiveness is gauged in terms of how successful her associates are in achieving their production goals. One production goal for each associate is to book 35 customers monthly to a new lease contract or to purchase and refinance their present vehicle. Another goal is that an associate must achieve a 40 percent success rate in having these customers purchase a warranty agreement on the vehicle. Regarding other departmental standards, associates must average (1) seven hours and 15 minutes each workday on line with customers, (2) fewer than 5 minutes with each customer contact, and (3) 30 or fewer seconds between calls.

Sharon's supervisory activities involve scheduling her associates' work, monitoring their calls (about 30 to 40 percent of her day), assessing their daily performance reports, resolving customer situations referred to her by lead associates, conducting a 20- to 30-minute monthly performance review with each team member, conducting a weekly staff meeting with her associates, preparing performance reports for her department head, meeting weekly with her department head to review performance results, and attending supervisory meetings called by her department head. She also interfaces with department heads other than her own, for instance, when recruiting a new associate (human resources), ordering equipment and supplies (purchasing), or having equipment repaired (facilities).

Learning Objectives

After reading and studying this chapter, you should be able to:

1. Explain why management is needed in all organizations.

2. Describe the different levels of management.

3. Discuss what managers do.

4. Explain the basic skills required for effective management.

5. Explain where supervisors come from.

6. Clarify the different relationships supervisory managers have with others.

7. Discuss the emerging position of supervisory managers.

8. Discuss some trends challenging supervisors.

EXHIBIT 1-1

Partial Organization
Chart for AutoFin
Southeast Division

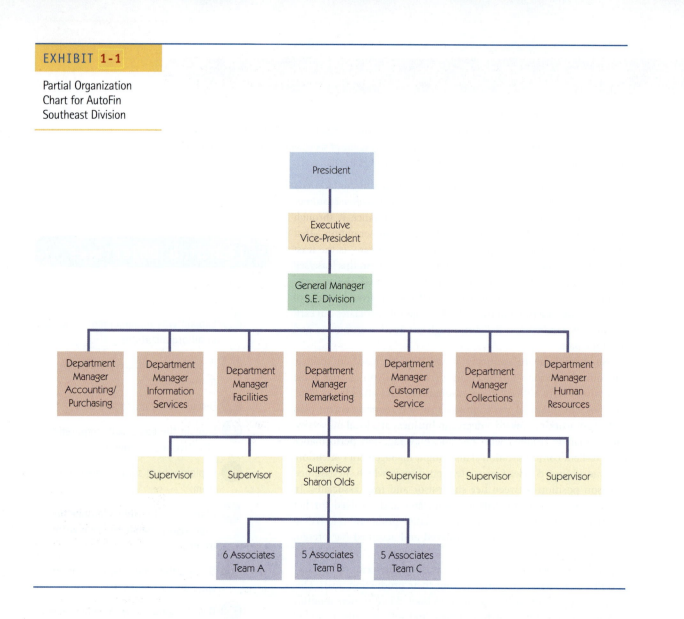

Sharon's department typifies important changes in technology and employee diversity that are shaping organizations today. Each associate has a cubicle, complete with computer and phone. A customer call list, contract information, and a format for easily reporting the result of each associate's calls are computer generated; progress and results are networked to Sharon's computer for immediate performance tracking.

Sharon's daily, weekly, and monthly performance reports are forwarded via computer format to her own department head. She and her associates are proficient in Word and Excel and use e-mail routinely throughout the day. Additionally, Sharon uses PowerPoint software to assist her presentations to employees and management. Sharon's present 16 associates represent today's growing organizational diversity. Her group is comprised of 11 males and 5 females; there are ten whites, four African-Americans, one Hispanic, and one Asian. They include a 23-year-old single male, a 35-year-old single mother of four, and a grandmother of seven in her late fifties.

The issue that most challenged Sharon the past year came when her department manager, under pressure from corporate headquarters, increased associates' production quotas.

Despite strong feelings of resistance by associates and supervisors, several supervisors said little at the meeting in which the departmental manager announced the change. Despite the fact that she had only recently been promoted to supervisor, Sharon was among the most outspoken of her fellow supervisors in making her feelings known. She was concerned that this might not be the best thing politically for her to do, and this meant walking a narrow line with her boss and even fellow supervisors who may have resented her being so outspoken when they were not. But this seemed not to be the case; in fact, several supervisors told Sharon they appreciated how she had gone to bat in voicing associates' feelings about the new standards.

This case illustrates well the many aspects of a supervisor's job and some of the many challenges that supervisors must face. Note that:

1. Sharon performs a broad set of duties, ranging from scheduling work, monitoring phone calls, having one-on-one performance reviews, and conducting meetings.

2. She interfaces with people from multiple groups, including her own personnel, her department head, personnel from other departments, fellow supervisors, and customers.

3. She uses a variety of skills ranging from computer know-how to the necessary diplomacy required when discussing poor performance with an associate.

Sharon faces a common challenge of supervisors—obtaining results through others. In a sense, her effectiveness is determined by how successful her personnel are. One way of looking at the supervisor's job, then, is to think of it in terms of "helping your people be as good as they can be." This case indicates some of the many changes taking place that impact the work of supervisors and managers at all organizational levels, the increasing use of technology, and workforce diversity. At no time has the job of supervision been recognized as being so important. Likewise, at no time has it been more challenging. In reading this material, you will be introduced in more depth to the roles and challenges of being a supervisor.

The Need For Management

1 Explain why management is needed in all organizations.

Whenever a group of people work together in a structured situation to achieve a common objective, they form an **organization.** The organization may be a student group, a business firm, a religious group, a governmental institution, a military unit, a sports team, or a similar group. The main objective of such organizations is to produce a product or provide a service. Other organizational objectives may be to provide satisfaction to members, employment and benefits to workers, a product to the public, and/or a return to the owners of the business (usually in the form of a profit). To reach these objectives, management must perform three basic organizational activities: (1) **operations,** or producing the product or service, (2) **marketing,** or selling and distributing the product, and (3) **financing,** or providing and using funds. These activities must be performed in almost all organizations, be they large corporations or small entrepreneur shops, whether they operate for profit or not for profit.

organization A group of people working together in a structured situation for a common objective.

operations Producing an organization's product or service.

marketing Selling and distributing an organization's product or service.

financing Providing or using funds to produce and distribute an organization's product or service.

What is Management?

Organizations are the means by which people get things done. People can accomplish more working together than they can achieve alone, but to combine and coordinate the efforts of the members of the organization, the process of management is required. Without management, people in the group would go off on their own and try to reach the organization's objectives independently of other group members. If small organizations lacked management, the members' efforts would be wasted. If management were absent in larger, more complex

Supervisors help their employees learn, grow, and develop, so that company objectives can be reached.

© Ryan McVay/Photodisc/Getty Images

management Working with people to achieve objectives by effective decision making and coordinating available resources.

human resources The people an organization requires for operations.

physical resources Items an organization requires for operations.

financial resources The money, capital, and credit an organization requires for operations.

organizations, objectives would not be reached and chaos would result. In summary, *managers are needed in all types of organizations.*

Management can be defined as the process of working with and through people to achieve objectives by means of effective decision making and coordination of available resources. The basic resources of any organization are **human resources,** which are the people involved; **physical resources,** which include buildings, furnishings, machinery, computers, equipment, materials, and supplies; and **financial resources,** such as money, capital, and credit. Exhibit 1-2 shows *the vital task of management: combining resources and activities into a productive system to attain organizational objectives.*

Consider the situation below:

Pete Bolton, entrepreneur, operates a one-person shoe repair shop. Pete performs all the necessary activities, including repairing shoes, serving customers, ordering equipment and supplies, maintaining equipment, keeping records, paying bills, and borrowing money. He does it all. Would you say that Pete is performing management?

Our position is that he is not. On the one hand, he certainly employs *physical* and *financial resources.* On the other hand, while he does interact with customers, they are not an employed resource, because they do not perform work. The only *human resource* that Pete utilizes is himself. Now consider a new scenario for Pete:

Business is so good that Pete leases the adjacent office and removes the wall, creating five times more floor space for the shop. He hires four employees: Three perform shoe repairs and one is a counter clerk/repairer. Whereas in the first situation he was a doer, performing all activities himself, in the second situation Pete must manage, guide, and direct *others* who perform tasks. The skills required for Pete to perform successfully in the new situation differ markedly from those required in the first. Pete must now perform "management."

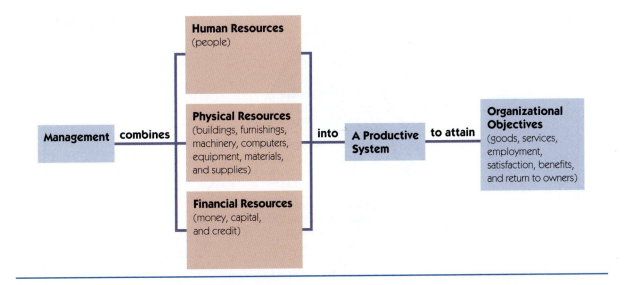

This simple example explains why many individuals perform successfully in non-management positions such as entrepreneurs, technicians, operators, and professionals but often fail when placed in positions of supervision. The material which you are reading will help you succeed in the second situation!

Levels of Management

Except in very small organizations, the different levels of management are usually based on the amount of responsibility and authority required to perform the job. Individuals at higher levels of the organization have more authority and responsibility than those at lower levels. **Authority** is the right to tell others to act or not act in order to reach objectives. **Responsibility** is the obligation that is created when an employee accepts a manager's delegated authority.

Large organizations usually have at least three levels of management, plus a level of operative employees. These levels are generally referred to as (1) *top management,* (2) *middle management,* and (3) *supervisory management.* In large organizations, there may be multiple levels of top and middle management.

2 Describe the different levels of management.

authority The right to tell others how to act to reach objectives.

responsibility The obligation of an employee to accept a manager's delegated authority.

✔ SELF-CHECK

In the chapter preview, for example, note that five levels of management exist at AutoFin: the president/CEO and executive vice-president levels comprise top management, the general manager and department managers comprise middle management, and supervisors comprise the supervisory management level.

EXHIBIT 1-3

How Management
Authority and
Responsibility Increase
at Higher Levels

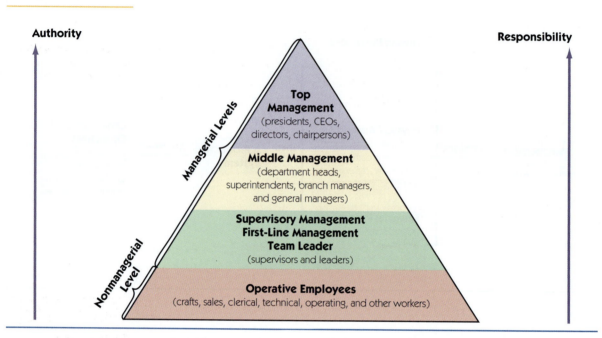

Exhibit 1-3 shows that authority and responsibility increase as one moves from the nonmanagerial level into the managerial ranks and then into the higher managerial levels. The titles and designations listed are only a few of those actually used in organizations.

Although the duties and responsibilities of the various management levels vary from one organization to another, they can be summarized as follows. **Top management** is responsible for the overall operations of the entire organization or oversees a major segment of the organization or a basic organizational activity. **Middle management** is responsible for a substantial part of the organization (perhaps a program, project, division, plant, or department). Finally, **supervisory management** has control over the operations of a smaller organizational unit (such as a production line, operating unit, office, or laboratory). Managers in this last group, such as Sharon Olds' group, are in charge of nonmanagerial, or rank-and-file, employees and are the managers with whom most employees interact.

Our focus is primarily upon the first level of managers, who may be called *supervisory managers* or simply *supervisors*. It is this group which is the organization's primary link with most of its employees. At BP Group, the large multinational energy company, they number 10,000 and are called first-level leaders, overseeing operations at retail outlets, managing crews at chemical plants, refineries, or drilling platforms, or supervising professionals in R&D, human resources, marketing or accounting. About 75 percent of BP employees report to them and as one BP executive states "in aggregate their decisions make an enormous difference in BP's turnover, costs, quality, safety, innovation and environmental performance."[1]

top management
Responsible for the entire or a major segment of the organization.

middle management
Responsible for a substantial part of the organization.

supervisory management
Controls operations of smaller organizational units.

What Do Managers Do?

3 Discuss what managers do.

It is now time to see what managers do that makes them so necessary to an organization's success. First we examine the functions managers perform. Then we look at some roles managers play. Note at this point that not all managers spend the same amount of time performing each management function or playing each role.

Functions Performed by Managers

Managerial functions are the broad classification of activities that all managers perform. There is no single, generally accepted classification of these functions, but we believe that five separate, but interrelated, basic functions must be performed by any manager at any level in any organization. Successful managers perform these functions effectively; unsuccessful ones do not. The functions are as follows:

managerial functions Broad classification of activities that all managers perform.

1. Planning
2. Organizing
3. Staffing
4. Leading
5. Controlling

As shown in Exhibit 1-4, these functions reflect a broad range of activities.

EXHIBIT 1-4

The Management Functions in Action

Primary Function	Examples
Planning	Determining resources needed
	Setting daily, weekly, monthly performance objectives
	Developing work schedules
	Anticipating and preparing for problems before they occur
Organizing	Making sure members understand roles and responsibilities
	Deciding who is best suited to perform a given task
	Assigning tasks to team members
	Coordinating members' activities
Staffing	Interviewing and selecting potential employees
	Securing needed training to upgrade members' skills
	Helping employees grow and develop through coaching, job rotation, broadening of assignments
Leading	Communicating relevant information to members
	Coaching, encouraging, supporting members
	Praising, recognizing, rewarding for work well done
	Building employee acceptance of change
Controlling	Observing and monitoring employee performance
	Ensuring employee compliance with standards, procedures, rules
	Identifying and resolving crises, problems that occur
	Following up to ensure implementation of decisions

Planning. **Planning** involves selecting goals and future courses of action and deciding how to achieve the desired results. It also encompasses gathering and analyzing information in order to make these decisions. Through planning the manager establishes goals and objectives and determines methods of attaining them. All other basic managerial functions depend on planning, because it is unlikely that they will be successfully carried out without sound and continuous planning.

> Note that Sharon Olds's important activities involve planning and scheduling her employees' work.

Organizing. Deciding what activities are needed to reach goals and objectives, deciding who is to perform what task, dividing human resources into work groups, and assigning each group to a manager are tasks that make up the **organizing** function. Another aspect of organizing is bringing together the physical, financial, and human resources needed to achieve the organization's objectives.

Staffing. The process of recruiting, selecting, developing, promoting, and paying and rewarding people to do the organization's work is called **staffing.** This basic function is sometimes regarded as a part of the organizing function, but we think it is important enough to be considered separately.

Leading. The **leading** function involves guiding, influencing, and motivating employees in the performance of their duties and responsibilities. It consists of coaching and empowering employees, facilitating their activities, communicating ideas and instructions, and motivating employees to perform their work efficiently. Typically, middle managers and supervisory managers spend a larger proportion of their time in leading—that is, "working with their people directly"—than do top managers.

Controlling. The **controlling** function involves comparing actual performance with planned standards and taking corrective action, if needed, to ensure that objectives are achieved. Control can be achieved only by setting up standards of performance, checking to see whether they have been achieved, and then doing what is necessary to bring actual performance in line with planned performance. This function must be executed successfully to ensure that the other management functions are effectively performed.

> Note that Sharon Olds spends a large part of her workday monitoring associates' phone calls and evaluating progress toward their work goals.

How the Functions Are Related

Although the five management functions must be performed by managers in all types of organizations and at all management levels, they may be performed in different ways and given different emphasis by various managers. One or more functions may be stressed over another at a particular level. For example, planning is done most often by top management, and leading and controlling are common among supervisory managers. Yet the functions are interrelated, interactive, and interdependent, as shown in Exhibit 1-5. Although they may be performed in any order, the functions tend to be performed in the sequence indicated by the numbers in the exhibit.

Roles Played by Managers

The preceding discussion of the management functions might lead you to believe that the manager's job is orderly, well organized, systematic, and harmonious. But this is just not so. In performing these functions, managers engage in a great many varied, disorganized, fragmented, and often unrelated activities. These activities may last for a very short time or may extend over a longer period.

planning Selecting future courses of action and deciding how to achieve the desired results.

organizing Deciding what activities are needed to reach goals and dividing human resources into work groups to achieve them.

staffing Recruiting, training, promoting, and rewarding people to do the organization's work.

leading Guiding, influencing, and motivating employees in the performance of their duties and responsibilities.

controlling Comparing actual performance with planned action and taking corrective action if needed.

EXHIBIT 1-5

How the Management
Functions Are Related

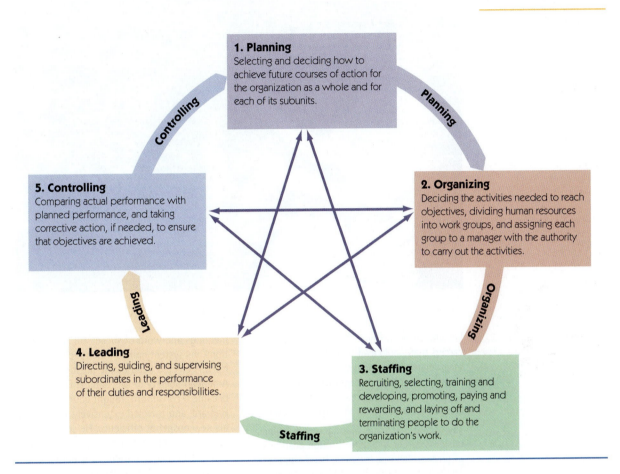

1. Planning
Selecting and deciding how to
achieve future courses of action for
the organization as a whole and for
each of its subunits.

2. Organizing
Deciding the activities needed to reach
objectives, dividing human resources
into work groups, and assigning each
group to a manager with the authority
to carry out the activities.

5. Controlling
Comparing actual performance with
planned performance, and taking
corrective action, if needed, to ensure
that objectives are achieved.

4. Leading
Directing, guiding, and supervising
subordinates in the performance
of their duties and responsibilities.

3. Staffing
Recruiting, selecting, training and
developing, promoting, paying and
rewarding, and laying off and
terminating people to do the
organization's work.

Taylor's "Scientific Management" and Fayol's "Management Principles"

Management: Key Pioneers

Historically, evidence of early management practice is easy to find. It was required to organize and build the Roman Empire and other civilizations. China's Great Wall, Egypt's pyramids, and other massive architectural feats stand today as concrete examples of successful management. The same can be said of the great amount of planning and organization required in building massive, effective organizations, including governments, religious institutions, and armies.

Early approaches to managing consisted primarily of trial and error. Businesses were small, entrepreneurial ventures with personal oversight by owners or foremen, each achieving efficiency in his or her own most effective way. In the mid-1800s, the advent of the factory system changed that approach. Inventions of machinery and tools caused production to shift from "made by hand" to "made by machine" and enabled mass production. In the United States, the expansion of transportation (railroads) and communications (telegraph, telephone, and postal systems), the development of Western frontiers, and the building of mechanized plants created larger organizations and the need for more systematic management. It was during this changing of the organizational landscape toward larger organizations in both the United States and Europe that two key figures, American Frederick W. Taylor (1856–1915) and

In the mid-1800s, goods that were "made by hand" began to be mass produced. This shift led to new thinking about productivity and managing people as evidenced by Frederick Taylor and his "scientific management."

Frenchman Henri Fayol (1841–1925), began careers that would lead them to be considered major pioneers in management. Both were engineers, but their careers focused on two distinct management areas: Taylor at the operating level, Fayol at the executive level.

Taylor and Scientific Management. Taylor's business career took him through positions of physical laborer, foreman, head engineer, and private consultant until his death in 1915 at age 59. It was during his work at Midvale Steel, a large Philadelphia foundry, and later at Bethlehem Steel, that he began to research ways to improve efficiency. Operating in a production environment with few substantiated "rules of thumb," Taylor systematically conducted numerous experiments involving efficiency. These included time study; determining physical weight loads that workers could efficiently handle during a day; efficiencies of equipment, such as optimum shovel head size; and many others. His theme was that through proper work methods, workers could produce more work while earning higher pay, benefiting both employers and workers. Taylor's systematic approach was called "Scientific Management," and through papers presented at professional

meetings and word of successful applications, his system gained much recognition. He was elected head of the prestigious American Society of Mechanical Engineers, became a consultant, taught courses at Harvard, and traveled extensively, presenting his new gospel of efficiency. He spawned a number of other "efficiency" associates who themselves gained national popularity, including Carl Barth (inventor of the slide rule), Frank Gilbreth (motion study), and Henry Gantt (production charts).

Taylor's books, *Shop Management* and *Principles of Scientific Management*, laid the groundwork for his system. His "Scientific Management" distinctly shaped management practice during the critical period when American industry was shifting from smaller, manager-owner firms to larger-scale operations. Ford Motor Company, for example, used Taylor's ideas in building its Highland Park, Michigan, plant, which opened in 1910.

Fayol and Management Principles. Like Taylor, Frenchman Henri Fayol began his career in technical work when, following his graduation as a mining engineer, he joined a large iron mining/foundry operation, Commentary-Fourchambault, in 1860.

Earning a reputation for developing ways to fight underground fires, Fayol was promoted to several management positions and, in 1888, was named managing director, today's equivalent of CEO. When he took over, the company was in severe financial straits and its key mineral/ore deposits severely depleted. Fayol succeeded in turning the company's fortunes around. It was during his long experience as a top manager of a full-scale, fully integrated enterprise of 9,000 employees that Fayol developed his ideas about management. Unlike Taylor's operational focus, Fayol built a theory of management from the perspective of an executive. He felt that management was sufficiently important that it should be studied and theories developed; then, this being done, it could be taught and studied in universities. The body of management theory he developed included "principles" of management, including principles for planning, organizing, staffing, and controlling. He felt that all managers in all organizations must perform certain basic management functions, very similar to the functions just presented in this chapter.

Like Taylor, Fayol was a writer and paper presenter at meetings. His major work, *General and Industrial Management*, was published in 1916, nine years before his death in 1925. Unfortunately, it was not until the 1940s that an English translation of his book would lead to proper recognition of his work in the United States. Many of Fayol's ideas form the framework for contemporary management theory, most notably those dealing with the planning and organizing functions.

Sources: Frederick W. Taylor, *The Principles of Scientific Management* (New York and London: Harper and Brothers, 1911); Henri Fayol, *General and Industrial Management*, trans. Constance Storrs (New York: Pitman, 1949; originally published in French, 1916); Daniel Wren, *The Evolution of Management Thought*, 3rd ed. (New York: John Wiley and Sons, 1987), especially Chapters 7, 11, and 12, which discuss Taylor, and Chapter 10, which discusses Fayol.

In carrying out these activities, managers play **roles** as if they were actors, and these roles change rapidly and frequently. A landmark management study identifies ten roles, grouped as follows: (1) interpersonal roles, (2) informational roles, and (3) decision-making roles.[2] Exhibit 1-6 shows how each might be carried out by Sharon Olds (opening case).

> **roles** Parts played by managers in the performance of their functions.

Like managerial functions, these roles are given varying degrees of emphasis by managers in different organizations and at different levels in the same organization. Managers vary in how they interpret the roles, the time they devote to them, and the importance they assign to them. With training and experience, supervisors can learn to perform these duties effectively.

Skills Required for Effective Management

> **4** Explain the basic skills required for effective management.

You may be wondering at this point what basic skills managers need in order to perform the managerial functions and play the managerial roles most effectively. Although many skills are needed, a few of the most common ones follow:

1. Conceptual skills
2. Human relations skills
3. Administrative skills
4. Technical skills

The relative importance of these skills varies according to the type of industry in which managers work, the organization to which they belong, their level in the managerial ranks, the job being performed, and the employees being managed. Exhibit 1-7 shows an estimate of the relative importance of these skills at different management levels.

EXHIBIT 1-6

Roles Played by Managers

Role	What Is Involved	Examples
Interpersonal Roles		
Figurehead	Representing the unit as its symbolic head.	Greeting departmental visitors, attending meetings and ceremonies, representing company on community boards.
Leader	Helping personnel reach organizational and personal goals.	Motivating, encouraging, supporting associates; providing feedback about performance; building morale.
Liaison	Maintaining relationships between the unit and outsiders.	Meeting with departmental heads and other supervisors.
Informational Roles		
Monitor	Seeking out useful information that is especially relevant for the unit/organization.	Attending professional meetings, learning about forthcoming changes.
Disseminator	Providing relevant information to appropriate organization members.	Routing reports and information to associates and others; copying departmental head on memos sent to associates.
Spokesperson	Representing employees to supervisors and vice versa; representing the unit to others.	Representing the department at weekly meetings; speaking out against changes that adversely affect associates.
Decision-Making Roles		
Entrepreneur	Tackling problems; seeking changes to improve unit.	Introducing new equipment, encouraging improved methods, promoting innovation by associates, taking risks.
Disturbance handler	Responding to crises/ problems that arise.	Resolving associate conflicts, soothing associates' resistance to change.
Resource allocator	Allocating the unit's resources.	Preparing a budget, deciding which associates receive new equipment, which are offered overtime work.
Negotiator	Negotiating differences with employees, managers, and outsiders.	Negotiating with a difficult customer, bargaining for favorable terms with associates, other departments, own department head, and others.

Source: "Roles Played by Managers," adapted from *The Nature of Managerial Work* by Henry Mintzberg. Copyright © 1973 by Henry Mintzberg. Reprinted by permission of Henry Mintzberg.

Conceptual Skills

conceptual skills Mental ability to become aware of and identify relationships among different pieces of information.

Conceptual skills involve the ability to acquire, analyze, and interpret information in a logical manner. All managers need to understand the environments in which they operate, as well as the effects of changes in those environments on their organization. In other words, managers should be able to "see the big picture." Top managers particularly need strong conceptual skills, because changes affecting the organization tend to be more

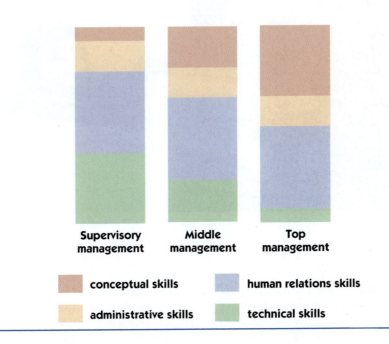

Supervisory
management

Middle
management

Top
management

conceptual skills   human relations skills

administrative skills   technical skills

important at their level than at other managerial levels. Around a third of their time is spent using conceptual skills.

Human Relations Skills

Human relations skills consist of the abilities to understand other people and to interact effectively with them. These skills are most needed in performing the leading function because they involve communicating with, motivating, leading, coaching, empowering, and facilitating employees, as well as relating to other people. These skills are important in dealing not only with individuals, but also with people in groups and even with relationships among groups. These skills are important to managers at all levels, but especially to supervisory managers, who spend almost one half of their time using human relations skills.

human relations skills
Understanding other people
and interacting effectively.

Administrative Skills

Administrative skills are the skills that permit managers to use their other skills effectively in performing the managerial functions. These skills include the ability to establish and follow policies and procedures and to process paperwork in an orderly manner. By lending *coordination, order,* and *movement* to tasks, administrative skills underlie the ability some people have to "make things happen" and "get things done." These skills are very similar to those possessed by good students, who are well organized and get things done efficiently.

administrative skills
Establishing and following
procedures to process paperwork in an orderly manner.

Supervisors often use both their human relations and their technical skills in discussions with employees.

© Royalty-Free/CORBIS

Technical Skills

Technical skills include understanding and being able to supervise effectively the specific processes, practices, or techniques required to perform specific duties. Technical skills are more important for supervisors than for top managers, since supervisors are closer to the actual work being performed. They must often tell—or even show—employees how to perform a job, as well as know when it is done properly.

A head nurse in a hospital, for example, must have some degree of technical understanding of proper equipment use, nursing procedures, medication, chart maintenance, and other important aspects of a nurse's job. We are not saying that the head nurse, or any other supervisor, must necessarily be a technical expert, but that a supervisor needs a basic understanding of the work being done in order to perform the managerial functions and roles effectively.

The four skills we have just discussed form the basis for a wide variety of important management actions. For example, effective time management requires *conceptual* and *administrative* skills to prioritize activities and efficiently dispose of required paperwork; being an effective trainer requires the *technical* skills or an understanding of the subject matter and the *human relations* skills of being sensitive and able to communicate effectively with a trainee; political know-how requires *conceptual* and *human relations* skills to identify the potential implications of actions and to build strategic relationships.

In summary, effective supervisory management requires all of the skills—conceptual, human relations, administrative, and technical. The appropriate mix, however, depends on the level of management and the circumstances surrounding the managerial situation.

✔ SELF-CHECK

Which of the four skills are reflected when a supervisor performs these tasks? (1) Prepares a to-do list for next week. (2) Monitors a newly hired associate's phone conversation with a customer. (3) Conducts a weekly performance review meeting with a new employee. (4) Completes her unit's daily performance report.

The Transition: Where Supervisors Come From

5 Explain where supervisors come from.

Each year several hundred thousand nonmanagers become supervisors or managers. Teachers become principals, ministers become pastors, nurses become head nurses, salespersons become sales managers, and skilled operators or technicians become supervisors. Most of these positions are filled by current employees.

Internal promotions make sense for at least three reasons. First, an inside candidate understands the organization and its culture. Also, if promoted within the same department, he or she will know the tasks required, the personnel, fellow supervisors, and likely the new boss. Second, management has firsthand knowledge of the employee's track record and can use this as a predictor of success. Third, to promote someone internally serves as a reward and as an incentive for those employees who have an interest in management and demonstrate management potential.

Unfortunately, organizations commonly make two crucial mistakes when selecting supervisors. One is to automatically select the best present performer. Although the best performer may have excellent technical skills, as you saw earlier, other skills, especially human relations skills, are also important.[3] Frequently, outstanding technical performers have unreasonably high expectations or little patience with non-producers. Moreover, they may find it difficult to let go of their old positions, at which they were so good. Instead, they continue to perform their unit's operating work, neglecting the supervisory responsibilities of their position.

> One of the authors was scheduled to interview a maintenance supervisor of a large paper manufacturer. His assistant informed the author that he was running late for the interview because of an equipment breakdown. An hour or so later he entered the office, sleeves rolled up, with grease covering his hands. "Sorry about missing the appointment; I'll be right with you after I wash up," he said. The author learned from this supervisor's crew that for this supervisor, almost every breakdown was a "major one." He micromanaged, insisted on being notified of every development, and continually took over his technicians' jobs, especially the most challenging ones. His crew members had little opportunity for skill development and little initiative. As one stated, "Our best work is done when he [the supervisor] is out of the plant, like on vacation."

Another crucial mistake made by organizations stems from inadequately preparing the employee to assume a supervisory position. Unfortunately, it is common to hear a supervisor say that the transition to supervisor went like this: "When I left work on Friday, I was a lab technician. With absolutely no training or warning, on Monday morning I learned I was a lab supervisor." Ideally, an organization should take great care when identifying potential candidates for supervisory positions and, once candidates are chosen, should help new supervisors make the transition. Before a permanent position is assigned, promising potential supervisors can be identified, assessed, and trained. Thus, such candidates may fill in as temporary supervisors when the supervisor is absent because of illness or vacation, or may occupy a "lead" position that actually entails some supervisory responsibility. Fortunately, organizations are doing a much better job nowadays of identifying people with supervisory potential and preparing them through appropriate training to help them make a successful transition.

> Note in the preview that Sharon Olds had occupied a lead associate position, which became her stepping-stone for the advancement to supervisor.

Supervisory Relationships

6 Clarify the different relationships supervisory managers have with others.

If we are to understand the role of supervisory managers in organizations, we must look at some of the relationships they have with different individuals and groups. For example, supervisors are legally a part of management and interact upward with other members of

EXHIBIT **1-8**

The Supervisor's Network
of Relationships

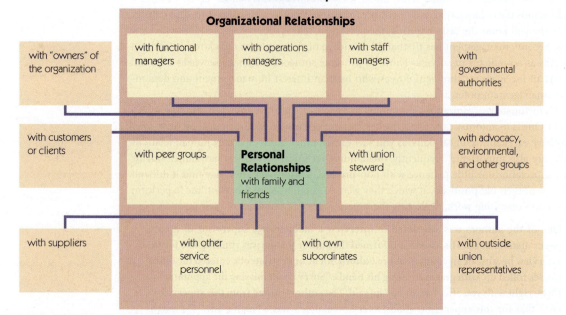

External Relationships

Organizational Relationships

- with "owners" of the organization
- with functional managers
- with operations managers
- with staff managers
- with governmental authorities
- with customers or clients
- with peer groups
- **Personal Relationships** with family and friends
- with union steward
- with advocacy, environmental, and other groups
- with suppliers
- with other service personnel
- with own subordinates
- with outside union representatives

Relationships network The major individuals and groups with whom the supervisor interacts.

management. But they are often not accepted as peers by those managers, who usually have more education, come from outside the organization, and have higher social status and position. Before their promotion, supervisors typically worked as peers with those they now supervise.

The three major types of relationships that supervisors have, as shown in Exhibit 1-8, are (1) personal, (2) organizational, and (3) external. These comprise the supervisor's relationships network, the major individuals and groups with whom the supervisor interacts.[4]

Personal Relationships

At one time it was believed that managers and employees left their personal problems at home when they entered the workplace. We now recognize that people bring their problems— as well as their pleasures—to their jobs. Supervisors' relationships with their families and their friends determine their attitudes and frame of mind as they perform managerial duties. Their attitudes, in turn, influence the relationships they have with other people, both inside and outside the organization.

Organizational Relationships

Within the organization, supervisory managers have varied and often conflicting relationships with several organizational entities. As shown in Exhibit 1-9, these are: the supervisor's employees, the supervisor's peer group supervisors, the union steward, and the supervisor's managers.

EXHIBIT **1-9**

The Flow of Supervisors'
Organizational
Relationships

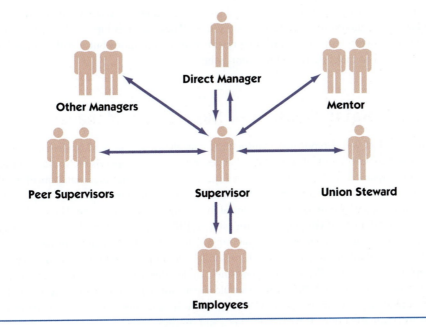

Supervisor-to-Employee Relationships. Supervisory managers must relate to their own employees and to people from other units who perform some type of service for them. As Exhibit 1-9 illustrates, a manager-to-employee relationship exists where the supervisor facilitates and directs nonmanagerial personnel.

Relationships with Peer Supervisors and Union Steward. There are essentially two sets of horizontal relationships: those with other supervisory managers and those with the union steward or other representative(s) of the employees. Supervisors need the feeling of support and reinforcement that comes from associating with other supervisors who are considered their equals or peers. Yet the relationship can result in competition or even conflict if they seek to be promoted to the same job at the next higher level.

In a unionized organization, employees select a **union steward** to represent them in their dealings with management. Although the steward is a supervisor's peer—legally, if not organizationally—he or she does represent the supervisor's employees. Therefore, the association between the supervisor and the union steward may be competitive or even combative. This association provides supervisors with a challenge but can also be frustrating. For example, a supervisor will probably attempt to motivate employees to improve productivity, whereas a union steward may encourage them to maintain the status quo for fear that their jobs will be eliminated.

union steward A union
member elected by other
members to represent their
interests to management.

Supervisor-to-Manager Relationships. Supervisors have a *reverse* manager-to-employee relationship with their immediate manager. As a result of downsizing, reengineering, empowering, and similar new managerial approaches, this relationship is being upgraded. In addition to a supervisor's direct manager, staff managers in other departments, such as legal and research, may also tell supervisors what to do. Functional executives, such as the controller and the human resource manager, may also interact with supervisors in handling certain activities. Often, supervisors have an upper manager who serves as mentor and acts as advocate, teacher and advice giver.

Mentor An experienced manager who acts as an advocate and teacher for a younger, less experienced manager.

External Relationships. Supervisory managers must also deal with people outside the organization. Some of the people who must be served or catered to are the owners of the business, customers or clients, suppliers, higher-level union representatives, governmental authorities, and leaders of environmental and advocacy groups. These relationships can be quite difficult and frustrating for supervisors, who represent their organizations but usually do not have the authority to make decisions and enforce them.

7 Discuss the emerging position of supervisory managers.

The Emerging Position of Supervisory Managers

Peter Drucker, world-renowned management consultant, author, and academic, correctly predicted 20 years ago that important changes in the role of supervisors would occur as a result of organizations' quest for improved quality. He noted that top management would, of necessity, conclude that the commitment and involvement of rank-and-file employees in improving quality would make them central in leading the quality charge. The result would be greater authority or empowerment for rank-and-file employees to make key decisions on their own, including such things as planning, determining the resources to best perform their jobs, and interfacing directly with personnel who impact their job, such as customers, suppliers, and service department personnel. Under this scheme, Drucker reasoned, the supervisory role would shift. No longer would supervisors effectively manage by fear and the pressure of "my way or the highway" management. Instead, they would assume more supportive, facilitating roles as leaders, teachers, and coaches.

Several other trends have fueled the shift in supervisory roles that Drucker predicted. One is the trend toward leaner organizations with fewer levels of management. Another is organizations' present commitment to helping employees at all levels grow and develop. The resulting shift in the role of supervisory managers looks like that shown in Exhibit 1-10.

EXHIBIT 1-10

Changing Views of Supervisor's Job

4AST 10-15yRS

Traditional View of Supervisor's Job	Emerging View of Supervisor's Job
Supervisor-focused work unit	Team-focused work unit
Dominant role	Supportive role
Technical skills emphasis	Facilitation skills emphasis
Seeking stability	Encouraging change
Telling, selling skills	Listening skills
Personal responsibility for results	Shared responsibility for results
Personal problem solving	Team problem solving
Narrow, vertical communication	Broader, horizontal, external communication
Fear, pressure used to motivate employees	Pride, recognition, growth used to motivate employees
Autocratic decision style	Participative decision style

No matter what type of role supervisors play, their goals are the same—getting out production, maintaining quality, holding down costs, maintaining high morale, and otherwise serving as management's representative while also acting as a spokesperson for employees. Although the knowledge and skills required today to perform most supervisory jobs have greatly increased from, say, 25 years ago, the central objective has remained the same—to obtain quality and quantity production while maintaining good human relationships.

A study of supervisors in two plants within the same company illustrates this point.[5] One plant followed traditional organizing practices: The supervisor had authority to supervise, to determine working conditions, to plan the work and schedule it, and to control it. In the other plant, "team advisors" were used instead of supervisors, with the focus being on facilitation rather than traditional direction of the work teams. As it turned out, "exceptional" and "average" supervisors at both plants, whether they were called supervisors or team advisors, exhibited characteristic behaviors.

"Exceptional" supervisors:

1. Were competent, caring, and committed both to getting the job done and to supporting their employees.

2. Pushed for high quality, provided clear direction, and motivated employees with timely, accurate feedback.

3. Willingly shared information with personnel, even if the system didn't require it.

4. Were committed to teamwork and employee participation in the department's decisions.

5. Shared skills and knowledge willingly and saw their role as one of coach rather than driver.

6. Understood what was involved beyond their own units, from the broader perspectives of the plant.

7. Took the initiative in implementing changes and new approaches.

Supervisors considered only "average" in the two differently organized plants also exhibited similar behaviors. These supervisors:

1. Set narrowly defined goals and had more specific performance standards.

2. Were less attuned to the plant's overall goals and focused more narrowly on their own unit.

3. Provided less information or feedback about performance to their work groups.

4. Were less flexible, less innovative, and less willing to change.

5. Maintained tighter controls and were uncomfortable practicing participative management.

Note that the "exceptional" supervisors exhibited behaviors that were more consistent with the emerging view of the supervisor's job (Exhibit 1-10).

Some Current Trends Challenging Supervisors

8 Discuss some trends challenging supervisors.

As shown earlier, today's supervisors must be prepared to adjust to the many current trends that will challenge their best performance. Among the more significant of these trends are (1) dealing with a more diverse workforce, (2) emphasizing team performance, (3) coping with exploding technology, (4) adjusting to occupational and industry shifts, (5) meeting global challenges, (6) improving quality and productivity, (7) improving ethical behavior, and (8) responding to crises.

Dealing with a More Diverse Workforce

http://www.dol.gov/

http://www.bls.gov/cps/

Diversity refers to the wide range of characteristics that distinguish employees, such as sex, age, race, ethnic origin, and other factors. At no time in our history has our workforce been so diverse, and this trend is expected to continue. Our comments here focus only on broad trends regarding gender, race, ethnicity, and age.

According to the Department of Labor, in 2005, white males represented 44.6 percent of all U.S. workers. However, the shifting U.S. population calls for decreasing numbers of whites. By 2014, of an additional 13 million (28%) people who will be added to the workforce, only about 28 percent will be white males. Hispanic employment will have increased by 30 percent, Asian employment by 28 percent, and African-American employment by 15 percent. Overall, women will account for almost 48 percent of the total workforce by 2014.[6] Although men and women are entering the workforce at about the same rate, men, who have been in the workforce longer, are retiring at a faster rate. Thus, like racial and ethnic minorities, women will continue to occupy many types of jobs and positions that were previously the domain of men, including supervisory and management positions.

Providing opportunities for women is particularly challenging, as there appears to be a **glass ceiling** in many organizations. These ceilings are considered invisible barriers that limit the advancement of women into higher levels of the organization. Thus, supervisors will be expected to design programs to attract and to develop women and minority employees and to provide them with a full range of opportunities for growth and development, the same as they do for all other employees.

http://www.general
motors.com/company/
community_ involvement/
diversity

Along with changes in gender, race, and ethnicity, the workforce is aging, as is the rest of the U.S. population. Those in the 55 or older age group made up 16 percent of the 2005 workforce, but their number will increase by more than 10 million employees and comprise 21 percent of the projected workforce by 2014.[7] Being able to effectively manage such diverse individuals requires greater supervisory skills than was the case with the more homogeneous work groups of past decades.

More diverse work groups are becoming the norm in today's organizations.

© Getty Images

Emphasizing Team Performance

As organizations seek to equip employees to function on their own, less direct supervision is required. This **empowerment** results in supervisors increasingly working with work groups or teams. These teams make suggestions for improvements in activities to make things run smoothly and to accomplish goals effectively.

When supervisors work with these teams, their roles are changed. No longer are they "bosses"; instead, they become leaders, facilitators, or **team advisors,** who share responsibility with the team for maintaining cost, quality, and prompt and effective delivery of products. Therefore, supervisors must provide further training to their teams in order to manage the production process more effectively.

empowerment Granting employees authority to make key decisions within their area of responsibility.

team advisors Share responsibility with team for cost, quality, and prompt delivery of products.

Coping with Exploding Technology

Most working Americans now earn their living by creating, processing, utilizing, and distributing information, and the computer revolution shows no sign of slowing. As innovations in computer and other communications technology have displaced thousands of workers who used different skills, new opportunities are opening up for those who have the required education, training, and temperament. Conversely, employees with the older skills are being replaced in the workplace.

Computer-based information technologies continue to revolutionize how organizations function, impacting how tasks are performed, customers served, and people supervised.

Note that Sharon Olds was skilled in Microsoft Word, PowerPoint, and Excel computer software and used e-mail regularly to communicate with her department head, employees, and others in the organization.

The primary effect of exploding technology on supervisors will be the need to keep personally abreast of changes that can potentially improve effectiveness, improve training of employees, and overcome their resistance to change. Change brings with it uncertainty, and because most people resist that which is uncertain, overcoming employee resistance to technological change becomes an increasing part of the supervisor's job.

Adjusting to Occupational and Industry Shifts

The previously mentioned technological advancements, along with cultural and marketing changes, have resulted in shifts in occupation and industry mixes. First, there is a declining emphasis on the traditional industries, with a concurrent shift toward more people-related activities such as services and marketing. Along with these shifts, there has been a **reinvention** of many organizations in which they have dramatically changed their size, organizational structure, and markets. Many of the large companies have also been **reengineering** their activities. A common reengineering approach is to ask, "If we blew this place up and started over, what would we do differently to improve cost, quality, service, or speed? What should we eliminate entirely? What can we do that would make things easier for our customers?" Not only are manufacturing companies reengineering, but so are many service companies, such as Sears and Taco Bell. These and other activities resulted in another trend, called **downsizing,** in which an organization strives to become leaner and more efficient by reducing the workforce and consolidating departments and work groups.

Some of the best-known companies, such as Motorola, American Express, 3M, and Honda, have been reinvented or reengineered. The results often included the elimination of 10 to 20 percent of a company's jobs, especially at the management level. This means that frontline workers—and their supervisors—must handle more diverse tasks, think more creatively, and assume more responsibility. On the downside, though, those same people must work harder and therefore are under more pressure.

reinvention Organizations dramatically changing such elements as their size, organizational structure, and markets.

reengineering Rethinking and redesigning processes to dramatically improve cost, quality, service, and speed.

downsizing Striving to become leaner and more efficient by reducing the workforce and consolidating departments and work groups.

In an effort by organizations to avoid health care and other costs associated with maintaining a large workforce, and to aid in transitions during downsizing, temporary workers have been in much demand. In 2005 General Motors, as part of its downsizing, announced plans to cut 113,000 employees "as soon as possible," using temporary employees to ease the transition. Temporary services firms, such as Manpower and Kelly, grew to a record 2.8 million employees in September 2005. Moreover, the Bureau of Labor projects this trend to continue, with employment service firms creating 1.57 million new jobs through 2014, making it the U.S. economy's number one job producer during this ten year period.[8] Supervisors face numerous challenges when integrating temporaries into their teams of permanent employees, who often view temporaries as obstructing their own overtime, commissions, or higher pay. Temporaries themselves know little about the company and often show little inclination to be included as team members, knowing the assignment is only for a few days, weeks, or months.

Meeting Global Challenges

As business activities have become more global, those interested in supervisory management need to understand that they may have to operate in a one-world market. In fact, we estimate that up to one-half of all college graduates will work in some type of international activities in the future. And while we usually think of product exports as autos, movies, or computers, exports of financial information and other services are growing even faster. Citibank, for example, has branches in 46 countries; its parent, Citicorp, operates in over 100 different countries.

Supervisors have to become familiar with all the capabilities of technology in order to make good business decisions and guide their employees in its effective use.

© VSTOCK/Alamy

Many U.S. production facilities have relocated to countries like Mexico. This trend will likely extend into the foreseeable future and will continue to have an effect on management ideologies and style.

A result of the global challenge is the large number of U.S. businesses, such as Random House, Magnavox, Wilson Sporting Goods, Uniroyal, and Chrysler, that are foreign owned. This changing ownership may lead to differing cultures and management styles, especially at supervisory levels. U.S. production facilities have also moved to Mexico, South America, Asia, and other countries where low wages and high productivity lead to a competitive advantage. When supervisors move to those areas to supervise local workers, or when a foreign company acquires a domestic company, supervisors must learn to adapt to cultural differences and find ways to adjust to nontraditional styles.

Improving Quality and Productivity

No organizational theme has run deeper in the past decade than has the search for improved quality and productivity. Global competition has been the primary force behind this interest. The view of quality being embraced today reflects a comprehensive organizational approach to customer satisfaction through continuous improvement in organizational processes.[9] Almost all major firms have adopted some form of quality management focus that addresses not only such processes as product design and manufacturing, but also marketing, purchasing, human resource management, and others. The supervisor, as management's direct link with employees, plays an important role in an organization's quality initiatives. It is the supervisor who is challenged to find ways to gain employee commitment to high-quality performance.

Equally important as achieving better quality is achieving improved productivity, which is a measurement of the amount of input needed to generate a given amount of output. As productivity is the basic measurement of the efficiency of people and processes, it becomes a challenge for supervisors to improve through having people work better and smarter.

Improving Ethical Behavior

The recent downfall of major corporations, such as Enron, Arthur Andersen, Tyco, WorldCom, HealthSouth, and South Korea's Daewoo has dramatically called attention to the issue of organization ethics.[10] Although the problems in these companies resulted primarily from the behaviors of upper-level managers, the vulnerability of organizations to ethical misdeeds was clearly exposed. The result is that organizations have raised the "ethics" bar for all employees and management levels—including supervisors—for a wide range of issues, not just financial ones. These include accuracy and truthfulness in reporting results, employee discrimination and sexual harassment, responsibility for supporting employee development, and due vigilance in reporting what can be viewed as unethical requests and behavior by others.

In this environment, supervisors will likely continue to face **ethical dilemmas** in which they are not sure of the correct action in a given situation involving themselves or their employees.[11]

Responding to Crises

Dealing with crises—events that have major negative or potentially negative impact on entire organizations or on individual managers or supervisors—have always been part of managerial life. Recently, however, the scope of such events has been dramatically increasing. As the first management interface with operating employees, supervisors are particularly challenged to maintain production and morale during such times.

One such crisis has been the extensive organizational downsizing that has occurred across a wide variety of industries and in major organizations, such as General Motors, Procter & Gamble, IBM, AT&T, Sara Lee, and the U.S. government. In many cases, crises have been associated with economic slowdown and recession; in others, they are the result of mergers/acquisitions; in the cases of Enron and WorldCom, the crisis was caused by illegal mismanagement. A single act of terrorism—the World Trade Center attacks of September 11, 2001, resulted in the indirect or direct loss of 55,000 jobs. Hurricane Katrina, which hit Louisiana, Mississippi, and Alabama in 2005 negatively impacted 145,000 businesses and 2.5 million employees.[12]

Add to these extraordinary crises those associated with technological outages, equipment breakdowns, job accidents, incidents of workplace violence, sudden loss of key suppliers/customers, and one can view the supervisor's role as increasingly one of addressing workplace crises.

Final Note: The Supervisor and Leading

In pre-1990 years, managers who were adept at planning, organizing, staffing, and controlling—and not so effective in leading—could function effectively. Unlike the relatively stable environment then, today's management challenges make effective "leading" essential. Managers and supervisors must do more with fewer personnel, integrate more diverse team members, ask personnel to reach increasingly higher performance levels, and to continuously implement change. No longer do they rely on authority as the primary means to achieve these, but on influence and persuasion. In short, their leadership is being tested at much higher levels than ever before, and the results have not been satisfactory, according to many critics of U.S. business who say "we need more leaders and fewer managers." What they really mean, given the new, dynamic environment, is that we need managers at all levels who are better at performing leadership.

Note the title of this book: *Supervisory Management: Inspiring, Empowering, and Developing People*. While coverage is provided of the other four management functions—planning, organizing, staffing, and controlling, the largest number of chapters are devoted to leading. These include a chapter on leadership itself, and also on communicating, motivating, coaching, resolving conflict, implementing change, and managing teams, all of which are essential leadership tools.

1 Explain why management is needed in all organizations.

Management is needed whenever people form organizations. An organization is a group of people in a structured situation with a common purpose. People form organizations because they realize that they can achieve more by working together than they can alone.

Management is the process of working through people to achieve objectives by making effective decisions and by coordinating the development and use of scarce human, financial, and physical resources.

2 Describe the different levels of management.

Large organizations usually have at least three levels of management. Top management oversees the overall operations—or a major segment of the organization or one of the basic organizational activities; middle management is responsible for a smaller part, such as a division or department; and supervisory management controls a smaller organizational unit.

3 Discuss what managers do.

Managers at all levels do essentially the same things, but to different degrees. First, they perform the same functions—namely, planning, organizing, staffing, leading, and controlling. In performing these functions, managers engage in many varied and often unrelated activities that require them to play different roles. In playing interpersonal roles, a manager may act as a figurehead, a leader, or a liaison between different groups. Informational roles include acting as a monitor, disseminator, and/or spokesperson. Finally, decision-making roles require the manager to be an entrepreneur, a disturbance handler, a resource allocator, and/or a negotiator.

4 Explain the basic skills required for effective management.

Effective managers need various skills in order to perform their functions and play their roles. Conceptual skills are needed in acquiring, interpreting, and analyzing information in a logical manner.

Human relations skills involve understanding other people and interacting effectively with them. Administrative skills provide the ability to get things done by using other skills effectively. Technical skills consist of understanding and being able to supervise the processes, practices, or techniques required for specific jobs in the organization.

5 Explain where supervisors come from.

By far most supervisory positions are filled through internal promotion. This has several advantages. Insiders understand the organization and its culture, and when promoted within their own department, the tasks, personnel, and other supervisors are familiar as well. Managers know something about the potential supervisor's capabilities through his or her track record. Also, internal promotion serves as a reward and incentive for present employees who desire to move up. Organizations can help to ensure a successful transition to supervision by identifying, assessing, and training potential supervisors and observing how they perform in temporary supervisory assignments.

6 Clarify the different relationships supervisory managers have with others.

Supervisory managers are involved in at least three sets of relationships. First, they have personal relationships with their families and their friends. Second, they have sometimes conflicting organizational relationships with lower-level employees, fellow supervisors,

IMPORTANT TERMS

administrative skills
authority
conceptual skills
controlling
diversity
downsizing
empowerment
ethical dilemmas
financial resources
financing
glass ceiling
human relations skills
human resources
leading
management
managerial functions
marketing
mentoring
middle management
operations
organization
organizing
physical resources
planning
reengineering
reinvention
relationships network
responsibility
roles
staffing
supervisory management
team advisors
technical skills
top management
union steward

and higher levels of management. Third, they have external relationships with outsiders, such as business owners, customers or clients, suppliers, union representatives, governmental authorities, and leaders of environmental and advocacy groups.

7 **Discuss the emerging position of supervisory managers.**

The role of supervisory managers has drastically changed during the past 25 years. In the traditional role, supervisors had strong technical expertise, had much authority over employees, and were key problem solvers. Pressure was often the tool used to motivate employees. The emerging role of supervisors has resulted from organizational trends toward greater organizational emphasis on quality, empowerment of employees, downsizing of management ranks, and commitment to employees' growth and development. These trends have given employees authority to plan their own work, to determine the resources they need, and to resolve job problems themselves. While still responsible for achieving results, supervisors have shifted toward leading, facilitating, and supporting employees, in contrast to the dominant, authority-laden traditional role.

8 **Discuss some trends challenging supervisors.**

As the supervisory position grows in importance, it is becoming more complex because of many trends that are challenging supervisors' abilities to perform their jobs. The more important trends challenge supervisors to (1) deal with a more diverse workforce, (2) emphasize team performance, (3) cope with exploding technology, (4) adjust to occupational and industry shifts, (5) meet global challenges, (6) improve quality and productivity, (7) improve ethical behavior, and (8) respond to crises.

QUESTIONS FOR REVIEW AND DISCUSSION

1. Why do people form organizations?
2. Identify the five functions every manager must perform and briefly explain each.
3. Why is management needed in organizations?
4. What are the three levels of management found in most large organizations? Describe each, giving its responsibilities.
5. Identify the four skills that managers need. Can someone be weak in one of these skill areas and still function effectively as a supervisor? Explain.
6. How are most supervisory positions filled? Explain why this is so.
7. What are the three types of supervisory relationships? Explain.
8. Identify each of the trends challenging today's supervisors and explain how each impacts supervisors.
9. What are some reasons why "leading" is such a critical skill for supervisors and managers today?

Skill Builder 1-1

The Personal Interest Inventory

Directions: Each of the following questions is worth a total of 3 points. For each question, assign more points to the response you prefer and fewer points, in order of preference, to the others. For example, if one response receives 3 points, the other two must receive 0; if one receives 2, then the others must receive 1 and 0; or each may receive 1 point. Enter your scores in the Score Matrix.

1. Which activity interests you most?

____a. Working with your hands

____b. Working with people

____c. Reading books

2. Which skills would you invest time in learning?

____a. Research and writing

____b. Organizing and leading

____c. Crafts and art

3. Which job activities would you enjoy most?

____a. Counseling and coaching

____b. Building and doing

____c. Thinking and planning

4. Which trait is most characteristic of you?

____a. Helper

____b. Doer

____c. Scholar

5. Which would you most enjoy doing?

____a. Talking with people

____b. Writing a book

____c. Building a house

6. How do you prefer to use your spare time?

____a. Outdoor projects

____b. Social activities

____c. Thinking

7. Which of these traits is most important to you?

____a. Physical coordination

____b. Ability to deal with people

____c. Mental ability

8. Which jobs most reflect your interests?

____a. Teacher, social worker, counselor

____b. Engineer, surveyor, craftsman

____c. Researcher, historian, author

9. Which ability is your strongest?

____a. Communication skills

____b. Creative thinking

____c. Physical skills

10. Which tasks do you perform best?

____a. Operating and maintaining

____b. Communicating and motivating

____c. Developing and planning

11. Which occupation interests you most?

____a. Pilot

____b. Judge

____c. Politician

12. Which of the following is most interesting to you?

____a. Helping others

____b. Thinking things through

____c. Using your hands

13. Which skills could you learn with the least effort?

____a. Leading and negotiating

____b. Artwork and handicrafts

____c. Language and theoretical reasoning

14. What tasks appeal to you most?

____a. Developing new theories

____b. Helping people with problems

____c. Developing a skill

15. What assignment appeals to you most?

____a. Working with ideas

____b. Working with people

____c. Working with things

16. Which is your greatest attribute?

____a. Creativity

____b. Competence

____c. Sensitivity

17. For which occupation do you have a natural talent?

____a. Counselor

____b. Builder

____c. Scientist

18. Which subject interests you most?

____a. Practical arts

____b. Philosophy

____c. Human relations

19. To which group would you prefer to belong?

　___a. Scientific society

　___b. Outdoor group

　___c. Social club

20. How do you like to work?

　___a. In a group, discussing and recommending solutions

　___b. Alone, using ideas and theories

　___c. Alone, using tools and materials

Score Matrix

Question	Things	People	Ideas
1.	a.	b.	c.
2.	c.	b.	a.
3.	b.	a.	c.
4.	b.	a.	c.
5.	b.	c.	a.
6.	a.	b.	c.
7.	a.	b.	c.
8.	b.	a.	c.
9.	b.	c.	a.
10.	a.	b.	c.
11.	a.	c.	b.
12.	b.	c.	a.
13.	b.	a.	c.
14.	c.	b.	a.
15.	c.	b.	a.
16.	c.	a.	b.
17.	b.	a.	c.
18.	a.	c.	b.
19.	b.	c.	a.
20.	c.	a.	b.
	TOTAL	TOTAL	TOTAL

Instructions: The Personal Interest Inventory should give you some insight into the strengths you would bring to a management position. Basically, if you enjoy an activity, it is likely to be something that you do well. The three areas shown in the Score Matrix—things, people, and ideas—correspond to the following skills, which managers must use in doing their job:

Things:　　Technical skills

People:　　Human relations skills

Ideas:　　Conceptual skills

1. After scoring your inventory, break into groups of three to five and discuss your profiles. To what extent are they similar? Different? Are any of the areas dominant in the group? Underrepresented? Discuss.

2. Generalize about the kinds of supervisory jobs that might call for

   a. High technical skill

   b. High human relations skill

   c. High conceptual skill

3. Are your answers on this inventory consistent with the type of management job that you have in mind? If there are inconsistences, what do they mean?

Source: Based on an exercise designed by Billie Stockton, Anita Bullock, and Anne Locke, Northern Kentucky University, 1981.

Effective and Ineffective Supervisors

group activity

Instructions

1. Think of all the supervisors for whom you've ever worked—part-time or full time. If you have not worked for a supervisor, consider some of your teachers or perhaps a coach.

2. Select two—one who was most effective and one who was least effective—and list the behaviors of each.

3. In groups of three to five classmates, share your lists and discuss. Were there common behaviors? Select a spokesperson to present to the class your discussion results.

CASE

Coach X: Effective Hospital Administrator?*

Case 1-1

Assume that you are a member of the search committee that is evaluating applicants for the position of administrator of a 300-bed, community-owned hospital in your city. In examining the applicants' resumes you note that most have had experience in health care settings, many having previous experiences as administrators or assistant administrators.

One application, however, is quite different. It is from one of the most successful college football coaches in the country, someone we will call X. Being a sports fan, you have seen this person many times on national television as his teams have consistently placed in the top-ten NCAA ratings. He has won five national championships in the past 15 years. His school leads major colleges in athlete graduation rates; throughout his 30-year coaching career, his programs have not been charged with a single NCAA violation. He has won national coach-of-year title four times. He has mentored countless assistant coaches who themselves have become successful. His former players have been among the NFL's biggest stars. He has charisma and is a gifted motivational speaker. No one is more highly respected in the profession. Serving also as athletic director the past five years, he oversees a $57-million budget, 400 employees, and the University's athletic department is one of the most profitable in the country. His university's sports teams annually win the award given to the university having the best overall team performance across all sports. He has served with distinction as head of the National Association of College Coaches, and is often selected to represent his peer coaches on important NCAA issues. Presidents Bush and Clinton have named him to important presidential commissions. He has often been courted by Democrats and Republicans as an easily winnable gubernatorial or U.S. Senate candidate. Why is he interested in the position of head administrator of the hospital? In his application, he states that it was always his ambition to change careers by age 55. While acknowledging his lack of experience in the health care field other than

*Any association of Coach X as presented in this case with a real person or persons is coincidental.

through hospital stays with family, players, and friends, he would love the challenge of hospital management.

Instructions:

1. Respond to the following question: "Would X be someone whom you would consider as a viable potential candidate for the hospital administrator position, despite his limited technical expertise?

    _____Yes _____No   Why?

2. Suppose that the position being sought was that of supervisor of the hospital's computer technology department. Would your answer be the same? Why?

3. In groups of four to six, discuss your answers, and be prepared to report highlights of your discussion to the overall class.

Planning and Organizing

2 Fundamentals of Planning

Effective planning is critical to personal and professional success, whether you are going on a camping trip or working as a supervisor for a company like Dixon, featured in the chapter preview.

If you don't know where you're going, any road will get you there.

—AUTHOR UNKNOWN

After you have made up your mind just what you are going to do, it is a good time to do it.

—JOSH BILLINGS

Preview

Now that you have seen some of the roles played by supervisors and some of the challenges they face, it is time for you to see how they play these roles and meet these challenges. That is what this chapter is about. But first, let's see how one supervisor faced this problem.

Changes at Dixon

Harold Marshall, newly promoted general manager of the Dixon Division of Computronix, Inc., was addressing a meeting of Dixon's 35 department heads, superintendents, and supervisors. The Dixon Division was one of the oldest in the Computronix system and one of the least cost effective. In fact, there were rumors that it would gradually be phased out of operation. Most people at the meeting were seeing Marshall for the first time, although his reputation had preceded him. At age 32, he had gained widespread exposure as manager of the company's "experimental" plant in Fresno, California. That plant utilized totally new technology and many innovative management techniques.

Marshall began:

Ladies and gentlemen, it's good to meet many of you for the first time. We are faced with an important challenge—to increase the efficiency of this plant—and it's going to take dedication and commitment. I've promised Mr. Alexander [the vice-president] that I'll give it my best, and together we can show progress that will make top management commit itself to capital spending that will again make our division a top producer in the company.

If we're going to improve, our management system must change drastically. At Dixon, we have been practicing "defensive" management. That is, we react to problems when or after they occur. We've been good at doing that. But to be effective today, we must become far better at planning our future—setting goals and objectives, developing ways to reach them, and making sure we achieve them. Our industry cannot fly by the seat of its pants as we've done in the past. Each and every one of us is going to have to become adept at planning—for the division, for each department, and for each work unit. This is especially true of our supervisory level, for that is where the organization succeeds or fails. In the past, top management has done most of your planning for you, but now things will have to change.

Under the new unit planning system that we will establish, each of you will be required to commit to writing a plan for your operating unit, to be signed by you and your manager, with copies sent to the next higher level. The plan will contain five major objectives for your unit for the next six months. Each objective will be specific and include actual figures, such as "to reduce labor costs in my unit by 12 percent in the next six months." These objectives should cover the most critical areas of your operation and, of course, will require your own manager's approval.

Additionally, your unit plan must include the steps you'll need to take in order to achieve each objective, along with a timetable and names of employees responsible for each step. It should also identify the major potential impediments to reaching each objective, as well as your contingency plans for addressing these potential impediments. Finally, the plan should identify the process you'll use to monitor progress toward achieving the objectives.

Those of you who know me know that I am a firm believer in effective planning at all levels. I'm confident that implementing such a planning system—along with good follow-through—can help us make Dixon the most profitable division in the Computronix system.

Marshall continued to speak for about 15 minutes on such topics as the need to involve employees in the planning system, the importance of delegation, and the need for effective teamwork.

He closed with an announcement that workshops would be held for all managers and supervisors to acquaint them with specific details of the new unit planning system.

We wish Marshall well in his attempt to turn Dixon around. Note the emphasis he places on effective planning. He is correct in his assessment of the role of supervisory management. Many managers see themselves as being strictly "fire fighters"—handling first this problem, next another, and then another. He is also correct in his view that supervisors at all levels must become more proficient at planning—perhaps the most neglected function of management at all levels.

Planning, involves selecting future courses of action for your organization and deciding how to achieve the desired results. This chapter builds on that definition. We focus on the first of the management functions—planning—and show that much planning must precede effective empowerment of employees and achievement of improved quality.

Some Important Points about Planning

① Discuss some of the more important points about planning.

Suppose you and a group of friends decide to take a weekend camping trip. Effective planning requires answers to the following kinds of questions: What constraints impact the group, such as the distance you can travel or the funds you have available? What activities most interest the group, such as hiking, boating, fishing, or mountain biking? What camping sites are available to choose from, and which activities are offered at each? What supplies and equipment will be needed, and does the group have the means to obtain them? Only after questions such as these are answered can you do more effective planning. Then your group can decide when and where to go, what time to leave, who will bring what, and perhaps even schedule your planned activities. Your plan should also anticipate future contingencies such as weather and occupancy of sites. Should rain be forecast, might you postpone the trip to a later date? If not, might you bring rain gear or have games available for indoor use? Might you reserve a site in advance or, if not, have a nearby backup site in mind?

As you can see, the trip's effectiveness depends greatly on the quality of planning that you and your group put into it. Supervisory planning works much the same way. Supervisors do planning—both routine and detailed—as an ongoing part of their jobs. This may include plans for scheduling work, developing and living within budgets, making job assignments, and so on. They must also plan for major events that happen infrequently, such as when a department manager of a major department store plans for an annual inventory count or when a pizza store manager knows a week in advance that she must deliver 300 freshly baked pizzas to a convention of 600 people.

Basic Steps Involved in Planning

② Explain the steps involved in planning.

Planning means deciding what will be done in the future; in other words, planning is forward looking. A manager must have a lot of discipline to set aside the time needed to solve present problems and to plan for the future. As you can see, much planning is intellectual: it is a "between the ears" activity that involves hard work. Effective managers must use conceptual, human relations, administrative, and technical skills. Planning is normally an

EXHIBIT 2-1

The Three Planning Steps

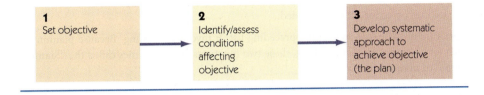

example of a conceptual skill. But it also requires other skills, especially in order to get the plans adopted and implemented.

Planning covers a wide variety of activities, from simple to complex, and from short to long term. But in all cases, the three basic planning steps are as follows:

1. Setting an objective, or goal.

2. Identifying and assessing present and future conditions affecting the objective.

3. Developing a systematic approach by which to achieve the objective (the *plan*).

These are shown in Exhibit 2-1.

Three additional steps must also be taken in order to effectively achieve the objective or goal established in step 1, though they are not exactly planning steps. These include the following:

4. Implementing the plan (organizing, leading, staffing).

5. Monitoring the plan's implementation (controlling).

6. Evaluating the plan's effectiveness (controlling).

These last three steps illustrate how closely planning is related to the other managerial functions, especially controlling.

The *first step in planning—setting objectives or goals—*addresses the issue of what one hopes to achieve. Notice in the chapter preview that Marshall's new planning system would require each manager to develop a plan that addresses five major objectives that his or her unit seeks to achieve.

The *second planning step—identifying and assessing present and future conditions affecting objectives—*recognizes important variables that can influence objectives. In the camping trip example given earlier, these would include such factors as equipment needed, weather, and site availability. Since planning involves the future, certain assumptions about the future must be made.

The *third step of planning is the developing of a systematic approach to achieve the objective.* This third step becomes the *Plan*. It addresses such issues as the what, when, who, where, and how of the plan. The plan's complexity and importance are major factors in determining how formal and detailed this final step must be. For example, a plan to build a new 200-bed–wing expansion for a hospital would be much more formal and detailed than a plan to shut down a paper-making machine for routine maintenance. Many daily plans are routine, however, and are carried about in supervisors' heads rather than being committed to paper.

Planning Is Most Closely Related to Controlling

Of the managerial functions, planning is probably most closely related to controlling. As you will see in more detail in a later chapter, the steps in controlling are as follows:

1. Setting performance goals, or norms.
2. Measuring performance.
3. Comparing performance with goals.
4. Analyzing results.
5. Taking corrective action as needed.

Note carefully the first step in the preceding list. It involves planning! Because planning is such an integral part of controlling, these two functions are sometimes called the **"Siamese twins" of management.**

"Siamese twins" of management
Planning and controlling.

Many Managers Tend to Neglect Planning

Poor planning results in disorganized and uncoordinated activities, thus wasting time, labor, and money, but since thinking is often more difficult than doing, many managers—including supervisors—tend to slight planning. It is very tempting to forgo thinking about the future in order to get busy performing a task or solving present work problems. The result is frequently unsatisfactory, as shown in Exhibit 2-2.

As Harold Marshall, the new Dixon general manager mentioned earlier in this chapter, pointed out, it's not unusual for a supervisor to spend his or her day fighting one "fire" after another—seemingly never catching up. Consider the following example:

> **Henrietta Green, one of my supervisors, had a hectic schedule and was about to be driven up a wall. She said: "Today I had three no-shows because of the weather, and my department is absolutely swamped. I'm pitching in myself, but I've also got to conduct a tour for some of our home office staff personnel after lunch. I'm supposed to meet with our industrial relations people on a case that goes to arbitration next week. To cap it off, Barbara Brown is asking for a transfer out of the department and wants to talk about**

EXHIBIT 2-2

Lack of Planning

EXHIBIT 2-3

The Nonplanner's Cycle

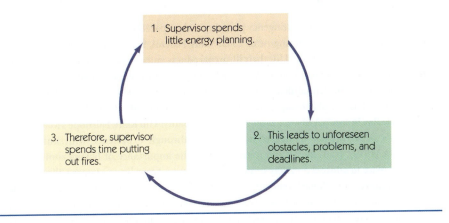

1. Supervisor spends little energy planning.

2. This leads to unforeseen obstacles, problems, and deadlines.

3. Therefore, supervisor spends time putting out fires.

it today. She and two of the other workers can't get along. This afternoon, I've got to have some important figures ready for the cost accounting department. On top of all this, I'm supposed to supervise my 19 people, three of whom are new hires who are just being broken in. What a day! But recently, they all seem to be like this."

Is it any wonder that this supervisor forgoes planning when her typical daily schedule is so demanding? But, ironically, many of the short-run crises that confront supervisors could be greatly eased by proper planning. As shown in Exhibit 2-3, when a supervisor devotes too little time to planning, short-run problems are likely to result, including impossible deadlines, unforeseen obstacles, crises, and crash programs. These problems preoccupy the supervisor, leaving little time to devote to planning—and the cycle goes on and on!

Contingency Planning Anticipates Problems

It is important for supervisors to build flexibility into their plans by preparing contingency plans. **Contingency planning** means having anticipated solutions in advance for problems or changes that may arise and being prepared to deal with them smoothly when they do arise. Consider the following examples:

> When the X-ray unit in the radiology department went down, Nurse Ratchett knew exactly whom to contact and how to divert patients to the X-ray machine in the hospital's emergency room.

> Three weeks earlier, Charlie Fay had been relieved of his regular duties for a few days so that he could be trained as a backup forklift operator. Although not as expert as Willie Burns, Fay performed smoothly on the forklift when Burns was absent twice in one week.

You might think of contingency planning as the responses to the "what if . . . ?" questions that describe serious events. Thus, contingency planning separates effective managers from ineffective ones. Proper anticipation of a problem may prevent it from happening. If you are to be a good contingency planner, you will need to ask yourself the following questions and find answers to them:

contingency planning
Thinking in advance about possible problems or changes that might arise and having anticipated solutions available.

1. What might happen that could cause problems within my area of responsibility?

2. What can I do to prevent these events from happening?

3. If these events do occur, what can I do to minimize their effect?

4. Have similar situations occurred in the past? If so, how were they handled?

Consider the emphasis on contingency planning and preparedness after Hurricane Katrina hit the Gulf Coast region in August of 2005. Many Federal, State, and local governmental entities were harshly criticized for their ill-preparedness and response to the storm and the devastation that occurred. Due to increased public scrutiny, government at all levels is addressing future potential disasters and developing more effective emergency response plans (ERP). The city of Fairhope, a resort, retirement community situated along the shores of Mobile Bay in south Alabama, is one such municipality. Tim Kant, Fairhope's Mayor, and the city's departmental managers have learned through experience with hurricanes Frederick (1979), Ivan (2004), and Katrina (2005) the importance of having contingency plans in place to address a variety of possible problems. According to James Gillespie, the city's Administrative Superintendent, "the public sector has to deal with expectations that are different from those in the private sector. A municipality must aim to accommodate and assist all citizens, which involves proactively developing an emergency response plan for the worse scenario imaginable and devising alternative options based on that position. Dedication and love for your town is what drives city employees—you have to take care of your town and plan for your citizens, you can't afford to wait and react."

As Gillespie states, "the city hires people to do a job with the caveat that they must be willing to operate outside their job descriptions when an emergency arises. For example, Gas Department Superintendent, Steve Seay's first responsibility is to the check the gas system for leaks. Afterwards, his employees assist the Electric Department or Department of Public Works in their cleanup efforts. During these natural disasters, municipal employees also must put their personal needs aside for the greater good even though it is an emotional time. City managers felt they should be able to respond to the community and do a good job of understanding and responding to the employees' needs. Therefore, a series of contingency plans were developed that would enable the city to respond to both citizens and employees. Local businesses and residents were contacted to coordinate lodging, meals, and gas supplies. In the event that city employees and their families would not be able to reside in their homes in the aftermath of a storm, hotel rooms with air conditioning powered by generators were secured for employees and their families. An arrangement was made with a local restaurant to provide hot meals, and gas supplies were stored at a local farm in the event that local fuel supplies became short or depleted. These alternative action plans proved to be critical during Hurricane Ivan (2004). The newly formed living arrangements resembled a command center. The department heads were all together, which facilitated planning, communication, and teamwork. It was also a load off the minds of the employees knowing their families were safe and taken care of, allowing them to focus on their job of getting the city up and running again. Two days before Hurricane Katrina made landfall, Public Works Director, Jennifer Fidler, held a meeting to share expectations and responsibilities and identify critical and noncritical employees. "The idea was that only critical employees would be required to be here during the storm." Thus, noncritical employees could make plans to evacuate their families first.

Having confidence in your employees when non-routine events occur is critical for timely response. Fairhope Mayor, Tim Kant, has confidence in his directors and superintendents to get the job done. As Dan McCrory, Superintendent of the Water & Sewer Department, states, "It is like in the military after an attack, the commander tells the noncommissioned officers (NCOs) what needs to be done and then gets out of the way and lets them go, because they know the system and what to do." After Ivan, it took approximately 7 days to restore power and two weeks for Fairhope to really get back on-line. The improved turn-around time was due in part to the implementation of an organizational contingency plan. As Dan further asserts, "The government is known for red tape, but during emergencies, participation and empowerment are critical for timely response." To combat "red tape" during emergencies, Fairhope altered its chain of command to facilitate timely decision-making in the field. Rather than having ten people report directly to the mayor, the "Fab Four," as they are referred to, was devised. The "Fab Four" included Aaron Norris (Electrical Department Superintendent), Tommy Long, James Gillespie (Administrative Superintendent), and Chris Browning (Police Chief), who were responsible for communicating with the mayor and providing updates. This leadership team set goals, devised plans, and directed efforts, such that during Katrina (2005) the high school gym was converted into a makeshift hospital to effectively respond to some of the Louisiana and Mississippi communities' medical needs.

According to Chris Browning, "It is far worse to not make a decision—preplanning is the key to everything." Planning for contingencies helps organizations be more flexible, adaptable, and responsive overall. When Chris coordinated the purchase of bottled water supplies, the goal was to be ready for the next hurricane. However, due to pre-planning, the city was ready when an unexpected sewer leak caused residents to be without water service for several days. During this time, city employees handed out bottles of water to residents until water main was restored.[1]

A variation of contingency planning is **scenario planning,** which involves anticipating alternative future situations and developing courses of action for each alternative. Scenario planning has a long-term focus and is typically associated with planning at upper levels within organizations. Front-line managers are becoming more involved with this type of planning with the continuing emphasis on utilizing participatory management approaches. Thus, scenario planning is a necessary tool for most managers' today.[2] Consider the City of Fairhope again and what they now have to be prepared for that were not really critical issues 15 years ago.

scenario planning
Anticipating alternative future situations and developing courses of action for each alternative.

As Fairhope's Police Chief, Chris Browning notes, "Fairhope has in place general policies and procedures, but what if an issue is not addressed in the book—you have to think outside of the box. An officer's supervisor must be able to make a decision and know the chief will support it." To enhance the police department's flexibility and response in the field, Chris uses a disaster planning control tool similar to a yes/no command flow chart when he plans for future critical incident scenarios. Once a possible scenario has been identified, such as a gunman on the loose in city's hospital or one of the schools, the disaster planning command center is used to establish responsibilities, devise reporting relationships, identify assigned areas, preset critical contact information, and allocate vehicles for transportation. Next, critical incident drills are performed to simulate a gunman on the loose. Every police officer was shown and knew his/her responsibility. Chris' actions were initially criticized by some of the members of the force, but the officers soon realized the significance of scenario planning when a real situation arose; in less than six minutes, the police were at the scene and ready to respond to a gunman loose in Thomas Hospital. As Chris shares, "Research shows that you respond under stress to the way you've been trained." The disaster command planning center concept has been so successful for Chris that other department managers like Dan McCrory have picked up on it—"it provides preplanning information at your fingertips! Fairhope is in the vector for jumbo jets flying to Brookley Field. If a plane crashed in Fairhope, we would need fire, morgue, triage, and other support from Daphne and Mobile, Alabama. The command center has been very useful in helping us think through what we would do if this situation actually happened."[3]

Planning Differs at Different Management Levels

3
Explain how planning differs at top, middle, and supervisory management levels.

strategic planning Has longer time horizons, affects the entire organization, and deals with its interface to its external environment.

mission Defines the purpose the organization serves and identifies its services, products, and customers.

objectives The purposes, goals, and desired results for the organization and its parts.

strategies The activities by which the organization adapts to its environment in order to achieve its objectives.

operational planning Consists of intermediate and short-term planning.

Management planning differs according to the level of management at which it occurs, as shown in Exhibit 2-4. Top managers are more involved in **strategic planning**, which has longer time horizons, affects the entire organization, and deals with the organization's interaction with its external environment. Strategic plans include these:

1. The **mission,** which defines the fundamental purpose the organization attempts to serve and identifies its services, products, and customers.

2. The overall **objectives** that drive the organization, such as profitability, customer satisfaction, employee relationships, environmental protection, or other critically important ends to be sought.

3. **Strategies,** the activities by which the organization adapts to the important factors that comprise its external environment, including consumers, customers, suppliers, competitors, and social, political, economic, and technological conditions.

Middle and supervisory level managers are more concerned with operational planning. **Operational planning** consists of intermediate and short-term planning that facilitates achievement of the long-term strategic plans set at higher levels. As shown in Exhibit 2-4, these plans "operationalize" the plans made at higher levels and are much narrower in scope and much shorter term than those formed at higher levels. As one supervisor related:

> **Planning? Sure, I spend time planning. But most of my department's goals, objectives, and schedules are handed down to me from above. My planning is more along these lines: How can I get better performance from my work group members? How can I cut down turnover and absenteeism? Given my group's workload for the week, or for the day, what's the best way to attack it? Whom should I assign to various jobs?**
>
> **Take last week, for example. Four of my people were out—two sick and two on vacation—and I had to do a lot of planning in order to figure out who'd work where and when.**

EXHIBIT 2-4

Planning at Three Management Levels

Level	Planning Periods	What Is Planned
Top managers	Strategic long-term intermediate-range plans of 1 to 5 or more years	Growth rate Competitive strategies New products Capital investments
Middle managers	Intermediate- and short-range plans of 1 month to 1 year	How to improve scheduling and coordination How to exercise better control at lower levels
Supervisors	Short-range plans of 1 day, 1 week, 1 to 6 months	How to accomplish performance objectives How to implement new policies, work methods, and work assignments How to increase efficiency (in costs, quality, etc.) Employee and supervisor vacations

Companies in earthquake-prone areas such as Japan and California must have contingency plans for providing supplies, parts, and other necessities in case of disaster.

Things seemed to go a lot more smoothly because I'd put in some time anticipating the problems. I've learned to plan on having a few people out "sick" on the opening day of hunting season!

As you can see, all managers need to plan, regardless of their position in the hierarchy. Although planning at the supervisory level generally is less complex and involves less uncertainty than planning at higher levels, it is still crucial that such planning be done effectively.

✔ **SELF-CHECK**

What are some other examples of events that supervisory managers must plan for?

http://www.whirlpoolcorp.com/whr/ics/story/value.html

http://www.amazon.com

http://www.benjerry.com/our_company/our_mission/

Importance of Setting Objectives

Objectives are crucial to effective planning. As one of the opening quotations in this chapter implied, only if you first know where you are heading can you effectively plan to get there.

What Are Objectives?

As previously stated, objectives are the goals that provide the desired purposes and results for an organization and its parts. Plans are aimed at achieving objectives. They answer the question "What do I want to accomplish?"

Is there a difference between an *objective* and a *goal*? Management experts disagree on this matter. Some say that goals are broad and nonspecific, whereas objectives are narrow and specific. Others reverse the distinction just given. Still others do not distinguish between the two. Since the terms *goal* and *objective* are often used interchangeably, we will treat them as synonyms in this book.

Objectives Serve as a Stimulus for Motivation and Effort

If you follow organized sports, you know that athletes frequently have objectives they try to achieve. For example, baseball players may strive to hit .300; basketball players may attempt to average 20 points; and football quarterbacks seek to average 50 percent pass completions. A weekend golfer may step up to the first tee with an 85 in mind. A Friday-night league bowler may shoot for an average of 150. Just as athletes are motivated by goals or objectives, so are people in the world of work.

Richard Ost owns three of the smallest drugstores you've ever seen.

They are located in Philadelphia's "most bombed-out and burned-up neighborhoods." Yet he does more than $5 million worth of business a year—more than twice the rate of average drugstores. He succeeded by becoming "culturally competent." He labels prescriptions in Spanish for his Hispanic customers. He's also loaded some 1,000 common regimens in Spanish into his computer. With a single keystroke, any one of these can be printed in Spanish rather than English.

Richard recently bought a second location with an Asian clientele. Soon he was filling more than 400 prescriptions a day—half in English, 30 percent in Spanish, and 20 percent in Vietnamese.[4]

In summary, objectives provide a stimulus for effort; they give people something to strive for. If Ost had no set goal—if he simply planned to go out and sell—he'd have no benchmark for telling whether he was doing well or poorly.

4 Explain how the hierarchy of objectives works.

hierarchy of objectives
A network with broad goals at the top level of the organization and narrower goals for individual divisions, departments, or employees.

Hierarchy of Objectives

In any organization, objectives are first needed at the top-management level. Once top management has determined broad objectives or goals, other levels of the organization, including supervisory management, reflect these in objectives or goals of their own, thus creating a **hierarchy of objectives.** Exhibit 2-5 presents a hypothetical hierarchy of objectives for Computronix, the firm described in this chapter's preview.

Computronix's overall organizational objectives are increased profits, improved market share, new product introductions, and cost effectiveness, as well as others not mentioned. Note how one of these, the cost-effectiveness objective, is reflected at progressively lower organizational levels. At the division level, Dixon's objectives address cost effectiveness by seeking a 5 percent reduction in production costs and implementing a new inventory control system. The Dixon maintenance department reflects the plant's 5 percent production cost reduction through the objectives of reduction of equipment downtime and objectives reflect the maintenance department head's objectives, and so on down the line. The diagram in Exhibit 2-5, though simplified, shows how the individual worker can be linked to top corporate levels through objective setting.

Unified Planning through Objectives

unified planning
Coordinating departments to ensure harmony rather than conflict or competition.

A major advantage of organizational objectives is that they give managers at lower levels guidance in developing their own operational plans and coordinating their own activities. Ideally, top management's objectives should give tactical plans at lower levels unity of purpose. **Unified planning** means ensuring that plans at all organizational levels are in harmony, rather than at cross-purposes, with one another. Unified planning is especially important where coordination is required among departments or work units. Many supervisors are extremely dependent on other departments in accomplishing their own objectives. As shown in the following example, lack of unified planning at Computronix's Dixon Division has led to difficulties!

EXHIBIT 2-5

Hierarchy of Objectives
for Computronix

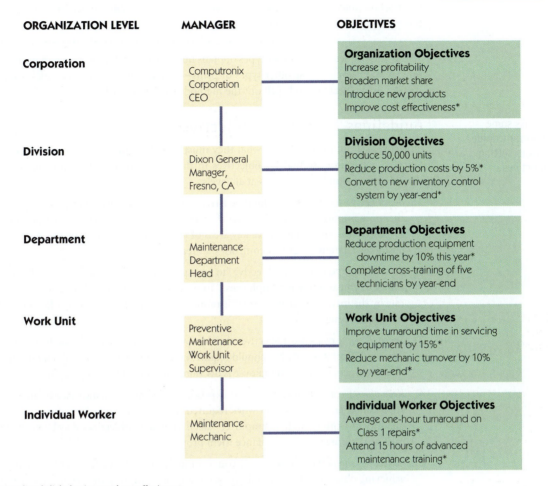

ORGANIZATION LEVEL	MANAGER	OBJECTIVES
Corporation	Computronix Corporation CEO	**Organization Objectives** Increase profitability Broaden market share Introduce new products Improve cost effectiveness*
Division	Dixon General Manager, Fresno, CA	**Division Objectives** Produce 50,000 units Reduce production costs by 5%* Convert to new inventory control system by year-end*
Department	Maintenance Department Head	**Department Objectives** Reduce production equipment downtime by 10% this year* Complete cross-training of five technicians by year-end
Work Unit	Preventive Maintenance Work Unit Supervisor	**Work Unit Objectives** Improve turnaround time in servicing equipment by 15%* Reduce mechanic turnover by 10% by year-end*
Individual Worker	Maintenance Mechanic	**Individual Worker Objectives** Average one-hour turnaround on Class 1 repairs* Attend 15 hours of advanced maintenance training*

*Objectives directly linked to improved cost effectiveness.

"This is ridiculous! They are trying to cut me down," stormed Juan Fernandez, supervisor of the processing department at the Dixon Division. The division was under the gun to reach its monthly production quota, and Fernandez' department absorbed a lot of the pressure. Fernandez continued: "If *we* don't process quota, the division doesn't make quota. It's as simple as that. But those jerks in maintenance are killing me. Last week, they were supposed to shut me down for PM [preventive maintenance]. But what happened? Absolutely nothing! They couldn't get to me because they were caught shorthanded. You tell me why they had to send three of their technicians to a training school last week. I built my whole departmental schedule around last week's being slack. They knew I was scheduled for PM last week. There's no way they're shutting me down for even 1 minute during the next 3 weeks."

Dixon has a problem here! Fernandez doesn't want to shut down for maintenance, but he risks some downtime later if his equipment doesn't receive the proper preventive maintenance.

The lack of unified planning at lower levels may cost Dixon its objectives. It has already strained the relationships among personnel in the plant.

✔ SELF-CHECK

What action would you take now if you were Juan Fernandez? What should be done to prevent this type of situation in the future?

....

As you will see shortly, other types of plans may also be established to aid in unified planning at lower levels. These other types of plans—policies, procedures, and rules—are more specific than objectives and spell out the methods used at lower levels.

5 Discuss some important guidelines in setting objectives.

Guidelines for Setting Objectives

Objectives set out for employees what they must do to make their performance acceptable. Since all supervisors should set objectives in their departments, the following guidelines should prove helpful to managers at all levels.

1. *Select key performance areas for objectives*. Since objectives focus attention and effort, the more important areas will suffer if there are too many objectives. Instead of having 15 objectives, select four or five key areas of performance, such as quality, quantity, customer relations, and cost controls, that really count!

2. *Be specific, if possible*. The objective "to have good quality" probably means different things to you and to your employees. "To produce parts with a 99 percent acceptance rate by the inspection department" is more specific, and it gives the worker a tangible measure of progress.

3. *Set challenging objectives*. Objectives should not be set so low that they can be met through "average" effort. Instead, they should require some stretching, but they should not be so difficult to achieve that an employee is discouraged from attempting to achieve them.

4. *Keep objective area in balance*. Effort expended in one performance area frequently affects another. The quality of work required influences the quantity of work, and the quantity of work may affect employee safety. Therefore, objectives may be needed in each of these areas so as to balance them properly.

5. *Objectives should be measurable*. If you want to determine whether employees are achieving objectives, there should be some way of measuring the extent to which they are being attained.

6. *Involve employees in setting objectives*. What do employees consider the key performance areas of their job? What do they think is a challenging but fair objective in a given area? When possible, ask these questions. There are times, however, especially during periods of financial difficulties and other crises, when it is not feasible or desirable to involve employees in objective setting.

7. *Follow up*. Once objectives have been set, supervisors tend to let up. Frequently only the supervisor knows the results of a worker's performance. Discuss progress with employees. Sharing results and discussing employees' progress will improve their commitment and demonstrate your own.

✔ SELF-CHECK

Note the quality objective in guideline 2: "to produce parts with a 99 percent acceptance rate by the inspection department." Do you see any problems with making this the only objective? Explain.

....

Types of Plans

6 Differentiate the various kinds of standing and single-use plans.

Once objectives have been set to determine *what* needs to be accomplished, plans can be developed to outline *how* the objectives can be attained. Basically, these plans fall into two categories: *standing plans*, and *single-use plans*.

Standing Plans

Standing plans, or **repeat-use plans,** are those that are used repeatedly over a period of time. The three most popular types of standing plans are *policies, rules,* and *procedures.*

standing plans or repeat-use plans Plans that are used repeatedly over a period of time.

policy Provides consistency among decision makers.

Policies. A **policy** is a guide to decision making—a sort of boundary on a supervisor's freedom of action. That is, it's a way to provide consistency among decision makers. For example, suppose that an *objective* of Computronix (recall the chapter preview) is "to operate our divisions so as to achieve high safety." Note that this objective tells the "what." A *policy* for achieving this objective at the various divisions could be that "all flammable substances will be stored and handled in a manner consistent with federal, state, and local regulations." Another policy might be: "Each division shall emphasize safety performance of employees through a well-designed promotional campaign." Within the Dixon Division of Computronix, an overall policy established by Marshall might be: "Each operating department shall hold safety meetings at least once every three months to encourage adherence to rules and solicit employee safety suggestions." Other examples of policies are shown in Exhibit 2-6.

Supervisory managers fit into the policy picture in two key ways. First, they play an important part in implementing organizational policies that have been established by higher management. Second, they create policies within their departments as guides for their own work groups. Here are some examples:

1. *Absence notification.* "Employees who will be absent should notify me in advance, assuming this is feasible."

2. *Decision making.* "You are encouraged to make decisions on your own within your area of responsibility."

✔ SELF-CHECK

What are some other examples of supervisory policies? Can you think of any examples of policies established by the teacher of this course?

. . . .

EXHIBIT 2-6

Examples of Policies

Compensation policy: "This company shall establish and maintain wages on a level comparable to those paid for comparable positions in other firms in the community."

Overtime policy: "Supervisors shall offer overtime opportunities first to the most senior employees in the department."

Grievance policy: "Each employee shall have an opportunity for due process in all disciplinary matters."

Purchasing policy: "Where feasible, several sources of supply shall be utilized so as not to be solely dependent on one supplier."

Supervisory policy: "Managers shall periodically hold group meetings with employees for the purposes of discussing objectives, explaining new developments that may affect employees, responding to questions, and, in general, encouraging more effective and accurate communications within the organization."

Policies established by upper-level managers should be put into writing, since they must be enforced at operating levels by supervisors. Also, they often form the basis for legal proceedings against the organization and its management. Supervisory policies like the ones just mentioned, however, may be communicated orally. Some policies may be unwritten, implied, or based on past practices because "that's the way things actually happen."

It was Mary Hicks's first week on the job. Her supervisor, Clara Sanchez, had been very helpful in showing her the ropes. Each day, Mary had shown up for work a few minutes before starting time—just to make sure she was on time. She noticed, however, that at least a third of the employees drifted in 5 to 10 minutes late. This was true not only in her department, but also in others throughout the building. On asking one of her coworkers about this, she was told, "Yeah, they don't get really upset about 5 or 10 minutes, just so it's not the same person all the time."

The preceding example describes a practice that has become so widespread that supervisors may treat it as a policy. Supervisors must keep in mind that action or even inaction may come to be thought of as policy by employees and serve as a guide to their behavior.

Policies are relatively permanent but should not be "set in stone." Circumstances change, and management must from time to time reexamine the appropriateness of its policies.

rule A policy that is invariably enforced.

Rules. Like policies, rules provide guidance. But a **rule** is stronger than a policy in that the guidance given by a rule is final and definite. Rules are inflexible and *must* be obeyed, under threat of punishment. If you work in an organization that has the rule "No smoking on the premises," you cannot smoke, and that is that. Note the difference between a policy and a rule as shown in the following examples:

1. *Policy:* "Employees who violate the no-smoking rule are *subject to discharge*."

2. *Rule:* "Employees who violate the no-smoking rule are *automatically discharged*."

Why distinguish between rules and policies, especially when the distinction is sometimes a fine one? First, as a supervisor, you must know when you do not have flexibility. Second, too many rules can result in overmanagement. Taking too much discretion away from the employees leads them to say, "Well, let me look in the rule book and see what I'm supposed to do."

Rules are inflexible requirements and are much stronger than guidelines. It is important for supervisors to know when they can be flexible in promoting the objectives of their company and when they have to enforce rules.

Although rules have an important place in organizations, their overuse can lead to problems. When there are too many rules, supervisors lose their individualism and may use the rules as crutches. Or they may offer weak, apologetic reasons when they enforce the rules. For example, consider the following dialogue:

Supervisor: "Catherine, I'm sorry to have to write you up for punching in 3 minutes late."

Catherine: "But you know I was actually here 10 minutes early and just forgot to punch in. I was at my desk all the time. I can't afford to get laid off half a day for being written up."

Supervisor: "Sorry, Catherine. It doesn't seem fair to me, either, but I've got to stick by the rule book. A rule's a rule."

Procedures. The need for procedures arises when an organization or a department requires a high degree of consistency in activities that occur frequently. Procedures are established to avoid "reinventing the wheel" and to ensure that an effective sequence is followed. A **procedure** outlines the steps to be performed when a particular course of action is taken. Organizations have procedures for obtaining leaves of absence, ordering parts through central purchasing, taking weekly inventory, processing an employee's grievance, and so on.

procedure Steps to be performed when a particular course of action is taken.

✔ SELF-CHECK

Can you think of a procedure for a regular activity that takes place in each of the following organizations: airline, hospital, retail store, college? Procedures used in driving a car? Preparing a payroll?

Single-Use Plans

Single-use plans are developed to accomplish a specific purpose and are then discarded. Unlike policies, rules, and procedures, single-use plans detail courses of action that won't be performed on a repetitive basis. Examples of single-use plans are programs, projects, budgets, and schedules. These plans are more numerous and diversified than standing plans.

single-use plans Developed to accomplish a specific purpose and then discarded after use.

Programs. We hear and read about programs daily—such as your city's pollution control program, a voter registration program, and so on. A **program** is a large-scale plan that involves a mix of objectives, policies, rules, and smaller projects. A program outlines the specific steps to be taken to achieve its objectives and the time, money, and human resources required to complete it. It is essentially a set of single-use plans carried out over a period of time. Other examples of programs are as follows:

program A large-scale plan composed of a mix of objectives, policies, rules, and projects.

1. A tourism marketing program undertaken by your state.

2. A research program undertaken by drug producer Pfizer to develop vaccines for major diseases, such as AIDS and Parkinson's.

Projects. A **project** is a distinct, smaller part of a program. For example, a state's tourism program involves many projects, such as selecting a tourism committee, benchmarking several states with outstanding tourism programs, promoting public attractions, and upgrading the welcome centers that greet transit visitors on interstate highways. Each project has its own objectives and becomes the responsibility of personnel assigned to oversee it.

project A distinct part of a program.

http://www.gpo.gov/usbudget/

budget A forecast of expected financial performance over time.

schedule A plan of activities to be performed and their timing.

gantt chart Identifies work stages and scheduled completion dates.

Budgets. Most individuals, families, or organizations use some form of budgeting. A well-planned budget serves as both a planning and a controlling tool. Simply stated, a **budget** is a forecast of expected financial performance over a period of time. A departmental budget covers such items as supplies, equipment, scrap, overtime, and personnel payroll.

Schedules. A **schedule** is a plan showing activities to be performed and their timing. Scheduling techniques range from a simple note or appointment book used to schedule your day to sophisticated schedules for such major challenges as building a new plant or launching a space shuttle. Two scheduling approaches with which you should be familiar are the Gantt chart and PERT network.

The **Gantt chart** is a visual progress report that identifies work stages or activities on a vertical axis and scheduled completion dates horizontally. It is named after its developer, Henry Gantt, a management consultant who introduced the basic idea in the early 1900s. Since then, Gantt charts have been used extensively as a planning tool. Exhibit 2-7 illustrates a simplified Gantt chart. Note the specific activities that proceed from contract negotiation to job start-up and the scheduled times for each. Also note that one activity, long lead purchasing, can be carried on simultaneously with development of a manufacturing schedule. In actual practice, Gantt charts may include movable strips of plastic to represent bars, with different colors to indicate scheduled and actual progress. At a glance, a manager or supervisor can see whether a project is on time, ahead of schedule, or behind schedule. While the Gantt chart is helpful as a planning tool, it does not show directly how the various activities involved in a job depend on one another. It is in showing such dependencies of activities that PERT network analysis can be helpful.

EXHIBIT **2-7**

Example of Gantt Chart Showing Activities Needed in Production Start-Up

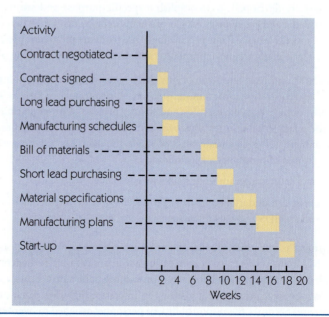

Program Evaluation and Review Technique (PERT) is a management scheduling tool that shows relationships among a network of activities and events to determine the completion time of a project. Typically, PERT is used on highly complex, one-time projects, such as building a skyscraper or completing the prototype of a new jet aircraft, and requires the use of a computer. However, its principles are relevant for many supervisors, especially in planning and scheduling various aspects of their jobs.

Let's examine a PERT chart that can be applied at the supervisory level. Suppose that you are a maintenance supervisor and your department has to overhaul an important machine. You have determined that the following activities must be done to complete the job:

A. Remove the machine from its foundation.

B. Haul the machine to the repair shop.

C. Dismantle the machine.

D. Order and receive new replacement parts from the manufacturer.

E. Repair the machine.

F. Test-run the machine.

G. Build a new machine foundation.

H. Move the repaired machine to the factory floor.

I. Secure the machine to the new foundation.

Now, assume that you are asked to estimate when the machine can be ready for use again. The PERT network of events and activities involved in your analysis is shown in Exhibit 2-8. The numbered squares represent events at which the different activities to complete the job *begin* and are *completed*. For example, Event 2 marks the completion of activity A and the beginning of activities B and G. The lines represent the activities to be performed. The hours represent your estimate of how long each activity will take to complete based on your experience or on information supplied by others.

Note that the estimated completion time for the job is 62 hours. This total time is obtained by adding the hours necessary to complete the series of activities that comprise the *longest* route, in terms of time, to complete the job. This route is called the **critical path.** The series of activities on the critical path include A, B, C, D, E, F, H, and I. These are the activities that determine the completion time for the job. Activity G is not a critical step in the network because it can be begun and completed independently of activities B through I and is not included on the critical path.

7 Draw a simple PERT chart

Program Evaluation and Review Technique Shows relationships among a network of activities to determine the completion time of a project.

critical path The series of activities in a PERT network that comprise the longest route, in terms of time, to complete the job.

EXHIBIT **2-8**

PERT Network for Completing Machine Overhaul

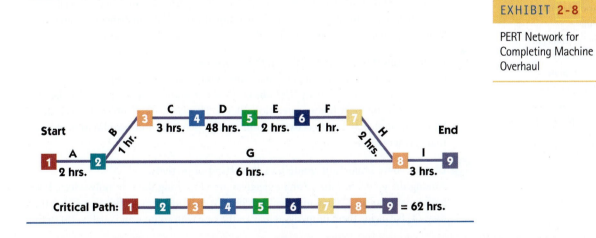

A major advantage of PERT networks, even for simple problems, is that they graphically display the dependent parts of a total job. The supervisor thus has a better grasp of the total job to be completed.

✔ **SELF-CHECK**

Suppose that it takes you 4 hours rather than the 2 hours estimated to repair the machine (activity E) as shown in Exhibit 2-8. Will this cause your project to be completed later than planned?

CHAPTER REVIEW

1 **Discuss some of the more important points about planning.**
Supervisors do planning as an ongoing part of their jobs. They must include planning for scheduling work, developing and living within budgets, and making job assignments.

2 **Explain the steps involved in planning.**
Planning is deciding what will be done in the future. The three planning steps are (1) setting an objective or goal, (2) identifying and assessing present and future conditions affecting the goal, and (3) developing a systematic approach to achieving the goal. Properly done, planning helps managers accomplish the four other management functions of organizing, leading, staffing, and controlling. Of these functions, planning is most closely linked to controlling. In fact, they are sometimes called the "Siamese twins" of management. Because it is a difficult and time-consuming process, many supervisors tend to neglect planning. Instead of planning, they scurry about solving one problem, then another, seemingly too busy to plan anything. Effective planning anticipates many problems so that they are more easily handled when they occur. Contingency planning is thinking about anticipated problems in advance, and having potential solutions available.

3 **Explain how planning differs at top, middle, and supervisory management levels.**
Planning differs for top-, middle-, and first-level management. Top managers spend a greater proportion of their time developing strategic long-term and intermediate-range plans of one to five or more years. Strategic plans include the organization's mission, objectives, and strategies and interfacing with its external environment. Middle-level and supervisory managers perform operational planning—intermediate-range and short-range plans of 1 year to 1 day—that operationalize strategic plans.

4 **Explain how the hierarchy of objectives works.**
Objectives are crucial to effective planning. Once established, objectives provide a stimulus for individual effort. The objectives set at one management level reflect the objectives of the next higher operational level. This network of objectives is called a hierarchy of objectives. Objectives permit unified planning and coordination at lower management levels.

5 **Discuss some important guidelines in setting objectives.**
Among the guidelines for setting objectives are (1) setting them in only selected, key performance areas; (2) making them specific; (3) making them challenging rather than easy; (4) balancing them properly, as may be the case with volume and quality; (5) stating

IMPORTANT TERMS
budget
contingency planning
critical path
Gantt chart
hierarchy of objectives
mission
objectives
operational planning
policy
procedure
program
Program Evaluation and
    Review Technique
    (PERT)
project
rule
scenario planning
schedule
"Siamese twins" of
    management
single–use plans
standing plans or
    repeat-use plans
strategic planning
strategies
unified planning

them in measurable terms; (6) involving employees in setting them; and (7) following up on results.

6 **Differentiate the various kinds of standing and single-use plans.**

After objectives have been established, plans can be developed throughout the organization. Standing, or repeat-use, plans direct action that deals with recurring situations. They include policies, rules, and procedures. A policy is a guide to individual decision making. Policies allow some flexibility, whereas rules are final and definite as to what action must be taken. A procedure outlines the steps that should be taken to complete a given action, such as applying for vacation leave or processing a grievance. Single-use plans are one-time plans that are discarded on completion. Examples of these are programs, projects, budgets, and schedules.

7 **Draw a simple PERT chart.**

Two important types of schedules are Gantt charts and PERT charts, each of which provides a visual display of activities to be performed and the time frames involved.

QUESTIONS FOR REVIEW AND DISCUSSION

1. What are the three basic steps in planning? Why do supervisors tend to slight the planning function?

2. How does planning differ among top, intermediate, and supervisory management levels?

3. What are some guidelines for setting objectives?

4. What is meant by a hierarchy of objectives? Explain.

5. What is the difference between a policy, a rule, and a procedure?

6. What is a Gantt chart? How does it differ from a PERT chart?

7. What is contingency planning? Explain.

8. Distinguish between objectives and strategies.

Testing Your Planning Skills

Skill Builder 2-1

group activity

Harold Marshall, general manager at Computronix's Dixon Division, has just named you as chairperson of the first annual blood drive, to be conducted at the plant site. A strong believer in the company's participation in community affairs and himself a member of the local Red Cross board of directors, Marshall has committed the division's 500 employees to the blood drive. Your committee will set the exact dates for the drive, which is to be held in 3 or 4 months. As chairperson, you have been assigned a team of four other company employees to plan and implement the project. All members are highly respected, competent people, representing a true cross section of the employees: One is a production worker who is president of the local union; another, an engineer, represents the professional segment; the human resources manager represents the management group; and a payroll clerk represents the administrative office group. Marshall was given your name by your boss, who expressed confidence in your ability to lead a successful donor campaign at the plant. At 27, you are the youngest person on the committee and anxious to do a good job. You have called the first committee meeting, which you have advertised as a "preliminary planning meeting," to identify key factors that must be planned for in order for the committee to meet its objective: having a successful blood drive at Computronix.

Instructions:

1. Make a list of what you consider the key planning issues to be identified by the committee at this initial planning meeting.

2. Of the items on your list, which two or three do you believe are the most crucial? Why?

3. Identify major problems that could prevent accomplishment of your objective. What contingency planning could be done to avert them or minimize their impact?

4. To help in your preparation for the planning meeting, identify six to ten steps that you feel will be needed to achieve a successful blood drive. These steps might be such things as

   a. Determine a date.

   b. Identify a location.

   c. Secure commitment from Red Cross.

   Draw a PERT chart that shows the sequence and relationship of the activities identified. (You need not be concerned with the length of time needed for each activity.)

5. Compare your responses to questions 1, 2, 3, and 4 with those of other students. To what extent do they agree with you?

Determining Priorities

group activity

Assume that you are a high school principal. Organizationally, 12 teachers, five coaches, your assistant, and an assistant principal report to you. The assistant principal supervises another eight teachers, four clerical workers, a custodian, a librarian, a counselor, and the cafeteria dietitian.

Listed below are a number of activities you performed during the past week.

a. Prepared a 15-minute speech to deliver to your school's PTA.

b. Met a sales representative from a local computer company to discuss possible purchase of computer equipment.

c. Filled in as a substitute teacher for an 11th-grade math teacher, who left school ill at lunchtime.

d. Met with the student homecoming committee to acquaint them with the guidelines for homecoming activities.

e. Prepared your list of yearly objectives and budget requests that must be submitted to the city superintendent's office.

f. Met with a group of four parents to discuss their complaints about unreasonably high demands by one of your teachers.

g. Listened to councilwoman Judith Johnson, who spoke to a civics class on "Your City Government."

h. Toured the school halls during changes in class periods.

i. Interviewed two final candidates for a woman's basketball and volleyball coaching position.

j. Discussed with the football coach next week's homecoming game against a crosstown rival.

1. Indicate how you would classify these in priority: MI (most important), RI (relatively important), or RU (relatively unimportant). Be prepared to defend your choices.

2. What additional information about the principal's activities may have helped you establish your priority listings? How would this information have helped?

3. Meet with groups of three to five other students to compare your choices of priorities. Discuss these and be prepared to report your results to the class.

CASE

Setting Performance Objectives

Case 2-1

Jane Persons supervises the word processing center at Computronix, which consists of seven word processors. Work done by this section consists of word processing various reports and correspondence as required by other departments and handling all photocopying for the plant. Persons had just attended a meeting with the other section heads and heard Edna Strong, the administration department head, talk briefly about the new planning system in store for the Dixon Division. As Strong heard it from Marshall, the plant manager and all department heads and supervisors would be required to identify five key performance areas in their departments. These were supposed to be areas that had a significant impact on performance.

It was the meeting with Strong that puzzled Persons. Strong had asked her to come up with the five key performance objectives for her word processing section. Persons said: "I can understand how our sales group or production groups can have specific objectives. But I can't see how our

section can have anything like that. What am I supposed to come up with? Something like 'We will process 9,500 pages in the next year' or 'At least 99.5 percent of our pages will be error-free'?

This whole unit planning system seems like a lot of 'wheel spinning' to me. My people know their objectives without this planning stuff. Their objective is to do a good job at getting the required word processing done for these other departments as quickly as possible."

Answer the following questions:

1. Do you agree with Jane Persons's view that the new planning system is "wheel spinning"? Why or why not?

2. Are there some key performance areas that Persons could identify for her action? What are they?

3. To what extent does Persons's last sentence meet the criteria discussed in the text under "Guidelines for Setting Objectives"?

3 Decision Making, Problem Solving, and Ethics

AP Photo/Coeur d'Alene Press, Jason Hunt

Ethics, an extremely important aspect of supervisory decision making, are the standards used to judge whether behavior is inappropriate.

It is management's public responsibility to make whatever is genuinely in the public good become the enterprise's own self interest.
—PETER F. DRUCKER

Ethics is a code of values which guide our choices and actions and determine the purpose and course of our lives.
—AYN RAND

All the analyst really requires for the solution to a problem is: first, the painstaking assembly of all the phenomena; second, exhaustive patience; and third, the ability to comprehend the whole problem with a fresh and unbiased imagination.
—ELLERY QUEEN

The Advancing Landscape Architect

Bobby Jones was hired as a landscape architect for Lane Corporation five years ago. His duties include supervising a crew of 23 groundskeepers who are responsible for maintaining the corporate grounds. Because the work requires physical stamina and is performed mostly outdoors, the majority of the groundskeepers are men, although there are four women employed.

Brenda Lewis was hired by Jones 6 months ago. During her initial interview with Jones, she was told that she would be expected to perform the same duties as the male groundskeepers. However, once she was employed, she was assigned to work with a second female worker in the greenhouse. The two other female groundskeepers were assigned to caring for the indoor plants in the corporate offices.

Brenda's duties consisted mainly of transplanting seedlings and watering plants. When she indicated to Jones that she would like to be given the opportunity to work outdoors with the rest of the crew, she was told that she was needed to work in the greenhouse because it was more suited for females and that she could not be expected to work like a man, mowing lawns and planting shrubs.

Jones frequently came by the greenhouse to see how the two female employees were doing. Although Lewis had been employed for six months and Maria Taylor had been there a year, Jones never called them by name. He always addressed them as "Babe" or "Honey." As he was giving them instructions, he had a habit of putting his arm around their shoulder or running his fingers through their hair. He always made a point to tell them his latest joke—usually one with sexual overtones.

On several occasions Jones insisted that Lewis help him deliver new plants to the grounds crew for planting. On these trips she rode with him in a golf cart. When the cart hit a bump or made a turn, Jones would put his hand on Lewis's leg to steady her. When she protested, he insisted he was just concerned for her safety.

In addition, Jones gave Lewis a book dealing with insecticides and told her that she would need to learn the information in order to work safely with the various chemicals stored near the greenhouse. He suggested that perhaps they should study the book together at her apartment after work.

At this point Lewis went to Jones's supervisor and filed a complaint of sexual harassment against Jones. She stated that she had never welcomed any of his "advances." When he put his arm around her shoulder, she pulled away. She did not laugh at his jokes, and she objected to his putting his hand on her leg. She also rejected his offer to study with him after work. She stated that she was afraid to tell him how she really felt because he was her supervisor, and she feared he would fire her.

Source: Prepared by James D. Powell, Professor of Management, University of North Texas, Denton, Texas. Adapted from *Human Resource Management*, 1st ed., by Megginson/Franklin/Byrd. Copyright © 1995. Reprinted with permission of Cengage Learning Custom Solutions, www.cengage.com/custom.

Learning Objectives

After reading and studying this chapter, you should be able to:

1. Explain the role of decision making in the supervisor's job.

2. Discuss why supervisors need to make so many decisions.

3. Define decision making and identify at least four elements involved.

4. Discuss how decisions are made.

5. Name some factors to keep in mind when making decisions.

6. Decide whether to use the individual approach or the group approach when making decisions.

7. Discuss some ways of improving decision making.

8. Explain the role of ethics in the supervisor's decision making.

We will discuss the subject of decision making in considerable detail. Decisions must be made about people, processes, and priorities, to name just a few issues! Keep the supervisor's problem in mind, because we will return to his situation throughout the chapter.

1

Explain the role of decision making in the supervisor's job.

Role of Decision Making in Supervisory Management

Managers must make decisions whenever they perform any of the five management functions—planning, organizing, staffing, leading, and controlling. Without decision making, the entire management system would cease to exist. For example, in *planning*, the supervisor must decide which objectives to seek, which policies to establish, and what rules to institute. In *organizing*, choices must be made as to who gets what authority and how duties and responsibilities are grouped. In *staffing*, decisions must be made concerning employee selection, placement, training and development, performance appraisal, compensation, and health and safety. In *controlling*, if actual performance does not conform to planned performance, decisions must be made about how best to bring them together. The function of *leading* entails deciding how best to communicate with and motivate employees.

The decisions that managers make often must be made quickly—and frequently with little information, or even conflicting information. Then, those decisions must be carried out in order to achieve the department's objectives!

Decision Making: The Heart of Supervisory Management

Decision making is central to the supervisor's job. Supervisors must continually decide what is to be done; who is to do it; and how, when, and where it is to be done (see Exhibit 3-1). As we will show throughout the chapter, although these decisions may be discussed separately, they are interrelated. One decision is affected by, and builds on, previous ones. For example, what your department produces determines what types of production facilities are needed. Decisions about production, in turn, influence the types of employees needed and the training and compensation they should receive. All of these decisions affect the amount of resources budgeted for the department.

2

Discuss why supervisors need to make so many decisions.

Why Supervisors Need to Make So Many Decisions

Supervisory managers—even more than managers at other levels—are involved in directing employees' behavior toward achieving the organization's goals, as well as those of the employees themselves. Supervisors must make more decisions more frequently—and often more quickly—than other managers, since they're operating on a production-oriented, day-by-day, person-to-person basis. These decisions involve a variety of activities, as the following example illustrates.

Wilma Malone, nursing supervisor at Alquippa Medical Center, had been at work for only 3 hours, but she had already made several major decisions. For example, she had

1. **Signed up to attend a 1-day course on time management, to be offered the following week;**

2. **Assigned performance ratings to five of her new nurses on their performance appraisal forms;**

3. **Approved vacation requests for two nurses in her department;**

4. **Referred to the floor physician a patient's request to be taken off a prescribed medication;**

EXHIBIT **3-1**

Decision Making is the
Heart of Supervisory
Management

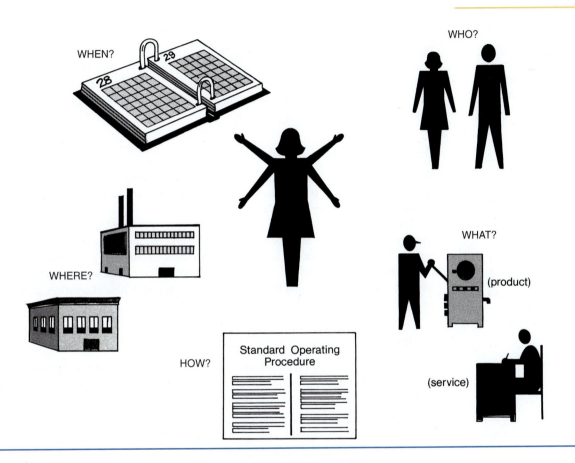

WHEN?

WHO?

WHERE?

WHAT?

(product)

HOW?

Standard Operating
Procedure

(service)

5. Resolved a dispute between one of the nurses and a floor orderly;

6. Selected Jane Moore to serve as her replacement when she was to take her vacation in 3 weeks; and

7. Requisitioned supplies needed by her department.

In addition, she made a handful of other minor decisions. The young trainee assigned to Malone said, "Are you always this busy, or is it just because it's Monday morning?" Malone replied, "It's all a normal part of a supervisor's job."

Employees look to their supervisors for more direction, assistance, guidance, and protection than do subordinates of managers at higher levels. Also, in general, supervisors spend more time socializing with others in the organization since they have more employees than other managers. All of these activities require decision making.

One basic truism of management is that the lower the level of management, the greater the **span of management,** which is the number of immediate employees a manager can supervise effectively. Therefore, supervisors make decisions that affect not only their own behavior, but also that of many other people.

span of management
The number of immediate
employees a manager can
supervise effectively.

✔ STOP & THINK

What was Jones's span of management in the chapter preview? Do you think that span was too great, just right, or too little for this type of business? Explain.

<table>
<tr><td>

3

Define decision making and identify at least four elements involved.

</td></tr>
</table>

What Is Decision Making?

It is now time to define decision making, discuss its characteristics, look at some selected types of decisions, and consider some differences between decision making and problem solving.

Decision Making Defined

Have you known people who couldn't ever make up their minds? They might say, "I really don't know what to do. If I do this, such and such will happen. If I do that, then something else might happen." They just can't make decisions.

The word *decide* comes from a Latin word meaning "to cut off." When you make a decision, you first consider a matter causing you some uncertainty, debate, or dispute, and then make a choice or judgment that more or less results in a definite conclusion. You cut off further deliberation on the matter. Thus, **decision making** is the conscious consideration and selection of a course of action from among two or more available alternatives in order to produce a desired result.

decision making
Considering and selecting a course of action from among alternatives.

Elements Involved in Decision Making

There are several facts you should know about decision making. The most important ones are (1) a decision may not be needed, (2) decisions involve the future, (3) the process is a conscious one, and (4) there must be more than one alternative solution.

A Decision May Not Be Needed. A wise decision maker begins by asking "Is a decision needed?" It may seem strange to include this question in a discussion of decision making, but it's important. In many supervisory situations, no decision is needed, and decision making would be in vain. If a given event is inevitable or if higher management is going to act in a certain way regardless of the supervisor's wishes, then making a decision is a waste of time. Some things cannot be changed regardless of the supervisor's wishes or actions.

> "You really have guts, Will," said Carol Sheffield to Will Hauser, office supervisor for Gridtronics, Inc. "You didn't waste a lot of time with competing bids or even looking at what different software packages can do. Don't you feel uncomfortable getting the vice-president to approve a $10,000 purchase? What if he wants some evidence that you really shopped around?"
>
> "Well," said Hauser, "that's a good question, I suppose. But there's more to the story. Getting competing bids and spending a lot of time evaluating different systems would have been a waste of my time. A 'decision' really wasn't needed. The guy I bought that piece of equipment from is the vice-president's son!"

Decisions Involve the Future. Surely you have heard others say "If only I had done this, then that wouldn't have happened." They assume that if they had made a different decision, it would have resulted in a happy marriage, a rapid promotion, or a killing in the stock market. It is said that hindsight is 20/20, but the supervisor's world is no place for Monday-morning

EXHIBIT 3-2

Decision-Making Process

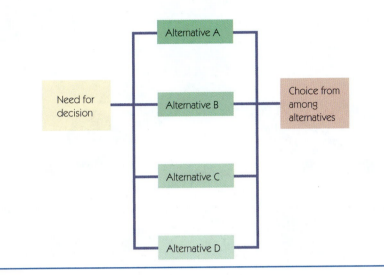

quarterbacking. Rather, it's a place to prepare for today or tomorrow. Because a supervisor's decision making is oriented toward the future, it always contains an element of uncertainty.

Decision Making Is a Conscious Process. Decision making involves a conscious process of selection. No decisions are needed about breathing or digestion, because these are unconscious, reflexive actions. In making a decision, the individual consciously (1) becomes aware of a want that needs to be satisfied, (2) seeks relevant behavioral alternatives, and (3) evaluates them as a basis of choice, as shown in Exhibit 3-2.

Decision Making Involves More Than One Alternative. As indicated earlier, for a true decision to be made, there must be two or more available alternatives to choose from, including the possibility of doing nothing. Frequently, there are only two choices, as in a "yes or no" or "to do or not to do" situation. The decision to do nothing is sometimes the worst decision.

Most decision situations involve several alternatives with varying expected outcomes. You may not be aware of some of the alternatives and may not have decision authority over others. For other alternatives, you must estimate expected outcomes. You then evaluate each outcome in terms of its desirability. Sometimes there are no desirable alternatives. In such cases you have to decide between two undesirable ones.

✔ **STOP & THINK**

What are the possible alternatives that Jones's supervisor can choose in the situation described in the chapter preview?

Types of Decisions to Be Made

Although there are many ways of classifying decisions, we will discuss only one at this point—namely, categorizing decisions as either programmed or unprogrammed.

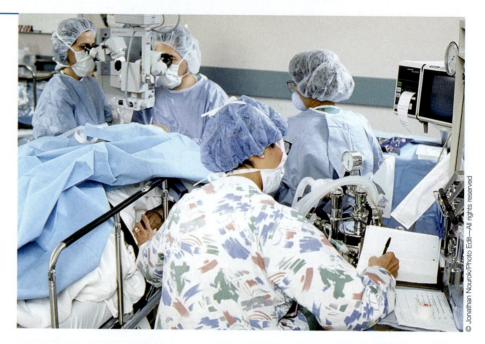

Imagining the numerous decisions required of a nurse working in a supervisory position in a hospital helps us understand what decision making is, the types of decisions that must be made in a workday, and how decision making and problem solving relate to one another.

programmed decisions
Routine and repetitive decisions.

Programmed decisions are those that are routine and repetitive. Since such decisions tend to be similar and must be made frequently, supervisors usually establish a systematic way of handling them. Here are some examples of this type of decision:

1. How to handle an employee who reports to work late or is absent without permission

2. How to schedule work, shifts, vacations, and other time variations

3. How to determine which employees need training and what type of training should be given to them

4. How frequently to do maintenance servicing of machinery and equipment

The effective supervisor handles these decisions in a systematic way and may even set up a decision framework, including guidelines such as policies, procedures, or rules to be followed.

unprogrammed decisions
Decisions that occur infrequently and require a different response each time.

Unprogrammed decisions are those that occur infrequently. Because different variables are involved, requiring a separate and different response each time, it is difficult to establish a systematic way of dealing with such decisions. Some examples of unprogrammed supervisory decisions include the following:

1. Whether to buy an important piece of machinery or equipment, especially an expensive, complex piece

2. How to react to a union representative who says that a grievance will be filed if you give a written reprimand to a certain worker for a work-related violation of safety rules

3. How to handle a severe accident or explosion

4. Whom to promote to a supervisory position

How Decision Making and Problem Solving Relate

In one of his educational films, Joe Batten, a well-known management consultant, has a manager say, "We have no problems here, just opportunities. Each problem should be considered an opportunity." Although we don't necessarily agree with that conclusion, it does give us a chance to show how decision making and problem solving are related. An **opportunity** is a set of circumstances that provides a chance to improve a situation or help reach a goal. A **problem** is an existing unsatisfactory situation causing anxiety or distress, which must be addressed.

opportunity A chance for development or advancement.

problem An existing unsatisfactory situation causing anxiety or distress.

Effective supervisors must be able to identify problems and their cause(s), to analyze complex and involved situations, and to solve problems by removing their cause(s). But placing too much emphasis on problems can prevent one from identifying opportunities. After all, solving a problem only eliminates or neutralizes a negative situation. Progress or advancement comes from seeking and identifying opportunities; recognizing the emotions, needs, and motivations of the people involved; and analyzing ways of satisfying them. Here are some examples of "opportunity" decision making at the supervisory level:

1. Replacing a piece of equipment that, while it is still functioning well, can be upgraded to increase efficiency.

2. Improving an already effective preventive maintenance system.

3. Cross-training employees to broaden their skills and raise morale.

4. Creating a new position for a highly skilled technician who has recently left the employ of a competitor.

5. Instituting the most innovative new processes and techniques.

✔ STOP & THINK

What other examples of "opportunity" decision making can you think of?

How to Make Decisions

Exhibit 3-3 shows that the decision-making process involves six basic steps. We have already mentioned most of them.

4 Discuss how decisions are made.

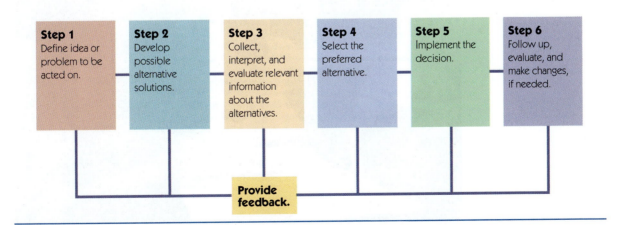

EXHIBIT **3-3**

Steps in Decision Making

| Step 1 Define idea or problem to be acted on. | Step 2 Develop possible alternative solutions. | Step 3 Collect, interpret, and evaluate relevant information about the alternatives. | Step 4 Select the preferred alternative. | Step 5 Implement the decision. | Step 6 Follow up, evaluate, and make changes, if needed. |

Provide feedback.

Step 1: Define the Idea or Problem

Peter Drucker once stated that a decision is only as good as the correct definition of the problem. In other words, the right cure for the wrong problem is just as bad as the wrong cure for the right problem. But it is not always easy to know what the problem is or which opportunity is the best one to seek. When you have a fever, it is only a symptom of the true problem—an infection or other disorder. Likewise, as a supervisor, you should remember that low morale, high turnover, many complaints or grievances, waste, and declining sales are not the real problem. They are only symptoms of the real problem.

If the decision to be made involves solving a problem, its cause, or the factors that are creating it, must be determined. Without identifying the cause (or causes), it is difficult to solve the problem, for you may be treating its symptom rather than the root cause(s).

✔ STOP & THINK

What do you see as the real problem facing Jones's supervisor in the chapter preview? What was/were the cause(s) of the problem?

Step 2: Develop Alternatives

alternatives Possible courses of action that can satisfy a need or solve a problem.

The second step is to develop alternative ways of solving the problem or taking advantage of the opportunity. **Alternatives** are possible courses of action that can satisfy a need or solve a problem. Several choices are usually available if you are able to identify and develop them. It is easier to choose from a few alternatives than from many, so reduce the number to as few as is feasible. Also, be aware that, if choices are limited, they may include only undesirable ones.

This is the stage in which you decide whether you should make the choice or channel it to some other person who has the authority or expertise to make it. If you decide that it is your "call," one choice is to do nothing, hoping that the problem will go away or solve itself

The importance of decision making resonates in company expenditures. Deciding who will travel on business and why can have a significant impact on overall company budgets.

PhotoAlto/Getty Images

in time. You must be careful, though, that this doesn't become an excuse for not making a difficult choice. If it does, you may get a reputation for being indecisive—the "kiss of death" to many promising supervisory careers.

Step 3: Collect, Interpret, and Evaluate Information about Each Alternative

Usually there are many sources from which to gather information affecting a decision. Sometimes standing orders, policies, procedures, and rules provide relevant information. In fact, these documents may have already made the decision for you—or at least may indicate how you should decide. Other sources of information include your own experience, company records and reports, discussion with the people directly and indirectly involved, and personal observations.

✔ STOP & THINK

In the chapter preview, where do you think Jones's supervisor can get the information he needs to make his decision? What additional information beyond that given would be helpful to him in reaching the best decision?

⑤ Name some factors to keep in mind when making decisions.

Perhaps you've heard the saying "Tell me what you want to prove, and I'll get you the data to prove it." The effective evaluation of alternatives involves looking *objectively* at the pros and cons of each one. Choices can be evaluated in many ways. The information can be written down on a type of balance sheet, as shown in Exhibit 3-4, with the reasons for each

EXHIBIT **3-4**

Evaluating Alternatives

alternative on one side and the reasons against it on the other. Or a process of elimination can be used in which the undesirable (or less desirable) choices are dropped.

Step 4: Select the Preferred Alternative

Finally, you reach the point where you must make a choice. You look at your conclusions from step 3 and then logically and rationally pick the alternative you think is most desirable for all concerned from objective, ethical, and practical points of view.

Selecting the preferred alternative involves cost/benefit analysis and risk analysis. Using the technique of **cost/benefit analysis,** you estimate what each alternative will cost in terms of human, physical, and financial resources. Then you estimate the expected benefits. Finally, you compare the two estimates. You choose the one with the greatest payoff, where the ratio of benefits to cost is most favorable.

Analysis of risk is inherent in decision making. **Risk** is the possibility of defeat, disadvantage, injury, or loss. Prudent decision makers try to minimize risk by effectively forecasting outcomes and considering all variables.

cost/benefit analysis
Estimating and comparing the costs and benefits of alternatives.

risk The possibility of defeat, disadvantage, injury, or loss.

✔ **STOP & THINK**

From the information you are given in the chapter preview, what decision should Jones's supervisor make? Why?

Step 5: Implement the Decision

Effective decision making doesn't stop when you choose from among alternatives. The decision must be put into operation. For example, you might need to obtain and allocate some equipment and supplies. Or you might need to develop methods and procedures. Or you might have to select, train, or even terminate some employees. This is a difficult part of decision making, because you must face and deal with people who may not like your choice. Many good supervisory decisions are ineffective because of the way they're implemented.

Step 6: Follow Up, Evaluate, and Make Changes—If Needed

This last step in the decision-making process involves exercising management's control function. It determines whether the implementation of the decision is proceeding smoothly and achieving the desired results. If not, and the decision can be changed or modified, it should be. If it can't be changed, then you must "live with it" and try to make it succeed.

6 Decide whether to use the individual approach or the group approach when making decisions.

Approaches to Decision Making and Problem Solving

Two approaches that are particularly useful in both decision making and problem solving are the Myers-Briggs Type indicator and the Vroom-Yetton model. The Myers-Briggs Type indicator is the better known and is used throughout the world.

The Myers-Briggs Type Indicator®

The 126-item **Myers-Briggs Type indicator** (**MBTI®**) helps identify an individual's personal style.[1] Although it measures eight dichotomies of personality types, we will concern ourselves with only the four internal dimensions: (1) sensing versus (2) intuition and (3) thinking versus (4) feeling. These four are directly related to decision making and problem solving. (The Myers-Briggs concept is based on the work of scholar-physician Carl Gustav Jung, born in Switzerland and a contemporary of Sigmund Freud. Isabel Myers and her mother, Katherine Briggs, further refined and added to the basic theory.)

According to Myers & Briggs, people who rely primarily on *sensing*, or becoming aware of things through the five senses, tend to be patient, practical, and realistic. Those who rely primarily on *intuition*, tend to be impatient, idea and theory oriented, and creative. Although everyone uses both ways of perceiving, Myers & Briggs indicates that at an early age we develop a preference for one method over the other. Therefore, we tend to use our favorite approach and slight the one we enjoy less. Thus, people develop a set of traits based on whether they prefer sensing or intuition, as shown in the top half of Exhibit 3-5.

People who trust and prefer *thinking*, or using a rational, logical process to come to impersonal conclusions, are quite skillful in dealing with matters that require logic, objectivity, and careful examination of facts. On the other hand, those who trust and prefer *feeling*, or using innate processes that take into account one's own and others' values and beliefs, tend to be adept at working with other people and successful in applying skills in interpersonal and human relations. Such people are normally tactful and appreciative and have the ability to empathize with other people's problems and feelings. The bottom half of Exhibit 3-5 compares thinking and feeling types.

Although experience and growth opportunities can help develop weaker dichotomies, most people have developed two of them more than others. The ideal is to maintain a balance by developing capability in all four. This is especially important for decision making, since all four dichotomies can be valuable in the decision-making method described earlier.

EXHIBIT 3-5

Characteristics of Different Personality Types

How do you prefer to take in information? The S–N Dichotomy

Sensing	Intuition
People who prefer Sensing like to take in information that is real and tangible—what is actually happening. They are observant about the specifics of what is going on around them and are especially attuned to practical realities.	People who prefer Intuition like to take in information by seeing the big picture, focusing on the relationships and connections between facts. They want to grasp patterns and are especially attuned to seeing new possibilities.
Characteristics associated with people who prefer Sensing:	*Characteristics associated with people who prefer Intuition:*
• Oriented to present realities	• Oriented to future possibilities
• Factual and concrete	• Imaginative and verbally creative
• Focus on what is real and actual	• Focus on the patterns and meanings in data
• Observe and remember specifics	• Remember specifics when they relate to a pattern
• Build carefully and thoroughly toward conclusions	• Move quickly to conclusions, follow hunches
• Understand ideas and theories through practical applications	• Want to clarify ideas and theories before putting them into practice
• Trust experience	• Trust inspiration

Continued

EXHIBIT **3-5**

Continued

How do you make decisions? The T–F Dichotomy

Thinking	Feeling
People who prefer to use Thinking in decision making like to look at the logical consequences of a choice or action. They want to mentally remove themselves from the situation to examine the pros and cons objectively. They are energized by critiquing and analyzing to identify what's wrong with something so they can solve the problem. Their goal is to find a standard or principle that will apply in all similar situations.	People who prefer to use Feeling in decision making like to consider what is important to them and to others involved. They mentally place themselves into the situation to identify with everyone so they can make decisions based on their values about honoring people. They are energized by appreciating and supporting others and look for qualities to praise. Their goal is to create harmony and treat each person as a unique individual.

Characteristics associated with people who prefer Thinking:

- Analytical
- Use cause-and-effect reasoning
- Solve problems with logic
- Strive for an objective standard of truth
- Reasonable
- Can be "tough-minded"
- Fair—want everyone treated equally

Characteristics associated with people who prefer Feeling:

- Empathetic
- Guided by personal values
- Assess impacts of decisions on people
- Strive for harmony and positive interactions
- Compassionate
- May appear "tenderhearted"
- Fair—want everyone treated as an individual

Note: While the names of some of the MBTI preferences are familiar words, the MBTI meaning of the preferences is somewhat different from everyday use. Remember:

- "Extravert" does not mean "talkative" or "loud."
- "Introvert" does not mean "shy" or "inhibited."

- "Feeling" does not mean "emotional."
- "Judging" does not mean "judgmental."
- "Perceiving" does not mean "perceptive."

Sensing, which helps in developing and facing facts as well as being realistic about the nature of the problem or opportunity, is helpful in step 1, recognizing a problem or opportunity. *Intuition,* on the other hand, is used in areas where creativity is needed to see possibilities and develop opportunities. It is therefore helpful in step 2, developing alternative courses of action.

Because *thinking* is impersonal and logically considers the consequences of cause and effect, it is helpful in step 3, evaluating the alternatives. *Feeling* comes into play when it is necessary to consider the values and ethics of others and the impact of the final decision on them. This provides sensitivity in selecting the preferred alternative implementing it.

Ideally, as a result of new experiences such as working in a team or being coached or through training, we can develop balance and function effectively in all dichotomies. Although she is retired now, a bank officer who developed such balance while we were consulting with her bank is profiled next.

A Well Balanced Meyers-Briggs Profile

Linda Dean Fucci was secretary/treasurer at Auburn National Bank in Auburn, Alabama. Her duties included investment portfolio management, shareholder relations, asset liability management, strategic planning, accounting procedures, budgeting, tax planning, and control. In 1994 her duties were expanded to include the departments of data processing, marketing, and electronic services. She was also promoted to senior vice-president of the bank's holding company.

After graduating from Southern Union Junior College with a grade point average (GPA) of 4.0, she completed flight training to the level of commercial pilot and flight instructor. Linda has always regretted not completing a bachelor of science degree in business, but this lack has not been a barrier to her career achievement. For example, she graduated from Louisiana State University's Graduate School of Banking of the South—one of the premier schools in the country for bankers on a fast career track—in 1986 with a GPA of 2.73 (out of 3.0). In a graduating class of 353 bankers, she not only ranked ninth in academic achievements but also was elected class president. The Alabama Senate passed a resolution of commendation for that achievement. Her previous bank president, William Walker, singled her out in a speech at a state banking meeting as the best chief financial officer, at the time, of any bank in the state.

Linda's decision-making style is intuitive-thinking. Although these two dimensions are her strongest, she is quite flexible. Through experience and effort, she has developed the sensing and feeling sides as well. In a confidential employee survey evaluating the effectiveness of the top-level Auburn National Bank officers, Linda received an excellent rating. Under the heading of "Additional Comments," one of the employees made this observation: "Linda is a great officer of the bank, representing us in a highly professional manner. She is a great manager and leader, earning a high degree of respect from her employees. She is my mentor. When I grow up, I want to be just like her."

Asked to describe her management philosophy and core values, Linda responded with the following impromptu remarks:

> Maybe because I came up through the ranks, I can remember what it was like to be at all different levels. I can remember being unsure of myself and how different reactions made me feel. I try not to reprimand when people make mistakes but to understand and teach. I try never to make them feel "stupid." I do not think that people make errors intentionally. . . .
>
> I think that people need to feel important. Sometimes all it takes is a title. I do not like to call people "clerks." Doesn't "funds management assistant" sound better than "clerk"?
>
> I try to provide my employees with as much knowledge as I can. I sincerely believe that shared knowledge is increased power. The more people in my department know, then the better they do their jobs and the better I, my department, and the whole organization look. I don't think anything makes me feel better than to teach someone something and then see them excel at putting it to use.
>
> Once my employees have learned enough to progress to a given level, I try to leave them alone to get their jobs done. I know they will make some mistakes, but I also think they will learn more this way.
>
> I try to give lots and lots of credit. Whenever I am praised for something done in my department, if others had a hand in it, I give them credit. On the other hand, I try not to pass on the blame. We deal with that back in the department.
>
> I try always to be honest with the employees in my department.
>
> I guess it all comes down to treating others the way I want to be treated; putting myself in their place and feeling how they feel; sensing what is difficult for them to say, to do, and trying to make it easier.
>
> I believe in participative management. I have seen it work in our institution. People are experts in different areas, and the pooling of that expertise creates an exceptional organization. People work harder for a plan they have had a part in than a plan simply dictated to them.

Source: Discussions and correspondence with Linda Dean Fucci.

Carl Jung saw type development as a lifelong, never-ending process. People grow and develop problem-solving and decision-making processes if they have the ability to learn from experience. In our profile of Linda Fucci (intuitive-thinking), we saw an example of development of the sensing and feeling dimensions. As a result, she has the ability to use the appropriate dimension at the appropriate time, thus gaining good balance and wholeness in problem solving and decision making.

The Vroom-Yetton Model

The **Vroom-Yetton model** provides guidelines on the extent to which subordinates are involved in decision making or problem solving.[2] This involvement may run the gamut from consensus decision making by a natural or self-managing work team, a committee, or an ad hoc task force to the manager making the decision with minimal or no involvement of others. The assistance of subordinates may occur at any of the decision-making steps.

The extent of employee involvement is a contingency call based on the situation, the quality of information available to the decision making, the importance of subordinates' acceptance of the decision, and the time to make the decision.

Participation. Exhibit 3-6 defines five alternative participation styles, as developed by Vroom and Yetton. There are two autocratic approaches (A and B), two consultative approaches (C and D), and one group consensus approach (E). These five approaches represent the varying degrees of participation by others a manager uses in decision making.

Appropriate Style. A manager can use a decision tree in determining which approach to use. One example of such a tree is shown in Exhibit 3-7. The questions shown at the top help the decision maker determine the characteristics of a given decision situation.

To use the model for a particular situation, you start at the left-hand side of the tree and work toward the right. When you encounter a box, answer the corresponding question and

---

EXHIBIT **3-6**

Managers' Participation
Styles for Making
Decisions

Participation Style	Description
A	You solve the problem or make the decision yourself, using the information available to you at the present time.
B	You obtain any necessary information from subordinates, then decide on a solution to the problem yourself.
C	You share the problem with the relevant subordinates individually, getting their ideas and suggestions without bringing them together as a group. Then *you* make the decision.
D	You share the problem with your subordinates in a group meeting, in which you obtain their ideas and suggestions. Then *you* make the decision.
E	You share the problem with your subordinates as a group. Together you generate and evaluate alternatives and attempt to reach agreement (consensus) on a solution. You can provide the group with information or ideas, but you do not try to press them to adopt "your" solution, and you are willing to accept and implement any solution that has the support of the entire group.

Note: A & B = autocratic, C & D = consultative, E = group consensus.

Source: Adapted and reprinted from *Leadership and Decision-Making,* by Victor H. Vroom and Philip W. Yetton, by permission of the University of Pittsburgh Press. © 1973 University of Pittsburgh Press.

EXHIBIT 3-7

Decision Tree, Governing
Group Problems

1	2	3	4	5	6	7
Is there a quality requirement such that one solution is likely to be more rational than another?	Do you have sufficient information to make a high-quality decision?	Is the problem structured?	Is acceptance of decision by subordinates critical to implementation?	Is it reasonably certain that your subordinates would accept the decision if you were to make it by yourself?	Do subordinates share the organizational goals to be obtained in solving this problem?	Is conflict among subordinately likely in preferred solution?

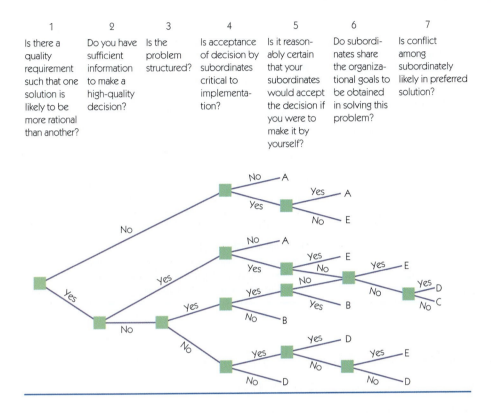

proceed to the next appropriate box. The decision style designation you finally reach will suggest which of the participation styles from Exhibit 3-6 you should probably use.

There are other parts of Vroom's and Yetton's theory that are too detailed to present here. This classic model has been the subject of much attention and is being tested and evaluated by many management researchers.[3]

Two cases at the end of this chapter will give you an opportunity to put the model to use. Although a model such as the one just discussed can help in selecting the best decision-making method, a manager's personal style also has a major impact on the method chosen. (The following Exhibit 3-8 shows how to use the model in making the decision on a student banquet date.)

Creative Problem Solving

More organizations and individual managers are involving subordinates in decision making and problem solving, particularly using styles similar to D and E in the Vroom-Yetton model. As a senior technician and union leader in a paper mill told one of the authors, "Management used to tell us what to do; now they ask us." One of the primary reasons for this trend is the concept of synergy.

EXHIBIT 3-8

The Vroom-Yetton Model:
Which Decision Style
to Use

Decision Problem

As president of the Student Management Club at State University, you must make a decision concerning a date for the annual student banquet.

Q1 Is there a quality requirement such that one solution is likely to be more rational than another?

Ans Yes. One solution is likely to be more rational since there are various dates that will be unsatisfactory because of competing activities.

Q2 Do you have sufficient information to make a high-quality decision?

Ans No. You may have certain information on competing dates for some officially scheduled university activites, but there may be some other kinds of activities going on that you are unaware of.

Q3 Is the problem structured?

Ans Yes. Selection of a given date for a banquet to be held within the next month is a well-structured decision problem.

Q4 Is acceptance of the decision by your subordinates critical to implementation?

Ans Yes. If the subordinates (and others) don't show up, the banquet is a failure.

Q5 Is it reasonably certain that the decision would be accepted by your subordinates if you were to make it by yourself?

Ans No. You might accidentally select a date that would not be suitable to your subordinates. For example, the day you select could be one on which subordinates have a major exam or term papers due the following day.

Q6 Do members share the view that the banquet date is important?

Ans Yes. Members have shown good attendance at meetings and consider the banquet the highlight of the year. Awards are presented, next year's officers announced, and so on.

Optimum Decision Style

As president, you should share the problem with members as a group, with the group generating and evaluating alternatives, and should attempt to arrive at a consensus decision.

The Concept of Synergy and some Processes of Creative Problem Solving

Synergy means that the whole is greater than the sum of the parts. This concept is especially applicable in the use of teams and ad hoc task forces in problem solving. Assume that an ad hoc task force of five persons is presented with a complex problem that has an impact on the entire organization. If the team reaches a synergistic solution to the complex problem, then mathematically synergy can be defined as $1 + 1 + 1 + 1 + 1 = $ more than 5.

Increasingly, this type of synergy is being achieved by teams throughout the world. This emphasis on synergistic teamwork is recognized in the United States by Rochester Institute of Technology's College of Business and *USA Today's* Quality Cup Awards. These awards are presented in five categories to teams that have made outstanding contributions in products or services. The categories are manufacturing, service, nonprofit, government, and organizations with fewer than 500 employees.

7 Discuss some ways of improving decision making.

Developing Creativity

Scientists generalize that the right hemisphere of the brain captures our intuitive impulses. If we think of ourselves as problem solvers/decision makers, the right side of the brain generates ideas and is where imagination originates. Right-hemispheric functions are frequent catalysts for solution alternatives.

Alternatively, the brain's left hemisphere functions in logical, analytical, and linear ways, allowing the decision maker to evaluate his or her intuitive, imaginative alternatives. This is where judgment enters into the process. Although the brain has a multifunctional capacity, the decision maker may allow his or her preferred brain functioning to dominate and can allow left-side evaluation and analysis to encroach on right-brain intuitive ideas prematurely.

To gain the maximum benefit from ad hoc task forces, quality circles, self-managing work teams, or any problem-solving effort, the brain's left-hemisphere functions must be restrained initially. The key to doing so is to make use of the concept of deferred judgment. This is the idea behind brainstorming, and the secret is to develop right-hemispheric skills and to use them appropriately. After the ideas are generated, it is helpful to use analytical brain functions to evaluate and judge which insights are good, cost-effective, and so forth. Using right-hemisphere functions as thought generators and following them with left-brained functions result in powerfully effective "whole-brained" creativity. Three techniques that are very useful in the idea generation process are brainstorming, the Crawford Slip technique, and the nominal grouping technique.

Brainstorming

One of the most effective techniques in creative problem solving is brainstorming. **Brainstorming** refers to a group of individuals responding to a question, such as "How can we improve communication?" without evaluating the ideas as they are generated. The ideas are thrown out no matter how silly they may appear and without regard to the rank of individuals or the value of any idea. Sorting out the value of respective ideas comes later. Larry Hirschorn, management consultant and writer, has suggested four excellent guidelines when using this powerful technique:

1. The group favors quantity over quality.
2. Team members refrain from judging anyone's contributions; they can ask questions later, in the evaluation part.
3. Team members avoid censoring.
4. Pride of authority is minimized; team members should feel free to offer variants and build on one another's ideas.[4]

Brainstorming is especially useful in developing alternatives during step 2 or the decision-making or problem-solving process. In most cases in creative problem solving, the team will draw from a number of alternatives in putting together the action plan. In addition to identifying possible solutions, brainstorming is also useful in these dimensions of creative problem solving:

- Defining all possible problems
- Redefining problems
- Determining all possible causes for a problem
- Listing all possible actions for implementing the chosen solution

Unfortunately, based on the observations of the authors, formally appointed committees and management meetings with subordinates rarely use brainstorming in their deliberation. For example, a faculty committee spent the allotted time for a meeting (two hours) debating the pros and cons of the second idea presented. On the other hand, ad hoc task forces and problem-solving teams tend to use brainstorming in a more creative and effective manner.

✔ STOP & THINK

Why do you think formal committees or a boss meeting with his or her subordinates seldom uses brainstorming in problem-solving endeavors?

The Crawford Slip Technique

The **Crawford Slip technique** was developed by Professor C.C. Crawford at the University of Southern California. It makes use of two elements that are important in achieving creativity—fluency and flexibility. **Fluency** is the ability to let ideas flow out of your head like water over a waterfall, and **flexibility** is the ability to use free association to generate or classify ideas in categories. Materials needed are a number of 3" x 5" scratch pads and a number of empty boxes distributed among the participants. The process starts by telling participants that they are about to engage in a new type of problem solving that will generate 50 to 100 new ideas.

For example, this technique was used with the top management of Baldor Electric Company, a very successful company listed on the New York Stock Exchange. Unfortunately, one of the large motors it produced was losing money. The following series of steps was initiated to deal with the problem.[5]

1. Participants were asked not to pause to evaluate ideas and not to generate such thoughts as "We've tried this before."

2. Every participant was given a 3" x 5" scratch pad.

3. In this technique, the leader presents a problem in how-to form. In the case of Baldor Electric, the problem presented was, "How can we reduce costs on our 300 series motors without affecting quality?"

4. Each person would write down as many answers to the problem as time would permit. After an idea was written on a slip, it was placed in the idea bank (box) anonymously.

5. After 10 minutes, the idea boxes were collected and task forces established. In the case of Baldor, there were three task forces. Idea slips were distributed to them like cards dealt from a deck.

6. Each task force was charged with arranging the ideas in categories, using judgment (left side of the brain) to throw out weak ideas and then developing the good ideas and presenting recommendations to the larger group.

The chief executive officer of the company then judged what ideas were most relevant to solving the problem and decided to implement them. Please note that although there was considerable participation in the process, *one person made the final decision*. In many instances, this is a desirable approach in using participative management.

Nominal Grouping Technique

The **nominal grouping technique (NGT)** also makes use of brainstorming, and we have found the technique very effective in developing creativity and generating useful information. Nominal grouping is a structured group technique for generating ideas through round-robin individual responses, group sharing without criticism, and written balloting. The authors have found it to be exceptionally beneficial to use nominal grouping in working with organizations. Exhibit 3-9 identifies the steps in nominal grouping when it is used in this manner. The following example illustrates the steps in the process.

Two of the authors were asked to participate in a management development program for a branch plant of a corporation headquartered in our home state. The plant, located in another state, was struggling to achieve a break-even point, and the executive vice-president hired us to conduct management training sessions. The authors were rotating training sessions and the report after the first session was that the "canned management training was similar to placing a Band-Aid on a festering boil." During the break, the employees complained about issues and problems the training program did not directly address. A consultation with the executive vice-president resulted in a change in strategy for the next session.

EXHIBIT 3-9

Steps in Nominal Grouping

Divide into groups of six or nine persons.

>*Without* interaction, list the strengths you feel are associated with Question I, then list the problems for Question 2. (Time: 6 minutes.)

Select a recorder.

 a. The recorder asks each member, one at a time, to read from his or her card one strength associated with Question I. *Example:* What are the strengths of this plant?

 b. The recorder writes each strength exactly as it is read.

 c. Those having the same strength should raise hands. The recorder checkmarks each strength once for each person raising a hand.

 d. When all Question I strengths are recorded, the procedure is repeated for Question 2 problems. *Example:* What are the problems preventing this plant from reaching its potential effectiveness?

Discuss the two lists. Clarify, defend, elaborate, or add other items as needed. (Time: 5 minutes.)

>*Without* interaction, each member lists on an index card the *five* items he or she considers most important with reference to Question I; do the same for Question 2.

The recorder collects and records the votes.

Using the nominal grouping process, the 25 participants (supervisors, managers, and staff personnel) were asked to respond to two questions:

1. What are the strengths of the plant?

2. What are the problems preventing this plant from reaching its potential effectiveness?

Twelve strengths were generated, and 55 problems were initially identified. Through nominal voting, the top five problems were prioritized; task forces from the participants were formed, and action plans were developed to solve the plant's more pressing problems.

✔ STOP & THINK

Since in this process only five problems were addressed, speculate on what happened to the majority of the other problems.

. . . .

If your answer was, "They dissipated," you are correct.

Developing and implementing the action plans were catalysts in shifting the plant from a low performer to a high performer within a year.

Ethical Considerations Play a Part

8 Explain the role of ethics in the supervisor's decision making.

Supervisors must be particularly concerned with ethical considerations when making decisions and solving problems. They should have a true concern for the well-being of others, both inside and outside the organization. Therefore, supervisors should not only obey all laws and conform to the ethical codes of practice established by their employer and society, they should also have a personal set of ethical principles that guides their actions. However, the difficult question is, what is and what isn't ethical?

Ethics are the standards used to judge the "rightness" or "wrongness" of one person's behavior toward others. As this concept of ethical behavior is the individual's personal *ethic*, it is the highest and most rigid level of behavior. The next highest level is adhering to professional and organizational *codes of ethics,* which are statements of what is and isn't acceptable behavior. The lowest level is the *legal level*, where we are all expected to adhere to the "law of the land."

In 2001, Sherron Watkins was vice-president of corporate development for Enron, one of the largest companies in America. She referred to her company as having an "electric atmosphere" with people "energized to change the world." However, on August 22, 2001, Watkins sacrificed all of this when she composed a memorandum to her chairman informing him of her misgivings about various questionable activities taking place in the upper echelon of the company.

From a simple natural gas pipeline business, Enron flourished with the help of trading chief Jeffrey Skilling and his financial adviser, Andrew Fastow. Watkins admired Enron's lack of a strict organization structure, which allowed entrepreneurs to be more creative and pursue various opportunities.

What happened to break the stride of this booming firm? Why should Sherron Watkins risk losing the company that had provided her with so much success and opportunity for creative ventures?

Sherron Watkins risked her reputation and her professional stability for what she felt was moral and good. What impact will her actions have on the management of North American companies?

© Ron Sachs/CORBIS

Watkins grew up in a rural town in Texas, graduated from the University of Texas in Austin with a degree in accounting, and began working at Arthur Andersen in New York. In 1993, she moved to Houston to take a job with Enron, where she quickly rose through the ranks as a result of her hard work and decidedly no-nonsense attitude.

In late June of 2001, Watkins began to work directly under Andrew Fastow, but while managing his records, she became exceedingly nervous about vague and improperly documented business arrangements. Watkins sent an anonymous note to her boss and Enron chairman, Kenneth Lay, expressing her concern about unethical activities happening at Enron. Later she arranged a meeting with Lay again expressing her disappointment and frustration that these unethical activities were happening at Enron. Lay promised to investigate.

However, a few months later, the company announced a $618 million third-quarter loss and was forced to file for bankruptcy in December. The repercussions were disastrous. Thousands lost their jobs, and many lost their life savings. Fastow faced criminal charges for money laundering, fraud, and conspiracy, and Lay was charged with insider trading. America's faith in free enterprise had been drastically eroded.

Were Sherron Watkins' actions worth the fallout? Since then, as one of America's most famous whistle-blowers, she has argued in published articles and speeches that her actions were not only justifiable, but ultimately beneficial. Watkins insisted that businesses must be judged on more than just the profits they create, and that "we need to reward the good, ethical ones." Although many people were hurt by her actions, she feels vindicated that her insistence on morality in business has lessened the chance that corruption will be rewarded.[6]

Finally, in March 2006 Sherron Watkins, testifying in the fraud and conspiracy trial of Lay and fellow former boss Jeff Skilling, stated that in the memo she wrote to Lay, . . . "I am incredibly nervous we will implode in a wave of accounting scandals. This was not just aggressive accounting, it was fraudulent accounting. I couldn't believe we had done it." In a later meeting with her, Lay had promised an investigation, but the probe was conducted by the lawyers and accountants who originally approved the questionable deals and who, not surprisingly, found them to be OK again. "I thought the investigation was bogus," she said. Further, she testified that she was not aware that in the days after her memo and meeting with Lay that Lay had sold $16 million in Enron stock to repay loans from the company. Also, it was only later, in an appearance before a congressional committee in Washington, that she found out the company almost immediately began looking into the possibility of firing her.

Lay and Skilling face multiple criminal charges that they knew of the financial fraud in Enron but hid it from investors so the stock price would not fall. They have denied wrongdoing and blamed the fall of Enron on Fastow.[7] Unfortunately, shortly after the trial Kenneth Lay died of a heart attack while on vacation. In the wake of Enron, the unethical business practices of other companies (WorldCom, Tyco, ImClone, etc.) came to light. WorldCom, for example, disclosed that nearly $4 billion in improper accounting was used to boost profits in one of the largest frauds in corporate history.

The corporate misdeeds of Enron, followed by a string of other company scandals, have brought heightened awareness of the devastating results of unethical business practices. In June 2002, President Bush conducted several hundred investigations. Justice Department spokesman Bryan Sierra stated, "Enron was certainly a wake-up call and the department made among its top goals to prosecute these cases, with the hope of restoring confidence in the marketplace."[8] In July 2002, President Bush created the Corporate Fraud Task Force.

(Before this 7e is published, there may be verdicts in the Enron case.)

Unfortunately, business leaders are not the only ones acting unethically. The following headlines and article appeared in the Mobile Register, Mobile, Alabama.

Charity Leaders' Pay Soars Under Jobs Program for Disabled

Nonprofits hiring workers with relatively mild impairments for contracts rather than the severely disabled—and new money rolling in is boosting chief executive officer (CEO) pay

When Congress created the nation's most ambitious jobs program for Americans with severe disabilities, the idea was straightforward and rich with compassion. Federal agencies would reserve contracts for small nonprofit workshops that hired epileptics, paraplegics, and the mentally retarded to make simple products such as mousetraps, blackboards, and first-aid kits. The disabled would gain a decent paycheck, some self-esteem, and a chance to learn skills that someday might land them a better job.

More than three decades later, the nonprofits increasingly are hiring workers who are mildly disabled, if at all, with aching backs, substance-abuse problems, and other maladies common in the American workplace. This new class of federally subsidized worker is getting the highest-paid jobs, while many of the most severely disabled toil for pennies an hour.

[However], their bosses are benefiting handsomely, with leaders at many of the program's biggest charities pulling in private sector–style compensation as the new money rolls in. At least a dozen earn $350,000 or more a year, and average pay and benefits for top executives at the program's largest nonprofits have grown more than three times faster than their workers' pay.

The program's key requirement—that 3 of every 4 hours of work is performed by people with severe disabilities—is policed under what's essentially an honor system. Oversight is so weak that the biggest contractor, a Texas nonprofit, amassed $834 million in government sales despite repeated findings that it couldn't document many of its workers' disabilities.

This radical reordering of the government's priorities comes at a cost. Many of the most severely disabled workers, who labor at charities with shoestring budgets, have been left behind.

"Like a lot of federal contracting, the big money drives it," said David Wiegan, who believes workers at his small nonprofit in McMinnville, Oregon, are simply too disabled to win many of the contracts now offered by the program. He said some bigger charities are drifting away from their social welfare missions, "I think they get sucked in, and I think they lose their sense of what's right and wrong when they're tempted by a lot of big dollars."[9]

This was certainly not the outcome that the federal program intended.

However, on the positive side of social responsibility and ethics, many corporations such as Mattel, Nike, and Home Depot are using their clout to improve working conditions around the world. Following are excerpts from *USA Today:*

Since launching its codes in 1997, Mattel has cut off several dozen suppliers and licensees whose factories fell short of Mattel's standards—a model for codes adopted recently by the International Council of Toy Industries. "We call it Zero Tolerance," says Senior Vice-president, Jim Walter. "If we find evidence of systematic violations, we are not going to do business with you."

Companies have come a long way since the 1980s, when public outrage against apartheid forced many to withdraw their investments in South Africa, and the 1990s, when apparel and footwear companies were attacked for sweatshop labor conditions in suppliers' plants. . . .

But corporations clearly are moving on the issue by adopting:

Codes of conduct. About 2,000 companies have joined the United Nations Global Compact, which urges businesses to embrace labor, human rights and environmental practices, from banning child and forced labor to using environmentally sound technologies. . . .

Social goals that boost business. In 2004 business professors Frank Schmidt and Sara Rynes at the University of Iowa looked at 52 studies on corporate social responsibility over a 30 year period. They found that well-run, profitable businesses also boasted solid social and environmental records. . . .

Critics such as David Vogel, a University of California, Berkeley, business professor and author of *The Market for Virtue*, says corporate social responsibility is overrated. Investors don't care, and consumers won't pay higher prices for environmentally safe goods. "Companies will make the world a better place as long as it doesn't cost too much," he says. "That's the limit of corporate responsibility."

Better monitoring. A decade ago, U.S companies had few people to inspect thousands of manufacturing sites. Their superficial audits "didn't get at the root causes of problems," says Auret van Heerden, executive director of the nonprofit Fair Labor Association.

Today, Van Heerden says, more corporations are strengthening their monitoring and teaching suppliers how to better run their plants and manage workers. . . .

The audits—by Mattel and Prakash Sethi, a business professor at Baruch College and founder of the International Center for Corporate Accountability—praise some plants but warn others to shape up or lose Mattel's business. "It's not empty rhetoric," Sethi says. "Vendors have a financial incentive to comply with Mattel's codes."

Nike also is a seasoned veteran of audits. In the 1990s, the company was a favorite target of activists because of foreign sweatshops run by its suppliers.

Now Nike inspects many of its 1,000 suppliers' factories worldwide. It grades them from A to D and warns poorly run sites to improve or get dropped, says Nike Vice-President Dusty Kidd. "Beyond the Policing," Kidd says, "factories need to manage their work and manage it well." Critics accuse the companies of compromising their values so that Chinese authorities will let them operate in the huge market. Despite the growing number of U.S. companies there, labor conditions and violence against workers have worsened, charges Sharon Hom, executive director of Human Rights in China. "Their presence alone will not lead to improvements," Hom says. As the China debate heats up, it's clear that companies' social responsibilities will loom larger everywhere as international trade grows.

"We're drafting rules of the road in the new global economy," says Michael Posner, executive director of Human Rights First. "We've made progress, but there's still a long way to go."

Source: Edward Iwata, "How Barbie Is Making Business a Little Better," *USA Today*, March 2, 2006, p. B1.

Model of Effective and Ethical Decision Making

The Bank of the Ozarks serves as an excellent example of ethical decision making and community involvement. Unlike many large banks, Bank of the Ozarks is geared toward relationship banking and giving back to the community where they operate. It is the amazing story of entrepreneurship and sound decision making of the bank's Chairman and CEO, George Gleason, the son of a business man who inspired George to think big and with an entrepreneurial spirit.

George received his undergraduate degree from Conway's Hendrix College and went on 3 years later to graduate, first in his class, from the University of Arkansas at Fayetteville School of Law. He wrote the top paper on the Arkansas Law Examination.

Bank of the Ozarks branch location.

© Joel Rafkin/Photoedit

After 2 years with a law firm, George decided to strike out on his own, realizing his career shift was risky. "With just $10,000 to his name, he managed to get a Little Rock bank to loan him $3.6 million to buy the Bank of Ozark. It was, he says, something 'only a single 25-year-old would be foolish enough to do.'" Gleason contacted the local businesses to introduce himself and, according to Kenneth Smith, now Bank of the Ozarks [chief financial officer] CFO, became known and respected in the community for his work ethic and aggressive approach to learning his new business. He studied bank regulation books all day, every day, to learn what he could do and couldn't do legally in the banking business.

Twenty-five years later Bank of the Ozarks boasts 52 branches in Arkansas and outposts in North Carolina and Texas—and new branches keep coming. Gleason's organization claims the fifth largest share of Arkansas banking market, and among Arkansas-chartered banks it has the second largest share.

In 1995, Gleason moved the headquarters of the bank to Little Rock with a strategy in mind. At the time financial institutions thought automation and internet was the way to go, but Gleason believed customers would still want personal contact and believed that "branches were not dead" and put his "de novo strategy" (Latin for once more or anew) to work. Instead of expanding through acquisitions, he believed Bank of the Ozarks could build a more stable corporate culture by building new locations from the ground up. "If two banks of size merge, there are two different cultures, two different ways of doing business, two different philosophies that have to come together. But by building one branch at a time, we may typically have 20 or 30 new employees with whom you can sit down and talk about your bank and your way of doing business."

Source: Scott A. Johnson, "George Granville Gleason II, *Arkansas Democrat Gazette*, March 1, 2006.

Gleason's de novo strategy and emphasis on relationships work well because while experts in the banking field expect a new office to take a year to get to the break-even point, the Bank of the Ozarks usually reaches this goal in only 6 months. This is due in large part to good personal relationships.

Obviously the Bank of the Ozarks has made an impression on the people in the markets in Arkansas. Based on FDIC deposit market share dating from June 30, 2003 to June 30, 2004, Bank of the Ozarks had the largest volume of internally generated deposit growth of any FDIC insured institution in Arkansas. During that 12-month period, deposits grew $241 million.[10] The Bank has plans for the *de novo* strategy in Texas and North Carolina.

A Business Model That Works

"Our continued success has come from the effective implementation of our growth and *de novo* branching strategy first implemented in 1994. Successful implementation of this strategy requires that we hire talented and experienced bankers, place them in prime locations in good markets, and arm them with products and services that enjoy a competitive advantage. Over the past 10 years we have proven this strategy works."

"While there are many important elements to successful implementation of this strategy, a key element is providing competitive advantage. We do this by providing our customers a compelling combination of products, great service and relationships with our bankers. Our customers want many of the products and services the "big" banks offer, but they also desire the friendly, personal service of a "hometown" bank and a personal relationship with their bankers. We have the products and the services we need to compete with the big banks, but more importantly we are deeply committed to developing personal relationships with our customers and providing exceptional service. Our customers, both large and small, are our future and we will keep that truth clearly in focus."

2005 and Beyond

"We are very pleased with our 2004 results, and we are excited as we look ahead to 2005 and beyond. Even after reporting to consecutive quarters of record net income and diluted earnings per share, we will not rest on past accomplishments. Our focus is clearly on the future as we believe our best opportunities are ahead."

"Our entire team worked hard to accomplish these 2004 results and we will continue to work hard. We welcome the new year and the challenges it brings. We want to make sure that Bank of the Ozarks continues to be, "The Right Bank at the Right Time" for all our customers and our shareholders."

Source: Bank of the Ozarks, Inc. Annual Report, 2004.

EXHIBIT 3-10

Bank of the Ozarks
Banking Offices

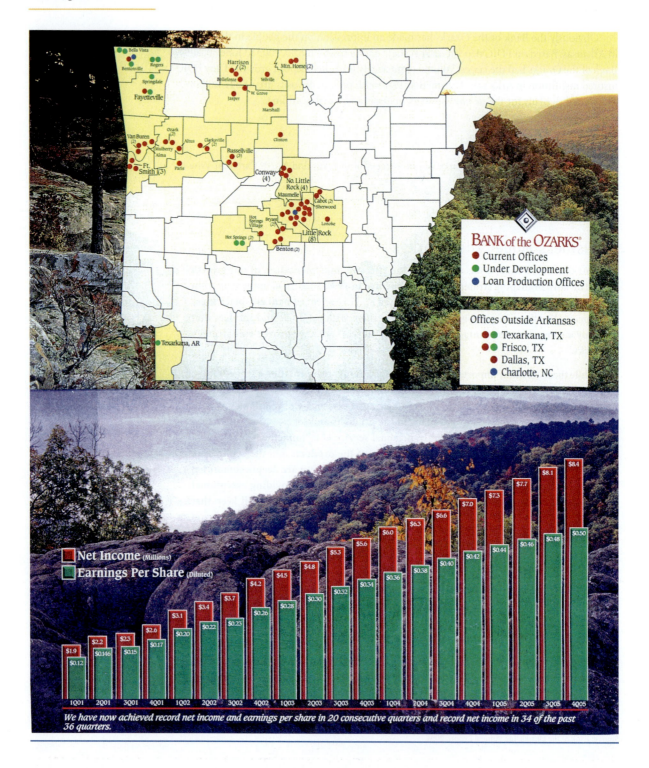

We have now achieved record net income and earnings per share in 20 consecutive quarters and record net income in 34 of the past 36 quarters.

EXHIBIT **3-11**

Bank of the Ozarks
Community Involvement

By combining our financial support and resources with caring employees who volunteer their time and talent, we strive to enrich lives and strengthen the communities we call home.

*The Bank of the Ozarks Run For their Lives 5K Race benefited six Arkansas youth ministries in 2005 providing $285,000 in net proceeds to **Young Life, Fellowship of Christian Athletes, LTCare, P.A.R.K., Ministry to the Inner City,** and **S.T.E.P.***

4-H Foundation • A Women's Place • ACORN (Association of Community Organizations for Reform Now) • American Association of Retired Persons • American Cancer Society • American Diabetes Association • American Heart Association • American Legion • American Lung Association of Arkansas • Argenta Community Development Corporation • Arkansas Arts Center Children's Theatre • Arkansas Black Caucus Foundation • Arkansas Black Hall of Fame Foundation • Arkansas Children's Hospital Foundation • Arkansas Department of Health • Arkansas Diabetes Association • Arkansas Economic Development Foundation • Arkansas Fallen Firefighters • Arkansas Future Farmers of America Foundation • Arkansas Leadership Prayer Breakfast • Arkansas Minority Business Development Roundatable • Arkansas Minoority Supplier Development Council • Arkansas Prostate Cancer Foundation • Arkansas Rice Depot • Arkansas State Board of Nursing Scholarship Found • Baptist Health Foundation • Baxter Regional Medical Center • Bend of the River Arts Council • Bethany Christian Services • Big Brothers Big Sisters • Black Community Developers • CARE for Animals • CARTI Foundation • Center for Healing Hearts and Spirits • Center for Youth and Families • Christian Commpetition • Community Service Clearinghouse • Conductive Education of Northwest Arkansas • Consumer Credit Counseling Services • Conway Human Development Volunteer Council • Crawford Sebastian County Community Development Corporation • Credit Counseling of Arkansas • Crisis Pregnancy Center of Central Arkansas, Inc. • Easter Seals Arkansas • Famil,y Service Agency • Frisco Family Service Center • Habitat for Humanity • Inner City FutureNet • Johnson County Community Foundation • Joshua Ministries • Junior Achievment of Arkjansas, Inc. • Junior Auxiliary • Keys to Success IDA • League of United Latin American Citizens • Lions Clubs • Livin It • Lonoke Country Council of Aging • March of Diames • Marion County Senior Center • Martin Luther King Commission • Maumelle Veterans Memorial Committee • Muscular Dystrophy Association • Museum of Discovery • National Conference for Community & Justice • Northwest Arkansas Economic Development District, Inc. • Ozark Area Youth Organization • Ozark Music Center • Ozark Rape Crisis Center • P.H.O.E.B.E (People Helping Others Excel By Example) • Philander Smith College • Pulaski technical College Youthbuild • Relay for Life • River Valley Food Bank • Rotary Club • Russellville Development Foundation • Saline Memorial Hospital • Single Parent Scholarship Found • Special Olympics Arkansas • St. Edward Mercy Foundation, Inc. • St Mark/East Wind Community Development Corp • The Downtown Partnership • Together—Jobs for the River Valley • Twin Lakes Community Foundation • Union Rescue Mission • United Way • Universal Housing • Urban Financial Services Coalition • Van Buren County Conservation Center • Waatershed • Women's Foundation of Arkansas • World Services for the Blind • Youth Home

Now a Brief Review of Performance for 2005

"While 2005 was a challenging year for many bank stocks, we feel our stock performed relatively well. According to Bloomberg, L.P., in 2005 our total return to shareholders, assuming reinvestment of dividends in Company share, was 9.8 percent for the year, compared to the NASDAQ Financial Index with a total return of 2.4 percent for the year and the NASDAQ Bank Index with a total return of −1.9 percent. We are even more pleased with our long-term performance. If you had purchased our shares on July 31, 1997, shortly after our initial public offering, held them through 2005 (approximately 8.4 years) and reinvested your dividends in Company share, your total return would be 840 percent, or 30.5 percent compounded annually. As substantial shareholders ourselves, we find these results to be very satisfying, . . . [and] look forward to pursuing new goals in 2006."

Source: Bank of the Ozarks, Inc., 2005 Annual Report.

A Winning Team

The steady growth of Bank of the Ozarks is due in large part to good business decisions (de novo strategy) and good personal relations. But during the growth and success, the Bank and its employees do not turn a deaf ear to the communities it serves (Exhibit 3-10).

Bank of the Ozarks employees volunteer thousands of hours to support community projects. As an example look no further than Angela Payne of the Clinton office. Angela met a family who had fled to Arkansas from St. Bernard Parish in Louisiana during Hurricane Katrina. In addition to attending to their urgent financial matters, she immediately arranged for donated medical care, housing, furnishing, and veterinary care for their pets and was even able to assist them in finding jobs in Clinton. The list of community endeavors is long; to name a few:

- Support new and existing businesses.

- Create affordable housing through loans and investments.

- Assist in establishing and repairing credit. One such program is the Crawford Sebastian Community Development Corporation's Credit Repair Program for which Bank of the Ozarks is the primary funding source.

- Provides financial support to hundreds of worthwhile organizations such as Ozarks Run for Their Lives 5K, Arkansas Art Center, Arkansas Symphony Orchestra, and many, many more.

CHAPTER REVIEW

This chapter focused on managerial decision making, which is the conscious selection of a course of action from among available alternatives to produce a given result. All employees, but especially managers, must make decisions.

Programmed decisions are routine and repetitive and enable management to develop a systemic way to make them. Nonprogrammed decisions occur relatively infrequently, and a separate decision must be undertaken each time.

The five steps in managerial decision making are (1) recognizing a problem or opportunity, (2) developing alternative courses of action, (3) evaluating the advantages and disadvantages of the alternatives, (4) selecting a preferred alternative and implementing it, and (5) evaluating the decision results.

The decision-making method used is also influenced by the decision maker's personal problem-solving type or style. According to the Myers-Briggs Type indicator, individuals have two ways of perceiving information and two ways of evaluating it. The four combinations of sensing-thinking, intuitive-thinking, sensing-feeling, and intuitive-feeling have a definite influence on problem solving and decision making. Ideally, a balance will be developed by using all four dimensions in decision making.

To what extent should a manager involve others in the decision-making process? The Vroom-Yetton model helps answer the question by examining the key characteristics of given decision situations and identifying various decision-making styles. A particular decision style can be selected on the basis of answers to questions about the characteristics of the given situation. Some techniques for involving others in creative problem solving are brainstorming, the Crawford Slip technique, and the nominal grouping technique.

The more effective supervisors use ethical value judgments in making decisions. Ethics are the standards used to judge the "rightness" or "wrongness" of actions or decisions when dealing with other people or organizations. Ethical value judgments have a wide range of consequences involving the decision maker, employees, stockholders, and the community in general, and, therefore, as much consideration should be given to people and their problems as to economical and financial factors.

IMPORTANT TERMS
managerial decision
  making
programmed decisions
nonprogrammed decisions
decision tree
creativity
Myers–Briggs Type
  Indicator (MBTI)
Vroom–Yetton Model
synergy
brainstorming
Crawford Slip technique
fluency
flexibility
nominal grouping
  technique (NGT)

QUESTIONS FOR REVIEW AND DISCUSSION

1. Peter Drucker states that a big decision-making error supervisors frequently make is failing to get a handle on a problem. Often, managers plunge in prematurely. Why do you think many managers make this common mistake?

2. Discuss the following statement: It's better for a manager to try to carry out a poor decision for the sake of worker confidence. You can't build worker confidence by continually admitting the poor decisions you make.

3. What are the pros and cons of decisions made by groups such as committees and task forces as compared to decisions made by one person?

4. Is it possible for someone to be a good decision maker but a poor supervisor? Explain.

5. One supervisor says that she finds procrastination to be a big help in her decision making. Do you agree or disagree? Why?

Coast Guard Cutter Decision Problem

Skill Builder 3-1

You are the captain of a 210-foot medium-endurance Coast Guard cutter, with a crew of 9 officers and 65 enlisted personnel. Your mission is general at-sea law enforcement and search and rescue. At 2:00 this morning, while en route to your home port after a routine two-week patrol, you received word from the New York Rescue Coordination Center that a small plane had ditched 70 miles offshore. You obtained all the available information concerning

the location of the crash, informed your crew of the mission, and set a new course at maximum speed heading for the scene to commence a search for survivors and wreckage.

You have now been searching for 20 hours. Your search operation has been increasingly impaired by rough seas, and there is evidence of a severe storm building to the southwest. The atmospherics associated with the deteriorating weather have made communications with the New York Rescue Coordination Center impossible. A decision must be made shortly about whether to abandon the search and place your vessel on a northeasterly course to ride out the storm (thereby protecting the vessel and your crew, but relegating any possible survivors to almost certain death from exposure) or to continue a potentially futile search and incur the risks it would entail.

Instructions: You have contacted the weather bureau for up-to-date information concerning the severity and duration of the storm. While your crew members are extremely conscientious about their responsibility, you believe that they would be divided on the decision of leaving or staying.

Review the decision processes in this chapter and decide which comes closest to what you would do if you were the captain in this situation. Circle your choice:

A   B   C   D   E

Source: Victor H. Vroom and Arthur G. Jago, *The New Leadership: Managing Participation in Organizations,* 1e, © 1988 Electronically reproduced by permission of Pearson Education, Inc., Upper Saddle River, New Jersey; pp 42–43.

| Skill Builder 3-2 | **New Machines Decision Problem** |

You are the manufacturing manager in a large electronics plant. The company's management has always been searching for ways of increasing efficiency. They have recently installed new machines and put in a new, simplified work system, but to the surprise of everyone, including yourself, the expected increase in productivity was not realized. In fact, production has begun to drop, quality has fallen off, and the number of employee separations has risen.

You do not believe that there is anything wrong with the machines. You have had reports from other companies that are using them, and the reports confirm this opinion. You have also had representatives from the firm that built the machines go over them, and they report that the machines are operating at peak efficiency.

You suspect that some parts of the new work system may be responsible for the change, but this view is not widely shared among your immediate subordinates—four first-level supervisors, each in charge of a section, and your supply manager. The drop in production has been variously attributed to poor training of the operators, lack of an adequate system of financial incentives, and poor morale. Clearly, this is an issue about which there is considerable depth of feeling within individuals and potential disagreement among your subordinates.

This morning you received a phone call from your division manager. He had just received your production figures for the last six months and was calling to express his concern. He indicated that the problem was yours to solve in any way that you thought best, but that he would like to know within a week what steps you plan to take.

You share your division manager's concern with the falling productivity and know that your people are also concerned. The problem is to decide what steps to take to rectify the situation.

Instructions: Review the decision processes in this chapter and decide which comes closest to what you would do if you were the manager in the above situation. Circle your choice:

A   B   C   D   E

Source: Adapted and reprinted from the book *Leadership and Decision-Making,* by Victor H. Vroom and Philip W. Yetton, © 1973. All rights controlled by the University of Pittsburgh Press, Pittsburgh, PA 15260. Used by permission of University of Pittsburgh Press.

Instructions: Indicate the response that comes closest to how you usually feel or act. If you really cannot choose, two answers being an absolute toss-up, leave that question unanswered. There are no correct or incorrect answers.

1. Which are you more careful about, (a) what people's rights are or (b) how people feel?

2. Which phrase do you feel best describes you, (a) having common sense or (b) having vision?

3. Are you more likely to be impressed by (a) principles or (b) emotions?

4. Which phrase best describes your preference as to how to get a job done, (a) using techniques that have proved effective in past situations or (b) experimenting with new and different approaches?

5. In making decisions, which is more important to you, (a) standards or (b) feelings?

6. Which do you think is worse, (a) not having a clear grasp of details or (b) not having a clear grasp of the big picture?

7. Do your friends see you as basically more (a) hardheaded or (b) warmhearted?

8. Are you basically more interested in (a) data or (b) ideas?

9. If another person says something that is incorrect, which would you normally do, (a) point out the error or (b) ignore it?

10. Which kind of person would you prefer as a roommate, (a) someone who's very practical, with both feet on the ground, or (b) someone who's always having new ideas?

11. Are you best described as (a) drawing conclusions in a logical, objective way or (b) drawing conclusions based on feelings or emotions?

12. In making decisions, are you more likely to decide based on (a) the real facts and data or (b) your hunches?

13. As a student, would you prefer taking (a) fact-oriented courses or (b) theory-oriented courses?

14. Which do you feel is the greater error, (a) to be too sympathetic or (b) to be too firm?

15. Assume that a party contains two rooms of people, and in each room are the same types of people. Which room would you be drawn to, (a) a room with sensible people or (b) a room with imaginative people?

16. Which of the following terms best describes you: (a) objective or (b) compassionate?

17. Which do you value more highly, (a) a strong sense of reality or (b) a strong imagination?

18. Which role has the greater appeal to you, (a) being a judge or (b) being a peacemaker?

19. In which of these activities have you more interest: (a) production or (b) design?

20. Would you describe yourself as (a) more firm than merciful or (b) more merciful than firm?

Score Sheet

Instructions: Record your answers to each question in the appropriate box. Then add the total number of checks in each column. If you have an equal number of points for Sensor and Intuitor, circle the Intuitor; if an equal number of points for Thinker and Feeler, circle the Feeler.

	a	b			a	b
2	___	___		1	___	___
4	___	___		3	___	___
6	___	___		5	___	___
8	___	___		7	___	___
10	___	___		9	___	___
12	___	___		11	___	___
14	___	___		14	___	___
15	___	___		16	___	___
17	___	___		18	___	___
19	___	___		20	___	___
TOTAL	___	___		TOTAL	___	___

```
S   I           T   F
E   N           H   E
N   T           I   E
S   U           N   L
O   I           K   E
R   T           E   R
    O           R
    R
```

Skill Builder 3-4

The $100,000 Investment Decision

Assume that a wealthy entrepreneur has provided a $2 million fund for the management department at your school, to be used in improving students' decision-making skills. The department has decided to use this course as the vehicle for student development in decision making.

Divide the class into teams of five to seven students. Each team is given $100,000 to invest for a period of five years. At the end of that period, a member of each team will have six months to liquidate the team's investment(s).

The $100,000 principal, along with 50 percent of profits, will be returned to the management department. The remaining 50 percent will be divided among team members. The department will cover any loss of principal up to $75,000.

Each team's assignment is as follows:

1. Following the steps of the decision-making process, reach a decision about what your investment(s) will be. Write out your reasoning for each step in the decision-making process and turn in the report to your instructor.

2. Be prepared to make a five- to ten-minute presentation to the rest of the class as to why your decision will reap the best return in five years.

At the end of the exercise, class members will vote on which team seems to have made the best investment decision (s).

Leadership

Self-Assessment Exercise 3.1, Delegating tasks to subordinates.

For each of the following questions, select the answer that best describes your approach to delegating tasks to subordinates. Remember to respond as you *have* behaved or *would*

behave, not as you think you *should* behave. If you have no managerial experience, answer the questions assuming you are a manager.

When delegating to a subordinate, I:

	Usually	Sometimes	Seldom
1. Explain exactly how the task should be accomplished.	____	____	____
2. Specify the end results I expect.	____	____	____
3. Feel that I lose control.	____	____	____
4. Expect that I'll end up doing the task over again myself.	____	____	____
5. Only delegate routine or simple tasks.	____	____	____
6. Clarify to subordinates the limits of their authority.	____	____	____
7. Establish progress report dates with the subordinate.	____	____	____
8. Inform all who will be affected that delegation has occurred.	____	____	____

Scoring Key and Interpretation   For questions 2, 6, 7, and 8, give yourself 3 points for *Usually,* 2 points for *Sometimes,* and 1 point for *Seldom.*

For questions 1, 3, 4, and 5, give yourself 3 points for *Seldom,* 2 points for *Sometimes,* and 1 point for *Usually.*

Sum up your total points. A score of 20 or higher suggests superior delegation skills. A score of 15 to 19 indicates that you have room for improvement. A score below 15 suggests that your approach to delegation needs substantial improvement.

Source: Stephen P. Robbins and Phillip L. Hunsaker, *Training in Interpersonal Skills,* (Prentice Hall, Upper Saddle River, NJ) 3rd ed., 2003, p. 181.

4 Fundamentals of Organizing

© Jim Craigmyle/CORBIS

No matter how small a business is when it begins, it needs to be effectively organized as it grows in order to be successful. To gain a broad understanding of organization, we'll follow the progress of John Moody's boat-trailer business as it grows from a one-person operation into a much larger one.

The only things that evolve by themselves in an organization are disorder, friction, and malperformance.
—PETER DRUCKER

Preview

John Moody's Growing Organization

Our story begins in a small Midwestern city of 75,000. Our main character is John Moody, 29, a high-school graduate and veteran, who has been working in a large paper mill on the outskirts of the city since his discharge from the service. John still holds the same semiskilled job at the operative level that he started with. His wife's relatives believe he is a lazy person with a low IQ who will never amount to much. Actually, John is quite an intelligent person, but his basic satisfaction in life comes from the challenge of building and creating things in his garage workshop. Although he assumes that he will never get rich, he feels his take-home pay is sufficient to take care of the necessities of life and to support his hobbies. Even though his job at the mill is not very challenging, he gets all the challenge he needs from tinkering around in his workshop.

Unfortunately, the country has begun to slide into an economic recession, which is adversely affecting the paper industry. Several mill employees, including John, are laid off because of excessive inventory buildup. John signs up for unemployment compensation and decides to spend time building a new boat trailer in his garage. He puts a lot of thought and effort into the task. The result is an excellent trailer—such a fine one that several of his friends talk him into building trailers for them for 20 percent more than his expenses.

Even at this price, his boat trailer sells for less than those sold in local stores. Before long, so many requests are coming in that John finds himself spending all his time in his garage. At this point, John decides to work full time building boat trailers as long as he can make a living doing so.

Learning Objectives

After reading and studying this chapter, you should be able to:

1. Understand the stages of organization growth.

2. Identify the advantages and disadvantages of the functional, product, and matrix departmentalization approaches.

3. Explain the principles of unity of command and span of control.

4. Describe the difference between line and staff.

5. Understand how to avoid excessive conflict between line and staff.

6. Explain the three types of authority found in organizations.

7. Distinguish between centralization and decentralization.

8. Discuss the benefits and costs of downsizing.

9. Understand the relationship between management philosophy, strategy, and newer forms of organization.

Organizing is one of the key functions of any manager or supervisor. In this chapter, we present concepts, principles, and a frame of reference for understanding this function. We do so by expanding on the John Moody preview case throughout the chapter to illustrate the stages of growth in most organizations and the principles of organizing.

Many first-level managers understand organization only from a narrow vantage point—their immediate department or perhaps one or two levels above them. We believe that it is equally important to be able to see and understand the organization from a much broader standpoint. The more completely supervisors understand the big picture, the better equipped they are to work effectively as key members of the management team. Consequently, organizing is presented from a broad, overall perspective in this chapter. Failure to understand the organizing function from a broader viewpoint can lead to the following problems:

1. Excessive violation of the unity of command principle.

2. Failure to develop additional departments or work groups when needed.

3. Unclear and improper assignment of duties and responsibilities to new employees.

4. Ineffective use of organizational units and inadequate development of human resources because of improper decentralization of authority.

5. Excessive and unhealthy conflicts between departments and between line supervisors and staff personnel.

1 Understand the stages of organization growth.

The Four Stages in Growth of an Organization

To see the organizing function of management in operation, let us study the growth and development of John Moody's hypothetical manufacturing business. Usually a business organization grows in four stages. Stage 1 is the one-person organization; stage 2 is the organization with assistants added; stage 3 is the line organization; and stage 4 is the line-and-staff organization. Not all organizations go through all of these stages. Many skip the first stage and go directly to stage 2. For clarity's sake, however, we'll discuss each stage.

Stage 1: The One-Person Organization

From our reading of the preview case, we see that John Moody's business is in the first stage of organizational growth—that is, a one-person operation (Exhibit 4-1). This means that John alone performs the three basic activities common to all manufacturing operations: financing, producing, and selling.

EXHIBIT **4-1**

John Moody's One-Person Organization

John Moody
Owner and Operator

Finance
Production
Sales

EXHIBIT 4-2

John Moody Hires
Assistants

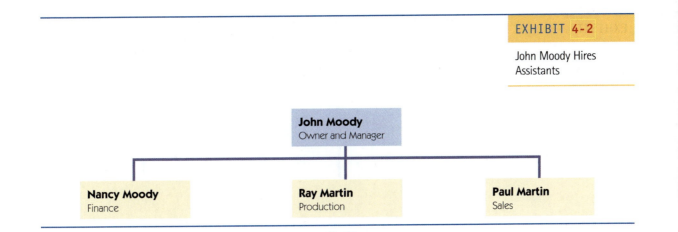

Stage 2: The Organization with Assistants Added

After 3 months, so many orders are coming in that John Moody cannot fill them. In the past few years, the federal government has built a number of dams near John's town, creating four new lakes in the region. Fishing has been good, and there is a large demand for boats and boat trailers. John is now making more money per day than he did when he was with the mill. To keep pace with the orders, he hires Ray Martin, a former army buddy, to help build the trailers. For a small monthly salary, John also hires his wife, Nancy, to keep books and handle the financial details. Before the month is out, Ray has mastered his job so well that he and John are producing more boat trailers than they have orders for. At this point, John and Ray start thinking about hiring someone as a salesperson. Ray's brother, Paul, has just graduated from college with a major in marketing. After hearing about John's business from John and Ray, Paul decides that it has possibilities. With the assurance of an opportunity to buy into the business in the future, Paul starts to work for John as a salesperson.

Exhibit 4-2 shows that John Moody has had to hire three assistants to help carry out the three primary activities of his business. This stage is a critical one; over 50 percent of new businesses fail in their first year of operation from lack of capital, ineffective management, or both.

Paul Martin proves to be an excellent salesperson, and the business continues to grow. To keep up with the increasing volume of orders, John hires additional people. Also, the business moves to a larger building. As Exhibit 4-3 shows, after two years John has 19 people working for him. His net income is such that Nancy has quit working, but John finds himself so busy that he cannot enjoy his higher income. More important, he feels that he is losing control of the business; the increased costs per trailer support this belief.

✔ STOP & THINK

Before reading further, look at the organization chart in Exhibit 4-3. Can you explain why John Moody is losing control of his business?

In desperation, John Moody asks the Martin brothers for advice about his problem. Paul Martin recalls that in one of his college courses, the instructor talked about the management principle of *span of control*. This principle holds that there is a limit to the number of people a manager can supervise effectively. In Paul's opinion, the solution is to select managers for the areas of finance, production, and sales.

EXHIBIT 4-3

John Moody's Organization after Two Years

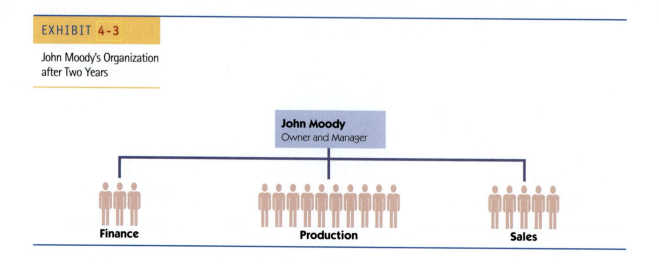

Paul's solution seems so simple that John Moody wonders why he didn't think of it himself. He places Beth Fields—his best accountant—in charge of finance, Ray Martin in charge of production, and Paul Martin in charge of sales.

Stage 3: The Line Organization

line organization
An organization concerned with the primary functions of the firm—in this case, production, sales, and finance.

Exhibit 4-4 shows that John Moody has selected a manager for each of the three major departments, and his span of control has been reduced from 19 to three employees. Beth Fields is responsible for two employees, Ray Martin for nine employees, and Paul Martin for four employees. In effect, John Moody's business is now structured as a **line organization.** This means that each person in the organization has clearly defined responsibilities and reports to an immediate supervisor.

There are two advantages to having a line organization at an early stage of a business organization's growth:

EXHIBIT 4-4

The Span of Control in John Moody's Line Organization

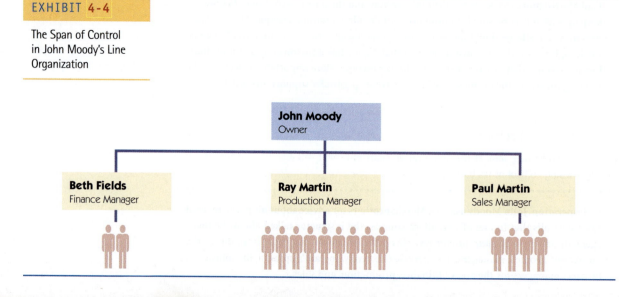

EXHIBIT 4-5

John Moody's Line
Organization after
Ten Years

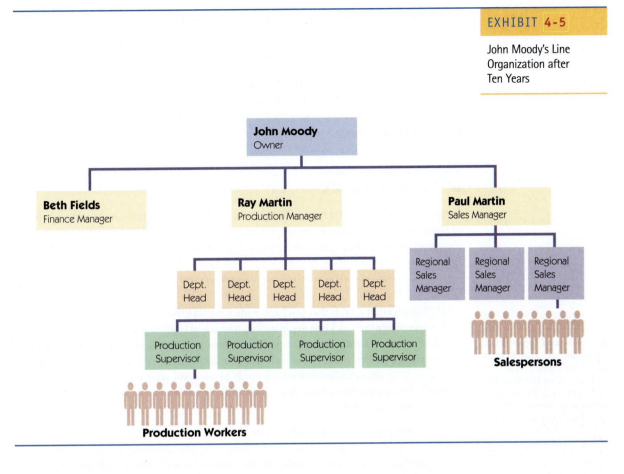

1. Quick, decisive action on problems is possible because authority is centralized—it is in the hands of John Moody and his three managers.

2. Lines of responsibility and authority are clearly defined. Everyone knows what his or her job and obligations are. Thus, evasion of responsibility is minimized and accountability is maximized.

As a result of the line organization and the capabilities of each manager, the unit cost of making each boat trailer is lowered. Under the leadership of sales manager Paul Martin, the business expands its sales territory to cover most of the states in the Midwest. As sales increase, production also increases. New people are added in both sales and production. The line organization develops to accommodate the increased growth. Keeping in mind the principle of span of control, John Moody adds new sections in production and sales whenever the volume of business justifies the new additions. He now also finds time to concentrate more on such tasks as developing plans for the future, coordinating the work of the three departments, and supervising his managers.

After 10 years, John Moody's business is employing over 150 people. During this period, John has promoted Ray Martin to be in charge of five production department heads. Exhibit 4-5 shows that this move has created an additional level of management in the production department. The department heads, in turn, are each responsible for four production supervisors. Each production supervisor is responsible for ten production workers. Similarly, John has made Paul Martin sales manager in charge of three regional sales managers, each of whom is supervising eight salespersons.

Stage 4: The Line-and-Staff Organization

Unfortunately, increasing sales require John Moody's business to add more people to meet production quotas, so the profit on each unit produced declines. Finally, Beth Fields, the head of finance, reports to John that each $1.00 in sales is costing $1.10. In other words, a boat trailer that the business sells for $300 is costing $330 to manufacture. Although the business is now financially sound, John is aware that, with the way things are going, it will not take long for the business to go bankrupt. He, therefore, decides to call in a reputable management consultant.

✔ **STOP & THINK**

Before reading the consultant's recommendations, decide what you think is the primary problem or problems causing manufacturing costs to increase in John Moody's business. The management consultant interviews managers from different levels in the company. After several days of investigation, the consultant makes the following report to John Moody:

line-and-staff organization
An organization structure in which staff positions are added to serve the basic line departments and help them accomplish the organization objectives more effectively.

My investigation reveals that you have made a mistake that many companies make: You are operating purely as a line organization, whereas at your stage of growth, you need to adopt a *line-and-staff organization*. This means that you need to hire several staff experts to perform some of the activities your line managers presently do. As it now stands, your organizational structure tends to overload your managers. They are, in effect, wearing too many hats. More specifically, I have found evidence of the following three kinds of inefficiency:

1. Your supervisors are doing their own hiring, firing, and disciplining. Consequently, you have no uniform way of screening, selecting, promoting, and disciplining employees. Moreover, a number of the supervisors are hiring friends and relatives for their departments, and other employees believe that favoritism is rampant throughout the company.

2. The several department heads independently purchase materials and supplies for their departments. This duplication of effort has caused excessive space and dollars to be tied up in raw materials inventory. In addition, this practice has opened the door for waste and pilferage of supplies and materials.

3. Your department heads and supervisors are involved in method and layout studies, maintenance and repair work, scheduling and dispatching, and, to cap it off, quality control—all on top of their primary jobs of supervising the work and motivating their employees. The old proverb that "a jack of all trades is master of none" is certainly borne out by the situation I find in your plant.

My primary recommendation, therefore, is that you hire a human resources specialist to screen and select new employees, a production control manager to do all the purchasing and inventory control, and an industrial engineering manager to do method and layout studies and the like. [Their relationship to the organization is shown in Exhibit 4-6.] By adding these three staff specialists, you will give your department heads and supervisors a chance to concentrate on their primary job of overseeing production and motivating their employees. Equally important, you should receive immediate benefits and cost savings by eliminating inefficiencies and installing improved ways of operating.

EXHIBIT 4-6

John Moody's Line-and-Staff Organization

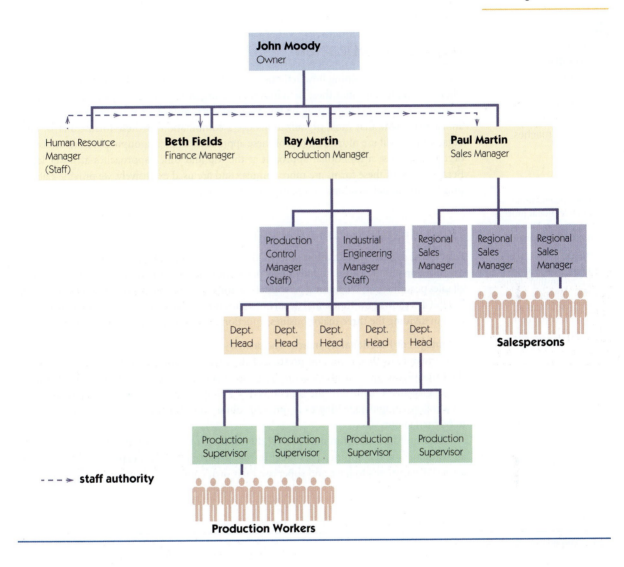

John Moody — Owner

Human Resource Manager (Staff)

Beth Fields — Finance Manager

Ray Martin — Production Manager

Paul Martin — Sales Manager

Production Control Manager (Staff)

Industrial Engineering Manager (Staff)

Regional Sales Manager · Regional Sales Manager · Regional Sales Manager

Salespersons

Dept. Head · Dept. Head · Dept. Head · Dept. Head · Dept. Head

Production Supervisor · Production Supervisor · Production Supervisor · Production Supervisor

- - - → **staff authority**

Production Workers

✔ STOP & THINK

What adjustments will the supervisors need to make to accommodate the consultant's recommended changes? Do you think these changes will help or hinder the supervisor in the job of motivating and managing his or her crew?

The consultant went on to report that, in the future, additional staff people would be needed if the company's rate of growth continued. He also stated that the company might want to consider diversifying by adding product lines that would require similar skills.

John Moody accepted the consultant's recommendations, and his line-and-staff organization went on to achieve not only record sales, but also record profits and growth. Ultimately, any growing business needs to pass into this fourth stage. Unfortunately, many do not, and some suffer the consequences of decline and bankruptcy.

2
Identify the advantages and disadvantages of the functional, product, and matrix departmentalization approaches.

Departmentalization

The process of determining how activities are to be grouped is called **departmentalization.** There are many ways that these activities may be organized. For example, types of departmentalization include organizing by function, product, service, process, territory, customer, and matrix. Note that most organizations use a combination of these forms; that is, most organizations will use more than one of these approaches in their groupings. However, usually organizations use a functional approach at the top and other approaches at lower levels. Because three of these forms are more complex and are used extensively, we provide elaboration for functional, product, and matrix departmentalization.

departmentalization
The organizational process of determining how activities are to be grouped.

functional departmentalization A form of departmentalization that groups together common functions or similar activities to form an organizational unit.

Functional Departmentalization

Functional departmentalization groups common functions or similar activities to form an organizational unit. Thus, all individuals performing similar functions are grouped, such as all sales personnel, all accounting personnel, all nurses, all computer programmers, and so on. Exhibit 4-7 shows how functional departmentalization would be used at the top management level in dividing the three major business functions—production, sales, and finance.

Advantages of Functional Approach. The primary advantages of the functional approach are that it maintains the power and prestige of the major functions, creates efficiency through the principles of specialization, centralizes the organization's expertise, and permits tighter top-management control of the functions. For example, having all library-related activities on a college campus reporting to a common "library director" permits unified library policy to be carried out.

This approach also minimizes costly duplications of personnel and equipment. Having all computers and computer personnel in one department is less expensive than allowing several departments to have and supervise their own computer equipment and personnel.

EXHIBIT **4-7**

Functional Departmentalization at the Top Management Level

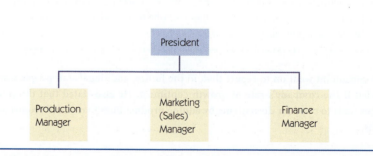

© S&G Photography/Alamy

Types of departmentaliza-tion can vary widely accord-ing to the activities being grouped. Sales organiza-tions, for example, often structure groups according to territories.

Disadvantages of Functional Approach. There are also many disadvantages to a functional approach. Some of these are that responsibility for total performance rests only at the top, and since each manager oversees only a narrow function, the training of managers to take over the top position is limited. Organizations attempt to remedy this by transferring managers so that they become "rounded," with experience in several functions. Coordination between and among functions becomes complex and more difficult as the organization grows in size and scope. Finally, individuals identify with their narrow functional responsibilities, causing subgroup loyalties, identification, and tunnel vision.

Product Departmentalization

At some point, the problems of coordination under a functional approach become extremely complex and cumbersome, especially when rapid, timely decisions must be made. The functional approach is slow and cumbersome because there is no single manager accountable for all the given activities, with the result that considerable coordination and communication are required before decisions can be reached. Consequently, some products that top management feels have the most potential may not receive the attention they deserve. And no one person is accountable for the performance of a given product line. What can be done to resolve this dilemma? One solution for many organizations is to shift to smaller, more natural semiautonomous miniorganizations built around specific products, each with its own functional capabilities. This is known as **product departmentalization,** in which all the functions associated with a single product line are grouped.

product departmentalization
A form of departmentaliza-tion that groups together all the functions associated with a single product line.

Some of the advantages of product departmentalization are that attention can be directed toward specific product lines or services, coordination of functions at the product division level is improved, and profit responsibility can be better placed. Also, it is easier for the organization to obtain or develop several executives who have broad managerial experience in running a total entity.

Some of the disadvantages of product departmentalization are that it requires more personnel and material resources, it may cause unnecessary duplication of resources and equipment, and top management assumes a greater burden of establishing effective coordination and control. What a disaster it would be for GM's next economy-priced Chevrolet to have a body style almost identical to GM's top-priced Cadillac Seville. Top management must use staff support to create and oversee policies that guide and limit the range of actions taken by its divisions.

Matrix Departmentalization

Matrix departmentalization is a hybrid type of departmentalization in which personnel from several specialties are brought together to complete limited-life tasks. It usually evolves from one or more of the other types of departmentalization and is used in response to demands for unique blends of skill from different specialties in the organization. The matrix structure is used not alone but in conjunction with other types of departmentalization. Say, for example, that a company had to complete a project requiring close, integrated work between and among numerous functional specialties. The project could be designing a weapons system or building a prototype for a supersonic aircraft. The traditional approaches to organization we have discussed do not easily provide for the flexibility to handle such complex assignments, which involve expertise from numerous functional areas of the organization. As shown in Exhibit 4-8, a project manager is given line authority over the team members during the life of the project.

EXHIBIT 4-8

Example of Matrix Departmentalization

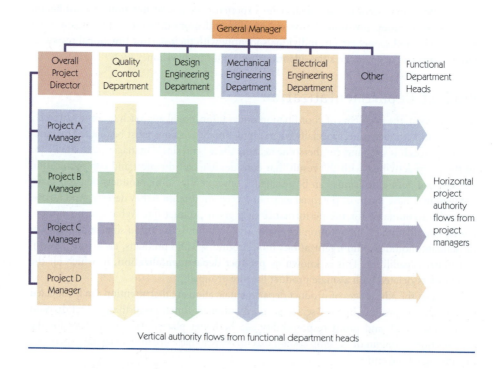

The matrix organization provides a hierarchy that responds quickly to changes in technology. Hence, it is typically found in technically oriented organizations, such as Boeing, General Dynamics, NASA, and GE, in which scientists, engineers, or technical specialists work on sophisticated projects or programs. It is also used by companies with complex construction projects. Under this system, team members' functional departments maintain personnel files, supervise administrative details, and assemble performance reports while their members are on assignment.

http://www.boeing.com

Advantages of the Matrix Approach. One advantage of the matrix approach is that it permits open communication and coordination of activities among the relevant functional specialists. Another advantage is that its flexibility enables the organization to respond rapidly to change. This response to change is the result of a self-imposed and professional desire to respond—not a response to a hierarchically managed change effort. The use of this approach is essential in technologically oriented industries.

Disadvantages of the Matrix Approach. One disadvantage of matrix departmentalization relates to the lack of clarity and coordination in assigned roles. Conflict may occur when the requirements of the project team result in decisions contrary to the philosophy and viewpoint of the home office. For example, a project team might want the authority to make most decisions on-site, while the home office wants tight control. Another possible source of conflict is the assignment of team members to more than one project; someone must determine how to allocate such team members' time on each project. Such situations require *facilitators*, who intervene to resolve clashes resulting from conflicting priorities.

> **Jean Johnson was a professor of management at Mid-Atlantic University.**
>
> **For the past year, she had been teaching in the management department and working half-time on an interdisciplinary project to improve the university computer system. For the life of the project, she had two bosses—the project director and the chairman of the management department.**
>
> **Until recently, this dual reporting had not caused any problem, but within the last month, the chairman of the management department had been putting increasing pressure on Jean to teach an additional course for the fall term. A professor had resigned suddenly, leaving the department shorthanded. The dilemma was that the computer study was nearing completion and required a major commitment of time and effort from all project members.**

In a matrix structure, who will decide on the members' advancement and promotion? Moreover, who will assign them to their next projects? Normally, the functional department head will make these decisions, based in part on reports received from project managers for whom the persons have worked. But functional specialists are often caught in the middle in disputes and torn between loyalties to project managers and to their functional department heads.

Finally, there are disadvantages relating to the temporary nature of assignments under this form of departmentalization. Psychologically, one may never feel that one has "roots" while drifting from one project to another—perhaps unrelated—project. Moreover, the close personal ties formed while working on a project team may be severed at the project's completion, in which case an individual's reassignment requires establishing a new set of working relationships with strangers.

Special Managerial Abilities Required. Because of the complexities of the matrix approach, managers should have special abilities in order to be successful. They should be adept at teamwork and coordination and also have facilitation skills.

Two Important Organizing Principles

Two important principles involved in the organizing function were illustrated in the case of John Moody's organizations. These are unity of command and span of control (or span of management). Let us now discuss these principles in detail.

Unity of Command

The **unity of command principle** states that everyone in an organization should report to and be accountable to only one boss for performance of a given activity. This supervisor should be responsible for evaluating performance, passing down orders and information, and developing employees to become better employees in the organization. It is to this person that employees should turn for help in carrying out their duties and should communicate any deviations, either positive or negative, in implementing their duties. In sum, the supervisor is responsible only for motivating his or her employees to achieve effective results and for taking action when employees deviate from planned performance.

Adherence to the unity of command principle is important for five reasons:

1. It prevents duplication and conflict when orders and instructions are passed down.

2. It decreases confusion and "passing the buck" because everyone—including managers—is accountable to only one person for a given assignment.

3. It provides a basis whereby a supervisor and his or her employees can develop a knowledge of each other's strengths and weaknesses.

4. It provides an opportunity for a supervisor and employees to develop supportive relationships and to realize their individual and group potential in achieving organizational objectives.

5. It promotes higher morale than is generally found in organizations that do not follow the unity of command principle.

Unfortunately, some managers only give lip service to this principle, although their organization chart seems to reflect it. One of the authors of this book was working with a branch plant of a large company to tailor a management development program. Among other things, this author was examining the leadership styles practiced by key managers and their effect on employees. To determine those leadership styles, the author interviewed managers at all levels. The results showed that the plant manager, though unusually capable and generally effective, made one mistake with his employee managers: He violated the unity of command principle by periodically conducting inspections throughout the plant and making on-the-spot suggestions to operative employees. Often, he made these suggestions when the employees' supervisor was not present. As a result, operative employees were following instructions that their immediate supervisors were unaware of. Moreover, employees would stop working on their assigned duties to carry out the instructions of the plant manager. This practice caused a problem for supervisors, as illustrated by Exhibit 4-9.

As a result of this one error, a serious morale problem had developed. Many of the plant manager's otherwise effective managerial practices were being undermined. When this situation was called to his attention, he was quite surprised. It seems that he had slipped into this habit without being fully aware of its long-range consequences. When this manager thereupon began passing his suggestions and instructions through lower-level managers, morale improved.

Although employees should have only one supervisor, they may, of course, have relationships with many people. For example, in a line-and-staff organization, line supervisors and department heads will have many contacts with staff personnel. These contacts are

Following the unity of command principle, the supervisor is solely responsible for motivating his or her employees to achieve company goals.

necessary so that both line and staff personnel can accomplish their duties. Later in this chapter, we will explain how these relationships can be developed without violating the unity of command principle. The important thing to remember is this: If a conflict results from a staff request and a line manager's command, the employee should have a single manager to turn to for clarification or a final decision.

EXHIBIT 4-9

Violating the Unity of Command Principle

Span of Control

span of control principle
States that there is a limit to the number of people a person can supervise effectively.

Before World War II, experts maintained that the span of control should be three to eight people, depending on the level of management. In those days, one of the first things an organizational consultant examined when a company was having problems was the span of control at various levels. Today the three-to-eight-people limit is no longer accepted as universally applicable. This is why we state the **span of control principle** simply as follows: There is a limit to the number of people a person can manage effectively. Just as you can span only a limited number of feet and inches with your arms, your mental reach can span only a limited number of the problems, situations, and relationships that make up the activities of management.

Narrower Span of Control at the Top. One thing we can say without qualification: The higher the managers are in an organization, the fewer people they should have reporting directly to them. There are at least three reasons for relating span of control to management level:

1. Top-level managers must solve a variety of different, nonrecurring problems. Much mental concentration is required to solve such problems.

2. Middle managers must spend much of their time doing long-range planning, working with outside interest groups, and coordinating the various activities of the organization. They cannot afford to be tied down by the excessive burden of supervision created when a large number of people report directly to them.

3. First-level managers, by contrast, tend to be concerned with more clearly defined areas of operation. Although they are responsible for a certain amount of coordination with other departments, most of their contacts are directly with their immediate employees. Hence, they are able to supervise more people than are higher-level managers.

Different Approaches to a Supervisor's Span of Control. Exhibit 4-10 depicts three different approaches to a supervisor's span of control, leading to quite different jobs for supervisors A, B, and C. Can we say that one of these approaches is best? No, because the correct size of a supervisor's span of control depends on a number of circumstances, as shown in Exhibit 4-11.

Companies that follow a policy of a narrow span of control are often hampered in achieving effective results. If an organization of, say, a thousand people rigidly adheres to a span of between three and seven, this tall, narrow organizational structure (with many, many management levels) will have some disadvantages. Numerous supervisory managers will be required, resulting in high payroll costs. Communication will have to pass up and down through many levels, increasing the possibility of distortion. Oversupervision may restrict decision making by employees and limit their opportunities to achieve their full potential. On the other hand, an advantage of tight control is that the work can be closely directed, so the company can hire relatively less skilled people.

Tendency toward Wider Spans of Control. Over the years, many companies have tended to broaden their span of control at all levels. There are at least four reasons for this trend:

1. Higher educational attainment, management and supervisory development programs, vocational and technical training, and increased knowledge generally on the part of the labor force have improved the abilities and capacities of both managers and employees. The greater the supervisor's capacity, the more people he or she can supervise.

2. Research indicates that in many situations *general* supervision is more effective than *close* supervision. A supervisor practicing general supervision delegates authority and supervises by results, whereas a supervisor practicing close supervision provides detailed instructions and often does the same type of work as the workers he or she is supervising.

EXHIBIT 4-10

Narrow, Wide, and Very
Wide Spans of Control

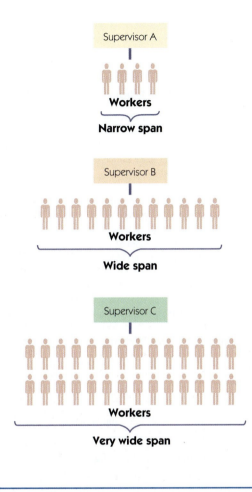

Supervisor A

Workers

Narrow span

Supervisor B

Workers

Wide span

Supervisor C

Workers

Very wide span

3. New developments in management have permitted businesses to broaden their span of control and supervise by results, without losing control. For example, by using a computer, an organization can process information more quickly and develop more efficient information-reporting systems.

4. Finally—and sometimes this is the primary reason—wider spans of control save the company money.

Relationships Between Line and Staff

Line personnel carry out the primary activities of a business, such as producing or selling products and/or services. **Staff personnel,** on the other hand, use their expertise to assist the line people and aid top management in various areas of business activities. Line departments, therefore, are like a main stream. Staff departments are like the tributaries serving and assisting the main stream, although they should not be thought of as being secondary to the line departments. Both line and staff people are important.

4 Describe the difference between line and staff.

line personnel Carry out the primary activities of a business.

staff personnel Have the expertise to assist line people and aid top management.

EXHIBIT 4-11

Factor	Narrow Span Indicated	Wide Span Indicated
How physically close are the people performing the work?	Dispersed, perhaps even in different geographical locations.	Very close, perhaps all in one physical work area in a building.
How complex is the work?	Very complex, such as development of a manned space station that will orbit the earth.	Rather routine and simple, such as an assembly-line operation.
How much supervision is required?	A great deal. So many problems arise that the supervisor needs to exercise close control.	Little. Workers are well trained and able to make normal job decisions easily.
How much nonsupervisory work is required of the supervisor?	Much. The supervisor spends much time planning, coordinating, and performing nonsupervisory tasks.	Little. Not much planning and coordination is required of the supervisor. The supervisor spends most of his or her time supervising employees.
How much organizational assistance is furnished to the supervisor?	Little. The supervisor may do his or her own recruiting, training, and controlling.	Much. The supervisor may be aided by a training department, quality control department, etc.

✔ STOP & THINK

Of the various jobs you've held, which were "line" and which were "staff"?

Once a business has reached the fourth stage of growth and is no longer a small organization, it becomes more complex and difficult to coordinate. A line and staff structure that places competent specialists in certain positions, such as human resources management, legal and governmental departments, research and development, and public relations, will help eliminate confusion, duplication, and inefficiency. However, a growing organization must be continually alert to pitfalls and potential trouble spots.

Conflicts between Line and Staff

One common problem in most large organizations is excessive conflict between line and staff personnel and between different departments. Differences in viewpoint between people and departments are natural, inevitable, and healthy, but excessive conflict can disrupt an entire organization. As shown in Exhibit 4-12, many line and staff contacts are normal.

There are many reasons excessive conflict can develop between line and staff personnel within an organization. Exhibit 4-13 summarizes some reasons for conflict between line and staff personnel.

✔ STOP & THINK

Before reading further, decide what you think might be done to decrease or eliminate the reasons for conflict between line and staff personnel.

EXHIBIT **4-12**

Line and Staff Contacts

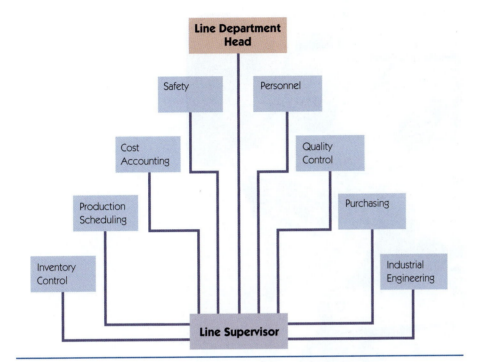

How to Avoid Excessive Line-Staff Conflict:
Delineating Authority

Although conflict between line and staff people is not likely to be completely eliminated, a major way to avoid it is to ensure that people clearly understand the authority/responsibility relationships between individuals and departments. There are three types of authority: advisory, line, and functional.

5 Understand how to avoid excessive conflict between line and staff.

EXHIBIT **4-13**

Some Reasons for Conflict between Line and Staff Personnel

- Staff personnel give direct orders to line personnel.
- Good human relations are not practiced in dealings between line and staff personnel.
- Overlapping authority and responsibility confuse both line and staff personnel.
- Line people believe that staff people are not knowledgeable about conditions at the operating level.
- Staff people, because of their expertise, attempt to influence line decisions against line managers' wishes.
- Top management misuses staff personnel or fails to use them properly.
- Each department views the organization from a narrow viewpoint instead of looking at the organization as a whole.

Behind-the-scenes functions of research (accounting, quality control, and safety) are found in many companies. What kind of authority would a staff person have working in this environment?

© Ed Young/CORBIS

6

Explain the three types of authority found in organizations.

advisory authority
Authority of most staff departments to serve and advise line departments.

line authority Power to directly command or exact performance from others.

functional authority A staff person's limited line authority over a given function.

Advisory Authority. The primary responsibility of most staff departments is to serve and advise the line departments. This type of authority is called **advisory authority** or the *authority of ideas.* However, some staff people may be so zealous in their efforts to sell their ideas to line personnel that they, in effect, hand out orders. If the line supervisor permits this to occur frequently, the unity of command begins here to break down.

Line Authority. The second type of authority, **line authority,** is the power to directly command or exact performance from others. Having this power to command does not mean that you will elicit effective performance simply by giving out orders. It does mean, however, that you are directly responsible for the results of a certain department or group of workers. Line authority is not restricted to line personnel. The head of a staff department has line authority over the employees in his or her department.

Functional Authority. The third type of authority, **functional authority,** is usually a restricted kind of line authority. It gives a staff person a type of limited line authority over a given *function,* such as safety or quality, regardless of where that function is found in the organization. For example, a staff safety specialist may have functional authority to insist that line managers follow standard safety procedures in their departments. The staff safety specialist may have top management's blessing to dictate to lower-level line managers exactly what they must do and must not do concerning any matter that falls within the realm of safety. A quality control inspector may tell a line worker that certain parts need to be reworked. A human resources specialist may say to a line supervisor that the latter cannot fire a certain employee. A cost accountant may notify line departments that certain cost information must be furnished weekly, and so on.

Can you think of some other common examples of functional authority?

••

Are you thinking that functional authority seems to violate the unity of command principle? It does! For this reason, it is important that all individuals clearly understand what functional authority is. Top-line managers have the major responsibility for defining the nature of functional authority. Moreover, it is important for line personnel to exercise their right to appeal to higher management levels when they have disagreements with staff personnel. Functional authority is necessary, but it can be dangerous if it is granted indiscriminately. Normally, it is given only to a staff area where there is a great deal of expertise and the staff expert's advice would be followed anyway.

Another way to avoid excessive conflict between line and staff people is to have effective communication between people and between departments. Key managers overseeing both line and staff people can improve the communication process by periodically bringing line and staff people together to discuss problems that cut across departmental lines. This example may inspire lower-level managers to do the same thing with their key employees. Thus, the danger of seeing only part of the picture will be minimized.

Decentralization versus Centralization

7 Distinguish between centralization and decentralization.

The concept of decentralization is closely related to the concept of delegation. Briefly, delegation is the process by which managers allocate duties and authority downward to the people who report to them and assign responsibility for how authority is used.

An example of delegation occurred when John Moody called in assistants to help him do a better job than he could do alone. He assigned his assistants duties in finance, production, and sales.

Both delegation and decentralization are concerned with the giving of authority to someone at a lower level. **Decentralization** is the broader concept, as it refers to the extent to which authority is delegated from one level or one unit of the organization to another. In a *decentralized* organization, middle and lower levels of management make broader, more important decisions about their units. In a *centralized* organization, upper management makes most of the important decisions that concern all levels or units within the organization.

decentralization The extent to which authority is delegated from one unit of the organization to another.

Factors Affecting Decentralization

No organization is completely centralized or decentralized. Decentralization is a relative concept and depends on a number of factors, including the following:

1. *Top-management philosophy.* Some top managers have a need for tight control. They put together a strong central staff and want to make the most important decisions themselves. Others believe in strong delegation and push decisions to the lowest levels of their organization.

2. *History of the organization's growth.* Organizations that have grown by merging with other companies or acquiring them tend to be decentralized. Those that have grown on their own tend to be centralized.

3. *Geographic location(s).* Organizations that are spread out, with units in different cities or regions, tend to be decentralized so that lower-level managers can make decisions that fit their territory or circumstances.

4. *Quality of managers.* If an organization has many well-qualified, well-trained managers, it will likely be decentralized. If it has few, top management will centralize and make the most important decisions.

5. *Availability of controls.* If top management has an effective control system—good, timely information about performance at lower levels—the organization will tend toward decentralization. Without a good flow of control information for monitoring results, it will tend to be centralized.

6. *The economy.* Generally, there is a tendency toward more centralization during poor economic times, such as a recession, and more decentralization during good economic times.

7. *Mergers, acquisitions, and joint ventures.* Unfortunately, many mergers, acquisitions, and joint ventures fail to achieve expected synergies and positive outcomes because they do not effectively plan and implement an early strategy to integrate different organization cultures, to evaluate old ways of operating, and, when appropriate, to develop new ways of functioning. Certainly, not dealing with decentralization versus centralization can have a negative impact on the organization and its managers and supervisors.

Effect of Decentralization on Organizational Structure

The degree to which an organization is decentralized will have a direct effect on the number of levels within the organization. The trend in the United States is toward reducing the number of levels of management and decentralizing. While Toyota, which is relatively decentralized, has only seven levels of management, this trend has not been followed with Ford and General Motors. As shown in Exhibit 4-14, Ford Motor Company, which is relatively centralized has 12 layers of managers and supervisors between the operational employees and the chairperson. GM is even more cumbersome.

click! http://www.toyota.com

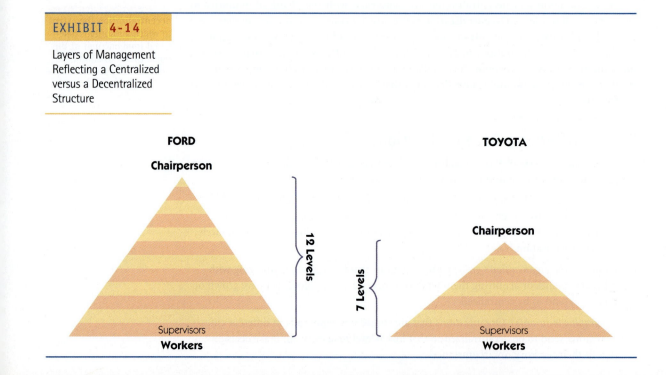

FORD — Chairperson — 12 Levels — Supervisors — Workers

TOYOTA — Chairperson — 7 Levels — Supervisors — Workers

IT'S TIME TO STORM THE SEASON *Experience the 255-hp Cadillac STS V6 and SRX V6 with available All-Wheel Drive, and the powerful 345-hp Escalade AWD. Or discover the stylish, award-winning Cadillac CTS. And every Cadillac comes with the security and safety of one year of OnStar.* Holiday gifts for only the most exclusive lists.*
THE CADILLAC SEASON'S BEST SALES EVENT

CTS   *Escalade*

General Motors print ad showing Cadillacs being driven in the snow.

General Motors' Bureaucracy and Cumbersome Structure

General Motors does well in the Midwest, but it has completely bombed in the coastal regions of the country. An example is the Miami region. In the late 1990s, years before GM's Cadillac Escalade became a hit, dealers in Miami suggested building such a luxury sport/utility vehicle. This idea was "shot down" by executives in Detroit, who said it would never work. GM later went on to sell more than 400,000 of the luxury SUVs.[1] The following highlights some of the problems and what GM is doing to try for a revival in Miami.

In December [2005], General Motors Corp. ran a series of ads across the U.S. showing Cadillacs being driven in snow. The decision to do so was made by the giant car maker's executives in Detroit, where on Christmas Day, temperatures hovered just above freezing.

The ads also ran in Miami, a vibrant car market where GM has bombed for the past 15 years. As Christmas dawned, temperatures there started climbing into the high 70's.

GM is struggling under a financial burden created by monumental pension and health-care obligations. But it's also having a hard time persuading Americans to buy its cars. One reason: GM's cumbersome and unresponsive bureaucracy, the one that ran the snow ads in Miami, has for years failed to connect with the tastes and expectations of consumers outside the company's Midwestern base.

In Miami, where no GM car is a top seller, GM started bilingual advertising much later than its rivals. Some of the ads it did run were duds. One wooed Miami's mostly Cuban-Hispanic population by showing a woman in a Mexican dress standing in front of the Alamo as GM Saturns raced around her. Another was built on the theme "Breakthrough"—a word that doesn't have a direct Spanish translation . . . .

GM employs 325,000 people, almost as many as the population of Miami itself. At various times there have been as many as six layers of management between top executives in Detroit and those in the field. GM's general manager for the Southeast has 38 teams reporting to him, overseeing relations with the region's 1400 dealers, among other things.

In addition to these geographic units, the company is divided along functional lines, with global groups overseeing areas such as marketing, product development and human resources. GM calls this "the matrix." To explain how the two chains of command interact, GM has produced a chart that shows them overlapping in a pattern that resembles a basket weave. It's a system that's confusing even to insiders, especially midlevel employees who often feel as if they have two bosses. Marketing ideas often get lost as they bounce between departments.

The design of GM's corporate headquarters, located in Detroit's Renaissance Center, reflects this bureaucratic inertia. Its four towers resemble massive, steel grain silos. To find colleagues in different departments, employees must sometimes take elevators to the ground floor and walk around an illuminated walkway to get to the other towers. New employees and contract workers get lost frequently. "We are a large company and we are all working independently to make things happen," says Sonia Green, a GM marketing executive charged with helping revive the company's business in Miami. "Unfortunately, we all work in little silos."

Since the mid 1980s, GM's overall U.S. market share has fallen by about 15 percentage points. Last year, the company reported a loss of $8.6 billion, the bulk of which stems from its U.S. auto business. The company has said it plans to slash costs, including cutting 30,000 jobs in the next couple of years, and has sliced benefits for both union and nonunion employees.

In an interview last year, GM's Chief Executive Rick Wagoner said it was critical that GM halt its two-decade-long slide in big coastal cities such as Miami. "We have a very specific strategy to address these markets, one by one, East and West," said Mr. Wagoner, who doubles as the head of GM's North American auto operations. As for the company's complex structure, he made few apologies, arguing that a global auto maker needs such a matrix-style organization. "People really have trouble because they want to know who's in charge," Mr. Wagoner said. "And the answer is going to be, increasingly: It depends."

Through a spokesman, Mr. Wagoner declined to be interviewed for this article. GM released a written statement instead, in which Mr. Wagoner praised GM's dealer network and product lineup and reiterated the company's intension to focus on these key markets. "We are pleased with the initial results from our efforts, and encouraged about the prospects for even more success," he said.

In early 2005, Mr. Wagoner flew to Miami for a "state of the business" briefing from a group of regional marketing managers. The presentation showed how GM lost about 11 percentage points of market share among Hispanics in South Florida between 1990 and 2000. Even as the local Hispanic population grew to encompass 60 percent of Miami's population. "It took you 5 years to see the decline?" Mr. Wagoner said [to the regional marketing managers], recalls Ms. Green, the GM marketing executive who was also visiting Miami at the time. There was silence in the room. "He was pretty harsh," she says.

What some executives in the room didn't say was that many people locally held Detroit responsible for the company's collapse in Miami. Local dealers and managers saw the decline firsthand but say their appeals to Detroit for help fell on deaf ears, a problem that was repeated across the country.

In the past, "We didn't have access to them, nor did they have access to us," says Lynn Thompson of Thompson Sales Co., Springfield, Mo. "It was: "we're running this company, we know what to do and we don't want your input." Now, Mr. Thompson says, things have improved: "They'll take some of our ideas and some of them they won't, but they'll ask." . . .

Image Makeover

GM has charged Ms. Green, the marketing executive, with rebuilding the company's image and sales among South Florida's Hispanic population. Her official title is director of diversity, marketing and sales for South Florida. A previous job was helping Avon Products Inc. sell better to Hispanics.

At GM, one of Ms. Green's first jobs was persuading the company to use in Miami something trendier than Cadillac's advertising theme song, Led Zeppelin's "Rock and Roll," which was a hit in the early 1970s.

"We never thought that Led Zeppellin was appropriate," Ms. Green said, "there are a lot of things that may not be appropriate in Miami." GM still uses the song for its national ads.

Instead, Ms. Green lined up Daddy Yankee, a Puerto Rican recording artist known as "The King of Reggaeton," to do a series of bilingual commercials for the launch of the Chevrolet Cobalt, a trendy compact, Reggaeton, a hot phenomenon, is a fusion of Caribbean and dance music.

When she met with her GM counterparts to plan the campaign, Ms. Green learned that few of her colleagues had heard of Daddy Yankee, a platinum-selling artist. She says no one had considered using GM's coup as a promotional tool to create some buzz around the campaign. When she played some Reggaeton for local dealers, Ms. Green says the reaction was poor. Latin "music all sounds the same to them," she says.

GM encourages dealers to attend seminars designed to make them more effective selling to Hispanic and black consumers. Because many immigrant Hispanic families like to bring their entire family to the showroom, dealers are urged to keep multiple chairs in offices that are used to finalize vehicle sales. . . .

David Borchelt, general manager of the Southeast region, says GM's retail sales volume in South Florida rose 8.4 percent in 2005, compared with the year earlier, mostly due to newly launched GM vehicles.

GM managers in Miami say they are feeling optimistic, in part because they can now talk directly to Detroit, "The whole organization is flatter than it used to be," says Doug Stevens, a sales manager in GM's Southeast region who has worked for GM for 32 years. "When I started out, there was no chance that I would have talked to the CEO or the vice president of sales and marketing."

Downsizing

8 Discuss the benefits and costs of downsizing.

In their book *In Search of Excellence,* Thomas Peters and Robert Waterman noted that one of the attributes of excellent companies is a simple organizational structure with a lean top-level staff. In a 1988 article, management theorist Peter Drucker predicted that by 2008 a typical large business would have half the levels of management and one-third the managers of its counterpart today.[2] Drucker's forecast is already coming true throughout the United States and Canada. **Downsizing** is the process of eliminating unnecessary levels of management and employees, thus reducing the number of staff personnel and supervisors.

downsizing Eliminating unnecessary levels of management.

Benefits of Downsizing

One of the major benefits of downsizing is the tremendous cost reductions that occur almost immediately. Perhaps even more important are the improvements that take place in the way the organization is managed. Turnaround time in decision making is speeded up, and usually communication improves in all directions. Moreover, the organization becomes more responsive to customers and provides faster product delivery. Downsizing also removes the tendency for each level to justify its existence by close supervision and by frequently asking for reports and data from lower levels. Without excessive interference and stifling of creativity at lower levels, line managers have more opportunity to develop and use their authority to make decisions affecting the bottom line. In the final analysis, all of these things translate into higher profits.

An illustration:

A. T. Kearney analyzed management layers among both highly successful companies and others whose performance was not above average in their industry. The 15 not-so-successful companies typically had at least four more organizational layers than the 26 successful ones. Interviews confirmed that more layers in the organization inhibit productivity because the decision-making process is slower and the chances are greater that opportunities will be lost.[3]

Costs of Downsizing

Downsizing has some costs that can wreck the prospect of higher profits if the process is not accomplished ethically and efficiently. Some companies downsize so rapidly and prune staff and middle management so much that they lose control. In addition, some companies are very insensitive in the way they go about downsizing, telling a number of loyal, effective managers that they are no longer needed. A heavy-handed approach can lead to morale problems with remaining employees for years to come. Some other potential disadvantages are increased workloads, diminished chances of promotion, and threatened job security for those remaining.

Perhaps the greatest costs are the least known—the social costs. Research shows that when employees lose their jobs because of downsizing, domestic problems increase. Fifteen percent lost their homes, despite an increase in the number of hours their spouses worked. Moreover, the suicide rate for laid-off workers is 30 times the national average.[4] Because of these costs, downsizing can never be painless, but thoughtful planning can minimize the pain.

Impact on Remaining Supervisors and Managers

Remaining managers and supervisors must adapt to fuzzier lines of authority and must develop skills in team building. In tall, narrow structures, middle managers and supervisors are accustomed to carrying out orders, and suddenly they must operate differently. As a first-line supervisor in an International Paper Company mill told one of the authors: "They used to tell us what to do; now they ask us." With the increasing emphasis on quality management, a supervisor has to function more as a coach, a facilitator, an expediter, and a team developer.

Ways to Get Beyond Downsizing

Without question, downsizing has a negative impact on employee morale, and, according to an American Management Association survey, just 45 percent of firms that have downsized have seen corporate profits increase.[5] Thus, it is important to look on downsizing not as an end in itself but as a means to an end. The way to get back to health is to focus on the remaining employees by developing a strategy of support for survivors and a strategic plan for growth and development for the organization.

However, it is important not to go back to a traditional management and organizational design based on principles of command, control, and compartmentalization.[6] This danger can be negated by (1) developing effective work teams and (2) using a process called *reengineering*.

Reengineering is a reaction to the way many organizations do work today using the traditional methods of command, control, and compartmentalization. In a world of rapid change, firms that focus on division or specialization of labor with a resulting fragmentation of work end up with vertical structures built on narrow pieces of a process. Consequently, decisions are slow, and people look upward to their department heads and bosses for answers, rather than looking horizontally to internal and external customers to solve problems and get answers.[7]

When Michael Hammer and James Champy, two of the world's leading experts on reengineering, were asked for a quick definition, they gave this answer: "It means starting over. . . . It means asking and answering this question: If I were recreating this company today, given what I know and given current technology, what would it look like?"[8] Their more formal definition of reengineering is "the fundamental rethinking and radical redesign of business processes to achieve dramatic improvements in critical, contemporary measures of performance such as cost, quality, service, and speed."[9]

Reengineering can be very expensive, and so firms should not use it for everything. If you have an unprofitable business, it may be better to close it, or, if quality is a problem, focus on improving the quality rather than starting over. The general guideline is to save reengineering for big challenges that really matter, such as new product development or customer service. Although by one estimate, 50 percent of reengineering efforts fail to achieve the goals set for them, when it is done properly, reengineering has a big payoff. For example, Union Carbide used reengineering to save $400 million in 3 years.[10]

As Hammer and Champy have documented, the following types of changes occur when a company has successfully reengineered business processes:

- Work units change from functional departments to process teams.
- Jobs change from simple tasks to multidimensional work.
- People's roles change from controlled to empowered.
- Job preparation changes from preparation to education.
- Focus of compensation shifts from activity to results.
- Advancement criteria change from performance to ability.
- Values change from protective to productive.
- Managers change from supervisors to coaches.
- Organizational structure changes from hierarchical to flat.
- Executives change from scorekeepers to leaders.

reengineering "It means starting over. . . . it means asking and answering this question: If I were creating this company today, given what I know and given current technology, what would it look like?"

http://www.xerox.com

Historical Insight

During the 1960s and 1970s, Dr. Rensis Likert and his team of researchers and consultants at the University of Michigan's Institute for Social Research Survey Research Center made tremendous contributions to management theory and practice. Likert's two best-known books, *New Patterns of Management* and *The Human Organization,* are considered management classics, and, in the opinion of the authors, many of the concepts are quite valid today.[11]

One concept that is especially relevant to this chapter is the researchers' conclusion that two causal variables affecting both intervening variables and results are (1) management philosophy and leadership behavior, and (2) organization structure. It follows that if, over time, an organization is having difficulties, they can be traced back to the causal variables where improvements and perhaps changes need to be made. Usually, the concept is shown as in Exhibit 4-15.

EXHIBIT 4-15

Variables

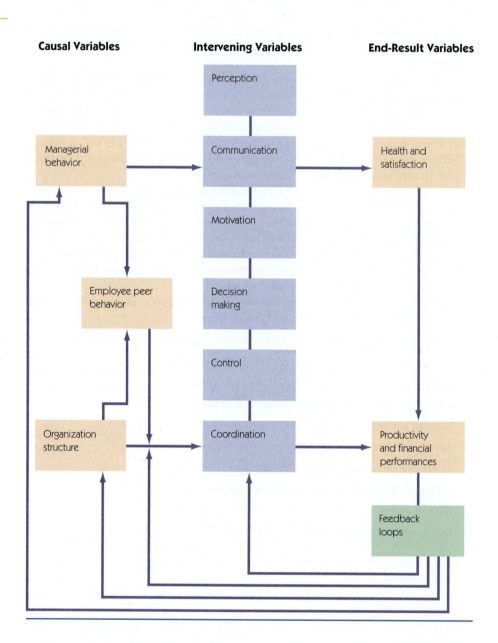

Causal Variables   **Intervening Variables**   **End-Result Variables**

Management Philosophy, Strategy, and Organization

Earlier in the chapter we discussed the impact management philosophy has on the organization. Management philosophy is particularly significant when we discuss the newer forms of organizations, involving more decentralization, empowerment, team development, quality improvement, and networking. In a world of rapid change and

9   Understand the relationship between management philosophy, strategy, and newer forms of organization.

Creation of the inverted pyramid has been attributed to Nordstrom. The retailer's empowerment of sales personnel has been extremely successful.

global competition, more and more firms are shifting to more decentralization, team development, and empowerment.

http://www.wcem.com
http://www2.ford.com

Exhibit 4-16 shows the *internal systems model* developed by Likert. The model groups the dimensions of a company's human organization into three broad categories of variables: *causal, intervening,* and *end result.*

1. *Causal variables.* These variables determine the course of developments within an organization and the results achieved by the organization. They include only those independent variables that can be altered or changed by the organization and its management. Causal variables include the structure of the organization, and management's policies; decision, business, and leadership strategies; skills; and behavior.

2. *Intervening variables.* These reflect the internal state and health of the organization. They include the loyalties, attitudes, motivations, performance goals, and perceptions of organization members and their capacities for effective interaction, communication, and decision making.

3. *End-result variables.* These are dependent variables that reflect the achievements of the organization, such as productivity, costs, scrap loss, and earnings.

You can see that causal variables affect intervening variables that, in turn, affect end results. Thus, an organization running into such difficulties as declining sales and profits or high turnover and absenteeism can usually trace the problem to deficiencies in variables of this sort: organizational structure or top management's policies, decisions, and leadership philosophies, strategies, and behavior.

Creative Organizational Leadership

A good example of creative organizational leadership can be found in the nonprofit International Association of Facilitators (IAF). This organization's primary purpose is to

EXHIBIT 4-16

Creative Organizational
Structure of IAF

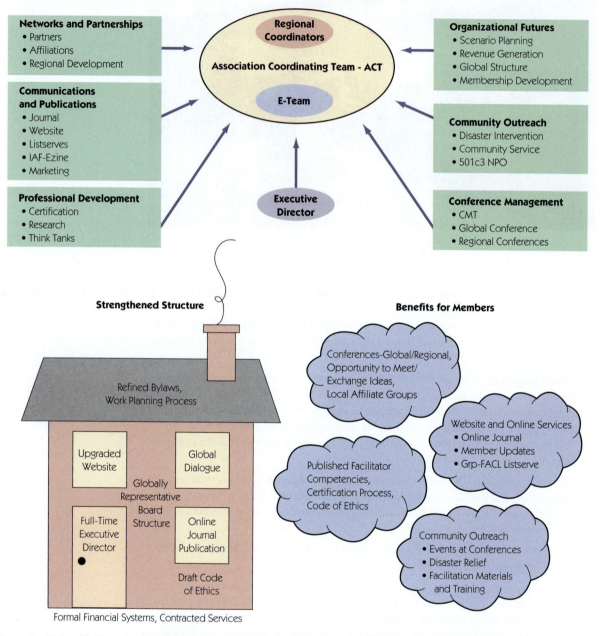

Networks and Partnerships
• Partners
• Affiliations
• Regional Development

Communications and Publications
• Journal
• Website
• Listserves
• IAF-Ezine
• Marketing

Professional Development
• Certification
• Research
• Think Tanks

Regional Coordinators

Association Coordinating Team - ACT

E-Team

Executive Director

Organizational Futures
• Scenario Planning
• Revenue Generation
• Global Structure
• Membership Development

Community Outreach
• Disaster Intervention
• Community Service
• 501c3 NPO

Conference Management
• CMT
• Global Conference
• Regional Conferences

Strengthened Structure

Refined Bylaws,
Work Planning Process

Upgraded Website

Global Dialogue

Globally Representative Board Structure

Full-Time Executive Director

Online Journal Publication

Draft Code of Ethics

Formal Financial Systems, Contracted Services

Benefits for Members

Conferences-Global/Regional,
Opportunity to Meet/
Exchange Ideas,
Local Affiliate Groups

Website and Online Services
• Online Journal
• Member Updates
• Grp-FACL Listserve

Published Facilitator
Competencies,
Certification Process,
Code of Ethics

Community Outreach
• Events at Conferences
• Disaster Relief
• Facilitation Materials and Training

Source: Graphic from The International Association of Facilitators (IAF) Website 2002—http://iaf-world.org. Reprinted by permission.

provide opportunities for members (facilitators) to meet and exchange ideas to improve competencies in helping groups and organizations. The IAF represents two areas we feel are very important to supervisors: conducting effective meetings and developing facilitation skills.

The IAF demonstrated creative leadership when it changed its own organization structure to meet the challenge of growth. To give you an idea of the transformation of IAF in the last few years:

In 1994: 75 founding members (all North America)

In 1998: 700 members

In 2002: 1,300 members (all over the world)

At the global IAF conference in 2002, the chair, Jo Nelson, presented the new structures shown in Exhibit 4-16. According to Nelson, "Transformation often feels like hitting the wall and going through it, coming out the other side as something totally new." The organization had to face a turning point in 2000 when its number of members outgrew its ability to manage them informally. Within 18 months, the organization added the formal structures shown in Exhibit 4-16 to increase effective participation.

We now turn to other organization forms that are influenced by management philosophy and leadership: the inverted pyramid and the wagon wheel.

The Inverted Pyramid

The creation of the **inverted pyramid** has been attributed to Nordstrom, a very successful specialty retailer. Nordstrom's structure is very flat with few levels and employs a bottom-up management philosophy. The sales and sales support personnel, who are in direct contact with the customer, make the key decisions. The chart portrays "helping hands" symbolizing that all other levels are there to help and support the sales personnel to better serve and satisfy the customer. Exhibit 4-17 shows Nordstrom's inverted pyramid and the helping-hand concept.

inverted pyramid
A structure widest at the top and narrowing as it funnels down.

The success of Nordstrom's management philosophy and empowered personnel is reflected in end results. During the past decade its sales have increased from $769 million (39 stores, 10,000 employees) to $3.4 billion (72 stores, 30,000 employees).[12]

EXHIBIT **4-17**

Nordstorm's Inverted Pyramid

Customers

Sales and Sales Support People

Department Managers

Merchandise Managers
Store Managers
Buyers

Board of
Directors

Source: Based on description found in Robert Spector and Patrick D. McCarthy, *The Nordstrom Way: The Inside Story of America's #1 Customer Service Company* (New York: Wiley, 1996).

The Wagon Wheel

Management consultant and author Nancy Austin points out that the **wagon** or **wheel** is even more unorthodox than the inverted pyramid. In her words, "there are usually three main parts to these innovative formats: the hub of the wheel; a series of spokes, which radiate from the hub; and, finally, the outer rim. Customers are at the center. Whether you call the hub 'customers,' 'customer satisfaction,' or 'customer delight'—as AT&T Universal Card Services does—at last, customers show up inside the chart! Next come the spokes— business functions (finance, marketing, engineering) or teams (new-product development, customer satisfaction, suppliers). Keeping it all together on the outer rim—where the rubber meets the road—are the chief executive and the board, who are placed there to make sure everybody has at his or her fingertips everything needed to serve customers. Here, too, managers are coaches and supporters, not naysayers and devil's advocates. The stubborn 'Us vs. Them' antagonism spawned by the old hierarchical mentality begins to even out a bit."[13]

CHAPTER REVIEW

IMPORTANT TERMS

advisory authority
decentralization
departmentalization
downsizing
functional authority
functional
  departmentalization
inverted pyramid
line-and-staff organization
line authority
line organization
line personnel
matrix departmentalization
product departmentalization
reengineering
span of control principle
staff personnel
unity of command principle
wagon wheel

1 Understand the stages of organization growth.

This chapter focused on concepts that give supervisory managers a better understanding of their organization. A continuing case illustrated several phases of organization growth, from a one-person organization to a line-and-staff organization. It is important for a growing company to evolve from a line organization to a line-and-staff organization. This evolution allows the company to take advantage of specialization in such areas as human resources, quality control, purchasing, maintenance, scheduling, and safety. It also allows line managers and supervisors to concentrate on supervising and motivating their employees.

2 Identify the advantages and disadvantages of the functional, product, and matrix departmentalization approaches.

The span of control principle emphasizes that there is a limit to the number of people a person can effectively manage. As one moves down the organization chart from top-management to supervisory management levels, the span of control should increase. The reasons for tying span of control to management level are (1) top management requires the freedom to solve a variety of different, nonrecurring problems; (2) higher-level managers must spend much of their time doing long-range planning, working with outside interest groups, and coordinating the various activities of the business; and (3) supervisory managers tend to be concerned with more clearly defined areas of operation.

3 Explain the principles of unity of command and span of control.

Two important management principles for organizations are unity of command and span of control. Following the unity of command principle is important because it prevents duplication and conflict when orders and instructions are passed down. It also decreases confusion and "passing the buck" and provides a basis for managers and their employees to develop a better understanding of what they expect of each other. Finally, it promotes higher morale than is found in organizations that excessively violate the unity of command principle.

4 Describe the difference between line and staff.

Though both line and staff personnel are important, their duties differ. Line personnel carry out the primary activities of a business, such as producing or selling products and/or services. Staff personnel use their expertise to assist the line people and to aid top management in various business activities.

5 Understand how to avoid excessive conflict between line and staff.

A line-and-staff organization sometimes leads to excessive conflict between line and staff departments. Conflict can be minimized by ensuring that people understand the authority/responsibility relationships between individuals and departments.

6 Explain the three types of authority found in organizations.

The three types of authority found in organizations are advisory authority (common in staff departments), line authority (direct command authority over employees), and functional authority (limited line authority in a narrow area of specialization). Another way to avoid excessive conflict is to have effective communication between people and between departments.

7 Distinguish between centralization and decentralization.

The concept of centralization versus decentralization is important in understanding organizations. Some factors that influence the extent of centralization or decentralization are top management's philosophy, the history of the organization's growth, its geographic location(s), the quality of managers, and the availability of controls. Computer technology has increased the ability of higher management to shift in either direction. The trend, however, seems to be in the direction of decentralization.

8 Discuss the benefits and costs of downsizing.

Many organizations are currently being streamlined by downsizing, or reducing the number of administrative levels. Although rapid downsizing can get out of control and there is unavoidable cost to the staff and supervisors who are laid off, the benefits to the organization in the form of cost reduction, faster decision making, and improved communication outweigh the costs. As a result of downsizing, supervisors often have more authority and responsibility, on the one hand, but they are called on to act more as leaders, coaches, facilitators, and team developers.

9 Understand the relationship between management philosophy, strategy, and newer forms of organization.

The newer forms that are being developed, the inverted pyramid and the wagon wheel, emphasize the role and importance of the customer and empowerment of employees who are close to the customer. Creative leadership is particularly valuable in developing innovative forms as a result of growth and new challenges.

QUESTIONS FOR REVIEW AND DISCUSSION

1. Outline the four stages of organizational growth, and relate them to an organization with which you are familiar.

2. What two important management principles affect the successful operation of a growing organization? Do you think John Moody's difficulties could have been avoided if he had understood these principles? Discuss the advantages and disadvantages of functional, matrix, and product departmentalization.

3. What is the relationship between levels of management and span of control? Explain the advantages and disadvantages.

4. Distinguish between line and staff functions. Are they always easily identified in various types of business enterprises? Justify the existence of both line and staff departments.

5. What conflicts may arise between line and staff personnel? What reasons can you give for these problems? How does effective communication ease the conflict?

6. What are the three types of authority? Do they all exist in all four stages of functional growth?

7. What are some factors that favor centralization or decentralization?

8. How can a company minimize the negative effects of downsizing?

9. What are the potential benefits and potential drawbacks of reengineering?

10. Discuss the relationship between management philosophy, strategy, and newer forms of organization. If you were the owner/manager of ten convenience stores in the same city, what type of structure would you use? If you were the owner/manager of ten CPA offices in various cities, what type of structure would you use?

Skill Builder 4-1

Proposed Change of Organization

group activity

Starting by himself in 1984, Jim Hardy built Hardy Pest Control until it operated in four states and employed over 1,000 persons. In 1996, Hardy hired Derek Temple as vice-president of marketing. Temple, exceptionally bright and articulate, had previously owned an advertising agency.

Before Temple was hired, all the employees in each local area reported to the local manager, and the service personnel were also the salespeople for the firm. The district managers were responsible for both operations and sales. Temple recommended that Hardy specialize by separating sales from service and placing all sales personnel under Temple.

Under this new arrangement, even though sales personnel operated from the local manager's office, they reported organizationally to a district sales manager, usually located in another city (see Hardy organization chart). The sales manager positions, since they were new, had to be staffed with office help and supplied with office space. The proposed new organization is shown as follows:

Prior to accepting the proposal, Jim Hardy decided to call in a management consulting firm to evaluate the proposal and suggest to him whether to accept or reject it.

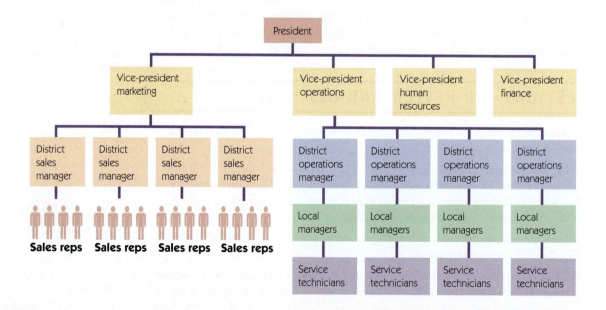

Divide the class into teams of five to seven students who will play the role of a consulting firm, and analyze the proposal.

Answer the following questions:

1. What do you see as the pros and cons of the new structure?

2. Based on your analysis, what is your recommendation to Jim Hardy?

Source: The Synergistic Group, consulting files, 6 Schwaemmle Drive, Mobile, AL 36608.

Reducing Costs in an Accounting Firm

Skill Builder 4-2

group activity

Divide the class into groups of five to seven students, each group representing the managing partners of an accounting firm. Have them discuss the following situation and report back to the class what their plan is, and how they would communicate it to employees.

> There are 30 employees in your organization, and for the past year, sales and profits have been down. In fact, for the past 6 months, the firm has been operating at a loss.
>
> Two months ago, a larger accounting firm acquired your firm in a friendly takeover. Its philosophy is to treat your smaller organization as a semiautonomous division of the accounting company, providing only general guidance and managing by results.
>
> The accounting company CEO has asked your group, the managing partners, to develop a plan to reduce costs. It is important to note that 90 percent of your budget goes to salaries. The accounting company CEO also wants to know how you will communicate the plan to employees.

Source: The Synergistic Group, consulting files, 6 Schwaemmle Drive, Mobile, AL 36608.

CASE

Conflicting Views

Case 4-1

Conflicts between departments occur frequently. In production facilities, these conflicts often arise between production and maintenance departments, as illustrated by the following comments:

Production Supervisor: What a job! Top management is breathing down my neck to get the work out. My people do a real good job, considering our equipment problems and how crowded we are. But what a problem I have with that crew from maintenance!

You'd think they owned the whole company, the way they carry on. They act as if they're doing you a big favor to do a repair job—letting you know how important they are and how they have to schedule their jobs. And they hate for you to tell them what's wrong with the equipment, as if they have to be the ones to do a "complete diagnosis." They always seem to drag their feet for me, and yet other production departments get things done right away. I've told the superintendent about their favoritism and cockiness, but it doesn't help.

Maintenance Supervisor: What a job! I've got production people running around here all day telling me what they've got to have done. I've got six mechanics, and sometimes we'll have 20 calls a day, not to mention our scheduled maintenance. So I try to assign priorities—that's the only way to survive. And then one of those @#$%&*! production supervisors takes his or her problem to the superintendent! What really burns me up is the abuse my people get from them. You try to do what's right, and some say you play favorites. I'd like to straighten that whole bunch of production yo-yos out!

Answer the following questions:

1. What concepts presented in the chapter are involved in this conflict?

2. What do you recommend be done to resolve the problem between the two supervisors?

3. Describe how a third party might work with the two supervisors to attempt to resolve the problem.

5 Delegating Authority and Empowering Employees

AP Photo/The Free Press, John Cross

Teaching is one significant way for leaders to empower their employees. In learning organizations, teams thrive when people are able to learn from each other.

The greatest challenge in life is to be who you are and to become what you are capable of becoming.
—ROBERT LOUIS STEVENSON

The second greatest challenge is to assist and empower other people to become what they are capable of becoming.
—THE AUTHORS OF THIS BOOK

Preview

LARRY S. BONINE, International Leader in Empowerment, Team Building, and Creating High-Performance Learning Organizations

Peter Senge in his influential Book, *The Fifth Discipline*, offers a very important insight and observation that is essential in understanding the "why" of effective delegation, empowerment, and team building.

> "Learning organizations are possible because, deep down, we are all learners. No one has to teach an infant to learn. In fact, no one has to teach infants anything. They are intrinsically inquisitive, masterful learners who learn to walk, speak, and pretty much run their households all on their own. Learning organizations are possible because not only is it our nature to learn, but we love to learn. Most of us at one time or another have been part of a great "team," a group of people who functioned together in an extraordinary way—who trusted one another, who complemented each others' strengths and compensated for each others' limitations, who had common goals that were larger than individual goals, and who produced extraordinary results. I have met many people who have experienced this sort of profound teamwork—in sports, or in the performing arts, or in business. Many say that they have spent much of their life looking for that experience again. What they experienced was a learning organization. The team that became great didn't start off great—it *learned* how to produce extraordinary results."[1]

The first chapter of Senge's book is titled, "Give me a lever long enough . . . and singlehanded I can move the world." Reflecting on that quote, Larry Bonine is the leader who comes to mind. This author first met Larry while serving as one of two facilitators for the first formalized public sector partnering project, the construction of the Oliver Lock and Dam on the Black Warrior River in Alabama.[2]

Larry is tall (6'4") and lanky, and even with a quick and ready smile, he conveys a certain commander/leadership aura and presence. During our work with the Corps of Engineers, we were told that Colonel Bonine was a West Point graduate and a sure bet to make General if he stayed in the military. It was not until later that we learned that Larry was not a West Pointer, but actually a graduate of Tennessee Tech University. He certainly looks like a West Pointer and has the charismatic/transformational leadership quality you would hope to find in a West Pointer. One of Larry's early role models was Raymond Cronwell, assistant professor of Military Science at Tennessee Tech, whose leadership and military bearing had a major positive influence on Larry's decision to make the Army his first career.

His first Battalion Commander, an autocratic, Theory X leader who believed people must be directed or threatened with punishment to get them to put forth adequate effort, also had a major influence on Larry; he learned what he did *not* want to be like as an officer. Fortunately, his next commander used just the opposite leadership style and provided a great positive learning experience for him. While serving as a company commander in Germany and Vietnam, Larry continued to be blessed with good commanding officers and role models.

Learning Objectives

After reading and studying this chapter, you should be able to:

1. Recognize the importance of delegation.
2. Explain what is involved in the delegation process, including authority, responsibility, and accountability.
3. Understand the role of authority.
4. Understand the role of power and why it is a great motivator.
5. Indicate ways to increase empowerment.
6. Recognize the benefits of delegation.
7. Understand why leaders fail to delegate and why employees may not welcome delegation.
8. How to face adaptive changes.
9. Indicate ways to achieve effective delegation and discuss the roles of various parties in achieving effective delegation.

When he first had the opportunity for a higher command and was given a choice of Battalion Commander or District Commander, he chose the district assignment. At the time, he was younger than anyone he supervised and had no experience building dams. Rather than trying to hide his inexperience, he confessed to the experienced personnel that he needed their guidance and wanted to know what he could do to help and empower them. They responded with a high degree of creativity and performance. Later Colonel Larry Bonine was District Engineer for the U.S. Army Corps of Engineers in Mobile, Alabama, the Corps' largest district, running from Panama to North Georgia. When Larry arrived to take command, the district had a reputation for being bureaucratic with excessive red tape and a lack of timely decision making. Bonine's leadership produced a number of initiatives that served as catalysts for change and renewal, not only in the Corps, but also in the construction industry in general.

Early in his tenure professional training and education were provided to all district employees in teamwork and leadership. The cultural change initiative was called the Mobile Team Express; all employees who achieved a certain level of training were presented, by the Colonel, a railroad engineers hat labeled "Mobile Team Express." The internal team building and partnering continues to this day.

It was the lack of teamwork that prompted Dan Burns, Chief of Construction of the Mobile district, to approach Colonel Bonine with the idea of trying partnering in the public sector. Partnering is a variation of team building and strategic planning that emphasizes shared leadership, open communication, and solving problems at the lowest level possible. As Burns explains the situation,

> **"Frequently, the time consumed between the initiation of a project and the final resolution of all administrative problems and financial responsibilities is two or three times the duration of the actual field work. Over 40 percent of my time as chief of construction has been involved in dispute resolution and conflict management; [we felt] there had to be a better way, [and so decided] to investigate the concept of partnering utilized in the private sector."[3]**

At the time Burns made these comments, the Corps had a backlog of disputes with contractors that many times would result in costly litigation. In the words of Larry Bonine:

> **"My first encounter with partnering came in 1988, while I was District Engineer for the Army Corps of Engineers in Mobile, Alabama. We had plans to construct the Oliver Lock and Dam, on the Black Warrior River in Alabama. The district Chief of Construction, Dan Burns, approached me with the notion to try private sector partnering as a tool to reduce claims and facilitate communication for the project. Although none of us had any experience with partnering, it sounded like a good idea. We tried it and the concept was a tremendous success. Later, I briefed the other District Engineers in the Corps on partnering. Colonel Chuck Cowan, then District Engineer in Oregon, picked up on the partnering concept and gave it the push it needed to become Corps policy. Enough can't be said to describe Chuck's impact on partnering. His personal energy and commitment, coupled with the enthusiasm of the construction industry in the Northwest, demonstrated [that] the time for Public Sector Partnering had arrived."[4]**

The second partnering effort was the construction and operation of a tactical and operational control center at Cape Canaveral. The partners were the Air Force Systems Command, Corps of Engineers, the Harris Company, and W & F Construction Company. At the initial workshop a major problem identified was the lengthy response time on cost-saving–value engineering proposals by the contractor. The average response time was 15 months, so the contractor rarely submitted cost savings ideas. The partners developed a plan to change the turnaround time from 15 months to 15 days.

The facilitator of the workshop recalls there was considerable skepticism by the Air Force and contractor participants that the command office of the Corps in Mobile would approve the plan. This skepticism was present despite the fact that lower level engineers from the Corps had participated in developing the action plan. Actually, this type of empowered, creative thinking, and problem solving by those most involved in the project was exactly what Larry Bonine and Dan Burns were expecting when they initiated partnering in the public sector. They strongly supported the plan, and in the first 3 months of the project approximately $400,000 in cost savings had been generated as a result of contractor-initiated engineering proposals. This high visability project turned out to be a group success.

As a result of partnering success in the Mobile district and other districts, commanding General Harry Hatch emphasized two major initiatives in the Corps of Engineers in the 1990s: (1) concern for the environment and (2) partnering. The Navy heard about partnering, visited Mobile, adopted their partnering model and approach, and used it in projects from Guam to the U.S. east coast. The Associated General Contractors of America were influenced by the Mobile model, developed partnering guidelines, and ultimately presented the Excellence in Partnering Awards for outstanding projects. These are just some of the reasons why, when I think of Peter Senge's quote, "Give me a lever long enough . . ." I think of Larry Bonine.

Larry retired from the Army Corps of Engineers as a full Colonel. Because of his excellent reputation and experience, he had a number of interesting opportunities but chose to work for an international engineering firm, Parsons-Brinckerhoff.

After several years with Parsons-Brinckerhoff, Larry received an offer to become Director of the Arizona Department of Transportation. He continued to lead through team building and partnering, and after 5 years, the Arizona Department was known as one of the country's leading learning organizations. During this time Larry and his leadership team would spend 2 days each month with his middle managers teaching and implementing enlightened leadership management concepts and practices. For example, the five disciplines of a learning organization (presented in Chapter 1) were taught and discussed thoroughly. These disciplines are systems thinking, personal mastery, mental model, building a shared vision, and team learning. Larry is quite proud that leaders from the Arizona department have been selected to head other organizations. Tom Warren was selected to head the Utah Department of Transportation and Mary Peters is a top executive in the Federal Highway Administration.[5]

Today, Larry is founder and President of the Pinnacle Leadership Group and continues to be an international leader in empowerment, team building, and creating high-performance learning organizations. His group accomplishes this by offering consultation services, designing in-house training and development courses, and offering a 2-and-half day leadership course in Scottsdale, Arizona. Comments from a recent participant attests to the value of the course and Larry's continuing influence as a change agent:

> *"Best leadership course I've been to . . . combines all the leadership training I've experienced in a 25-year military career with the best ideas of partnering . . . and packs it into a 2-and-half day program."*
>
> —ROBERT KEYSER, COLONEL, USA CORPS OF ENGINEERS, MOBILE DISTRICT COMMANDER

Concepts and Definitions

There are a number of leaders who are intelligent and well educated, yet, unlike Colonel Larry Bonine, do not practice true empowerment. The authors are convinced that mastering the art of delegation and empowerment is essential to a leader's growth, development, and effectiveness. Consequently, we want to start with concepts and definitions to ensure we understand the process of delegation and empowerment.

Delegating allows employees an opportunity to learn by doing. It also allows the supervisor to perform other tasks, and it improves control. As a result, more work gets accomplished!

© Chip Henderson/Index Stock

Role of Delegation. Delegation is the process by which leaders distribute and entrust activities and related authority to other people in the organization. The three key aspects of delegation are (1) granting authority, (2) assigning duties and responsibilities, and (3) requiring accountability.

- *Authority* is the right to do something. When authority is delegated, an individual or team is given the power or right to act in a specified manner in order to reach organizational objectives. For example, a department chair at a university is given the authority to recruit faculty members to fill vacant positions without the president of the university having to interview each candidate to make a final decision.

- *Assigning duties and responsibilities* occurs when key tasks associated with a particular job are specified. In mid-to-large size organizations, job descriptions provide information to employees about the important job-related tasks. Due to the dynamic nature of business today, managers may assign nontraditional duties and responsibilities. For example, production employees in a southeastern furniture manufacturing plant are given the responsibility of projecting a positive image of the company both on the job and in the community. Since the plant competes for most of its production personnel from the surrounding rural area with other manufacturers, a positive corporate image is a key differentiating factor.

- *Accountability* is the obligation that is created when an employee accepts the leader's delegation of authority. Accountability flows upward, such that the delegatee is responsible to the next higher level of management to effectively carry out the assigned duties and responsibilities.

Decentralization

Though closely related to the concept of delegation of authority, decentralization is the broader concept, in that it refers to the extent to which authority is delegated from one level or unit of the organization to another, rather than from one individual to another.

The Role of Authority

Since authority is constantly being used, its nature and role should be well understood. As mentioned earlier, **authority** is the *right* to do something or to tell someone else to do it, in order to reach organizational objectives. If no one in an organization had authority, employees could come to work and leave when they wanted to, they could carry out their assignments any way they wanted to, rather than the way prescribed by higher authority. Without a system of authority, an organization could not function. The following are some examples of higher authority in action.

> **A police officer gives a motorist a ticket for driving 45 mph in a 30-mph zone. The officer's authority derives from the city council.**
>
> **In 1999, Henry Ford III, as chairman of Ford Motor Company, fired Jaque Nasser as its president. Ford's authority came from the company's board of directors, which got its power from the stockholders.**
>
> **The department manager at Macy's assigned the work shifts for her personnel during the Christmas holidays. Her authority was delegated by the store manager.**

In each of these examples, the individual exercised the right to exert authority over others. That authority came with the position and resulted from delegation by a higher-level manager.

Sources of Authority

Basically, there are two contradictory views regarding the source of a manager's authority: the formal theory and the acceptance theory.

Formal Authority View. According to the **formal theory of authority,** authority is conferred; authority exists because someone was granted it. This view traces the origin of authority upward to its ultimate source, which for business organizations is the owners or stockholders. The head nurse in a hospital has authority granted by the nursing director, who has been granted it by the hospital board, which has been granted it by the stockholders (if a private hospital) or the public (if a public hospital). The formal theory is consistent with the definition of authority we presented in the previous section.

✔ STOP AND THINK

You may be reading the material in this book because it has been assigned by an instructor. What is the source of the instructor's authority to make such an assignment, to give exams, and to assign a grade in the course?

···

Acceptance of Authority View. The **acceptance theory of authority** disputes the idea that authority can be conferred. Acceptance theorists (chiefly behaviorists) believe that a manager's authority originates only when it has been accepted by the group or individual over whom it is being exercised. Chester Barnard stated this position. He wrote, "If a directive communication is accepted by one to whom it is addressed, the authority for him is confirmed

---

2 Explain what is involved in the delegation process, including authority, responsibility, and accountability.

3 Understand the role of authority.

or established."[6] Thus, acceptance of the directive becomes the basis of action. Disobedience of such a communication by an employee is a denial of its authority for him or her. Therefore, under this definition, the decisions about whether an order has authority lies with the person to whom it is addressed and does not reside in "persons of authority" or those who issue those orders, as the following example implies.

> Jan was a manager in a large publishing company that had initiated a participative management by objectives process. Jan's immediate supervisor asked her to set objectives for her area and develop a 1-year plan to accomplish those objectives. Jan consulted her employees and developed what she perceived as difficult but attainable objectives.

> When her boss reviewed the objectives, he discovered he disagreed and revised them drastically. He then called Jan in and dictated that she accept the altered objectives. Jan responded that the objectives would be impossible for her staff to achieve, and she could not in good conscience agree to them. At this point, Jan refused to accept her boss's authority, and, although her boss eventually capitulated, it caused some future difficulties in their relationship.[7]

✔ STOP AND THINK

Do you agree with Jan's position in this example? Why or why not? Assuming that Jan was correct in feeling that the revised objectives would be impossible to attain, how might she have handled the situation differently?

....

We have defined authority in line with the position taken by the formal theorists—that authority is a right a manager has been formally granted by the organization. As we will shortly point out, though, the acceptance theorists seem to confuse authority with power or leadership, which involves the ability of a manager to influence employees to accept his or her authority.

The behaviorists do, however, make the point that *to be effective*, managers are certainly very dependent on acceptance of their authority.

④ Understand the role of power and why it is a great motivator.

The Role of Power

The leader's possession of authority is not always sufficient in itself to assure that subordinates will respond as the leader desires. In such cases, a leader must use some other approach, as the following example illustrates.

> Mary Fleming was named supervisor of the Number 2 paper machine at the Northern Mill of a large national company.[8] She was the first female supervisor to be named to such a traditionally male position. The position carried much authority with it, but Mary was intelligent enough to realize that her authority alone would not get her workers to accept her and meet performance standards.

> Several of the employees tested her immediately by taking extended work breaks and making some snide remarks within her hearing about the department's "skirt supervisor." Mary ignored this behavior the first few days and felt that the worst thing she could do was to overreact and come on too strong. But the resistance persisted. Mary had a meeting with Carl White and Pete Antheim, the two senior members of the department, and asked for their advice about handling the situation. White and Antheim seemed flattered by being consulted and told Mary they'd handle the situation. The problems never recurred, and 6 months after the incident, Mary's group was highly supportive of her leadership, and the "female department head" issue had been forgotten.

A female supervisor in a traditionally male role may find her power tested by her subordinates.

We will now study this example with an eye toward the authority-power combinations illustrated in Exhibit 5-1. Mary used a leadership strategy that played a key role in getting her into quadrant 3, where she had both authority and power. **Power** is the ability to influence individuals, groups, events, and decisions and is closely related to leadership. In an earlier example in this chapter—where Jan refused to accept impossible objectives dictated by her boss—we see an example of quadrant 2 in operation. Jan's boss had considerable authority but little power to influence Jan to accept his edict. In other cases, staff personnel have little authority but much power to influence line managers (quadrant 4).

The belief of Sir Dahlberg Acton that "power tends to corrupt, and absolute power corrupts absolutely" is widespread in today's culture. In recent years, however, there has been an increasing awareness that power is not necessarily all bad—that the use of power may be essential for the effective accomplishment of individual, organizational, and social goals. Interest in power has also been generated by David McClelland's research showing that a high need for power is an important characteristic of successful managers.

How Power Is Obtained

As shown by J.R.P. French, Jr., and Bertram Raven in one of the earliest—and still most useful—studies, there are many sources from which power can be obtained.[9] Six of these sources have been translated into types of power, classified as follows:

1. **Reward power** arises from the number of positive rewards (money, protection, etc.) that a leader is perceived as controlling.

EXHIBIT 5-1

Authority-Power
Combinations

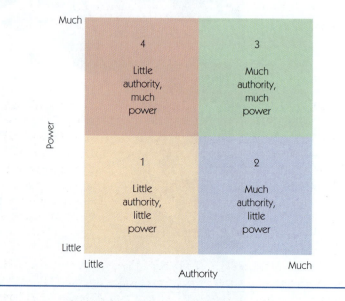

2. **Coercive power** results from people's perceived expectation that punishment (being fired, reprimanded, etc.) will follow if they do not comply with the orders of a leader.

3. **Legitimate power** develops from internalized values that dictate that a leader has an inherent right to influence subordinates. According to this view, one has an obligation to accept that influence simply because a person is designated boss or leader.

4. **Control-of-information power** derives from the possession of knowledge that others do not have. Some people exercise this type of power by either giving or withholding needed information.

5. **Referent power** is based on people's identification with a leader and what that "leader" stands for or symbolizes. Personal charisma, charm, courage, and other traits are important factors in the exercise of referent power.

6. **Expert power** results from a leader's expertise or knowledge in an area in which that leader wants to influence others.

Do not infer from this discussion that a given leader draws upon all of these types of power. Rather, each leader finds his or her own source of strength from many of these types. We can say that more effective leaders draw more on referent power and expert power, and practice more open communication in information sharing.

How Power Can Be Used

Some leaders believe that if a manager has power and shares it with others (delegates it), it is diminished. Actually, the best way to expand power is to share it, for power can grow, in part, by being shared. Sharing power is different from giving it or throwing it away—delegation does not mean abdication.

Effective leaders have a high need for power, but that need is directed toward the benefit of the organization as a whole. In addition, the need for power is stronger in these leaders than the need to be liked by others. Thus, as a leader you must be willing to play the influence game in a controlled way. This does not imply that you need to be authoritarian in action. On the contrary, it appears that power-motivated leaders make their subordinates feel stronger rather than weaker. A true authoritarian would have the reverse effect, making people feel weak or powerless.

The Role of Empowerment

5 Indicate ways to increase empowerment.

Empowerment essentially is the granting of authority to employees to make key decisions within their enlarged areas of responsibility. The driving idea of empowerment is that individuals closest to the work and to customers should make the decisions. Similar to Colonel Larry Bonine, another military leader who has been a model of progressive leadership in empowerment is Michael Abrashoff. In 1997, D. Michael Abrashoff was commander of the USS Benfold, "a $1 billion warship with the world's most advanced computer-controlled combat equipment, revolutionary radar technology, a stack of missiles capable of taking out precise targets on land, sea, or air, and a crack crew of 300 highly skilled, totally committed sailors." The ship spearheaded some of the most critical missions in the Desert Storm confrontation with Iraq.

Abrashoff's leadership led to the Benfold's being the best ship in the Navy. "In fact, the ship won the prestigious Spokane Trophy for having the best combat readiness in the fleet—the first time in at least 10 years that a ship of its class had received that honor." Some excerpts from an article describe the commander's philosophy and grass roots leadership principles and concepts he practices:

> **I divide the world into believers and infidels. What the infidels don't understand (and they far outnumber the believers) is that innovative practices combined with true empowerment produce phenomenal results.**

© Reuters NewMedia Inc./CORBIS

The USS Benfold, which engaged in critical missions during Operation Desert Storm in Iraq, was led by Commander Michael Abrashoff, who carried out successful delegation and empowerment in a very challenging environment.

He continues,

> I'm lucky, all I ever wanted to do in the Navy was to command a ship. I don't care if I ever get promoted again, and that attitude has enabled me to do the right things for my people instead of doing the right things for my career. In the process, I ended up with the best ship in the Navy, and I got the best evaluation of my career. The unintended benefit? My promotion is guaranteed.

> When you shift your organizing principle from obedience to performance, . . . the highest boss is no longer the guy with the most stripes, it's the sailor who does the work. There is nothing magical about it. . . . In most organizations today, ideas still come from the top. Soon after arriving at this command, I realized that young folks on this ship are smart and talented, and I realized my job was to listen aggressively to pick up all of the ideas that they had for improving how we operate. The most important thing a captain can do is to see the ship from the eyes of the crew.[10]

6 Recognize the benefits of delegation.

7 Understand why leaders fail to delegate and why employees may not welcome delegation.

Why Leaders Fail to Delegate

Many good and intelligent people have difficulty delegating authority when in leadership positions, particularly in the early stages of their career. Our culture has a major influence on why this occurs so frequently. In the formative years, success in school and in summer jobs depended primarily on the individual's efforts. Achievement and success did not come from inspiring, developing and working with other people. Grades were determined primarily by hard work and self-discipline. Moreover, those who went to college had a high need for achievement and usually chose difficult majors. The majority who chose such fields as accounting, finance, and banking usually had a keen sense of responsibility, were very conscientious, and were good with details. A survey of bank leaders attending the Louisiana State University Banking School indicated that most of the participants had personality types that incorporated these qualities. One class of sixty-five bankers was given a home-study problem of identifying their primary weakness which needed improvement to increase their effectiveness as a bank leader. They were also asked to develop and implement an action plan to turn the weakness into a strength. The weakness that appeared most frequently in the banking class was delegation. The Action Plan to improve delegation by a vice-president of lending is found in Exhibit 5-2.

✔ STOP AND THINK

How many people do you know who follow the guide "if you want it done right, do it yourself?" Do you follow this guide? What negative consequences will this trait have for effective delegation and empowerment if you are a leader?

· ·

The late industrialist Andrew Carnegie once said, "When a man realizes he can get others in to help him do something better than he can do it alone, he has taken a big step in his life." The following are some other reasons why many leaders have difficulty delegating:

- Many leaders like to control but feel that when they delegate they surrender some of their power and authority. Pfeffer, Cialdini, Hanna & Knopoff (1998) found that managers tended to assign higher evaluations of work quality to their employees when the managers, themselves, were more involved in the production.[11] Since empowerment dilutes work supervision, many managers may make inaccurate evaluations of their workers abilities, skills, and output.

- Some leaders do not delegate because of a lack of trust in others.

EXHIBIT 5-2

Action Plan of James
McKenney, Vice President
of Lending

I. Statement of my objective

    To greatly improve my efficiency and effectiveness in carrying out the delegation process with the leading officers reporting to me.

II. Analysis of the problem or objective

    A. At the banking school when we discussed the 16 problem styles (Myers-Briggs profiles and analysis), I discovered that the characteristics of my type can lead to being a very effective leader if a few potential blind spots can be overcome. It seems that those who are sensing/thinking types (as I am) are so conscientious that our attitude is "If you want it done right, do it yourself." This statement definately applies to me.

    B. When I was recently promoted to this position, the president of the bank gave me a number of positive reasons for my promotion. He also cautioned me that with my increased responsibilities, I could expect to get involved in activities as previously, but he wanted me to focus on developing the skills and knowledge of our loan officers and improve bottom line results.

    C. I realize that most of my life I earned good grades in high school and college because of individual effort. This carried over to my work habits as a loan officer, but I now realize that to be a successful supervisor, I need to develop my team and make use of coaching and empowerment.

III. Development of alternative solutions

    A. Start having biweekly meetings for one hour after banking hours.

        1. At our first meeting we will jointly develop objectives that enhance and reinforce the bank's financial goal.

        2. At our subsequent meetings we will review our progress and discuss any problem loans.

    B. Set up a participative individual management-by-objectives program. This plan will allow individual bank officers to set performance objectives that support our lending division's objectives. During this process I will play the role of coach and mentor, and after the initial meeting, set up performance review sessions with each officer every six months or as needed.

    C. Once every six months at our biweekly meeting we will conduct a brainstorming session to identify our strengths and any problems, issues, or missed opportunities we need to address.

    D. I will explore educational opportunities available for our officers including scheduling several officers for our state banking school or the Banking School of the South.

IV. Final action plan

    I have begun implementing all of the alternative ideas (A, B, C, and D in Section III). Prior to sending this to you, I met and discussed the ideas with our president and CEO. He was most enthusiastic and supportive and is presenting the concept to our executive committee for possible implementation in all divisions of our bank.

Source: This example is based on the experiences of Don Mosley, Sr., when he served as coordinator and instructor for the management and leadership segment of the Banking School of the South at Louisiana State University. The name is fictional to ensure no embarrassment to the actual banker.

- Closely related to the above point, since leaders are being held accountable for results, they don't delegate out of fear employees will make mistakes. Research by Yuki and Fu (1999) found that one determinant of managerial delegation was the strength of the manager-subordinate relationship. Managers delegated more to employees that they perceived to be competent, shared their task goals, and had longer tenure.[12]

- Others do not delegate because they are insecure and are afraid that their employees will do so well that they will be recognized and promoted ahead of the leader.

- A legitimate reason why some leaders don't delegate is they correctly assess that employees need more training, coaching, and experience in certain assignments.

Why Employees May Not Welcome Delegation

Of course, there are also reasons why employees may not welcome delegation:

1. **Ambiguous or Unclear Duties and Responsibilities.** When delegating authority, the manager must clearly communicate to the employee the duties and responsibilities,

the need and importance of the assignment, and why the employee was selected. In one case, the plant had been downsized so drastically that workers were being assigned responsibilities and duties that middle managers had previously performed. In this type of environment, change occurs rapidly, so there is always the chance that newly delegated responsibilities and duties will be poorly communicated which can lead to negative outcomes.

2. **Fear of Failure.** Even if assignments are communicated so the individual understands what their new duties consists of, other problems may arise. Many managers misdiagnose the job maturity level of their employees and assign them tasks that are too difficult. This mistake may result in the employee being unfairly criticized during their performance review or perhaps even fired. A company that one of the authors worked with in a consulting capacity which had a national presence and was growing rapidly promoted internally as a means of filling newly created positions and to motivate their existing employees. One individual was promoted to manager of his work department because he had excelled as an operating level employee and possessed the technical expertise that was needed. However, he had not had an opportunity to develop other skills needed in the new management position, such as team building, communication, conflict management, and leadership skills. His inability to employ a diverse skill set with his employees ultimately led to his being replaced as head of the work department.

3. **Increased Stress.** Finally, increased delegation can mean increased stress on employees. Even when effective communication and appropriate training is provided, employees may still resist delegation and empowerment. Management efforts to downsize or restructure the organization to be more competitive can lead to employee role overload. During the 1990s the following comments seemed quite common: "They call it empowerment and say we get a chance to be a real part of this organization. I call it doing more work for the same amount of money." Some employees prefer not to be empowered. As Hackman and Oldham's Job Characteristics Model points out, the level of participation an individual is comfortable with is not just dependent on effective job

Increased delegation can sometimes overwhelm employees.

Getty Images.

design, communication, and training. Meaningful participation also depends on that person's need for growth and development. Managers must assess an employee's job maturity level and need for growth when selecting an employee for delegation.[13]

Facing Adaptive Challenges

8 How to face adaptive changes.

A number of leadership experts have acclaimed the Ronald A. Heifetz book, *Leadership Without Easy Answers* as the most innovative and creative contribution to leadership studies in years.[14] In this book and in a follow-up article in the *Harvard Business Review* by Heifetz and Donald Laurie, a concept of adaptive challenges and work is presented. In their words:

> To stay alive, Jack Pritchard had to change his life. Triple bypass surgery and medication could help, the heart surgeon told him, but no technical fix could release Pritchard from his own responsibility for changing the habits of a lifetime. He had to stop smoking, improve his diet, get some exercise, and take time to relax, remembering to breathe more deeply each day. Pritchard's doctor could provide sustaining technical expertise and take supportive action, but only Pritchard could adapt his ingrained habits to improve his long-term health. The doctor faced the leadership task of mobilizing the patient to make critical behavioral changes; Jack Pritchard faced the adaptive work of figuring out which specific changes to make and how to incorporate them into his daily life.

> Companies today face challenges similar to the ones confronting Pritchard and his doctor. They *face adaptive challenges*. Changes in societies, markets, customers, competition, and technology around the globe are forcing organizations to clarify their values, develop new strategies, and learn new ways of operation. Often the toughest task for leaders in effecting change is mobilizing people throughout the organization to do adaptive work.

> Adaptive work is required when our deeply held beliefs are challenged, when the values that made us successful become less relevant, and when legitimate yet competing perspectives emerge. We see adaptive challenges every day at every level of the workplace—when companies restructure or reengineer, develop or implement strategy, or merge businesses. We see adaptive challenges when marketing has difficulty working with operations, when cross-functional teams don't work well, or when senior executives complain, "We don't seem to be able to execute effectively." Adaptive problems are often systemic problems with no ready answers.

> . . . But the locus of responsibility for problem solving when a company faces an adaptive challenge must shift to its people. Solutions to adaptive challenges reside not in the executive suite, but in the collective intelligence of employees at all levels, who need to use one another as resources, often across boundaries, and learn their way to those solutions.[15]

Achieving Effective Delegation and Empowerment

9 Indicate ways to achieve effective delegation and discuss the roles of various parties in achieving effective delegation.

When the authors conduct workshops regarding leadership, team building, and partnering, we start by asking participants, "What is the most effective way you learn that produces the most insight, growth, and development?" Although we received different answers, there is always a core group of people who respond by saying experience and, especially, mistakes are the best learning tools. We then ask what is the implication of saying, "we know of people who have had 1 year of experience 20 times?" Usually, someone correctly assesses that although those individuals have experience, they really haven't learned from that experience. Thus, the key to learning from experience, including both successes and failures, is to go through a disciplined reflection on that experience.

EXHIBIT 5-3

The Experiential
Learning Model

Experience = Do

The individual or team does something that results in success or a mistake.

Identify = Look

The individual or team, perhaps with the assistance of a coach or facilitator, identifies what happened.

Analyze = Think

Together they analyze what factors were involved in causing the success or failure.

Generalize = Grow

A conclusion is drawn and an attempt to discover principles that will help in future situations.

Exhibit 5-3 shows the experiential learning model and highlights the importance of using feedback to gain insights in learning from experience. The use of this model, particularly in a coaching or mentoring environmental, is very helpful for achieving successful delegation, empowerment, and end results.

Coaching and Teaching

Two of the most significant ways of empowering and developing people are coaching and teaching. This area is so significant to the leadership process that we have an additional chapter covering the topic, so at this point we will only introduce the process.

There are many different ways to coach and teach. The forthcoming story describes a way that may have been the catalyst for Dwight D. Eisenhower's becoming General of the Army and President of the United States. As a student at West Point, Eisenhower excelled as a football player until a football injury ended his career. After a bout with despondency, he regrouped and directed his energies to becoming head cheerleader. During this period, he was not known for excelling in his studies and graduated in the middle of his class.

Most of his initial assignments after graduation involved coaching the football team; from all reports he was a good coach. Fortunately, he was then assigned to Panama and reported to General "Fox" Conner, a graduate of West Point, who saw great leadership potential in young Eisenhower. In World War I Conner had served as General Pershing's operations officer in France and was considered one of the smartest men in the army.

After the war, in 1922, General Conner took command of the 20th Infantry Brigade in the Panama Canal Zone. He requested that Eisenhower be assigned to his command as executive officer, and his old boss, Chief of Staff, John Pershing, granted the request. The General was a great teacher and coach for Eisenhower, and since their duties were light, they spent a lot of time in a teacher/coach/student relationship.

Conner insisted that Eisenhower read serious military literature and forced the younger man to think about what he was reading by asking probing questions. Eisenhower read memoirs of Civil War generals, then discussed with Conner the decisions Grant and Sherman and the others had made. What would have happened had they done this or that differently? Conner would ask, What were the alternatives? Eisenhower was anxious to please; so anxious that he read *Clausewitz on War* three times—a difficult enough task to complete even once and made more difficult by Conner's insistent questioning about the implications of Clausewitz's ideas.

They also discussed the future. Conner insisted that there would be another war in twenty years or less, that it would be a world war, that America would fight with allies, and that Eisenhower had better prepare himself for it. He advised to try for an assignment under

Colonel George C. Marshall, who had been with Conner on Pershing's staff. Marshall, Conner insisted, "knows more about the techniques of arranging allied commands than any man I know. He is nothing short of genius." . . . Indeed, Conner's highest praise was "Eisenhower, you handled that just the way Marshall would have done."[16]

Many years later after Eisenhower was identified as a world class leader, he stated that his 3 years under Conner were "a sort of graduate school in military affairs . . . In a lifetime of association with great and good men, he is the one figure to whom I owe an incalculable debt." In fact, Eisenhower has stated frequently that Conner influenced him more than anyone he ever served under.[17]

In the fall of 1924, Eisenhower was transferred back to Ft. Mead to coach football. He was greatly disappointed because he had his heart set on attending the infantry school; however, the Chief of Infantry turned down his request without discussion. The infantry school was a prerequisite for the Command and General Staff School (C & GSS) at Ft. Leavenworth, Kansas, and only the best and brightest of officers were selected to attend. Finally, General Conner used his influence with the war department to get Major Eisenhower to the Command and General Staff School. Even then, the infantry command tried to discourage him. An aide to the Chief of Infantry wrote advising him to stay away from C & GSS because "you will probably fail," in which case the failure would make him useless as an infantry officer.[18] Eisenhower then wrote Conner expressing some self-doubts and asking his advice on how to prepare himself. In his reply Conner said, "you may not know it, but because of your 3 years' work in Panama, you are far better trained and ready for Leavenworth than anybody I know."[19]

Conner was right; Eisenhower persevered and through hard work, diligent study, and the development of a good mind, Eisenhower finished number one out of a class of 275 of the best young officers in the Army.

✔ STOP AND THINK

Do you agree or disagree on the importance of coaching and teaching in the empowerment and development of individuals? If you agree, identify and reflect on who influenced you the most in the role of coach, teacher, and mentor. Specifically, share with someone else how they influenced you.

. . . .

Reframing and Training. Related to coaching and teaching is the concept of reframing and training. This is also a way to face adaptive challenges at work. It helps organizations and individuals to change values and behaviors, and to identify new approaches and strategies. The essence of reframing is examining the "situation from multiple vantage points to develop a holistic picture. Effective leaders change lenses when they don't make sense or aren't working."[20] Leadership training and development have a major impact in getting leaders/managers to change.

Individual Introspection and Development

In the final analysis the motivation to change and improve effectiveness in delegation and empowerment rests with the individual. It is well documented in literature that many people in leadership positions have read widely to gain ideas for improving their own leadership and effectiveness. Common sense indicates that this would especially apply to reading autobiographies and biographies of successful people. Warren Buffett, Chairman of Berkshire Hathaway, and Bernadine Healy, former President and chief executive officer (CEO) of the American Red Cross, have this to say about Jack Welch's autobiography:

> *"Jack is the Tiger Woods of management. All CEOs want to emulate him. . . . They won't be able to, but they'll come closer if they listen carefully to what he has to say."*
>
> —WARREN BUFFETT, CHAIR, BERKSHIRE HATHAWAY

"An American treasure, Jack Welch teaches us how a leader with keen intellect, guts and honor can impart courage to people around him, weather unexpected storms, inspire performance, and take an organization to greater and greater heights. His formula challenges all of us and any institution striving for excellence."

—BERNADINE HEALY, M.D., FORMER PRESIDENT AND CEO, AMERICAN RED CROSS[21]

Benefits of Delegation

- **Employee Development.** Through delegation, employees can learn from their experiences. When a manager enables his or her employees to succeed and/or make mistakes on their own, a valuable learning opportunity has been created. The manager can assist the individual in analyzing the situation and evaluating the reasons for the success or failure, so the employee can grow from the experience.

- **Improved Control.** Contributing to the benefit of employee development, managers who delegate effectively emphasize results, not specific actions, and provide feedback when it is appropriate.

- **Improved Time Management.** Leaders that choose not to share their power may find they are so consumed with "putting out fires" that they have very little time to devote to truly important or long-term tasks. Conversely, managers who effectively delegate tasks to their subordinates have more time to spend on planning and trouble shooting.

- **Enhanced Power.** When employees are empowered, an environment is created resulting in more people being knowledgeable and concerned about the organization's objectives. This concern leads to a sense of responsibility or ownership in the work itself.

Seven Habits of Unsuccessful Executives

We want to conclude this chapter with some interesting insights from leadership theorist Sydney Finkelstein, Professor of Management at the Tuck School at Dartmouth College. He wrote an article, "The Seven Habits of Spectacularly Unsuccessful Executives." Two of the seven habits are directly related to the concepts covered in this chapter, and others are indirectly related. The seven habits are as follows:

1. They see themselves and companies as dominating their environment.
2. They identify so completely with the company that there is no clear boundary between their personal interests and the corporation's interests.
3. They think they have all the answers.
4. They ruthlessly eliminate anyone who isn't 100 percent behind them.
5. They are consummate spokespersons obsessed with the company image.
6. They underestimate obstacles.
7. They stubbornly rely on what worked for them in the past.[22]

✔ **STOP AND THINK**

Which two habits are directly related to the concepts in this chapter? Why?

Finkelstein goes on to say that "most of the great destroyers of value are people of unusual intelligence and talent. . . . Nearly all of the leaders who preside over major business failures exhibit four or five of these habits."[23]

In our chapter review the authors will discuss the two habits most directly related to concepts in this chapter and how they relate to all leaders, not just to high-level executives.

CHAPTER REVIEW

1 Recognize the importance of delegation.

The delegation process is a partnering process between a supervisor and employees, bosses, and colleagues. Experiential learning is an important part of delegation, allowing employees to grow and develop by "learning through experience." Effective delegation is essential to performing the supervisory management job successfully. In addition to developing people, delegation (1) allows the supervisor to do other things, (2) accomplishes more work, and (3) improves control.

2 Explain what is involved in the delegation process, including authority, responsibility, and accountability.

The process of delegation has three aspects: granting authority, assigning responsibility, and holding people accountable for results. Because accountability is essential to maintaining effective control over results, a person who delegates an assignment should not be able to escape accountability for poor results. Controls to ensure effective delegation can include personal observation by the delegator; periodic reports by the delegate; and statistical reports concerning output, costs, and grievances.

3 Understand the role of authority.

Authority is the *right* to do something or to tell someone else to do it, in order to reach organizational objectives. If no one had authority, employees could do just what they liked in no prescribed manner; they could come and go as they pleased. Without a system of authority, an organization could not function.

4 Understand the role of power and why it is a great motivator.

Power is the ability to influence individuals, groups, events, and decision and is closely related to leadership. Power can be used for good or evil by leaders. Successful leaders have (1) the ability to influence others and (2) a greater need for power than for being liked or needing to do tasks alone. They also believe that to expand power, they need to share it with other members of the organization through delegation and empowerment.

5 Explain the role of empowerment and indicate ways to increase empowerment.

The driving role of empowerment is that individuals closest to the work and to customers should make the decisions. When implemented properly, it becomes an important way to improve organizational performance. Coaching and teaching are important in carrying out successful empowerment. Also critical to the process is sharing information with everyone and, where appropriate, using self-directed work teams.

6 Name and explain the benefits of delegation.

The first of four benefits is *employee development*. The manager can assist the individual in analyzing the situation and evaluating the reasons for the success or failure, so the employee can grow from the experience. The second benefit is *improved control*. Managers who delegate effectively emphasize results, not specific actions, and provide

IMPORTANT TERMS
accountability
authority
coaching
delegation of authority
empowerment
experiential learning
job descriptions
parity principle
Peter principle
power
reframing

feedback when it is appropriate. *Improved time management* is the third benefit. Rather than leaders having their time consumed with "putting out fires," they can effectively delegate tasks to their subordinates and have more to time for planning and trouble shooting. And finally, the fourth benefit is *enhanced power*. When employees are empowered, an environment is created resulting in more people being knowledgeable and concerned about the organization's objectives, which in turn, leads to a sense of responsibility.

7 Understand why some leaders are reluctant to delegate and why employees may not welcome delegation.

Despite the benefits of effective delegations, some supervisors fail to do so for a variety of reasons. For example, because of his or her accountability to a manager, a supervisor may closely monitor or even perform an employee's work. Also, many leaders or supervisors like control and do not want to surrender their power and authority. On the other hand, many employees do not welcome delegation. They may feel the duties and responsibilities are not clearly communicated; they may not understand the importance of the assignment or why he was selected. Also, there is the *fear of failure* factor. Other problems may arise that the employee is not prepared to solve, leading to an employee being unfairly criticized. With more responsibility frequently comes *increased stress* to get the job done correctly. Therefore, some employees may still resist delegation and empowerment.

8 Learn how to face adaptive challenges.

Reframing and training, related to the concept of coaching and teaching is one way to face adaptive challenges at work. It helps organizations and individuals to change values and behaviors, and to identify new approaches and strategies.

9 Indicate ways to achieve effective delegation and discuss the roles of various parties in achieving effective delegation.

One of the solutions to ineffective delegation is to emphasize management training and development. This will reduce the probability that your organization will be subject to the Peter principle, which states that employees rise to their level of incompetence. However, effective delegation also requires knowing when to delegate, understanding how the delegation process operates, and taking the time to train employees. Although higher management should be supportive and the supervisor should delegate clearly, it is the responsibility of employees to function on their own and turn to the supervisor for help when there is a *major* problem.

QUESTIONS FOR REVIEW AND DISCUSSION

1. Discuss four reasons delegation is important.

2. Describe the process of delegation.

3. Explain the interrelationships among authority, responsibility, and accountability.

4. What is the principle of parity of authority and responsibility? How does it operate in practice?

5. Why do some supervisors fail to delegate effectively? If this situation were a common problem in an organization, what could be done to increase supervisors' skills in delegating effectively?

6. What are the roles played in effective delegation?

7. In what way or ways can higher management affect the delegation process?

8. In what way or ways can employees affect the delegation process?

9. Do you think Commander Abrashoff's approach and philosophy would be successful in the private sector? Why or why not?

10. Do you agree or disagree with McClelland and Burnham that power is the great motivator? Support your position.

11. How does a firm set boundaries to create autonomy and empowerment?

Do You Delegate As Much As You Can?

Skill Builder 5-1

By assigning duties in a more efficient way, delegating not only can create greater overall productivity, but also can reduce overload and burnout of managers. To learn whether you are a good delegator, answer "yes" or "no" to each of the following questions:

_____ Do you often work overtime?

_____ Do you take work home evenings and weekends?

_____ Is your unfinished work increasing?

_____ Are daily operations so time-consuming that you have little time left for planning?

_____ Do you keep control of all the details needed to do a job?

_____ Do you frequently have to postpone long-range projects?

_____ Are you distracted by constant emergencies?

_____ Do you lack confidence in your subordinates' abilities to shoulder more responsibility?

_____ Do you find yourself irritable and complaining when the work of your group doesn't live up to expectations?

_____ Do conflict, friction, and loss of morale characterize the atmosphere of your work group?

_____ Do your subordinates defer all decisions to you?

_____ Do you instruct your subordinates to perform certain activities, rather than accomplish certain goals?

_____ Do you feel that you're abdicating your role as a manager if you ask for your subordinates' assistance?

_____ Have subordinates stopped presenting their ideas to you?

_____ Do operations slow down much when you're away?

_____ Do you believe that your status and the salary you earn automatically mean that you have to be overworked?

If nine or more of your answers are affirmative, it's likely that you're not delegating enough. If so, identify the negatives, and work on eliminating them. Here are the most common reasons for not delegating:

- Lack of patience. (It takes longer to explain it than to do it myself.)

- Insecurity. (I'm so eager to prove myself that I refuse to delegate.)

- Inflexibility. (I'm convinced that nothing can be done properly unless I do it myself.)

- Inadequacy. (I'm afraid of being shown up.)

- Occupational hobby. (I'm so attached to some aspect of the job that I just don't want to give it up.)

Source: "Do You Delegate as Much as You Can?" *Nation's Business* 84, July 1996, pp. 9–10. © U.S. Chamber of Commerce. Reprinted with permission.

Delegating Tasks to Subordinates

For each of the following questions, select the answer that best describes your approach to delegating tasks to subordinates. Remember to respond as you *have* behaved or *would* behave, not as you think you *should* behave. If you have no managerial experience, answer the questions assuming you are a manager.

When delegating to a subordinate, I:

	Usually	Sometimes	Seldom
1. Explain exactly how the task should be accomplished.	____	____	____
2. Specify the end results I expect.	____	____	____
3. Feel that I lose control.	____	____	____
4. Expect that I'll end up doing the task over again myself.	____	____	____
5. Only delegate routine or simple tasks.	____	____	____
6. Clarify to subordinates the limits of their authority.	____	____	____
7. Establish progress report dates with the subordinate.	____	____	____
8. Inform all who will be affected that delegation has occurred.	____	____	____

Scoring Key and Interpretation   For questions 2, 6, 7, and 8, give yourself 3 points for *Usually,* 2 points for *Sometimes,* and 1 point for *Seldom.*

For questions 1, 3, 4, and 5, give yourself 3 points for *Seldom,* 2 points for *Sometimes,* and 1 point for *Usually.*

Sum up your total points. A score of 20 or higher suggests superior delegation skills. A score of 15 to 19 indicates that you have room for improvement. A score below 15 suggests that your approach to delegation needs substantial improvement.

Source: Stephen P. Robbins and Phillip L. Hunsaker, *Training in Interpersonal Skills,* (Prentice Hall, Upper Saddle River, NJ) 3rd ed., 2003, p. 181.

Theory X and Theory Y Attitudes

For each pair of statements distribute 5 points, based on how characteristic each statement is of your attitude or belief system. If the first statement totally reflects your attitude and the second does not, give 5 points to the first and 0 to the second. If it's the opposite, use 0 and 5. If the statement is usually your attitude, then distribution can be 4 and 1, or 1 and 4. If both statements reflect your attitude, the distribution should be 3 and 2, or 2 and 3. Again, the combined score for each pair of statements must equal 5.

Here are the scoring distributions for each pair of statements:

0–5 or 5–0   One of the statements is totally like you, the other not like you at all.
1–4 or 4–1   One statement is usually like you, the other not.
2–3 or 3–2   Both statements are like you, although one is slightly more like you.

1. ____ People enjoy working.
   ____ People do not like to work.

2. ____ Employees don't have to be closely supervised to do their job well.
   ____ Employees will not do a good job unless you closely supervise them.
3. ____ Employees will do a task well for you if you ask them to.
   ____ If you want something done right, you need to do it yourself.
4. ____ Employees want to be involved in making decisions.
   ____ Employees want the managers to make the decisions.
5. ____ Employees will do their best work if you allow them to do the job their own way.
   ____ Employees will do their best work if they are taught how to do it the one best way.
6. ____ Managers should let employees have full access to information that is not confidential.
   ____ Managers should give employees only the information they need to know to do their job.
7. ____ If the manager is not around, the employees will work just as hard.
   ____ If the manager is not around, the employees will take it easier than when being watched.
8. ____ Managers should share the management responsibilities with group members.
   ____ Managers should perform the management functions for the group.

To determine your attitude or belief system about people at work, add up the numbers (0–5) for the first statement in each pair; don't bother adding the numbers for the second statements. The total should be between 0 and 40. Place your score on the continuum below.

Theory X 0—5—10—15—20—25—30—35—40 *Theory Y*

Generally, the higher your score, the greater are your Theory Y beliefs, and the lower the score, the greater your Theory X. Leaders with theory Y beliefs find it easier to implement participative and empowerment strategies.

Source: From Leadership, Theory, Application, and Skill Development 1st edition by Lussier/Achua, 2001. Reprinted with permission of South-Western, a part of Cengage Learning, www.cengage.com/permissions.

CASE

Marion Dawson's Problem

Case 5-1

Marion Dawson was quite pleased when she graduated from community college with an associate's degree in business. While pursuing her degree, she had been employed as a worker with an international company specializing in fast foods similar to McDonald's, Wendy's, and Burger King. She was a very efficient worker and was soon elevated to handling the outside window sales where only the best employees were placed. She was also promised an opportunity to work for the organization upon completion of her associate's degree program. After graduation, Dawson entered the company's management training program. From there she was placed in a busy store location as assistant manager. As an achievement-oriented person, Dawson saw this as the first step toward her long-range goal of becoming a regional manager or having her own franchise some day.

In her position as assistant manager, things went well. Dawson was familiar with all operations, and she practiced close supervision, stayed on top of things, and really stressed high production and fast service. Six months later she was promoted to manager at another busy store that was the most profitable within the region. In fact, the previous manager had just been promoted to regional manager and was now Dawson's boss.

At this stage of her career, Dawson was well ahead of schedule in her long-range program of becoming a regional manager. She had anticipated spending a minimum of two years as an assistant manager before having an opportunity to advance to manager. Her next career objective of becoming a regional manager seemed well within reach, since the industry and company were growing at a rapid rate.

Dawson surmised that what had worked for her as an assistant manager would also work for her as a manager. She was not really concerned that the assistant manager and four supervisors who would be reporting to her were older and more experienced. After all, results were what counted. At her first meeting, she stressed her high expectations and set as an objective "to increase profits by 10 percent within 3 months." The yearly objective was to be a 20 percent increase. She indicated that she believed strongly in the management principle of follow-up. Not only would she be closely following up on their work, but she would expect them to do the same with store employees.

Two months later, overall profits in her store were down by 7 percent, and Dawson was beginning to worry. It seemed that the more she stressed profits and service and tried to follow delegated assignments closely, the more resistance she encountered. Although the resistance was not open, it was definitely present. In fact, she sensed hostility even from the part-time workers, a group with whom she had always been close.

At the end of 3 months, profits had decreased by 10 percent.

Instructions:

Meet in groups of six or seven people. Make a diagnosis of what the problem is, and identify the critical issues involved. Select one member of your team to present what the team thinks Dawson's boss should do. After all teams have presented, the class should vote on which approach offers the best solution.

CASE

The Autocratic Manager

Case 5-2

The plant manager of a paper mill has contacted your consulting firm to help diagnose why production has dropped in the last 18 months. Moreover, he wants a proposal from your firm on what can be done to turn things around. The partial organization chart indicates there are seven levels of management and the mill employs 410 people.

This mill is a key one in a company that has many mills located throughout the country. The manufacturing process goes through several stages before turning out finished products. There is a relatively large number of engineers employed, and most managers have an engineering background. The mill is unionized.

The plant manager has 4 years to go to retirement and wants to leave the firm with a reputation as a "manager who achieves effective results." He is a dynamic individual and has tended to use either an autocratic or a benevolent autocratic approach in managing. He took over the mill 6 years ago when production was low and a permissive management climate existed. He immediately shifted to a more autocratic management system and for 4 years production was high.

He is convinced that the reason for the current problem is that people at the foreman and supervisory level are not doing their jobs effectively. He thinks the solution is to develop detailed job descriptions for these positions and initiate a foreman management development program that will teach the foremen to get more work out of the unionized employees.

You suggest that interviews be conducted at different levels before making a diagnosis and developing a recommended plan of action. Below are the results of interviews discussing the question, "What problems are preventing this mill from reaching its potential effectiveness?"

Results of top management interviews:

a. The problem is that we must get commitment from foremen to management's higher performance expectations.

b. The greatest concern is abdication of responsibility by foremen. They fail to insist on top performance, and they tend to let employees do what they want. Once we get hourly people under control, we will see an improvement and increased production.

Results of middle management interviews:

a. Overmanagement from the top level to the supervisory level and undermanagement from the supervisory level down.

b. Too many levels of management.

c. Bypassing of middle management to supervise employees directly.

d. Dictatorial system of management in mill.

e. Supervisors and foremen oversupervised.

f. Foremen not given enough authority.

g. Fault-finding atmosphere in mill.

h. Employees will not accept foreman's job.

i. Up and down communication problems.

Results of interviews with foremen:

a. Inability to make decisions because authority is not delegated or is taken away.

b. If you do make a decision, you don't get backing from your bosses. Example: Night foremen have the ability

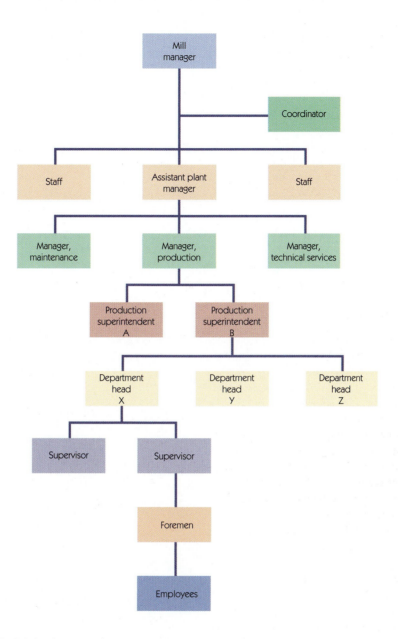

to make 90 percent of the decisions they are required to consult someone else about.

c. Too much pressure and threats from above.

d. Constant criticism when we have equipment or people problems, but no praise when we run above standard.

e. Low morale and poor attitudes. People cover their tracks and have the attitude that "it's everyone's problem but mine."

f. Communication problems, especially with higher management.

Instructions:

1. Why do you think the autocratic approach worked effectively for four years in this situation?

2. Diagnose the problems and/or issues facing this mill.

3. Develop a set of recommendations that you or your consulting team will present to the mill manager. Include suggestions regarding his leadership style. (Role-play the presentation, keeping in mind that the manager is paying your consulting fee.)

Source: Developed from the consulting files of the Synergistic Group, #6 Schwaemmle Dr., Mobile, AL, 36608.

Part **3**

Leading

6 Communication

AP Photo/Josh Reynolds

Bob Greim, manager at the *Boston Herald,* spends the majority of his day engaged in some form of communication.

No one would talk much in society if they knew how often they misunderstood others.
—JOHANN WOLFGANG VON GOETHE

When it comes to communication, my rule of thumb is it's not what you tell 'em but what they hear.
—RED AUERBACH

Too many people think they are wonderful with people because they have the ability to speak well. What they fail to realize is that being wonderful with people means being able to listen well.
—PETER DRUCKER

Preview

A Superintendent Speaks about His Job

Bob Greim manages the printing production end for the *Boston Herald,* a daily newspaper with a circulation of 263,000. His seven foremen directly supervise 70 to 80 print production employees. Bob talks about his job.

A newspaper is on a daily cycle. It's not like other industries where one project can take a month or three months or years. Our projects are a day long, and there is a very tangible outcome—the newspaper. Every 24 hours we must communicate with other departments, or else the product for that day—or the next day—will suffer. Other organizations have to share information, too, I know, but here, because of time issues, the importance of communicating well is magnified.

I need information from my subordinates. I work in the day; the production people work at night. When I arrive in the morning, I must receive reports from my night foremen that are detailed and clear. Otherwise, I cannot function nor can I respond to questions my superiors might have about the pressroom operation. I attend a daily meeting at 11 a.m. with other superintendents. If I am not adequately informed about nighttime activity and problems, I may not be able to participate intelligently at these sessions. I've been promoted internally here so I know that night workers typically go to sleep when their shift is over. Unless it's an absolute emergency I do not want to be phoning night employees for clarification until one or two in the afternoon. In an emergency I'd have to wake some folks up, but I want to be considerate. By not calling, I'm sending a message of sorts. I would be communicating a message beyond my questions if I were to regularly wake these people up in the middle of their nights.

Therefore, one of the key criteria for me in selecting my foremen is making sure I can count on them to communicate clearly and provide sufficiently detailed information. The other superintendents who attend the 11 a.m. meeting would say the same thing: They need information or they can't intelligently discuss the next day's paper at 11 a.m. Also, I leave reports for the foremen when I depart. I have to trust that they will read what I've written and will understand how to do what needs to be done.

Sometimes the discussion at 11 a.m. is irrelevant to my work, but there is still a value to the sessions. It helps me "feel their pain," if you know what I mean. I can understand what is going on in other units. Sometimes we, or at least I, get so caught up in my own department's responsibilities and problems that I don't think about the other parts of the paper. Each unit has its own issues and it's good for us to become sensitive to each other's needs in order to work cooperatively. Some people engage in finger pointing when there's been a glitch, but for the most part we realize that we're in this together. As I said previously, the paper comes out every day, so every day we have to combine Editorial, Circulation, Advertising, and Printing concerns. We have had some real success at the *Herald* and I'd like to think it's due, in part, to interacting well—up, down, and across.

Source: From *Organizational Communication* by Alan Jay Zaremba, p. 142. © 2003. Reprinted with permission of South-Western, a part of Cengage Learning, www.cengage.com/permissions.

Learning Objectives

After reading and studying this chapter, you should be able to:

1. Describe the five components of the communication process model.

2. Explain the forms of electronic communication technology.

3. Explain the different ways in which nonverbal communications influence supervisory communication.

4. Identify the three basic flows of formal communication in an organization.

5. Explain the managerial communication style matrix.

6. Identify and explain how organizational, interpersonal, and language barriers affect supervisory communication.

7. Identify five specific actions supervisors can take to improve their communications.

8. Show how a supervisor can use feedback to improve communication.

9. Define and illustrate active listening skills.

Communication is a critically important managerial skill. A typical workday finds supervisors assigning jobs, discussing coordination efforts with people from other departments, having discussions with their own bosses, attending meetings, listening to and counseling employees—the list could go on and on. Studies of managers and supervisors show that they spend 70–80 percent or more of their time directly communicating with others in meetings, on the telephone, online, or informally while walking around. Consider the management functions of planning, organizing, leading, and controlling—communication is essential in performing these. Moreover, the emerging supervisor role of teacher, leader, and coach depends heavily upon effective communication. Studies of managers and supervisors, like Bob Greim of the *Boston Herald*, reinforce how important communication skill is in performing their jobs successfully.[1]

What Is Communication?

Many supervisors think that communication is just a matter of "telling it like it is." When communication breakdowns occur, such supervisors are more apt to place the blame on others rather than themselves. Supervisors who have such an attitude fail to recognize the downside of such a narrow view of their communication responsibilities. To really understand a supervisor's role in communication, you must first learn about the basic communication process.

1 Describe the five components of the communication process model.

Communication Process Model

Rather than define communication in words, we will use a model that illustrates the communication process (see Exhibit 6-1). The five elements of the model are (1) message encoding (2) the channel, (3) message decoding, (4) feedback, and (5) noise.

The Sender Encodes the Message

Communication process model Model of the five components of communication and their relationships.

Encoding is the process by which a sender converts ideas into symbols, such as words or gestures that are capable of communicating. Each day, supervisors such as Bob Greim (Preview) send hundreds of encoded messages to their bosses, employees, other supervisors, personnel

EXHIBIT **6-1**

Communication
Process Model

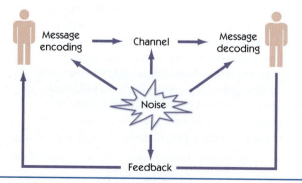

from other departments, and people outside the organization. Encoded messages consist not only of spoken and written words, but also nonverbal messages such as tone of voice, appearance, placing a watch on a desk and smiling or frowning, or showing up on time—or late—for an important meeting.

The Channel. The **channel** is the means used to pass the message. Channels include face-to-face communication, the telephone, written forms (such as memos, reports, newsletters, or e-mail), and group meetings. Note in the Preview the importance Greim placed on his 11 a.m. meeting of superintendents and on written messages to and from his foremen.

> One supervisor related how his crew was working on an important machine breakdown when the plant manager chewed him out for taking too long to complete the job. "I didn't mind getting chewed out as much as I minded the way he did it," said the supervisor. "It was via e-mail, and he copied the whole plant."

The Receiver Decodes the Message

Decoding is the process by which the receiver converts into an idea(s) the communication symbols encoded by the sender. Just as a sender's skill at encoding is important to effective communication, so also is the receiver's skill in decoding the sent message. Receivers give meaning to a message based on such factors as their interpretation of words, their familiarity with the subject matter, their perception of the sender's intent, their ability to listen, and the meaning they attribute to the sender's nonverbals.

Feedback

The message that we send in response to someone else's communication is called feedback. An advantage of the face to face communication channel is its immediacy and the number of feedback cycles allowed. Note in Exhibit 6-2 the information exchanged between the supervisor and Evan in just a matter of seconds, with each assuming the role of encoding,

sender Originates and sends a message.

message Words and/or nonverbal expressions that transmit meaning.

channel The means used to pass a message.

receiver The ultimate destination of the sender's message.

feedback The response that a communicator receives.

EXHIBIT 6-2

Communication Feedback

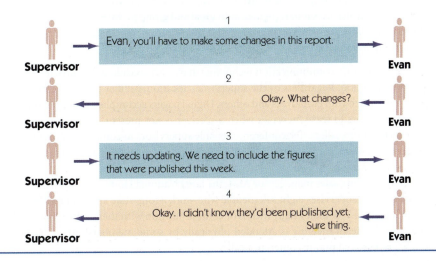

http://www.mars.com

decoding, and providing feedback. Most importantly, a supervisor's decision about the feedback needed to achieve the communication goal determines the appropriateness of the communication channel used, be it a one-to-one meeting, a larger group meeting, a voice or e-mail, or a handwritten note.

Noise

Noise consists of the potential barriers to effective communication in each phase of the communication process model. An example of noise at the "encoding" stage might be a supervisor's choice of words. Suppose your boss told you by voice mail that she just talked with an important customer and that you needed to follow up with the customer **"right away."** Does **right away** mean now, immediately after you hear the voice message? Or does it mean that you can do it several hours later in the day after closing an important sale or two with other customers? The nonspecific use of language is but one form of noise. Later in the chapter, you will learn more about "noise" when we discuss communication barriers.

② Explain the forms of electronic communication technology.

Electronic Communication Technology

Communication practices at the supervisory level are being greatly impacted by advancements in electronic communication technology. Just as computer fluency has become an essential employee requirement in many jobs, it has also become a prerequisite for more supervisory positions. Increasingly, supervisors are making use of electronically linked computer networks within their organization (intranets) and external to their organization (the Internet) to access information, transfer information, and, importantly, to communicate through e-mail. **E-mail** refers to documents created, transmitted, and read entirely on computer.

e-mail Documents created, transmitted, and read entirely on computer.

http://www.hotmail.com

> **Sharon Olds, remarketing supervisor for AutoFin, uses electronic communication extensively. She sends and receives daily more than 40 e-mail messages to people within her organization. These originate from and are sent to all levels. But even though she is physically housed near their cubicles in the immediate work area, Sharon frequently uses e-mail to communicate with her subordinates. E-mail allows her to be spontaneous, reduces the time involved in walking to see if someone is available, and enables easy record keeping. With a click of the Print button, she has a paper copy of the message. Sharon uses e-mail to pass on to her team members information about policy and procedure, but also uses it to recognize individual and group performance. She also uses PowerPoint software when making presentations to upper management and when conducting training classes.**

Advances in voice communication technology have also considerably impacted supervisory communication. Regardless of the supervisor's location, cellular phones enable him or her to keep in touch with employees and others. Digital pagers accomplish the same. Voice mail enables supervisors to leave messages when a receiver is not present, and to hear recorded voice messages from callers. Teleconferences enable supervisors to communicate with people in different locations simultaneously; videoconferences provide the additional benefit of visual communication.

Amanda Phillips, sales manager for ADT, the large National Home and Business Security System company, supervises eight salespeople who work a four-state area and reside in three different locations. Her major daily means of communication with them is by e-mail and cell phone; a weekly team meeting is attended physically by some members; others participate through a remote cell phone conference call.[2]

Importance of Nonverbal Messages

Nonverbal messages play a big role in communication. A classic study found that only about 7 percent of emotional meaning is communicated verbally; the other 93 percent is communicated nonverbally.[3] In other words, your impression of someone's emotions, such as anger, happiness, or fear, is formed more strongly from that person's tone of voice, facial expression, or other nonverbal means than from the words the person uses.

Supervisors have to be careful that their verbal and nonverbal signals are consistent and do not give the wrong impression. Moreover, supervisors can obtain much information from the nonverbal signals of others.

Basically, nonverbal signals, which can send positive or negative information, fall into seven categories:

1. **Voice signals.** Emphasis on certain words, pauses, or tone of voice. For example, can you say "Nice job, Evans" in such a way that it's actually a putdown?

2. **Body signals.** Slumped posture, clenched fist, or the act of kicking a piece of equipment.

3. **Facial signals.** Smile, frown, raised eyebrow, or degree of eye contact; note in Exhibit 6-3 how direction of one's eyebrows significantly changes the emotion conveyed.

4. **Object signals.** Office furniture, such as desks or chairs, plus carpet, plaques and awards on the wall, clothing or jewelry worn.

5. **Space signals.** Huddling close, being distant, or sitting beside someone.

6. **Time signals.** Being on time, being available, or saving time. An interview was scheduled for a potential medical school intern at Johns Hopkins Hospital. The interview was scheduled for 11 a.m., but transportation was affected by a severe snowstorm.

> **3** Explain the different ways in which nonverbal communications influence supervisory communication.

voice signals Signals sent by placing emphasis on certain words, pauses, or the tone of voice used.

body signals Nonverbal signals communicated by body action.

facial signals Nonverbal messages sent by facial expression.

object signals Nonverbal messages sent by physical objects.

space signals Nonverbal messages sent based on physical distance from one another.

time signals Nonverbal messages sent by time actions.

EXHIBIT 6-3

Nonverbal Communication

Set A: Basic happy face with changing eyebrows

Happy

Sheepish

Scheming

Set B: Basic sad face with changing eyebrows

Sad   Despondent   Angry

The student arrived at 1 p.m. for the interview, feeling his lateness would surely be acceptable. He was told, "What if a patient was in a life and death situation and you were on call and did not come in?" There was no formal interview and no intern position.[4]

touching signals Nonverbal messages sent by body contact.

7. **Touching signals.** Shaking hands, sympathetic pat on the back, or touching someone to gain attention.

✔ **STOP AND THINK**

Stephen Jobs, chief executive officer (CEO) of Apple Computer and Pixar Animation Studios, often dresses very casually at work. He frequently wears jeans. A coat and tie are exceptions rather than standard attire. Jobs explains this as his personal style. In what ways does a manager's attire communicate?

· ·

4 Identify the three basic flows of formal communication in an organization.

Flows of Communication

To put the supervisor's communication role in perspective, we need to examine the flows of communication in an entire organization. Here we will look at communication *within* the organization, rather than with outside groups such as customers, suppliers, or government agencies. Exhibit 6-4 shows that there are several directions in which formal communication flows: (1) downward, (2) upward, and (3) laterally or diagonally. A fourth flow is the flow of informal communication, commonly known as the *grapevine*.

EXHIBIT 6-4

Flow of Formal Communication in an Organization

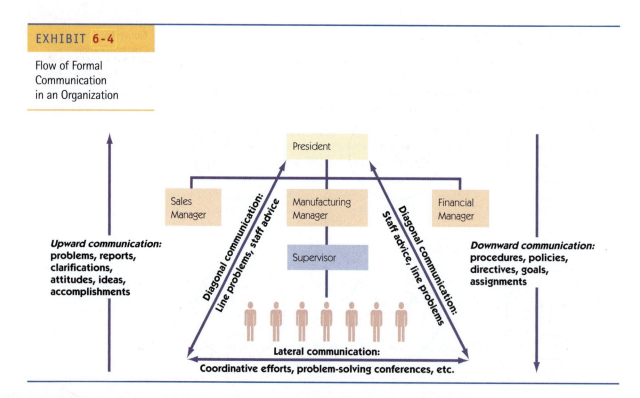

EXHIBIT 6-5

Communications You
Like to Receive from
Your Supervisor

Role clarifications. What's expected of you, how much authority and responsibility you have, and your job assignments.

Praise and recognition. A supervisor's commendations on a job well done, compliments about you in the presence of third parties, and expressions of appreciation.

Constructive criticism and feedback. Tactful criticism that demonstrates interest and implies a personal and professional concern on the part of the supervisor.

Demonstration of interest. Communications reflecting interest in your professional growth and development, efforts to work with you to do a better job, and giving you undivided attention during conversation (as opposed to lack of eye contact or partial attention).

Requests for information or assistance. Asking your opinion and advice, and consulting with you about relevant matters on the job.

Information that

a. Makes you feel important because you're "in the know"

b. Pertains to your department's progress, to other work team members, to plans for the department, and to contemplated changes

c. Pertains to aspects of the overall organization, such as sales, forecasts, objectives, outlook for the future, and general internal changes of which the supervisor is aware

d. Pertains to promotions, merit increases, desirable job assignments, and favors that can be granted by the supervisor

The Vertical Flows: Downward and Upward Communication

Downward communication originates with managers and supervisors and passes down to employees. Tremendous amounts of communication constantly flow in this direction. Examples of downward communication include announcements of goals and objectives, policies, decisions, procedures, job assignments, and general information.

> **A recent study of 336 organizations showed that up to two thirds of their employees do not understand or even know their organization's mission and strategies. About 30 percent of the organizations indicated that this information was only available to their upper management.**[5]

Studies show that employees consistently rate their direct supervisor as their preferred choice of communication channel. Exhibit 6-5 lists communications that employees *like* to receive from their supervisor. Take a few seconds to examine the list before reading further. Do any items on this list strike you as being more crucial than others? "Knowing where you stand" is listed by many employees as their single most important need.

Upward communication flows from lower to upper organizational levels, as shown in Exhibit 6-6. It may consist of progress reports on a job; requests for help or clarification; communication about employees' concerns, attitudes, and feelings; or ideas and suggestions for improvements on the job.

Unfortunately, many supervisors do not seek these forms of upward communication, especially progress reports, from their employees. Neither do they obtain information about their employees' true attitudes, feelings, or suggestions for improvements. Japanese managers

downward communication
Flows that originate with supervisors and are passed down to employees.

upward communication
Flows from lower to upper organizational levels.

EXHIBIT 6-6

Upward Communication
from Employees to
Management

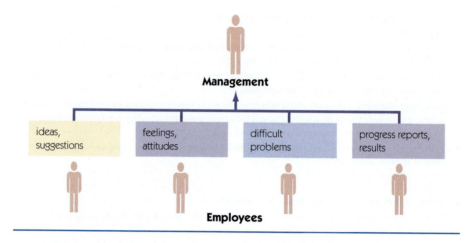

have a much better reputation than American managers for being receptive to workers' needs and opinions, especially in the area of job improvements. In 1 year, for instance, Toyota implemented over 60,000 new ideas that were received from workers at its five U.S. manufacturing plants.

In addition to requesting oral or written progress reports, other means of encouraging upward communication from employees include suggestion systems, an open-door policy, attitude and morale surveys, group or individual meetings at which employees are encouraged to speak up, and hot lines where employees can anonymously solicit answers to questions or report unethical practices.

One superintendent whom we know holds a weekly meeting of production supervisors to review work progress, discuss job changes, and resolve problems in the department. When issues are being discussed, he often makes sure that he gets others' opinions before giving his own. As he states, "I know personally that if this group knows how I feel about something, more of them will tell me what I want to hear. That's why I like to get their views first. Some of them will come right out and ask what I think, as if once I tell them, the discussion should end."

✔ STOP AND THINK

Dramatic changes are taking place to make the workforce much more diverse, including increasing percentages of foreign workers and of U.S. citizens of African-American, Hispanic, Asian, and Native American descent. In what ways do these changes impact the *downward communication flow* from manager/supervisor to work team members? The *upward communication flow* from team members to manager/supervisor?

⑤ Explain the managerial communication style matrix.

Managerial Communication Matrix. Now that you have a good understanding of the vertical communication flows, you can better understand each supervisor's communication

EXHIBIT **6-7**

The Managerial
Communication Matrix

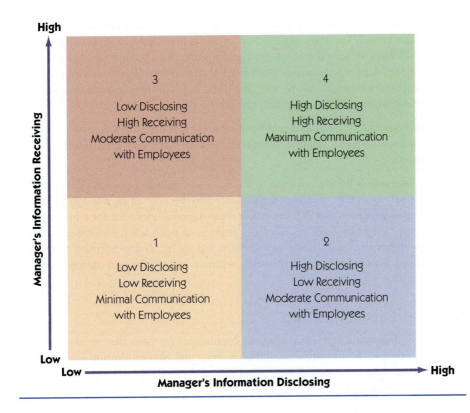

relationship with his or her team members. As shown in Exhibit 6-7, The Managerial Communication Matrix, a supervisor's basic communications with team members consist of disclosing information (downward communication) and receiving information from them (upward communication). A supervisor can be considered high as an information discloser and high as an information receiver (box 4), high in one but not the other (boxes 2 and 3), or low in both (box 1).

When you work for a high discloser, you hear frequently about performance expectations, standards, your boss's likes and dislikes, where you stand, and about the goings-on in the organization.[6] Low disclosers communicate less frequently and openly about such matters.

High information–receiving supervisors are accessible and maintain an environment that encourages feedback from employees. They are apt to spend much of their time listening to employees' discussions about performance progress, problems being experienced, and ideas and feelings about organizational and personal issues. In contrast, low information–receiving supervisors are less accessible and tend to create a less encouraging upward-communication environment.

What would you like your own supervisor's style to be? In our workshops and seminars, about 90 percent of managers and supervisors state a strong preference in working for a high discloser, high receiver (box 4). When given a choice of their own boss's style being either a high discloser, low receiver (box 2) or a high receiver, low discloser (box 3), most opt for a supervisor whose style falls in box 2. This choice reflects the importance managers place on knowing clearly their boss's performance expectations and his or her feelings about their performance. To determine where you fall on the matrix, complete Skill Builder 6-1, at the end of this chapter.

Lateral–Diagonal Flows

lateral–diagonal communication Flows between individuals in the same department or different departments.

Lateral–diagonal communication takes place between individuals in the same department or different departments. This form of communication has become more important than ever in the past 25 years for several reasons. First, organizations have become greatly specialized. Members of staff departments such as purchasing, human resources, cost accounting, maintenance, and others interact regularly with line personnel. This may be to provide services, coordinate, advise, and sometimes actually give directives.

> **In the preview, note the importance of Bob Greim's 11 a.m. daily meeting with superintendents from Editorial, Printing, Advertising, and Circulation to share information and concerns.**

A second reason is the increased use of teams. Cross-functional, problem-solving teams comprising personnel from different departments have become an increasingly necessary approach to address problems that cut across organizational lines. One form of employee empowerment is the use of self-managed or autonomous work teams *within* departments. These teams often meet as a group on a daily basis and are highly dependent on communications among their members as they budget, schedule, assign jobs, and control quality of their *own* work.

Informal Communication

informal communication Separate from a formal, established communication system.

The upward, downward, and lateral–diagonal communication flows that we have just presented are examples of formal communication. **Informal communication** is that which exists separately from the formal, established communication system. Some examples of informal communication are given below. Each example represents a social network channel

Coworkers having lunch together is a common setting for informal communication.

that you will not find listed in the company's organization chart. Yet, informal contacts such as these are a way of life and can be a valuable communication source for supervisors.

> Lisa, Diane, Fred, and Roberto carpool, since they all work for the same company and live about 35 miles away. Their driving time is usually spent talking about their departments, people who work at the company, and other job-related matters. Because they all work in different departments, they are very much "in the know" about a number of company matters long before the formal company communication channels carry them.

> Before seeing her boss about an important request, supervisor Mildred O'Neil dropped by to get Kathie Troy's opinion. Troy is a close friend of O'Neil's boss and would probably have some excellent advice for O'Neil as to how best to present her request.

The Grapevine. The best-known informal communication method is the grapevine, also called the *rumor mill*. It is called a **grapevine** because, like the plant it is named after, it is tangled and twisted and seemingly grows without direction. Yet some surveys have found the grapevine to be employees' major source of information about their company, and it has been found to be surprisingly accurate. In fact, the research of Keith Davis, an authority on human relations, has shown that in normal work situations, over 75 percent of grapevine information is correct.[7]

grapevine The "rumor mill."

Purposes Served by Informal Communication. Informal communication accomplishes a number of purposes. Among these are (1) providing a source of information not ordinarily available, (2) reducing the effects of monotony, and (3) satisfying personal needs such as the need for relationships or status. Some people, in fact, take great pride in their unofficial knowledge of company matters.

Living with Informal Communication. Effective supervisors realize that informal communication serves important purposes. A supervisor must be aware that, unless employees are informed through formal channels, the informal channels will take up the slack. Keeping employees well informed is the best way to manage the grapevine, although it can never be eliminated. It will tend to be especially active when employees are concerned about job security or status.

Barriers to Effective Supervisory Communication

Now that you understand the communication process, let's explore some typical communication barriers that a supervisor faces on the job. These barriers may be organizational, interpersonal, or language related.

6 Identify and explain how organizational, interpersonal, and language barriers affect supervisory communication.

Organizational Barriers

Three types of organizational barriers to communication are (1) layers of hierarchy, (2) authority and status, and (3) specialization and its related jargon.

Layers of Hierarchy. Have you ever asked someone to give a message to a third person and found that the third person received a message totally different from the one you sent? The same thing occurs in organizations. When a message goes up or down the organization, it passes through a number of "substations" at each layer. Each layer can add to, take from, qualify, or completely change the original message!

At higher levels of management, messages are usually broad and general. At lower levels, these broad messages must be put into more specific terms. That's frequently the fly in the ointment, especially when lower and top levels have a gap of understanding between them.

Authority and Status. The very fact that one person is a boss over others creates a barrier to free and open communication.

✔ **STOP AND THINK**

Do you recall your feelings, as a student in elementary or high school, when you were told to report to the principal's office? Even if you had done nothing wrong, you were probably still very anxious and defensive about the visit.

••

> The conference room patter before the superintendent walked in was loose and jovial. Some verbal horseplay occurred among the members, and there was kidding and joking. Some made very negative remarks about the major item on the agenda, which was a discussion of proposed changes in the company's system of performance evaluation. One person joked about another's being the one to tell the boss about the flaws in the new system, even though the boss strongly favored it. But when the boss walked in, the mood shifted dramatically. He did most of the talking; those in attendance listened attentively. Even when he asked for their opinions, he received only favorable comments about the proposal.

Since, as a supervisor, you must fill out employees' performance evaluations and determine rewards and penalties, employees will tend to give you the information that you are most likely to welcome. Information about frustrations, disagreements with your policies, job problems, below-standard work, and the like will tend to be withheld or changed to look more favorable.

Specialization and Its Related Jargon. The *principle of specialization* states that employees are more efficient when each performs just one task or only certain aspects of a task. For example, accountants do accounting work, salespersons sell, industrial engineers prepare efficiency studies, and safety specialists see to it that working conditions are safe.

Today's increased specialization, however, also creates problems. Specialists have their own technical language or jargon, interests, and narrow view of the organization. Many special terms used by accountants, computer technology personnel, marketing specialists, and other groups are completely foreign to people in other departments. This can severely hamper communication.

Interpersonal and Language Barriers

Even if the three organizational barriers just discussed do not exist, a supervisor's communication can still be distorted by interpersonal as well as language-related problems. Exhibit 6-8 lists a number of these barriers, some of which we will discuss.

perception How one selects, organizes, and gives meaning to his or her world.

Differing Perceptions. Perception is the process by which one selects, organizes, and gives meaning to his or her world. All of us have a special way of filtering things around us based on our culture, needs, moods, biases, expectations, experiences, and so on.

A major barrier to communication results from the increasingly diverse workforce. Broad differences in age, race, sex, education, nationality, and other factors result in quite different perceptions and interpretations of what is seen and heard, and they often result in different styles of communicating. This poses a much stronger communication challenge to supervisors than if all team members had similar backgrounds and shared similar characteristics with their supervisor.

One factor limiting our perception is that we can't grasp the whole situation at a given time. Some matters receive greater attention than others, while some matters receive none at all.

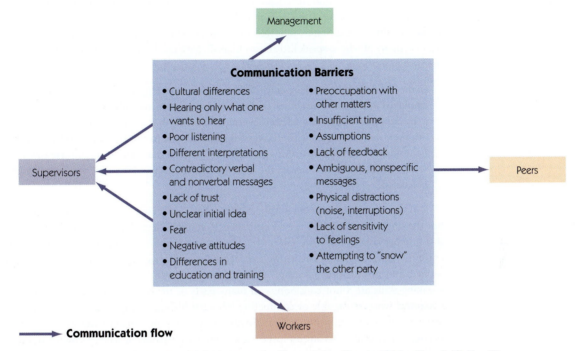

Source: *Business Communication Today*, 4/e by Bovee/Thill, (c) 1998. Reprinted by permission of Prentice-Hall, Inc., Upper Saddle River, NJ.

Those matters we do focus on usually serve some immediate purpose. A person's needs, moods, cultural and social influences, and attitudes all come together to determine which things are important and what they mean.

> In a factory accident, for example, the following persons might "see" the accident differently: the supervisor, who may have lost a valuable worker; the safety engineer, whose safety record may have been blemished; the fellow worker, who is the injured worker's best friend; the company physician, who attends to the injured worker; and the human resources manager, who is concerned with workers' compensation and finding a replacement for the injured worker. If these persons were to communicate about the accident, each would have a different version.

When we go about interpreting things around us, we have a tendency to put similar things in the same category, to make them easier to handle. This tendency is called **stereotyping.** Stereotyping poses a formidable communication challenge, given the increasing diversity of employees. There are strong negative stereotypes for various nationalities, races, religions, sexes, occupations, and other groups in our society. For example, a male manager may label all women as "emotionally weak," all union officials as "agitators," and all staff employees as "meddlers." Obviously, such stereotyping will have a strong influence on this manager's communications to and from these individuals. On the other hand, stereotypes may be favorable.

stereotyping The tendency to put similar things in the same categories to make them easier to deal with.

As a supervisor, you must be aware that your attitudes, biases, and prejudices—both positive and negative—strongly influence your communications with others.

Language-Related Factors

A primary communication barrier is posed by the lack of a common primary language. In 2003 more than 47 million Americans age 5 or older spoke a language other than English at home, almost 20 percent of the U.S. population![8] Spanish is the dominant second language spoken in the United States, followed by Chinese. The recent influx of immigrants from Mexico, many of whom speak little or no English, have created communication problems for many organizations.

In the Pacific Northwest, Hispanics comprise more than 60 percent of firefighting crews employed by private contractors. During a raging wildfire in southern Oregon, leaders of a fire crew got word to immediately evacuate a fire line that was being dug. The problem, however, was that all crew firefighters digging the line in the area were Hispanic, and none understood the instructions given in English. After much shouting and arm waving, someone was found to translate the message into Spanish and the crew was successfully evacuated.[9]

No one knows the specific number of U.S. workers having limited or no English skills, but the single fact that there are an estimated 10 million illegal Hispanic immigrants makes this number significant. Throughout the United States, they are employed in many smaller entrepreneurial organizations as well as larger ones in agriculture, trades, manufacturing, service, and not-for-profit sectors. Managers and supervisors with English- and Spanish-speaking skills are a hot commodity in many parts of the country, as are human resource personnel who are capable of conducting bilingual hiring, testing, orienting, training, and safety sessions. Sometimes managers themselves take the initiative to address the language barrier. Since most of his 50 employee organization is Hispanic, Bruce Frye, owner of Fresno, California, based Frye Roofing, went back to school to learn Spanish so as to improve his communications with personnel.[10]

Even when people speak the same language, though, language is still a major communication barrier. The fact that people interpret words differently can be traced to a lack of precision in the use of language. True, you can say that a drill press weighs 270 pounds, or that Sam Eggers is 5'11" tall, or that Judy Snead has completed ten years of service with the hospital. Language is precise in that regard, and we can verify it.

Suppose a supervisor colleague tells you that "Judy Snead is a good, loyal nurse." What does "loyal" mean to you? What your supervisor considers to be "loyal" (for example, turning down several job offers from competing firms) may be "complacent" or "unambitious" to you. A "good" nurse to you may be one who is a sympathetic listener and spends a lot of time talking with patients and being cheerful and friendly; to your fellow supervisor, a "good" nurse may be one who is knowledgeable and competent and goes about her or his work without trying to make much conversation.

Misinterpretation of the word "empty" by maintenance personnel led to 50–60 oxygen canisters labeled "empty" being shipped in the cargo hold of ValuJet Flight 592 en route to Atlanta from Miami on May 11, 1996. Unfortunately, the "empty" canisters were still highly volatile. They were routinely packed in cardboard boxes and stored in the plane's cargo hold without required safety measures. The canisters ignited in flight, causing the plane to crash in the Florida Everglades, killing 110 crew members and passengers. Subsequent investigations resulted in grounded ValuJet flights, adverse publicity, and severe financial repercussions for ValuJet, and a fine of $2 million for Sabretech, the airline maintenance firm responsible for shipping the canisters.[11]

http://www.daimler
chrysler.com

Growing diversity in the United States results in differing linguistic styles that can be barriers for effective communication. Supervisors need to be aware of these differences to effectively manage their employees.

Sometimes a supervisor uses imprecise language when more precise language is necessary. Suppose a supervisor tells an employee, "You must improve on your absenteeism, as it has been excessive. Otherwise, you'll be disciplined." What does the supervisor mean by "improve on your absenteeism" and "excessive"? What "discipline" does the supervisor have in mind? Skill Builder 6-2 reinforces our need to be specific in using language.

Another language barrier is the fact that words have multiple meanings and not all people have the same level of language skill, as exemplified in Exhibit 6-9. Many terms familiar to a veteran employee, for example, may be over the heads of a new crop of employees going through an orientation program. In some cases, people even try to "snow" others by using terms they know the others will not understand!

EXHIBIT 6-9

Multiple Interpretations of Words

FIX the machine to its foundation. (anchor)
FIX that nitpicking cost accountant. (give just due)
FIX the cash register. (repair)
FIXING to go to the storeroom. (getting ready to)
FIX our position regarding overtime policy. (establish)
FIX you up with that young engineer. (arrange a date)
A banquet with all the **FIXIN'S.** (special effects, side dishes)
FIX things up with the salespeople. (make amends, patch up a quarrel)
If we don't make quota, we're in a **FIX.** (a pickle, a bad position)
FIX the date outcome. (so that it's favorable, rig it)
FIX your hair before seeing the boss. (arrange, make orderly)
FIX the department meal on Friday. (cook, prepare)
FIX the company's mascot dog. (neuter)

Linguistic Styles. Linguistic styles greatly reflect the continuing diversity in the United States and the ways employees communicate at work. Linguistic style refers to typical patterns in their speech, including such factors as volume, speed, and pauses; being direct or indirect; asking questions; and using body language with speech. Differences in linguistic styles are important communication barriers, especially among different cultures, where the styles vary greatly. For example, Japanese workers tend to communicate very formally and show much respect toward their bosses. They also use lengthy pauses to assess what is said. Americans, on the other hand, often forgo formality and view pauses as signs of uncertainty or insecurity. Brazilians and Saudis favor closer physical speaking distances than do Americans. An American supervisor may find a Brazilian employee's desire for a close speaking distance aggressive, when, in fact, for the employee, it is a normal physical distance. Another cultural linguistic style difference involves eye contact.

> Several years ago, Barbara Walters interviewed Libyan leader Colonel Maummar Qaddafi for a national U.S. television audience. She was reportedly taken aback because during the interview he refused to look directly at her as he spoke. Walters considered this insulting, as if the intent was to demean her. Her reaction was attributable to differences in linguistic style of the two cultures. In Qaddafi's culture, not looking directly at her was a sign of respect.

Linguistic style may also vary among subcultures. Among some Native Americans, a child's continued eye contact with an adult is a sign of disrespect. Important differences exist between linguistic styles of American males and females, as shown in Exhibit 6-10. American males may find swearing and racy joke telling acceptable among themselves, but females might find this offensive. Furthermore, women's linguistic styles tend to be more indirect, expressive, and polite, whereas mens' styles are more direct and assertive. Women view conversation as a means for establishing a "connection" and intimacy with others; men see conversation as a negotiation through which they seek to establish or maintain status and independence.[12]

EXHIBIT 6-10

Linguistic Styles of Men and Women

A number of popular books about the different linguistic styles of men and women have been written in recent years. Among them are Deborah Tannen's *You Just Don't Understand: Women and Men in Conversation* and John Grey's *Men Are from Mars, Women Are from Venus*. Some of their ideas, greatly simplified, are shown here.

	WOMEN	MEN
Object of talk	Establish rapport, make connections, negotiate inclusive relationships	Preserve independence, maintain status, exhibit skill and knowledge
Listening behavior	Attentive, steady eye contact; remain stationary; nod head	Less attentive, sporadic eye contact; move around
Pauses	Frequent pauses, giving chance for others to take turns	Infrequent pauses; interrupt each other to take turns
Small talk	Personal disclosure	Impersonal topics
Focus	Details first, pulled together at end	Big picture
Gestures	Small, confined	Expansive
Method	Questions; apologies; "we" statements; hesitant, indirect, soft speech	Assertions; "I" statements; clear, loud, take-charge speech

Source: From *ACP-Business Communication Process & Product* 4th edition by Guffey. 2002. Reprinted with permission of South-Western, a part of Cengage Learning, www.cengage.com/permissions.

After examining Exhibit 6-8, which barriers do you believe are present between your instructor and members of this class?

Improving Supervisory Communications

As we've indicated, communication is too critical to your success as a supervisor to be left to chance. Improving your skills in communication will help you accomplish your "task" and "people" goals. Some specific things you can do are (1) set the proper climate with your employees, (2) plan your communication, (3) use repetition to reinforce key ideas, (4) encourage the use of feedback, and (5) become a better listener.

> **7** Identify five specific actions supervisors can take to improve their communications.

Set the Proper Communication Climate

A supervisor doesn't communicate in a vacuum. Communications take place within the entire supervisor–employee or supervisor–group relationship. A supervisor and his or her workers each bring a store of experiences, expectations, and attitudes to the communication event. These mental pictures strongly influence the meaning each person assigns to the messages sent and received. Thus, the setting is very important for good communication.

What type of setting best contributes to effective communication? We believe that two important factors are (1) mutual trust between the supervisor and employees and (2) a minimum of status barriers.

Establish Mutual Trust. Trust helps communication in two ways. First, if an employee trusts you, he or she is more willing to communicate honestly and openly. Second, if employees trust you, they are less likely to distort your motives and make negative assumptions about your communications. If you fight for your employees' interests by bargaining with higher management, if you discipline fairly and consistently, and if you respect your employees' abilities, you are more likely to be trusted by them. You'll be considered a source of help in reaching their goals.

Minimize Status Barriers. Status barriers consist of those factors that call attention to the fact that the supervisor ranks higher than his or her employees. Status barriers may be such things as dress, formality, office arrangement, and so forth. Generally, the best communication occurs in a setting where people are relaxed and comfortable and status differences are reduced. For example, the way a supervisor arranges his or her office furniture has much to do with establishing a relaxed setting, as shown in Exhibit 6-11.

> One supervisor says he likes to discuss certain sensitive matters away from his own turf so as to make an employee feel more comfortable and less nervous. By design, supervisors may communicate in the employee's work area or in a neutral situation such as over a cup of coffee or lunch.

> At Honda of America, Honda President Irimajiri Shoichiro wore no tie and ate in the company cafeteria. On the front of his white overalls, which were just like those everyone else in the plant wore, was his nickname, "IRI." He had no private office but worked at a desk in the same work area as the 100 others in his white-collar work group. This represented a distinct effort to diminish the status differences between himself and all other employees.

http://www.hondacars.com

EXHIBIT 6-11

Desk–Chair Arrangements
That Affect Formality

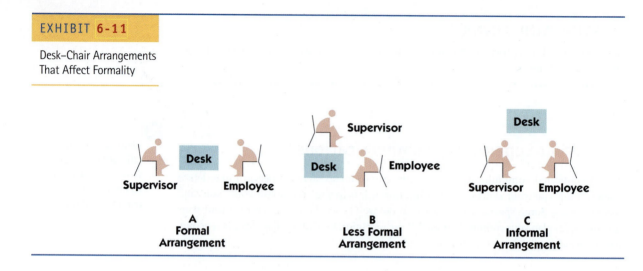

A
Formal
Arrangement

B
Less Formal
Arrangement

C
Informal
Arrangement

Plan for Effective Communication

How many times have you completely blown a communication situation by not being prepared for it? After it's over, you think "Now why didn't I say this?" or "I never should have said such and such."

Anticipate Situations. If you are a supervisor, many of your contacts will occur without much warning and may not allow much planning. Yet there are a number of situations you can anticipate. For example, you can give thought to the following situations before they occur:

1. Giving employees their performance evaluations.

2. Disciplining employees and making work corrections.

3. Delegating authority for a job and communicating job assignments and instructions.

4. Persuading employees to accept changes in the job or work environment.

5. Trying to sell an idea to your boss or to other staff members.

If you understand how complex good communications are, you'll be more aware of the existing barriers and try to minimize their effects. To be understood by your team members, you must put yourself in their shoes and try to see things from their viewpoint. An old North American Indian prayer expresses the thought this way: "Lord, grant that I may not criticize my neighbor until I've walked a mile in his moccasins."

Select the Proper Channel. Part of communication planning involves determining the appropriate communication channel, or medium, that you will use to convey your message. As mentioned earlier, your common options include a personal or group meeting, a telephone call, a memo or letter, an e-mail, or an electronic conference.

information richness The sheer amount of information that a communication channel carries.

Generally, supervisors and managers prefer face-to-face communication because that channel is high in **information richness**—the sheer amount of information that a communication channel carries. Face-to-face communication is the richest potential channel because it enables nonverbal messages and offers spontaneous feedback. The one-on-one, face-to-face setting is the richest communication form, followed by small-group meetings and telephone messages. Telephone messages have no visual contact, but still enable nonverbal information to be passed through tone of voice, inflection, pauses, and volume. A voice-mail message, however, loses much potential information richness because it lacks opportunity for immediate feedback.

Explaining company procedures and policies to employees helps establish mutual trust.

Lower information richness channels include the written communication forms: e-mails, memos, and letters. These channels lack nonverbal communication, and they do not provide a direct opportunity for spontaneous feedback. They are useful for delivering straightforward messages and presenting impersonal information, such as data, routine policy, and announcements, especially when a permanent record is useful. However, written messages are clearly less suited when the content deals with complex or emotional issues, or when clarification of the writer's intent is necessary to properly interpret a message's meaning. The e-mail message sent to 400 company managers by Neal Patterson, CEO of Cerner, a 3,000-employee software company, had a devastating effect. Some excerpts:

We are getting less than 40 hours of work from a large number of our KC-based EMPLOYEES. The parking lot is sparsely used at 8:00 a.m.; likewise at 5:00 p.m. As managers you either do not know what your EMPLOYEES are doing or YOU do not CARE. You have created expectations on the work effort which allowed this to happen inside Cerner, creating a very unhealthy environment. In either case you have a problem and you will fix it or I will replace you. NEVER in my career have I allowed a team which worked for me to think they had a 40-hour job. I have allowed YOU to create a culture which is permitting this. NO LONGER. . . .

You have allowed this to get to this state and you will fix it or I will replace you. . . You have 2 weeks. Tick Tock.[13]

Patterson later said he was "trying to light a match under them" and "expecting them to take it with a grain of salt." The message was leaked throughout the company intranet, then found its way to the Internet. Its harsh tone shocked thousands of employees and outside readers, especially financial analysts and investors. Within 3 days, the company stock dropped over 25 percent. Patterson later apologized to all, wishing he had never hit the Send button. But the damage had been done. The message to supervisors and managers is this: Be careful in choosing your message channel!

An important guideline is to select the channel that best suits your message. If you must communicate a personal, sensitive message where empathy and listening are required, such as one involving a transfer, promotion, or performance coaching, face-to-face communication is likely called for. On the other hand, if the message is straightforward or routine, involves much data or detail, or must serve as a record, then written communication is called for. A very important message may call for both written and spoken channels to be used together.

Consider the Receiver's Frame of Reference. Earlier we discussed how each of us has unique filters that influence the way we interpret the world around us. Obviously, the better attuned you are to your subordinates' and others' patterns of evaluation, the more effective your communications to and from them will be. Effective communication, then, requires you to step into the shoes of others and visualize situations from their perspective.

A supervisor must frequently ask questions like these:

1. How is this person *like* me?
2. How is this person *different* from me?
3. How is this person *similar* to other employees?
4. How is this person *different* from other employees?
5. How will this person react if I say such and such?

These questions are especially important given the increased diversity of employees. You don't find the answers to these questions by reading employees' biographical data from their personnel files. The only way to discover employees' different motives, needs, attitudes, and ways of interpreting things is to interact with them directly, be sensitive to these differences, and use effective feedback and listening techniques.

Reinforce Key Ideas through Repetition

Repeating a message plays an important part in communicating effectively. This is especially true when you have to communicate technical information or a direct order. Repetition, or redundancy, reduces the chance that incorrect assumptions will be made by the receiver. For example, you can state a complicated message in several ways, using examples, illustrations, or comparisons. You can also say the same thing several times, but in different words. Here, for instance, is how a supervisor might communicate an instruction to an employee.

> **Danny, we just got a telephone order for a 42-by-36–inch fireplace screen in our KL–17 series. I know you haven't done one up like it since last year, when that customer in Idaho gave us so much trouble. That's the same style this guy wants, with black and gold trim as shown in this catalog clipping. And you heard me right: He wants it 42 inches high by 36 inches wide—higher than it is wide. (*Hands Danny the written specifications for the screen.*) Can you get it out in the next week?**

Note how the supervisor used a past example and a catalog to clarify the style of the fireplace screen and how the supervisor repeated the required measurements, even though he also provided written specs.

8 Show how a supervisor can use feedback to improve communication.

Encourage the Use of Feedback

As mentioned earlier, feedback is the response given by the receiver of the message. Two ways a supervisor can encourage employees to provide feedback are (1) to create a relaxed environment and (2) to take the initiative.

Create a Relaxed Environment. Earlier in this section, we discussed the importance of establishing a favorable setting for communication. A relaxed setting is also required when the supervisor wants to obtain feedback from his or her employees. As a supervisor, you certainly should not look down on employees for asking questions or for openly stating their opinions, suggestions, or feelings on a subject. A defensive attitude on your part discourages feedback from employees. How you communicate also determines, to a large extent, the amount of feedback you will receive. For example, written instructions or memos don't allow for the immediate feedback that can be gained from face-to-face communication.

In ancient times, there was an Asian king who hated to hear bad news. Whenever a courier reported bad news or an unfortunate event to the king, the king became furious and had him beheaded. After three couriers bit the dust, the king began hearing only good news! The moral here for supervisors is that they must be receptive to all information, both good and bad, from their employees, or they, too, will be surrounded by a smokescreen.

Take the Initiative. Although the type of communication used and the setting for the communication are important in determining what feedback is obtained, the supervisor still must take the initiative in getting responses from the work group. For example, after giving a job assignment, you might ask "Do you have any questions?" or "Did I leave anything out?" An even better approach would be to say, "To make sure I've gotten my message across, how about repeating it to me?" Frequently this approach produces a number of clarifications that someone might otherwise be unwilling to request for fear of looking stupid. You must be careful, however, not to use a patronizing tone of voice or to put too much of the burden of understanding on the employee. Remember—effective communication is a two-way street. Finally, you can set the stage for further feedback with such comments as "If anything comes up later or if you have some questions, just let me know." A participative leadership style relies heavily on good two-way communication, which is a form of feedback. When a supervisor allows team members to make decisions or to express opinions, their responses are a form of feedback. This style helps the supervisor better understand the team members' thinking.

Feedback can also help you learn how to better send messages in the future. When you discover that your initial message wasn't clear or that your use of persuasion was not effective, you can refine future messages. A summary of tips about feedback appears in Exhibit 6-12.

EXHIBIT **6-12**

Tips about Feedback

- Generally, feedback is better where there is a trusting relationship between people. If a person doesn't trust you, he or she is not likely to level with you or share feelings very readily. As a result, you are told only what you want to hear instead of what you *should* hear. For example, the person may say, "Yes, sir, things are going okay on the Anders job," when in reality there is a lack of progress or some severe problem. Or the person may say, "I certainly agree with you, boss," when in reality the person doesn't agree with you at all but doesn't want to upset you or risk being chewed out.
- Some people give feedback readily, but others need some encouragement. Examples of the latter type are people who are timid, quiet, or insecure or have learned that "it's best to keep your mouth shut around here." *Asking* such people for their ideas, suggestions, or feelings may elicit feedback. For example, you can say, "Dale, how will this new policy affect your group?" or "What do you think about . . . ?"
- Complimenting people for providing feedback reinforces their willingness to *continue* providing feedback. When you say, "I appreciate your honesty in discussing this" or "Thanks, Joan, for raising some issues that need to be clarified," you are encouraging the other party to give feedback in the future.
- When you are giving instructions, it is a good habit to ask the listener if he or she has any questions. For example, you can ask, "Is this clear, Dick? Have you any questions?" Some supervisors end their instructions with "Now, Dick, let's see if we're together on this. In your own words, run by me what it seems I've just said." If the instructions are given over the telephone, you can say "Okay, Dick, read back to me those seven dates I just gave you so we can make sure we're together on this."
- When you have potentially negative feedback to give, it is helpful to begin by saying "Sarah, may I offer a suggestion about . . . ?" or "May I give you my impression of . . . ?" or "Can I share my feelings about . . . ?" This approach is less pushy, and the message will be received with less defensiveness than if you bluntly blurt out the negative information.
- Nonverbal signals and body language offer a wide variety of feedback. Frowns, nervous fidgeting, nods of the head, and other facial expressions and body movements give us a lot of information. Frequently, however, we overlook these signals completely because we are not looking at the other person or because we are absorbed in our own thoughts and messages.

Become a Better Listener

It has been said that Mother Nature blessed human beings with two ears and only one mouth as a not-so-subtle hint that, unfortunately, we often ignore. How to Be a Good Listener has become a popular subject and is being taught today in many elementary and high schools throughout the country. One of Dr. Stephen Covey's *Seven Habits of Highly Effective People* is "Seek first to understand, then to be understood."[14] Studies of managers show that on average they spend a larger percentage of their work day (about 60 percent) in listening than in the other communication forms—speaking, writing, or reading.[15] Test your listening skills by completing the test in Exhibit 6-13.

EXHIBIT 6-13

Rate Your Listening Habits

As a listener, how frequently do you engage in the following listening behaviors? Place a check in the appropriate column, and determine your rating based on the scale at the bottom of the page.

Listening Habit	Very Seldom 10	8	6	4	Almost Always 2
1. Faking attention, pretending to be interested when you're really not.	_____	_____	_____	_____	_____
2. Being passive—not asking questions or trying to obtain clarifications, even when you don't understand.	_____	_____	_____	_____	_____
3. Listening mainly to what a speaker says rather than his or her feelings.	_____	_____	_____	_____	_____
4. Allowing yourself to be distracted too easily.	_____	_____	_____	_____	_____
5. Not being aware of the speaker's facial expressions and nonverbal behavior.	_____	_____	_____	_____	_____
6. Tuning out material that is complex or contrary to your own opinion.	_____	_____	_____	_____	_____
7. Drawing conclusions, having your mind made up before hearing the speaker's full line of reasoning.	_____	_____	_____	_____	_____
8. Allowing yourself to daydream or wander mentally.	_____	_____	_____	_____	_____
9. Feeling restless, impatient, eager to end the conversation.	_____	_____	_____	_____	_____
10. Interrupting the speaker, taking over the conversation to get in your own side of things.	_____	_____	_____	_____	_____

Your total score: _____

90–100	Superior
80–89	Very good
70–79	Good
60–69	Average
50–59	Below average
0–49	Far below average

✔ STOP AND THINK

Our own research reveals that of the four communication skills (writing, speaking, reading, and listening) that managers and supervisors most frequently use, listening is the skill in which they have had the least training. Why do you think this is so?

Active Listening Techniques. A particular listening technique that places the supervisor in a receiver's role and encourages feedback from others is called **active listening** (also known as *feeling listening, reflective listening,* and *nondirective listening*). Basically, active listening requires the listener to make a response that tosses the ball back to the sender and says, "Yes, I understand; tell me more." It is used by psychologists, psychiatrists, counselors, and others when it is necessary to understand how someone feels and thinks. We think that active listening is of great value to supervisors as a method for encouraging more open feedback.

The **reflective statement** is a form of active listening in which you repeat the gist of the sender's message as you understand it.

Suppose the speaker is Joan Chavez, one of your team members. She tells you:

> **Chavez: "Say, I've got a little problem. It's about Klaric, our new guy. You asked me to help him transition into the team, but some have even asked, 'Where'd we dig this guy up?' He has no clue about fitting in, and the others seem to resent him for that. While he's technically okay, it's just that he doesn't seem to care about being part of the team."**

What is Chavez saying? How would you respond? An effective reflective statement would summarize, using your own words, what you think Chavez has just told you. For example, a reflective statement would be:

> **You: "So while he's competent, you feel that he's not making much progress fitting in as a team member."**

This statement allows Chavez to clarify her statement if needed, or to elaborate. A reflective statement can also go beyond the speaker's words and reflect your interpretation of the speaker's **feelings**. For example, picking up on Chavez's body language, facial expression, and tone of voice, you might have reflected her feelings by saying:

> **You: "So it seems that you're pretty frustrated about his not fitting in."**

Note that Chavez has not stated her frustration in the words of her message. However, your reading between the lines, combined with her nonverbal message, may strongly suggest it. In response to your reflective statement about her feelings, Chavez might further elaborate by saying:

> **Chavez: "Well, the thing that gets me most, I guess, is that I don't know how I could have messed up in evaluating him."**

Now you have gained further insight into the meaning intended by Chavez.

The **probe** is more specific than the reflective statement. It directs attention to a particular aspect of the speaker's message. For example, in the Klaric case, your response to Chavez could be any of the following: (1) "He doesn't seem to fit in at all?" or (2) "You say the other guys seem to resent him?" Note that these probes are more specific than the reflective statement, and they allow you to pursue what you feel may be important.

Other Listening Fundamentals. A number of other important techniques can help your listening effectiveness. These are presented in Exhibit 6-14. As you can see, good listening is hard work. But it is an essential tool for the supervisor!

9 Define and illustrate active listening skills.

active listening The listener makes a response so as to encourage feedback.

reflective statement The listener repeats, in a summarizing way, what the speaker has just said.

probe Directs attention to a particular aspect of the speaker's message.

EXHIBIT 6-14

Tips for Better Listening

- Try to avoid doing most of the talking yourself. Give the other person an opportunity to speak.
- Avoid distractions. Close your office door or move to a quieter area.
- Act interested in what the other person says. Don't doodle, write, or work on something else. Give the employee your full attention.
- Ask questions. As long as the questions aren't considered nosy or brash, this will help keep you interested and encourage the employee to give more details.
- Summarize what you think someone has said. "What you're saying is. . . . " This will reinforce what you have heard and enable the other person to correct any misunderstanding on your part.
- Be empathetic. Try to put yourself in the speaker's shoes.
- Don't lose your temper or show signs of being upset by what the speaker is saying. Try to listen with an open mind.
- Don't interrupt. Let the person finish speaking before you respond.
- Use active listening techniques—reflective statements and probes—to ensure your understanding of key points, to help the speaker talk, or to steer the conversation in certain directions.
- After an important conversation or meeting, jot down notes to yourself about the main points discussed.

IMPORTANT TERMS

active listening
body signals
channel
communication process
   model
downward communication
e-mail
facial signals
feedback
grapevine
informal communication
information richness
lateral–diagonal
   communication
message
object signals
perception
probe
receiver
reflective statement
sender
space signals
stereotyping
time signals
touching signals
upward communication
voice signals

CHAPTER REVIEW

1 Describe the five components of the communication process model.

Supervisors spend anywhere from 70 to 80 percent of their time in some form of communication. The communication process consists of five parts: message encoding, a channel, message decoding, feedback, and noise.

2 Explain the forms of electronic communication technology.

Among the new forms of electronic communication that are impacting communication at the supervisory level are e-mail, mobile phones, digital pagers, voice mail, teleconferencing, and videoconferencing.

3 Explain the different ways in which nonverbal communications influence supervisory communication.

"Meaning" lies in people rather than in words, and nonverbal messages communicate our emotions more strongly than words. Six categories of nonverbal communication signals are voice, body, object, space, time, and touching.

4 Identify the three basic flows of formal communication in an organization.

In any organization there is a tremendous volume of formal communication that flows in three directions: downward, upward, and laterally or diagonally. Downward communication includes announcements of goals, objectives, policies, decisions, procedures, job assignments, and general information. Upward communication consists of progress reports from employees; their requests for assistance; communication about their attitudes, feelings, and concerns; and ideas and suggestions for job improvement. Lateral–diagonal communication occurs between persons within a department or in different departments. It typically involves contacts between line and staff members and among team members in natural, cross-functional, and self-managed teams.

5 **Explain the managerial communication style matrix.**

The managerial communication style matrix reflects supervisors' behaviors toward disclosing information and receiving information. Supervisors who are high disclosers are active downward communicators to their employees. Supervisors who are high information receivers are open, accessible, and receptive to upward communication from their employees.

6 **Identify and explain how organizational, interpersonal, and language barriers affect supervisory communication.**

A number of organizational, interpersonal, and language barriers can hamper a supervisor's effectiveness in communication. Organizational barriers include the levels of hierarchy through which a message must pass, the authority and status of managers, and the jargon of specialized departments. Interpersonal and language barriers include people's differing perceptions, the general imprecision of language, and different linguistic styles.

7 **Identify five specific actions supervisors can take to improve their communications.**

There are several ways to improve supervisory communication. First, a supervisor should establish the proper setting when communicating with employees. The proper setting is a climate with a high trust level, where the supervisor is viewed as a source of help and where status barriers are minimized. Second, a supervisor should plan his or her communication. This involves determining in advance a communication strategy and channel choice that will enable the supervisor's communication objective to be reached. Third, a supervisor must consider the receiver's frame of reference. This requires looking at things from the receiver's view, which can be difficult. Fourth, a supervisor should use repetition to reinforce key ideas. Finally, a supervisor should encourage and induce feedback and become a better listener.

8 **Show how a supervisor can use feedback to improve communication.**

Two ways in which a supervisor can encourage employees to provide feedback are by (1) creating a relaxed communication environment and (2) taking the initiative to encourage feedback from others. A favorable feedback environment makes team members feel comfortable and relaxed and encourages open expression of their true feelings. Supervisors can take the feedback initiative by asking questions and creating situations which encourage or require their employees to communicate.

9 **Define and illustrate active listening skills.**

Active listening, known also as *feeling listening, reflective listening,* or *nondirective listening,* is a method of encouraging feedback from others. Two forms of active listening are reflective statements and probes. Reflective statements restate back to the speaker a summary of what the listener has heard the speaker express. Probes are more specific reflective statements that direct attention to a *particular* aspect of the sender's message.

QUESTIONS FOR REVIEW AND DISCUSSION

1. What are the five components of the basic communication process model? Define each. Identify some of the important forms of electronic communication discussed in the text.

2. Explain the six different ways in which nonverbal signals influence supervisory communication.

3. Identify the three major flows of communication in an organization.

4. Explain the managerial communication style matrix. What are some purposes served by informal communication?

5. What are some examples of linguistic style communication differences that you have experienced? Explain.

6. How does planning aid communication effectiveness? Can you give a personal example?

7. Explain how a supervisor can use feedback to improve communication.

8. Define and give an example of active listening.

Skill Builder 6-1

Assessing Your Information-Disclosing and Information-Receiving Style

Instructions: Please read the 16 items listed and circle the answer that best characterizes you.

To what extent do you:	Not much like you				Much like you
1. Make known your position on issues	1	2	3	4	5
2. Ask others for their advice about matters	1	2	3	4	5
3. Compliment/give recognition to others	1	2	3	4	5
4. Act friendly, approachable	1	2	3	4	5
5. Offer constructive criticism to others	1	2	3	4	5
6. Indicate willingness to explore differences of opinion	1	2	3	4	5
7. Keep people informed about things you know are going on	1	2	3	4	5
8. Invite feedback about your own behavior or thinking	1	2	3	4	5
9. Make clearly known your expectations of others	1	2	3	4	5
10. Try to avoid distractions when listening to others	1	2	3	4	5

To what extent do you:	Not much like you				Much like you
11. State your disagreement with opinions when they differ from your own	1	2	3	4	5
12. Hear out a position fully before making a judgment or decision	1	2	3	4	5
13. Provide adequate details when instructing or explaining	1	2	3	4	5
14. Ask questions of others to obtain information	1	2	3	4	5
15. Tell people when they've done something that irritates you	1	2	3	4	5
16. Keep an open mind to others' ideas and suggestions	1	2	3	4	5

Scoring: To calculate your information-disclosing score, add the results of items 1, 3, 5, 7, 9, 11, 13, 15 = _____ Information-Disclosing Score Total.

To calculate your information-receiving score, add the results of items 2, 4, 6, 8, 10, 12, 14, 16 = _____ Information-Receiving Score Total.

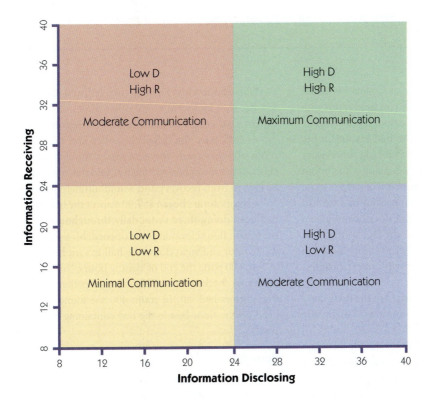

Listening Skills Practice

Skill Builder 6-2

For this exercise, three person teams will be used. One person will be the sender, another the listener, and the third an observer.

1. The sender speaks to the listener for 30 to 45 seconds on one of the following subjects:

   a. How I most like to spend my spare time.

   b. What I plan to be doing five years from now

   c. What I most like about my job, school, or life (select one)

   d. The type of person I best get along with

   e. What I think the ideal job would be and why

   f. Other topics selected by speaker

2. The listener responds, making a statement that reflects accurately the main ideas communicated by the sender.

3. The observer gives his/her critique of the listener's reflective statement, and the listener's nonverbal behavior while listening.

4. Sender, listener and observer jointly discuss steps 1, 2, and 3.

5. The three parties rotate roles and repeat steps 1, 2, 3, and 4. This should be done until each party has served at least once in each role.

CASE

Room 406*

Case 6-1

It was 4:56 p.m. on the surgical floor of Collins Memorial Hospital. Nurse Rhoda Fleming, an efficient head nurse with 15 years experience, was in charge of the floor that afternoon. As is the case in many hospitals, she had responsibility for several patients herself as well as assuming supervisory responsibilities over other floor nurses. Making a final room check of her own patients prior to the arrival of her 5:00 p.m. relief, in Room 406 she found Mr. Henry Youstra, who had undergone surgery the week before and not done well, had finally died. She pulled the sheet over the face of the body and made a mental note to tell her relief to empty the room for a new patient, bed space being especially important at this time in the hospital.

After finishing her check she returned to the floor desk. The evening shift supervisor, Anne Simmons, had already arrived, and was waiting at the desk.

"Hi, Anne. 406 just died, so that room's all set to go again. Too bad. We can certainly use the space, though."

"That's for sure. Has 411 had her shot yet? Dr. Alpers really climbed on me yesterday about it. You know how he is."

"No, not yet. You'd better do that right away."

"Does the office know that 406 is ready?"

"No , you'll need to call them after you get things taken care of."

Nurse Supervisor Fleming then left, and Simmons gave 411 her shot and went about other duties, dropping in on her own patients, and chatting with nurses on the shift.

At 5:45 p.m. she called the office and told them that room 406 was ready for occupancy, though she had not checked the room herself. She was told that a patient would be moved from recovery and would ultimately occupy 406.

Visitors' hours began at 7:00 p.m. at the hospital. As she had been doing three times daily throughout the week, as the fourth floor elevator doors opened, Mrs. Henry Youstra walked out and went down the hall to visit her husband.

At 8:00 p.m., the end of visiting hours, Nurse Supervisor Simmons checked each of her assigned patient rooms to see that visitors had left. In room 406 she found Mrs. Youstra dead on the floor beside the bed containing her husband's body.

Questions

1. Explain how "noise" impeded accurate communication between Shift Supervisors Fleming and Simmons in this incident.

2. What barriers to communication existed in the situation?

3. How might this miscommunication have been avoided?

*This case adapted from William V. Haney, *Communication Patterns and Incidents* (Homewood, IL: Richard D. Irwin, 1960), pp. 71–72.

CASE

Evaluating a Supervisor's Communication

Case 6-2

The interaction below is a dialogue between Ann Bishop, a medical records clerk with Community Hospital, and Jean Curtis, the administrative section head for whom she works.

Bishop: (enters Jean Curtis' office) You wanted to see me?

Curtis: Yes, I did, Ann. Come in and have a seat. (Rises to meet Bishop, shakes her hand, and offers her a chair. Both sit.)

As you know, I've been very pleased with your performance in archives since you joined us 6 months ago. You seem to have an excellent handle on everything we do there. An opening in the coding department has come up, and it would be an excellent opportunity. I want to see how you would feel about moving into coding. You are first choice, and that's what I want to discuss with you today.

Bishop: Into coding? Gee, I don't know; I really don't know much about coding. I don't know what to say....

Curtis: So I seem to have taken you by surprise....

Bishop: I mean, yeah, this is a surprise. I've not been here that long. I've heard a little about what they do in coding. I've heard stories about some of the charts having the wrong codes on them and people getting into trouble because of that. It seems like a lot more pressure and responsibility....

Curtis: So the extra responsibility involved in coding concerns you....

Bishop: Yes, that's an important factor to me in any job. Not that I don't mind some responsibility. It's just that it seems there's a lot more in coding than in archives.

Curtis: Well, Ann, you're right about that; it is more responsibility because having updated, accurately coded charts is very important to doctors, nurses, patients, and insurers. That's why we're careful about who we ask to work in coding.

Bishop: I like working in archives. I like the other clerks and we work together well. We work our lunch breaks out to cover for each other; we all pitch in and help when one of us gets overloaded. That's one thing I really like about working here—the cooperation.

Curtis: You're right; cooperation is very important in making a job more pleasant.

Bishop: Yeah, I really like that. At the last place I worked, nobody seemed to get along. I made more money than I make here, but getting along is more important to me than money. I know some people have left coding recently. Why is that?

Curtis: One left to work as a marketing assistant downstairs. Another married and moved out of the state. I've just finished writing her a letter of reference for a similar coding position in a hospital in her new location. The third didn't work out because of several reasons, including excessive absenteeism and marginal performance when she was here. The first two had been with us for over 5 years each and seemed very happy in the department. (Pause) So money's not the most important thing to you in a job?

Bishop: Oh, it's important, but there are other things—the people, the work, liking what I do. I guess money just isn't the only important thing.

Curtis: I think you're wise in looking at a job in ways other than just money. As a coder you would receive a $300 monthly increase, but it also would enable you to build a record of responsibility—this helped in landing the job in marketing for the person I just mentioned. It would also provide a stepping stone for you if you wanted to work in our legal records department.

Bishop: I don't know. It's just that I know the archives, I know what's expected of me there, and I know pretty much all there is to know about it. And I really was trained well before getting started. I've really felt comfortable there.

Curtis: So, you're not sure you will feel as comfortable in coding?

Bishop: Yeah, I'm concerned about that. I just started really feeling comfortable in archives. . . .

Curtis: We certainly would want you to be comfortable before putting you on your own in coding. You'd work with Stephanie Koval, one of the senior coders, for 2 or 3 days to get the hang of things. And we wouldn't turn you loose until you felt comfortable about your performance. In fact, since you seem to have some reservations that are understandable, we could let you try the job for two weeks and see how things go. Would that help any? I think you're ideally suited, but I don't want you to feel that I'm pressuring you.

Bishop: So you're saying you understand some of my concerns. . . .

Curtis: Yes, Ann, I think I do. And they're certainly normal. So why don't you give this some thought? I told Koval I'd be talking with you, so feel free to ask her any questions, or if you need to see me about anything further on this, please do. You've impressed us with your work in archives and that's what has led to today's meeting. Will you be able to let me know something by this Friday about giving coding a two-week trial?

Bishop: I really like working here, Ms. Curtis, and I'm pleased by the confidence you have in me. The chance to switch jobs is a surprise to me . . . I just wasn't expecting it. You've given me some things to think about, so a few days will be fine. I'll let you know something by Friday.

Instructions:

1. What communication barriers do you feel likely existed in this interaction? Why?

2. What uses of active listening responses by Curtis can you find in the interaction? By Bishop?

3. Assign Curtis' communication approach a score of 1 (very poor) to 5 (excellent). Why did you assign this score?

4. What might Curtis have done differently?

7 Motivation

© Royalty-Free/CORBIS

Supervisors play a key role in motivating their employees.

Give me enough medals and I'll win you any war.
—NAPOLEON BONAPARTE

Journalist: "Your Eminence, the Vatican is such a huge place. About how many people work here?"
Pope: "About half, my son."
—ANONYMOUS

Sharon Olds: People Motivator

Since Sharon Olds became a supervisor at AutoFin 2 years ago, her department has consistently reached or exceeded its production quotas. When she took over her present supervisory position, Sharon knew that she faced a strong challenge given the diverse ages, education levels, marital statuses, cultures, and needs of her personnel. Her department ranked in the middle of the pack from a performance standpoint. She felt that AutoFin was a solid organization to work for, with very good pay and benefits. Job security was excellent, assuming an employee met or came close to production quotas, which, although difficult, could be attained with hard work. Working conditions were excellent once employees became accustomed to spending 95 percent of their work time on the phone with customers.

Sharon felt the biggest difference she could make was to soften the impersonal, bottom-line attitude of upper management. "Although an excellent company to work for, AutoFin is very bottom-line oriented. While our success comes from our people, top management is seen as impersonal and numbers oriented," Sharon says. "They give an impression of being less concerned with their employees. I see my job as not only being concerned about my department's numbers, but also having my people feel good about themselves. Motivating people to feel good about themselves and our department is an important key to my job."

A summary of some of Sharon's interactions reveals how she approaches the task of motivating her personnel:

1. Sharon uses weekly staff meetings as an opportunity for her associates to grow and learn from each other. For example, at each meeting, she has three or four members report to the larger group about a particular customer contact that began on a negative note and was turned into a positive outcome by the associate.

2. Sharon actively works at finding ways to encourage and support her newest associates. After listening in on one particularly difficult conversation in which her newest associate handled a sour, rude customer in a patient, highly professional manner, Sharon e-mailed the associate: "Jan, we should use the tape of your Miami phone call as the textbook example in effective communication. Great job!"

3. Sharon works hard at recognizing outstanding employee performance. When one associate set a weekly record for booked customer lease contracts, Sharon e-mailed her lauding the achievement and copied the department manager and other associates in the department. Sharon also congratulated the associate personally on her accomplishment, and, at the weekly associates' meeting, Sharon led the team in giving her a round of applause.

4. Sharon finds a variety of ways to give recognition. When one associate shared at a team meeting suggestions for improving the customer database, Sharon e-mailed the suggestion to her own boss and recommended that all departments adopt the suggestion, crediting the employee for the suggestion. Sharon also championed the idea with her

Learning Objectives

After reading and studying this chapter, you should be able to:

1. Identify the three levels of employee motivation.

2. Explain the relationship between performance and motivation.

3. Understand and explain Maslow's hierarchy of needs theory and the principle underlying his theory.

4. Differentiate between Herzberg's dissatisfiers and motivators.

5. Understand and explain expectancy theory.

6. Explain how supervisors can use goal-setting theory to motivate employees.

7. Define equity theory.

8. Define and explain reinforcement theory.

9. Explain how generational differences affect motivation.

10. Identify five steps to motivating employees.

fellow supervisors. The recommendation was eventually implemented, and Sharon persuaded her boss to send a personal letter of appreciation to the employee.

5. Sharon particularly enjoys coaching and helping her lead associate learn the ropes. He is eager to learn and wants ultimately to become a supervisor. Sharon often seeks his advice and will delegate to him special assignments which give him an opportunity to learn more about the department. When Sharon was out with the flu, she missed a special meeting of supervisors with the department manager; she asked her lead associate to attend in her place. She could tell that he was quite pleased to do this.

6. While she is eager to praise for good performance, Sharon will not back off from addressing performance problems. But she does so tactfully and with concern for her associates' feelings. Several weeks ago her 57-year-old associate, one of the highest producers in the department, achieved only one-half of her daily quota on Monday and again on Tuesday. When Sharon approached her to discuss it, instead of first bringing up the matter, Sharon began with some small talk. The employee herself brought up the issue with, "I guess you see where I've gotten off to a slow start this week. . . ."

7. Sharon is extremely sensitive about the best way to treat her associates. When one walked in 20 minutes late for the second time in a week, Sharon noted his hurried entrance, but withheld acknowledgment or eye contact. She talked with him within the hour about his tardiness, preferring not to address it immediately. During the eventual discussion, Sharon listened patiently to his explanations, which she considered plausible. She reinforced the reasons why punctuality was important and insisted that he be on time. The next day when the employee arrived on time, Sharon made sure she saw him, greeting him with a friendly "good morning," and asked if she could fix him a cup of coffee.

8. Sharon works hard to make her associates feel part of the team and to share team identity. At meetings, her language consists of "we" and "us." Two weeks ago, she ordered sandwiches and pizza and treated the associates to lunch in the conference room. Since her employees take lunch in two shifts, half went one day, the other half the next. Sharon intentionally avoids bringing up work-related issues at such events, preferring that they be strictly social occasions. She and her lead associate felt the lunches were effective in establishing camaraderie, and Sharon plans to do this once every year or so.

Motivation: Some Fundamentals of Understanding Human Behavior

motivation Willingness to work to achieve the organization's objectives.

The chapter preview demonstrates that understanding and motivating employees is the core of effective supervision. Perhaps you've heard people say that no one can motivate someone else. They mean that **motivation** comes from within. It is the result of a person's individual perceptions, needs, and goals. We define motivation as the willingness of individuals and groups, as influenced by various needs and perceptions, to strive toward a goal. In organizations with enlightened management, there is an attempt to integrate the needs and goals of individuals with the needs and goals of the organization. In the chapter preview, we saw that Sharon is trying to create compatibility between employees' needs and those of her company.

The quest for high quality and quantity of work, safety, cost effectiveness, compliance with company policies and procedures, and punctuality are important issues that supervisors face each day. For example, cost of absenteeism rose to $660 per employee in 2005, about $25,000 annually for small companies and more than $10 million for larger organizations.[1] A global study of 85,000 employees in 18 countries across four continents showed that only 14 percent considered themselves "highly engaged"—that is, they felt involved and enthusiastic about their work. The most engaged workers were found in Mexico, Brazil, the United States, and Belgium, in that order. Countries in which workers reported the least engagement were Japan and Italy. Separately, a Gallup poll of U.S. workers showed that 54 percent were only "moderately engaged" and 19 percent so negatively engaged that their companies might be better off when they call in sick.[2]

In our management seminars supervisors and managers are asked to anonymously rate on a scale from 1 (lowest) to 10 (highest) the motivational level of employees whom they supervise. The ratings are turned in and written on a flipchart or board. Only rarely do scores higher than 8 appear; the average tends to be in the 5 to 6 range. When asked why ratings tend to be so mediocre, participants respond with comments such as "People today just don't seem to care as much," or "Some employees just want their paycheck and will do just enough to get by," or "There's no pride or commitment to their work."

Few social scientists would deny that people often act emotionally, but many would dispute that most people behave irrationally and unpredictably. They would argue that if more people understood the *why* of human behavior, other people's behavior would seem more rational and predictable. Why don't some people have pride in their work? Why do they just do enough to get by? Why are others outstanding performers? The answer lies in their motivation.

Historical Insight

The Hawthorne Studies

You may already be familiar with Frederick Taylor's "scientific management" approach which emphasized efficient employee work methods as the basis for achieving higher performance. In the late 1920s and early 1930s, other researchers discovered the importance played by employees' psychological attitudes toward their work.

The Hawthorne Studies were conducted at the Hawthorne Plant of Western Electric, a Chicago plant of 30,000 employees, that was the manufacturing arm of giant AT&T. The studies began in 1924 as an experiment to determine whether increases in lighting would affect worker productivity. Researchers studied two groups of workers, one called the research group, the other the control group. In the research group, lighting levels were increased in stages over a period of months. In the control group, lighting levels remained the same. Researchers were confused to note that not only did productivity increase steadily throughout the study period for the research group, it also increased for the control group where no lighting changes had been made! Perplexed, the researchers introduced a new lighting variable in the research group; they reduced lighting to levels below those at which the experiment began. They were again stumped by a continued productivity increase. Baffled, the researchers regrouped. What was going on here to cause the higher performance?

Further research conducted at Hawthorne yielded some answers. In another study, six 15- and 16-year-old girls agreed to participate in the research and were put to work producing relay assemblies, a telephone component. The work area was separated from other plant areas to enable researchers to observe the employees and keep detailed records. For $2\frac{1}{2}$ years, a series of changes in the girls' working conditions were introduced, including shorter workdays and workweeks, periodic rest breaks, free lunches and snacks, and changes in starting and quitting times. And, perhaps you have guessed the results. Throughout the entire $2\frac{1}{2}$ years, their output increased from 2,400 to 3,000 relays weekly per worker. Moreover, their attendance and morale also increased steadily.

What do you think was causing these improvements? Subsequent experiments and an extensive interview program with workers throughout the plant attributed the improvements to psychological factors within the experimental groups. By being singled out to participate in the experiments, the workers selected felt "special" and important, causing them to operate under motivational conditions quite unlike other Hawthorne workers. Management had directed attention toward them, and their results became more meaningful. An important result of the Hawthorne Studies was the discovery of a powerful motivational force that ushered in the beginning of the human relations era of management.[3]

EXHIBIT **7-1**

The Three Levels
of Motivation

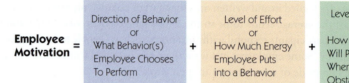

| **Employee Motivation** = | Direction of Behavior or What Behavior(s) Employee Chooses To Perform | + | Level of Effort or How Much Energy Employee Puts into a Behavior | + | Level of Persistence or How Hard Employee Will Pursue Behavior When Faced with Obstacles |

Levels of Motivation

1

Identify the three
levels of employee
motivation.

Broadly, when we say that someone is or is not motivated to engage in a certain behavior, we can refer to three distinct, but sometimes related, levels as shown in Exhibit 7-1.[4] One level is the direction in which the individual behaves. Does an employee behave in desirable ways?

> **Does an AutoFin associate spend 95 percent of his or her time on the phone with customers? Does he or she key into his or her computer the result of each contact as it occurs, as desired by management? Does he or she attempt to sell a warranty agreement to each customer who extends a lease? Does he or she cooperate with other employees by providing information they may need about a customer he or she initially contacted?**

Employees might be very
motivated under ideal work
conditions, but in the face
of adversity, obstacles, or
roadblocks, motivational
persistence will come
into play.

© Bryan Allen/CORBIS

Note that the direction of an employee's behavior may be unfavorable from the supervisor's perspective. An AutoFin associate may spend 15 percent of his or her time making personal calls or reading the newspaper instead of contacting customers. He or she may try to sell warranty agreements to only 50 percent of his or her contacts. She or he may choose *not* to share information that would be helpful to his or her colleagues. It is not enough for a supervisor merely to identify and communicate the desired practices; supervisors must meet the challenge of motivating employees to actually perform the desired behaviors.

A second motivation level relates to *how hard* the individual works to perform the behavior(s). While an employee may be aware of the need for the behavior, how much energy and effort does he or she exert to properly perform it?

> **John B. is keenly aware that safety is an important part of his job as a welder at Inland Marine's Yard 2. Yet, he often overlooks securing his safety harness when he works at heights over 3 feet above ground, despite the fact that this safety requirement is widely known and regularly discussed at weekly safety meetings held by his supervisor. Because he is experienced, John feels that this requirement is often a nuisance, so he usually "forgets." He'd rather put his energy into welding, which is what he is paid to do, he says. As John's supervisor states, John just isn't motivated to be conscientious in following established safety rules.**

For many supervisors, it is this second motivational level that provides the biggest challenge, getting employees to work hard, to put effort into what they do. A men's department manager complains that salespeople only go through the motions to keep their areas neat and orderly. "They know it, they just don't do it as well as they should." A restaurant manager keeps watch, making sure her bartenders do not spend too much time talking with friends at the bar; a branch bank manager laments her tellers who don't try very hard to make eye contact with customers, smile, call the customer by name, or attempt to cross-sell a certificate of deposit or loan.

The third and final level responds to the motivational level of *persistence*. In the face of adversity, obstacles, or roadblocks, how hard does an employee keep trying to produce a behavior? The employee may be highly motivated when conditions for the behavior are favorable, but what happens in the face of adversity or roadblocks? When an employee isn't feeling well in the morning, will she call in absent? If she shows up, will she still persevere and perform the job well? If her equipment acts up, will she be motivated to find a makeshift way to get the work done?

> **Frito Lay is filled with tales of salespeople going to extraordinary efforts to meet their customers' needs. These include braving the fiercest of weather to ensure their daily contacts with stores that they serve, or going to great lengths to help a store clean up after a hurricane or fire. Letters about such acts pour into Dallas headquarters.[5]**

http://www.frito-lay.com/

Intrinsic and Extrinsic Motivation

Intrinsic motivation is that behavior which an individual produces because of the pleasant experiences associated with the behavior itself. Employees who are intrinsically motivated feel satisfaction in performing their work. This satisfaction may come from any of several factors, including enjoying the actual work done, the feeling of accomplishment, meeting the challenges, etc.

intrinsic motivation
Behavior that an individual produces because of the pleasant experiences associated with the behavior itself.

> **Anne Marie Bains has strong intrinsic motivation in her work as a pharmaceutical sales representative. She enjoys interacting with the professionals she calls on—nurses and physicians—and talking with them about her products. She enjoys traveling and the freedom of planning her calls. But the highlight is the actual time she spends communicating with the health care professionals—getting to know them on a professional basis, gaining their confidence, and sharing with them information about her company's products.**

By contrast, **extrinsic motivation** is performed not for its own sake, but rather for the consequences associated with it. The consequences can include such factors as the pay, the benefits, the job security, or working conditions.

> **Lincoln Hammons is a loan collector for a local bank. While he dislikes "putting the squeeze" on people, as he calls it, he can earn a nice bonus by exceeding his production goals. He also works in a nice air-conditioned office, and the bank's location is only 10 minutes from his home.**

Lincoln is extrinsically motivated. It's not what he *does* in his job that he finds satisfying, but the indirect factors of pay, benefits, and working conditions.

The Motivation–Performance Link

2 Explain the relationship between performance and motivation.

Many supervisors make a mistake in assuming that an employee's performance is directly related to an employee's level of motivation. Initially, one might conclude that the more highly motivated an employee is, the higher will be that employee's performance. This is not necessarily the case. Unquestionably, direction of behavior, level of effort, and persistence affect an employee's performance; however, the motivation–performance link is just not that simple.

As shown in Exhibit 7-2, an individual's skill/ability level also influences performance.

An employee with low motivation and exceptional skill may be able to outperform a more highly motivated, less-skilled employee. Also, an employee's performance depends largely on what we call "organizational support." We all are familiar with sports examples of highly motivated players whose "performance" is below par, but the poor performance is not necessarily attributed to them: the National Football League (NFL) quarterback who last year was an all-star, but this year has three rookie offensive linemen and no pass protection; the outstanding pass receiver who this year is handicapped by a rookie quarterback; the pitcher whose infield leads the majors in errors. It works similarly in business organizations. The level of organizational support, including resources and assistance provided, often influences performance.

To attribute an employee's low performance to low motivation or high performance to high motivation overlooks the fact that there are many other causes of performance besides just motivation level.

EXHIBIT 7-2

Factors Affecting an Individual's Job Performance

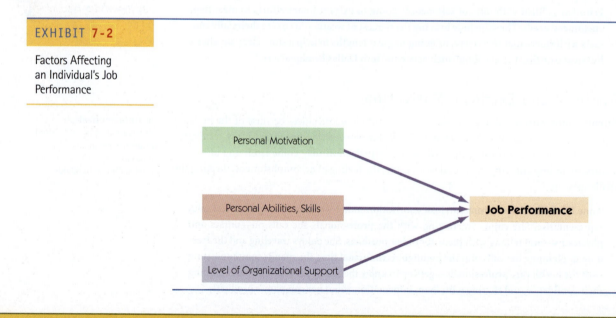

We conclude this discussion by stating that, *things being equal, employees who are more highly motivated will have higher performance.* But things are seldom truly equal, which challenges the supervisor's diagnostic skills when examining the true cause of a performance-related problem.

Since the 1960s, much research has been done on the behavior of people at work. Some significant theories have been developed that are important to anyone in a position of leadership who wants to avoid unnecessary friction arising from human relationships in an organization. For a person of action, such as a supervisor who has to work with and through people, an understanding of motivation theory is essential. Kurt Lewin, famous for his work in the study of groups, once said that there is nothing so practical as good theory. The remainder of this chapter will focus on the important theories of motivation, with emphasis on their application to effective supervision.

Maslow's Hierarchy of Needs Theory

3   Understand and explain Maslow's hierarchy of needs theory and the principle underlying his theory.

One theory that is particularly significant and practical was developed by psychologist Abraham H. Maslow and is known as the hierarchy of needs. Of all motivation theories, it is probably the one best known by managers. The key conclusion drawn from Maslow's theory is that people try to satisfy different needs through work.[6]

Principles Underlying the Theory

The two principles underlying Maslow's **hierarchy of needs** theory are that (1) people's needs can be arranged in a hierarchy, or ranking, of importance, and (2) once a need has been satisfied, it no longer serves as a primary motivator of behavior. To understand the significance of these principles to Maslow's theory, let us examine the hierarchy of needs shown in Exhibit 7-3.

hierarchy of needs
Arrangement of people's needs in a hierarchy, or ranking, of importance.

EXHIBIT **7-3**

Maslow's Hierarchy of Needs

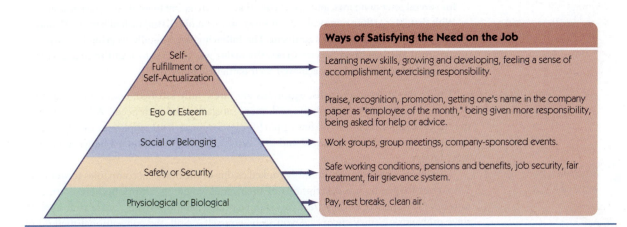

	Ways of Satisfying the Need on the Job
Self-Fulfillment or Self-Actualization	Learning new skills, growing and developing, feeling a sense of accomplishment, exercising responsibility.
Ego or Esteem	Praise, recognition, promotion, getting one's name in the company paper as "employee of the month," being given more responsibility, being asked for help or advice.
Social or Belonging	Work groups, group meetings, company-sponsored events.
Safety or Security	Safe working conditions, pensions and benefits, job security, fair treatment, fair grievance system.
Physiological or Biological	Pay, rest breaks, clean air.

physiological need The need for food, water, air, and other physical necessities.

Physiological or Biological Needs. At the lowest level, but of primary importance when they are not met, are our **physiological** or **biological needs.** "Man does not live by bread alone," says the Bible, but anything else is less important when there is no bread. Unless the circumstances are unusual, the need we have for love, status, or recognition is inoperative when our stomach has been empty for a while. But when we eat regularly and adequately, we cease to regard hunger as an important motivator. The same is true of other physiological needs, such as those for air, water, rest, exercise, shelter, and protection from the elements.

safety need The need for protection from danger, threat, or deprivation.

Safety or Security Needs. When the physiological needs have been reasonably well satisfied, **safety** or **security needs** become important. We want to be protected from danger, threat, or deprivation. When we feel threatened or dependent, our greatest need is for protection or security. Most employees are in a dependent relationship at work, so they may regard their safety needs as being very important. Arbitrary or autocratic management actions such as favoritism, discrimination, or the unpredictable application of policies can be a powerful threat to the safety of any employee at any level.

social need The need for belonging, acceptance by colleagues, friendship, and love.

Social or Belonging Needs. **Social** or **belonging needs** include the need for belonging, for association, for acceptance by colleagues, and for friendship and love. Although most supervisors know that these needs exist, many assume—wrongly—that they represent a threat to the organization. Fearing group hostility to its own objectives, management may go to considerable lengths to control and direct human efforts in ways that are detrimental to cohesive work groups.

When employees' social needs, as well as their safety needs, are not met, they may behave in ways that tend to defeat organizational objectives. They become resistant, antagonistic, and uncooperative. But this behavior is a *consequence* of their frustration, not the cause.

ego need The need for self-confidence, independence, appreciation, and status.

Ego or Esteem Needs. Above the social needs are the **ego** or **esteem needs.** These needs are of two kinds: (1) those that relate to one's self-esteem, such as the need for self-confidence, independence, achievement, competence, and knowledge; and (2) those that relate to one's reputation, such as the need for status, recognition, appreciation, and respect from one's colleagues.

> **During World War I, General Douglas MacArthur, a 38-year-old brigadier general, had recently been named commander of a battlefield brigade in Europe. On the eve of a major battle in France, he met with the battalion commander. In an effort to inspire the men, MacArthur asked that when the signal was given to start the charge, the commander, a major, be the first one out to lead the charge, in front of his men. MacArthur said, "If you do this, your battalion will follow you, and you will earn the Distinguished Service Cross, and I will see that you get it." MacArthur then paused, looked at the major for several long moments, and said, "I see that you are going to do it. You have it now." With that, MacArthur removed from his own uniform his Distinguished Service Medal and pinned it on the major's uniform. The following day, proudly wearing his as yet unearned Distinguished Service Cross, the major was the first to lead the charge, his troops behind him, and they achieved their battlefield objective.[7]**

Unlike the lower-level needs, ego needs are rarely fully satisfied, because people, once they have become important, always seek more satisfaction of such needs. A few years ago, the typical organization offered few opportunities for lower-level employees to satisfy their ego needs. However, well-managed and innovative companies are doing a better job in this regard today.

Southwest Airlines is continuously ranked as one of the best U.S. companies to work for. Employees frequently use descriptions of their employment as, "Working here is truly an unbelievable experience. They treat you with respect . . . empower you . . . use your ideas to solve problems . . . they encourage you to be yourself."[8] Still, the conventional method of

http://www.south west.com/

organizing work, particularly in mass-production industries, gives little consideration to these aspects of motivation.

Self-Fulfillment or Self-Actualization Needs. At the top of Maslow's hierarchy are the **self-fulfillment** or **self-actualization needs.** These needs lead one to seek realization of one's own potential, to develop oneself, and to be creative.

> John B., age 64, is about 3 years from taking company retirement. He enjoys woodworking and has become quite good at it, his bowls and carved figures having won several awards at arts fairs. John is one of the most knowledgeable technical service representatives in the company, but continually turns down overtime work on weekends. "The extra money just isn't worth it to me anymore," he says. "I'd much rather spend my time working in my shop or showing my work at an arts and crafts show." John recently was asked on short notice to be flown over a weekend to a customer location to help resolve a difficult problem, which that site could not resolve. He accepted. As he stated, "It wasn't the money, it was the fact that nobody else could resolve it and I looked forward to the challenge."

It seems clear that the quality of work life in most organizations provides only limited opportunities to fulfill these needs, especially at lower organizational levels. When higher-level needs are not satisfied, employees compensate by trying to further satisfy lower-level needs. So the needs for self-fulfillment may remain dormant.

✔ **STOP AND THINK**

Reflect on the examples of motivation described in this chapter's preview. Which need levels of employees are reflected in each of these?

Qualifying the Theory

Maslow's theory is a relative rather than an absolute explanation of human behavior. You should be aware of the following four important qualifiers to his theory:

1. Needs on one level of the hierarchy do not have to be completely satisfied before needs on the next level become important.

2. The theory does not pretend to explain the behavior of the neurotic or the mentally disturbed.

3. Some people's priorities are different. For example, an artist may practically starve while trying to achieve self-actualization through the creation of a great work of art. Also, some people are much less security oriented or achievement oriented than others.

4. Unlike the lower levels, the two highest levels of needs can hardly ever be fully satisfied. There are always new challenges and opportunities for growth, recognition, and achievement. A person may remain in the same job position for years and still find a great deal of challenge and motivation in his or her work.

> Bob Buschka, a computer programmer for a large bank in a Midwestern state, has held his position for 20 years and would like to remain in that position. He enjoys programming and is looked on as one of the top programmers in banking in the area. The bank sends him to various schools to keep him growing and developing on the job.

> "Bob's a remarkable person," says his boss. "He's passed up promotions into management to keep his present job, he's so into it. We know what a gem he is, and we do everything we can to give him lots of room to operate—special key projects, training and developing new programmers, and keeping up with the new applications to our industry."

Herzberg's Theory

In the 1960s, a researcher named Frederick Herzberg conducted in-depth interviews with 200 engineers and accountants from 11 different firms in the Pittsburgh, Pennsylvania, area.[9] Those interviewed were asked to recall an event or series of related events that made them feel unusually good and unusually bad about their work and how much the event(s) affected their performance and morale. Prior to Herzberg's study, a common assumption was that factors such as money, job security, and working conditions were all strong positive motivators, and pretty much worked the same way: If these things were not satisfied at work, people would be negatively motivated; if they were satisfied, they would be positively motivated. Herzberg's findings disproved this assumption and helped us better differentiate among various motivational factors.

Dissatisfiers and Motivators

Herzberg found that two different lists emerged, one for factors that made the engineers and accountants feel unusually good, the other for those that made them feel unusually bad. Basically, he found that what people said most affected them negatively, or *dissatisfied* them (called **dissatisfier** or **hygiene factors**) about their jobs, were things such as low pay, low benefits, unfavorable working conditions, poor job security, and poor company policy/administration.

The things that *turned them on* (called **satisfier** or **motivator factors**) tended to be recognition, advancement, achievement, challenging work, being one's own boss, and the work itself (see Exhibit 7-4). A recent survey of 372 managers seemed to reinforce Herzberg's theory, as 76 percent said that personal achievement and job enjoyment *most* motivated them, in contrast to only 30 percent who cited financial rewards.[10] Note that the satisfier/motivator factors are found at the highest levels of Maslow's hierarchy, whereas the dissatisfier/hygiene factors are at the lower levels.

4
Differentiate between Herzberg's dissatisfiers and motivators.

dissatisfier factors Factors that employees said most affected them negatively, or dissatisfied them about their job, including low pay, low benefits, and unfavorable working conditions.

satisfier factors Factors that employees said turned them on, such as recognition, advancement, achievement, challenging work, and being one's own boss.

EXHIBIT 7-4

Herzberg's Satisfier/Motivator and Dissatisfier/Hygiene Factors

Satisfier/Motivator Factors

+ Recognition	"The boss says I've done a good job."
+ Advancement	"I was promoted to team leader."
+ Challenging work	"I solved a really tough job problem."
+ Being one's own boss	"I was given a free hand to do my job."
+ Work itself	"I got to design the new system."

Dissatisfier/Hygiene Factors

− Pay	"I'm not paid fairly for what I do."
− Benefits	"This company doesn't pay tuition or medical benefits."
− Working conditions	"It's so hot in the plant it's often unbearable."
− Job security	"With the seasonal work I never know for sure if I'll have a job."
− Company policy/administration	"We have so much red tape to go through."

Try to answer Herzberg's survey questions yourself. Think about a particular job you have held in the past or presently hold. If you haven't had a job, think of your schoolwork.

1. What specific incident or event (singular or recurring) gave you the most satisfaction?

2. What caused the most dissatisfaction?

Herzberg reasoned that the dissatisfier factors are what people take for granted about their jobs, so their presence is not particularly stimulating. For example, consider an employee who said that the most dissatisfying thing about his job was that the plant was too hot. Assume that the company addressed this issue and installed a cooling system throughout the plant. Six months later would this employee be likely to say that one of the most satisfying things about the job was the cool plant? Not likely.

Conversely, factors that cause *strong dissatisfaction* do not tend to be such things as the lack of responsibility or challenge in a job or absence of recognition. If a company seeks to eliminate dissatisfaction it must address factors including wages, working conditions, and security. Note that supervisors often have greater ability to influence motivator factors such as recognition, assigning challenging jobs, and empowering employees than they do hygiene factors of pay, benefits, working conditions, job security, and company policy. A recent study of the Irish health sector examined it from Herzberg's perspective. It found that health sector managers have limited control over employees' pay, job security, and work load, much of this being determined by the "system." But although they have a greater degree of control over motivational factors of achievement, recognition, and responsibility, the study concluded that managers were not effectively using these motivational tools.[11]

Link to Intrinsic and Extrinsic Motivation

Earlier in the chapter we discussed the subject of intrinsic and extrinsic motivation. Note that the factors associated with positive motivation were intrinsic to the job, whereas those causing job dissatisfaction were extrinsic to it. When people felt good about their jobs, it was usually because something had happened that showed they were doing their work particularly well or were becoming more expert in their professions. In other words, good feelings were keyed to the specific tasks that they performed, rather than to extrinsic factors such as money, security, or working conditions. Conversely, when they felt bad, it was usually because something had happened to make them feel that they were being treated unfairly.

The crux of Herzberg's theory is that dissatisfiers and satisfiers are each important in their own way. Dissatisfier factors, such as good pay, benefits, working conditions, and job security, must first be addressed by management as a motivational base so as to prevent employee dissatisfaction. Once dissatisfaction is removed, management will get more "bang for its motivational effort" by focusing on employees' opportunities for responsibility, recognition, advancement, and challenge in their jobs.

More than 20 years ago, Walter Vaux was a young chemical engineer toiling in the lab when his boss walked in. "You're doing a wonderful job," he remembers the supervisor saying. "I'm so glad you're part of the department." It was just a few words, but the input was such a valuable motivator that Vaux, now retired, still talks of the lesson he learned—it takes more than cash. "Many other bosses have just taken my contributions for granted and felt that their response was more money. The real motivator was genuinely realizing my successes and telling me so."[12]

Qualifying Herzberg's Theory

Herzberg's results have been replicated in other studies involving nonprofessionals such as food service workers, assembly-line workers, and others. However, there are some important qualifications to Herzberg's theory that you should bear in mind:

1. Money *can* be a motivating factor, especially when it is tied to recognition and achievement.

2. For some people, especially professionals, the absence of motivating factors such as recognition, advancement, and challenge can constitute dissatisfaction.

3. Critics contend that a built-in bias of Herzberg's findings is that when asked about something on the job that is positive, a person is biased toward mentioning something in which his or her behavior is the focal point, such as a feeling of achievement, meeting a job challenge, and so on. Conversely, when asked about dissatisfiers, a person is likely to mention extrinsic factors over which he or she has no control, such as pay or working conditions.

Despite these qualifications, we feel that Herzberg's theory is valuable as a general guide to understanding behavior at work.

5

Understand and explain expectancy theory.

expectancy theory Views an individual's motivation as a conscious effort involving the expectancy that a reward will be given for a good result.

Other Theories of Motivation

This section explores some other theories of motivation with which you should be familiar. These include expectancy theory, goal-setting theory, equity theory, and reinforcement theory.

Expectancy Theory

The theories of Maslow and Herzberg focus primarily on the individual and his or her needs as dominant employee motivation factors. **Expectancy theory** is more dynamic. It views an individual's motivation as a more conscious effort involving the interplay of three variables:

Motivating employees through rewards is one aspect of expectancy theory.

EXHIBIT **7-5**

Expectancy Theory

Motivation = Expectancy that increased   ×   Probability that a performance   ×   Value attached to
            effort will lead to a given   level will lead to a given   reward
            performance level   reward
            (Effort → Performance link)   (Performance → Reward link)

(1) expectancy that effort will lead to a given performance result; (2) probability of reward(s) associated with the performance result; and (3) the value of the reward to the individual.[13] Expectancy theory states that most work behavior can be explained by the fact that employees determine in advance what their behavior may accomplish and the value they place on alternative possible accomplishments or outcomes. Some writers have termed this a "payoff" or "What's in it for me?" view of behavior. Developed by Victor Vroom of the University of Michigan, expectancy theory is illustrated in Exhibit 7-5.

Let us take a look at how Vroom's theory operates. Suppose that Maria's boss says, "If you are able to complete the project by Monday, Maria, I'll recommend you for a promotion to supervisor. I realize that it will mean your putting in some heavy work without pay, but think about it and let me know your answer." There are three important factors involved. As shown in Exhibit 7-6, one is the Effort → Performance relationship—Maria's expectancy that if she puts in the extra effort, she can realistically complete the project by Monday. The second factor is the Performance → Reward relationship—the likelihood that if she does complete the project by Monday, Maria will actually be promoted to supervisor. In other words, does Maria's supervisor really have the influence to get her the promotion? The final factor is the value Maria places on being promoted to supervisor. Suppose the last thing in the world she wants is the responsibility and pressure of being a supervisor!

EXHIBIT **7-6**

Applying Expectancy Theory

1. Hire people who have adequate skill levels.
2. Set clear, recognizable performance goals.
3. Make sure employees know what is expected.
4. Continually stress employee training and skill development.
5. Use performance feedback and coaching to help employees gain skills.
6. Have employees share knowledge and expertise with others.
7. Give employees special jobs or assignments that stretch their abilities.
8. Celebrate performance successes.
9. Reward performance achievement.
10. Develop trust in your commitments by others; do not overpromise rewards.
11. Emphasize multiple rewards such as praise and recognition, being assigned desired work, receiving special training, attending a conference.
12. Determine what different individuals value as rewards (financial, social, being in the know, learning a new skill, etc.) and help make these happen.

In expectancy theory, then, the three factors of the Effort → Performance link, the Performance → Reward link, and the value of the reward all interface to determine someone's motivation.

Note that the perceptual process plays a critical role in maximizing employee motivation, according to expectancy theory:

1. An employee must *perceive* that he or she has the ability and appropriate support level to achieve the targeted performance level;

2. An employee must *perceive* that if he or she does reach the performance level, he or she will receive the reward; and

3. An employee must *perceive* the reward to be something valued.

The writers are familiar with one Chicago manufacturer that used tickets to cultural and social events as rewards for a program that tried to improve daily attendance among its hourly workforce. The program had little impact. As one manager stated, rewards with a more targeted appeal, such as free dinners at Chicago restaurants or tickets to professional sporting events, would have been stronger motivators. Often, however, employees may not grasp this reward potential of assignments given by their supervisors. American Express managers are taught to "label and link" when delegating or giving assignments. This means telling why the assignment is important to the individual receiving the assignment.[14]

Eileen Rogers of Allegra Print and Imaging Company in Scottsdale, Arizona, keeps a supply of $2 bills on hand. Whenever a client expresses satisfaction with an employee's behavior, Rogers gives the employee a $2 bill and delivers a compliment in front of the entire team. "The funny thing . . . no one spends it," she says. Many post the bills near their desks, and one star employee is close to wallpapering her area with them.[15]

As shown in Exhibit 7-6, supervisors can do a number of things to apply the principles of expectancy theory. Here are three basic ways: (1) they can help employees reach desired performance levels through training and coaching (the Effort → Performance link); (2) they can deliver on their commitments (the Performance → Reward link); and (3) they can reward performance in ways that are meaningful to employees (the reward). Exhibit 7-7 illustrates a wide range of rewards that managers can provide. Note that many of these are absolutely free.

Each of Sharon Olds' sales remarketing associates has a sales goal to book 35 monthly customers to a new lease contract or to purchase and refinance their present vehicle. At that point, a financial incentive kicks in. Sharon works especially hard on the Effort → Performance aspect of expectancy theory by helping associates to be confident that if they work hard, they will actually achieve the 35 customer rate and higher.

Among the tools Sharon employs are continuous sales training of her associates, publicizing achievement levels and success stories, and performance feedback and coaching. "I do my best to make them feel that they have the right stuff and my support to succeed. It is especially important for new associates to know that if they work hard each day, they will achieve the necessary successes with customers. My full-timers have done it before and know that they can get there, so my job is more one of encouraging them and rallying them."

Sharon also works hard to reinforce the rewards received by top performers. She knows that the financial incentive is an important reward for most, but for others it is the fact that they have achieved a high level of success. "That's why I like to make it a big deal when someone gets there, like e-mailing everyone in sight about it," she says. "For many, that is as satisfying or more satisfying than the extra money."

EXHIBIT 7-7

Manager's List of
Potential Rewards

Raises and bonuses

Social functions

Outings

A night on the town

A nice meal or lunch courtesy of the manager

Lunch as a group that the manager buys

Dinner

Day off or time off

Picnics for teams

Tickets to sports, special events

Direct oral praise to individual, one to one

Direct praise to individual in presence of others

Direct praise/recognition at group events

Peer recognition

Letters of recognition to file or place where customers can see them

Passing on customer compliments and commendations in voice mail or in writing

Written praise

Certificates and plaques

Shirts, phones, pins, hats, cups, jackets, and so on, all with the name of the company on them

Opportunity to attend conference, special training course

A parking space

Additional responsibilities

Personal call or visit from CEO or senior executive

New furnishings or equipment

Being assigned more favorable jobs

Allowing people to bid on projects/tasks they prefer

Source: Reprinted from Peter Meyer. "Can You Give Good, Inexpensive Rewards? Some Real-Life Answers," November-December 1994, pp. 84–85. Copyright © 1994, Reprinted with permission from Elsevier.

Goal-Setting Theory

Task goals, in the form of clear and desirable performance targets, form the basis of Edwin Locke's **goal-setting theory** of motivation.[16] Goals are important not only in the planning process, but as an important motivational factor as well. Locke's basic premise is that task goals can be highly motivating—if they are properly set and if they are well managed. Performance goals clarify the expectations between a supervisor and an employee, between coworkers and subunits in an organization. They also establish a frame of reference for task feedback and provide a foundation for self-management. In these and related ways, Locke believes goal setting is of primary importance in enhancing individual motivation and job performance, and has spent much research since the 1970s substantiating that theory.

Listed here are the major ways in which a supervisor can use goal setting as a motivational tool:

1. Set specific goals. Specific, concrete goals consistently lead to better performance than general ones, such as "do your best," or no goals at all.

6

Explain how
supervisors can
use goal-setting
theory to motivate
employees.

goal-setting theory The
theory that task goals,
properly set and managed,
can be an important
employee motivator.

2. Set challenging but reasonably difficult goals. Be careful, though, not to set goals that an employee feels he or she has very little, if any, chance to reach. Several years ago, one professional football team posted in the dressing room the following offensive team goals: "Never allow our quarterback to be sacked; always score when inside the red zone (opponent's 20-yard line); never give up a fumble." Because they were unattainable, these goals were likely perceived as meaningless by the team's offensive players.

3. Ensure timely feedback to employees about goal achievement. This may be easier in certain situations, such as sales or production work, than in others.

4. Where practical, strengthen employees' commitment by allowing them to participate in goal setting. A key step in MBO—Management by Objectives—is involving employees in establishing their own key performance goals.

5. When multiple goals are established, make sure employees understand their priorities. For example, is meeting a quality goal more important than meeting a quantity goal or cost-effectiveness goal?

6. Reinforce goal accomplishment. When people reach or exceed goals, ensure timely rewards and recognition.

At the company Christmas luncheon in 2004, T. Paul Bulmahn, Chairman of ATP Oil and Gas, a 55-employee, Houston, Texas, offshore development company, wanted his company to grow. So he tried something he'd not done before. He gave his employees a special challenge: triple daily production by the end of 2005 and boost the reserve replacement rate by 200 percent and everyone would go to Sweden and get new Volvo 760s. No kidding!

While it would surely be a challenge, employees committed to the task. But the progress they made through fall 2006 took a turn for the worse when Hurricanes Rita and Katrina devastated the company's Gulf of Mexico operations. So Bulmahn extended the time frame another quarter—till March 2006. And darn if they didn't put forth a Herculean effort and achieve their goals!

Employees were ecstatic. Thirty-nine of the 55 employees with their spouse or a friend flew to Sweden with Bulmahn and selected Volvos; the others opted instead for a cash payment of $25,000. Bulmahn stated that he issued the challenge because the company had reached a point that it needed to move forward. Achieving the challenging goal of tripling production in a little over a year, has put ATP in another league, he said. And doing it without an acquisition is unheard of.[17]

7

Define equity theory.

Equity Theory

Employee motivation can also be viewed in terms of how fairly or "equitably" an employee feels he or she is rewarded as compared to others. **Equity theory** states that when people find themselves in situations of inequity or unfairness, they are motivated to act in ways to change their circumstances.

Two factors determine whether one is in an equitable situation. One is the inputs, such as skill, education, experience, and motivation, that an employee brings to the job situation. The second consists of the rewards that a person receives for performance, including pay, advancement, recognition, or desirable job assignments. Think of equity theory, then, as an input/output comparison that responds to this question: Given what I bring to a job as compared to what others bring, are the rewards that I receive fair as compared to theirs? If you asked this question of yourself and answered no, according to equity theory you would likely act to reduce the inequity in several ways. Three options are as follows:

1. You can try to *increase your reward level* by making a case with your supervisor or relevant others, appealing to higher management, or filing a grievance;

2. You can *decrease your input level* by putting in less job effort, taking longer breaks, or being less cooperative; or

3. If you cannot restore equity in your present job, you can *leave the situation* by asking for a transfer or seeking a position with another employer.

Equity theory typically addresses broad, overall organizational issues such as pay and benefits, working conditions, and advancement. However, equity theory is quite relevant to individual supervisors. First, some supervisors may be in a position to influence employee pay and promotion when supervisors feel that these are inequitable. Second, supervisors can provide rewards through job assignments, assignment of newer resources, and recognition. In these and other situations, the message is clear: Employees must feel that rewards are equitably distributed; otherwise, they will be motivated to reduce the inequity.

Reinforcement Theory

Reinforcement theory uses rewards and punishments that follow a person's behavior as a way to shape that individual's future behavior.

Based on the law of effect, it holds that behaviors that meet with pleasant consequences tend to be repeated, whereas behaviors that meet with unpleasant consequences tend not to be repeated. To the extent that a supervisor has a degree of control of the reward and discipline system for employees, he or she has some control over the law of effect. Suppose that a worker's attendance has been spotty recently. Reinforcement theory can work in two ways: (1) You can *positively reinforce* (praise, reward) the worker's favorable behavior (showing up on time), thereby encouraging him or her to repeat it, or (2) you can *discourage* the worker's unfavorable behavior through punishment (scolding, writing a disciplinary warning, assigning nondesirable work duties), thereby encouraging him or her not to repeat it.

Advocates of reinforcement theory argue strongly that positive reinforcement often is more effective than punishment in getting people to behave in desired ways.

> Take, for example, an employee who gets punished for not treating a customer well. When the employee is called on the carpet, she might not necessarily know what specifically she must do to improve. Moreover, she might not be in a situation where she feels like listening, even if told. She might respond by associating "customer" and "punishment" and try to avoid customers altogether.

> On the other hand, if, when the employee does something right and the supervisor says, "I couldn't help but notice how patient and understanding you were in helping that customer work out her refund; I wanted to compliment you," then we are likely to get an employee out looking for customers to treat well. The specific behaviors (patience, understanding) lead to rewards that satisfy a person's need to enhance his or her self-image.[18]

Positive reinforcement, when properly applied, can be a very powerful motivator. Organizations and their supervisors have available a wide range of potential reinforcers, as listed earlier in Exhibit 7-7. Note that in addition to the more obvious raises and bonuses, a wide range of nonfinancial rewards was included.

Unfortunately, one of the lowest-cost tools is also one of the least used—and least correctly used. That is the simple "thank you," according to Malcolm Baldridge Award Examiner and management consultant Kevin McManus. He encourages supervisors to do a

8 Define and explain reinforcement theory.

reinforcement theory Based on the law of effect, holds that behaviors that meet with pleasant consequences tend to be repeated, whereas behaviors that meet with unpleasant consequences tend not to be repeated, and rewards and punishments are used as a way to shape the individual.

http://www.hp.com

Thank You Assessment (TYA) of their own behavior by asking to count the number of times they hear a sincere "thank you" or "I appreciate that" from him/her in a given time period. As McManus states:

> **Failing to use this simple tool sends a powerful message to people, just as effectively using it does... We spend lots of money trying to learn better ways to motivate people through the use of gift certificates, plaques, and tickets to sporting events given out to only a select group of people. At the same time, we fail to say "thank you" to each of our people every day in a manner that means something to them... Saying "thank you" is free and it is a form of recognition that can be distributed at any time.[19]**

One recent survey showed that 75 percent of employees felt that praise from the boss was the strongest motivator they receive. An independent study conducted by management search firms wanted to find out why upper-level managers left their jobs. The leading reason, given by 34 percent of respondents, was "limited praise/recognition," compared to only 25 percent who said "compensation."[20] Recall how Sharon Olds used praise and recognition to reinforce associates when they performed their jobs well. Indeed, when praise is properly used, it is one of the most effective reinforcers a supervisor has; see Exhibit 7-8.

EXHIBIT 7-8

How and When to Praise

Bob Nelson, author of *1001 Ways to Reward Employees,* says the form of reward rated number one by employees is verbal appreciation or praise from their immediate boss. Written appreciation or praise ranked number two. Below are some guidelines regarding the effective use of praise.

1. **Praise should be genuine.** Often employees see through praise as simply a carrot used to motivate. Some supervisors compliment employees primarily when an upper manager is present to cast the supervisor in a good light. For praise to be meaningful, the employee must feel it is intended as appreciation or recognition by the supervisor, with no additional conditions attached.

2. **Praise should be specific.** Assume that an employee has made a presentation at a safety meeting. After the meeting the supervisor says, "That was a terrific presentation, Anne. Thanks." While that *is* praise, there is no communication about the reason the behavior was praised. *More effective praise* would be "Anne, thanks for making the safety presentation. Your statistics and survey results were presented in a way that everyone could understand. And you are so good on your feet, in front of a group. I really appreciate your making us all aware of the need for continued safety awareness."

3. **Give praise for better than expected performance.** While recognition for expected results is important, especially in cases where you supervise below-average performers, some supervisors are too lavish in their praise of the expected and ordinary. When an employee who is always on time is greeted by his supervisor with "John, you're on time today, you're doing great," he may wonder what's really going on here and what the big deal is. In building a team of top performers, supervisory praise and recognition is especially important for better than expected results, such as putting out extra effort, exceeding performance goals, or going the extra mile.

4. **Praise should be timely.** To maximize its reinforcement potential, praise should be closely linked to the behavior. If you discussed yesterday with an employee his or her lack of punctuality, the time to recognize his or her punching in on time today is *today*, not the end of the week. You might make it a point to be near the clock and casually say "Thanks, Pete," which is sufficient to get the reinforcement across.

5. **Give praise for its own sake, not as a secondary motive.** When employees feel that praise is being used as a secondary motive, such as to soften their acceptance of another issue, it may be seen as superficial. Sometimes supervisors sandwich employee criticism with praise. They open with brief praise, then comes the "but" or "however" followed by criticism, which is the real purpose of the communication. Sometimes supervisors use praise to buffer bad news, such as when they disclose a turned-down promotion or reassignment. Positive conditional praise has its place, such as when coaching a new employee, but when viewed as an attempt to soften acceptance of another issue, praise is likely to be resented.

Source: Bob Nelson, *1001 Ways to Reward Employees* (New York: Workman Publishing Co., 1993).

The Different Generations: Some Insights for Motivation

9
Explain how generational differences affect motivation

A generational looking glass can be a valuable tool in learning how people differ in the attitudes they bring to work and what they value. Academics and practitioners agree that generation members share certain commonalities of thinking and behavior. Shared economic conditions, world events, pop culture, social experiences, education, and parenting, give each generation its own personna. While a generational perspective may not give you a complete picture of a given individual, it can certainly be helpful. Exhibit 7-9 highlights differences among the generations.

With the recent entry of Generation "Y" employees—those younger than age 27—into the working world, the workforce for the first time contains four generations.[21] The generations, and their present percentage of the work force, are:

EXHIBIT **7-9**

Characteristics of Different Generations

	Traditionalists	Baby Boomers	Generation X	Generation Y
Age in 2007	Pre 1945 Age 63–	1945–1964 Age 43–62	1965–1980 Age 27–42	1981–Present Age 1–27
Formative Events	Great Depression World Wars	Post war prosperity	Globalization Downsizing Tech boom	Networking 9-11 World terrorism Internet
Qualities	Loyal Self-sacrificing	Competitive Optimistic	Independent Individualistic Enterpreneurial Lack loyalty	Diverse Skilled Demanding Sophisticated
Assets	Wisdom Experience Persistence	Social skills	Tech skills Educated	Multi-tasking Work ethic

Lack	Technology
	  skills
		Technology
		  skills
			Social skills	Direction
				Focus
				Interpersonal
				  skills

Value	Family Patriotism	Material success Free expression Equity	Skill more than title Work-life balance	Patriotism Family Respect
Style	Directive Take Charge Do what's right	Respect authority Micromanage Proactive Work hard	Skeptical Reluctant to network Outcome focused Bend rules as needed	Plunge right in Negotiate Blend work/play Measure own success

Strategies For Managing	Respect their experience
	Value their loyalty
	Use their knowledge/
	  experience to help
	  others
		Give important roles
		Value their
		  contributions
		Show respect
		Minimize conflict
			Provide autonomy
			Give quick feedbacks
			Update their tech
			  skills
			Give credit for
			  results
				Train/upgrade
				Assign meaningful
				  work
				Use in teams
				Promote positive,
				  open environment.

Source: Adapted from Susan P. Eisner, "Managing Generation Y," **SAM Advanced Management Journal** 70, Autumn, 2005, v. 70, pp 4–13.

Traditionalists, born before 1945 (10%)

Baby Boomers, born between 1945 and 1964 (45%)

Generation Xers, born between 1965 and 1980 (30%)

Generation Yers, born in 1980 and later (15%)

Traditionalists, children of the depression and World War, were typically raised in a home with a stay-at-home parent. Imbued with strong family values, traditionalists themselves had a parent stay at home to raise their own children. Loyal and self-sacrificing, they value hard work, get satisfaction from a job well done, and tend to stay with a company a long time.

Baby Boomers were raised in a period of prosperity in the 1950s and 1960s. The largest generation in history, they were the center of their parents' lives, likely having a stay-at-home parent. They are socially skilled, ambitious, and driven to succeed, which for them is often measured materialistically. They believe in growth, change, and expansion. Boomers grew up to want the best for themselves and their families, and seek it through hard work and long hours. They, too, show loyalty toward employers, and often have a "live to work" reference frame. They dislike authoritarianism and laziness; having paid their dues through hard work and loyalty, they feel particularly dismayed in today's era of downsizing and reengineering.

Generation Xers, children of the workaholic Baby Boomers, did not see as much of their parents as earlier generations. In many cases, both their parents worked; a tripling divorce rate also meant about half were raised in a one-parent home. Xers learned to function on their own, being highly independent, self reliant, and individualistic. This generation loves freedom and room to grow. Growing up, they heard their parents' laments about layoffs, downsizing, and managers who didn't treat their parents well. They view the employment relationship as one based on service for dollars paid, rather than loyalty, even if it means frequent employer changes. Xers do not believe in paying their dues to achieve success; to them success means following the opportunity. While they possess strong technical skills, they lack the social skills of their parents' generations, not being particularly adroit at networking. They thrive on autonomy that allows them independence to handle their jobs as they see fit; thus, they respond poorly to being micromanaged.

Generation Yers have been raised in a time of economic expansion, prosperity, and the Internet. Electronic communication has enabled them to see and learn more at an early age than any preceding generation. They are the most diverse, highly educated, and technically literate generation. As the first truly global generation, Yers have some values consistent with traditionalists, including patriotism, valuing family and home, a strong sense of morality and commitment to volunteer service. They like intellectual challenge and strive to make a difference. Emotionally mature, Yers have lived with strong social stressors ranging from pressures to excel in school to parental divorce, to being products of one-parent homes. Of all the generations, one expert says, the Yers are the most willing to "rock the boat."

Because organizations have been run by **traditionalists** and **boomers,** large corporations' strict rules of engagement especially clash with Yers' values of openness and flexibility. They are accustomed to handling information, getting immediate results, and want freedom rather than rigid controls and standardized ways of doing things. Teachers and parents allowed them to freely speak their minds, so why not ask a supervisor questions such as "Why do I need to do it that way?" Growing up with instant messaging and live views of the Gulf and Iraqi wars on their televisions, Gen Yers are the ultimate stimulus junkies. They want instant feedback, rapid results, and jobs that offer excitement as well as a paycheck.[22]

You can see in Exhibit 7-9 some of the specific actions that supervisors and organizations can take that may have special impact on individuals of a given generation. For example, traditionalists may be strongly motivated by an opportunity to mentor a younger employee or help train other team members; the opportunity to attend a technology training class might be highly valued by younger Gen X or Gen Y employees. In the next section, you will learn some important principles for motivating that cut across all generation types. Peter Sheahan, a most sought after international speaker on Generation Y, says there are three things all generations, and especially Generation Yers want in a motivating work environment. These are as follows:

1. Having their supervisor's respect;

2. Feeling like they are making a real contribution—their work must have an impact; and

3. Having control—"Gen Yers want to customize their careers just like lattes are customized by coffee shops." This may range from flexible work hours to rotation among job assignments.[23]

10

Identify five steps to motivating employees.

Lessons from the Theories: Five Steps to Motivating Employees

Our intent in this chapter has been to explain a number of popular theories of motivation that can help you understand why people act as they do. You have noted the commonalities and close relationships among many of the theories.

Based on these theories, we feel there are a number of things a supervisor can do to help create a motivating environment for employees. Moreover, these five actions apply broadly to supervisors in all types of organizations. These supervisory actions are as follows:

1. Help make employees' jobs interesting.

2. Provide clear performance objectives.

3. Support employees' performance efforts.

4. Provide timely performance feedback.

5. Reward employees' performance.

Help Make Employees' Jobs Interesting

Recall Herzberg's finding that employees believed the most satisfying things about their jobs included feeling a sense of accomplishment, challenge, or responsibility. Granted, it is more difficult to make dull, repetitive jobs more interesting, especially when you cannot alter an assembly line or change the nature of work being done. But you can do a number of things to make even dull, unchallenging jobs more interesting. Might you be able to rotate jobs/tasks? Might you assign team members to special projects that give them a break from the usual grind? Have them train a new employee? Learn skills to prepare them for a more advanced job? Make a safety presentation at a safety meeting? Might you elicit their help in resolving problems which you face, such as cost or deadline overruns, relationships with other departments, or ways to improve quality? As a supervisor, it is worth your effort to make employees' work provide opportunities for intrinsic satisfaction.

✔ **STOP AND THINK**

If you are currently a supervisor, what actions could you take to help make your employees' jobs more interesting? If not currently a supervisor, select a job you have held that you considered dull and uninteresting. What actions could your supervisor have taken to make the job more interesting?

Provide Clear Performance Objectives

In line with expectancy and goal-setting theories, make sure employees clearly understand what is expected of them. If possible, set concrete, specific, challenging goals as discussed in

Direct praise is one way to reward employee performance.

Blend Images/Getty Images

goal-setting theory. Moreover, if these are not set by the system itself or by your own manager, try to obtain your employees' assistance in determining these. Employees are more likely to commit to goals they have had a hand in setting.

Support Employees' Performance Efforts

View yourself as a coach whose job is to support your team members. Help them through intangibles such as building confidence and encouraging them, but also support them in tangible ways through the resources you provide, through your responsiveness to their needs, by obtaining additional training for them, and so on. Be viewed not only as their best cheerleader, but as someone who delivers tangible support also.

Provide Timely Performance Feedback

Performance feedback is the fuel that employees need to sustain their effort. While the job itself may provide feedback to them, it is important that you acknowledge their progress. While reason would say this is easier to do in favorable situations, our experiences with managers and employees indicate it is not. Many employees state that they know things must be going well only because they *do not* hear from their supervisor. Managers must give favorable as well as unfavorable performance feedback. Note that we are not talking here about the feedback that accompanies an employee's 6- or 12-month formal review, but the feedback that occurs on a daily, regular basis. Team or departmental progress should be posted in high-visibility areas where everyone can see it regularly—from CEO to hourly employees.[24]

Reward Employees' Performance

Be liberal with rewards, making sure they are earned. Reinforce your high performers through the reward system available to you, such as merit increases, praise, recognition, or opportunities to take on a more challenging job. Be creative with rewards, remembering that rewards are valued differently by different individuals.

1 **Identify the three levels of employee motivation.**

The three levels of employee motivation are (1) the direction of an employee's behavior, (2) the level of effort, and (3) the level of persistence. Direction of behavior relates to those behaviors the individual chooses to perform. Level of effort dictates how hard the individual is willing to work on the behavior. Level of persistence refers to the individual's willingness to pursue the behavior despite obstacles or roadblocks.

2 **Explain the relationship between performance and motivation.**

While motivation is an important contributor to employee performance, it is not the only one. Also involved are an employee's skill and ability, and organizational support in the form of physical resources and assistance. We conclude that other things being equal, employees who are more highly motivated will have higher performance records.

3 **Understand and explain Maslow's hierarchy of needs theory and the principle underlying his theory.**

The principle underlying Maslow's theory of a hierarchy of needs is that needs are arranged in a hierarchy of importance and that, once a need has been satisfied, it is no longer a primary motivator. The lower-level needs include physiological, security, and social needs, and the higher-level needs are esteem and self-fulfillment.

4 **Differentiate between Herzberg's dissatisfiers and motivators.**

Herzberg's research discovered that motivators are those factors that have an uplifting effect on attitudes or performance, whereas dissatisfier/hygiene factors are those that prevent dissatisfaction but do not motivate by themselves. Motivators are recognition, advancement, achievement, being one's own boss, and the challenge associated with the work itself. Dissatisfiers include pay, benefits, working conditions, job security, and company policy/administration. Motivators relate to the two highest levels of the Maslow hierarchy, self-fulfillment and esteem. Dissatisfiers are related to lower-level physiological and security needs.

5 **Understand and explain expectancy theory.**

Expectancy theory views an individual's motivation as a conscious effort involving three variables: (1) expectancy that a given effort can achieve a given performance result; (2) probability that achieving the given performance result will lead to a reward; and (3) the value of the reward to the individual. Supervisors can apply expectancy theory by rewarding performance in ways that are meaningful to employees, by helping employees reach desired performance levels through coaching and training, and by delivering rewards as promised to employees.

6 **Explain how supervisors can use goal-setting theory to motivate employees.**

The basic premise of goal-setting theory is that task goals can be highly motivating if properly set and well managed. To maximize their motivational impact, performance goals should be specific and difficult, but achievable. Ideally, employees should participate in the goal-setting process and, if multiple goals are involved, should understand their priorities. Performance feedback about progress toward goal attainment should be provided as well as timely rewards and recognition when goals are achieved.

IMPORTANT TERMS

baby boomer generation
dissatisfier (or hygiene) factors
ego (or esteem) need
equity theory
expectancy theory
extrinsic motivation
Generation X
Generation Y
goal-setting theory
hierarchy of needs
intrinsic motivation
motivation
physiological (or biological) need
reinforcement theory
safety (or security) need
satisfier (or motivator) factors
self-fulfillment (or self actualization) needs
social (or belonging) need
Traditional generation

7 **Define equity theory.**

Equity theory states that when people feel they are rewarded inequitably as compared to others, they will act in ways to change their circumstances. They may do this by (1) attempting to increase their reward level, (2) decreasing their input level, or (3) seeking to leave the situation by requesting transfer or leaving their employer.

8 **Define and explain reinforcement theory.**

Reinforcement theory uses rewards and punishment that follow an individual's behavior as a way of shaping future behavior. It is based on the law of effect, which holds that behaviors that meet with pleasant consequences tend to be repeated, whereas behaviors that meet with unpleasant consequences tend not to be repeated.

9 **Explain how generational differences affect motivation.**

The four generations are Traditionalists, born before 1945; Baby Boomers, born between 1945 and 1964; Generation X, born between 1965 and 1980; and Generation Y, born in 1980 or later. Generalizations based on the common experiences shared during a generation's formative years enable insights into their values, behaviors, and what is likely to motivate them. Traditionalists, the oldest generation, tend to be loyal, hard working, value family, and get satisfaction from jobs well done. Workaholic Baby Boomers are ambitious, driven to succeed, and often materialistic; Generation X, raised to fend for themselves, are highly independent, technologically competent, and thrive on autonomy and freedom. Generation Y, the new workforce entrants, are the Internet generation. Technologically savvy, they are the ultimate networkers, like instant results and feedback, open communications, and value flexibility.

10 **Identify five steps to motivating employees.**

Supervisors, in general, can take five specific steps to motivate employees. They can (1) help make employees' jobs more interesting by enabling greater challenge, accomplishment, or responsibility; (2) provide clear performance objectives; (3) support employees' performance efforts through training, coaching, and assistance; (4) provide timely performance feedback to employees; and (5) reward employees generously for performance accomplishment.

QUESTIONS FOR REVIEW AND DISCUSSION

1. Identify and explain the three levels of employee motivation. Give an example of each for one of the situations below:
   - Customer associate at Home Depot
   - Bagboy at grocery chain
   - Carpenter for construction company

2. Explain the relationship between motivation and job performance. Can you identify a situation in which a factor other than your skill or motivation level impacted your performance?

3. Briefly outline Maslow's theory of the hierarchy of needs. What need levels are addressed by each of the following:
   - Being promoted from operator to supervisor
   - Setting a new record for individual performance
   - Being selected to attend a special training course

4. In what ways did Frederick Herzberg's research concerning employee motivation correlate with Maslow's hierarchy of needs?

5. In a management seminar taught by one of the authors to supervisors in a large ship-yard, one supervisor commented: "We have very little opportunity to 'motivate' employees. All monetary factors—starting pay, yearly merit increases, and bonuses based on the yard's profits—are controlled by upper management, with no input from supervisors. We don't have anything to motivate with." Do you agree or disagree with this supervisor? Why?

6. What are the elements of goal-setting theory? Explain.

7. What relationship, if any, do you see among expectancy theory, goal-setting theory, equity theory, and reinforcement theory? Explain.

8. What are some important characteristics of each of the following generations?

    a. Traditionalist

    b. Baby Boomer

    c. Generation X

    d. Generation Y

9. Identify five important steps to motivating employees.

Career Exercise: What Do You Want from Your Job?

Skill Builder 7-1

Assume that you could create the ideal job for yourself. Examine the 12 items shown below and rank these from most important to least important. In other words, what single item of the 12 is most important to you? Number that item 1. Follow a similar process until you have ranked all items.

Your Priority Rank	Ideal Job Factor
_____	a. First-class working conditions
_____	b. Opportunity to achieve wide recognition for job performance
_____	c. Working in the city/area of your choice
_____	d. A super-competent boss
_____	e. Guaranteed job security (lifetime employment)
_____	f. Exceptional advancement opportunity
_____	g. Salary 20 percent higher than the industry average
_____	h. Challenging, interesting job that you really like
_____	i. Professional, supportive colleagues
_____	j. Working for a prestigious, nationally known organization
_____	k. Outstanding fringe benefits
_____	l. Excellent opportunity to grow and develop job skills

Instructions:

1. Now that you have completed the ranking, to what extent, if any, do your results reflect Maslow's needs theory? Herzberg's motivation–hygiene theory?

2. Meet with a group of four to six classmates and compare your rankings. To what extent were the rankings similar? Dissimilar? What might account for any different rankings given by your group?

3. Present a report to the class that summarizes the results of your group's discussion.

Skill Builder 7-2 | Classifying Managerial Rewards

Listed here are 15 actions that an organization's managers can take, each of which addresses one or more potential needs on the Maslow hierarchy. Some have been taken from Exhibit 7-7, "Manager's List of Potential Rewards," but others have been added.

Instructions:

1. For each item, identify the levels on the Maslow hierarchy of needs that the action addresses.

2. Select three items that you personally feel would be most important for you at the present time.

3. In small groups, discuss your results for items 1 and 2. To what extent did your team members agree on the three items? Why were there differences? Be prepared to report your results to the rest of the class.

Action	Maslow Need Level(s) Addressed
1. Day off or time off	
2. Personal call or visit from CEO or senior manager	
3. "Employee of the Month" parking space	
4. Direct oral praise from supervisor	
5. Opportunity to attend special training course	
6. Name in company newsletter	
7. Additional responsibilities	
8. Special task force assignment	
9. Company outing, picnic	
10. Being assigned favorable tasks	
11. Opportunity to attend special seminar	
12. New title, new office, new equipment	
13. Direct praise to individual in presence of others	
14. Receiving bonus for reaching production goal	
15. Being given more responsibility	

Skill Builder 7-3 | Applying Motivational Theory

Assume you are a manager of a 30-employee chain restaurant. Your personnel consist of an assistant manager, cooks and food preparers, kitchen personnel, a host/hostess, waiters, table bussers, and bartenders. Give an example of how you can use each of the following motivational theories to motivate your employees:

a. Expectancy theory

b. Goal-setting theory

c. Reinforcement theory

d. Equity theory

CASE

Nucor, The Surprising Performance Culture of Steelmaker Nucor

In the early afternoon, three Nucor electricians got a call from their Hickman, Arkansas, plant colleagues. The Hickman mill's electrical grid had failed, which meant the mini-mill couldn't melt the usual auto parts, appliances, and mobile home parts that it uses to produce steel. But why should an outage in Arkansas concern anyone at plants in other Nucor locations? Here's why. At Nucor, steelworker production bonuses are based not only on what their own mill does, but how others fare also. When a grid goes out, it hurts all. That's why when Hickman's electrician colleagues called for help, people didn't need top management to tell them to go; they responded on their own. Two from the company's South Carolina plant boarded the first plane they could get to Memphis. Arriving at 11 p.m., they rented a car and drove 2 hours directly to the Hickman mill. The third electrician, from the company's Decatur, Alabama, plant was in Indiana, visiting another Nucor site. He immediately drove to Hickman. Combined with Hickman staff they camped out on site and worked 20-hour shifts to mobilize the plant in 3 days—much less than the anticipated week. They received no extra pay for their effort.

Why would they do such a thing? It's because of Nucor's unique way of motivating their workforce and the strong family bond throughout its employment ranks. First, there's pay. Nucor steelworkers make only about $10 hourly, compared to the typical steelworker's $16–$21 hourly. Managers also earn salaries as much as 20 percent below what competitors pay. But what a difference incentives can make! Based on production incentives for their mills, Nucor's steelworkers took in $79,000 in pay and incentives in 2005. Then, in 2005 they participated in company profit sharing, topped by a $2,000 one-time bonus that marked the company's record earnings year. That brought the total to $99,000. A worker's incentives are tied not only to quality production in their own mill, but also to that of other mills and overall company profits. They can track their performance each week, so they know exactly where they stand.

But it's more than just dollars that make Nucor special. The company became the darling of the late 1980s when its unique "pay for performance" system was implemented under then CEO Ken Iverson. Iverson insisted on a culture that would result in employees feeling like owners. In addition to their pay system, Iverson empowered employees to make critical decisions, implement their ideas, and take risks. The rest is history.

Operating in a single North Carolina location then, and in an underdog role to U.S. Steel and other giants, the lean mini-mill company today has 13,000 employees in ten locations and is the U.S.'s largest steel producer with revenues of $13 billion and its past 4 years' 387 percent return to shareholders has beaten almost all companies listed in the Standard and Poor stock index.

The Nucor culture also includes some symbolic things, like every employee's name being placed on the cover of the annual report. And sure, there's something egalitarian—present CEO Daniel DeMicco flying commercial jets rather than having his own, finding his own parking space in the headquarters lot like every other employee, or making the coffee when it's his turn. In 2005, when the average CEO pay of big companies averaged 400 times that of the hourly employee, at Nucor, DiMicco's was 24 times that of his steelworkers.

Plant managers' incentives are based on the company's overall return on equity, rather than specific results from their own mill. As one stated, "At Nucor, it's not my plant versus someone elses, as they're all 'our' plants. When one plant has a problem it's everyone's problem."

Questions

1. What are the most relevant concepts from the chapter that are reflected at Nucor? Comment specifically about the following:

   Maslow's Hierarchy of Needs

   Herzberg's Motivation–Hygiene theory

   Expectancy theory

   Equity theory

   Goal-Setting theory

Source: Nanette Byrnes and Michael Arndt, "What You Can Learn From a Company That Treats Workers Like Owners. Inside the Surprising Performance Culture of Steelmaker Nucor," *Business Week*, May 1, 2006, pp. 56–62.

8 Leadership

© Stock Connection Distribution/Alamy

Supervisors may adopt different managerial styles in an effort to influence their employees to achieve company goals.

Leadership is of the spirit, compounded of personality and vision; its practice is an art.
—SIR WILLIAM SLIM

Leadership is action, not position.
—DONALD H. MCGANNON

Preview

Kenny: An Effective Supervisor

The most effective supervisor encountered by one of the authors of this textbook was named Kenny, and he was maintenance supervisor in a chemical plant of an international corporation.* The author was called in as a consultant because the plant was suffering from the results of the ineffective, autocratic leadership of a former plant manager. Such leadership at the top had adversely affected all levels, resulting in low morale and losses from plant operations.

In gathering data about the plant through interviews, questionnaires, and observations, the consultant discovered that one maintenance crew, unlike the rest of the departments in the plant, had very high morale and productivity. Kenny was its supervisor.

In the interview with Kenny, the consultant discovered that Kenny was a young man in his early thirties who had a two-year associate's degree from a community college. The consultant was impressed with his positive attitude, especially in view of the overall low plant morale and productivity. Kenny said that the plant was one of the finest places he'd ever worked and that the maintenance people had more know-how than any other group he had been associated with. Kenny's perception of his crew was that they did twice as much work as other crews, that everyone worked together, and that participative management did work with them.

The consultant was curious about why pressure and criticism from the old, autocratic manager seemed not to have had any effect on Kenny's crew. The crew gave the consultant the answer. They explained that Kenny had the ability to act as a buffer between upper management and the crew. He would get higher management's primary objectives and points across without upsetting his people. As one crew member described it:

The maintenance supervisors will come back from a "donkey barbecue" session with higher management where they are raising hell about shoddy work, taking too long at coffee breaks, etc. Other supervisors are shook up for a week and give their staff hell. But Kenny is cool, calm, and collected. He will call us together and report that nine items were discussed at the meeting, including shoddy work, but that doesn't apply to our crew. Then he will cover the two or three items that are relevant to our getting the job done.

Unfortunately, Kenny did have a real concern at the time of the consultant's interview. He was being transferred from the highest producing crew to the lowest producing one. In fact, the latter was known as the "Hell's Angels" crew. The crew members were a renegade group who were constantly fighting with production people as well as with one another. The previous supervisor had been terminated because he could not cope with them.

In the course of this chapter, we will return to Kenny and what happened with the renegade crew.

*The company would not permit use of its name.

Learning Objectives

After reading and studying this chapter, you should be able to:

1. Describe factors that affect the leadership style used.

2. Discuss and explain two frequently used leadership models.

3. Determine which leadership style is most appropriate in different situations.

4. Contrast heroic supervisors with developmental supervisors.

5. Contrast transformational leadership with transactional leadership.

6. Discuss how to inspire self-confidence, develop people, and increase productivity.

7. Explain why emotional intelligence is so important for effective leadership.

209

Do you think Kenny can turn things around in a year with the renegade crew? Why or why not?

. . . .

One thing we need to say about motivation is that it cannot take place in a vacuum. For things to happen, effective leadership must be exhibited. This chapter focuses on effective leadership. We don't want the chapter preview to give you the idea that being an effective leader is easy. Today many supervisors and managers use a less effective leadership style than they could be using, often because they don't have the necessary skills or don't even realize the benefits of using other styles. They don't realize that the most effective style in one situation may not be the most effective in another. Hence, this chapter addresses such questions as the following:

1. Why do some leaders use one style and other leaders use another?

2. What effects do different styles have on employee productivity and morale?

3. What style is most appropriate in a particular situation?

4. Should a particular style be used consistently, or should the style be changed as circumstances change?

Such questions are vital for an organization, since supervisory leadership is one of the primary determinants of organizational performance and productivity.

Leadership: What Is It All About?

leadership Influencing individual and group activities toward goal achievement.

Leadership is defined as a process of influencing individual and group activities toward goal setting and goal achievement. In the chapter preview, Kenny successfully influenced his group toward the achievement of effective results, whereas the former supervisor of the "Hell's Angels" had not. This chapter provides insights and concepts that will assist supervisors in successfully leading their work groups.

1 Describe factors that affect the leadership style used.

Factors Affecting Leadership Style

Three factors, or variables, have a major impact on the choice of leadership style. These are (1) Theory X or Theory Y management philosophy, (2) the followers' readiness level, and (3) the situation faced by the supervisor. As Exhibit 8-1 shows, these factors are interrelated.

Theory X or Theory Y Management Philosophy. A supervisor's management philosophy is basically determined by his or her assumptions about the nature of people. Whether they are aware of it or not, most supervisors have a philosophy that influences their style in working with and through people. This philosophy is affected by several factors. Three critical factors interact to influence a supervisor's view of the nature of people and consequently shape his or her philosophy:

1. The supervisor's family and early school environment;

2. The supervisor's experience and training in the area of leadership;

3. The supervisor's present work environment, including the type of work and the general management system.

Kenny had a very supportive and happy home environment. His father was a big influence and served as a role model. He always stressed to Kenny that he should treat people as he would want to be treated.

EXHIBIT 8-1

Factors Affecting Choice
of Leadership Style

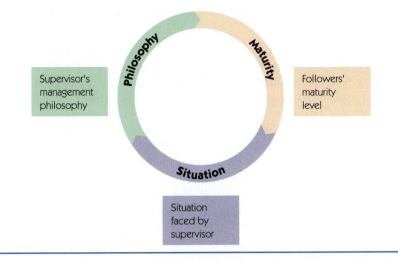

Supervisor's
management
philosophy

Followers'
maturity
level

Situation
faced by
supervisor

One of the most widely publicized approaches to the study of management philosophy is Douglas McGregor's concept of Theory X and Theory Y.[1] On the basis of his consulting and research work in industry, McGregor outlined two contrasting sets of assumptions about the nature of people. A manager's leadership style is influenced by the set of assumptions to which he or she subscribes.

Following are the most significant assumptions of **Theory X**:

1. The average human being has an inherent dislike of work and will avoid it if possible.

2. Because of this human characteristic—dislike of work—most people must be coerced, controlled, directed, or threatened with punishment to get them to put forth adequate effort toward the achievement of organizational objectives.

3. The average human being prefers to be directed, wishes to avoid responsibility, has relatively little ambition, and, above all, seeks security.

4. The average human being cannot be trusted.

Supervisors who accept Theory X assumptions will be more inclined to prefer a structured, autocratic leadership style.

The basic assumptions of **Theory Y** are as follows:

1. The expenditure of physical and mental effort in work is as natural as play or rest.

2. External control and the threat of punishment are not the only means of bringing about effort toward organizational objectives. People will exercise self-direction and self-control in the service of objectives to which they are committed.

3. Commitment to objectives is a function of the rewards associated with their achievement.

4. The average human being learns, under proper conditions, not only to accept but also to actively seek greater responsibility.

Theory X The average person has an inherent dislike of work and wishes to avoid responsibility.

Theory Y Work is as natural as play or rest.

5. The capacity to exercise a relatively high degree of imagination, ingenuity, and creativity in the solution of organizational problems is widely, not narrowly, distributed in the population.

6. Under the conditions of modern industrial life, the intellectual potential of the average human being is only partially utilized.

7. The average human being believes that she or he is a winner, so treat her or him like a winner.

Supervisors who hold Theory Y assumptions will be more inclined to prefer a supportive, participative leadership style when the situation calls for it. This last point is important because some people have misconstrued Theory Y by assuming that it always dictates a supportive, participative approach. Although a leader holding Theory Y assumptions about people might prefer a participative approach, the theory does not preclude a tough-minded approach or decisions. For example, Henri Fayol, one of the pioneers of management thinking, used the term "commanding" for what today we call "leading." One of Fayol's principles of command (leadership) is to eliminate the incompetent. However, he indicates that before you take that step, you attempt to develop competence in the employee through training, coaching, counseling, etc. If these strategies do not work, you eliminate the individual through firing, and everyone knows the action was fair and warranted. This illustration reflects a Theory Y set of assumptions, and the outcome reflects a tough-minded decision.

Edgar Schein, an international expert on organization culture and process consultation, has stated, "Show me an organization that has a key leader with Theory X assumptions about people, and I predict they will eventually screw things up."[2] The authors agree with Schein. The former plant manager in the chapter preview was Theory X oriented and was a casualty of Henri Fayol's principle of command—eliminate the incompetent.

✔ STOP AND THINK

Which of these Theory X or Y assumptions did Kenny hold concerning his people? Also, what views did he hold regarding his boss and the new plant manager?

What if the renegade crew decides not to cooperate with Kenny and its members continue to be poor performers? Should Kenny continue to be supportive and use Theory Y strategies? Why or why not?

readiness level The state of a person's drive or need for achievement.

The Followers' Readiness Level. Readiness level is the state of a person's drive and need for achievement. It results from his or her experience, education, attitudes, and willingness and ability to accept responsibility. These readiness variables should be considered only in relation to a specific task to be performed.

The readiness concept is expressed by the following formula:

$$\text{Readiness} = \text{Ability} + \text{Willingness}$$

If followers are less ready, the leader should use a different style than if followers are more ready. Unfortunately, some supervisors fail to take into consideration the readiness level of their employees.

After Kenny was assigned to the new crew, he had to make a decision on the leadership strategies he would use in dealing with them. His initial diagnosis was that the crew had the ability to do the work but lacked the willingness because of a poor attitude.

Through discussion with members of the "Hell's Angels" crew, the consultant learned that the first day on the job Kenny called a meeting, shut the door, and conducted a "bull session" that lasted over 2 hours. Among other things, he told them about his philosophy and the way he liked to operate. He especially stressed that he was going to be fair and treat everyone equally. The crew members were allowed to gripe and complain as long as they talked about matters in the plant, while Kenny played a listening role without arguing with them. In the course of the session, Kenny expressed his expectations of the crew. They, in turn, told him they would do it his way for 2 weeks to see if he "practiced what he preached."

As you may have surmised by now, Kenny's leadership made the difference. Before the year was out, his new crew was the most productive in the plant.

The Situation Faced by the Supervisor. Common sense dictates that the situation faced by a supervisor should have a major influence on his or her leadership style. A platoon leader directing troops in combat, an airline pilot who suddenly has engine trouble, or a supervisor faced with an immediate safety crisis would certainly not call for a group meeting and get people involved to deal with the emergency.

The nature of the work and the types of assignments must be considered in assessing a situation. Research scientists who perform creative and complex jobs, for example, require more freedom to operate than do workers who perform repetitive, assembly-line work. Finally, a leader's choice of style is influenced by how her or his unit is progressing. For example, a football team with outstanding potential that loses the first three games would get a different leadership response from its coach than a team that had won its first three games.

Two Leadership Models

Of the many theories and theoretical models regarding leadership, we have selected two that are especially applicable for supervisors. These are (1) Robert Blake and Anne Adams McCanse's well-known Leadership Grid® and (2) Paul Hersey and Kenneth Blanchard's Situational Leadership® Model. Probably more supervisors have been trained using these models than any others. More than a million people have been trained in both the Situational Leadership and Grid models in 40 countries worldwide.[3] Clearly businesses see these two models as more practical than the theory-based models.

Leadership Grid. The **Leadership Grid®** in Exhibit 8-2 (originally published as the Managerial Grid by Robert Blake and Jane S. Mouton) shows that a leader has two concerns: production and people.[4] "Concern for Results" is plotted on the horizontal axis of the grid, while "Concern for People" is plotted on the vertical axis. Although the exhibit identifies seven basic leadership styles, theoretically there are 81 combinations of "concerns" that could be plotted by using the nine-point system in the grid.

If a supervisor is primarily concerned with production and shows little concern for people, he or she is a *9,1* leader (9 in concern for production results and 1 in concern for people). The 9,1 leader is one who structures the work, delegates as little as possible, and usually is an autocrat in getting work accomplished. This style is called **authority compliance** or *task management.*

Conversely, the supervisor who shows primary concern for people and little concern for production is a *1,9* leader. The 1,9 leader is supportive and somewhat permissive, emphasizing the need to keep employees happy and satisfied. Leaders of this type tend to avoid pressure in getting the work done. This style is called **country club management.**

The *5,5* leader uses a **middle of the road management** style—this leader places some emphasis on production and some emphasis on people. Usually the unstated agreement in this style is "if you give me reasonable production, I will be reasonable in my demands on you."

The *1,1* leader reflects the poorest of all styles, called **impoverished management.** Supervisors using this type of leadership have completely abdicated the leadership role. If any significant work gets done, it is due to the initiative of people working for this leader. In actuality, the leader has retired on the job!

2
Discuss and explain two frequently used leadership models.

Leadership Grid®
Categorizes leadership styles according to concern for people and concern for production results.

authority compliance
The leader's having a high concern for production results and using a directive approach.

country club management
High concern for people.

middle of the road management Places equal emphasis on people and production.

impoverished management
Little concern for people or production.

EXHIBIT 8-2

The Leadership Grid
Figure

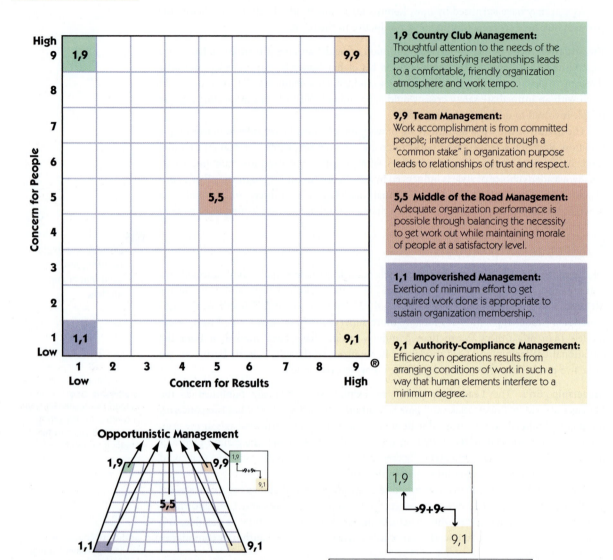

1,9 Country Club Management:
Thoughtful attention to the needs of the people for satisfying relationships leads to a comfortable, friendly organization atmosphere and work tempo.

9,9 Team Management:
Work accomplishment is from committed people; interdependence through a "common stake" in organization purpose leads to relationships of trust and respect.

5,5 Middle of the Road Management:
Adequate organization performance is possible through balancing the necessity to get work out while maintaining morale of people at a satisfactory level.

1,1 Impoverished Management:
Exertion of minimum effort to get required work done is appropriate to sustain organization membership.

9,1 Authority-Compliance Management:
Efficiency in operations results from arranging conditions of work in such a way that human elements interfere to a minimum degree.

Opportunistic Management

In Opportunistic Management, people adapt and shift to any grid style needed to gain the maximum advantage. Performance occurs according to a system of selfish gain. Effort is given only for an advantage for personal gain.

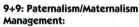

9+9: Paternalism/Maternalism Management:
Reward and approval are bestowed to people in return for loyalty and obedience; failure to comply leads to punishment.

Source: The Leadership Grid® figure, Paternalism Figure and Opportunism from *Leadership Dilemmas—Grid Solutions,* by Robert R. Blake and Anne Adams McCanse (Formerly the Managerial Grid by Robert R. Blake and Jane S. Mouton). Houston: Gulf Publishing Company (Grid Figure: p. 29, Paternalism Figure: p. 30, Opportunism Figure: p. 31). Copyright 1991 by Scientific Methods, Inc. Reproduced by permission of the owners.

The 9,9 leader believes that the heart of directing work lies in mutual understanding and agreement about what organizational and unit objectives are and about the proper means of attaining them. This type of leader has a high concern for both people and production and uses a participative approach called **team management** to get the work done.

team management High concern for both people and production.

✔ STOP AND THINK

Which style do you think Blake and associates advocate as the style that works best?

. . . .

If your answer was the 9,9 style, then you are correct. Blake and associates strongly believe that the 9,9 style is the way to manage in leadership situations. They cite the many managers and supervisors with whom they have worked, regardless of political, religious, or business practices, who have concluded that a 9,9 (team management) leader is using the ideal style.

Hersey and Blanchard's Situational Leadership. It sounds as if we have leadership licked, doesn't it? You may have concluded that the best approach is a high concern for both production and people. But not so fast—a number of people disagree, saying that there is *no one best approach for every situation,* but only a best approach for a given situation.

One of the most popular situational approaches is called the **life-cycle theory of leadership.** It draws heavily on leadership research conducted at Ohio State University. In these studies, leadership behaviors and strategies in a number of different organizations were examined. The researchers concluded that many leadership behaviors fall into one of two areas—task behaviors or relationship behaviors. **Task behaviors** involve clarifying the job; telling people what to do, how to do it, and when to do it; providing follow-up; and taking corrective action. **Relationship behaviors** involve providing people with support, giving them positive feedback, and asking for their opinions and ideas.

These two concepts, along with the concept of the readiness level of followers, are central to understanding the Hersey-Blanchard model.[5] Recall that the readiness level of followers is assessed in relation to their ability to do a *specific* job or task. It encompasses their desire for achievement, experience, education, attitudes, and willingness to accept responsibility. Now that we have a few building blocks, let's examine Hersey and Blanchard's situational leadership model, as shown in Exhibit 8-3.[6]

The Hersey-Blanchard **Situational Leadership® Model** shows the relationship between the readiness of followers and the leadership style based on task and relationship behaviors of leaders. The model consists of four labeled blocks, or quadrants, with a curved line running through each quadrant. At the bottom of the model is a scale showing various ranges of readiness: high, moderate, and low. The direction of the arrow on the readiness scale and the direction of the arrow on the task behavior axis indicate that the higher the degree of readiness, the lower the degree of task behavior required.

To use this model, first identify the readiness level of the members of your work group (high, moderate, or low) on the readiness scale. Keep in mind that this point represents your assessment only in regard to their ability to carry out a *specific* task or assignment. Then draw a vertical line. The point where it intersects the curved line will fall within one of the four quadrants, and the label on that quadrant gives the most effective leadership style for the particular situation.

Hersey and Blanchard use the model to explain not only leadership in dealing with adults, but also parents' leadership in raising children. Let's first illustrate the model using a family situation.

3 Determine which leadership style is most appropriate in different situations.

life-cycle theory of leadership Leadership behaviors should be based on the readiness level of employees.

task behaviors Clarifying a job, telling people what to do and how and when to do it, providing follow-up, and taking corrective action.

relationship behaviors Providing people with support and asking for their opinions.

Situational Leadership® Model Shows the relationship between the readiness of followers and the leadership style.

EXHIBIT **8-3**

The Hersey-Blanchard
Situational Leadership®
Model

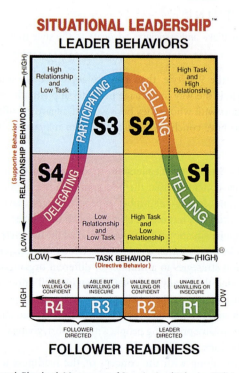

SITUATIONAL LEADERSHIP™
LEADER BEHAVIORS

✔ STOP AND THINK

Assume that a 4-year-old boy is to walk to a birthday party. Although the party is in the neighborhood, it is two blocks away and there are two busy streets to cross. Diagnose the leadership style the child's mother would use to get her son to the party.

If you responded that a high-task and low-relationship style is appropriate, then you are correct. The task involves some danger (crossing busy streets), and the follower is less ready. Hence, the mother should use a structured, high-task approach, accompanying the child and perhaps even holding his hand as they cross the streets.

The four quadrants in the top portion of Exhibit 8-3 can be translated into four basic leadership styles: (1) structuring and telling, (2) coaching and selling, (3) participating and supporting, and (4) delegating. The **structuring and telling style** (S1: high task and low relationship) usually works best with new or less-ready employees and with individuals or groups whose performance is slipping. For example, if a department's costs have increased considerably beyond the standard, then a highly structured, close leadership style would be called for to correct the situation. Thus, the structuring and telling style would be used with an individual or a group that is relatively low in readiness with respect to a given task.

structuring and telling style Used with individuals or groups relatively less ready for a given task.

The **coaching and selling style** (S2: high task and high relationship) is best used with individuals or groups that have potential but haven't completely mastered their assignments. For example, a high school football coach with young but talented players should probably use this approach. The coach would have a high concern for both task accomplishment (coaching) and convincing the players through positive reinforcement that they have the ability to win (selling).

An appropriate style to use as individuals or groups mature is the **participating and supporting style** (S3: high relationship and low task). The leader should use more participative management in getting ideas and should involve the followers in setting objectives and solving problems. Think of Maslow's hierarchy of needs theory: As employees gain experience and competence, they have a need for more support for and involvement in their work.

The **delegating style** (S4: low relationship and low task) is one of the more difficult styles for a supervisor to use even when individuals or groups working under the supervisor are exceptionally ready and capable. A primary reason is that the supervisor is held accountable for results and therefore is reluctant to involve employees in her or his work. Perhaps you have heard the expression "If it ain't broke, don't fix it." This saying sums up why the wise supervisor will leave well enough alone as long as results are satisfactory. But what happens when conditions change?

> **coaching and selling style** Used with individuals or groups that have potential but haven't realized it fully.
>
> **participating and supporting style** Best used with ready individuals or groups.
>
> **delegating style** Used with exceptionally ready and capable individuals and groups.

✔ STOP AND THINK

Suppose you are a supervisor and have a skilled, capable worker who has never caused you any difficulties. For 3 years she has been a productive person in your department. Since she has proved to be a capable person, you would probably be using a delegating style in regard to her work. However, in the past 2 weeks her work has steadily deteriorated. Projects are late and the work, when completed, is of poor quality. As her supervisor, what leadership style would you use in this situation?

You certainly would not continue to delegate, would you? Most supervisors would shift all the way to a coaching and selling style or even to a structuring and telling style. Depending on what the problem is, either style could be appropriate. This situation shows how a leader might use a different style with an individual or a group, depending on the situation.

Tannenbaum and Schmidt's Leadership Continuum

Robert Tannenbaum and Warren Schmidt are two writers who take a situational viewpoint toward leadership.[7] Their **continuum of leadership behavior,** shown in Exhibit 8-4, is especially useful when a supervisor is considering the degree to which employees should be involved in decision making. The figure is a rectangular block representing a continuum of power, which is divided by a diagonal line into two distinct parts: (1) use of authority by the supervisor and (2) the area of freedom for employees. The more authority the supervisor has, the less freedom there is for employees. Conversely, the more freedom employees are given, the less authority the supervisor uses. The continuum also indicates the range of available behaviors from which the supervisor can draw.

> **continuum of leadership behavior** The full range of leadership behaviors in terms of the relationship between a supervisor's use of authority and employees' freedom.

Tannenbaum and Schmidt maintain that each situation calling for a decision may require a different approach. The path the leader chooses to follow should be based on a consideration of the following three types of forces:

1. *Forces in the leader.* These include the leader's value system, confidence in employees, leadership inclinations, and feelings of security or insecurity.

2. *Forces in the employees.* These include the employees' need for independence, need for increased responsibility, knowledge of the problem, attitude toward and interest in tackling the problem, and expectations with respect to sharing in decision making.

EXHIBIT 8-4

Continuum of Leadership
Behavior

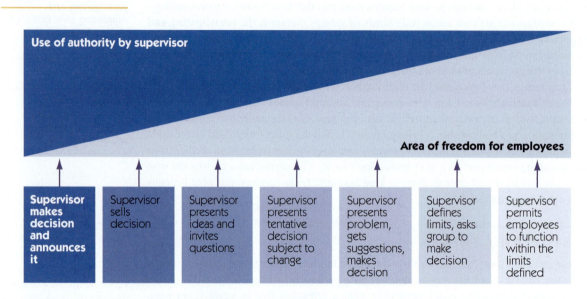

Use of authority by supervisor

Area of freedom for employees

Supervisor makes decision and announces it	Supervisor sells decision	Supervisor presents ideas and invites questions	Supervisor presents tentative decision subject to change	Supervisor presents problem, gets suggestions, makes decision	Supervisor defines limits, asks group to make decision	Supervisor permits employees to function within the limits defined

3. *Forces in the situation.* These include the type of organization, the group's effectiveness, the pressure of time, and the nature of the problem itself.

These three types of forces can be compared to the three factors affecting leadership (discussed at the beginning of the chapter and shown in Exhibit 8-1). For example, a supervisor's management philosophy is greatly influenced by his or her value system.

The key point to remember is that the successful supervisor is skilled in assessing the appropriate behavior to use in a given situation. Utilizing this approach, how would you deal with the following stop and think question?

✔ STOP AND THINK

As the result of a dramatic upward shift in sales, the XYZ firm has to rearrange vacation schedules. The previous supervisor consulted individually with employees and, when possible, gave them their first or second choice of vacation time. Because of time pressure, this approach would take too long now. Donna Douglas, the current supervisor, has a lot of confidence in her group of employees. They have a good work record. Drawing from the continuum of leadership behavior, what approach would you recommend that she use in rearranging vacation schedules?

Is One Leadership Style Best?

As we indicated, research supports the thesis that there is no one best style for all situations. However, Hersey and Blanchard and others recognize that, in most situations, the appropriate style is either coaching and selling or participating and supporting. So we can learn a lot from the Blake and associates thesis regarding the payoffs from utilizing a participative, team approach to managing.

The long-run trend in U.S. industry is for supervisory managers to use more participative styles, although they initially resist the move toward more participation.[8] An explanation for this trend is that employees are becoming better educated and their lower-level needs have been relatively well satisfied. It is only through tapping the higher-level needs, then, that significant motivation will occur. We believe the next three leadership approaches to be discussed are the most affirming of supervisors who hold a Theory Y set of assumptions regarding people. We also believe these approaches are the most rewarding for the employees, the organization, and the supervisors in arriving at win–win outcomes. Although there is some overlap, there are enough differences that we present them individually. The approaches are developmental leadership, transformational leadership, and servant leadership.

Developmental Leadership

4 Contrast heroic supervisors with developmental supervisors.

We noted earlier in the chapter that there is no one leadership approach that is effective in all situations, and that a contingency approach is called for to achieve effective results. In many environments, however, with educated personnel, a contingency diagnosis calls more and more for an approach known as *developmental leadership* that is especially effective in managing groups.

Developmental leadership is an approach that helps groups to evolve effectively and to achieve highly supportive, open, creative, committed, high-performing membership. To understand developmental leadership better, let us first examine what David Bradford and Allen Cohen called "heroic management."

developmental leadership An approach that helps groups to evolve effectively and to achieve highly supportive, open, creative, committed, high-performing membership.

Heroic Managers

Heroic managers are those who have a great need for control or influence and want to run things. If they are dynamic and capable, they may do an effective job and produce good results, particularly in the short run. However, it is critical that they do not overcontrol and stymie the development of subordinates. They are depicted very heroically in films, especially those dealing with the Wild West. Some examples are the trail boss who gets the wagon train through to its destination and the sheriff who takes care of the bad guys.

heroic managers Those managers who have a great need for control or influence and want to run things.

From interviews with managers providing their views of what a good leader is like, Bradford and Cohen developed the following list of characteristics of heroic managers:

1. The manager should know at all times what is going on in the department. (In westerns, when asked for information, the trail boss always seems to know what is going on.)

2. The manager should have enough technical expertise to supervise subordinates. (The really good trail boss cannot only outdraw and outshoot anyone around but also handle troublemakers quite effectively with his bare fists.)

3. The manager should be able to solve any problem that comes up or at least solve it before the subordinate does. (If the trail boss cannot handle any problem that arises, he loses face and his leadership position is undermined.)

4. The manager should be the primary (if not the only) person responsible for how the department is working. (The trail boss has total responsibility for the welfare of the group, so shared leadership is out of the question.)

Desirable though these characteristics are, if carried to extremes, they can lead to overcontrol and lack of development of subordinates, as shown in Exhibit 8-5. Therefore, what is needed is an orientation that focuses on *building heroes* rather than *being a hero*.

Effective leaders like Carol Boote, CEO of Autodesk, understand that their job is not to be a hero but to cultivate heroes among their employees.

Developmental Managers

Building heroes is the goal of developmental leaders. Bradford and Cohen's model of the manager as a developer has three interrelated components: (1) building a shared-responsibility team, (2) continuously developing individual skills, and (3) determining and building a common department vision.[9]

Building a Shared-Responsibility Team. In talking about building a shared-responsibility team, we are really talking about shared leadership. Instead of using meetings primarily for reporting and providing information to the group, developmental leaders deal with real issues and actual problem solving.

✔ **STOP AND THINK**

Refer to the continuum of leadership behaviors shown in Exhibit 8-4. Which behaviors would support building a shared-responsibility team?

••

Developing Individual Skills. The second component of developmental leadership, continuous development of individual skills, is closely interconnected with the first. One of the best opportunities for individual development is offered by an effective team that deals with real issues. It is no secret that many effective top executives derived considerable development from serving on committees or task forces tackling tough issues. In addition, developmental leaders encourage and seek out opportunities for their people to attend various developmental courses of either a technical or a managerial nature and to increase both knowledge and skills continually.

Shaping a Common Vision. Many times, the final component, determining and building a common group vision, is the first step in a manager's movement toward developmental leadership. Bradford and Cohen refer to this as developing the work group's *overarching goal*, which is supportive of the mission and overall goals of the organization. They go on to say

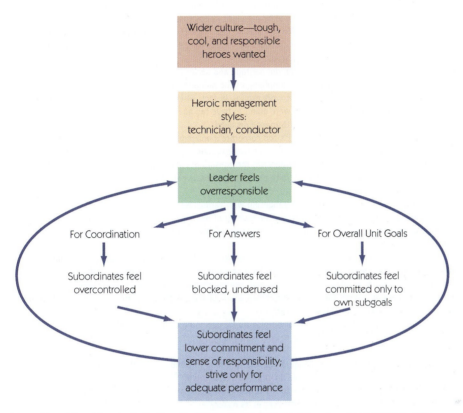

Source: Adapted from *Managing for Excellence*. David L. Bradford and Allen R. Cohen, Copyright © 1984, John Wiley & Sons, reprinted by permission of John Wiley & Sons, Inc.

that creating a tangible vision makes group members excited about where they are going. Exhibit 8-6 explains how one heroic manager evolved into a developmental leader.

Transformational and Transactional Leadership

Transformational leadership is one influential theory and way of looking at leadership that has emerged in more recent years; it is closely related to team leadership.

John MacGregor Burns[10] and Bernard Bass[11] were the first to identify and explore the differences between transactional and transformational leadership. Both authors make the case that transformational leadership is a paradigm shift to a more visionary and empowering leadership style, particularly needed in a world of rapid and turbulent change. As Burns states, "the result of transforming leadership is a relationship of mutual stimulation and elevation that converts followers into leaders and may convert leaders into moral agents."

Transactional leadership is a more traditional leadership approach and is similar to an exchange process. For example, a supervisor may implicitly or explicitly get this message

5 Contrast transformational leadership with transactional leadership.

transformational leadership
Converts followers into leaders and may convert leaders into moral agents.

transactional leadership
Leaders identify desired performance standards and recognize what types of rewards employees want from their work.

EXHIBIT **8-6**

International Paper's
Turnaround Artist
Bob Goins

In the fall of 1982, Bob Goins was considered to be one of International Paper Company's (IP) top-performing mill managers. Based on IP's criteria, the mill he managed in Bastrop, Louisiana, was consistently best in its peer group. But Goins was not satisfied. He felt that he had taken the mill about as far as it would go—from a productivity standpoint. In Goins' words, "I could try various things at getting production and performance pumped up, but shortly thereafter the air would go out."

As a heroic manager, Goins had a "can do" attitude and decided that next year was going to be a better year. This turned out to be a self-fulfilling prophecy, as the mill just had a great year. It was accomplished by Goins putting excruciating pressure on the work groups. In fact, when he sensed that they were at a breaking point, he pulled back and told them they were going to have fun again. Unfortunately, without the pressure and his intimidation style, the groups' performance declined.

Fortunately, around this same time, IP's top corporate management was initiating a number of strategies to change its culture. Among these was a series of two-day monthly meetings of a group of IP mill managers with representatives of an Atlanta consulting firm. The consultants played primarily a listening-facilitating role, allowing the groups unlimited brainstorming opportunities. Eventually the group developed a philosophy statement for the primary mill facility.

During this period, Goins started experimenting with various ways to allow people in the mill to do their own jobs. Among other things, Goins reduced the number of management levels in the mill. He used a shared-responsibility and joint problem-solving approach with what he calls the "lead team"—the group reporting directly to him.

One of the things he was most proud of at Bastrop was the initiation of team activity at the operative level. These area teams were organized into small groups for problem solving. Although each team had a trained facilitator, each selected its own leaders and own problems. The teams were made up of volunteers, and people rotated on and off the teams. Sometimes, after solving a particular problem, a team would disband, but sometimes it worked throughout the year.

The outcome of all this experimentation was a mill operating at historic performance levels and the transformation of Bob Goins from a heroic, benevolent autocrat to a developmental, participative manager.

Goins was next offered the challenge of managing IP's largest mill—one with a recent bitter strike and lockout. Not long after Goins took the job, an engineer commented, "I've heard a number of managers preach participative management, but Bob is the best I've seen at implementing it in a mill." After two years, Goins had IP's largest mill performing better than ever in its history.

Goins' next assignment was to the company's Texarkana mill—one that IP's higher management felt had never realized its potential. This turned out to be his greatest challenge. In the past, management had thrown people and extra supervision at production problems. Goins quickly found that empowering lower levels with decision-making and problem-solving authority did not motivate people to get the job done. They still deferred to foremen and higher levels for decision making and problem solving.

Goins' diagnosis was that the employees certainly had the ability but had been working a long time in a culture of top-down management, with an emphasis on telling people what to do rather than asking them and sharing leadership. Over a two-year period and without firing anyone, the following things happened:

1. There was a reduction of management levels in finished products and maintenance.
2. As a result of transfers and retirements, seven of the ten direct-reports are new.
3. High-performance, self-managing work teams are being used in several areas of the mill, and they operate the day shift without a foreman, reporting only to an area supervisor.
4. The mill is placing a high priority on training employees so they can operate effectively in a shared-leadership environment.

Oh, incidentally, Goins' developmental style and use of empowerment through shared leadership have been the catalyst behind the highest production level in the history of IP's Texarkana mill. Bob is now retired but his legacy is continuing to positively influence International Paper's culture.

click!
http://international
paper.com

Source: Conversations and correspondence with Bob Goins and other managers from his company.

Being familiar with various leadership styles will help to inspire self-confidence and increase productivity of a work group.

across: "If you give me reasonable production, I will keep higher management off your back." Let us first examine transformational leadership and then transactional leadership.

Transformational Leadership

Bass and others have taken Burns' general framework and applied the concepts to the field of management. Their research has resulted in identifying a number of past and current transformational leaders. A recent study found three factors that were an integral part of being a transformational leader—charismatic leadership, individualized consideration, and intellectual stimulation.

> **The most important factor of transformational leadership is *charismatic leadership.* To receive a high score on this factor, a leader would need to instill pride, respect, and esprit de corps and have a gift of focusing on what is really important, as well as a true sense of mission. The second factor, *individualized consideration,* indicates that the leader uses delegated assignments to provide learning and development and gives personal attention to individuals. The third factor, *intellectual stimulation,* indicates that the leader has vision and presents ideas that require rethinking of past methods of operation and allows for development of new ways of thinking.**

Some leaders who have scored exceptionally high on the charismatic leadership factor are Lee Iacocca, R. David Thomas (founder of Wendy's), George Patton, John F. Kennedy, Dr. Martin Luther King, Jr., Ronald Reagan, Sam Walton (founder of Wal-Mart), and Jack Welch (former chief executive officer of General Electric). While charisma is important for effective leadership, it may be exercised to meet objectives that do not benefit society—Adolf Hitler and Saddam Hussein are cases in point.[12]

Research today reveals that transformational leaders are not limited to only world-class leaders. For example, Kenny in the chapter preview demonstrates many of the characteristics of this type of leader.

http://www.wendys.com

Transactional Leadership

Of course, not everyone can be a transformational leader, and there are many leaders who fall into the category of transactional leaders. These leaders identify desired performance standards and recognize what types of rewards employees want from their work. They then take actions that make receiving these rewards contingent on achieving performance standards. In essence, this exemplifies an exchange process, a quid pro quo or "I'll do this if you'll do that." The transactional leader operates within the existing culture and employs traditional management strategies to get the job done. Transactional leadership is based on the premise that the leader can positively reward or reinforce employees for their completion of the bargain. For example, if a leader utilized a management-by-objectives system and was able to reward employees who met or exceeded their objectives, this approach would work quite well.

> **A number of effective leaders demonstrate both transformational and transactional leadership behaviors. One example is Franklin D. Roosevelt, who "illustrated a balance with respect to transformational and transactional leadership. . . . Roosevelt played the consummate transformational leader with his inspiring addresses, encouragement of intellectual solutions, and fireside chats. He also played the consummate transactional politician in the give-and-take of the balance of powers among executive, legislative, and judicial functions."[13]**

Comparison of Transactional and Transformational Leadership. One who believes that some people have the ability to grow and develop through levels of leadership and become transformational leaders is George McAleer, former air force pilot and now on the faculty of the National Defense University's Industrial College of the Armed Forces. McAleer agrees with Bass' thesis that transactional leadership can result in lower-order improvements, but if one wants higher-order improvements, transformational leadership is needed. This is the challenge that faces select military officers who are chosen to spend a year at a senior service college such as the Industrial College in Washington, D.C. This year is critical in one's military career: Out of this select group, approximately one in five will become a general or an admiral in the next 5 to 10 years.

In McAleer's words, "What made them successful up to this point in their career may not necessarily be the best avenue for them to proceed over the next several years. That's the formidable task my colleagues and I have at the Industrial College. Part of the challenge is encompassed in a course entitled 'Strategic Decision Making.'"[14] The challenge is to convince these officers that the leadership style that will serve them best in the future as strategic decision makers is transformational. One way to convince them is to contrast the two leadership styles as shown in Exhibit 8-7.

Servant Leadership

Although the concept of **servant leadership** has been around for centuries, only recently has it been seriously taught in management and leadership courses. In fact, few supervisory books even mention the concept. Today, however, it is once again recognized as a very powerful and useful concept and philosophy.

The Paradox of Servant Leadership

Bennett J. Sims, Bishop Emeritus of the Episcopal Diocese of Atlanta and president of the Institute for Servant Leadership, provides a beautiful description of the nature of this paradox:

---

(6) Discuss how to inspire self-confidence, develop people, and increase productivity.

---

servant leadership Define success as giving and measures achievement by devotion to serving and leading. Winning becomes the creation of community through collaboration and team building.

EXHIBIT 8-7

Contrasting Leadership
Approaches

Transactional	Transformational
Characteristics	
Exchange Process	Relations Orientation
Evolutionary Ideas	Revolutionary Ideas
Within Existing Structure	Emerges in Crisis
Reactive	Proactive
Motivation	
Contingent Reward (Extrinsic)	Inspiration; Recognition (Intrinsic)
Power	
Traditional	Charismatic
Focus	
Outcomes	Vision
Leader	
Specifies Talk	Consultant, Coach, Teacher
Clarifies Roles	Emphasis on Empowering the Individual
Recognizes Needs	Gives Autonomy; Good Listener; Informal
Manages by Exception	Accessible; Model of Integrity
Employees	
Seek Security; Needs Fulfilled	Transcend Self-Interests for the Organization
Separate Organization from Individual	Do More than They Are Expected to Do
Outcomes	
Expected Performance	Quantum Leaps in Performance

Source: George McAleer's presentation at APT Type and Leadership Symposium, Crystal City, VA, March 5–7, 1993.

> **The idea of paradox in the abstract is murky, but in a *person* it can shine like moonlight on tranquil water. Paradox will always need incarnation—embodiment—in order to be real. Logic falls short as a persuader.**
>
> **Consider the paradox of servant leadership. A servant is one who stands below and behind, while a leader's position is above and ahead. Logically then, it is impossible to make these two positions fit a single point in space or in the make-up of one person. But paradox, like servant leadership, is not bound by logic. When paradox is understood as a formula for great truth, then the opposite of a great truth becomes another great truth. Servant and leader combine to form an ideal blend of personal attributes in *toughness* and *tenderness*.[15]**

When one of the authors first read this passage by Sims, he immediately thought of an officer he served under in the army. Captain Paul J. Padgent had won a battlefield commission in Korea and was the most highly decorated officer or enlisted man in the 82nd Airborne Division. He wore a pearl-handle revolver and was tough and had exceptionally high expectations and standards for members of the infantry rifle company he commanded. His troops believed they were the best and would follow him anywhere. An example from a 3-month, peacetime, simulated battle in southern Louisiana swamps and forests gives us a clue to his troops' devotion and loyalty. Most of the company commanders had small tents where officers were served individually on plates. Their troops went through a long mess line being

EXHIBIT 8-8

A Distant Drum

Joining the United States Marine Corps at age seventeen was the single most important choice I have made for my life. I graduated from boot camp, then from technical school with honors. I was meritoriously promoted and given my choice of duty stations. This was the first real accomplishment I had achieved on my own, and I knew that I didn't even really put forth much effort. It was then that I realized there was a whole world of opportunity available for me, and I was determined to go after a better way of life. I chose El Toro, California, as my duty station. I was proud to be a Marine, and I worked hard in my assigned unit.

I learned innumerable lessons throughout my military service, but the main ones were ingrained during boot camp (the dreaded "Parris Island"), and I live by them still:

1. Tell the truth.
2. Do your best, no matter how trivial the task.
3. Choose the difficult right over the easy wrong.
4. Look out for the group before you look out for yourself.
5. Don't whine or make excuses.
6. Judge others by their actions, not their race, culture, religion, or sexual orientation.

I cannot think of even one important situation in life which cannot be made better by applying these six creeds. I have tried to instill these lessons into my own child, and I am proud to say I believe he lives by them as well.

The exceptional men and women I met and worked with during my military service are still an inspiration to me. I feel a special kinship with each and every marine I meet.

Source: Cherl Templet, My Leadership Autobiography, March 1, 1999. A requirement in an MBA Leadership course taught by Donald C. Mosley, Spring Semester 1999, University of South Alabama, Mobile, Alabama.

served on their mess kits. But in our company the officers were at the end of the line and followed the troops, and if any item was short, the officers missed it, not the troops. Incidentally, at the end of this 3-month field exercise, Captain Padgent's company was singled out as the top-performing company by the umpires.[16]

The United States Marine Corps has a history of training its troops, officers, and non-commissioned officers by placing the well-being of the group before the individual. This notion is an important part of servant leadership and is expounded on in an excerpt from a leadership autobiography by a former student. The excerpt is reprinted in Exhibit 8-8.

Characteristics of Servant Leadership

The person to whom we owe the greatest debt for providing us with insights into servant leadership is Robert K. Greenleaf, retired executive with AT&T. Prior to his retirement, he served seven years as director of management research and led an internal consulting group concerned with the values and growth of people. After his retirement, he worked as a consultant for businesses, foundations, professional societies, church organizations, and universities.[17] Greenleaf makes the important point that the servant leader wants to serve first and then lead. The servant leader focuses on meeting the needs of others and responding to problems first by listening. Greenleaf believes that leaders who empathize with others provide a climate in which followers have the ability to grow and develop. In the chapter preview, this was one of Kenny's great strengths as a leader. Greenleaf also makes the point that leaders "who empathize and who fully accept those who go with them on this basis are more likely to be trusted."[18] Again referring back to the chapter preview, the big challenge facing Kenny in his new assignment is gaining the trust and improving the performance of the "Hell's Angels" crew.

Larry Spears is a scholar who has studied Greenleaf's original writings for a number of years. He is also chief executive officer (CEO) of the Greenleaf Center for Servant Leadership. He has identified ten characteristics of servant leadership, which are shown in Exhibit 8-9.

EXHIBIT **8-9**

Ten Characteristics of
Servant Leadership

1. **Listening.** Leaders have traditionally been valued for their communication and decision-making skills. Servant-leaders reinforce these important skills with a focus on listening intently and reflectively to others in order to identify and clarify the will of a group of people.

2. **Empathy.** Servant-leaders strive to understand and empathize with others. They accept and recognize others for their unique gifts and spirits. One assumes the good intentions of coworkers and does not reject them as people.

3. **Healing.** Learning how to help heal difficult situations is a powerful force for transforming organizations. Servant-leaders recognize that they have an opportunity to help make whole those people and institutions with whom they come in contact.

4. **Persuasion.** Another characteristic of servant-leaders is a reliance on persuasion, rather than using one's positional authority, to make organizational decisions. Servant-leaders seek to convince others, rather than coerce compliance. They are effective at building consensus with groups.

5. **Awareness.** General awareness, and especially self-awareness, strengthen the servant-leader. Awareness aids one in understanding issues involving ethics and values, and it enables one to approach situations from a more integrated, holistic position.

6. **Foresight.** The ability to foresee the likely outcome of a given situation is a characteristic that enables the servant-leader to understand the lessons from the past, the realities of the present, and likely consequences of a decision for the future. It is deeply rooted within the intuitive mind.

7. **Conceptualization.** Servant-leaders seek to nurture their abilities to dream great dreams. This means that one must be able to think beyond day-to-day management realities.

8. **Commitment to the growth of people.** Servant-leaders believe that people have an intrinsic value beyond their tangible contributions as workers. As such, servant-leaders are deeply committed to the personal, professional, and spiritual growth of everyone within an organization.

9. **Stewardship.** Greenleaf's view of organizations is one in which CEOs, staff members, and trustees all play significant roles in holding their institutions in trust for the greater good of society. In effect, everyone has a responsibility for being a good steward within an organization.

10. **Building community.** Servant-leaders seek to build a sense of community among those within an organization.

Source: Larry C. Spears, "Creating Caring Leadership for the 21st Century," *The Not-For-Profit CEO Monthly Letter* 5, No. 9, July 1998 (The Robert K. Greenleaf Center for Servant Leadership, 921 East 86th Street, Suite 2000, Indianapolis, IN). Reprinted with permission.

✔ **STOP AND THINK**

Do you think training in servant leadership would be useful for business organizations? Why or why not?

http://www.greenleaf.com

Core Leadership Functions

The best of the contemporary leadership studies and books support the value of working toward developmental, transformational, and servant leadership. Also, as we saw in the chapter preview with Kenny, leadership of this nature is not restricted to the highest levels of management, but can occur at any level. Seven leadership functions reinforcing the transformational approach are valuing, visioning, coaching, empowering, team building, promoting quality, and listening with empathy. The effective leader is value driven and is

© Matthew Borkoski/Index Stock Imagery

able to implement these functions. Brief descriptions of the core leadership functions are as follows:

Valuing. Having a good grasp of the organization's values and being able to translate these values into practice and elevate them to higher levels.

Visioning. Having a clear mental picture of a desired future for the organization or organizational unit.

Coaching. Helping others develop the knowledge and skills needed for achieving the vision.

Empowering. Enabling others to move toward the vision.

Team building. Developing a coalition of people who will commit themselves to achieving the vision.

Promoting quality. Achieving a reputation for always meeting or exceeding customer expectations.

Listening with empathy. Clarifying where others are coming from and acceptance of others even with imperfections. Anyone can lead perfect people if perfect people are to be found.[19]

Throughout, we emphasize the importance of values, visioning, empowering, promoting quality, listening with empathy, coaching, and team building. Note the commonality between the core functions and the characteristics of servant leadership and effective leadership.

One who effectively demonstrates the core leadership functions is Maureen McNamara, hospital administrator extraordinaire. Being a hospital administrator is a difficult job today. The industry, in the eyes of one experienced observer, is 10 years behind other industries in employing enlightened leadership and management practices.[20]

At age 16 and in her first job as a candy-counter girl in a movie theater, Maureen demonstrated her ability to link commitment with action. One of the world's leading experts on leadership, Joan Goldsmith, states, "By committed action, we mean that people are willing to take a stand, put their integrity on the line, and sacrifice time, energy, and resources to

click!

http://www.academy. umd.edu

achieve a goal."[21] Maureen demonstrated this quality. When the candy counter in the theater was not being run efficiently, she stepped in and took over the management of the entire operation and within 6 months had improved efficiency. She continued to use her skills for committed action and for linking intentions and goals throughout her career. The following life events—educational achievement and career changes—summarize some of these pursuits.

Maureen attended the Katherine Gibbs secretarial school. The skills she mastered there proved invaluable in her early career, her first job being administrative assistant with the American Mathematical Society. While there, she developed and improved processes and systems for the society. Maureen went on to earn a B.S. degree in business from the University of Rhode Island and an MBA degree from Bryant College.

Maureen took a position at Brown University and worked her way through a number of positions in the medical school and at the affiliated hospital. She progressed from management assistant in the department of microbiology and molecular basic science to the dean's office in charge of faculty affairs to assistant administrator for the Department of Medicine. She was then promoted to associate vice president of operations for the hospital, then to senior vice president of operations, and finally to chief operating officer of the Medical College and hospital. The hospital at that time had 1,500 employees and a budget of $125 million.

Through these positions Maureen gained insights regarding organization politics and organization inertia and noticed that organizations did not leverage their resources. Each move around the medical school and hospital system gave her increased responsibility, and no matter where she was, she felt she could improve the system and bring people on board.

Her greatest opportunity and challenge came when she was made chief operating officer. She states that she was fortunate to have a chief executive officer who was involved in community and statewide affairs and who allowed her to run the operation. Throughout her career she confronted issues and problems and took the responsibility for initiating action to solve them.

When going into positions of greater responsibility, it is very important for a leader to know his or her own strengths and to be aware of areas needing help and improvement. Maureen believed her strengths and the reasons for her success were:

- her ability to see the big picture;

- her ability to see connections;

- her ability to create a vision and mobilize resources to achieve it;

- her ability to inspire others to achieve and grow to an extent they never thought possible;

- her integrity, as well as her direct, candid, straightforward manner;

- her commitment to always challenge individuals and the organization.

The areas where she perceived she needed help and needed to improve were:

- asking for help (early in her career she was reluctant to bring others in when she needed help; later this weakness was turned into a strength when she brought in an outside facilitator in organization development [to be discussed later]);

- listening empathetically;

- being overly impatient when things did not move or change as fast as she would like.

Her goal and vision were to develop a team approach in delivering health care. In the process of doing so she wanted to shift the management system to a participative culture and eliminate the undesirable aspects of bureaucracy.

Shortly after being made chief operating officer, Maureen faced a major challenge. The union was trying to organize the maintenance and engineering department employees. Maureen had no anti-union feelings; rather, she felt that most unions came into existence to protect employees against poor and arbitrary management practices. She wanted a chance to talk with the 35 employees who made up the department. Prior to meeting with them, she studied the files and backgrounds of each employee. At the meeting she played primarily an active and empathetic listening role. Based on the relationships she built and the approach she took, the union was unsuccessful in two organizing attempts.

Over time, Maureen developed a close relationship with the employees and used their input and participation in an organization development (OD) change program she initiated early in her 10-year stay in senior management.

In developing a strategy for the OD change program, she worked closely with Cynthia Bielecki, an excellent and very bright internal staff person in human resources. They decided to bring in an outside consultant to assist them in formulating a shared-leadership approach to improving and managing the organization. They brought in Keith Krewson, who had worked in organization development all of his life and was then in his early 70s. He assisted them throughout the change effort and became a trusted mentor for Maureen.

The following are a few of the innovative steps initiated in the change effort.

1. They wanted to do the organization change from within by giving employees ownership of the change process.

2. They communicated very early their expectations and goals through oral and written communication and continued to communicate throughout the process.

3. They invited people to apply for two teams—the clinical redesign team and the administrative redesign team.

4. They had a big party to launch the program and made clear the ground rules and the need to bring in the various stakeholders.

5. The teams went on a retreat into the mountains for team building and action planning.

6. Maureen made herself available to answer questions and had weekly sessions to communicate what was happening.

The outcome was a revitalized organization that became more efficient and effective in delivering patient health care.

While getting her education and advancing in her business career, Maureen married and had three children (a career all its own) who are now grown and successful. She has also had a happy marriage for 37 years.

Earlier we presented what leadership expert Joan Goldsmith said about leaders linking commitment with action. She elaborates, "Committed action is sustained over time . . . and [is] focused on achievement. To encourage committed action, linking leaders radically expand participation and the range of options for organizational direction."[22]

Goldsmith's words summarize the success of Maureen McNamara as a leader and team builder. Today, she has her own firm named Bridgework, whose slogan is "Connecting businesses and their leaders to a better future."[23]

✔ STOP AND THINK

Since most of Maureen's experience has been in hospital administration, do you think she would be a successful consultant in another industry such as a large hotel or bank? Why or why not?

....

Emotional Intelligence

The foundation of successful leaders is a concept called emotional intelligence. As Daniel Goleman, a leading researcher, states, "I.Q. and technical skills are important, but emotional intelligence is the sine qua non of leadership." Goleman and other researchers have found that emotional intelligence not only pinpoints outstanding leaders, but also can be linked to strong performance. In fact, numerous studies demonstrated that emotional intelligence proved to be twice as important as technical skills and I.Q. as an ingredient of excellent performance in a leadership role.[24]

Emotional intelligence refers to an assortment of skills and characteristics that influence a person's ability to succeed as a leader. Exhibit 8-10 provides definitions and hallmarks of the five components of emotional intelligence at work.

Amy Joe Rathje was working in Chicago for "the worst manager she ever worked for," and she was miserable. Her boss never used positive reinforcement, only negative motivation. After being subjected to a lecture stressing that Amy Joe and her husband were "dumb to allow this [her pregnancy] to happen," Amy Joe resigned and went to work for the Lexus Company. She was transferred to Atlanta where she worked for Jay Emery, the "best manager she has worked for."

> **7** Explain why emotional intelligence is so important for effective leadership.

> **emotional intelligence**
> An assortment of skills and characteristics that influence a person's ability to succeed as a leader.

EXHIBIT **8-10**

The Five Components of Emotional Intelligence at Work

	Definition	Hallmarks
Self-Awareness	The ability to recognize and understand your moods, emotions, and drives, as well as their effect on others	Self-confidence Realistic self-assessment Self-deprecating sense of humor
Self-Regulation	The ability to control or redirect disruptive impulses and moods The propensity to suspend judgment— to think before acting	Trustworthiness and integrity Comfort with ambiguity Openness to change
Motivation	A passion to work for reasons that go beyond money or status A propensity to pursue goals with energy and persistence	Strong drive to achieve Optimism, even in the face of failure Organizational commitment
Empathy	The ability to understand the emotional makeup of other people Skill in treating people according to their emotional reactions	Expertise in building and retaining talent Cross-cultural sensitivity Service to clients and customers
Social Skill	Proficiency in managing relationships and building networks An ability to find common ground and build rapport	Effectiveness in leading change Persuasiveness Expertise in building and leading teams

Source: Daniel Goleman, "What Makes a Leader?" *Harvard Business Review,* November–December 1998, p. 95. Copyright © 1998 by the Harvard Business School Publishing Corp. All rights reserved. Reprinted by permission.

At that time, Jay was customer satisfaction manager for the southern region; presently, he does dealer development for Lexus. Amy Joe states that she learned more from him than she did from her college education.

> "He not only took an interest in us as individuals, but he also looked out for the entire team. For example, when I first went to work for him, I was still in my pregnancy. The first thing he did when we met was congratulate me and say how happy he was we would be adding to our family. Some days during this period he would say 'you look tired; why don't you go home early today?' I rarely did, but I sure was motivated to give my best effort for this man and Lexus.
>
> "Jay always stood behind us and empowered us to make our own decisions. He never told us we were wrong but kept asking us questions to help us [see a problem at different angles]. Most impressive, he did not focus on himself, but looked out for the well-being of the team. He believed his success was based on how well the team performed."

Both Jay Emery and Amy Joe score quite high on the components of emotional intelligence and servant leadership. Amy Joe states that she enjoys her work with Lexus: "The company lets you do the right things for the right reasons. They uphold my ethical and moral values and are truly customer oriented."[25]

Interviews with Mel Johnson, service manager at the Mobile, Alabama, Lexus dealership, resulted in both Jay and Amy Joe receiving A evaluations on the components of emotional intelligence. Mel states that Amy Joe leads by example and carries out the Lexus philosophy when working with customers and dealers. An interview with Jeff Matherne, finance and sales manager, resulted in Amy Joe's receiving As on three components and A+ on two. Jeff stated that she has a genuine concern for the customer, having more concern for a customer's problem than the expense for Lexus in solving it. Moreover, "She provides service and attention to our dealership over and beyond the call of duty and her job description."[26]

✔ **STOP AND THINK**

For which of the two components of emotional intelligence do you think Jeff Matherne gave Amy Joe the A+? (Answer is in endnote 22).

··

Emotional intelligence is having a large impact in assessing and evaluating leadership and leaders by researchers and historians. A good example is Doris Kearns Goodwin's work about Abraham Lincoln's presidency. She states that when he arrived in Washington, he did not have much political experience, but Lincoln had emotional strengths that made him a natural.

"As it turned out, unbeknownst to the country at the time, Lincoln was a towering political genius—not because he had mastered the traditional rules of the game, but because he possessed a remarkable array of emotional strengths that are rarely found in political life. He had what we would call today a first-class emotional intelligence."

"To appreciate the magnitude of Lincoln's political success, it helps to understand just how slight a figure he appeared to be when he arrived in Washington. 'Never did a President enter upon office with less means at his command.' Harvard professor James Russell Lowell wrote in 1863. 'All that was known of him was that he was a good stump-speaker, nominated for his availability—that is because he had no history.' His entire national political experience consisted of a single term in Congress that had come to an end nearly a dozen years earlier and two failed Senate races. He had absolutely no administrative experience and only one year of formal schooling. Newspapers described him as a 'third-rate Western lawyer and a fourth-rate lecturer, who cannot speak good grammar.'"

"In contrast, his three chief rivals for the Republican nomination were household names in Republican circles. William Henry Seward had been a celebrated Senator from New York for

Emotional intelligence was a major factor in Abraham Lincoln's political success.

more than a decade and Governor of his state for two terms before he went to Washington. Ohio's Salmon P. Chase, too, had been both Senator and Governor, and had played a central role in the formation of the Republican Party. Edward Bates was a widely respected elder statesman from Missouri, a former Congressman whose opinions on national matters were still widely sought. All three men, knowing they were better educated, more experienced and more qualified than Lincoln, were stunned when he received the Republican nomination and went on to win the election."[27]

Yet he placed all three defeated candidates in his cabinet. It was a dangerous risk but Lincoln made sure that he did not have only "yes" men in his cabinet, but some of the best minds in the country. In the introduction to her award winning book, *Team of Rivals: Political Genius of Abraham Lincoln*, Doris Kearns Goodwin states:

> "... This, then is a story of Lincoln's political genius revealed through his extraordinary array of personal qualities that enabled him to form friendships with men who had previously opposed him; to repair injured feelings that, left untended, might have escalated into permanent hostility; to assume responsibility for the failures of subordinates; to share credit with ease; and to learn from mistakes. He possessed an acute understanding of the sources of power inherent in the presidency, an unparalleled ability to keep his governing coalition intact, a tough-minded appreciation of the need to protect his presidential prerogatives, and a masterful sense of timing. His success in dealing with the strong egos of the men in his cabinet suggests that in the hands of a truly great politician the qualities we generally associate with decency and morality—kindness, sensitivity, compassion, honesty, and empathy—can also be impressive political resources."[28]

The Influence of Emotional Intelligence at Roadway Express— a Trucking Company

Current researchers and consultants are also publishing important work showing how to change the culture using emotional intelligence. Ellen Van Oosten of Case Western Reserve and

Lincoln was able to work with people who opposed him. His cabinet included all three of the men he defeated for the Republican nomination.

© Bettman/CORBIS

Richard Boyatzis, an early collaborator with Daniel Goleman, give us the story of Roadway Express:

Frank Sims was standing on Roadway Express's shipping dock, watching one of the company's trucks drive away with goods for Specialty Glassware (a pseudonym), one of Roadway's large customers. Frank was worried. The damage problems had been mounting and he was worried about how this might be affecting Roadway's customers. As he walked to his office, Frank began to recall a workshop on emotional intelligence (EI) he had attended recently. Simply recalling the workshop immediately put Frank in a better state of mind: Instead of worrying about the damage and an angry customer, he started to ask himself how he could use what he learned in the workshop to do something constructive and important. As he watched another truck being loaded, an idea began to take shape. What, he wondered, if Roadway's dockworkers and drivers understood how important loading the trucks was for their company? Immediately, he started thinking about how he could engage people in solving the customer's problems.

The dock crew was surprised that the customer's top management would put so much effort into helping them understand the glassware business. He felt good knowing how their efforts fit into the big picture, how important the glassware products were, and how well Specialty Glassware served its own customers' needs. It made them want to be more careful and find ways to help Specialty Glassware succeed. Later on, workers would describe these meetings to new hires as an example of why Roadway was a great place to work.

Leaders like Frank Sims are among the many who can raise the human spirit and make their organizations better. They do so by using their emotional intelligence to create an atmosphere in which people want to do and be their best. . . . we describe how emotionally intelligent leaders ignite organizations and people to perform better. The article also provides the not insignificant hope that, though EI-based leadership may be rare, it can be developed.[29]

Roadway is a trucking company with more than 20,000 employees and 379 terminals in the United States and Canada. It had a traditional structure that was hierarchical and primarily command and control in the competitive trucking industry. Inspired by Frank Sims' experience higher management began to look for ways to improve its financial performance.

They developed a partnership with Case Western Reserve University and designed a tailored program with the following objectives:

- Increasing leaders' self-awareness and emotional intelligence;

- Positioning leaders to develop leaders at every level;

- Developing the capabilities of the leadership team to achieve breakthrough performance; and

- Broadening the participants' understanding of issues that are crucial for long-term economic performance.

A 9-day program, designed and delivered over 6 months to key company leaders, including the president, focused on emotional intelligence, strategy, system thinking, marketing, finance, and appreciative inquiry process for leading change.

Over the next 3 years they produced the following results:

- Saved Roadway $6 million

- Decreased the number of injuries by 43 percent annually; and

- Decreased the number of accidents by 41 percent annually.[30]

The leadership program focuses on helping supervisors identify areas for behavioral change and gives them opportunities to apply new habits on the job. They are also provided coaches to assist them in mastering five discoveries as shown in Exhibit 8-11.

EXHIBIT 8-11

Boyatzis' Theory of Self-Directed Learning (Goleman, Boyatzis, and McKee, 2002)

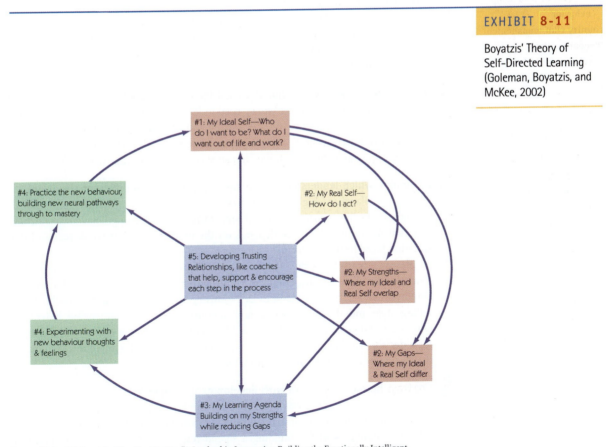

Source: Richard E. Boyatzis, Ellen Van Oosten, "A Leadership Imperative: Building the Emotionally Intelligent Organization", Ivey Business Journal, January/February 2003, Volume 67, Number 3, p. 3.

The culture has changed dramatically, right down to the drivers and mechanics. An example cited in the article noted how a mechanic and driver teamed up to save Roadway $130,000 on one route. Applied to 379 terminals and many routes, it does not take long to see the impact of this one change.

In conclusion, Roadway feels like a new company in an old business. Its people are excited about being leaders, and have expanded the ways in which they can make a personal impact. Inspiration and energy have become contagious. A new culture has emerged, one in which people are motivated and innovative. The new Roadway is surpassing many of its competitors in revenue and net profit growth through savvy acquisitions and cost savings during a period that has not been kind to the industry. Roadway's experience is a powerful example of how emotional intelligence can ignite excitement and inspire better performances from everyone in your organization.[31]

CHAPTER REVIEW

IMPORTANT TERMS

authority compliance
coaching and selling style
continuum of leadership
    behavior
country club management
delegating style
developmental leadership
emotional intelligence
heroic managers
impoverished management
leadership
Leadership Grid®
life-cycle theory of
    leadership
middle of the road
    management
participating and supporting
    style
readiness level
relationship behaviors
servant leadership
Situational Leadership®
    Model
structuring and telling style
task behaviors
team management
Theory X
Theory Y
transactional leadership
transformational leadership

1 **Describe factors that affect the leadership style used.**

Leading is a process of influencing individual and group activities toward goal setting and goal achievement. How well this process is carried out has a major impact on both performance and morale.

Three interrelated variables have an impact on the choice of leadership style. These are (1) the supervisor's management philosophy, (2) the followers' readiness level, and (3) the situation faced by the supervisor. The followers' readiness level must be evaluated only with regard to carrying out a specific task or assignment.

2 **Discuss and explain two frequently used leadership models.**

Two leadership models that are widely used in leadership training programs are Blake and associates' Leadership Grid® and Hersey and Blanchard's Situational Leadership Model. The Leadership Grid® plots five basic leadership styles. The one Blake and associates recommend as the ideal leadership style is the team management style.

3 **Determine which leadership style is most appropriate in different situations.**

Hersey and Blanchard highlight four basic leadership styles: structuring and telling, coaching and selling, participating and supporting, and delegating. They make a strong case that the ideal style to use depends on the maturity level of employees and the situation faced by the supervisor.

Research tends to support the Hersey and Blanchard position that there is no one best style for all situations. However, with the increasing readiness and education of employees today, there is a trend in U.S. industry toward using both the coaching and selling style and the participating and supporting style in influencing individual employees and groups. Tannenbaum and Schmidt maintain that each situation calling for a decision may require choosing a solution that balances the three forces found in the leader, the employees, and the situation.

4 **Contrast heroic supervisors with developmental supervisors.**

Heroic supervision often leads to overcontrol and lack of group development.

By contrast, developmental supervision involves the group by using the three interrelated components of (1) building a shared-responsibility team, (2) continuously developing individual skills, and (3) determining a department vision in the form of an overarching goal.

5 **Contrast transformational leadership with transactional leadership.**

While research supports the thesis that no one leadership style is best for all situations, transformational and transactional leadership styles have emerged as two influential theories. Three important factors of transformational leadership are charismatic leadership (instilling pride, respect, and esprit de corps), individualized consideration (delegating assignments and giving personal attention), and intellectual stimulation (requiring rethinking of past methods and developing new solutions).

Transactional leadership is a more traditional approach. The transactional leader operates within the existing culture, positively rewarding and reinforcing employees for jobs well done.

6 **Discuss how to inspire self-confidence, develop people, and increase productivity.**

No one single leadership style or model provides a magic formula for inspiring self-confidence, developing people, and increasing productivity. However, by being familiar with all styles, using good common sense, and developing a contingency/situational leadership approach, one can become an effective leader who does realize the preceding objectives. Servant leadership is particularly valuable in inspiring self-confidence, tapping higher-level needs, and developing people.

7 **Explain why emotional intelligence is so important for effective leadership.**

Research has shown that emotional intelligence is a foundation for successful performance as a leader. There is clearly an assortment of skills and characteristics that influence a person's ability to succeed over the long term. These characteristics and skills were shown in Exhibit 8-10 and were demonstrated in the leaders profiled in this chapter. They were sorely lacking in the executives shown to be crooks.

QUESTIONS FOR REVIEW AND DISCUSSION

1. What is meant by leadership?

2. Briefly discuss the major factors that may influence the choice of an individual's leadership style. Correlate these factors with different leadership styles.

3. Discuss how a supervisor would determine the readiness level of an employee.

4. What leadership actions fall under the category of task behaviors, and what actions fall under the category of relationship behaviors?

5. Do you agree or disagree with Blake and associates that there is one best leadership style? Support your position.

6. In his early fifties, Bob Goins modified his leadership style from heroic to developmental. If you were trying to motivate managers to change as Goins did, how would you go about it? Do you think the majority of supervisors have the ability to modify their style? Why or why not?

7. Can you identify any transformational leaders from your own experience or reading? Please list the reasons why you placed them in the category of transformational leader. If you cannot identify someone, do you agree with the leaders identified in this chapter— John F. Kennedy, Martin Luther King, Jr., and George Patton? Why or why not?

8. What traits or characteristics appeal to you the most regarding servant leadership?

9. Of the various leadership approaches discussed in the chapter, which one would you most prefer your boss to use in working with you and your group? Explain your reasons.

10. How does transactional leadership differ from the telling and structuring style of Hersey and Blanchard?

11. What are the components of emotional intelligence, and why is emotional intelligence important for effective leadership?

12. Can emotional intelligence be taught to aspiring leaders and integrated into their philosophy and approach? Why or why not?

Skill Builder 8-1

The Debate Question

group activity

In general, are women or men more transformational in leadership approach? Judy Rosener, in her article "Ways Women Lead," makes a case that, in general, women tend to be more transformational in leadership approach than men, who tend to be more transactional in approach. The comparison of the transactional and transformational leadership approaches found in Exhibit 8-7 should be referred to in completing the following instructions.

Instructions:

1. Have your class ask for five volunteers to form a team to debate on the side that, in general, women are more transformational in approach than men. Conversely, ask for five volunteers to take the opposite side. Allow a week for the two teams to prepare their respective cases. Two suggested starting reference sources are as follows: Judy Rosener, "Ways Women Lead," *Harvard Business Review,* Jan.–Feb. 1990, pp. 119–125; and "Ways Men and Women Lead," *Harvard Business Review,* Jan.–Feb. 1991, p. 150.

2. After the week, the teams should present their cases in the form of a debate. A suggested format for the debate is to allow the affirmative team 15 minutes to present their case, followed by the opposing team, which also gets 15 minutes. Then, allow the affirmative team up to 5 minutes for rebuttal and the opposing team up to 5 minutes for rebuttal.

3. Who do you believe won the debate? Explain your reasoning.

Skill Builder 8-2

Diagnosing and Selecting the Appropriate Leadership Style

In each of the following situations, choose the appropriate leadership style.
Afterward, your instructor will give you the best and worst answer for each situation.

1. The interdepartmental task force that you manage has been working hard to complete its division-wide report. One of your task force members has been late for the last five meetings. He has offered no excuses or apologies. Furthermore, he is way behind in completing the cost figures for his department. It is imperative that he present these figures to the task force within the next three days.

   a. Tell him exactly what you expect, and closely supervise his work on this report.

   b. Discuss with him why he has been late, and support his efforts to complete the task.

   c. Emphasize when the cost figures are due, and support his efforts.

   d. Assume he will be prepared to present the cost figures to the task force.

2. In the past, you have had a great deal of trouble with one of the people you supervise. She has been lackadaisical, and only your constant prodding has brought about task completion. However, you have recently noticed a change. Her performance has improved,

and you have had to remind her of meeting deadlines less and less. She has even initiated several suggestions for improving her performance.

   a.   Continue to direct and closely supervise her efforts.

   b.   Continue to supervise her work, but listen to her suggestions and implement those that seem reasonable.

   c.   Implement her suggestions and support her ideas.

   d.   Let her take responsibility for her own work.

3.   Because of budget restrictions imposed on your department, it is necessary to consolidate. You have asked a highly experienced member of your department to take charge of the consolidation. This person has worked in all areas of your department. In the past, she has usually been eager to help. Although you believe that she has the ability to perform this assignment, she seems indifferent to the importance of the task.

   a.   Take charge of the consolidation yourself, but make sure you hear her suggestions.

   b.   Assign the project to her, and let her determine how to accomplish it.

   c.   Discuss the situation with her. Encourage her to accept the assignment in view of her skills and experience.

   d.   Take charge of the consolidation and indicate to her precisely what to do. Supervise her work closely.

4.   Your staff members have asked you to consider a change in the work schedule. In the past, you have encouraged and supported their suggestions. In this case, your staff members are well aware of the need for change and are ready to suggest and try an alternative schedule. Members are very competent and work well together as a group.

   a.   Allow staff involvement in developing the new schedule, and support the suggestions of group members.

   b.   Design and implement the new schedule yourself, but incorporate staff recommendations.

   c.   Allow the staff to formulate and implement the new schedule on their own.

   d.   Design the new schedule yourself, and closely direct its implementation.

Source: W. Alan Randolph, *Understanding and Managing Organizational Behavior* (Homewood, Ill.: Richard D. Irwin, 1985), pp. 255–257. A complete 20-item Leader Behavior Analysis II questionnaire is available from the Ken Blanchard Companies at 1-800-728-6000.

Leadership Characteristics and Skill Assessment

Skill Builder 8-3

This survey is designed to provide feedback and self-assessment regarding your servant leadership characteristics and your emotional intelligence at work. Read each item listed and decide to what extent you exhibit each characteristic using the following five-point scale:

1—very weak   2—fair   3—average   4—very good   5—excellent

_____   1. At work I strive to build community within my group.

_____   2. I do a good job in understanding the personalities of other people, and I usually understand where they are coming from in discussions and problem solving.

_____   3. I accept the good intentions of others and recognize their unique gifts.

_____   4. In working with other people, I am trustworthy and have integrity.

_____ **5.** In general, I place the interests of my group and customers ahead of my own self-interest unless there is an ethical conflict.

_____ **6.** I am confident in the work I am doing and have a self-deprecating sense of humor.

_____ **7.** I try to listen intently and reflectively to determine where a person is coming from and/or the will of the group.

_____ **8.** I tend to pursue goals with optimism, energy, and persistence.

_____ **9.** I am committed to the growth and development of people.

_____ **10.** I have developed the skills and feel confident in building and leading teams.

_____ **11.** I rely on persuasion and discussion rather than coercion in team building.

_____ **12.** I am committed and dedicated to providing service to clients and customers.

Instructions: Add your individual scores and divide by 12 to obtain your average.

Scoring scale interpretation:

4.5–5.0	A	Excellent
4.0–4.4	B	Moderately high
3.5–3.9	C	Average
3.0–3.4	D	Below average
2.9	F	Very weak

It would be valuable to have members of your group evaluate you and to compare your self-evaluation with the evaluation from your group.

CASE

Kenny's Leadership: A Further Analysis

Case 8-1

In the chapter preview, we presented Kenny, an effective leader. Clues to his success may be found in the following comments made about him by his old crew, his new crew (the former "Hell's Angels" group), the plant's production manager, and Kenny's boss, the plant's maintenance manager.* It should be noted that both the production manager and the maintenance manager are relatively new to their positions and are not part of the former "autocratic management system." As you read these comments, review what you have learned in the preceding chapters and summarize the principles, points, and concepts from the text that Kenny puts into practice as a leader.

Maintenance Manager, Kenny's Boss:

- He's very knowledgeable in the maintenance area.

- He has considerable self-confidence.

- He interacts with people in the plant more than other supervisors do and works well with people from other departments.

- He has the ability to motivate his crew and gets along well with them.

- He functions well as a leader in one-on-one situations and in conducting crew meetings. For example, in both cases he lets people know how they stand and provides them with feedback, and together they discuss ways of improving performance.

- He's better organized than most supervisors, and there's less confusion in his department than elsewhere in the company.

Production Manager:

- He doesn't give the production people any hassle. He doesn't ask a lot of questions about why production wants it done. Instead, he tells the production people what needs to be done—and why.

- He's a team player—and he wants to get the job done.

*Except for minor editing, the comments are presented as they were made to Donald Mosley.

- He's good with people—a great leader—and his crew work well together.
- He's conscientious—he does his job, does it right, and wants others to do the same.
- He goes out into the plant with his people, and he's there with them when they need help and advice.
- His crew doesn't give planners and coordinators a lot of static about what they put into a memo.

Kenny's Old Crew:

- He's fair.
- He has a good attitude and a positive outlook.
- He's concerned about and looks out for the welfare of his people.
- He keeps crew problems within the crew and doesn't run to upper management with every little detail.
- He has a broad-based knowledge of our work; people feel confident about his decisions.
- He's a good intermediary between upper management and the crew.
- He gets points across without getting the crew upset.
- When things are tight, he doesn't mind helping his men with the actual work.
- He has a level personality—he doesn't show much emotion.
- He's very supportive of his crew.

Kenny's New Crew (the Former "Hell's Angels"):

- He treats us fairly and equally.
- He takes up for the crew and his men.
- He doesn't threaten you and doesn't come back after a bad job and nit-pick and tell you what you did wrong. He takes a positive approach to solving problems.
- He can be trusted.
- He helps you with your personal problems.
- He's competent at what he does and relates the competency to us.
- He places his employees really well. We're not all like oranges—some are like apples—but he places us where we can do our best.
- He lets us work at our own pace— actually makes us want to work harder.
- He never appears to get angry; he's always the same—cool, calm, and collected.
- He's helpful on the job. He's there, but he's not there—doesn't hang over you, telling you what to do and how to do it. Instead, he wants results but lets us get them our own way.
- He seems to enjoy work and being around us.
- He listens to anything we have to say.

Answer the following questions:

1. How do you explain Kenny's acceptance by so many other people and the respect they have for him?

2. Can all supervisors operate the way Kenny does—and be effective? Explain your answer.

3. Given Kenny's effectiveness in his present job, would you recommend promoting him into high levels of management? Explain.

4. Review the characteristics of servant leadership in Exhibit 8-9 and transformational leadership in Exhibit 8-7. Which characteristics apply to Kenny?

9 Group Development and Team Building

Daniel Acker/Bloomberg News/London

The Ritz-Carlton hotel chain is one of the best business examples of effective change management and organizational development.

The essence of [collaboration] is working with people rather than over people or under people.
—MARY PARKER FOLLETT

There is nothing permanent except change.
—HERACLITUS

Preview

The Ritz-Carlton Hotel Corporation

This chapter preview could easily have been placed in a discussion of leadership, because it involves transformational leadership. The case is a classic "textbook" example of effective management and organizational development.

In 1850, Cesar Ritz was born in Neiderwald, Switzerland. "Blessed with virtues of ambition, courage and taste, Ritz strived for excellence in everything he did, and when he entered the hotel industry, his ideals were not to be compromised." After working as a waiter at Voisin, then the most fashionable restaurant in Paris, Ritz teamed with the renowned French chef Auguste Escoffier, with whom he had worked in several of Europe's famous hotels. While both were employed at the Carlton Hotel in London, Cesar Ritz went to Paris to find a place for a hotel of his own.

After selecting the perfect location for his hotel, Ritz contacted Marnier La Postolle, an old friend and the originator of the liqueur Grand Marnier, who gladly loaned him the money to open his hotel. June 1898 marked the opening of the Ritz of Paris of the Place Vendome, with, of course, Escoffier as *chef de cuisine*. The hotel, conceived by Cesar Ritz according to his own standards of perfection, initiated the European deluxe hotel industry.

Ritz's idea was to create not a "grand hotel" but a new and original one, a home that would equal the comforts, security, and service that discriminating patrons would provide for themselves—a nonhotel.

Cesar Ritz insisted on certain criteria that would be the foundation for the Paris Ritz and all future hotels bearing the Ritz name: a central location, preferably overlooking a public park or square; comfortable and attractive rooms; food and beverage services second to none; and a wine cellar that would appeal to the finest connoisseurs. Combining all of these elements, Ritz still considered the most crucial aspect of his "perfect" hotel to be service. In order to provide the finest service and quality, the number of employees was to exceed the number of guests.

Both Ritz and Escoffier had an interest in the Carlton Hotel in London. They combined their efforts and established the Ritz-Carlton Company to give rights to the Ritz-Carlton name internationally. Under the supervision of Cesar Ritz, hotels developed all over the world, including New York City, bearing the Ritz-Carlton name, but few were able to survive the rigid standards established by Cesar Ritz.

The preceding sentence highlights the problem. Despite the Ritz-Carlton tradition, a number of the properties bearing the name failed to maintain the consistency and standards of excellence of the original founders. This changed in 1983, when the current Ritz-Carlton Hotel Company acquired the rights to the name and bought the Ritz-Carlton in Boston. The hotel chain today owns outright only a few of the properties, but the company's 11,500 employees manage all 30 of the Ritz-Carlton properties located around the world. Under the transformational leadership of Horst A. Schulze, president and chief operating officer,

Learning Objectives

After reading and studying this chapter you should be able to:

1 Identify the stages of group development.

2 Compare the advantages and limitations of groups.

3 Describe the variables that determine a group's effectiveness.

4 Determine what is involved in team building.

5 Describe what made team building successful at Resort Quest.

6 Describe the GE approach.

7 Describe what made team building successful in the nonprofit area.

8 Describe how to work with self-managing work groups.

the company's 30 properties have met or exceeded the standards of excellence of the original founders. Evidence of this achievement is reflected in the following:

1. In 1992, the Ritz-Carlton was selected best hotel chain in the United States by the Zagat U.S. Travel Service.

2. In 1992, Horst Schulze was chosen Corporate Hotelier of the World by *Hotels Magazine.*

3. In 1992, Ritz-Carlton became the first hotel company to win a Malcolm Baldrige National Quality Award (established by Congress in 1987 to promote quality management).

4. In 1994, the company was rated by *Consumer Reports* as the number one luxury hotel chain in the world.

At present, most Ritz-Carlton hotels are located within the United States; however, 10 or 12 new developments will be located outside the United States.

After a consulting trip to Honolulu in June 1994, one of the authors took a week's vacation and stayed at the Ritz-Carlton Kapalua, on the island of Maui. We had never stayed in a Ritz-Carlton and were curious to see if it lived up to its reputation. Afterwards we rated our stay a 10 on a 10-point scale. Here are just a few reasons why:

- *A basket of fruit was in our room upon arrival.*

- *A minor problem was presented to a staff member who solved it without fanfare. Later we found out that any staff member to whom a guest presents a problem is empowered to solve that problem.*

- *On two occasions when we asked for directions regarding a location on the hotel's 32 acres, we were not simply given directions; we were escorted there.*

- *The food was consistently excellent in all three of the hotel's restaurants.*

Horst Schulze is given the credit for catalyzing the chain's reputation for quality and service. In regard to the awards received, Schulze has stated, "We are not resting on the momentary glory or satisfaction of these awards. We have embarked, and have worked diligently the last 3 years, on total quality management (TQM). We know that through TQM we will continuously improve our product and services. It is our intention to not only serve you with genuine care and comfort, but to fulfill all your needs in our hotels and give you complete service excellence all of the time.

"Today every employee, from housekeeper to server to manager, is committed to the ultimate dream and vision through TQM: 100 percent guest satisfaction." Although the hotel's corporate managers have used consultants such as Joseph M. Juran and Stephen Covey in their search for excellence, they have created their own version of total quality management. According to Sue Musselman, assistant to the vice-president of quality, it was pursuit of the Malcolm Baldrige Award that gave the organization the quantum leap in improving processes and services.

Just a few of the tailored features of the Ritz-Carlton's focus on quality, service, and guest satisfaction are as follows:

1. President Schulze participates in employee orientation programs at each new hotel.

2. In the 2-day orientation program for new employees, Rebecca Powell, the training manager, emphasizes that "you serve but you are not servants"; rather, "you are ladies and gentlemen serving ladies and gentlemen."

3. In addition to the orientation program, 100 more hours of training are provided to employees.

4. When processes are improved or reengineered in one hotel, the information and concepts are shared with all hotels.

5. Every worker is empowered to spend up to $2,000 to fix any problem a guest encounters.

EXHIBIT 9-1

The Ritz-Carlton Credo

The Ritz-Carlton Basics

THREE STEPS OF SERVICE

1

A warm and sincere greeting.
Use the guest name, if and when possible.

2

Anticipation and compliance with guest needs.

3

Fond farewell. Give them a warm good-bye and use their names, if and when possible.

"We Are Ladies and Gentlemen Serving Ladies and Gentlemen"

THE EMPLOYEE PROMISE

At The Ritz-Carlton, our Ladies and Gentlemen are the most important resource in our service commitment to our guests.

By applying the principles of trust, honesty, respect, integrity and commitment, we nurture and maximize talent to the benefit of each individual and the company.

The Ritz-Carlton fosters a work environment where diversity is valued, quality of life is enhanced, individual aspirations are fulfilled, and The Ritz-Carlton mystique is strengthened.

THE RITZ-CARLTON
CREDO

The Ritz-Carlton Hotel is a place where the genuine care and comfort of our guests is our highest mission.

We pledge to provide the finest personal service and facilities for our guests who will always enjoy a warm, relaxed yet refined ambience.

The Ritz-Carlton experience enlivens the senses, instills well-being, and fulfills even the unexpressed wishes and needs of our guests.

The Ritz-Carlton Credo

1. The Credo is the principal belief of our Company. It must be known, owned and energized by all.

2. Our Motto is: "We are Ladies and Gentlemen serving Ladies and Gentlemen." As service professionals, we treat our guests and each other with respect and dignity.

3. The Three Steps of Service are the foundation of Ritz-Carlton hospitality. These steps must be used in every interaction to ensure satisfaction, retention and loyalty.

4. The Employee Promise is the basis for our Ritz-Carlton work environment. It will be honored by all employees.

5. All employees will successfully complete annual Training Certification for their position.

6. Company objectives are communicated to all employees. It is everyone's responsibility to support them.

7. To create pride and joy in the workplace, all employees have the right to be involved in the planning of the work that affects them.

8. Each employee will continuously identify defects (M.R. B.I.V.) throughout the Hotel.

9. It is the responsibility of each employee to create a work environment of team work and lateral service so that the needs of our guests and each other are met.

10. Each employee is empowered. For example, when a guest has a problem or needs something special, you should break away from your regular duties to address and resolve the issue.

11. Uncompromising levels of cleanliness are the responsibility of every employee.

12. To provide the finest personal service for our guests, each employee is responsible for identifying and recording individual guest preferences.

13. Never lose a guest. Instant guest pacification is the responsibility of each employee. Whoever receives a complaint will own it, resolve it to the guest's satisfaction and record it.

14. "Smile—We are on stage." Always maintain positive eye contact. Use the proper vocabulary with our guests and each other. (Use words like—"Good Morning," "Certainly," "I'll be happy to" and "My pleasure.")

15. Be an ambassador of your Hotel in and outside of the workplace. Always speak positively. Communicate any concerns to the appropriate person

16. Escort guests rather than pointing out directions to another area of the Hotel.

17. Use Ritz-Carlton telephone etiquette. Answer within three rings with a "smile." Use the guest's name when possible. When necessary, ask the caller "May I place you on hold?" Do not screen calls. Eliminate call transfers whenever possible. Adhere to voice mail standards.

18. Take pride in and care of your personal appearance. Everyone is responsible for conveying a professional image by adhering to Ritz-Carlton clothing and grooming standards.

19. Think safety first. Each employee is responsible for creating a safe, secure and accident free environment for all guests and each other. Be aware of all fire and safety emergency procedures and report any security risks immediately.

20. Protecting the assets of a Ritz-Carlton Hotel is the responsibility of every employee. Conserve energy, properly maintain our Hotels and protect the environment.

Patrick Mene, director of quality, has reported that employees do not abuse this privilege. "When you treat people responsibly, they act responsibly."

Are employees achieving President Schulze's goal of 100 percent guest satisfaction? In the eyes of one customer, they are. "They not only treat us like a king when we hold our top-level meetings in their hotels, but we just never get any complaints," said Wayne Stetson, the staff vice-president of the convention and meetings division of the National Association of Home Builders in Washington, D.C.

The Ritz-Carlton credo—found in Exhibit 9-1 and carried by each employee—explains in more depth the chain's success. This is a hotel that has created a culture where the employees practice their credo.[1]

In 1995, Marriott International bought 49 percent interest in the Ritz-Carlton Hotel Corporation for $200 million in cash and assumed debt. In 1998, Marriott bought the rest, and under Marriott's leadership, the high standard of excellence was continued so that in 1999, the company again won the Malcolm Baldrige National Quality Award and was announced as the first service company to be a repeat winner, one of the reasons being the firm's close attention to the customer. "Ritz-Carlton maintains a database on the preferences of nearly one million of its customers, detailing their likes, dislikes, family and personal interests, preferred credit card, etc. Each employee is responsible for identifying and recording guest preferences. The goal is to customize service and thereby create a lasting relationship with the customer."[2]

In 2003, Ritz-Carlton Hotel Company of Atlanta moved to Chevy Chase, Maryland, to be closer to its parent company, Bethesda-based Marriott International.[3] Currently Ritz-Carlton has 51 hotels worldwide and is continuing to do well. As they say in the business world, "they walk their talk."

Historical Insight—The Hog Comeback

A historical insight into a proactive approach to managing change is the amazing story of Harley-Davidson, an American icon which almost went under in the 1980s.

This story also highlights the importance of leadership, empowerment, and team building in turning a crisis into a success.

Harley-Davidson, written off in the 1980s as another casualty of Japanese superiority, is running full throttle once again. The demise and resurgence of the 90-year-old motorcycle company has become a story told again and again in boardrooms of corporate America and in business schools throughout the United States.

The Harley story begins in the 1970s, when AMF Corporation still owned the company. In response to the surging popularity of motorcycles late in the decade, Harley tripled production over a short 4-year period, in the process deferring styling and engine performance upgrades. However, in the rush to get more motorcycles out the door, the company suffered a noticeable decline in quality. Engines came off the line leaking oil, lacking parts, and evidencing serious vibration problems. The once great American motorcycles were simply no competition to high-quality, fully equipped Japanese bikes. As a result, market share fell from 40 percent in 1979 to 23 percent in 1983.

Former chief executive officer (CEO) Vaughn Beals and a group of top Harley executives decided to kick-start the company one more time with a buyout of AMF in 1981. As Beals explains, "We were being wiped out by the Japanese because they were better managers. It wasn't robotics, or culture, or morning calisthenics and company songs." Under the direction of Beals and managers from every department, a strategic planning audit was conducted. Harley management used the audit results to determine company strengths, weaknesses, opportunities, and threats, and developed a long-range, 10-year plan—something the company had never done before. The audit revealed the importance of quality in every aspect of the firm.

Harley managers became quality obsessed. They implemented a new quality and inventory control system based almost entirely on employee participation—both in its planning and in its implementation. Employees were

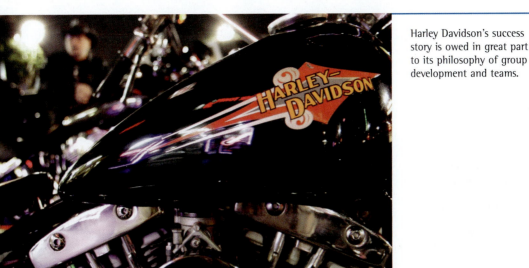

Harley Davidson's success story is owed in great part to its philosophy of group development and teams.

REUTER'S/Mario Anzuoni/Landov

taught statistical techniques and were empowered to manage their own work. Plant managers were trained in team leadership techniques, replacing the old domineering style of bosses. In an effort to build new relationships with current and prospective customers, Harley executives began sponsoring and participating in weekend cross-country Harley rallies. During these outings, managers would listen to what other Harley riders had to say. Customer feedback provided managers with ideas that led to engine and styling improvements.

It wasn't long before Harley employees had formed the Harley Owners Group, more popularly known as the HOGs, the name riders affectionately call their Harleys. HOGs began sponsoring motorcycle events almost every weekend somewhere in the United States. Today, over 100,000 members participate in the nationally advertised events, frequently held to support charity causes. As Harley began recouping market share and, more importantly, customer loyalty, the Japanese motorcycle manufacturer, Honda, was faltering. When Honda tried to start a rival club, it never got off the starting line and dropped out of the race.

By 1993, Harley had taken command of 60 percent of the big cycle market (1,200cc and larger), and profits and stock prices doubled. The Harley motorcycle once again led the ranks as a symbol of American ingenuity and quality craftsmanship. Under the direction of CEO Richard Teerlink, Harley-Davidson became one of America's most admired corporations. Speaking to the Academy of Management, Teerlink emphasized that the company's continual challenge was to keep open communication channels and use all the abilities and ideas of its employees. Additionally, the company operates as a unified team with a "whole company" perspective among the individual departments—engineering, manufacturing, marketing, and design. These objectives enable employees to focus on quality and keep the company running smoothly and efficiently at the same time.[4]

Teerlink retired as CEO in 1999, but spends his time providing "messages for managers who might be wrestling with change in their own companies." He goes on to say, "Leadership isn't a person, but a process to which everyone must contribute." In creating a partnership with the company's workforce, Harley-Davidson used an approach based on a Chinese proverb: "Tell me, I'll forget; show me, and I may remember. But involve me, and I'll understand."

In 2003, Harley not only is continuing its financial success, but also has achieved a high reputation among U.S. firms for corporate sincerity, ethics, and standards.[5] In a Harris Interactive Survey, it ranked second only to the maker of No More Tears baby shampoo and Band-Aids.[6]

Forces Causing Change

Numerous factors affect an organization. Continuously changing forces leading to or causing change originate both outside and within the organization, as shown in Exhibit 9-2. You might compare this situation to yourself. You must respond to such external stimuli as the condition of the weather, the requirements of your daily work schedule, and the different needs arising each day. Also requiring responses are the internal stimuli, such as your hunger level, the state of your health, or your attitude. A similar situation exists when we substitute an organization for yourself.

external change forces
Forces outside the organization that have a great impact on organizational change. Management has little control over these numerous external forces.

External Change Forces. Management has little control over the strong impact of numerous **external change forces.** Yet an organization depends on and must interact with its external environment if it is to survive. Specifically, resources, profits, and customers for products and services are all from the outside. Therefore, any force that impacts or changes the environment affects the organization's operations and brings about pressures requiring a change response. External forces—from technological advancements to consumers' changing requirements—cause an organization to alter its goals, structure, and methods of conducting business.

✔ STOP AND THINK

Suppose you were the director and owner of a 30-bed nursing home. What are some kinds of external change factors that might have an impact on your organization?

· ·

Experts have theorized that basic changes are needed in today's organizations. These changes are a move away from (1) a short-term to a long-term perspective, (2) a focus on ends rather than the means, and (3) an emphasis on the individual over the community.[7]

internal change forces
Pressures for change within the organization such as cultures and objectives.

Internal Change Forces. Change forces also come from within. **Internal change forces** may result from different organization goals or new challenges, as in the case of the Ritz-Carlton Hotel Company. Or they may be caused by new quality initiatives, changing technologies, or employee attitudes. For example, shifting the goal from short-run profit to long-term growth directly impacts the daily work of most departments and may lead to a reorganization that will streamline overall operations. Changing to automated equipment and robots to perform work previously done by people will cause changes in work routine and just-in-time supplies. Altering incentive programs and personnel policies and procedures may result in different

---

EXHIBIT 9-2

External and Internal Change Forces

External change forces

Educational · Cultural · Social · Natural resources · Economic · Technological · Political/legal → Organization

Internal change forces

Worker activities/abilities/attitudes · Objectives · Policies · Organizational structure → Technology, resources

hiring and selection procedures. Employee attitudes about child and/or parent care, insurance needs, or flexible working hours may change daily business practices.

External and internal forces for change are often interrelated, not isolated from one another. At times, this linkage results from the changes in values and attitudes affecting people within the system. Some of these changes from within are from people who have entered the organization. For example, many of the changes now occurring in organizations are the result of the increasing availability of a highly trained workforce, including the need for increased flexibility and responsiveness of the organization to employee needs and a flattened hierarchy allowing greater responsibility to be placed with front-line workers.

Planned Change

For management to plan for change, it must decide what needs to be changed in the organization. In general, management seeks to change things that prevent greater organizational effectiveness. **Organizational effectiveness** results from activities that improve the organization's structure, technology, and people so it can achieve its objectives.

organizational effectiveness
The result of activities that improve the organization's structure, technology, and people.

The nature of the problem causing the organization to be less than ideally effective determines the choice of the particular technique used to achieve change. From a choice of alternatives, management must determine which one is most likely to produce the desired outcome. Diagnosing the problem includes defining the outcome that is desired from the change. In general, the desired outcome is either improved employee behavior or activities that will result in improved performance. This can be achieved by changing the organization's structure, technology, and/or people (Exhibit 9-2).

This classification of organizational elements in no way implies a distinct division among elements. According to the systems concept, a change in one element is likely to affect other elements. In general, the more change that is required, the more likely it is that management will change all three elements.

Management must decide the desired outcomes and the type of change programs to use to change the specific organizational element—including those activities needed to get the work done effectively (Exhibit 9-3). Changing the organization's *structure* involves modifying and

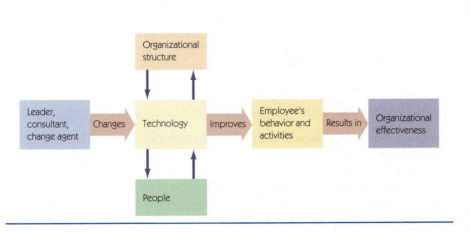

EXHIBIT 9-4

Different Responses
to Change

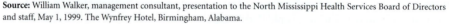

Source: William Walker, management consultant, presentation to the North Mississippi Health Services Board of Directors and staff, May 1, 1999. The Wynfrey Hotel, Birmingham, Alabama.

rearranging the internal relationships. This includes such variables as authority–responsibility relationships, communications systems, work flows, and size and composition of work groups.

Changing the organization's *technology* may require modifying such factors as its tools, equipment, and machinery; research direction and techniques; engineering processes; and production system, including layout, methods, and procedures. Changing technology may result from or contribute to changing tasks to be performed. Products and other inputs may be altered. For example, mechanization changes the nature of work performed.

Changing the organization's *people* may include changing recruiting and selection policies and procedures, training and development activities, reward systems, and/or managerial leadership and communication.

Supervisors and employees are likely to support change if they perceive the change as being directed at the real cause of the problem, as being an effective solution, and as not affecting them adversely. Most importantly, those who participate in a change process respond entirely differently than those merely affected by it. Exhibit 9-4 shows these different responses to change.

Next, we turn to the study of group dynamics, which will provide greater insight into creating a climate of positive change.

Importance of Work Groups

synergy The concept that two or more people working together in a cooperative, coordinated way can accomplish more than the sum of their independent efforts.

To achieve synergy and, we hope, to gain the most from the employees, organizations require groups. **Synergy** means that the whole is greater than the sum of the parts. This is especially applicable when using teams and ad hoc task forces. Assume that a five-person ad hoc task force is given the opportunity to solve a problem that has an impact on the entire organization. If the team reaches a synergistic solution to the problem, then synergy can be mathematically defined as $1 + 1 + 1 + 1 + 1 =$ more than 5. It is important for supervisors to understand the basic concepts of group or team development because work groups or teams produce the synergistic effect needed for management to reach its goals.

What Are Groups?

Groups have been defined in various ways. The definition we prefer is that a **group** is two or more people who communicate and work together regularly in pursuit of one or more common objectives. This highlights the point that at least two individuals must work together to constitute a group. If a group becomes too large, interaction among all members is difficult. This leads to the evolution of smaller groups. Remember, one finding of the Hawthorne Studies was that groups can be either supportive of organizational goals or opposed to them overall.

group Two or more people who communicate and work together regularly in pursuit of one or more common objectives.

Types of Groups

Groups in organizations are either formal or informal. Formal groups are those created by the organization. The most common example is the group formed by a manager and his or her immediate team members. Informal groups evolve out of the formal organization but are not formed by management. Neither are they shown in the organization's structure. An example would be a friendship group that enjoys discussing sports during lunch.

Formal Groups. **Formal groups** are deliberately formed by management and are often shown on the organizational chart. For example, command groups are formal groups composed of staff who report to a designated manager, such as a group of vice-presidents for worldwide marketing. Committees and task forces are additional examples of formal groups. Later in this chapter, we examine the increasing use of self-managing work teams, another example of formal groups created by management. Exhibit 9-5 illustrates how one manager can be a member of several different groups while employed by one organization.

formal group A group prescribed and/or established by the organization.

Informal Groups. **Informal groups** evolve out of employees' need for social interaction, friendship, communication, and status. While not a part of the formal organization, an informal group can sometimes be the same as a formal work team. The group members might give more allegiance to the informal leader than to the formal manager.

Other types of informal groups cross formal work team boundaries and are based on common interests. An informal interest group may come together to seek increased fringe benefits or attempt to solve a particularly broad-based software problem. Another type of informal group is a friendship group. Its members also have common interests, but they are more social in nature. Such groups could include a running team, a band, or the people who gather to chat during a break.

In general, informal groups provide a valuable service by helping members meet affiliation and social needs. Ideally, management tries to create an environment in which the needs and objectives of informal groups are similar to the needs and objectives of the formal organization.

informal group A group that evolves out of the formal organization but is not formed by management or shown in the organization's structure.

How Groups Develop

B. W. Tuckman developed a model of small-group development that encompasses four stages of growth.[8] A desirable feature of this classical model—which basically has been followed by later researchers[9]—is that it examines the stages in terms of task functions and interpersonal relations, both essential concerns of any group.

1 Identify the stages of group development.

Stages of Group Development. The stages of group development defined by Tuckman are (1) forming, (2) storming, (3) norming, and (4) performing. There is some overlap between the stages, and the length of time spent in each stage can vary; however, the central concept is that a group will usually remain in a stage until key issues are resolved before moving to the next stage. Sometimes a group appears to have resolved key issues but really has not.

http://www.onepine.info/ mgrp.htm

EXHIBIT 9-5

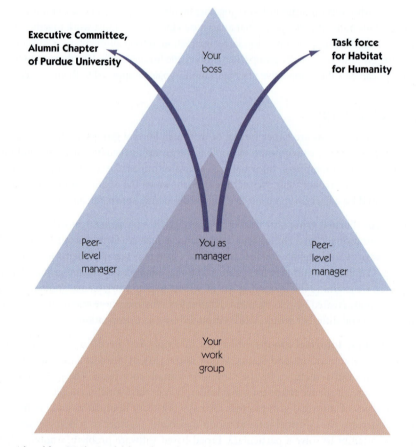

**Executive Committee,
Alumni Chapter
of Purdue University**

**Task force
for Habitat
for Humanity**

Your
boss

Peer-
level
manager

You as
manager

Peer-
level
manager

Your
work
group

Source: Adapted from W. Alan Randolph, *Understanding and Managing Organizational Behavior* (Homewood, Ill.: Richard D. Irwin, 1985), p. 385.

In this case, after moving to the next stage, the group will have to shift back to the earlier stage to resolve the unsettled issue. The characteristics of each stage follow.

Stage 1: Forming. Forming is the stage in which members first come together and form initial impressions. Among other things, they are trying to determine the task of the group and their role expectations of one another. In this stage, members depend on a leader to provide considerable structure in establishing an agenda and guidelines, since they tend to be unsure of what is expected of them.

Stage 2: Storming. The storming stage is typically a period of conflict and—ideally— organization. Conflicts arise over goals, task behaviors (that is, who is responsible for what), and leadership roles. Relationship behaviors emerge, in that people have strong feelings and express them, sometimes in a hostile manner.

It is a mistake to suppress conflict; the key is to manage it. If a group gets through stage 2 successfully, it becomes organized and begins developing norms, rules, and standards.

Stage 3: Norming. Norming is a stage of developing teamwork and group cohesion and creating openness of communications with information sharing. Members feel good about one another and give each other positive feedback, and the level of trust and cooperation is usually quite high. These desirable characteristics of team development result from establishing agreed-on goals and finalizing the processes, standards, and rules by which the group will operate.

If the issues of the earlier stages have not been resolved, the group can regress. Later in this chapter, we will discuss norms in more detail.

Stage 4: Performing. Performing is the stage in which the group shows how efficiently and effectively it can operate to achieve its goals. Information exchange has developed to the point of joint problem solving, and there is shared leadership.

As one organizational behavior text points out, "Some groups continue to learn and develop from their experiences and new inputs. . . . Other groups—especially those that have developed norms not fully supportive of efficiency and effectiveness—may perform only at the level needed for their survival."[10] Thus, group development, like individual development, is a continuing process.

Evaluating Groups

Groups, whether formal or informal, are a fact of organizational life. In this section, we discuss some important advantages and limitations of groups.

Advantages of Groups. Among the major advantages of groups are that they (1) provide members with opportunities for need satisfaction and (2) may function more effectively than individuals.

Provide Opportunities for Need Satisfaction. Group membership provides an opportunity for members to satisfy security and relationship needs as well as higher-level esteem and self-actualization needs. Group membership can be highly satisfying. For example, being viewed as a member of a high-performing problem-solving task force brings out feelings of pride.

2 Compare the advantages and limitations of groups.

Employees who work in groups often find they are able to accomplish more than they can by working alone. In addition, working in a group can be a satisfying social experience.

© Photonica/Getty Images

At times, a task you perceive as drudgery may actually turn out to be less distasteful when you are working together in a group.

May Function More Effectively Than Individuals. Synergy is the concept that two plus two can equal five. This is one of the major potential advantages of groups. The combination of members possessing different perspectives, experiences, and job skills can often work in a team's favor. Moreover, individuals operating as a group may feel a collective responsibility that often leads to higher motivation and commitment.

Limitations of Groups. Among the general limitations of groups are that they may (1) encourage social loafing, (2) diffuse responsibility, and (3) be less effective than individuals.

Encourage Social Loafing. *Social loafing* is the term used to describe "taking a free ride" when working with others as a team. We have all known team members who did not pull their weight as part of a team writing a group term paper or putting together a classroom presentation. Generally, social loafing occurs because some members genuinely believe that their contributions to the group are not that significant or they hope for a free ride. Free riders are reinforced when they receive rewards or recognition on an equal basis with those who have carried the greater load.

Diffuse Responsibility. The diffusion of responsibility among members of a group is somewhat related to social loafing and is also one of its major causes. Because each person may be expected to do only a part of a project, no one person may feel totally responsible. Diffused responsibility may result in groups' assuming positions that individual members would not take if held individually accountable. The "Oh, what the heck" attitude, as well as the idea that "they" will handle it, leads to more liberal risk taking. This also means that the more mundane, routine, and undesirable group tasks may be neglected by individual members in the hope that someone else will complete them.

May Be Less Effective Than Individuals. While the concept of synergy is an attractive argument in favor of group effort, the sad fact is that sometimes two plus two equals three. One classic study showed this effect dramatically. One would expect a group of three pulling on a rope to exert three times the pulling power that each could attain separately. Such was not the case: Groups exerted a force only two and a half times the average of individual performance.[11]

Thus, as a result of social loafing, diffusion of responsibility, and other factors, groups may not necessarily be more productive and effective than individuals.

3 Describe the variables that determine a group's effectiveness.

Determining Group Effectiveness

What are the key factors determining the effectiveness of groups? Exhibit 9-6 highlights the essential variables affecting group satisfaction, goal accomplishment, and productivity. As the model demonstrates, there is a cause-and-effect relationship between leadership (the causal variable), group characteristics (the intervening variables), and the end result variables. Variables affecting group effectiveness are (1) group size, (2) member composition and roles, (3) norms, and (4) group cohesiveness.

Group Size. Without question, the size of the work group has an impact on a group's effectiveness. The size of a group depends to a large extent on its purpose. Organizations can take a contingency approach to determining a manager's span of control, which influences the size of the natural group. With the increasing use of committees, task forces, quality circles, and self-managing work teams, we need additional guidelines for determining the size of these types of groups. Exhibit 9-7 provides some guidelines on the effects of size on group leadership, members, and group processes.

EXHIBIT 9-6

Model of Group
Effectiveness

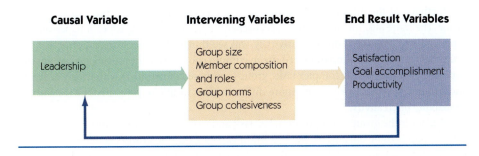

Causal Variable   **Intervening Variables**   **End Result Variables**

Leadership

Group size
Member composition
and roles
Group norms
Group cohesiveness

Satisfaction
Goal accomplishment
Productivity

It has been our experience that the ideal size for a problem-solving group is five to seven members. As Exhibit 9-7 highlights, with this size, there is less chance for differences to arise between the leader and members, less chance of domination by a few members, and less time required for reaching decisions. In partnering workshops, we usually use ad hoc task forces of five to seven to study an issue and report back to the larger group with a recommended plan of action. Almost invariably, the action plan is accepted with only minor modifications. The one time we ran into difficulty was when we used a larger group—14 people—to develop a partnering agreement. In that instance, the reported agreement was later sabotaged by a

EXHIBIT 9-7

Possible Effects of Size
on Groups

	Group Size		
Category/Dimensions	2–7 Members	8–12 Members	13–16 Members
Leadership			
1. Demands on leader	Low	Moderate	High
2. Differences between leaders and members	Low	Low to moderate	Moderate to high
3. Direction by leader	Low	Low to moderate	Moderate to high
Members			
4. Tolerance of direction from leader	Low to high	Moderate to high	High
5. Domination of group interaction by a few members	Low	Moderate to high	High
6. Inhibition in participation by ordinary members	Low	Moderate	High
Group Process			
7. Formalization of rules and procedures	Low	Low to moderate	Moderate to high
8. Time required for reaching judgment decisions	Low to moderate	Moderate	Moderate to high
9. Tendency for subgroups to form within group	Low	Moderate to high	High

Source: Adapted from ORGANIZATIONAL BEHAVIOR, 10th edition by Hellriegel/Slocum/Woodman, page 208. Copyright © 2004. Reprinted with permission of South-Western, a part of Cengage Learning, www.cengage.com/permissions.

subgroup of the original group of 14. Their complaint was that the agreement had been rushed through by two of the more dominating members. On the other hand, one study has found that 14 members are the ideal size for a fact-finding group.[12] This shows once again that the ideal size depends on the group's purpose.

Member Composition and Roles. The composition of a group has considerable impact on productivity. At the minimum, the ability of members to carry out the mission is a major factor. The more alike members are in age, background, value systems, education, personality type, and so forth, the more similarly they will see things. The literature suggests that for tasks that are relatively simple and require maximum cooperation, homogeneous groups are superior.[13] Conversely, for complex tasks, groups composed of members with widely differing backgrounds are superior because more different ideas would be generated, increasing the probability of creativity.

Whatever the group's composition, key task and maintenance roles must be carried out if the group is to be effective (Exhibit 9-8). In carrying out the group's activities, members tend to shift back and forth between these roles naturally. This is especially true in problem-solving groups and in regular work teams where the formal leader is skillful in getting everyone to participate.

EXHIBIT **9-8**

Task and Maintenance
Roles in Groups

Effective Roles		Ineffective Roles
Work or Task* Functions	**Group Maintenance* Functions**	
Initiating. Proposing tasks or goals; defining need for action; suggesting a procedure or an idea for a course of action.	*Consensus testing.* Checking with the group to see how much agreement has been reached, or how near it is to a united conclusion.	*Displays of aggression.* Deflating others' status; attacking the group or its values; joking in a barbed or semiconcealed way.
Information giving. Offering facts; providing relevant information; giving an opinion.	*Harmonizing.* Attempting to reconcile disagreements; reducing tensions; getting people to explore differences.	*Blocking.* Disagreeing/opposing beyond "reason"; stubbornly resisting group wishes for personal reasons; using hidden agenda to thwart the movement of a group.
Information seeking. Requesting facts; seeking relevant information; checking on meaning; asking for suggestions or ideas.	*Gate keeping.* Helping to keep communication channels open; facilitating the participation of others; suggesting procedures that permit sharing remarks.	*Dominating.* Asserting authority or superiority to manipulate group or some of its members; hindering others' contributions; controlling through flattery or other forms of patronization.
Clarifying. Interpreting ideas or suggestions; defining terms; clarifying issues before group; clearing up confusions.	*Encouraging.* Being friendly, warm, and responsive to others; indicating by facial expression or remark the acceptance of others' contributions; giving others opportunity for recognition.	*Playboy behavior.* Making a display, "playboy" fashion, of one's lack of involvement, "abandoning" the group while still physically in it; seeking recognition in ways not relevant to group task.
Summarizing. Pulling together related ideas; restating suggestions after group has discussed them; offering a decision or conclusion for group to consider.	*Compromising.* When one's own idea or status is involved in a conflict, yielding status; admitting error; disciplining oneself to maintain group cohesion.	*Avoidance behavior.* Pursuing special interests not related to task; staying of subject to avoid commitment; preventing group from facing up to controversy; filibustering.
Reality testing. Making a critical analysis of an idea; testing an idea; testing an idea against some data to see if the idea would work.	*Sharing feelings.* Sensing feelings, moods, relationships within the group; sharing feelings with other members; sharing observations on group processes.	*Sniping.* Ridiculing opinions and ideas of others by word or action; personal criticism.

*The distinction between "task" and "maintenance" roles is somewhat arbitrary. Some of these terms could be classified in either column.

Many members in a problem-solving group will play several task or maintenance roles. Unfortunately, there are ineffective roles or behaviors, such as dominating, that can have a negative impact on group effectiveness (see Exhibit 9-8). The skill is for the leader to operate so that members share the leadership role and ineffective behaviors are minimized. Exhibit 9-9 is a questionnaire allowing individual members of a group to assess how well they function in helping the group achieve its goals and in minimizing ineffective behaviors.

Norms. **Norms** are generally thought of as rules of behavior developed by group members to provide guidance for group activities. Norms, standards, and action plans in an effective team are highly interrelated and are supportive of the organization's goals. However, if a group is not well led, negative norms will result, working against the organization's goals.

norms Rules of behavior developed by group members to provide guidance for group activities.

EXHIBIT **9-9**

Assessing Your Behavior as a Team Member

Instructions: Select a team you are currently working with or have worked with in the recent past. Assess your behavior on each item for the team that you selected by using the following scale.

1	2	3	4	5
Almost Never	Rarely	Sometimes	Often	Almost Always

Place the appropriate number value next to each item.

Task-oriented behaviors: In this team, I . . .

_____ 1. initiate ideas or actions.

_____ 2. facilitate the introduction of facts and information.

_____ 3. summarize and pull together various ideas.

_____ 4. keep the team working on the task.

_____ 5. ask whether the team is near a decision (determine consensus).

Relation-oriented behaviors: In this team, I . . .

_____ 6. support and encourage others.

_____ 7. harmonize (keep the peace).

_____ 8. try to find common ground.

_____ 9. encourage participation.

_____ 10. actively listen.

Self-oriented behaviors: In this team, I . . .

_____ 11. express hostility.

_____ 12. avoid involvement.

_____ 13. dominate the team.

_____ 14. free ride on others.

_____ 15. take personal credit for team results.

Total scores of 20–25 on task-oriented behaviors, 20–25 on relations-oriented behaviors, and 5–10 on self-oriented behaviors would indicate that you are probably an effective team player.

Source: From ACP Organizational Behavior/NAU 10th edition, p. 210 by Hellriegel/Slocum/Woodman, 2005. Reprinted with permission of South-Western, a part of Cengage Learning, www.cengage.com/permissions.

An example of a negative norm is an informal leader in a construction team sending the message "Don't rush the work—they'll just give you more to do."

The critical role of leadership is especially important in influencing positive norms. An example of a positive norm is the informal leader in the marketing group sending the message "Make sure it looks nice—we want to be proud of our work." Business ethics are similar to norms in that they provide guides to behavior. The top leadership of an organization has significant influence on ethical normative values of groups as well as individuals.

Group Cohesiveness. The mutual liking and team feeling in a group are called **group cohesiveness.** As we have already seen, size plays a major part in the cohesiveness of a group. Another major factor is the frequency of communication.

In the partnering workshops we have conducted, communications were frequently issue-oriented. This led to the development of group cohesiveness. Agreement on overall goals, with the processes and plans to achieve those goals, also enhances group cohesiveness.

Conversely, the major factors preventing group cohesiveness are dysfunctional conflicts, internal power struggles, and failure to achieve goals. However, sometimes a group will be very congenial, agree on goals, and feel like a team, yet fail in its mission.

Three other concepts that play a key role in healthy group development are listening, supporting, and differing. How many times have you been in a group discussion and been cut off in midsentence? How many times have you been thinking about the point you want to make next rather than listening to the other person? Sometimes we find ourselves responding to another person's idea or suggestion with the thought, "That's a great idea—I would never have come up with that." At those moments, it is important to give positive feedback in support of the suggestion if we want to create a supportive group environment for generating ideas. Finally, and perhaps most important for creativity in groups, is the creation of an environment in which people can disagree without being disagreeable. In Skill Builder 9-2, you will have an opportunity to solve an unfamiliar problem first on your own and then in a small group. While working in the small group, make a conscious effort to carry out the concepts of listening, supporting, and differing.

4 Determine what is involved in team building.

Different Approaches to Team Building

Now that you have an insight into groups and group dynamics, we focus on teams and team building. Many supervisors are now shifting to the role of team leader, so we will use that term through the chapter. A **team** is a collection of people who must rely on group cooperation if the team is to experience the most success possible and thereby achieve its goals.[14] Experience has demonstrated that successful teams are "empowered to establish some or all of a team's goals, to make decisions about how to achieve those goals, to undertake the tasks required to meet them, and to be mutually accountable for their results."[15]

Unfortunately, a number of teams do not achieve their optimum success and potential. This is often caused by the team leader's leadership style being too autocratic or too permissive in managing the group. Consequently, several of the characteristics of an effective team are lacking. These characteristics are shown in Exhibit 9-10. The following sections illustrate how these characteristics of an effective team are implemented through the use of organizational team building.

Teams and organizations may not be successful because they fail at one or more of the following concepts, first identified by the renowned leadership expert, John W. Gardner:

1. effective leadership at the top of the team and/or organization,

2. effective recruitment of good and talented people,

3. the creation of an environment so good and talented people grow and develop.

EXHIBIT 9-10

Characteristics of
an Effective Team

Clear Purpose	The vision, mission, goal, or task of the team has been defined and is now accepted by everyone. There is an action plan.
Informality	The climate tends to be informal, comfortable, and relaxed. There are no obvious tensions or signs of boredom.
Participation	There is much discussion, and everyone is encouraged to participate.
Listening	The members use effective listening techniques such as questioning, paraphrasing, and summarizing to get out ideas.
Civilized Disagreement	There is disagreement, but the team is comfortable with this and shows no signs of avoiding, smoothing over, or suppressing conflict.
Consensus Decisions	For important decisions, the goal is substantial but not necessarily unanimous agreement through open discussion of everyone's ideas, avoidance of formal voting, or easy compromises.
Open Communication	Team members feel free to express their feelings on the tasks as well as on the group's operation. There are few hidden agendas. Communication takes place outside of meetings.
Clear Roles and Work Assignments	There are clear expectations about the roles played by each team member. When action is taken, clear assignments are made, accepted, and carried out. Work is fairly distributed among team members.
Shared Leadership	While the team has a formal leader, leadership functions shift from time to time depending on the circumstances, the needs of the group, and the skills of the members. The formal leader models the appropriate behavior and helps establish positive norms.
External Relations	The team spends time developing key outside relationships, mobilizing resources, and building credibility with important players in other parts of the organization.
Style Diversity	The team has a broad spectrum of team-player types, including members who emphasize attention to task, goal setting, focus on process, and questions about how the team is functioning.
Self-Assessment	Periodically, the team stops to examine how well it is functioning and what may be interfering with its effectiveness.

Source: Glenn M. Parker, *Team Players and Teamwork* (San Francisco: Jossey-Bass/John Wiley & Sons, 1991), p. 33. Used with permission of the publisher.

To gain insight into how effective these concepts and characteristics are we examine team building in various types of organizations.

Team Building in the Sales and Service Sector

The hospitality industry has for some time been one of the fastest growing service sectors in the United States and around the world. One of the many players nationally is a company called Resort Quest, which specializes in selling, managing, and renting properties in beach and ski resorts. Although Resort Quest has long been active in the Destin and Sandestin beach areas of Florida, in 2000 they moved into the Perdido Key area (sometimes called the Lost Key), which is located between Gulf Shores, Alabama, and Pensacola, Florida.

The hospitality industry is one of the fastest growing service sectors in places like Perdido Key, Florida.

© Jeff Greenberg/Photoedit.

In 1973, only two resort condominiums were in Perdido Key. When Resort Quest placed sales agents on the key in 2000, there were over 100 resort properties and more were being built. This story is about the development and achievements of a small sales team and what we can learn from their experience.

Leadership at the Top

Pete Mulry is the leader at the top of the sales unit at Perdido Key. Rather than thinking of himself as a traditional hierarchical leader, who exerts power and influence from above, Pete operates as a team leader using shared leadership and serving as a facilitator/coach with the sales team in the achievement of results, which are outstanding. The Perdido Key office has the highest gross sales and profits with the least number of independent sales agents in the entire company. Overall in 2005, there were 130 sales agents in Resort Quest with four of the top fifteen in sales located in the Perdido Key office.

The background of Pete Mulry provides some interesting insight as to his current success as a team teacher/coach/facilitator. Pete is very dynamic and has spent most of his career as a coach/teacher. He coached baseball, basketball and football in the Tampa area and was quite successful. He had also completed course work in counseling through the doctoral level when he decided to make a career change.

He went to work for Diversified Marketing. With this company, he had the opportunity to manage his own business or move into a sales management leadership program. Pete started out by learning to sell door to door and moved very rapidly from sales into managing his own business, other businesses and, finally, managing the entire company as the number two man.

When he started in Gulf Shores with Diversified Marketing, there were three sales offices, and when he left 10 years later there were 54 locations. He left Diversified Marketing when he saw the company taking a different direction than where he wanted to go, which was into real estate sales and development. As a leader he learned that helping enough people get to where they want to go, will lead to win-win outcomes and synergistic results. He also observed that excessive micro-management could keep some young leaders from reaching their potential or even cause them to fail.

When Pete became the leader of the Perdido Key sales team, it was struggling. In a short time, it became an effective, cohesive team with outstanding results, due in large part to Pete's being the causal variable in recruiting, creating a climate for growth, and coaching. This led to significant improvements in communications and teamwork.

Recruitment of Good People

Most of the sales agents have had successful careers and experiences prior to joining the Perdido Key sales team. The two I have singled out, one woman and one man, have contrasting personalities and are outstanding individuals, as well as team contributors, and are recognized as outstanding mentors. They willingly share information and knowledge with other members of the team.

Kathy. At our first meeting, Kathy came across as personable, dynamic, and knowledgeable. According to the experienced agents at Resort Quest, Kathy's strengths are a positive attitude, outstanding knowledge of the amenities of over 100 properties on Perdido Key, and great people skills. Her educational background includes a B.S. in Mechanical Engineering from Florida State University. She told the author that she was surprised at how much her engineering background had helped her in selling condos.

Her first job was with Proctor and Gamble in research as a product development engineer. She left Proctor and Gamble with an outstanding performance record, including several patents that she developed in the feminine product area, and had proved to herself that she could be successful in a large international company.

Mike Ricketts. As retired military Mike is an ideal team player. He embraces and carries out the core values of developing teamwork, team cohesion, cooperation and support. At the same time, he is an outstanding individual contributor to the overall sales goals of the Perdido team. Mike is willing to go the extra mile to provide outstanding customer service. One customer mentioned to Mike that he would like an overall perspective of the Key, rather than just studying photographs. Mike, who is a pilot, rented a plane and flew the customer over the entire area for an overall view. The customer still calls from New York City once a month for recommendations from Mike on real estate investments.

Mike has exceptional integrity, and is always honest and genuine in his beliefs and actions, and is focused on meeting clients' needs. Once a week he visits all his listed properties to ensure they are in good condition.

The Creation of an Environment for Growth and Development

Many people will tell you that one of the most difficult tasks in sales is to develop true teamwork and sharing of information. There is a limited supply of potential customers, and each salesperson's compensation directly relates to what they sell. It is perceived that they are competing with each other and that it is in their best interest to keep information about prospects or sales techniques to themselves. Several of the Perdido Key sales team have been in organizations where secrecy prevails and cut throat competition exists. It is refreshing to be in an environment where information is shared and people help each other. They cover for each other in emergencies and nonemergencies. On many occasions, individual and team successes are celebrated by the entire team.

One team member stated that Pete Mulry has the uncanny ability to select people who have the desire to succeed. If they leave the team, they usually do so with a positive attitude about their experience at Resort Quest. One person who left for a better opportunity was

5 Describe what made team building successful at Resort Quest.

Matt Callan, a former Marine pilot, who thanked the team prior to leaving, saying "it has been a great life and learning experience being in this group."[16]

First, Pete Mulry brought in an outside facilitator, Tim Duncan, to assist in team building. Duncan held some coaching sessions with the team as a whole as well as with individuals of the team. Based on his experience as a teacher/coach and his insights from his doctoral program, Pete was confident that this step "would help us let down our barriers and our fear of competition." Team members learned to listen and to connect and communicate. Over time they began to feel a part of the team and to develop ways to help each other. They moved from the platinum rule of "treat people as they want to be treated" to the golden rule, "treat other people as I want to be treated."

✔ **STOP AND THINK**

If you were the team leader, would you make it mandatory for the independent sales agents to attend team meetings or allow voluntary attendance?

....

Team Building in the Large Company Sector

We have chosen to study General Electric (GE) because it is still considered one of the most admired companies in the world.

⑥ Describe the GE approach.

The GE Approach to Team Building

In one of the most significant books of this century (according to Warren Bennis), Mayo and Nohrid identify the 100 greatest business leaders of the 20th century. They do so by identifying three distinct paths that the best leaders forge to greatness—entrepreneurial innovation, savvy management, and transformational leadership—and they explore the contextual factors that leaders must "read" correctly in order to succeed. Their survey results in Jack Welch's being ranked seventh on the list of 100. Exhibit 9-11 summarizes the context-based leadership.[17] Exhibit 9-12 shows the survey results of why some individual leaders should be considered great.

Although most of the 100 executives are classified in the entrepreneurial profile, Jack Welch is the hallmark of the leader profile. "His ability to transform General Electric from a faltering industrial conglomerate into a financial, product and service powerhouse is the essence of great leadership."[18]

Exhibit 9-12 suggests criteria used for executives to be considered great. One of the themes of this book is the emphasis on development of others. Though Welch did not score high on the survey, he would be the exception. The current CEO of GE, Jeffery Immelt, emulates Welch's approach to team building, as do many other chief executives influenced by Jack Welch. Larry Bossidy, a disciple at GE, used what he learned to turn Allied Signal around. Bob Nardelli, the current CEO of Home Depot, was a product of GE and was number two being considered to replace Welch as president of GE. Since it is suspected that Jack Welch would make the final decision on who would replace him as CEO, it is interesting to see what he has to say about the current president of Home Depot, Bob Nardelli.

Today Nardelli, the man best known for coming up short in the most public succession story in business—the race to replace Jack Welch—wears the mantle of leader at Home Depot with confidence. "He is really the best manager, execution wise, I've ever encountered," says Welch. "His real ability is to motivate lots of people around a mission, excite them about it, and make it happen."[19] He also knows about the value of emotional intelligence and that means he listens, often without needing to set the agenda. We will focus on Jack Welch, one of the most influential leaders during the 20th century.

EXHIBIT 9-11

Context-Based
Leadership

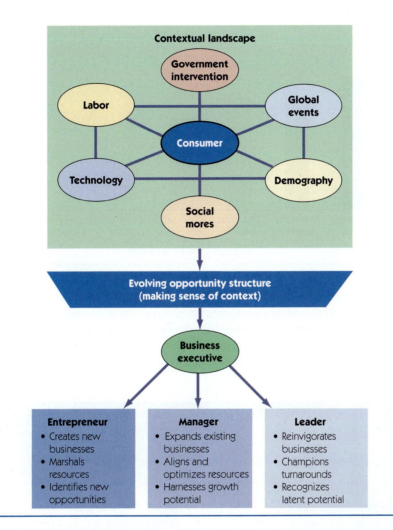

GE's Fight with Bureaucracy

In 1981, at the age of 45, Jack Welch took over the reins of GE from the popular and well-thought-of chairman and CEO Reginald H. Jones. Under Jones' leadership, earnings per share, adjusted for inflation, had risen an average of 4.9 percent a year as compared to 1.9 percent a year under his predecessor, Fred Borch. A major reason for the high regard for Jones was that GE had moved from a state of chronic cash shortage to one of tremendous financial strength. On the other hand, Jones' thirst for information and control led to the building of a bureaucracy, causing decisions to be reviewed at many levels.

Almost immediately after taking office, Jack Welch went to war with the bureaucracy that had developed during Jones' tenure. In the process, the world's tenth largest industrial corporation has been remade and revitalized. During this time, Welch has gained a reputation as a tough and ruthless manager.

EXHIBIT 9-12

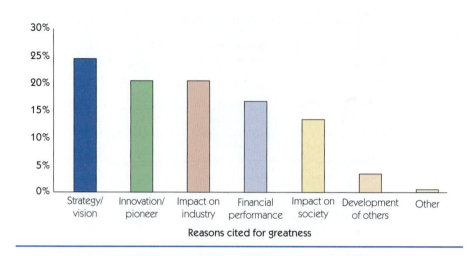

A key question is, Has it been worth it? If you were to ask one of the over 100,000 workers whose jobs were eliminated through layoffs, attrition, or sales of businesses, you would get one answer. If you were to ask stockholders who have seen earnings per share rise from 4.9 percent under Jones to 7.6 percent under Welch, you would get another answer. What kind of man is it who has streamlined the company from 100 business units down to 14?

Jack Welch is recognized as one of the most inspiring leaders in business during the 1990s. He adroitly managed change and team building during his tenure at General Electric. Jeffrey R. Immelt, pictured on the right, succeeded Welch following his retirement in 2001.

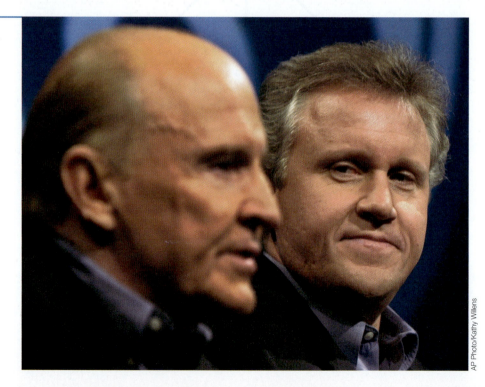

AP Photo/Kathy Willens

Welch was an only child whose father was a hardworking railroad conductor. Like many prominent leaders, Jack considers his mother the dominant influence in his life and his earliest role model. It was she, he says, who influenced his core values: "She always felt I could do anything. It was my mother who trained me. She wanted me to be independent. Control your own destiny—she always had that idea. Saw reality. No mincing words. Whenever I got out of line, she would whack me one. But always positive. Always constructive. Always uplifting." These core values have been translated into a GE strategy of ranking either first or second globally in the markets it serves. The strategy has succeeded, as 12 of GE's units are considered market leaders.

In the 1990s, Jack Welch was considered one of the stars of American industry. His newsletter in GE's annual report was a much anticipated event by business leaders, stockholders, and scholars, who read it reaching for creative ideas. In the 1993 annual report, he stated:

> **We are betting everything on our people—empowering them, giving them the resources and getting out of their way—and the numbers tell us that this focus has not only pointed us in the right direction, but it is providing us with a momentum that is accelerating.**

> **With the objective of involving everyone, we use three operating principles to define the atmosphere and behavior at GE:**

> > *Boundaryless* **. . . in everything we do;**
> > *Speed* **. . . in everything we do;**
> > *Stretch* **. . . in every target we set.**

Welch went on to give us examples of boundaryless behavior—a woman in the appliance division of GE in Hong Kong helping NBC to develop a satellite television service; on a broader scale, labor and management becoming partners to transform the unprofitable appliance parts complex in Louisville to profitability.

In the process of reorganizing, delayering, and reenergizing GE, Welch did not rest on past accomplishments but was continually on the warpath against inefficiencies caused by the excessive bureaucracy he inherited. One company campaign, called Work Out, was designed to win the hearts and minds of all 300,000 GE employees worldwide. GE visualized Work Out as a fluid and adaptable concept, not a program. Work Out generally starts as a series of regularly scheduled "town meetings" that bring together large cross sections of GE's people from manufacturing, engineering, customer service, hourly, salaried, and higher and lower levels. The initial purpose of these meetings was simple—to remove the more troublesome aspects of bureaucracy, such as multiple approvals, unnecessary paperwork, excessive reports, routines, and rituals. Ideas and opinions were often, at first, voiced hesitantly by people who never before had a forum—other than the water cooler—to express them. After a short time, the ideas began to come in a flood—especially when people saw action taken on the ones already advanced.

With the desk largely cleared of bureaucratic impediments and distractions, the Work Out sessions began to focus on the more challenging tasks of examining the myriad of processes that make up every business, identifying the crucial ones, discarding the rest, and then finding a faster, simpler, better way of doing things. Next, the teams raise the bar of excellence by testing their improved processes against the very best from around the company and from the best companies in the world.

During Jack Welch's early years as CEO, a number of people called him one of the most unfeeling, ruthless CEOs in America. Today, many people say he was a statesman and one of the most visionary of all America's CEOs.

Six Sigma

Along with Work Out, a second major thrust of Jack Welch's efforts to transform GE was his quality improvement initiative, Six Sigma.

Developed at smaller companies and perfected at two large ones, Motorola and Allied Signal, Six Sigma is a specific methodology designed to slash the number of defects in a company's end-to-end process of producing, improving, selling, distributing, and servicing its products.

Six Sigma was inaugurated at the company in late 1995 with 200 projects. It grew to 6,000 by 1997. By the time of his farewell annual meeting address in 2001, Welch was prepared to declare that "Six Sigma, originally focused on reducing waste and elevating the quality of our products and processes within the company, has delivered billions of dollars to GE's bottom line in savings."[20]

Tough Love—Evaluating Performance

Jack Welch was known for his tough-love style, both in evaluating business units and individuals. His philosophy was based on recruiting and hiring really outstanding people, creating a performance-based environment in which they could grow and develop, and rewarding those who succeeded. The tough part involves the company-wide performance reviews that result in the bottom 10 percent of GE's workforce being escorted out the door each year.[21] The new president, Jeffrey Immelt, is a follower of Welch's 10 percent rule and in this area will "go about running GE in much the same way."[22] Welch's philosophy on hiring, firing, and rewarding employees is shown in Exhibit 9-13.

GE used a process called differentiation in its evaluation process. Finding a way to differentiate people across a large company is not an easy process. In Welch's words:

> Over the years, we've used all kinds of bell curves and block charts to differentiate talent. These are all grids that attempt to rank performance and potential (high, medium, low). We've also led the charge into "360-degree evaluations," which take into account the

---

EXHIBIT **9-13**

Welch on Hiring, Firing, and Rewarding Employees

- Successful leaders must make very difficult decisions about the people who work for them. The "easy way out" is to treat everyone the same in terms of pay, promotions, and job security—but follow such an approach and your organization will flounder. The top performers will leave or throttle back on effort when they see that no matter how well they do, they will be paid just like everyone else. The average performers will see no incentive to try harder. And the poor performers will likely never leave. They have nowhere to go. They'll just drag you down.

- Despite possible confrontations and charges of favoritism, giving all employees similar raises is bad for an organization. It is unfair to those who have excelled. The challenge for leaders is to devise a true meritocracy that sets out clear goals for people and gives everyone a chance, but not a guarantee of success. Leaders must ensure that those they reward the best truly are the best, and not just the ones most adept at "impressing the boss."

- "Making the numbers" by itself is not enough to secure pay raises and promotions. Leaders must insist that key players in their organizations also share the values and embrace the culture of that organization. Capable people can at the same time be disruptive and destructive forces, poisoning the work environment and driving other potential star employees out the door.

- Leaders must deftly use the carrots and sticks of pay, promotion, and dismissal to boost productivity and inspire stellar performance. Meritocracy, not bureaucracy, is what you must implement to make your organization excel.

Source: James W. Robinson, *Jack Welch and Leadership* (Roseville, Calif.: Prima Publishing Co., 2001), p. 147. Reprinted by permission of author James W. Robinson, a senior official with the U.S. Chamber of Commerce.

EXHIBIT 9-14

Jack Welch's Vitality
Curve for Differentiation

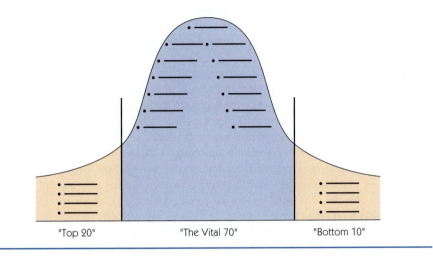

"Top 20"   "The Vital 70"   "Bottom 10"

views of peers and subordinates. We were always groping for a better way to evaluate the organization. We eventually found one we really liked. We called it the vitality curve [see Exhibit 9-14]. Every year, we'd ask each of GE's businesses to rank all of their top executives—top 20 percent, vital middle 70 percent, and finally the bottom 10 percent. The underperformers generally had to go.

Making these judgments is not easy, and they are not always precise. . . . Year after year, differentiation raises the bar higher and higher and increases the overall caliber of the organization. . . . [The top 20 percent] are people who are filled with passion, committed to making things happen, open to ideas from anywhere, and blessed with lots of runway ahead of them. They have what we call "the four Es of GE leadership"—very high *energy* levels, the ability to *energize* others around common goals, the *edge* to make tough yes-and-no-decisions, and finally the ability to consistently *execute* and deliver on their promises.[23]

Chuck Abraham's Insights

Chuck Abraham is a great admirer of Jack Welch and gives us some insight into how Jack Welch creates excellence in leadership and team building. Chuck spent 17 years with GE and when he left, he was a Global Business Manager of the medical division. Currently he is CEO of Orametirx and Chairman of the Board of NSITE.

Chuck sent his resume to GE while a senior at Mississippi State University. After two interviews, he was hired. GE was looking for people who could be on a fast track and could accept greater responsibility and challenge. Chuck made the initial interviews because of his high grades and outstanding personality. His father suggested that being an Eagle Scout as a youngster did not hurt as one of the interviewers asked a number of questions about scouting and what he had learned from it.

Chuck spent 7 years in sales in the medical division. He moved on to be the regional sales manager of the Boston region, where he really got to know Jack Welch.

During this period Jack Welch paid a visit to Sam Walton because Walmart had developed a quick market intelligence response making it possible to exploit opportunities or solve problems within 1 week's time. Jack brought this information back to GE and called a meeting of his vice-presidents to discuss it and to get their recommendations. Chuck's boss could not attend and sent Chuck to represent him. At the meeting all the vice-presidents presented rather complex plans and suggestions for the quick market response effort. Chuck was the last to speak and closed with "have fun and make decisions." At that point Jack Welch jumped up, slammed his fist on the table and said, "that's what I want us to do."

Shortly after his presentation, Chuck was named manager of the Boston region, which at the time was the lowest performing division on all measures. Chuck brought in some new people and early in his tenure threw a party on one of the beaches. At the party they had fun, but also they set goals to reach much higher standards. After 1 year, under Chuck's leadership, Boston was the second highest performing division.

Chuck had opportunities to meet individual bosses with Jack Welch, and quickly realized that Jack prefers the give and take of discussion and does not like "yes" people. He focuses on results and on evaluations; the excellent performers receive circles (○) around the trotter matrix (sales volume). The poor performers receive boxes (□), which are called coffins, and if they stay too long in that category, they soon are not with GE.

Chuck never felt fear, enjoyed the intensity of working in a competitive environment, and was asked to give several presentations at general meetings at GE. His appreciation of Jack Welch as an excellent leader and change agent, led to his being selected as Global Business Manager and assigned to the Paris office.

A manager from another company who had worked with GE managers told me that he sensed an element of fear in their working relationships with Welch. This was not the case with Chuck.

Chuck does not feel the fear factor is a problem, if one does his job. He goes on to describe Jack as having an incredible energy level and in a large room everyone feels his presence. His intellect can go from global and economic analysis to discussing a specific product or problem in detail. He also has the ability to rally 450,000 people around a vision and energize them to achieve.

✔ **STOP AND THINK**

Do you agree with Jack Welch and General Electric about eliminating the bottom 10 percent each year? Why or why not.

· ·

7 Describe what made team building successful in the nonprofit area.

A Nonprofit Approach to Team Work and Team Building

The Providence Hospital and Sacred Heart Hospital Cancer Centers provide a good example of effective teamwork in every aspect of patient care. There are seven doctors of varying specialties at the Center; this author interviewed three, Dr. Michael Meshad, Dr. Thadeus Beeker, and Dr. Nicole Angel.

Dr. Michael Meshad received his medical education and training at the University of Alabama, in Birmingham, Alabama. He served in special forces in the military and was a paratrooper. He enjoys an excellent reputation as an oncologist with an outstanding personality and sense of humor. He was one of the first to see the potential for the Center.

Dr. Thadeus Beeker, a graduate of Wake Forest University where he played baseball, later received his medical degree from Vanderbilt University. Dr. Beeker was recruited because he has some special talents needed in Mobile. He is the only doctor south of Birmingham, Alabama, who is qualified to do stem cell transplants obtained from the patient's body as well as other complex treatments. He has the reputation of being on the cutting edge in cancer research and diagnosis. He also treats the whole person and is very interested in receiving feedback on how well the patients are doing and how they can do better. Dr. Beeker facilitates communications between doctors, nurses, and staff concerning treatment for cancer patients. One professional who is not under the direct supervision of the Cancer Center, but who has worked with the patients' families, is impressed that Dr. Beeker has asked her to attend his patient visits and has asked her for suggestions on the treatment of the whole person.

Dr. Nicole Angel joined Dr. Meshad and Dr. Beeker in part because she was attracted by Dr. Meshad's reputation and his vision for the Center. She likes all her coworkers and likes the fact that they work as a team. In addition she states "the nurses are the best I have ever worked with." One experienced nurse stated "the doctors trust and respect the nurses, and the patients love the doctors."

The nurses are no small part of this successful team effort. Gail Havard was selected to be Patient Care Manager of the 17 nurses in the Cancer Center and is well received by her former team members. They can depend on her to help them when they are busy, and she is very supportive in working with the team. Gail serves as a mentor to the younger nurses, and as coach and advisor regarding diet and the handling of side effects from the high dose chemotherapy. Being a cancer survivor herself, she gives helpful tips, concerning living with cancer, not found in the cancer literature. Gail uses a participative style and consults with and involves her nurses in the decision making process for new hires. The doctors give Gail excellent evaluations. The outcome is a great nursing team that is both efficient (doing things right) and effective (doing the right things).

To summarize these observations made over a period of 6 months, through many conversations with doctors, nurses, and staff:

1. The Cancer Center's top priority is taking care of patients.

2. On a scale of 1 to 10 communication among nurses, between doctors and nurses, and team, the scores are 9 or 10.

3. The nurses know each job and are able to cover in emergencies or just to help out.

4. The nurses do not hesitate to approach any doctor if they need guidance or prescriptions.

5. Regular meetings are held with the doctors and nurses to discuss opportunities for better patient care.

6. A staff member is provided to interview all patients regarding care, treatment, positives, and any complaints.

Providence Hospital, through its affiliation with nationally established Ascension Health, has worked with Sacred Heart Hospital in Pensacola, Florida, to develop the Cancer Center's treatment program. Then the Cancer Center sought an affiliation with M.D. Anderson in Houston to give Mobile patients access to advice and treatment from the well-known "Andy" Center. The patients will be able to access a second opinion from M. D. Anderson and will have opportunities to participate in clinical trials being conducted at M.D. Anderson and seek records of cancer cases and treatments to determine their best options for treatment. The M.D. Anderson Cancer Center is one of 60 national cancer centers designated by the federal National Cancer Institute to receive additional research funding and to offer more advanced care to cancer patients. Within 24 hours of a local patient's diagnosis, the Cancer Center's physicians will be able to hold a conference with Anderson physicians to discuss the diagnosis and treatment. If a patient needs to go to Houston, his medical information will already be in the system, and the Cancer Center can facilitate the trip.[24]

The affiliation with Ascension Health, M.D. Anderson, Providence Hospital, and the Sacred Heart Cancer Center team is a giant step to bring better diagnosis, timely treatment, and care to cancer patients through effective teamwork.

Self-Managing Work Teams

Today management is undergoing a transformation, partly because of self-managing work teams that tend to operate by member consensus rather than management direction. Europe has been in the forefront of experimenting with self-managing work teams, but managers in Canada and the United States are increasingly using teams as building blocks in a corporate renaissance. Estimates suggest that over 500 U.S. manufacturing plants use some form of self-managing work teams. Illustrated here is the experience of a small southern plant.

> **A small parts plant is owned by a large corporation and employs 320 workers. Most of the self-managed work teams consist of eight to 12 members who select their own leader. At the next level are coordinators, who work with several teams. The coordinators report to an upper-management group called the support team. The coordinators operate primarily as developmental leaders. Their basic leadership practice is to encourage the teams to do things themselves—to be self-managing. Under this structure, there are productivity gains of significantly more than 20 percent.[25]**

8

Describe how to work with self-managing work groups.

Even companies that rely on an appointed leader make use of some empowerment concept of self-managed work teams. Michael Lloyd Odom who received IBM's Global Project Manager of the Year award is a prime example (only 25 worldwide received this award).

One of Mike's projects was running into some difficulty, and he was receiving a lot of negative feedback about one of the team members. Although this team member had good technical skills, he was insecure, and with the layoffs, he feared he was going to lose his job. If there was a problem on the project, he would point a finger and accuse other team members of being at fault. As a consequence, a lot of defensive behavior was taking place within the team.

Mike called the problem employee in, and, in essence, held up the mirror and gave him the feedback Mike was receiving from other team members. He also urged the employee to bring any issue or problem to the team as a whole and not to criticize individual members. He emphasized winning or losing *as a team*. He also called in other team members, one at a time, and asked for support in changing this employee's attitude and helping him become a team player. The problem employee was able to turn it around and the project was successful, meeting or exceeding objectives.[26]

Lessons Learned by Mike Odom

1. "Despite the first-time layoffs in IBM history in 1992 and 1993, IBM values its people as a key asset. It places a high priority on development of its people. I share the strong belief that people are your greatest asset."

2. "You need to understand the principles of managing a project."

3. "To be successful you have to build a good team; picking a good team is the first step."

4. "You need to be a good coach and work with people to help them understand what it takes to be successful."

5. "A key thing is to understand you are not alone. We are a lot smarter as a team than we are as individuals."

6. "Attitude can make all the difference in the world, not only from the standpoint of the team leader, but from the standpoint of all team contributors."

7. "A team leader management style can make the difference between a high-performing team and a team that just gets the job done."

8. "I think having good coaching skills is even more important than good technical skills in project management."

An American Company's Experience in India

Ron Moore has a B.S. degree in Industrial Management from the University of Alabama and an MBA from the University of Illinois. Although currently retired, he had a reputation as an outstanding team builder with Cummins in the United States. He became plant manager of a joint venture to build engines for the Indian market. Cummins has had a presence in India since 1963.

Some of the things Moore has learned about successful team work in the U.S. are as follows:

1. There has to be top management support and dedication.

2. The plant has to be organized for success and get people involved; there has to be structure and expectations focused on quality and production.

3. Initiate a process of job rotation so that everyone on the team knows all the jobs.

4. The improvement process has to be real and sustainable. Train and utilize a full-time facilitator to nurture and serve as a facilitator for the teams.

5. Give each team 30 minutes a week to talk and discuss issues or opportunities as a team.

Moore's plant was in eastern India, and although there are cultural differences, both India and the United States are democratic and the people reporting directly to Moore speak both Hindu and English. Although the people at the lower levels do not speak English, they are achievement oriented and want to succeed. The teams in India show success similar to that in the United States. As a result of that success, Ron spent 3 years as plant manager and then another 3 years as Division President of all of Cummins' operations in India.

CHAPTER REVIEW

1 **Identify the stages of group development.**

The focus turns to the development of work groups and the types—formal and informal—and stages of development. Formal groups are those formed by management. Informal groups are those that are not part of the official organizational structure and evolve out of employees' affiliation needs. An examination of synergy tells us that two or more people working together in a cooperative way can accomplish more than the sum of their independent efforts, and in order to achieve synergy, it is important for a group to move through all four stages of group development: forming, storming, norming, and performing.

2 **Compare the advantages and limitations of groups.**

The primary advantages of groups are that they (1) give members an opportunity for needs satisfaction and (2) may function more effectively than individuals. Some limitations are that they may (1) encourage social loafing, (2) diffuse responsibility, and (3) be less effective than individuals.

3 **Describe the variables that determine a group's effectiveness.**

Group effectiveness is determined by (1) group size, (2) member composition and roles, (3) norms, and (4) group cohesiveness.

IMPORTANT TERMS

adaptive challenges
external change forces
formal group
group
group cohesiveness
informal group
internal change forces
norms
organizational effectiveness
proactive (planned)
   process of change
self-managing work teams
synergy
team

④ Determine what is involved in team building.

Teams are successful if they have effective leadership at the top, effective recruitment of talented people, and an environment permitting good people to grow. The supervisor relies on group cooperation to establish the team's goals and to make decisions to achieve these goals.

⑤ Describe how to work with self-managing work groups.

Self-managing work teams have an impact on transforming organizations. Although some individuals and teams occasionally have difficulty coping with increased managerial responsibility, in general, employees in self-managing work teams are more satisfied, and production and quality show improvement. However, any company shifting to a participative team approach needs to ensure that the reward system is supportive or the move could backfire.

⑥ Describe what made team building successful at Resort Quest.

The leader at the top of the sales team recruited good people and created a climate for growth. This led to improvement in communication and achieved outstanding results.

⑦ Describe the GE approach.

GE found a transformational leader in Jack Welch, who greatly changed the culture of GE by dealing with the undesirable aspects of bureaucracy. To accomplish this, Welch and GE adopted such change initiatives as Work Out and Six Sigma, and changed the performance and reward system.

⑧ Describe what made team building successful at Sacred Heart Cancer Center, located at Providence Hospital.

Communication between doctors, nurses, and staff is very good. The nurses know each task and can cover for each other in emergencies. Doctors and nurses hold regular meetings to discuss how to provide better patient care.

QUESTIONS FOR REVIEW AND DISCUSSION

1. Is change as pervasive as the authors claim? Explain.

2. What are some of the primary reasons people resist change? What are some of the ways a team leader can ensure that change is accepted or at least not resisted?

3. What major changes in the last ten years have had considerable impact on organizations? Do these changes provide support for or make a case against the use of team building in organizations? Defend your position.

4. Compare and contrast formal groups and informal groups. Explain the importance of leadership in both types of groups.

5. If groups have so many limitations, why are they so popular?

6. Of the factors affecting group effectiveness, do you think there is any order of importance? If so, rank the factors 1 through 4 and explain why you chose to rank them in that order.

7. Identify conditions and organizations where self-managing work teams would *not* be the way to organize. Then identify conditions and organizations where self-managing work teams *would* be the way to organize.

8. How would you deal with an informal leader in a task force who seemed to be totally opposed to the group's objectives?

The 7 Habits of Highly Effective People

Skill Builder 9-1

Obtain Stephen Covey's book and review the seven habits he discusses. Review the story of Pete Mulry leader of the sales unit at Perdido Key for Resort Quest, and identify the habits utilized by Pete Mulry. Finally, examine your own way of functioning and note how many of the habits you are using. Are there some you could improve to increase your effectiveness? If so, how would you go about it?

Creating an Organizational Culture

Skill Builder 9-2

Assume you start your own business sometime after graduation. It can be any business of your choice that has a good opportunity for growth. After 10 years, the business has become quite successful and now employs 102 people.

1. Identify the business you have chosen.

2. Assume that initially you believed there is a positive correlation between having a strong culture and business success. Identify the specific actions you have consequently taken over a ten-year period to develop a strong organizational culture.

"Win as Much as You Can" Tally Sheet

Skill Builder 9-3

The detailed instructions for completing this exercise will be provided by your instructor. Basically, for 10 successive rounds you and your partner choose either an X or a Y on the scorecard. The payoff for each round depends on the pattern of choices made in your group. The payoff schedule is given at the bottom of the scorecard provided.

　　You are to confer with your partner in each round and make a joint decision. In rounds 5, 8, and 10, you and your partner may first confer with the other partnerships in your group before making your joint decision.

	Round	Your Choice (Circle)	Cluster's Pattern of Choices	Payoff	Balance
	1	X　Y	__X __Y		
	2	X　Y	__X __Y		
	3	X　Y	__X __Y		
	4	X　Y	__X __Y		
Bonus Round Payoff × 3	5	X　Y	__X __Y		
	6	X　Y	__X __Y		
	7	X　Y	__X __Y		
Bonus Round Payoff × 5	8	X　Y	__X __Y		
	9	X　Y	__X __Y		
Bonus Round Payoff × 10	10	X　Y	__X __Y		

Payoff Schedule

4 Xs:	Lose $1.00 each
3 Xs:	Win $1.00 each
1 Y:	Lose $3.00 each
2 Xs:	Win $2.00 each
2 Ys:	Lose $2.00 each
1 X:	Win $3.00
3 Ys:	Lose $1.00 each
4 Ys:	Win $1.00 each

If there is no objection to a modest wager, each partnership may want to place a bet, ranging from 10 cents to a dollar, on the outcome of the game. The winner collects the money at the end of the exercise.

Source: Adapted from an exercise by William Gellermann, Ph.D., in J. Pfeiffer and J. Jones, *Structured Experiences for Human Relations Training*, Vol. II, published by University Associates, 1974.

CASE

The Shift to Team Leadership

Case 9-1

group activity

You work for a company interested in initiating a team leadership training program, and your plant manager has appointed you to an ad hoc task force to study the feasibility of implementing such a program in your plant. In one of the company's other plants, however, supervisors resisted team leadership, giving the following reasons:

1. Lack of time

2. Leader mind-set ("It's the leader's job to make the major decisions.")

3. Lack of trust in employees

4. Lack of confidence in employees' abilities or judgment

5. Potential for major negative consequences ("too risky," "too costly")

6. Leader's belief that the leader knows best

7. Leader's concern that developed employees will erode leader's base of power ("They're not dependent anymore.")

8. Leader's perception that employees don't desire development ("They don't really care; they only want to do the minimum required.")

Instructions:

1. Divide the class into teams of three to six students.

2. Each team should brainstorm ways to overcome supervisors' predicted resistance to developmental leadership.

3. Each team is to outline an initial training agenda for the developmental leadership program to present to the plant manager.

4. The teams are to present their analysis and recommendations to the plant manager (represented by the instructor or a designated class member).

5. Vote with your class to determine which program appears to have the best chance of success. (*Note:* Students may not vote for their own team's program.)

Part **4**

Skill Development

© Ingram Publishing/Alamy © The Image Bank/Getty Images AP Photo/Justin Sullivan

10 Meetings and Facilitation Skills

AP Photo/Justin Sullivan

Expert facilitation can help any organization be more successful, whether military or civilian.

Meetings are places where minutes are taken, but hours often wasted.
—ANONYMOUS

"You know you're in a bad meeting when you look out the window on a sunny summer day wishing you were the person sitting on the mower."
—ANONYMOUS

Chuck Dansby, Facilitator "Extraordinaire"

Facilitators are being called on increasingly to help groups and organizations become more effective. One of the best facilitators around is Chuck Dansby, total quality management supervisor with the Navy's Public Works Center in the San Francisco Bay area. Some public works representatives have suggested that a number of awards received by the center could not have been achieved without expert facilitation. The most prestigious of these awards was the Meritorious Unit Commendation Award issued by the Secretary of Defense.

After graduating from Chattanooga State Technical Institute, Chuck spent 12 years in the Navy, ending his tour as a First-Class E6 Petty Officer. In 1988, he joined the Public Works Center, and in 1991 he was named the first quality improvement coordinator. During this time, the center was going through a period of expansion, and Chuck soon found himself operating a quality improvement department with a staff of seven people. Chuck and his team made, as their primary task, helping units and groups to permanently improve their processes. Even though Chuck and his group were in a staff capacity with no command authority, the following comments reveal why various managers called on him for assistance and what they said about him as a facilitator.

- Lt. Commander Bryan Johnson asked for Chuck's assistance when he needed to get the environmental group and construction group to work more effectively together. He states, "Chuck was very helpful in teaming with me to get key people to talk through issues and concerns and in getting the groups to cooperate in achieving objectives." He especially appreciated Chuck's ability to ask questions, getting people to brainstorm and rethink alternatives. Program Manager Steve Worthington echoes these observations and states, "Chuck is an excellent listener and is very good at getting people to 'see the big picture.'"

- Security Officer Mike Shanlas states, "He gets people to rethink their ways of operating and does it by asking questions. In this manner, people stay focused on the process, and they come out with improved ways of operating. People become indebted to him because he helps them to succeed; he does not set people up for failure."

- Contract Manager John Teetsov gives insight as to the ideal quality of a facilitator when he states that Chuck can come into an unfamiliar area and "not knowing the business, can extract the right ideas and answers. Very importantly, he does things in a manner so that the group feels that they are being helped rather than manipulated."

Learning Objectives

After reading and studying this chapter, you should be able to:

1. Explain how technology is enhancing meetings.

2. Explain the four basic purposes of meetings.

3. Differentiate between the leader-controlled approach and the group-centered approach used in meetings.

4. Identify the advantages and disadvantages of meetings.

5. Describe the actions that a supervisor can take before, during, and after a meeting to make it effective.

6. Explain the process of consensus decision making in meetings.

7. Define group facilitation.

8. Explain the role of group facilitator.

9. Differentiate between process consultation and other models of consultation.

10. Specifically identify what can be done to make teleconferencing more effective.

Chuck has attended a number of schools while with the Navy, but the one that had the greatest impact on him as a future effective facilitator was W. Edward Deming's 4-day workshop on continual quality improvement. Deming and the course taught Chuck the value of asking the right questions. Today, the Navy's Public Works Center is going through a process of downsizing. To carry out this process in a fair and humanistic manner, Chuck is being called on for his expert facilitation skills in meeting the Public Works Center's greatest challenge.

Source: Conversations and correspondence with Chuck Dansby and others with the Navy's Public World Center, San Francisco Bay area.

Today's supervisors increasingly are being called on to function effectively in meetings, both as leaders and participants. This requires that a supervisor understand certain fundamentals about small group behavior and have certain facilitation skills. The first part of this chapter addresses important information about meetings, including their purposes, approaches, and advantages and disadvantages, and some important principles of conducting effective meetings. The second part of the chapter addresses specifics of group facilitation, the skills attributed to Chuck Dansby in the chapter preview.

1 Explain how technology is enhancing meetings.

The Changing Technology of Meetings

There is no question that advances in technology are altering the meeting landscape for many organizations and supervisors. As greater numbers of employees work at sites some distance from their supervisor, and perhaps even at home, electronic meetings have become a necessary and valuable communication tool. Computers—including laptops and computer software—cell phones, and videoconference equipment have broadened the communication media available. Meetings conducted through e-mail or Web-based computer software are becoming standard for many organizations and will increase as these tools become more simple and cost effective.

Technology changes are also serving as support tools for face-to-face meetings. PowerPoint software enables high-quality visual presentation; other packages support participant participation through voting, immediate electronic tabulation, and display of results. Another enables electronic display of a working agenda, can record the disposition of each agenda item discussed, including action taken, names of persons responsible for action, dates for completion, and so on. These are visually displayed for all at the meeting to see. McKinsey and Company and Allstate use software packages at their meetings to allow participants'

Meetings have become an organizational fact of life.

© Tom McCarthy/PhotoEdit, Inc.

spoken comments at a meeting to be instantly displayed on a computer hooked up to a large overhead projector. Resulting discussion/comments can be identified, linked or edited onscreen, and serve as an immediate basis for meeting minutes.[1] High-tech support tools will continue to impact meeting effectiveness, for all types of meetings, be all members physically present in the same room or whether they be electronically linked.

For the vast majority of managers and supervisors, the face-to-face meeting remains the setting that is most utilized. While it is the setting that forms the backdrop of this chapter, most principles presented apply to electronically-linked settings also.

Purposes of Meetings

Meetings in today's organizations are a fact of organizational life. Estimates are that time spent in meetings ranges from several hours to several days weekly, depending on the organization and position.[2] Depending on the study, estimates suggest there may be as many as 20 million meetings held daily in U.S. organizations.[3] At 3M, for instance, the average manager reports spending 1 to $1^1/_2$ days weekly in meetings. Unfortunately, 3M managers judge up to half of this time as wasted![4] So much time is devoted to meetings that some organizations, including Nestlé USA, have established a policy of scheduling 1 day weekly when no meetings are held so as to allow personnel time to "get their work done."[5] Indeed, we have all experienced meetings that are unproductive because irrelevant information is presented, key people are missing, meeting leadership is poor, and nothing meaningful is achieved. To supervisors and most organization members, though, meetings are indeed a fact of organizational life. At Intel, meetings are considered so important that every employee completes an in-house course on effective meetings. In fact, former chief executive officer (CEO) Andy Grove was himself a course instructor.[6]

Exhibit 10-1 shows that meetings generally are called to achieve one or more of the following purposes: (1) to give information, (2) to exchange information, (3) to obtain facts about a particular situation, and (4) to solve a problem.

EXHIBIT **10-1**

Purposes of Meetings

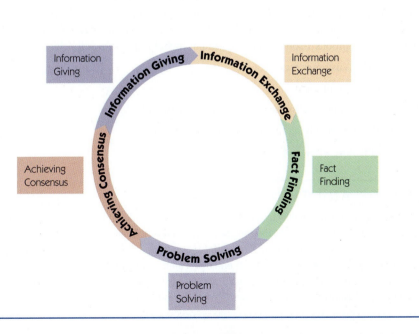

Information Giving

The **information-giving meeting** is held to make announcements of new programs and policies or to update information on the present ones. Generally, it is closely controlled by the leader or those who are called on to provide information to the group, frequently by means of committee reports. There tends to be little feedback from group members unless they have questions to ask or points to clarify about the information presented. Normally this is the easiest type of meeting to conduct, since its format is highly structured and lends itself well to large groups.

Information Exchange

The **information exchange meeting** is called to obtain information from group members and to allow them to provide information to one another.

> At the *Boston Herald,* a daily 11 A.M. meeting of editorial, advertising, circulation, and production superintendents is held to present a status report on the next day's paper. This daily exchange ensures that key managers are knowledgeable about issues that might affect them during the day and helps them get the paper out smoothly.[7]

Fact Finding

Only relevant facts about a problem or situation should be sought in a **fact finding meeting.** The meeting leader focuses not on finding solutions but rather on understanding the problem or situation. A supervisor might begin such a meeting as follows: "I called this meeting to discuss the high cost overruns we've been experiencing during the past month. I want to find out as much as I can about your perspective on the causes of this situation. Later, we can consider some steps we can take to reduce these costs." Once the facts have been uncovered, the supervisor will have a better understanding of the situation.

Problem Solving

Typically, the **problem-solving meeting** combines the other purposes of information giving, information exchange, and fact finding. Considered the most challenging of the meeting types, this type of meeting is held to identify the major elements of a problem, to discuss and evaluate alternative solutions, and ultimately to make a decision as to the proper action to take. Topics of problem-solving meetings might include any of the following:

1. Improving customer service
2. Reducing absenteeism
3. Determining production schedules or job assignments
4. Finding and remedying the causes of project delays
5. Implementing a new policy in the best way

✔ STOP AND THINK

Lois Kelly, founder and principal of Meaning Maker, a major marketing consulting firm, and former senior vice-president of one of the largest public relations firms in the world, says, "Meetings have become 'let me show you my PowerPoint presentation.' The best thing that can happen in corporate America is that there is a ban on PowerPoint. To me a meeting is a place where there is interaction and something gets decided and learned. I have sat through so many meetings where people just go through their slides."[8] What do you think about Kelly's assertion?

Approaches Used at Meetings

The interactions that take place at meetings vary greatly. Much depends on the purpose of the meeting and the meeting leader's personal style. One of two approaches is generally used in conducting meetings: (1) a leader-controlled approach or (2) a group-centered approach.

Leader-Controlled Approach

The **leader-controlled approach,** in which the leader clearly runs the show, is often used at information-giving meetings or when the large size of the group prohibits an open flow of information among members. The leader opens the meeting, makes announcements, or calls on those who have information to present. If anyone in the group has questions to ask or comments to make, he or she addresses them to the leader. The leader may answer the questions or bounce them to someone else. Exhibit 10-2 illustrates this approach. Should a stranger walk in after the meeting has begun, she or he would have no difficulty identifying who is in charge.

One advantage of this approach is that it is generally easier on the leader, because the fairly rigid structure means that there are few surprises. Another advantage is that this approach allows a large amount of material to be covered quickly. It also lends itself to larger groups.

William Pagonis, chief of operations for Sears, Roebuck, requires attendees to stand during his regular briefings. Pagonis boasts that he can cover more material in a 15-minute stand-up meeting than he could in a 2-hour seated version.[9]

An obvious disadvantage of the leader-controlled approach is that it discourages a free flow of information. The fact that comments from the group must go through the leader means that spontaneous, direct remarks may go unmade. The creativity that results from the "piggybacking" of ideas is stifled. Another disadvantage is that members have no real opportunity to get sensitive and emotional issues out in the open and blow off steam.

3 Differentiate between the leader-controlled approach and the group-centered approach used in meetings.

leader–controlled approach Used at meetings of large groups in which the leader clearly runs the show and the open flow of information is impeded.

EXHIBIT **10-2**

Interaction in the Leader-Controlled Approach

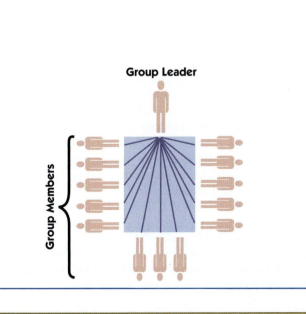

Group Leader

Group Members

EXHIBIT 10-3

Interaction in the Group
Centered Approach

Leader

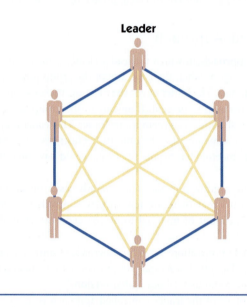

Group-Centered Approach

In a **group-centered approach,** group members interact more freely with one another, as shown in Exhibit 10-3. The meeting leader does not dominate the discussions; neither does he or she simply sit back and allow the group to formulate its own direction. Quite the contrary; the leader uses facilitation skills to keep the meeting moving by directing/redirecting focus, asking for clarification, making sure that everyone speaks, summarizing the group's position, testing for consensus, moving the group to the next issue, and so on.

The advantages of the group-centered approach stem from the greater interaction that occurs at the meeting. First, it results in a better understanding of members' viewpoints. Second, if the purpose of the meeting is to solve a problem, the free flow of information may contribute to a better decision. Third, when people can express their emotions or disagreements, they feel better.

One disadvantage of the group-centered approach is that the meeting takes up a great deal more time than does the leader-controlled approach. Another disadvantage is that the increased interaction among members means that the leader's skills are tested more severely. The leader must determine when to move the discussion of a topic along. He or she must make sure that everyone gets a chance to speak and that discussions stay close to the subject. Also, since the leader must deal with diverse personalities, he or she must know how to handle emotions that may arise. A third disadvantage is that this approach is not well suited to large groups because of its interpersonal nature.

Which Approach Should You Use?

Which approach is better for you, as a supervisor, to use? There is no best answer to this question. The answer depends on such factors as the meeting's purpose, the size of the group, the ability of the group members, the amount of time allowed for the meeting, your skills, and the subjects to be discussed. Remember that you can shift from one approach to the other at a single meeting, depending on the nature of the items on your agenda.

> Yoshi Tanabe's approach at meetings suits his purposes. Take Wednesday's meeting, for instance. The first item on his agenda was the new vacation scheduling procedure. At this point Tanabe was the expert in the room. He made a 3- to 4-minute presentation on the new procedure and then fielded questions from the group.
>
> The next topic on the agenda was the need to develop and submit to higher management a plan for the department's participation in the company's 10-year anniversary open house for members of the community. Tanabe used a more open approach for the discussion of this topic. It took up about 20 minutes, with much interaction among the group. Within this time, Tanabe and the group came up with a plan for the department's role during the open house.

Advantages and Disadvantages of Meetings

4 Identify the advantages and disadvantages of meetings.

Some supervisors despise attending and conducting meetings. They prefer to communicate on a one-to-one basis. But because meetings are a fact of life for supervisors, it is appropriate at this point to consider the advantages and disadvantages of meetings. Then, in the remainder of the chapter, we will provide pointers on how to make meetings more effective.

Advantages of Meetings

Meetings save time, ensure that the supervisor's communications are consistent, and permit a formal exchange of important information and ideas. Let's explore how these advantages work.

Save Time. Suppose you, as a supervisor, have a group of employees whose jobs are *not* performed in the same work area (as is the case with outside sales, delivery services, maintenance, or patient care). In order to communicate on a one-on-one basis, you would have to move from one location to another during the work period. By having a meeting, you can save a great deal of your personal time that would otherwise be spent tracking down each of your employees.

Moreover, when minutes of the meeting are distributed to members, they serve as a permanent record of what has occurred or been agreed on. In this way, they save time that might otherwise be needed to clarify or repeat what was said.

Ensure Consistency of Information. Meetings provide an opportunity for all present to hear the same message. If you communicate separately with each of your team members, you may present the information more effectively to some than to others. Also, some of your team members may ask questions or make comments that help clarify the communication or add a slightly different flavor to it. With one-on-one contacts, the grapevine goes to work, especially if there is a long lapse of time between when you talk with the first team member and when you talk with the last team member.

Permit Formal Exchange of Information. Sometimes individual members of a work group have information that *must* be shared with all the other group members. This is particularly true when a problem confronts the work group. In a meeting, a comment made by one member frequently triggers an important idea in another member. This exchange can lead to solutions that might not have been thought of by any one member.

The degree of formality inherent in a meeting can be used to advantage by a supervisor. For example, suppose that you, a supervisor, have been told by the plant manager that production must be increased by 15 percent over the next year—otherwise the plant will be closed. Presenting this information to your work group in a meeting conveys the seriousness of the situation and dramatizes the impact of the message.

Disadvantages of Meetings

Meetings may result in watered-down decisions, may not be cost effective, and may be too impersonal. Let's see how these disadvantages arise.

Many Are Unnecessary. Many supervisors claim that they waste too much time in unnecessary meetings. Yet they themselves hold many meetings perceived by their members as unnecessary. Meetings interrupt members' work day, may take them away from higher priority tasks, and compete with other activities, such as deadline-driven tasks, and can add significantly to job stress. Is the structure provided by a meeting essential to achieving your purpose? Could it be achieved as effectively through other means, such as by telephone, e-mail, or memo? Do all members of your group need the information or just a few? At Intel, most conference rooms are lined with posters reminding those present to adhere to guidelines for effective meetings. Among the posters, one asks, "Is This Meeting Necessary?"[10]

May Not Be Cost Effective. Meetings are more expensive than most people realize. When employees are attending meetings, they are not doing their normal jobs. Suppose ten people, with an average annual salary of $60,000, attend a 1-hour meeting. The cost of the meeting includes not only their salaries for that hour, but also costs for vacations, holidays, sick leave, medical insurance, Social Security, travel time, and so on. As shown in Exhibit 10-4, the cost of the meeting is $438. The meeting must therefore provide information important enough to justify the cost associated with it. And Exhibit 10-4 does not include the costs associated with time spent planning for the meeting or traveling.

May Water Down Decisions. Unless a meeting is properly conducted and its members are committed to effectiveness, the decisions made at the meeting may simply reflect the *average* input of members, rather than the ideas of the best members. Sometimes opinions voiced by the group's brightest or best-informed members may not be accepted by the majority. At other times, knowledgeable members may suppress their own disagreements simply for the sake of harmony.

May Become Too Impersonal. Meetings may not allow the personal interaction required for many sensitive issues. On a one-on-one basis, employees may communicate readily to their supervisor. But because a meeting involves a more formal setting with many people present, some employees will be reluctant to speak up.

EXHIBIT 10-4

Meetings Cost!

Many managers overlook the cost of meetings. The following table approximates hourly costs for employees at four salary levels. The hourly rates include only salary and normal benefits. They do *not* include costs of meeting planning and preparation time, travel time/costs, follow-up costs, and the like.

Salary/Benefit Hourly Meeting Costs

Salary	Number of Participants				
	25	10	8	6	4
$100,000	$1,825	$730	$584	$438	$292
80,000	1,460	584	467	350	234
60,000	1,095	438	350	263	175
40,000	730	292	234	175	117

Making Meetings Effective

This section presents some ideas that should help you conduct more effective meetings. Some of the actions discussed should be performed *before* the meeting, some *during* the meeting, and some *after* the meeting. As a prelude to this section, we invite you to complete Exhibit 10-5.

Factors to Consider Before the Meeting

Important premeeting steps will ensure an effective meeting; (1) have a clear purpose and (2) preplan the meeting.

5 Describe the actions that a supervisor can take before, during, and after a meeting to make it effective.

EXHIBIT 10-5

Scoring Your Meeting Leadership

How would you rate yourself as a meeting leader? For each of the 12 items below, circle the response that comes closest to how you view your own meeting conduct. If you do not conduct meetings, assess the meeting leadership of your own boss, or another leader of meetings that you normally attend.

	Strongly Agree	Agree	Disagree	Strongly Disagree
1. I assess whether a meeting is the most effective use of everyone's time before calling it.	1	2	3	4
2. I have in mind a specific objective for each meeting that I call.	1	2	3	4
3. I plan in advance the details of my meetings, such as who should attend, materials to distribute, meeting place, etc.	1	2	3	4
4. Where time allows, I plan and distribute an agenda in advance of my meetings.	1	2	3	4
5. My meetings stick to the published agenda without too much straying.	1	2	3	4
6. I do not monopolize discussion in meetings.	1	2	3	4
7. I maintain balanced participation among all meeting members.	1	2	3	4
8. I encourage discussion of all sides of issues without showing my bias.	1	2	3	4
9. Participants would say that I keep a meeting moving toward its objectives.	1	2	3	4
10. At the end of a meeting, I summarize the key ideas presented/actions taken.	1	2	3	4
11. I maintain and circulate meeting minutes.	1	2	3	4
12. I follow up in a timely manner on actions taken during meetings.	1	2	3	4

Scoring: Sum your circled responses.

Score of 12–15 = Excellent
            16–19 = Very Good
            20–24 = Good
            25–29 = Average
            30–48 = Below Average

Have a Clear Purpose. Assuming that a meeting is necessary, you should have a clear purpose for it. Otherwise you will waste everyone's time, including your own. Earlier, you noted that meetings can serve any of several purposes: (1) to give information, (2) to exchange information, (3) to obtain facts, and (4) to solve a problem. Having a clear purpose responds to the question that participants ask themselves: "Why are we here?" Having a clear purpose also enables other premeeting plans to be developed to support the purpose.

✔ STOP AND THINK

What are the pros and cons of having regular weekly meetings at an established time?

· ·

Preplan the Meeting. Many meetings are doomed from the start because of poor initial planning. Perhaps another group has reserved the conference room, for example. Or the bulbs in the overhead projector are burned out. Or the people present at the meeting weren't notified that they should bring certain needed information. Or the leader simply hasn't done his or her homework! Proper planning requires you to do some work before the meeting begins. Such work might include the following:

1. Make sure that the people who are to attend the meeting have adequate advance notice (unless it's an emergency meeting).

Prior to a meeting, check to see if the visual aides you intend to use function properly.

Photodisc/Getty Images

2. Make sure that key people will be able to attend.

3. Develop and distribute copies of the meeting agenda in advance. This will enable people to bring essential documents with them or to gather information that may prove helpful. See Exhibit 10-6 for agenda planning insights.

EXHIBIT **10-6**

Agenda Planning

Having a well-planned agenda is a critical starting point toward effective meetings. Many organizations have provided meeting "templates," which serve as guides for creating effective agendas. The template may reflect the components of a well-planned agenda and provide an actual physical design that can be used. The sample agenda below illustrates the details of a well-planned agenda for a fact-finding and decision-making meeting.

Sample Agenda

Date:	March 5, 2005	Location:	3rd floor conference room
Meeting called by:	Beth Shapiro	Attendees:	See distribution list
Facilitator:	Beth Shapiro Alice Chang	Please read:	Attached memo from Beth on expectations, deadlines, etc.
Note taker:	Bill Smith	Please bring:	Memo, So. Am. Strategy Plan

Objectives

- Review past efforts at launching products in South America
- Identify problems or obstacles to product introduction
- Determine possible approaches to overcoming problems
- Assign tasks and establish deadlines

Agenda

Time	Topic	Responsibility
8:30–8:40	• Introductions and review of agenda	Beth Shapiro
8:40–9:00	• Review of past launches in So. America (presentation)	Mario Cisneros
9:00–9:45	• Potential problems and solutions (brainstorming)	Alice Chang
9:45–10:00	• Assignment of action items	Beth Shapiro

Additional Information: This meeting will be the first of two. For this one, the goal is to surface all ideas, so each person should come prepared to contribute. At the end of the brainstorming session, we will decide as a group which solutions to pursue and will assign tasks to the appropriate team members.

Note that the agenda indicates three specific people other than the meeting leader who will have a formal role in the meeting: (1) a note taker (the basis for meeting minutes), (2) a presenter other than the leader, and (3) a resource person who will serve as facilitator for the brainstorming session.

Here are some other helpful agenda planning insights:

1. If possible, distribute an agenda several days before a meeting.

2. Allow an opportunity for members to add topics to the agenda.

3. Indicate the time allotted for agenda topics. This will help time management during the meeting.

4. Where the list of agenda topics is long, begin with routine items.

5. In longer meetings, controversial topics should be addressed sufficiently early in the agenda while group energy is high. Placing controversial items at the end of an agenda when discussion time is limited may give the impression that you are manipulating the group.

6. Build a break into meetings that last longer than 90 minutes. This will allow members to network, address other work-related items, and use the restroom as needed.

Source: Sample Agenda adapted from Deborah J. Barrett, **Leadership Communication**: (New York: McGraw-Hill/Irwin, 2006, p. 216. Other information from http://www.3com/meetingnetwork/reaingroom/meetingguide_anatomy.html)

4. Let people know in advance if they will be expected to provide information or make a report.

5. Check to see that the meeting room is arranged as you desire and that the visual aids you intend to use function properly.

6. Form a general idea of how long the meeting should last. You may want to indicate this to those who will attend. It is easier to predict the length of information-giving and information exchange meetings, however, than that of meetings held for fact finding or problem solving.

Factors to Consider During the Meeting

When the meeting time arrives, you can take a number of steps to help ensure the meeting's success. Among these are (1) starting the meeting on time, (2) designating someone to take minutes, (3) clarifying your objectives and expectations, (4) keeping the meeting on the desired topic, (5) encouraging participation, and (6) making sure there is closure.

Start on Time. Eli Mina, author of *The Complete Handbook of Business Meetings*, says that starting on time is a cardinal meeting principle.[11] There may be occasions when one or two employees do not arrive on time for a meeting. To avoid unnecessary delays, the supervisor should begin the meeting as scheduled. If a supervisor consistently waits for late arrivals, attendees may get the message that it's okay to be late, and successive meetings will start later and later. Such delays waste the time of those who arrive promptly.

Designate Someone to Take Minutes. Especially for information exchange, fact-finding, and problem-solving meetings, it is helpful to have someone record the important points discussed and agreed on at the meeting. These points are then outlined in a document called the **minutes** of the meeting, copies of which are distributed after the meeting. If no one takes minutes, those attending the meeting would be well advised to take notes on their own.

minutes A written record of the important points discussed and agreed on at a meeting.

Clarify Your Expectations. Earlier in this chapter we stated that a meeting was generally called to serve one or more of the following purposes: to give information, to exchange information, to obtain facts, or to solve a problem and make a decision. As the leader of the meeting, make sure that you introduce each item on the agenda by stating your purpose for including it. For example:

1. "I'd like to *give you some information* about . . . ." [information giving]

2. "Attached to the agenda that I sent each of you was the memo from Human Resources regarding the new benefits. I'd like to *get your reactions* to these new benefits." [information exchange]

3. "The purpose of this meeting is to review the recent changes in our billing policy and their impact on collections. Your input will give me an idea of the success or failure of our new billing policy. In your experience, what has been *the effect of* the billing policy?" [fact finding]

4. "I'd like to get your ideas on what we can do to show our department in its best light during our open house. After hearing your ideas, *I'll put together our plan.*" [problem solving and decision making]

5. "The branch manager wants to know what our department's position is on switching to a week of four 10-hour days, as we discussed in our meeting last week. I can go any way you want to on this. *What do we want to do?*" [decision making]

In each example, the supervisor spelled out and clarified his or her expectations regarding an item on the agenda. Take special notice of examples 4 and 5, in which the supervisor carefully outlined the role of the group in the decision-making process.

Provide Leadership. Ineffective leadership ruins many well-prepared meetings. The supervisor must be prepared to demonstrate leadership in the following ways:

1. *Keep the meeting moving.* Don't allow a meeting to drag on and on, and don't stray too far from the topic being discussed. If people wander from the topic, you might say, "We seem to have drifted from our major issue. Let's go back . . ."

2. *See to it that most or all members contribute to the discussion.* Don't allow one or two people to dominate the meeting. If this happens, call on others first for their comments or reactions.

3. *Summarize the apparent position of the group from time to time.* You might say, "Do I read the group properly? You seem to be saying that . . ."

4. *Address various problems related to participant behavior.* Exhibit 10-7 shows how to deal with some inappropriate behaviors.

Encourage Two-Way Communication. In most meetings the leader's job is to facilitate openness and interaction among group members. This is particularly important when the leader uses the group-centered approach. The leader must be an alert listener and be skilled in helping individuals in the group to express themselves. A key skill is the ability to use questions to involve individual members or the entire group in the communication process. Exhibit 10-8 shows some questioning techniques that can be used by the meeting leader.

Work to Achieve Consensus Decisions

Given the current trend toward participative management, a particularly important concept is that of consensus decision making.

Consensus is frequently misunderstood. It does not mean that members **agree** with the decision; it means that they agree to **accept** it, even though they may not personally favor it. The following example illustrates consensus.

> Charles Evans couldn't win support from other team members regarding his position on the team's recommendation about a company parking lot policy. Evans favored a process that allocated preferred parking places for key personnel in the company—some by seniority, some by position. Most other team members favored a process that had no preferred parking.
>
> The team leader stressed the need for a consensus decision that all members could accept. Charles spoke openly about why he felt his approach was best, responded to questions raised by other team members about his position, and raised many questions about their position. The team leader had given him extra time to survey how other companies in the community handled the situation. Finally, after all issues seemed to have been fully discussed, the team leader said, "I sense that after our full examination of the issue, while not unanimous, the group favors a system that will operate as an open, first-come, first-served system. Is this correct?" No one dissented. She continued, "That, then, is what we will send to the president. Charles, thank you for helping us to more fully explore all aspects of the system that we're recommending. Can you accept the team decision?" Evans reflected, "It was a fair process. I presented my views; they just think differently on this one." He said, "Yes, I can support it, even though I disagree with it." "Good," said the team leader, "We have reached consensus."

Consensus is more difficult when members have personal stakes in decision outcomes and when there is much member diversity. Such is often the case with cross-functional teams. Consensus is not always achievable; some members openly state their intent not to support the group's decision. Perhaps they feel that others do not listen meaningfully to dissenting views or that attacks are made on personality rather than position. At times, the

consensus The acceptance by all members of the decision reached.

6 Explain the process of consensus decision making in meetings.

EXHIBIT 10-7

Type	Behavior	Suggested Response
Hostile	"It'll never work."	"How do others feel about this?"
	"That's a typical engineering viewpoint."	"You may be right, but let's review the facts and evidence."
		"It seems we have a different perspective on the details, but we agree on the principles."
Know-It-All	"I have worked on this project more than anyone else in this room. . . ."	"Let's review the facts." (Avoid theory and speculation.)
	"I have a Ph.D. in economics, and . . ."	"Another noted authority on this subject has said . . ."
Loudmouth	Constantly blurts out ideas and questions.	Interrupt: "Can you summarize your main point/question for us?"
	Tries to dominate the meeting.	"I appreciate your comments, but we should also hear from others."
		"Interesting point. Help us understand how it relates to our subject."
Interrupter	Starts talking before others are finished.	"Wait a minute, Jim. Let's let Jane finish what she was saying."
Interpreter	"What John is really trying to say is . . ."	"Let's let John speak for himself. Go ahead, John, finish what you were saying."
	"John would respond to that question by saying . . ."	"John, how would you respond?"
		"John, do you think Jim correctly understood what you said?"
Gossiper	"Isn't there a regulation that you can't . . . ?"	"Can anyone here verify this?"
	"I thought I heard the V.P. of Finance say . . ."	"Let's not take the time of the group until we can verify the accuracy of this information."
Whisperer	Carries on irritating side conversation.	Walk up close to the guilty parties and make eye contact. Stop talking and establish dead silence. Politely ask the whisperers to wait until the meeting is over to finish their conversation.
Silent Distractor	Reads newspapers, rolls eyes, shakes head, fidgets.	Ask questions to determine the distractor's level of interest, support, and expertise. Try to build an alliance by drawing him or her into the discussion. If that doesn't work, discuss your concerns with the individual during a break.
Busy-Busy	Ducks in and out of the meeting repeatedly, taking messages, dealing with crises.	Schedule the presentation away from the office. Check with common offenders before the meeting to make sure interruptions during the planned time will be minimal.
Latecomer	Comes late and interrupts the meeting.	Announce an odd time (8:46) for the meeting to emphasize the necessity for promptness. Make it inconvenient for latecomers to find a seat, and stop talking until they do. Establish a "latecomers' kitty" for refreshments.
Early Leaver	Announces, with regret, the need to leave for another important activity.	Before starting, announce the ending time and ask if anyone has a scheduling conflict.

Source: "Ten Deadly Sins of Poor Presentation" from *Presentation Plus* by David Peoples, pp. 52–54. Copyright © 1988. John Wiley and Sons Inc., New York. Reprinted by permission of publisher.

EXHIBIT 10-8

Questioning Techniques
for Leaders of Meetings

- *Clarifying or elaborating on a point made by someone.*
  Example: "Are you saying that . . . ?" or "Alice, would you mind giving us a little more detail about the situation? When did it happen?"
- *Calling on someone who is reluctant to talk.*
  Example: "Pete, you've been through more maintenance shutdowns than most of us. What do you think about all of this?"
- *Getting specific facts.*
  Example: "Exactly what were our production figures last month? Can someone give us those figures?"
- *Examining possible alternatives.*
  Example: "What are the pros and cons of converting to the new system?" or "Would we be able to keep up our quality under the new system?" or "What would happen if . . . ?"
- *Initiating group discussion.*
  Example: "What is your reaction to this new vacation policy?" or "Does this new policy affect anyone here?"
- *Obtaining more participation from the group.*
  Example: "We've heard two alternatives. Are there any more?"
- *Guiding the meeting tactfully in certain directions.*
  Example: "We seem to have already discussed this issue pretty thoroughly and agreed on a course of action. Is everyone ready to move on?"
- *"Testing the water" as to the group's feeling.*
  Example: "What would be your reaction if we went to the system we've been discussing? Would you support it?"

team decision is hurried, the dissenter feels too strongly pressured, or takes the position, "If it's not my way, I won't support it, period." Sometimes members will appear to accept the group's decision, but work to sabotage it or divorce themselves from it once the group leaves the meeting room.

Consensus is more likely when a group's members:

1. Openly state their true feelings, ideas, and disagreements.

2. Examine their different views fully.

3. Try to understand underlying reasons behind their differences on an issue.

4. Actively listen to and seek to understand other members' positions.

5. Focus on issues rather than on personalities.

6. Avoid actions that polarize members or lock them into positions. This may be the case with voting or taking sides, especially in early stages of discussion.

Many companies teach skills in consensus decision making to all their employees and team leaders. At Saturn, for example, team members go through a minimum of 92 hours of training in problem-solving and people skills, teaching team members to reach a consensus point they call "70 percent comfortable, but 100 percent supportive."[12] Following discussion of alternatives (or causes), it is sometimes helpful in gaining consensus to determine a group's priorities, especially when several alternatives are available. One approach is the "dot plan." Alternatives are recorded on a flip chart or board. Each team member is given the same number of adhesive dots—say five—in three colors. One color represents high priority, another medium priority,

Information exchange meetings between domestic and overseas representatives of international companies can greatly enhance the success of their products and services.

and another low priority. Members then post their assigned dots to the different items. Some teams allow only one dot from one person on any one item, others may allow more passionate advocates to assign more than one. Following posting, a team can easily visualize how its members feel about alternatives. A variant is the "10-4" method used by teams at Bowater Carolina, the large newsprint manufacturer. Under this option, instead of colors, each member may assign a total of 10 points to items but no more than four to a single item. This achieves the same purpose as the dot listings. An example is shown in Exhibit 10-9.

Get Closure on Items Discussed. At many meetings that the authors have observed, an item will be discussed, but then the leader will go on to the next item on the agenda, leaving everyone to wonder what has been concluded.

closure Successfully accomplishing the objective for a given item on the agenda.

Achieving **closure** means reaching a conclusion with respect to a given agenda item that has been discussed. In the following example, notice how a department head achieves closure for a particular agenda item.

> **Martha Briem, a department head, presented comparative information showing that her department had a quality-rejection rate that was 10 percent higher than that of other departments in the company. She asked for her supervisors' input about possible actions. The discussion lasted about 25 minutes. Then she asked each supervisor to come up with a plan for improving product quality in his or her area and to make a 5-minute presentation at a meeting to be scheduled in 2 weeks.**

Item for 10-4 Team Scoring: "Possible Ways to Increase Teamwork in Our Department"

a) Change incentive system so that it reflects part individual, part department results

   3, 1, 2, 1 = 7

b) Include teamwork as an item on performance evaluation system

   2, 3, 1, 3, 4, 4, 3, 4, 3, 4 = 31

c) Develop system for recognizing when someone has been a good team player

   4, 4, 4, 4, 3, 4, 4, 4, 2, 4, 3 = 40

d) Include teamwork related behaviors as part of everyone's job description

   2, 2, 2, 3, 1, 1, 2, 2 = 15

e) Cross train members so that they better understand all jobs in the department

   4, 1, 2, 3, 2, 2, 1, 1 = 16

f) Rotate positions occasionally so that members perform each other's jobs

   2 = 2

Key: letter = alternative   numbers = each member's allocation of 10 points; maximum of four points can be awarded to a single alternative.

Factors to Consider After the Meeting

Even though the meeting is over, your work isn't finished. Follow up by making sure that the minutes (if any) are distributed and that any important decisions or responsibilities assigned to specific individuals are carried out.

Distribute Copies of the Minutes. Distributing copies of the minutes of the meeting is important for the following reasons:

1. The minutes serve as a permanent record of what has been agreed on and committed to at the meeting.

2. The minutes identify topics on the agenda that have not been dealt with completely or that have been suggested for a future meeting.

3. The minutes permit a smooth transition, allowing you to take up where you left off at the next meeting.

Follow Up on Decisions Made. It is crucial that the supervisor follow up on any actions that were agreed on and any decisions that were made during the meeting. The follow-up may consist of personal observations or visits. It may also involve reports that keep the supervisor informed of progress regarding the agreed-on commitments.

> **"Oh, I make it a point to follow up on my meetings," stated Luis Santos. "We have a pretty active crowd who say what they think. If I feel that someone has really gotten ticked off or hurt by what was brought up at the meeting, I'll make it a point to try to smooth things out on a one-on-one basis. I also go one-on-one with somebody who said something I wanted to follow up on if I didn't feel the meeting was the place to do it."**

More and more organizations are using facilitators to help make their meetings more effective, and they are training team leaders in group facilitation. We examine this important area next.

What is Group Facilitation?

7 Define group facilitation.

Group facilitation is a process of intervening to help a group improve in goal setting, action planning, problem solving, conflict management, and decision making in order to increase the group's effectiveness. Although an outside facilitator can be helpful, as we saw in the chapter preview, the ideal is for managers and supervisors to gain facilitation skills and utilize shared leadership in carrying out the process.

group facilitation The process of intervening to help a group improve in goal setting, action planning, problem solving, conflict management, and decision making in order to increase the group's effectiveness.

As organizations cope with the world of increasingly rapid change, the need for facilitation to improve their effectiveness increases. Examples run the gamut from empowering employees, developing shared visions, and creating self-managing work teams to changing to a more participative organizational culture. It is hard to imagine successful change efforts in the areas of total quality management, reengineering, partnering, mergers, or downsizing without some form of facilitation.

Role of the Facilitator

8 Explain the role of group facilitator.

In our discussion of group dynamics and conducting meetings, you were introduced to facilitation challenges and suggestions for handling inappropriate behavior at meetings. A good foundation for being an effective facilitator requires experience and knowledge, not only of dynamics of the group but also of decision making, problem solving, communications, motivation, and leadership. In addition, the core skills shown in Exhibit 10-10 are essential.

Process Consultation

9 Differentiate between process consultation and other models of consultation.

Among the many roles facilitators must play is that of process consultant. In fact, process consultation skills are identified as being among the core skills of an effective facilitator. This role involves sitting in on team or task force meetings, observing the group's process, and intervening, if needed, to help the group function more effectively. Skill Builder 10-4 is designed to help you better understand when and how to intervene. Increasingly, facilitators are being used in major change efforts of total quality management, reengineering, and partnering. In essence, a facilitator becomes a consultant. The following sections describe three consultation models, and we draw extensively from author/consultant Edgar Schein in comparing them.

It is important to keep in mind that the effective facilitator is primarily a helper and wants the group to achieve long-term development and continuous process improvement. Exhibit 10-11 highlights this emphasis by showing the distinction between basic facilitation and developmental facilitation.

EXHIBIT 10-10

Core Skills for the Effective Facilitator

- Communication skills—listening and asking the right questions.
- Leadership skills—participative management and developmental leadership.
- Problem-solving skills.
- Group dynamics skills.
- Conceptual and analytical skills.
- Conflict management skills—principled negotiation.
- Process consultation skills—intervention and diagnostic insights.

EXHIBIT 10-11

Basic and Developmental Facilitation

Characteristic	Basic Facilitation	Developmental Facilitation
Group objective	Solve a substantive problem or problems.	Achieve group goals along with solving substantive problems while learning to improve processes.
Facilitator role	Help group temporarily improve its processes.	Help group permanently improve its processes.
	Take primary responsibility for managing the group's processes.	Help group assume primary responsibility for achieving goals and managing processes.
Outcome for group	Emphasize dependence on facilitator for solving future problems.	Reduce dependence on facilitator for solving future problems.

Source: Roger M. Schwartz, *The Skilled Facilitator: Practical Wisdom for Developing Effective Groups,* Table 1.1, p. 7, adapted as submitted. Copyright © 1994 Jossey-Bass Inc., Publishers. Reprinted by permission of John Wiley and Sons, Inc.

Purchase-of-Expertise Model. The most widely used form of consultation is the purchase of expert information. The organization, or someone within the organization, decides there is a need to call on an expert to help solve a problem or add a service. For example, someone to initiate an organizational attitude survey or introduce a performance evaluation system may be called. An individual who specializes in conducting marketing surveys or initiating

An effective facilitator is primarily a helper.

© BananaStock/Alamy

total quality improvement programs may also be needed. Schein points out that this model frequently produces a low rate of implementation of the consultant's recommendations. Further, this model is based on many assumptions that have to be met for it to succeed, and therein lies its weakness. The assumptions are as follows:

1. The manager has correctly diagnosed the organization's needs.

2. The manager has correctly communicated those needs to the consultant.

3. The manager has accurately assessed the capabilities of the consultant to provide the information or the service.

4. The manager has considered the consequences of having the consultant gather such information and is willing to implement changes that may be recommended by the consultant.

Another weakness is the fact that the model is based on a "tell and sell" method by the expert and there is no "ownership" or commitment by the client.

Doctor–Patient Model. A relationship between a consultant and an organization can be likened to that of a doctor and a patient. When an organization suffers symptoms such as declining sales or profits, low morale, or high turnover, a consultant may be brought in to check these problems. After the "checkup," the consultant prescribes what the organization needs to do to "get well" again. As Schein points out, this model places a great deal of power in the hands of the consultant in that he or she makes a diagnosis and also prescribes a treatment. The success of the model then depends on the following:

1. The initial client has accurately identified which person, group, or department is "sick."

2. The "patient" has revealed accurate information.

3. The "patient" accepts the prescription that is, does what the "doctor" recommends.[13]

process consultation
A consultation model that involves others in making a joint diagnosis of the problem and eventually provides others with the skills and tools to make their own diagnoses.

Process Consultation Model. In contrast to the other models, **process consultation** involves others in making a joint diagnosis and eventually provides others with the skills and tools to make their own diagnoses. Also, even though the consultant may be an expert in the area of consultation, he or she refrains from solving the problem for the client. The emphasis is on facilitating the process so the client learns problem-solving skills. Although the facilitator may make suggestions or raise questions that broaden the diagnosis or develop more alternatives, the client makes the ultimate decision and develops the action plan or remedy. A summary of the underlying assumptions of the process consultation model follows:

1. Clients/managers often do not know what is wrong and need special help in diagnosing what their problems actually are.

2. Clients/managers often do not know what kinds of help consultants can give to them; they need to be informed of what kinds of help to seek.

3. Most clients/managers have a constructive intent to improve things, but they need help in identifying what to improve and how to improve it.

4. Most organizations can be more effective if they learn to diagnose and manage their own strengths and weaknesses.

5. A consultant probably cannot, without exhaustive and time-consuming study or actual participation in the client organization, learn enough about the culture of the organization to suggest reliable new courses of action. Therefore, unless remedies are worked out jointly with members of the organization, who do know what will and will not work in their culture, such remedies are likely either to be wrong or to be resisted because they come from an outsider.

6. Unless the client/manager learns to see the problem for himself or herself and thinks through the remedy, he or she will not be willing or able to implement the solution. More important, he or she will not learn how to fix such problems should they recur. The process consultant can provide alternatives, but decision making about such alternatives must remain in the hands of the client.

7. The essential function of process consultation, or PC, is to teach the skills of how to diagnose and fix organizational problems. In this way, the client is able to continue on his or her own to improve the organization.[14]

How do facilitators determine whether or not they are being effective? One group that facilitates partnering workshops always asks the participants to evaluate both the effectiveness of the workshop and the facilitator(s). The following comments demonstrate that the facilitator provided good process consultation skills.

"The facilitators did an excellent job in serving as catalysts for dialogue."

"The facilitator took the time to help each person or group with problem solving and with staying focused."

"The techniques of the workshop leader improved communications and helped us to solve our problems in a collaborative manner."

"The facilitator provided good, constructive, visionary thinking and identified personal and group blind spots."

"The facilitator was collaborative, but firm enough to keep things focused and keep things moving."

"The facilitator's people skills were exceptional. He was genuinely interested in the individual and group needs, which made the workshop most effective."

"The facilitator achieved the goal of allowing *us* to solve our problems."

"The facilitator kept us focused without inhibiting the interaction of the participants."[15]

In two of the skill builders at the end of the chapter, you will have an opportunity to develop your process consultation and facilitation skills. Again, more and more team leaders (supervisors) are asked to play facilitator roles that previously were the domain of outside consultants.

Facilitating Teleconferencing

Sometimes because of the expense of bringing people from distant locations to a meeting, a facilitator needs to set up or make arrangements for a teleconference. Susan Fox, executive director of the Society of American Archivists, has developed some excellent tips for facilitators in both profit and nonprofit organizations. They are presented in Exhibit 10-12.

10 Specifically identify what can be done to make teleconferencing more effective.

Leadership Strategies: The Facilitation Company

The International Association of Facilitators (IAF), a nonprofit organization, provides opportunities for members (facilitators) to meet and exchange ideas to improve competencies in helping groups and organizations. The membership grew from 75 founding members in 1994 to over 1,300 members in 2002.

The authors' experiences in working with organizations in partnering, team building, and organization development is that having effective internal facilitators is critical for success.

EXHIBIT 10-12

Preparation

1. *Decide who will be in on the call.* The first thing you need to consider is who should participate in the call. Usually conference calls address a specific issue that requires discussion leading to consensus. Think about including members who hold information relevant to the topic at hand. This may or may not include the obvious participants. You will also want to include key representatives from constituencies potentially affected by the outcomes resulting from the call.

2. *Establish a clear set of desired outcomes.* Ask yourself these kinds of questions:
   - Is this call necessary?
   - Can the issue wait?
   - If not, what needs to occur as a result of our discussion?
   - How quickly?
   - Who should be involved?
   - What will be the chief result?

3. *Create and distribute an agenda.* Once you have the rationale and desired outcome firmly established, develop an agenda and either fax or mail it to participants well in advance of the call, if at all possible. Remember to include clear instructions about how to dial into the call.

   All meetings, regardless of how they are convened, require an agenda. Don't try to cover too much ground. Keep the topic tightly focused, communicate your desired outcomes, and give each major agenda item a time limit. Cover minor items up front so that you can quickly move to items of substance. Conclude the agenda with next steps, which can be agreed on at the conclusion of the call.

Facilitation

Remember that a conference call is a cross between a face-to-face meeting and a telephone conversation. You will therefore need to draw on a number of skills. For example, similar to a face-to-face meeting, greet participants as they "check in," and engage those who are waiting for the quorum in small talk. Hold logistical and substantive topics until everyone is on line.

1. *Designate a timekeeper and note taker.* Once you have a quorum, ask one participant to be the timekeeper and another to take notes. You will, of course, take notes yourself, but having additional help will keep you focused on facilitation rather than dictation.

2. *Ask members to identify themselves each time they speak.* Because participants can't actually see one another, self-identification ultimately makes the discussion flow more easily. If a member forgets to identify himself or herself, take it upon yourself to make the identification as quickly and as unobtrusively as possible.

3. *Call on the silent.* Lack of visual clues can easily result in people stepping in on each other's conversation or, more likely, in one or two members dominating the discussion. It's up to you to provide balance and to call on those who remain quiet. You will need to ascertain whether their silence is the result of agreement, disagreement, or shyness.

4. *Poll each member.* It's up to you to solicit full participation. If you take a vote, register each participant. In fact, poll each member each time you reach a decision point. Bottom line, never assume.

5. *Watch the clock.* As in any meeting, work with your timekeeper. Groups naturally gravitate toward less difficult issues, which can quickly waste valuable time. Keep the discussion moving toward substantive issues and outcomes.

6. *Consider alternatives for difficult issues.* You may discover that the more difficult issues cannot be resolved on the telephone. If the group cannot reach consensus or engages in a heated disagreement, it may well be that a conference call is not the best communication mechanism for that particular issue. Acknowledge that fact and either give members time to reflect and eventually convene a second call or, if necessary, find another way to meet and work things out.

7. *Review assignments and close positively.* End the call on a positive note, then reiterate the tasks and deadlines and the individuals assigned to carry them out. Congratulate your colleagues on their fine work, and thank them for their time.

Continued

EXHIBIT **10-12**

continued

Follow-Up

As soon as the call is complete, prepare the to-do list with the deadlines and designees and send it out immediately. Within the week, if not sooner, gather your notes from the call and summarize the proceedings for all participants. Most of us tend to quickly forget what we say and promise to do, so this point can't be emphasized strongly enough.

It also helps to solicit feedback about how participants viewed the usefulness of the call. Did it accomplish its aims? Are there areas in which you can improve your facilitation skills? Most of us are unaware of our own telephone habits, and this kind of feedback can be enormously helpful.

Source: Tips for Facilitating Teleconferencing, Copyright © 1999. Reprinted with permission of Gale, Cengage Learning, www.cengage.com/permissions.

The effective facilitators, in most instances, come from the supervisor/team leader ranks and are closest to where the real work of the organization takes place, whether it is constructing a building, making a product, or providing a service.

Thus, there are a number of firms that either provide training for facilitators who then return to their own organizations or provide facilitator consultants who work with organizations in-house. One of these firms that is impressive in its philosophy, knowledge, and skills is Leadership Strategies, Inc.

The founder and managing director of the company is Michael Wilkinson, a high-honors graduate of Dartmouth College with a B.A. in mathematics and social sciences. After graduation, Michael spent 8 years with the information technology division of Ernst and Young's Management Consulting Group before starting Leadership Strategies 10 years ago. Following is a brief summary of Michael's many accomplishments.

Courtesy of Leadership Strategies

Michael Wilkinson, founder and manager of Leadership Strategies, is the author of a workshop that focuses on the ten fundamental principles of facilitation, as seen in Exhibit 10-12.

Michael is the founder and managing director of Leadership Strategies. While active in client assignments, his primary focus is setting the direction for the company, developing new products, and establishing strategic relationships.

He is the primary author of the firm's highly acclaimed course, The Effective Facilitator, a 3-day intensive workshop that teaches the ten fundamental principles for facilitation groups in strategic planning, process improvement, issues resolution, etc.

Michael is a much-sought-after consultant and trainer. He has worked on strategic planning, analysis, and training assignments for some of the country's largest organizations, including BellSouth, Bethlehem Steel, Centers for Disease Control, Data General, Georgia Pacific, KPMG Peat Marwick, Sears, Roebuck, Southwestern Bell, Southern Natural Gas, and Unisys Corporation.

Source: Adapted from http://www.facilitationcompany.com/michaelw.htm, accessed January 2003.

Michael's associates give him high marks in his role as managing director. One describes him as a dynamic, incredible leader and motivator who is the epitome of a successful entrepreneur. Although the company's home base is in Atlanta, Georgia, it operates throughout the world and has offices in London and Australia. According to another associate, Michael is a genius at building a business, having strong organization skills and being very intuitive. Michael's leadership style is very effective in that he really delegates, allowing each person to flourish and maximize his or her skills.

Michael himself says he has been blessed with two special gifts or talents. One, he has strong analytical skills, and two, he has the ability to follow a process orientation in leading people to understand how to do something better. Moreover, he believes that fundamental principles are repeatable when using process consultation to reach goals.

Michael cites as an example a commission he is working with to end homelessness in Atlanta within 10 years. He believes that by following a process approach and following certain principles, the commission will be successful in this endeavor.[16]

✔ STOP AND THINK

Do you think the Atlanta commission with Michael as a facilitator can achieve its goal? Why or why not?

∙∙

Exhibit 10-13 identifies the characteristics of Leadership Strategies' facilitators and also the characteristics and best practices they teach in their courses. A profile of one of the firm's facilitators, Susan Nurre, follows.

Susan Nurre is a senior manager with Leadership Strategies, Inc., a firm specializing in teaching leadership training classes in group facilitation, consulting, strategic planning, project planning, team building, and management excellence. The organization also provides clients with professional facilitators to lead sessions in strategic planning, process improvement, information need analysis, and issue resolution.

As a senior manager, Ms. Nurre works in the role of trainer, facilitator, and consultant by interacting directly with such clients as American Airlines, Southwestern Bell, Computer Sciences Corporation, and Tandy Corporation.

For over 20 years, Ms. Nurre has worked with clients to determine their needs from systems requirements to organizational change readiness. In addition to facilitation, Ms. Nurre has experience in assessing organizational culture, soliciting customer feedback, developing and implementing communication strategies, managing projects and team members, and developing and delivering training. Her varied experiences have

EXHIBIT 10-13

The Facilitators at
Leadership Strategies, Inc.

At Leadership Strategies, Inc. (LSI), our philosophy is to model the techniques and best practices that we teach in our courses. With their dynamic style and extensive facilitation experience, it's no surprise that our facilitators are consistently rated Excellent by over 95 percent of attendees. Our facilitators are carefully selected on the basis of the target characteristics that separate the great facilitators from those that are merely competent. We also specifically look for facilitators who bring a broad range of experiences to the table to meet the needs of clients in a variety of business industries as well as in the nonprofit sector. Our facilitators' backgrounds include Information Technology, Business Management, Education, Consulting, Human Resources, Training, and Customer Service. Here are the characteristics that make our facilitators stand out:

1. **Enjoy working with people** and have a genuine desire to help people feel good about themselves and achieve their desired results.
2. **Think quickly and logically,** and have the ability to analyze comments, understand how they relate to the topic, and develop appropriate responses.
3. **Communicate clearly and expressively** by making specific, concise points, and using appropriate levels of energy to build excitement and enthusiasm.
4. **Practice active listening** skills by engaging a speaker, listening attentively, and asking probing questions.
5. **Convey warmth to others** by using smiles, praise, and gestures in one-on-one and group interactions.
6. **Demonstrate self-confidence and leadership** when working with others, and are the people others look to for direction and counsel.
7. **Have a process orientation,** with an interest in finding methods to improve the way things are done, looking beyond the narrow focus of a job to the greater scope of the organization.

Once selected, our facilitators go through an in-depth certification process involving practice sessions, structured one-on-one feedback, and supervised facilitation experience. This rigorous approach helps us to ensure that every facilitator delivers a consistent, high-quality session every time. In addition, LSI facilitators adhere to a set of guiding principles focused on creating a positive environment and delivering superior service to our customers.

Source: From "About Our Facilitators." Reprinted by permission of Leadership Strategies—The Facilitation Company. Visit us on the web at: www.leadstrat.com.

Courtesy of Leadership Strategies

Susan Nurre has a successful career in facilitation and leadership training.

added to her ability to consult with project sponsors and stakeholders to best determine the impact of business change on their organization and developing the interventions required to minimize that impact.

A Certified Professional Facilitator, Ms. Nurre is active in the International Association of Facilitators and the Southwest Facilitators Network. In 1993, she created and continues to publish *The Facilitator*, a quarterly professional magazine.

Source: Adapted from http://www.facilitationcompany.com/snurre.htm, accessed January 2003.

CHAPTER REVIEW

1 **Explain how technology is enhancing meetings.**

Electronic technology is enhancing meetings dramatically. As greater numbers of employees work at sites distant from their supervisor, electronic technology, such as cell phones, videoconferences, and the computer have become valuable meeting tools. Moreover, face to face meetings are being enhanced through various computer software meeting-support programs, which include on-the-scene display of discussion points made, voting by members, actions taken, and on-the-scene meeting minutes.

2 **Explain the four basic purposes of meetings.**

Meetings can serve four general purposes: (1) to give information, (2) to exchange information, (3) to find facts, and (4) to solve problems. Group consensus is an important process in many meetings, especially in problem-solving meetings where decisions are made by the group.

IMPORTANT TERMS

closure
consensus
fact-finding meeting
group-centered approach
group facilitation
information exchange
    meeting
information-giving meeting
leader-controlled approach
minutes
problem-solving meeting
process consultation

3 **Differentiate between the leader-controlled approach and the group-centered approach used in meetings.**

With a leader-controlled approach to a meeting, the leader clearly runs the show and conducts a very structured meeting. The advantages of this approach are that it lends itself better to established time frames, has more predictable outcomes, and is more appropriate for large groups. With a group-centered approach, there is more interaction among members. This approach permits greater understanding, and the exchange of ideas is more apt to generate creative solutions.

4 **Identify the advantages and disadvantages of meetings.**

The typical supervisor frequently must conduct meetings with his or her work group. Meetings have the following advantages over one-on-one contacts: (1) they save time, (2) they allow all present to hear exactly the same message, and (3) they lend a degree of formality. The disadvantages of meetings are that (1) they may result in watered-down decisions, (2) they may not be cost effective, and (3) they may become too impersonal.

5 **Describe the actions that a supervisor can take before, during, and after a meeting to make it effective.**

A number of actions can help to make meetings more effective. *Before* the meeting, the supervisor should determine whether a meeting is necessary, establish a clear purpose for the meeting, and plan it. *During* the meeting, the supervisor should start promptly, designate someone to take minutes, clarify his or her expectations, provide leadership, encounter two-way communication, and see to it that closure is achieved on the items discussed. *After* the meeting, minutes of the meeting should be distributed, and agreed-on commitments should be followed up.

6 **Explain the process of consensus decision making in meetings.**
Group consensus means that members agree to accept the decision made by the group, even though not all of them may agree with it.

7 **Define group facilitation.**
Group facilitation is a process of intervening to help a group improve in goal setting, action planning, problem solving, conflict management, and decision making in order to increase the group's effectiveness.

8 **Explain the role of group facilitator.**
Among the many roles facilitators play is that of process consultant. In carrying out that role, the effective facilitator is primarily a helper and wants the group to achieve long-term development and continuous process improvement.

9 **Differentiate between process consultation and other models of consultation.**
In contrast to other approaches, process consultation involves others and eventually provides others with the skills to diagnose and solve their own problems.

10 **Specifically identify what can be done to make teleconferencing more effective.**
Teleconferencing can be made more effective by following these guidelines:

1. Include as participants those with information concerning the topic of the call and those affected by the outcome.

2. Establish desired outcomes and keep the call short.

3. Since the participants cannot see each other, involve all members and ask each to identify himself or herself before speaking; poll each member to ensure full participation.

4. Consider alternative solutions for difficult issues and the possibility of another call or another way to meet.

5. Review the tasks and deadlines and the individuals responsible for working on them.

6. Finally, close on a positive note.

QUESTIONS FOR REVIEW AND DISCUSSION

1. Explain some of the ways that technology is impacting meetings.

2. Name the four basic purposes of meetings. Of these, which generally requires the most skill on the part of the leader?

3. Differentiate between the leader-controlled approach and the group-centered approach used in meetings.

4. What are the advantages and disadvantages of meetings?

5. Describe the actions that a supervisor can take before, during, and after a meeting to make it effective.

6. Discuss the purpose of group facilitation and the role of the facilitator.

7. How does process consultation differ from other models of consultation?

Achieving Group Consensus

group activity

The table below lists the qualities most valued in a leader. These qualities appear in no special order and do not represent an all-inclusive listing. You will be asked to rank these according to your personal view of what is most important to what is least important.

Quality	Rank
a. intelligent	____
b. caring	____
c. dependable	____
d. inspiring	____
e. mature	____
f. forward-looking	____
g. courageous	____
h. honest	____
i. fair-minded	____
j. competent	____

Instructions:

1. Complete your personal ranking of the ten qualities listed. Rate as "1" your most important, "2" your second most important, and so on, with "10" being the least important.

2. Break into groups of seven to nine persons. The group will select a leader and two observers, who will follow additional instructions outlined below.

3. As a group, reread the discussion on the consensus process.

4. *The allotted time for this instruction is 30 minutes.* As a group, your leader will conduct a team meeting in which the team uses a consensus approach that results in a team ranking of the items. Make sure you fully explore differences of opinion among your members about the way your team will proceed to develop its ranking, as well as selection of what the team feels is #1, #2, etc. Try to avoid voting, which tends to restrict discussion of an issue. Make sure that all members "buy into" decisions of the group. *It is not necessary that you complete the ranking in the time permitted for the task.* It is more important that you reach consensus on that which you *do* achieve rather than totally complete the ranking of items. If you complete half or more of the items in the time allowed, the likelihood is that you have sacrificed consensus to do so.

Instructions to the leader:

Your team will have 30 minutes to work on the task. Remember, do not forge ahead without full discussion of all relevant issues. The consensus process takes time; make sure differences are fully explored and consensus achieved before moving along to the next issue. Your effectiveness as a leader and as a team is not based on how many items you rank, but rather the extent to which you effectively lead your group toward consensus.

Instructions to observers:

1. Your task is to observe the meeting, taking notes. Evaluate (a) the effectiveness of the leader's behavior in conducting the meeting and (b) the extent to which consensus was actually achieved by the group. Complete the leader assessment scale below.

		Good	Fair	Weak
a.	Clearly established the objective of the meeting.	_____	_____	_____
b.	Kept discussion relevant.	_____	_____	_____
c.	Made sure everyone participated.	_____	_____	_____
d.	Used questioning techniques effectively.	_____	_____	_____
e.	Kept the meeting moving along.	_____	_____	_____
f.	Helped the group fully examine issues.	_____	_____	_____
g.	Summarized key points thoroughly.	_____	_____	_____
h.	Achieved closure for each item on the agenda.	_____	_____	_____
i.	Maintained "consensus" approach within the group.	_____	_____	_____

2. After the instructor calls time, or when the meeting is complete, whichever comes first, report your observations to the group. (Keep the report to five minutes.)

Effective/Ineffective Meetings Survey

Skill Builder 10-2

Likely you have been a participant in numerous meetings, perhaps in your job, or as a member of a social group or student organization. Some of these have been effective, others less so.

Instructions

1. Identify a specific meeting in which you have participated that you would consider highly effective. Make a written list of the reasons why you considered the meeting "highly effective."

2. Identify a meeting in which you participated that you would consider "highly ineffective." Make a written list of the causes why you considered the meeting "highly ineffective."

3. From teams of 3-5 persons, compare your lists with those of other members and discuss the two lists.

4. Select a spokesperson to present to the overall group a summary of your team's lists and discuss.

Meeting Facilitation Challenges

Skill Builder 10-3

Assume that you are the supervisor leading your work team in addressing an important issue. Each situation below represents an incident that crops up during the meeting.

1. Two of your team members, Jean Morton and Taylor Lester, are hard-nosed people who often compete for attention. They often argue with each other as a way to get the spotlight. This meeting you're conducting is no exception. After stating the problem and requesting alternatives from the group, you have a good idea who the first two to

make comments will be. Morton gives the first alternative. Lester gives his alternative, which is, of course, quite different from Morton's. Morton mounts a counterattack by defending her own proposal. As she speaks, you can see by Lester's body language that he is preparing his own counteroffensive.

2. One of your team members, Ernie Statler, is especially long winded. He always stretches what could be said in 10 seconds to a minute or more. The meeting has now lasted about 10 minutes and Statler has already spoken four or five times. You can see the boredom on everyone's face as he interrupts another member and gets set to talk again. You must intervene.

3. As your meeting moves along, Ann Stiles and Harry Curran have become distracting. They have whispered a few comments to each other, and you have noted some other team members' raised eyebrows and glances cast in their direction. Harold Rodriguez, one of your quiet, softspoken members, has the floor as Stiles and Curran continue their private conversation. It's time you intervened.

4. It's now about 35 minutes into the meeting, and someone in the group makes a comment about the upcoming big football game tomorrow between the state's two large college archrivals. Several members chime in with comments. Your group has some strong fans pulling for each school; several members are going as a group to see the game. They would obviously rather talk football than the subject at hand. You need to have them refocus.

5. At the start of the meeting you told the group that you could live with any decision they made. It's now about 45 minutes into the meeting and your team has fully discussed four workable alternatives. You feel one alternative is the best, but you can truly live with any of the alternatives offered. You say, "Well, we seem to have done a good job discussing the alternatives; let's see if we can now make a decision." At that point, one of the members asks which of the alternatives you favor.

6. Based on the team's responses, considerable time has been spent discussing the pros and cons and the best choice of the four. It appears that seven of your nine members favor alternative 3. The other two members favor alternatives 2 and 4. You feel that everyone has had a chance to speak up and hear each other out. You say, "It appears that, having heard from everyone on this issue, this group strongly favors alternative 3. Is this alternative workable with everyone?" Rasheed Khan, one of the dissenting members, states, "No, it's not okay with me. I'm firmly convinced it's not workable. I refuse to vote for something I don't think is best."

Instructions:
1. Indicate how you would handle each situation by writing down the exact words you would say.

2. In groups of four to six students, compare your responses to each situation. Select one for each situation that your group feels is best and read it to the rest of the class.

Skill Builder 10-4   ### Developing Skills as a Facilitator/Consultant

group activity

In preparation for this exercise, reread the section on process consultation.

Keep in mind that the primary role of the facilitator/consultant is that of helper to an individual, a group, or an organization.

Instructions:

1. Each member of the class is to identify a problem or issue on which he or she needs help. It may be that you need help improving your study habits and grades. It may be that you are having a problem at work with your boss or with someone who works with you or for you. The guideline is that it must be a real problem or issue and that you "own" the problem.

2. The class is to be divided into groups of three. Each member of the trio will take turns being the client and receiving help from the other two members. The client will start the process by stating the issue or problem and will have 20 minutes to receive help.

3. The other two members will ask questions to clarify, expand on, and sharpen the diagnosis. In carrying out the questioning, the facilitators will play an active listening role and ask questions that not only help them in understanding the problem, but also aid the individual being helped to better understand. Examples of such questions would be: "When did you first start having this problem? Can you expand on the history of your relationship with this coworker?"

4. Ask the client what steps, if any, have been initiated to solve the problem.

5. Move into a joint problem-solving framework where all three of you engage in brainstorming ideas on how to deal with the problem.

6. Put together an action plan using the best ideas on specific actions the client can take to solve the problem.

Facilitator Training

Skill Builder 10-5

group activity

Assume you are in training to become an external facilitator/consultant and are faced with the following situations:

Your Task

First you are to choose the correct answer from the three alternatives and write the letter (a, b, c) that corresponds to the answer provided under the heading "Your Answer." You will have 10 minutes to complete the task.

Team Task

You will be assigned to a small team of trainees to develop a team answer. Although the team will arrive at its answer through consensus, remember that consensus does not always mean unanimity. It means everyone has an opportunity to have his or her views considered before a choice is made. You will have 30 minutes to complete the team task.

How would you handle the following situations if you were the facilitator?

1. You are the facilitator at a workshop with 35 participants. The participants have agreed on a common set of goals, and they have also identified five issues they need to deal with to achieve their goals. Five ad hoc subgroups of seven participants have been assigned to develop a plan to solve one of the top issues. The first step in the problem-solving process is to clearly state the problem. The members of one of the subgroups approach you as facilitator and state that they are having difficulty defining the problem and need your help.

   a. Tell them to do the best they can. (Your logic is that people learn from experience—success as well as failures.)

   b. Ask a few questions, and then write your version of the problem on the flipchart.

c. Suggest that each person write a statement of the problem and then record all of them on the flipchart to see if one stands out or if there is a central theme.

Your Answer _____ Team's Answer _____ Expert's Answer _____

2. You are facilitating a 2-day workshop between the Navy and a contractor regarding the environmental clean-up progress of a Pacific island. Several former Navy personnel now work for the contractor. Toward the end of the first day, during a break, a public works civilian from the Navy approaches you and expresses a concern that a former Navy captain, who now works for the contractor, always begins a suggestion or recommendation with the following comment: "When I was Captain of XYZ installation and we were faced with this situation, we did so and so."

a. Do nothing.

b. As facilitator, talk with the former captain and level with him about the concern of a member of the Navy's group. Suggest he make recommendations without mentioning his former leadership positions in the Navy.

c. As facilitator, mention the problem to the former captain's boss with the contractor. Leave it to him to decide whether or not he wants to say anything to the former captain.

Your Answer _____ Team's Answer _____ Expert's Answer _____

3. You are facilitator for a group of 25 participants of two organizations who must work together to complete a major task such as building a dam. The two groups are having difficulties. As facilitator, you have taken them through a process where the group has identified and prioritized five issues they need to work on to ensure they will achieve their goals. After this task is completed, the group takes a short break before they start work on the priority issues. During the break, a key manager of one of the organizations comes to you and says that unless the lack of trust issue is addressed, very little progress will be made in resolving the other issues.

a. Tell the key manager to trust the process and that by working on the five prioritized issues, team building will occur and trust will develop.

b. Prior to reconvening, have a short meeting between four of the leaders, two from each organization, to gain their opinion on adding the trust issue to the list. Have the key manager present his case to them, and you, as facilitator, point out that developing trust is an important factor in successful teamwork and task accomplishment.

c. When the group reconvenes, you as facilitator add the trust issue to the list to be worked on.

Your Answer _____ Team's Answer _____ Expert's Answer _____

4. Assume you are facilitating a quarterly improvement meeting between representatives from the production and maintenance departments of a chemical plant. There are seven participants: four from production and three from maintenance. The meeting has become bogged down and is not making progress because of the strong views of two participants—one from production and one from maintenance. It appears to you that although both views have merit, neither participant is hearing what the other is saying, and each is strictly focusing on his or her own viewpoint.

a. Intervene and remind the participants of the time constraints and suggest they move on to something else.

b. Intervene and request to hear the views of the other participants.

c. Intervene by asking the production representative to summarize the maintenance representative's viewpoint to be sure the viewpoint was understood correctly by the production representative; then reverse the process.

Your Answer   *Team's Answer*   *Expert's Answer*

_____   _____   _____

5. Assume you are the facilitator/consultant for two medical firms located in a U.S. city with a population of 300,000 people. The firms are considering a merger; there are a number of win–win outcomes from such a merger (lower costs, better offices and facilities, more complete medical coverage, etc.). You are facilitating an initial, exploratory meeting with eight doctors, four from each firm. After 3 hours, the meeting is running into difficulties, despite several interventions by you to get things on track. The problem is that one of the doctors in the first firm is, from a leadership standpoint, very Theory X oriented and is strongly against the merger. It is obvious he basically does not trust the other doctors, and by voice tone and verbal and nonverbal actions, he is behaving in a very autocratic manner.

a. Take a long break and have each group meet for an hour to decide if they really want to pursue the merger.

b. Intervene by giving a short theory input on Theory X and Theory Y management philosophies, and for this discussion, suggest that a participative shared leadership style should prevail.

c. Intervene by having all eight members respond on a 3 × 5 card to the following instructions:

   ■ Evaluate on a five-point scale how well we've done in focusing on substantive issues and ways to achieve our joint goals of better patient care, service, and profits.

   ■ Evaluate on a five-point scale how well we have done in carrying out good group dynamics of listening, supporting good ideas, sharing leadership, and differing without being disagreeable.

   ■ Post the results and use as a basis for the group to discuss how to improve the group's functioning and progress.

Your Answer   *Team's Answer*   *Expert's Answer*

_____   _____   _____

6. Assume you are the facilitator for a national sales organization that is changing its culture to a team approach from that of an individual entrepreneurial approach. The theme of the 2-day workshop is "working together to grow stronger."

   After the national sales director reviews the overall company objectives and history, each regional team prioritizes issues, problems, and opportunities that they need to address to achieve overall company objectives. Next, each regional team works on an action plan involving the top-ranked item.

   As facilitator, you visit the four regional breakout rooms and are quite pleased that three of the four regional teams are progressing quite well and demonstrating most of the characteristics of an effective team—shared leadership, good participation and listening, etc. Unfortunately, the last regional team is having difficulty. After observing for some time, it is apparent the problem lies with the regional manager. He is doing 80 percent of the talking, cutting people off in midsentence who offer suggestions, and forcing his own viewpoint.

a. As facilitator, suggest that they brainstorm ideas and write them on the flipchart before evaluating them.

b. As facilitator, take over the leadership of the group by "playing traffic cop" and directing the flow of who talks when.

c. Privately provide some coaching to the regional manager on how the session could be more productive.

Your Answer	Team's Answer	Expert's Answer
_____	_____	_____

7. This situation is a bonus question and provides an opportunity to find an answer comparable to, or even better than, the expert's answer. The instructor, with class input, will decide if a bonus is deserved.

You have been asked as an outside facilitator to assist the chairperson of an appointed task force involving a department of the federal government. This department is moving into a new federal building under design and construction. The task force has been charged to determine such interior design questions as size and type of offices, paint color, size and number of conference rooms, and so forth.

The task force consists of ten government employees and has had two meetings. There was no progress made in the meetings, however, primarily because of two disruptive task force members. One of the disruptive individuals is very skeptical about any new, innovative ideas and is playing the role of devil's advocate (challenger), to the point of causing frustration and unproductive meeting progress. The other individual obviously has no interest in being on the committee and has done paper work during both meetings.

What advice would you give the meeting chairperson regarding how to handle this situation?

Your Answer	Team's Answer	Expert's Answer
_____	_____	_____

Source: This skill builder was developed by the Synergistic Group, 6 Schwaemmle Drive, Mobile, AL 36608.

CASE

The Quiet Meeting

CASE 10-1

Debbie Ronson, sales supervisor, was just opening a meeting she had called for members of her department. Debbie did most of the talking for the first 5 minutes, recounting her group's performance over the past week. Then she asked, "Are there any questions?" No one responded.

Debbie then changed subjects. "As you know, in 2 weeks we'll be going to a new format for scheduling our calls. This was outlined in the memo from the vice-president, copies of which I sent to each of you. This is going to alter your calling schedules and significantly change the way we've been doing things. I have some ideas on how we can best work into this new system. But before getting into that, I'd like to see if anyone here has any ideas . . . [pause]. Anyone care to contribute anything?" No one in the group responded.

Debbie continued, "Well, here's what I think we should do . . . ." She then spent eight minutes outlining her plan.

After the meeting was over, Debbie discussed it with one of her fellow supervisors. "I don't know what it is," she said, "but I can never get my people to say much at meetings. I try to give them a chance, but I always end up doing most of the talking. It seems they're either shy or disinterested, but I really don't know if that's the reason or not. I just wish they'd contribute their ideas."

Instructions:

1. What might be some reasons for participants not saying much at Debbie's meetings?

2. Assume that you are a facilitation consultant. What advice would you give Debbie for encouraging participation in future meetings?

11 Coaching for Higher Performance

© The Image Bank/Getty Images

As a coach, a supervisor helps employees reach their highest level of achievement.

We grow because we struggle; we learn and overcome.
—R. C. ALLEN

The mediocre teacher tells; the good teacher explains; the superior teacher demonstrates. The great teacher inspires.
—WILLIAM A. WARD

My ultimate goal for every player is performance at the highest possible level.
—DON SHULA, COAUTHOR, *EVERYONE'S A COACH*

Preview

Coaching in Action

Manager: Jeff, thanks for coming. I know you're getting ready for our 1-week Supervisory Skills course at the Training Center next week. I like to meet with participants before and after each course to discuss how I can help. Having looked over the outline and completed the pre-course assignments, what would you most like to get from the course?

Jeff: Well, one thing I need to do better is to delegate tasks. Sometimes I'm too eager to do things myself. I guess it's just hard to let go.

Manager: You've only been a supervisor for 6 months, Jeff, so that's not unusual. It's especially challenging to someone with your strong technical skills.

Jeff: I'm afraid if you were to ask my technicians, they'd probably say I spend *too* much time still working on the challenging system breakdowns, rather than delegating the jobs to them. I guess it's my insecurity in supervision. . . .

Manager: So, you'd like the delegation session to help overcome some of this insecurity about your technicians. . . .

Jeff: Well, I wouldn't say it's so much insecurity about them, as it is about me. I guess I'm insecure about some of the younger, less-experienced ones. However, my key people are really talented professionals. Some know a lot more than I do about phases of our system. What bothers me is I feel like I'm getting behind in my own technical expertise in installing and debugging our systems. That's why I may assign a job, then follow up on it too closely. They probably see it as a lack of trust, when in fact, it's just my personal need to learn as much as I can to keep my own skills up.

Manager: I see what you're saying now. You feel as if you're losing some of your technical edge and miss doing the troubleshooting yourself. . . .

Jeff: Yeah, that's pretty much it. . . .

Manager: It seems as if that comes with your first management job. Technical expertise is a big plus, but it can also get in the way of your own employees' development.

Jeff: Yeah, so that's why in looking over the pre-course materials, being able to delegate better was one of the skill areas that jumped at me.

Manager: That's an excellent insight, Jeff. Our new culture is shifting to managers and supervisors becoming facilitators and developers and away from being the technical hub of expertise in our departments. Our job now is to allow our people to run with the ball and help them do it. There's going to be a premium for supervisors and managers who can do this successfully. When we put this course together, we strongly emphasized empowerment and delegation. Did any other areas particularly interest you? [The discussion continued for another 10–15 minutes.]

Learning Objectives

After reading and studying this chapter, you should be able to:

1. Explain the concept of coaching.

2. Identify the four major coaching functions.

3. Describe important skills used in coaching.

4. Differentiate between general and pinpointed coaching statements.

5. Describe an "I" message.

6. Explain the extent to which a supervisor should counsel an employee about personal problems.

Introduction to Coaching

Did you ever play an organized sport, such as football, basketball, soccer, or volleyball? Or take individual lessons in piano, karate, or math? In each case, you had a coach whose goal was to improve your performance. Golfer Tiger Woods, tenor Andrea Bocelli, and President Bush have coaches. So do many top managers who employ professional coaches to help them with anything from better managing their time to softening an abrasive personality.[1] In fact, executive coaching has become a $1 billion industry.[2] The essence of supervisory coaching—just as in those situations—is helping individuals become more effective performers. In the dialogue that began this chapter, Jeff's manager is performing coaching—helping Jeff grow and learn new skills as a supervisor. The manager will also perform coaching during the follow-up meeting with Jeff after he returns from the course. That is the objective of this chapter: to help you learn more about coaching and the skills required to perform it effectively.

Tiger Woods is successful, in part, because of good coaching. Employees within an organization can benefit from the same type of coaching and support. Both the employee and the organization benefit from the employee's success.

© Peter Byrne/EMPICS/Landov

Think of **coaching** as the interpersonal process that supervisors and managers use to help individuals continually reach their highest levels of performance.[3] It is a personal activity, a one-to-one relationship that starts when a new employee joins the team and continues throughout his or her tenure in your work unit. It may seem that new employees would be the primary focus of supervisory coaching. However, this is no longer true, given today's goals of *continuous* performance improvement. Supervisors continually coach individuals to help them achieve increasingly higher levels of performance throughout their careers. As one well-known coaching expert puts it:

> **Coaching is the process by which managers stay in touch with subordinates. All the walking around in the world will not help managers to get the best from their employees unless they are walking around as coaches. Coaching is "eyeball to eyeball" management. Every conversation between managers and employees is potentially a coaching conversation. It is a chance to clarify goals, priorities, and standards of performance. It is a chance to reaffirm and reinforce the group's core values. It is a chance to hear ideas and involve employees in the processes of planning and problem solving.[4]**

coaching Supervisors helping individuals to reach their highest levels of performance.

Coaching Is Performance Linked

The focus of coaching conversations is employee performance. The underlying assumption is that through effective coaching, the supervisor can help an employee become an increasingly effective performer, as shown in Exhibit 11-1. If a topic has a present or future impact on an employee's performance, then it should be considered suitable for a coaching situation. Some situations, such as helping an employee learn a new skill or addressing a problem of substandard work, are more obviously performance linked. Others are less directly performance related, such as helping an employee to prepare for advancement or to better understand and overcome insecurities. Notice the wide-reaching range of coaching situations shown in Exhibit 11-2 and how each is in some way performance linked. Quite a broad list, isn't it?

In the 1940s, a number of large organizations experimented by employing professionals to serve as organization-wide counselors. Their job was not to give advice, but essentially to become the organization's primary vehicle to listen to employees' job-related, personal, and emotional problems. Granted, it helped employees to vent their feelings about job frustrations

EXHIBIT **11-1**

Performance-Linked Coaching

EXHIBIT 11-2

Examples of Coaching
Situations

- Assigning a new challenging task; reviewing results.
- Determining with an employee his/her training needs.
- Showing an employee how to perform a task.
- Discussing a plan for employee career advancement.
- Listening to an employee's fears of job cutbacks.
- Providing an employee insight into company politics.
- Helping an employee adapt psychologically to job changes.
- Discussing poor employee performance.
- Helping an employee manage stress.
- Discussing how a long-term, excellent employee can reach an even higher performance level.
- Conducting a disciplinary interview.
- Discussing a problem of poor work or failure to follow organization rules/policy.
- Conducting a performance appraisal.
- Allowing an employee to "blow off" some emotional "steam."

and conflicts as well as personal problems, but the success of these programs was limited because the counselors worked outside of the formal chain of command. Today, while a number of large organizations employ full-time counselors, it is the individual supervisor who is considered the "first line" of counseling. She or he is best able to help an employee adjust to working conditions, work load and assignments, and employee–supervisor relationships. A team member's problems often affect his or her work performance (as well as the performance of others), attendance, and relationships on the job. Therefore, the supervisor has an immediate concern in these matters and assumes the legitimate role to address such employee problems. Supervisors cannot resolve personal problems such as poor health, substance abuse, or financial matters. However, the supervisor must at least understand the problem and urge the employee to seek adequate help if such a problem has the potential to negatively impact the employee's job performance. The supervisor's role in these situations is discussed later in the chapter.

Current Emphasis on Coaching

Coaching gained momentum in the quality-driven 1990s and today is increasingly becoming the trademark in "best of class" organizations.[5] As the supervisor's role has evolved into one of being a developer of people and a facilitator whose job is to help team members maximize their potential, effective coaching is recognized as a powerful supervisory skill.

Because organizations and work units have become more culturally diverse, managers and supervisors must understand their people as individuals, considering their needs, competencies, goals, attitudes, insecurities, and concerns. Coaching becomes an important vehicle by which a supervisor understands team members, which in turn better allows the supervisor to target his or her coaching efforts. Organizations recognize that coaching efforts should be tailored to the individual being coached. Coaching directed toward the younger, more insecure employee, who must learn many job essentials, differs dramatically from coaching directed toward the senior employee, who values advancement to the next level. And note: coaching is not limited in that it is only directed toward "B" and "C" level employees, but toward top performers also. [6]

Why Supervisors Reject Coaching

Coaching appears to be a natural activity; however, in actual practice many supervisors neglect their coaching role. First, many lack confidence. They may feel uncomfortable counseling employees and embarrassed to discuss problems of substandard performance.[7] There is always the risk that confronting a performance problem with an employee will create more problems than it resolves. The supervisor may have to deal with an employee's excuses, anger, or hurt feelings; the quality of a good relationship may be jeopardized. Ignoring a performance problem in the hope that it will resolve itself is often seen as a more desirable alternative.

Second, many supervisors view coaching as a passive process. They are more inclined through experience, and perhaps the expectation of their own managers, to have ready answers for everyone's problems and to deal with performance matters expeditiously. As one supervisor related in one of our coaching seminars:

> **When somebody's not doing his job, you get on his or her case and he or she had better shape up. There's no way I can see myself sitting around saying "Oh, really." My own boss would think I've lost it. I've always been direct with people—you tell them exactly what they're to do, see that they do it, and get on them when they don't. This is the best way to handle it.**

We are all products of our past. Our parents told us what to do when we were young, as did our teachers. For those of us with military service experience, platoon leaders took over the telling. Then, when we went to work, our bosses told us what to do. When we become supervisors, it is only natural that we tend to become "tellers," which is an active, expeditious way to handle things. However, today's supervisory environment has changed considerably. The supportive relationship required for effective coaching involves more open, two-way communication and greater emphasis on the supervisor's listening skills. However, as you will see throughout this chapter, coaching behavior always distinctly addresses continually improving performance.

Third, supervisors reject coaching because it takes considerable time. Faced by many pressures, supervisors are not prepared to abandon their heroic fire-fighting pace. Many are so immersed in managing "details" that they cannot effectively spare the time that coaching on the personal, one-to-one level requires.

✔ STOP AND THINK

Had the supervisor in the chapter preview *not* conducted the coaching situation with Jeff, the consequences would not have been grave. Jeff would still have completed the supervisory course, and Jeff seems to be someone who would have taken the classes seriously. But what were some of the advantages to the supervisor's having the pre-course coaching session with Jeff?

• •

The Coaching Functions

> **2** Identify the four major coaching functions.

There are different ways to understand effective coaching. One is to examine *why* someone conducts a coaching session—that is, the *function* that coaching intends to serve. Another is to examine what *skills* a coach uses during a coaching session. We will examine the functions first, then the skills. Coaching serves four fundamental functions: (1) tutoring, (2) mentoring, (3) confronting/challenging, and (4) counseling.[8]

An important coaching function, tutoring is the guidance offered by a supervisor to help employees master the skills necessary to perform their jobs.

Tutoring

tutoring Helps a team member gain knowledge, skill, and competency.

Tutoring involves a large range of coaching situations that help a team member gain knowledge, skill, and competency. Tutoring encourages team members to learn, grow, and develop. The goal is to avoid complacency with present skill levels and to develop a commitment to continuous learning. It also encourages members to put into practice those skills that are learned.

✔ STOP AND THINK

Note in the chapter preview that tutoring was the primary function being performed. The manager supported Jeff's attendance at the training course and drew out the major needs that Jeff hoped the course would address. The coach also established a follow-up meeting to review the course and discuss Jeff's plans for implementing the skills learned.

http://www.mentoring.org

Mentoring

mentoring Helps develop careers in others.

Mentoring is the coaching activity that helps develop careers in others. Mentoring may teach political savvy, understanding of the organization's culture, and the ways to advance one's career. It may also mean the following:

1. Helping an employee see the potentially negative impact of behavior he or she is considering.

2. Understanding how to approach and gain influence with powerful organization members.

3. Learning who key players are in given circumstances.

4. Understanding how relevant past or current events should impact the team member's actions and behavior.

Successful supervisory coaches help team members make key organizational contacts and develop their own networks. They aid in giving good career guidance, and they keep a watchful eye out for effective development of their team members' careers.

It is estimated that supervisors perform formal mentoring in about 75 percent of the companies listed as *Computerworld's* "Top 100 Best Places to Work." At companies such as Harrah's Entertainment, Lincoln Electric, and Avon Cosmetics, employees receive heavy doses of training to keep them challenged, satisfied, and employed. Mentoring comes into play by being more personal, practical, and job specific than training. It shows people short-cuts to using the skills learned in formal training. Or, as one manager puts it, mentoring shows people where the rocks and land mines are—how to avoid the mines and step on the rocks in moving toward career goals.[9]

✔ STOP AND THINK

In what way was mentoring involved in the chapter preview?

· ·

Confronting/Challenging

The **confronting/challenging** coaching function is most directly performance related. Supervisory coaches establish clear performance standards, compare actual team member performance against those standards, and address performance that does not meet those standards. Through confronting/challenging, successful coaches help less-than-successful performers become successful and challenge successful ones to reach even higher levels.

Often, supervisors who are good, sensitive listeners and effective tutors and mentors experience difficulty in confronting and challenging team members regarding performance issues. They may find it uncomfortable to establish clear, concrete performance standards and to talk directly about performance. They may not be willing to address performance problems when a team member's behavior falls below standard. Confronting/challenging sessions, when finally held, may be superficial and apologetic, and may skirt the poor performance problem. So important is this issue, we will discuss confronting/challenging in greater detail later in the chapter.

> **confronting/challenging** Establishes clear performance standards, compares actual performance against them, and addresses performance that doesn't meet those standards.

Counseling

Counseling is the coaching function whereby the supervisor helps an individual recognize, talk about, gain insight into, and solve either real or perceived problems that affect performance. The manager's role is essentially to help the individual determine his or her own course of action. Many supervisors feel inept and poorly trained to deal with employees' personal problems. Perhaps the most common mistake is the tendency to give advice rather than to help an employee think through, understand, and develop alternatives to problems.

In conducting counseling, it is especially important to show sensitivity and to help a team member understand how personal problems impact, or potentially impact, job performance. It is also important to help a team member gain confidence in his or her ability to handle problems. In serious cases—such as drug abuse, financial problems, or health issues—this would mean recommending that the individual seek help through the company's employee assistance program or an outside professional.

You can gain more insight into the four coaching functions by examining the different outcomes associated with each function, as shown in Exhibit 11-3.

> **counseling** Supervisors helping an individual recognize, talk about, and solve either real or perceived problems that affect performance.

EXHIBIT 11-3

Outcomes of the Four
Coaching Functions

http://www.workteam
coaching.com/books.htm

Tutoring

1. Increased technical know-how
2. Increased understanding of processes and systems
3. Increased pace of learning
4. Movement to expert status
5. Commitment to continual learning

Confronting/Challenging

1. Clarification of performance expectations
2. Identification of performance shortcomings
3. Acceptance of more-difficult tasks
4. Strategies to improve future performance
5. Commitment to continual performance improvement

Mentoring

1. Developing political understanding/savvy
2. Sensitivity to the organization's culture
3. Expanded personal networks
4. Increased sensitivity to key players' likes/dislikes
5. Greater proaction in managing own career

Counseling

1. Accurate descriptions of problems and their causes
2. Technical and organizational insight
3. Ventilation of strong feelings
4. Commitment to self-sufficiency
5. Deeper personal insight about own feelings and behavior
6. Changes in point of view

Source: Adapted from Dennis C. Kinlaw, *Coaching for Commitment* (San Diego, Calif.: Pfeiffer & Company, 1993), pp. 22–23.

✔ STOP AND THINK

Reexamine Exhibit 11-1. Which functions—tutoring, mentoring, confronting/challenging, and counseling—are reflected by some of the coaching situations described?

All four functions have much in common and are often combined in a single coaching session. For example, when a new employee is struggling to perform, a single coaching session may involve confronting/challenging, counseling, and tutoring. Many of the skills and processes involved in all four functions are similar—the need for sensitivity, listening, and movement toward some form of closure.

Coaching and Understanding Diversity

Today's organizations reflect considerably more employee uniqueness and diversity than in past years. And perhaps in no other supervisory activity is recognition of individual differences as important to success as in coaching. Because coaching requires a highly personal, one-to-one relationship, a supervisor's ability to relate to and understand an employee's needs, sensitivities, and uniqueness and to reflect these concerns in his or her interactions is crucial to successful coaching.[10]

Sharon Olds, marketing supervisor at AutoFin, supervises 16 associates. Her department reflects the wide diversity of employees found in organizations today. There are 11 men and four women; ten Caucasians, four African-Americans, one Asian, and one Hispanic. Their ages range from 23 to 59; three are single, never married; four are single and divorced or widowed. Half are college graduates, four never attended college, and four have completed some college or are presently attending college part time. Six different religions are represented, not to mention the differences in individual values, needs, interpersonal styles, and cultures. "I always thought that a correct saying was that you treat people the same way that you would like to be treated, or you treat people the same. I've learned that that's not true. Some people are so different. I have to be consistent and fair, but a key to being a good supervisor is being able to relate differently to the individual needs of my people."

The Coaching Skills

3 Describe important skills used in coaching.

When a supervisor initiates a formal coaching session, he or she should have an objective to achieve and establish a basic framework for the session, adapted to the coaching function and the circumstances. However, the coaching process largely involves a number of spontaneous interactions that occur in a relaxed, personal setting. Many coaching interactions are initiated by the team member rather than the supervisor, and these may include requests for help, advice, or informal discussion of a work-related matter. In some cases, such as those of a personal nature, work may not be directly involved.

A supervisor must create a supportive atmosphere that encourages contact. He or she must maintain a climate that makes people feel welcome, respects their views and feelings, and shows patience when communicating with them. A supportive climate exists when a supervisor understands what team members want to accomplish and when members are encouraged to try new approaches without fear of reprisal. It is difficult for many individuals to approach their supervisor for advice or to acknowledge job-related or personal problems that affect their job. Supervisors must establish an open, receptive communication climate, and effective listening is a critical coaching skill.

Coaching: The Core Skills

The core coaching skills are discussed in the following sections. No single coaching session will necessarily involve all, or even most, of these. As you read through these skills, note the importance of an atmosphere of respect and understanding and a clear need for an outcome of the coaching effort.

Acknowledging. **Acknowledging** is showing through a range of nonevaluative verbal responses that you have listened to what the employee has stated. These comments may range from a brief "uh-huh," "oh," "hmmmm," or "I see," to longer phrases like "I can understand that" or "So that's how it happened." The acknowledging skill is designed to bounce the communication ball back to the employee and allow him or her to further develop the information.

acknowledging Showing by nonevaluative verbal responses that you have listened to what the employee has stated.

Attending. **Attending** is showing through nonverbal behavior that you are listening in an open, nonjudgmental manner. In attending, your body language, such as alert posture, head nods, eye contact, and facial expressions, conveys full interest and attention. Nonattending behavior would include blank stares, nodding off, being distracted, glancing at your watch, or exhibiting other body language that displays uneasiness or disagreement with the topic being discussed. Effective attending behavior clearly communicates "I am interested and I am listening."

attending Showing through nonverbal behavior that you are listening in an open, nonjudgmental manner.

Affirming. **Affirming** is communicating to an employee his or her value, strengths, and contributions or other positive factors. An example might be "You have made excellent progress learning the new system." Or "It always amazes me how quickly you catch on." Or "I've always valued your willingness to share your feelings with me about things. It's good knowing you'll level with me about the proposed changes."

affirming Communicating to an employee his or her value, strengths, and contributions.

Confirming. Confirming is making sure that an employee understands what has been said or agreed upon. The coach can do this by summarizing and repeating the key points or by requesting the person being coached to do so. The coach might ask, "How about going over these steps in your own words and telling me how you would proceed?" Confirming may also occur with an eye to the future: "How about modifying your estimates as we've discussed, using the highest quality materials available, and let's take a look at this at 3 p.m. tomorrow."

Pinpointing. Pinpointing is providing specific, tangible information. For instance, "You did a poor job on the write-up" is a vague, general statement that covers wide territory. It is not as helpful as "The write-up used figures that were three years old, contained over 20 spelling and typographical errors, and lacked a specific recommendation."

Probing. Probing is asking questions to obtain additional information or exploring a topic at greater length, such as the following: "So you feel your group is ready to take on more responsibility. In what ways have they signaled this?" or "So you would do it differently next time, given what you now know. Just what would you do differently?"

Reflecting. Reflecting is stating in your own words your interpretation of what the employee has said or feels, such as "So you feel that you should have received more help from your teammates on this?" or "It seems like you're really upset with them for not helping out."

Resourcing. Coaches should act as resources for their team members. **Resourcing** can be done by providing information, assistance, and advice: "I really wouldn't recommend bypassing Mason on this. It cost someone his job about five years ago when he did it." or "Talk to the human resources people. They should be able to answer your question." or "Let me show you how to do that."

Reviewing. At the end of a coaching session, reinforcing key points to ensure common understanding is the skill of **reviewing.** This can be done by the coach as follows: "Let's pull this together. It seems we've identified three things you'll do with the survey data. First, you'll send your supervisors their individual results and the overall company results. Then you'll conduct one-on-one meetings with them to discuss their results. Following this, they'll develop a written plan, accepted by you as to what they'll do to improve." Or, "Let's make sure we're together on this. How about summarizing what you'll do with the survey results?"

Summarizing. Summarizing is pausing in the coaching conversation to summarize key points. "Let's see if I understand you. You believe two factors have hurt your sales performance: (1) our promotion strategy was changed and (2) extra committee work has taken time away from your sales calls."

Note that some skills, such as acknowledging and attending, relate to the *atmosphere* or environment of the coaching session—its openness and the fact that the coach is interested and is listening. Other skills such as pinpointing, probing, and resourcing are more directly tied to the *content* of the session, the issue(s) involved.

Coaching for Improved Performance: Confronting and Challenging

One of the things supervisors must do, but often do poorly, is address performance problems. Many managers do it in a blunt, threatening way that may cause resentment. Too often, they blame, lecture, put down, warn, or coerce a person in attempting to make that person improve. It is questionable whether a good chewing-out is the best way to do this. Supervisors are not mind readers, and until you can understand the reason for poor performance, you cannot adequately coach someone to improve. It simply is not coaching to call someone in, read the

EXHIBIT 11-4

Suggestions for
Confronting Poor
Performance

1. Describe the performance situation in specific detail.
2. Seek and listen to the team member's point of view.
3. Get agreement on the problem.
4. Try to get the employee's involvement in determining a solution.
5. Agree on a plan of action to improve performance.
6. Summarize the agreement and reinforce the changed behavior.
7. Plan for follow-up, if needed.

riot act, and send him or her away. Often, the result is no change, a half-hearted change, or resentment at having been called "on the carpet." By contrast, some supervisors dislike discussing poor performance and are reluctant to bring it up. They avoid confronting a poor performer only to find that the poor performance escalates, making the inevitable coaching meeting involve more serious stakes than if it had occurred earlier. An employee's poor performance can relate not only to actual on-the-job work performance, but to other types of behavior as well, such as attendance, safety, attitude, and adherence to various company rules and policies.

While individual situations may differ, the suggestions for dealing with substandard performance contained in Exhibit 11-4 are often effective.

It is essential that the issue of poor performance be addressed by the supervisor early in the meeting. Your comments should pinpoint the issues specifically. For example, instead of telling an employee "Your job performance is poor," it is more informative to say, "You reached only 75 percent of your work goal" or "You have been absent three times in the past 2 weeks." In this way, the employee is given something concrete. Here are some further examples:

4 Differentiate between general and pinpointed coaching statements.

General	**Pinpointed**
1. Your attendance is poor.	1. You have missed a day in each of the past four pay periods.
2. You need to cooperate better with department heads.	2. Company policy is to give department heads the cost information when they request it.
3. You need to follow our safety rules.	3. This morning I saw you performing the job without wearing your safety goggles.
4. You haven't made the progress that you'd agreed on.	4. You and I agreed that you would complete the first draft by today, but you tell me you need two more days.

Note that a number of steps shown in Exhibit 11-4 require you to listen and/or to actively involve the team member in the discussion, especially step 2: seek and listen to the team member's point of view; step 3: get agreement on the problem; step 4: try to get the employee's involvement in determining a solution; and step 5: agree on a plan of action to improve performance.

Exhibit 11-5 illustrates a supervisor conducting a confronting/challenging coaching session. Note the supervisor's use of the steps involved in confronting poor performance, as well as many of the skills of pinpointing, acknowledging, reflecting, resourcing, and summarizing.

EXHIBIT 11-5

Script of Confronting/
Challenging Coaching
Session

Sup 1	Bob, I wanted to talk with you because I have a problem. I'd thought after we last talked about quitting time that you understood our policy and that you intended to stick to it. So, I was surprised yesterday to see you'd left a little after 5 and not 5:30. I'm upset about it.
Wkr 1	Chuck, I've been trying hard not to leave before 5:30. I hadn't left early in about 2 months until this emergency.
Sup 2	You've had a good record recently. So yesterday was something special?
Wkr 2	I had a call in the middle of the afternoon from the guy I ride with in my neighborhood. Said he had to leave a little before 5:30, and if I wasn't out on the street, he'd have to leave me.
Sup 3	Put you in a bind, huh.
Wkr 3	You're right about that. Once when he was sick I took the bus, and it took me an hour and a half to get home.
Sup 4	So you hated to use that alternative, huh.
Wkr 4	Yep. It only takes about 30 minutes driving with him.
Sup 5	So you were torn between losing time getting home and sticking with our rule.
Wkr 5	Yeah, I looked around for you in the afternoon; you can ask Art. You were out of the office and I couldn't find you. Fifteen minutes didn't seem like such a big deal since I'd had a good record recently.
Sup 6	So you hoped I'd approve, if you could ask me.
Wkr 6	I was sure of it.
Sup 7	Apparently, you felt it was very important for you to go home and not miss your ride, even to the point of breaking a rule and our agreement.
Wkr 7	Well, it was a rare emergency that happens from time to time. Seems like a few minutes don't matter that much. I'm here working sometimes 20 minutes early in the morning.
Sup 8	I understand that. You're always here on time, and I appreciate that. But we have two policies— one for getting here on time and one for staying till 5:30—and both must be kept.
Wkr 8	I wouldn't expect this to happen again, at least only very rarely.
Sup 9	I felt that [way] after we had our last talk, Bob, but then something came up and it's happened again.
Wkr 9	I told him then that I have to stay until 5:30, so he usually waits, except for yesterday. At least he called me.
Sup 10	Can you think of something you might do to avoid this happening in the future? Because this rule is not to be broken unless there is an emergency more serious than this. I don't consider this to be the type of emergency that would warrant your leaving early. Can you think of anything you could do to keep it from happening again?
Wkr 10	I could make sure that you know I'm leaving early, if he ever needs to leave again.
Sup 11	That solution doesn't satisfy me—I don't think I could agree. I don't think I could give my permission for this.
Wkr 11	Not even for 10 or 15 minutes?
Sup 12	Not for that. We need a solution that will satisfy you and satisfy me and the company policy.
Wkr 12	Maybe I'd have to ride a bus on those days.
Sup 13	In other words, you can take a bus if you have to.
Wkr 13	Yeah, but it seems to me that the hour and a half it takes is a long time for just 10 or 15 minutes. Seems unreasonable to me, the policy, that is.
Sup 14	Seems to you like, if you keep the policy most of the time, it's all right to break it once in a while.
Wkr 14	It seems that way to me.
Sup 15	If the 20 people working on our department took the same approach, almost every night someone would be leaving early. I wouldn't feel that would be fair. Would you?

Continued

EXHIBIT 11-5

continued

Wkr 15	Well, no. Maybe I could find someone right here who could drive me home on those days. I wouldn't even mind catching the bus and then walking a little way.
Sup 16	Think that would solve it, huh?
Wkr 16	Yes, but how would I go about finding someone?
Sup 17	I'll bet Mr. Barrows has a list in the Human Resources department.
Wkr 17	O.K., I'll drop over there today.
Sup 18	Bob, it's important that I can count on you to keep the rules by working through until 5:30. Thanks for discussing this with me, and I appreciate your working it out.

Source: Adapted from Thomas Gordon, *Leader Effectiveness Training (L.E.T.)* Copyright © 1977, 2001 Penguin Putnam. Reprinted by permission of the author.

The exchange also illustrates how, even while willing to listen to the employee's views, the supervisor remains focused on the performance issue.

Tom Gordon, a well-known writer on leadership and interpersonal issues, advocates the use of what he calls "I" messages when we want to effectively alter someone's behavior.[11] He says there are three major parts of an **"I" message:**

- *Feelings:* Indicate how you feel about the effects of the behavior (angry, embarrassed, frustrated, concerned, etc.).

- *Behavior:* Identify the specific behavior (absenteeism, not keeping appointments, not meeting quota, etc.).

- *Effect:* Spell out the end result of the behavior (poor example for others, making the work unit look unproductive, inconvenience to others in the unit, etc.).

When you send an "I" message, you make an appeal rather than a demand that the other person change. Note in the following examples that the focus is the *behavior,* its *effect,* and how it makes you *feel.* While no one likes being told his or her behavior is causing a problem, framing your displeasure in an "I" message addresses the problem more openly and tactfully and is more likely to pave the way toward a resolution in an objective, supportive manner.

5. Describe an "I" message.

"I" message An appeal, rather than a demand, that the other person change.

"You" Message	"I" Message
You neglected to proofread that report, you should know better than to let a report go out like that.	When I noticed the many typos in the report, I was really upset. It makes our unit look careless and unprofessional.
You know I expect you to attend our regular meetings. You need to attend them from now on.	When you don't attend our regular meetings, I'm concerned that we miss your expertise and insight.

In using the "I" message, it is important to keep in mind the coaching skills from the previous section. Your goal as a supervisor is to correct the inadequate performance in a way that shields the employee's ego *and* maintains a positive relationship between you and the employee. Thus, the session should focus on the employee's *performance* rather than personality—in other words, the problem and not the person. Your use of "I" messages can be an important tool in focusing on the employee's behavior rather than on the employee's ego.

✔ **STOP AND THINK**

Refer to Exhibit 11-5. Can you identify the supervisor's use of an "I" message?

6

Explain the extent to which a supervisor should counsel an employee about personal problems.

Coaching: The Counseling Function

Counseling, one of the four coaching functions, involves a broad range of emotional areas, ranging from an employee's frustrations, insecurities, anger, and resentment to lack of commitment. The problem can be attributed to real or perceived factors and can be work related or personal. Basically, the objective of counseling is to help an employee better understand himself or herself and, when needed, to develop a plan of action to resolve the issue. The coach's job is to help the individual more fully discuss and understand the problem being experienced. Feelings, emotions, and attitudes may be exchanged. As shown in Exhibit 11-6, counseling attempts to identify and help both supervisor and team member better understand those "below-the-surface" factors that are influencing or may potentially influence the team member's performance. In counseling, the listening-related skills of attending, acknowledging, reflecting, and probing are especially essential.

A coach often has no advance notice as to when counseling is needed; these coaching opportunities are usually initiated by the team member. On other occasions, a team leader will plan to perform one of the other coaching functions, for instance, tutoring or confronting/challenging, when the need for counseling arises. The leader must be sufficiently flexible to shift gears and address counseling, as pointed out below.

> What started as a routine tutoring session for supervisor Rosa Bender turned out quite differently when she learned that Rudy Colquitt, a new technician, felt ignored by senior people in the department. Bender temporarily dropped her tutoring agenda and devoted about 10 minutes to reflecting and probing why Colquitt, the youngest and newest member of the team, felt this way. Learning that he felt slighted because senior employees

EXHIBIT 11-6

Iceberg Model
of Counseling

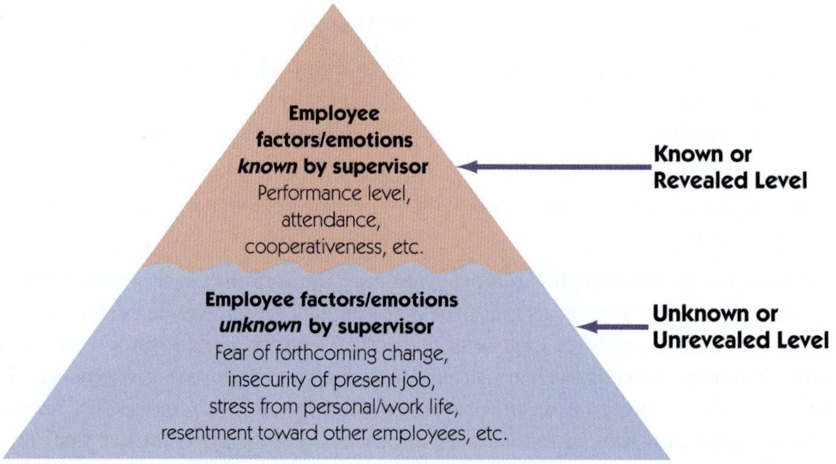

Employee factors/emotions known by supervisor
Performance level, attendance, cooperativeness, etc.
→ **Known or Revealed Level**

Employee factors/emotions unknown by supervisor
Fear of forthcoming change, insecurity of present job, stress from personal/work life, resentment toward other employees, etc.
→ **Unknown or Unrevealed Level**

offered him little help, Bender helped him understand that senior employees, while likely supportive, were independent performers who thoroughly immersed themselves in their own work. Although perhaps they hadn't offered help, they would gladly help if asked.

Colquitt agreed to ask senior employees for help when he needed it and to communicate to Bender his degree of success. Satisfied that this addressed the immediate counseling issue, Bender then shifted back to the tutoring session she had originally planned.

Areas of Employee Counseling

Counseling is involved in virtually all aspects of the supervisor–employee relationship. It begins with the hiring phase and does not end until the employee leaves the company. Certain areas, though, are more likely to necessitate counseling than others.

Job Performance. We have already indicated that counseling is often used in combination with the other four coaching functions. It is especially important in the area of job performance. Numerous factors, many of which the supervisor is unaware, influence employees' job performance. A good rule of thumb is to always be prepared to engage in counseling when addressing below-standard employee performance, especially for employees who have in the past had no performance difficulties or who have only recently engaged in negative job behavior. This would include performance changes in quality and quantity of work, absenteeism, adherence to policy and rules, and changes in cooperativeness and relationships with others, including the supervisor.

Physical and Emotional Illness. Another common need for counseling arises because of physical and emotional illness. In some cases, these are initially addressed by the supervisor as performance problems, but in many cases they may be initiated by the employee. Although the team leader must play a supportive, listening role in counseling, it is imperative that the employee clearly see the impact or potential impact of such problems upon performance.

> When Avery Williard showed up late, his supervisor coincidentally happened to be present at Williard's work area. While Williard appeared quite uncomfortable and embarrassed, his supervisor expressed surprise because Williard was never late. It was then that the supervisor smelled alcohol. He asked Williard to join him in his office. Williard acknowledged that he had been drinking a lot lately because of "problems at home," but pledged he would not do it again. His supervisor listened patiently, noting that Williard didn't volunteer particulars. He praised Williard for his excellent work and dependability over the years, but reminded him that should it happen again, he would have no choice but to formally discipline him. Seeing that Williard was in no condition to work, his supervisor sent him home after setting a meeting for the next day. This meeting was to reinforce (1) his support for Williard and (2) the fact that Williard's behavior could not be tolerated again on the job. He also planned to strongly suggest that Williard consider referral to the company EAP (Employee Assistance Program) as a source of help.

Often it is difficult for a supervisor to diagnose an employee's substance abuse, especially when it is not accompanied by performance slippage. Behavior that differs from the norm may be the telltale sign. Note in Exhibit 11-7 many behaviors—increased accidents, need for increased rest breaks, frequent off-the-job emergencies, deteriorating personal appearance, and overreaction to criticism are some indicators that substance abuse may be involved.

As in the preceding situation, supervisors are increasingly called on to counsel employees with many forms of physical and emotional problems. These problems range from substance abuse and job stress to debilitating physical illnesses, such as cancer, heart disease, and AIDS. Moreover, the rash of corporate downsizings, mergers, and financial and ethical mismanagement has created unparalleled emotional anxiety, as reflected by present and former employees who commit acts of physical violence against employers.

Sometimes superiors must counsel employees with emotional or physical illness or who have personal problems.

© Brand X Pictures/Alamy

Personal Problems. To what extent should a supervisor counsel an employee with personal problems, such as financial, health, or marital problems? The answer depends largely on the extent to which the problem impacts present or future job performance. If it affects job performance, it is essential that the supervisor use counseling to understand the nature of the problem, if for nothing more than to help the employee appreciate the need for professional assistance. However, a supervisor should tread carefully before becoming entwined in personal problems for several reasons:

✔ **STOP AND THINK**

Note in Exhibit 11-5 that in order to fully address the performance issue (employee leaving work early), the supervisor helped the employee address his personal problem (transportation after work).

1. Employees may feel resentful or embarrassed after "opening up" and disclosing highly personal matters. This may jeopardize their future job relationship with their supervisor.

EXHIBIT 11-7

Profile of Typical
Substance Abusers

- Four times more likely to have on-the-job accidents than nonabusers
- Four to six times more likely to have off-the-job accidents than nonabusers
- Five times the number of workers' compensation claims as nonabusers
- Five times the number of medical claims as nonabusers
- Two and a half times more absenteeism/tardiness than nonabusers, especially on Mondays and Fridays and before and after holidays
- Take extended breaks and lunch hours
- Have numerous restroom breaks
- Experience frequent off-job emergencies
- Experience frequent colds, flu, upset stomach, headaches, etc.
- Dramatic change in personality or work performance during the day, especially after breaks
- Deteriorating personal appearance and ability to get along with others
- Tendency to overreact to real or imagined criticism
- Experience difficulty handling instructions
- Depressed or anxious disposition
- Work at 67 percent of potential

Sources: Janet Gemignani, "Substance Abusers: Terminate or Treat?" *Business & Health* 17(6), June 1999, pp. 32–37; Laura A. Lyons and Brian H. Kleiner, "Managing the Problem of Substance Abuse . . . Without Abusing Employees," *HR Focus* 69(4), April 1992, p. 9; Peter Ellis, "Substance Abuse and Work," *Occupational Safety & Health* 30(13), March 2000, pp. 38–41.

2. If the supervisor makes too concerted an effort to probe into more than an employee cares to divulge, it will be resented.

3. If the supervisor gives advice on personal problems—such as marital difficulties, problems with children, or buying and selling property—and the results turn out unsatisfactorily, the supervisor will be blamed. Also, the supervisor and/or the company may be open to legal damages.

In general, supervisory counseling should be restricted to factors that affect job performance. Supervisors work hard to develop trusting, supportive relationships and are often placed in a position of counseling team members in problem areas only peripherally related to job performance. To reject the counseling opportunity outright may be perceived as lack of interest. The supervisor can always listen sufficiently to determine the nature of the employee's problem and then steer the individual toward a professional or other source of help. That is where the EAP enters the picture.

http://www.EAP
consultants.com

Role of EAPs in Counseling

From a handful of programs begun in the 1940s to address alcoholism, **Employee Assistance Programs (EAPs)** have emerged to extend professional counseling and medical services to employees confronted by unresolved personal or work-related problems.[12] These may include counseling for substance abuse, emotional illnesses, marital issues, divorce or stress.[13] Many companies have broadened the counseling services available through their EAPS; at Comcast, employees and their families may receive counseling assistance in such wide ranging areas as help with weight loss, smoking, budgeting, taxes, estate planning, legal matters

Employee Assistance Programs (EAPs)
Professional counseling and medical services for employees with unresolved personal or work-related problems.

EXHIBIT 11-8

Most of the time we like to think we are in control of our lives. All of us, however, occasionally experience personal crises that may cause us to feel out of control. These crises may be due to health problems, financial or legal difficulties, or emotional problems. Because we care about our employees, an Employee Assistance Program (EAP) has been implemented. The EAP will provide confidential, professional counseling and referral to employees who seek assistance with personal problems. Realizing that an employee may be affected by a family member's personal problem, the EAP is also available to the families of our employees.

What the EAP is:
- *Voluntary:* Employees or family members can contact the program directly. Participation in the program is always voluntary.
- *Independent:* The EAP is administered by Human Affairs Inc., a national company that provides assistance programs to many companies across the country.
- *Confidential:* Because of the two components mentioned above, EAP participants are assured that any information revealed to EAP staff will be held in the strictest professional confidence.
- *Professional:* All EAP staff are licensed Masters level therapists and counselors.
- *Free:* All counseling and referral services provided by the EAP are free to employees and their families. If an EAP counselor does recommend that employees consult a special outside resource, the counselor can let employees know what part of that service may be covered by their other medical benefits.
- *Accessible:* EAP counselors are available for emergency situations 24 hours a day, 7 days a week. Appointments are made for non-emergency situations during day or evening hours.
- *A Valuable Resource:* The EAP can serve as a resource concerning counseling, information, and management consultation to employees, supervisors, and family members.

What the EAP is NOT:
- *A Branch of Human Resources:* The EAP is not designed to replace any personnel or management procedures.
- *A Refuge for Poor Job Performance:* Participation in the EAP will not protect employees from disciplinary action.

Procedures
- *Self-Referral:* An employee or an immediate family member may use the service by contacting Human Affairs Inc. directly in complete privacy whenever they would like to consult with the counselor. Self-referrals are both anonymous and completely confidential. Self-referrals will not affect job security or promotional opportunity.
- *Supervisor/Management Referral:* A supervisor may recommend that an employee contact Human Affairs Inc. when there is a job performance or conduct problem which has not responded to ordinary supervisorial techniques. Whether or not the employee decides to contact Human Affairs Inc., it is the employee's responsibility to perform satisfactorily on the job; and if problems go unresolved and performance continues to deteriorate, disciplinary action up to and including discharge may result. Participation in the EAP is not a guarantee that these actions will not continue to occur, but improved performance often results from problem resolution.

The Company sincerely hopes that all staff and their dependents who might benefit from this service will take advantage of it.

Source: "Purpose of Company E.A.P.," *Personnel Policy Briefs,* Sample Issue, n.d., p. 2., as found in Leon C. Megginson, Geralyn McLure Franklin, and M. Jane Byrd, *Human Resource Management* (Houston, Tex.: Dame Publications, Inc.), 1995, p. 296.

and even buying a car or house.[14] In cases where an EAP does not exist, a supervisor may refer an employee to counseling services provided within the community, most of which have public mental health or social service professional counseling available. Surveys show that over 75 percent of companies with over 500 employees have EAPs in place, and close to 30 percent of small firms of 25 employees or fewer are providing EAP services.[15] Exhibit 11-8 gives you a good idea of the counseling services offered by one company's EAP.

Where present, the EAP can be a big help to supervisors by handling referred cases at a professional level. Studies of EAP programs at Abbott Labs and McDonnell Douglas show that employees who participated had fewer absentee days and fewer terminations than other company employees in general.[16] Thus, it is in the supervisor's best interests to encourage employees to participate when necessary. Supervisors typically are given training and policy guidance in how and under what conditions to refer employees to a company's EAP, should one exist.

CHAPTER REVIEW

1 Explain the concept of coaching.

Coaching is the interpersonal process used by supervisors and managers to help individuals continually reach their highest levels of performance. Coaching is performance oriented, whether it helps a new employee gain new skills or accept challenges or a seasoned employee to reach even higher levels of performance. The current emphasis on coaching reflects the changing role of supervisors as facilitators and developers of people.

Despite its importance, supervisors tend to experience difficulty in practicing effective coaching. Many lack the confidence in their communication skills, especially listening, to be an effective coach. Others see it as too passive and prefer to provide answers to employees rather than to work jointly with them to develop their own answers to problems. Still others are uncomfortable in spending the large amount of time that effective coaching takes.

2 Identify the four major coaching functions.

There are four coaching functions. Tutoring helps a team member gain knowledge, skill, and competency. Mentoring develops political savvy, an understanding of key players, and the way to advance one's career. Confronting/challenging focuses directly upon performance itself—from setting clear objectives to follow-up meetings that discuss results. It can address performance problems and inspire top performers to continue to grow and improve. Counseling helps an individual recognize, talk about, and thereby gain insight into his or her real or perceived problems that may affect performance.

3 Describe the important skills used in coaching.

Coaching is a one-to-one relationship that utilizes such skills as acknowledging, attending, affirming, confirming, pinpointing, probing, reflecting, resourcing, reviewing, and summarizing.

4 Differentiate between general and pinpointed coaching statements.

In coaching designed to confront/challenge an employee with a performance problem, supervisors should pinpoint, in specific, concrete language, the employee's performance level, rather than using general terms.

5 Describe an "I" message.

"I" messages, which indicate the problem behavior, its effect, and the supervisor's feelings, can be an effective way to focus on the performance problem. For example: "Your lunch break was in excess of an hour and a half. I was embarrassed when the plant manager came by looking for you on two occasions and found other people covering your work area."

IMPORTANT TERMS

acknowledging
affirming
attending
coaching
confirming
confronting/challenging
counseling
Employee Assistance
   Programs (EAPs)
"I" message
mentoring
pinpointing
probing
reflecting
resourcing
reviewing
summarizing
tutoring

6 **Explain the extent to which a supervisor should counsel an employee about personal problems.**

In general, supervisors should restrict their counseling to factors that affect an employee's job performance. Many personal problems, such as physical and emotional health, substance abuse, and financial and family problems, however, actually impact or may impact future performance. The supervisor should focus counseling on the performance-related aspects of the problem. Many firms today have an Employee Assistance Program (EAP) to which supervisors can refer troubled employees.

QUESTIONS FOR REVIEW AND DISCUSSION

1. What is meant by coaching?

2. Of the four major coaching functions—tutoring, mentoring, confronting/challenging, and counseling—which do you feel is most difficult? Why?

3. Describe the following coaching skills and give an example of each:

    a. attending

    b. affirming

    c. resourcing

    d. reviewing

4. Give an example of a "general" coaching statement as contrasted to a "pinpointed" coaching statement. Which is more effective and why?

5. What is an "I" message? Why is it an effective way to confront someone's behavior? Give an example.

6. To what extent should a supervisor counsel an employee about the employee's personal problems?

7. What is an EAP?

Skill Builder 11-1

Given everyone's addiction to good health, physical fitness has experienced much popularity. One of the fastest growing professions has been that of personal fitness trainer. Consider the fitness trainer's job: Listen to the client's goals, outline a program of activities that will achieve the client's goals, and then, through coaching, help the client to achieve them. Once the client has learned the basics, the trainer's job essentially becomes one of encouraging, supporting, and giving feedback. You know the language: "That's it," "All the way down, now," "Tighten up a bit," "Way to go," "You can do it," "That's great," "Terrific," "That's the way to push yourself," "Hold that form, come through for me," "That's ok, you showed improvement, we'll get it next time," and so on.

Instructions:

Break into teams of four to six members. Select a spokesperson and discuss the following questions:

1. In what way are the roles of personal trainer and manager/supervisor similar? Dissimilar?

2. In what types of circumstances can all or most of the coaching behavior of personal trainers be applied to the manager/employee relationship? Give examples.

3. Have any team members worked for a manager/supervisor who functioned much like a personal trainer? In what ways?

4. Following discussion, the spokesperson will present to the class results of the team's discussion.

Practicing "I" Messages

group activity

In reading this chapter, you learned that an "I" message consists of (1) how someone's behavior makes you feel, (2) what the specific behavior is, and (3) the effect of the behavior. The following three situations show a need for an "I" message.

a. Four of your employees share a single telephone line. You are aware that one of them, Harry R., is especially long-winded on the phone and talks for as long as 15 minutes. This prevents others from placing outgoing calls and ties up the line, preventing customers from getting through.

b. It is a requirement that waiters at the upscale restaurant you manage wear white shirts and ties. One waiter has been loosening his tie, dropping the knot about 2 inches, and unbuttoning his shirt collar.

c. Coffee breaks for your office staff are normally 15 minutes. When someone occasionally takes a few minutes longer, it's not a big deal. But lately, one staff member has had three consecutive days when the break exceeded 20 minutes.

Instructions:
1. Write a hypothetical "I" message for each of the three situations.
2. Gather in groups of three to five students and share answers.
3. From your answers, select some good examples and present them to the rest of the class.

Practicing Coaching Responses

Assume the role of shipping supervisor at Apex Company. One of your employees, Jason, has been an excellent performer for the past 5 years. However, during the past 2 weeks, Jason has not seemed himself. He was operating a forklift when a careless accident caused about $2,000 in damages. Moreover, Jason has punched in late twice. When you discussed these incidents, he apologized, attributing his tardiness to car trouble. Normally outgoing and energetic, he has appeared tired and edgy. Usually one of the liveliest contributors at meetings of your group, he said nothing at yesterday's safety meeting. During afternoon break on the loading dock today, Spud, another employee, made a joking comment about Jason's favorite college football team, which had been beaten handily by its cross-state rival this past weekend. Jason responded angrily with an expletive, then got up and left the area. Another employee commented, "What's been eating Jason, anyway?" Everyone shrugged their shoulders. You decide to have a coaching meeting with Jason.

It is about 2 hours later. Jason has just walked into your office. You stand, acknowledge him, and close the door behind him. Jason takes a seat and as you move to sit down, he says, "So you wanted to see me about something."

a. **In the space below, write the opening statement you will make to Jason that pinpoints the reason for the meeting.**

Assume that following your statement, a discussion with Jason lasts for several minutes. He is very soft-spoken and avoids eye contact. Then he looks you in the eye and says, "I'm glad I have this chance to talk with you. I feel like so much is going on with me lately. I guess I've just taken on more than I should . . . and I don't know what to do about it."

b. **In the space below, write the statement you will make to Jason that demonstrates reflecting.**

Assume that the discussion continues. Jason is quite talkative now, volunteering information about financial problems brought on by a house addition, his son's college expenses, and a recent auto accident that cost him $750 to cover the deductible on his policy. To meet his financial needs, Jason tells you he has been moonlighting for 30 hours weekly as a security guard at a local hotel. He has gotten little sleep the past 2 weeks. He now worries that he can't sustain the pace, because his job performance at Apex is being affected. He says, "I know I haven't been much of a contributor around here lately."

c. **In the space below, write the statement you will make to Jason that demonstrates affirming, but also reinforces the need for him to improve performance.**

During the remaining discussion, Jason commits to making his present job performance his number one priority, despite his short-term financial needs. You discuss several alternatives that would allow him to do both, two of which he proposed: (1) reduce his hotel hours, with most of them being worked on weekends, and (2) getting a loan from the company credit union or a bank. A third idea—taking his 2-week vacation now, which would allow him to work his full hotel hours for 2 weeks—was one you suggested he consider. You tell him you would look into waiving the normal 2-week vacation notice. You also suggest he consider making an appointment with the company's EAP office, which can arrange for financial counseling for employees. Jason expresses interest in this.

You agree to let Jason know tomorrow about the vacation matter and to be available as needed to discuss things further should Jason need to talk. You note that Jason picks up his hard hat, which was placed on the floor, and says: "Well, I feel much better having talked with you about this. It's taken a lot off my mind, and it's helped me think some things through. Thanks for being so patient."

d. **In the space below, write the statement you will make to Jason that demonstrates confirming/summarizing and closes the meeting.**

e. **Meet with other students and compare your responses.**

Critiquing a Coaching Meeting

The following exchange took place between Charlene Rowe, human resources manager, and one of her senior team members, Leonard Busche.

Rowe 1: Come in, Leonard, have a seat. [Leonard sits down.] I suppose you're wondering why I wanted us to get together.

Busche 1: Yes, I guess I am, Charlene.

Rowe 2: Leonard, yesterday something happened that I want to know your feelings about. It's about the quality steering report I asked you to put together for my committee meeting yesterday afternoon.

Busche 2: [Somewhat defensively] What about it?

Rowe 3: To be quite frank, Leonard, I was too embarrassed to distribute it at the meeting. It just wasn't up to your usual standards. For one thing, it seemed superficial in that it described only a few of the programs we'd benchmarked, rather than all seven. Since this will be the major document the committee will be using as a reference, we needed coverage of *all* the visits we've made. Also, some of the most important processes were not included—like J&J's 360-degree feedback system and Motorola's team incentives.

Busche 3: [only half joking] Gee, it seems as if I may need a union steward in here with me. [Leonard is a salaried, nonunion employee.]

Rowe 4: No, Leonard, I don't mean to give that impression. It's just that this job isn't like you at all, and that concerned me. You've always done exceptional work in putting together material like this for me. For all I know, it might have been my own fault, a misunderstanding between us. I wanted to meet and get your perspective on the situation.

Busche 4: Well, there isn't much to say. I guess I should have figured it wouldn't be of much help. [Getting a little emotional] I wasn't tickled about it either.

Rowe 5: You weren't pleased with it yourself?

Busche 5: No, I wasn't. Charlene, that report would have taken about 8 to 10 hours for me to do it up right. Do you know how long I had? About 4 hours, that's all. I couldn't do much in 4 hours.

Rowe 6: So you didn't get to put in the time on the report. . . .

Busche 6: No, I didn't. In fact, you weren't the only one embarrassed by it. But I can't promise it'll be the last lousy job. . . . I just can't handle everything that comes my way. I know we're a service department [human resources], but we're not the little outfit we were 5 years ago. I just can't keep up.

Rowe 7: It sounds as if the quality report is only part of the problem.

Busche 7: That's exactly what I'm saying. I'm expected to do everybody's odds and ends besides my regular job in training and safety. I've got the two accidents we're investigating from 2 weeks ago and all that paperwork. We're approaching our deadlines on the new training manuals. I'm heading up the newsletter committee that puts out our first edition next month. Then, you gave me the quality report with 1-week's notice. I would have gotten it done, but last week Bushman [VP and general manager] asked me to be his facilitator. I had to put in some 8 hours observing his meetings with the budget committee. So the quality report was lousy, I know. But if things continue as they are, it won't be the last. I hate it more than you do.

Rowe 8: Leonard, you know how we've all come to expect so much from you. Granted, we are a service department, but in retrospect, I wish you'd confided in me about this. I could have simply pushed back my quality committee meeting, which is what I essentially did, anyway. What can we do to help you?

Busche 8: How can we help? [Flippant] Oh, give me an assistant.

Rowe 9: Is additional help the answer?

Busche 9: I don't know the answer to that. I think what's really got me upset is Bushman. He didn't *ask* me to facilitate, he *told* me to. I should have turned him down, but I guess I haven't got the guts to say "no" to a vice-president. But then, I didn't want to let you down, either.

Rowe 10: I think it's terrific that Bushman values your abilities. Politically, it's in both of our interests for you to act as Bushman's facilitator. That is, if you want to do it.

Busche 10: Oh, I don't mind facilitating for Bushman. He needs a lot of help and he knows it. It would normally be a real compliment for me; it was just the timing that was bad.

Rowe 11: Leonard, you have a lot of things going on that I didn't know about. Maybe I'm the one who has to do some changing. I can see why, given your schedule the past 2 weeks, taking on that quality project was too much. It wasn't fair to you. Leonard, I need to feel confident that your work for me from now on will be what I can count on. What can we do to prevent this from happening again?

Busche 11: I could probably do a better job of letting you know what I've got going on. I could also be more honest with you. I just hate saying I can't do something, especially to my boss. You probably didn't know the newsletter was eating up my time last week, as were the safety problems. I guess I could keep you more up to date. I could also be more direct and tell you if I honestly don't have the time to take something on and do a good job. But it's hard for me to say no.

Rowe 12: O.K., let's give this a try. You'll give me a brief typed report on projects other than your normal training and safety activities. If you're skeptical about a commitment request from outside the department, you'll discuss it with me before taking it on. You're also agreeing to level with me about whether you have time to commit to special projects that I throw your way. We'll try this process for a month and see what happens. Is that acceptable?

Busche 12: Yep, that sounds acceptable. Hopefully, I'll not get caught up in a bind like this again.

Instructions:

1. What type of coaching function was reflected in Rowe's meeting with Busche?

2. In terms of effectiveness on a 1–10 scale, with 1 being "poor" and 10 being "excellent," what score would you assign to Rowe's handling of the session? Why?

3. Identify specific transcript comments by Rowe that reflect the following coaching skills: (a) reflecting, (b) pinpointing, (c) probing, (d) affirming, (e) confirming.

4. To what extent did the meeting reflect the seven suggestions for confronting poor performance (Exhibit 11-4)?

5. Meet with a group of three to five other students, discuss your answers, and be prepared to report these to the rest of the class.

Skill Builder 11-4

Conducting a Coaching Meeting: Role Plays

In this exercise, you will break into small groups as determined by your instructor. The entire group should read the role for the manager/supervisor and the employee. One person should be designated to perform each role, the others being observers. Several minutes planning time should be allowed for players and observers to study their roles before beginning the actual coaching meeting.

General Instructions for Observers

Following each role play, you will lead a discussion of the manager's effectiveness in handling the performance coaching meeting. Use the pre–role play planning time to review some of the important coaching principles presented in the chapter to help evaluate the manager's performance. The following questions give insight into your critique of the meeting:

1. What do you feel was the objective of the meeting?

2. Were the steps in Exhibit 11-4, "Suggestions for Confronting Poor Performance" followed? Were any done especially well? Which might have been improved?

3. Which of the "Core Coaching Skills" such as acknowledging, attending, affirming, etc., did the manager use in the meeting?

4. To what extent do you feel that the manager achieved the objective of the meeting?

Coaching Meeting 1: Assistant Principal and Teacher

(a) Role for Assistant Principal (to be read by all)

You are assistant principal at an elementary school. Twelve teachers report to you. One is Jan Wilson, who has been with you for 3 years. Jan teaches fourth grade. She has an excellent record as a teacher and is very well liked by her students' parents.

A well-known rule at your school deals with teacher absences—when a teacher will miss classes because of illness or emergency, your office should be notified so that a substitute teacher can be employed. Earlier in the year, Jan failed to show up for class and did not notify you until later in the day. You scurried to cover Jan's class and when Jan returned the following day, you reminded her of the notification policy. You learned that her absence related to a family emergency with one of her elderly parents.

Yesterday, it happened again. A teacher from an adjacent classroom notified you that Jan's class was unattended. Again, you had to exert much energy finding a temporary replacement for the rest of the day. Jan did leave a short voice mail at 10:30 a.m. yesterday for you in which she apologized for the inconvenience and said that she would be back in class today. No reason for her absence or late notification was offered.

Today, you made it a point to pass Jan's classroom shortly before class began. You asked if everything was OK, to which Jan responded, "Yes, thank you." You then asked Jan to drop by your office at 3:15 p.m. following dismissal of classes.

Instruction: In a few minutes, you will conduct a performance coaching session with Jan.

(b) Role for Teacher Jan (to be read by all)

Background facts for your role are presented in the "Role for Assistant Principal" as outlined in "a" above. In a few minutes you will meet with your Assistant Principal. You expect that the subject will relate to your class absence yesterday. To develop your role, take a few minutes to determine a reason why you may have missed class, and why you didn't notify the assistant principal earlier. Remember, you are a talented, conscientious teacher who has a good relationship with other teachers and your assistant principal. During the role play you may have to adapt your role as the discussion ensues.

Coaching Meeting 2: Restaurant Manager and Server

(a) Role for Manager (to be read by all)

You are manager of a well-known national casual dining restaurant in your area. You are reviewing customer comment cards that have been mailed by customers to your regional office, tabulated, and then forwarded to you each month. Results are compared to goals set for such important criteria as quality of service, food quality, and other factors. About 200 comment cards were returned to you from the past month. Your goal for server ratings is to average 85/100; during the past month your restaurants' customers rated your 15 servers an average of 81/100. These ranged from a high of 95 to a low of 68.

Kelly's score of 68 is clearly poor! A new server like Kelly (presently in her second month) sometimes scores lower than more seasoned servers, but Kelly's is the lowest you have seen in the past year. Most customers rated her as "excellent" or "good." But Kelly bombed on five of 17 customers' cards, being rated as "unacceptable." Four of these found fault with Kelly's language—one labeling it as "foul mouthed," another as "profane." One mentioned some four-letter words attributed to Kelly: "hell," "damn," and "crap." This troubles you. Kelly's training has emphasized how important courtesy, pleasantness, and most asssuredly nonoffensive language by servers is as part of a "quality" experience for your customers.

Much business is with Sunday and Wednesday churchgoers and with families with small children, so four-letter language is totally inappropriate. In her interview with you, Kelly displayed excellent interpersonal and rapport building skills. Presently majoring in leisure services at the local university, she saw the server position as an excellent opportunity to help understand customer service.

While you are clearly disappointed in the comment cards from Kelly's customers, and with its impact on your restaurant's goals, Kelly has promise of becoming an excellent server. But she must clearly clean up that language. You will conduct a coaching meeting with Kelly when she shows up for work this evening.

(b) Role for Server Kelly (to be read by all)

Read the background facts for your role as a server as presented in the "Role for Manager" outlined in "a" above. In a few minutes you will meet with your manager, who has asked to see you. Take a few minutes to decide how you will respond in the role play to the likely things that your manager will bring up in the meeting. During the role play, you may have to adapt your role as the discussion proceeds.

12 Managing Conflict, Stress, and Time

© Ingram Publishing/Alamy

Too much conflict can result in tremendous loss of human, as well as financial, capital.

Nothing in life is to be feared. It is only to be understood.
    —MARIE CURIE

Everything that irritates us about others can lead us to an understanding of ourselves.
    —CARL JUNG

Difficulties are meant to rouse, not discourage. The human spirit is to grow strong by conflict.
    —WILLIAM EMERY CHANNING

The Entrepreneur

Sam Hinton Construction (SHC) is a small, entrepreneurial firm in a mid-sized city situated in the south-eastern United States. SHC is run by Sam, the owner. Sam began the remodeling and repair business out of necessity when he couldn't find anyone to perform the needed work on his own home. External environmental changes, specifically the real estate and housing boom occurring across the nation due to monies being shifted from the stock markets to better investment opportunities in real estate, were impacting many communities just like Sam's. Add to this trend the impact of several years of active hurricane seasons in the south-eastern region of the country, and it is no surprise that construction supplies—skilled labor, materials, equipment, and management—were harder and harder to obtain for reasonable prices. Based on this and other data, Sam saw an opportunity for a planned career change, and after talking the situation over with his wife, Ellen, he decided to make the transition and start his own business. Sam's initial vision for his small company was to make money to support his family while meeting the needs of his customers in a cost-effective way. Sam lacked significant up-front capital, relying on his family's savings to start operations, so marketing efforts were limited to advertising in the local yellow pages. Once under way, he relied heavily on word-of-mouth to grow his small firm. He was a one-man show that was determined to make the venture successful.

He was not as experienced as his competitors, so he took every opportunity to read, observe, learn, and acquire the competencies necessary for his new profession. Initially, Sam chose work opportunities on the basis of his personal experiences with his own home. Thus, he was confident in the accuracy of his materials and labor estimates and his ability to complete a quality job, on time. Sam's initial strategy paid off, because other contractors did not seem to want to fool with the small-sized jobs. Those that did were not reputable. However, as his business grew, he found himself bidding for work that he was not as familiar or comfortable with. More and more of Sam's training occurred on the job. Sam won a bid to remodel an older home built prior to 1950, which included extensive plumbing and structural work. Unfortunately, he underestimated the types of work, amount of time, and supplies needed to complete the job and was forced to use a significant amount of his savings to finish the job.

Sam soon began building this "learning cost" into future bids to ensure he stayed afloat and remained in a positive cash flow position. His estimates for more complex projects were more like guestimates and tended to be higher than competitors' proposals. Sam decided to strategically reposition his small firm to survive. To justify the dollar difference to potential customers, Sam sold his firm as a quality renovating and remodeling operation—"You can go with the low bid, but you get what you pay for. My price is higher, because I pay attention to the details."

He really liked getting new work and prided himself on his ability to interact and communicate with his potential clients. Sam also believed that he was quite adept at seeing the "vision" for a given project. For example, he could take a customer's rough ideas and create a detailed drawing of what the completed work would look like. Even if the clients were not sure what they wanted, Sam found that through dialogue and listening to his customers, he could better understand their wants and needs.

Learning Objectives

After reading and studying this chapter, you should be able to:

1. Identify the causes of conflict.

2. Discuss conflict management styles and identify when each would be appropriate.

3. Describe principled negotiation.

4. Explain why modern life makes us particularly vulnerable to stress.

5. Describe both the costs and the benefits of stress.

6. Explain the major causes of stress.

7. Compare and contrast Type A behavior and Type B behavior.

8. Elaborate on personal ways to cope with stress.

9. Discuss some ways to effectively manage time.

Sam was committed to providing his customers with the best service possible. As he generated additional work, he worked more hours to complete projects. Sam would routinely arise at 4:30 a.m. to begin his day. The first order of business was making sure that he had the proper materials and equipment for the job each day. Over time he had gotten much better at planning such that he rarely had to stop and leave the site for additional supplies. Because of his improved planning and efficiency, he found he finished jobs much more quickly than before, but he still felt as if he was always one step behind where he needed to be. Sam typically knocked off around 4:30 p.m., so that he could visit with potential clients. The early evening hours were spent providing bids to secure future work. Once he arrived home, it was time for a quick bite before doing paperwork, tracking costs, and preparing estimates.

While Sam felt he had learned quite a bit during the past year and believed he had an effective strategy in place, he often found that he was stretched too thin managing the work and finances and filling the pipeline with new jobs to manage the schedule, produce quality work, handle customers, and continuously develop his knowledge. As the months passed, Sam's wife, Ellen, noticed he was not as easygoing as he once had been, and she rarely got a chance to visit with him on the weekends, much less during the week. Ellen was also becoming concerned about his health. He rarely slept through the night anymore, often getting up several times a night. She was shocked one night when she awakened to find him at his desk at 2:00 a.m. buried in receipts and bills. In addition to problems sleeping, Sam was developing bad eating habits. Ellen knew he often worked through lunch to complete various stages of his projects, but now he rarely had time for evening meals. Ellen believed that Sam's sleep deprivation and poor eating habits were partly to blame for his increasingly short temper. Uncharacteristically, Sam was more on edge, flying off the handle at the smallest incidents. Ellen's feelings were confirmed when she got off the phone with one of Sam's clients. The client had called quite unhappy with the way the project was going. The seams in the crown molding were unacceptable, the paint runs were unsightly, and when the client approached Sam about the imperfections, he got very gruff and defensive. As the customer complaints mounted, Ellen realized Sam was overwhelmed.

We have seen in the chapter preview that excessive stress can result in intrapersonal and interpersonal conflict, which is often very disruptive and damaging. A supervisor/team leader/entrepreneur must possess a variety of skills and two of the most critical are stress and conflict management. When stress is excessive, one's behavior can become dysfunctional. However, we must keep in mind that a certain amount of conflict and stress is healthy, because it can lead to more effective decision making.

For example, intrapersonal stress can motivate an individual to proactively make life changes for the better. When a certain amount of conflict is present, the status quo is examined. Individuals grapple with various solutions through their analysis of the situation. In many cases, this evaluation leads to better decisions.

<table>
<tr><td>**1**</td><td>Identify the causes of conflict.</td></tr>
</table>

Causes of Conflict

A supervisor/team leader must have a basic understanding of the causes of conflict before he or she can determine what is functional or dysfunctional. This section looks at some of the causes.

1. **Different goals or objectives.** If departments or individuals within an organization are working toward different goals, then conflict is almost always dysfunctional. It is important to develop a common set of goals that everyone supports.

2. **Communication.** Misunderstandings due to semantics, unfamiliar language, or ambiguous or incomplete information will surely lead to conflict.

3. **Structure.** Competition for scarce resources, power struggles between departments with conflicting objectives or reward systems, or interdependence of two or more groups to achieve their goals occur with organizational changes such as downsizing.

4. **Personal.** Incompatibility of personal goals or social values of employees with the role behavior required by their jobs will lead to conflict as will certain personality characteristics, such as authoritarianism or dogmatism. Individual stress can also be a source of intrapersonal and interpersonal conflict.

5. **Change.** Fears associated with having to accomplish a task differently, job security, or the loss of personal power and prestige can cause abnormal behavior. Change can be threatening. Even change that is perceived to be positive can cause conflict when individuals are responsible for new duties and tasks.

✔ **SELF-CHECK**

How many of the previous causes of conflict were operative in the chapter preview?

....

Historical Insight

Mary Parker's Integration Process

One of the first to focus on conflict in organizations from a research/consultant standpoint was sociologist Mary Parker Follett (1869–1933). Ignored for a time, her ideas are found in many management and psychology textbooks today. One of her contributions was her analysis of how to deal with conflict. She believed that any conflict of interest could be resolved by (1) voluntary submission of one side, (2) struggle and victory of one side over the other, (3) compromise, or (4) integration (today we call it joint problem solving).

Her preferred solution was the **integration process,** whereby everyone wins, as opposed to a win–lose situation, or a watered-down compromise by which neither side gets what it wants. An example Follett gave to illustrate the concept of integration was an incident that occurred when she was working in a small room in the Harvard library. The other person in the room wanted the window open, while Follett wanted it closed. After discussion, integration was achieved when they opened a window in the next room. This solution was not a compromise, since both got what they wanted: The other person got fresh air, and Follett did not have a cold draft on her back.

Follett also believed that the essence of collaboration and teamwork was creating the feeling of working *with* someone rather than *over* or *under* someone—the notion of "power with" rather than "power over."

integration process
A conflict resolution strategy in which everyone wins.

Source: Oliver Sheldon, *The Philosophy of Management* (New York: Pitman, 1939; originally published in 1923), p. 2.

Conflict Management Styles

Individuals must cope with all forms of interpersonal and intergroup conflict. It is important to properly diagnose the conflict situation so that it can be dealt with in the most effective manner. Exhibit 12-1 is a diagram of five conflict-handling styles that are based on the concern an individual has for oneself and for others. The five styles, which were influenced by Mary Parker Follett's original model, are as follows:

2
Discuss conflict management styles and identify when each would be appropriate.

- **Avoiding.** Avoiding is an unassertive, uncooperative style in which the individual's concern for self and others is low. It is a useful style when dealing with trivial issues or when the negative consequences of confrontation outweigh the need for resolution.

EXHIBIT 12-1

Interpersonal Conflict
Management Styles

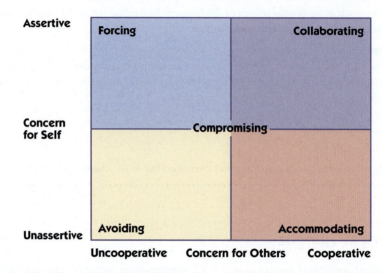

Source: Adapted from Thomas Ruble and Kenneth Thomas, "Support for a Two-Dimensional Model of Conflict Behavior," *Organizational Behavior and Human Performance,* vol. 16 (1976), p. 145. Used with permission of Elsevier.

- **Accommodating.** Accommodating is an unassertive, cooperative style in which the individual's concern for self is low while the concern for others is high. The accommodating approach downplays the parties' differences. It is an appropriate style to use when the issue is more important to the other party or the other party is right.

- **Forcing.** Forcing is an assertive, uncooperative style in which the individual's concern for self is high while the concern for others is low. This approach uses power to resolve conflict. A forcing style is useful in an emergency situation, where quick decisions are necessary. It is also useful for correcting unethical behavior.

- **Compromising.** Compromising is a somewhat assertive, cooperative style in which the individual has a moderate amount of concern for both self and others. The objective is to find a middle ground. The compromising style is appropriate when the parties have reached an impasse due to mutually exclusive goals.

- **Collaborating.** Collaborating is an assertive, cooperative approach in which the individual has a high concern for self and others. Collaboration is a problem-solving style. It is effective when dealing with conflict "head on," trying to surface all of the pertinent issues, and attempting to interpret differing points of view.

http://www.cri.cc/

Conflict management theory today supports collaboration as the appropriate approach to resolve conflict. Since collaboration in many cases leads to win–win outcomes, it is easy to discern why collaboration advocates support this approach as "the model" for handling conflict.

During the 1970s and 1980s, the contingency movement gained momentum. Proponents of this theory maintained that collaboration in all situations is unrealistic. For example, a management student, who is a member of a local emergency response team, made the following observation when conflict management styles were covered in class.

Conflict management styles must be adapted to fit the situation at hand.

Her unit was activated shortly after a tragic train wreck occurred. The emergency response team prepares for these types of situations regularly. However, unanticipated problems arise that must be dealt with effectively as quickly as possible in order to save lives. Although the team members may utilize the collaborative approach during the planning stages, they do not have time to rely on this method while in the field. She indicated that the approach most often used by the team in the field was the forcing style, because it was the most effective.

The avoiding, accommodating, forcing, and compromising conflict management styles are usually best used when dealing with tactical, day-to-day, short-term problems, whereas collaboration (and compromising, to a limited extent) is a conflict management style more appropriate for ad hoc task forces and long-term strategic problems.

✔ SELF-CHECK

In the chapter preview, what would be the preferred primary conflict management style for Ellen to use when approaching Sam about making changes in his life? Why?

Using Principled Negotiation to Resolve Conflict

3 Describe principled negotiation.

A real breakthrough in conflict management and resolution is found in the concepts proposed by Roger Fisher and William Ury of the Harvard negotiation project. They emphasize that, whether negotiation involves a peace settlement among nations or a business contract, people often engage in *positional bargaining*. This common form of negotiation involves proposing and then giving up a sequence of positions. The idea is to give up things that are not important. Hence, proposals are "padded" initially. For this form of negotiation to succeed, it must meet three criteria of fair negotiation: "It should produce a wise agreement if agreement is possible; it should be efficient; and it should improve, or at least not damage, the relationship between the parties."[1]

When people bargain over positions, they tend to back themselves into corners defending their positions, which results in a number of either win–lose or lose–lose outcomes. Moreover, arguing over positions often endangers an ongoing relationship by straining and sometimes shattering relationships. In a marriage this results in divorce, and in business the result can be the breakup of an otherwise successful operation. Many negotiations involve more than two parties, and in these cases positional bargaining compounds the problem of negotiating an agreement.

In their work with the Harvard negotiation project, Fisher and Ury developed an alternative to positional bargaining that they call **principled negotiation,** or negotiation on the merits. The four basic components of principled negotiation are as follows:

principled negotiation
Negotiation on the merits.

1. Separating the people from the problem.

2. Focusing on interests, not positions.

3. Generating a variety of possibilities before deciding what to do.

4. Insisting that the result be based on some objective standard.

EXHIBIT **12-2**

Contrast of Positional Bargaining and Principled Negotiation

Problem Positional Bargaining: Which Game Should You Play?		Solution Change the Game— Negotiate on the Merits
Softball	**Hardball**	**Principled**
Participants are friends.	Participants are adversaries.	Participants are problem solvers.
The goal is agreement.	The goal is victory.	The goal is a wise outcome reached efficiently and amicably.
Make concessions to cultivate the relationship.	Demand concessions as a condition of the relationship.	**Separate the people from the problem.**
Be soft on the people and the problem.	Be hard on the problem and the people.	Be soft on the people, hard on the problem.
Trust others.	Distrust others.	Proceed independent of trust.
Change your position easily.	Dig in to your position.	**Focus on interests, not positions.**
Make offers.	Make threats.	Explore interests.
Disclose your bottom line.	Mislead as to your bottom line.	Avoid having a bottom line.
Accept one-sided losses to reach agreement.	Demand one-sided gains as the price of agreement.	**Invent options for mutual gain.**
Search for the single answer: the one *they* will accept.	Search for the single answer: the one *you* will accept.	Develop multiple options to choose from; decide later.
Insist on agreement.	Insist on your position.	**Insist on using objective criteria.**
Try to avoid a contest of will.	Try to win a contest of will.	Try to reach a result based on standards independent of will.
Yield to pressure.	Apply pressure.	Reason and be open to reason; yield to principle, not pressure.

Source: "Positional Bargaining: Which Game Should You Play?" chart from *Getting to Yes,* 2e by Roger Fisher, William Ury and Bruce Patton. Copyright © 1981, 1991 by Roger Fisher and William Ury. Reprinted by permission of Houghton Mifflin Co. All rights reserved.

Consultant facilitators for a number of joint ventures and partnerships involving multiple parties have noted that educating the joint venture parties in the concepts of principled negotiation has resulted in a high percentage of win–win resolutions in dispute settlements. Exhibit 12-2 illustrates the difference between positional bargaining and principled negotiation. Notice that in positional bargaining, one can either play "hardball" or "softball."

Overcoming Interpersonal Conflicts

The authors are convinced that principled negotiation is an excellent approach for dealing with conflicts among departments within an organization or resolving conflicts in joint ventures or partnerships. Perhaps a more pervasive challenge is managing interpersonal conflicts. This challenge has been accelerated because of fears of downsizing, mergers, and unknown organizational futures. Job insecurity fueled by these fears produces fertile ground for conflict. Dysfunctional interpersonal conflict can lead to a variety of negative outcomes, including poor morale, low productivity, increased absenteeism, and higher turnover. In fact, in exit interviews, 50 percent of individuals list unresolved conflict as their primary reason for leaving.[2]

Industrial psychologist and trainer Dr. Jack Singer makes a strong case that human resource professionals and supervisors must learn conflict resolution strategies and teach them to other employees. He recommends a three-step program for assessing and implementing a conflict resolution strategy, as shown in Exhibit 12-3. As evidenced by the following example, conflict assessment and training can be quite effective.

When Fernando Costa became divisional manufacturing manager at MM Kembla Products in Kembla, Australia, relationships between management, supervisory, and shop floor personnel had broken down, and interactions often resulted in confrontation. "Dialogues were nonexistent and threats were the acceptable way of putting a position forward. Any issue—no matter how trivial—would be addressed through union representatives," says Costa. The company decided to offer conflict resolution training, and, 2 years later, the benefits are evident. "There is a total change in the way people talk to each other today," Costa says. Union representatives no longer use abusive language to intimidate management, and management addresses problems more effectively, using the conflict resolution techniques they learned. Employees can resolve some issues without involving senior management, and without increasing tensions on the floor."[3]

Many interpersonal conflicts occur when one person finds another person's behavior uncomfortable, bullying, or irritating. Robert Bramson has identified basic types of difficult behavior, three of which are particularly troublesome when trying to resolve conflicts. Exhibit 12-4 identifies these three types and gives suggestions for coping with them.

http://www.stress.org

What is Stress?

A number of concepts presented earlier in this chapter lend insight into how to manage stress. Organizations and supervisors can suffer serious consequences if stress is not understood and managed. We now examine the topic in more depth.

4

Explain why modern life makes us particularly vulnerable to stress.

Definition of Stress

For many years the medical community failed to take stress seriously. One of the reasons for this failure was the lack of an adequate definition of stress and of research into its effects.

EXHIBIT 12-3

STEP 1. EVALUATING CONFLICT STYLE

Several self-assessment questionnaires have been developed over the years that are geared toward offering participants insight into how they react in typical conflict situations. Consider using them. The insight they provide allows you to understand what "buttons" get pushed when a person is provoked, and becomes useful as a tool to reevaluate and enhance one's behavior.

STEP 2. IDENTIFYING CONFLICT BEHAVIORS

Nonproductive Behaviors. Confronting, dominating, defending, using sarcasm and hostile humor, repressing emotions, insisting on being right, stonewalling, blaming.

Neutral Behaviors. Avoiding, cooling off, apologizing, giving in, backing off to avoid confrontation.

Positive Behaviors. Active listening, empathizing, disarming, inquiring, using "I feel" statements, recognizing how internal dialogue impacts emotional reactions. The goal is to eliminate negative and neutral behaviors and practice positive confrontation reduction skills until they become new habits.

STEP 3. LEARNING POWERFUL CONFRONTATION REDUCTION SKILLS

Active Listening. The key to all interpersonal communications is genuine listening, as opposed to defensive listening, where you plan your retort *while* the other person is talking to you. To begin to really listen, set up a role-playing environment.

First, paraphrase what the other person says in your own words, without judging, agreeing, or disagreeing. Listen to and reflect upon the content, needs, and feelings of the other person.

Second, ask for feedback to determine whether you interpreted correctly. If you have not, ask for clarification.

Third, once you are sure you grasp the message and feelings of the other person, respond.

Fourth, the other person then should listen and paraphrase for you. This process continues until you have both clarified your positions.

Empathizing. This involves putting yourself in the other person's shoes and trying to see the world through his or her eyes, taking into account cultural, racial, gender, and experiential differences.

Disarming. The fastest way to defuse an argument is to find some truth in what the other person is saying, even if you do not agree with the basic criticism or complaint. For example, saying "*I can understand* how you'd feel angry with me since you believed that I started the rumor" acknowledges and validates the angry person's feelings without actually agreeing with what was said. This opens the door to clarification.

Inquiring. By asking for clarification of ideas, needs, and feelings *you* signal a feeling of working toward mutual understanding and compromise.

"I Feel" Statements. Expressing yourself with such statements as "I feel angry because you seem to be avoiding me" is much more productive than the accusatory, "*You* made me angry and it's *your* fault that I've had a bad day at work today." In the first scenario, *you* take responsibility for your own feelings and share them; in the second, you escalate the confrontation by blaming and putting the person on the defensive.

Source: Resources, Aberdeen Woods Conference Center, 201 Aberdeen Parkway, Peachtree City, GA 30269-1422. (Vol. 3, Issue 3, November 1997). Jack N. Singer, *Personality Collisions,* pp. 5–6.

stress Any external stimulus that causes wear and tear on one's psychological or physical well-being.

Stress can be defined as any external stimulus that causes wear and tear on one's psychological or physical well-being.[4]

Stress researchers point out that modern men and women sometimes react to the strains of work and everyday life the same way our primitive ancestors did. In the days of the caveman, when there was danger, a chemical reaction in the body geared our ancestors to either fight or flee. The problem for some modern men and women is that their bodies still react the same way to external stimuli, causing them to maintain a constant fight-or-flight readiness. The anxiety is similar to that of soldiers in combat, and it causes wear and tear on our bodies.

EXHIBIT **12-4**

Coping with Difficult
Behavior

Hostile-Aggressives: Hostile-aggressive behavior occurs when individuals bully other people by bombarding them with cutting remarks, or by throwing a tantrum when things do not go their way. Their focus is on attacking the other party in a conflict. Openly emotional, they use these displays to create discomfort or surprise in their adversaries. Underlying their behavior is a strong sense of "shoulds," internal rules about the way things ought to be. A key to dealing with hostile-aggressive behavior is to recognize the behavior and not to be drawn into it yourself.

HOSTILE-AGGRESSIVES:

- Stand up for yourself.
- Use self-assertive language.
- Give them time to run down.
- Avoid a direct confrontation.

Complainers: Complainers gripe constantly but never take action about what they complain about, usually because they feel powerless or they do not want to take responsibility. You may want to hear complainers out and let them know you understand their feelings, but do not get drawn into pitying them. Use a problem-solving stance. For instance, a manager might say, "Joan, what do you want the outcome of our meeting to be? What action needs to be taken?" This focuses the complainer on solutions, not complaints.

COMPLAINERS:

- Listen attentively.
- State the facts without apology.
- Acknowledge their feelings.
- Use a problem-solving mode.
- Avoid complaining with them.

Clams: Clams are silent and unresponsive when asked for opinions. They react to conflict by closing up (like their namesakes) and refusing to discuss problems. The challenge in coping with clams is getting them to open up and talk. Open-ended questions are invaluable, as is patience in allowing them their silence for a reasonable time.

CLAMS:

- Ask open-ended questions.
- Ask more open-ended questions.
- Be patient in waiting for a response.
- If no response occurs, tell clams what you plan to do, because no discussion has taken place.

Source: Adapted from *Coping with Difficult People* by Robert M. Bramson, copyright © 1981 by Robert Bramson. Used by permission of Doubleday, a division of Random House, Inc.

Jane Coleman was driving to work during the morning rush hour. An irresponsible driver nearly caused an accident by cutting into her lane. By the time Jane arrived at work, she was already tense; the problem was compounded when she discovered that one of her key employees was out with the flu. Two emergencies during the day caused her to end the day anxious and exhausted.

Many of us face situations similar to Jane's. Note that stress can be caused by an external stimulus, such as driving on the freeway, or by conditions on the job. An excellent definition of job stress is "a condition arising from the interaction of people and their jobs and characterized by changes within people that force them to deviate from their normal functioning."[5] Under normal conditions, our bodies and minds are in a state of equilibrium (see Exhibit 12-5). As a result of occurrences on or off the job, however, our equilibrium may be disrupted. In attempting to recover from this imbalance, we function differently and sometimes generate a fight-or-flight chemical reaction. Obviously, Jane, as a supervisor, cannot leave her job or pick a fight with someone, but the chemical reaction in her body occurs anyway. Exhibit 12-6 illustrates how stress takes its toll from a medical perspective.

EXHIBIT 12-5

Equilibrium and
Disequilibrium

5

Describe both
the costs and the
benefits of stress.

The Costs of Stress

It has been estimated that two thirds of all visits to physicians can be traced to stress-related symptoms. It is, for example, a major contributor to heart disease, cancer, lung problems, accidents, cirrhosis of the liver, and suicide. Even the common cold and skin rashes are sometimes related to a person's experiencing prolonged and severe stress. Industry leaders are aware that such symptoms play a major role in absenteeism, accidents, and lost productivity.

Certainly a person under severe and/or prolonged stressful conditions cannot function as effectively as a person leading a more balanced life. We are not implying that stress is all negative, however, because a certain amount adds zest to life.

The Positive Aspects of Stress

Some amount of stress is necessary to accomplish anything meaningful. The teams that play in the Super Bowl are certainly in a stressful situation. Anyone who has played a sport or spoken in front of a large group has been in a stressful situation. Without question, moderate amounts of stress improve performance. For example, difficult but attainable objectives motivate better than easy objectives. People who seek types of work and leisure that engage their skills find life zestful and interesting. The secret is to involve oneself in challenging work and active leisure

EXHIBIT 12-6

How Stress Takes Its Toll

Like its more severe cousin depression, ordinary stress is harmful to the body as well as the mind. Stress comes in two forms, each with its own biochemistry: **acute** (a response to imminent danger, it turbocharges the system with powerful hormones that can damage the cardiovascular system) and **chronic** (caused by constant emotional pressure the victim can't control, it produces hormones that can weaken the immune system and damage bones).

1. A stress response starts in the brain...
When the brain detects a threat, a number of structures, including the hypothalamus, amygdala and pituitary gland, go on alert: they exchange information with each other and then send signaling hormones and nerve impulses to the rest of the body to prepare for fight or flight.

Pituitary gland
Amygdala
Hypothalamus

2. ...and the body unleashes a flood of hormones...
Adrenal glands react to the alert by releasing epinephrine (adrenaline), which makes the heart pump faster and the lungs work harder to flood the body with oxygen. The adrenal glands also release extra cortisol and other glucocorticoids, which help the body convert sugars into energy. Nerve cells release norepinephrine, which tenses the muscles and sharpens the senses to prepare for action. Digestion shuts down.

3. ...that can cause significant damage.
When the threat passes, epinephrine and norepinephrine levels drop, but if danger comes too often they can damage the arteries. Chronic low level stress keeps the glucocorticoids in circulation, leading to a weakened immune system, loss of bone mass, suppression of the reproductive system, and memory problems.

Muscles tense
Lungs ventilate faster
Arteries widen
Heart beats faster
Stomach, digestion shuts down
Adrenal glands release hormones

Source: *Time,* Special Issue, "How Your Mind Can Heal Your Body," January 20, 2003, pp.68–69. Copyright © 2003, Time Inc. Reprinted by permission.

accompanied by sufficient rest and retreat. Life is full of stressors that can stimulate, energize, and aid in such positive outcomes as individual health and high productivity. We call the constructive dimensions of positive stress *eustress*, which can be a powerful motivator. Examples of eustress include going to an athletic event or participating in sports.

Major Causes of Stress

6
Explain the major causes of stress.

A number of factors contribute to individual stress. Among these are (1) life events, (2) personal psychological makeup, and (3) organizational and work-related factors. Especially in the case of organizational and work-related factors, the result is likely to be burnout.

Life Events

Stress occurs whenever we face situations that require changes in behavior and a higher level of activity. It would be impossible to list all of the situations that place stress on human beings, since the mere fact of living does so. However, researchers have identified major life events, both positive and negative, that require drastic changes in a person's behavior. If many of these events occur within a year's time, a person becomes particularly susceptible to unpleasant physical or psychological consequences of excessive stress.

Traffic is an external stimulus that can act as a common stressor. What is one example of an internal stimulus?

Digital Vision/Getty Images

life event Anything that causes a person to deviate from normal functioning.

Exhibit 12-7 lists a number of stress-provoking life events. A major **life event** is anything that causes a person to deviate from normal functioning. The events are ranked in order of impact on a person's life. The death of a spouse has the most impact; change in the number of family get-togethers causes the least stress. To obtain your score, record the points for each event you experienced in the past year. Add the events' points to get your total; anything above 300 points is the change level. Steps and action plans can be initiated to offset a high score and thus avoid adverse consequences. We discuss this later in the chapter.

> Patrick Hogan was a 34-year-old supervisor who seemed to have it all. He had a good job, was happily married, had two children, and was on top of the world. At work, he was highly productive and outgoing and was considered a leading candidate for advancement.
>
> In the course of a year, several events occurred in Patrick's life that completely disrupted his patterns of living. A long-time friend enticed him to invest in a steak house that the friend would operate. The restaurant lost money, and the friend left town, leaving Patrick responsible for the bank note. To save his investment, he started moonlighting at the restaurant, not getting home many nights until 1 a.m.
>
> While Patrick was struggling with the restaurant, his mother died after a lingering illness. Two weeks after the funeral, his wife had an accident and was confined to bed with a slipped disk. For the first time in his life, Patrick had to prepare meals, wash clothes, and care for the children while at the same time carrying on with his regular job and struggling with the restaurant. At work, Patrick's behavior changed drastically. He was impatient with his employees and lost his temper quickly. He became depressed and found it difficult to reach decisions about matters that he had previously handled decisively.

✔ SELF-CHECK

Based on the description of what happened in Patrick Hogan's life within the past year, calculate his score from the life event table. Assume you are his supervisor and Patrick comes to you to talk about his situation. What advice would you give him?

EXHIBIT 12-7

Sources of Stress

Life Event	Points
Death of a spouse	99
Divorce	91
Marriage	85
Death of close family member	84
Fired at work	83
Pregnancy	78
Marital separation	78
Jail term	72
Personal injury or illness	68
Death of close friend	68
Retirement	68
Change of financial state	61
Spouse begins or stops work	58
Marital reconciliation	57
Christmas	56
Change in health of family member	56
Foreclosure of mortgage or loan	55
Sex difficulties	53
Addition of new family member	51
Change to different line of work	51
Business readjustment	50
Mortgage over $10,000 (Present-day amount of $80,000)	48
Change in residence	47
Change in number of arguments with spouse	46
Change in responsibilities at work	46
Begin or end school	45
Trouble with boss	45
Revision of personal habits	44
Trouble with in-laws	43
Vacation	43
Change in living conditions	42
Son or daughter leaving home	41
Outstanding personal achievement	38
Change in work hours or conditions	36
Change in school	36
Minor violations of law	30
Change in eating habits	29
Mortgage or loan less than $10,000 (Present-day amount of $80,000)	27
Change in sleeping habits	27
Change in recreation	26
Change in church activities	26
Change in number of family get-togethers	15

Adapted from "The 1990s Stress Scale," ALBUQUERQUE JOURNAL, December 16, 1991, p. B1.

Any major life event, even a positive one, can provoke stress since it causes an individual to deviate from normal functioning.

Stone/Getty Images

7

Compare and contrast Type A behavior and Type B behavior.

Personal Psychological Makeup

Americans have long been noted for their emphasis on work. The United States has a justifiable reputation as a country where individuals, through hard work, can achieve considerable economic success. Some people, however, have become so caught up in the work ethic that work becomes the end itself rather than the means to an end. New Zealanders say that "Americans live to work and New Zealanders work to live." Our point is that some Americans have become workaholics, and this excessiveness has behavioral consequences that take a toll over a period of time. Researchers have identified two basic types of behavior characterizing people in our society: Type A and Type B.

Type A behavior A behavior pattern characterized by (a) trying to accomplish too much in a short time and (b) lacking patience and struggling against time and other people to accomplish one's ends.

Type A Behavior. Cardiologists Meyer Friedman and Roy Rosenman first defined the term **Type A behavior.** Individuals who exhibit Type A behavior tend to try to accomplish too many things in a short time. Lacking patience, they struggle against time and other people to accomplish their ends. As a consequence, they become irritated by trivial things. Type A people also tend to be workaholics. Because of their psychological makeup they may be subject to stress over prolonged periods. For this reason, Type A people have a much higher risk of heart disease than do Type B people.[6]

Type B behavior A behavior pattern characterized by (a) tending to be calmer than someone with Type A behavior, (b) devoting more time to exercise, and (c) being more realistic in estimating the time it takes to complete an assignment.

Type B Behavior. People exhibiting **Type B behavior** tend to be calmer, to take more time to exercise, and to be more realistic than Type As in estimating the amount of time needed to complete an assignment. Type Bs also worry less and, in general, desire more satisfaction from their work.

Studies of Type A and B behaviors indicate that 60 percent of managers and supervisors fall into the category of Type A people (see Exhibit 12-8). Many supervisors respond to all events as if they were emergencies or life-threatening situations. Managers and supervisors who exhibit extreme Type A behavior patterns tend to practice close supervision and find it difficult to delegate. They are concerned that errors might reflect on past achievements, and so they become excessively task oriented.[7]

EXHIBIT 12-8

Behavior-Type Quiz

To find out which behavior type you are, circle the number on the scale below for each trait that best characterizes your behavior.

Casual about appointments	1	2	3	4	5	6	7	8	Never late
Not competitive	1	2	3	4	5	6	7	8	Very competitive
Never feel rushed even under pressure	1	2	3	4	5	6	7	8	Always rushed
Take things one at a time	1	2	3	4	5	6	7	8	Try to do many things at once, think about what I'm going to do next
Slow doing things	1	2	3	4	5	6	7	8	Fast (eating, walking, etc.)
Express feelings	1	2	3	4	5	6	7	8	"Sit on" feelings
Many interests	1	2	3	4	5	6	7	8	Few interests outside work

Total score: _____ Total score multiplied by 3: _____

The interpretation is as follows:

Number of Points	Type of Personality
Less than 90	B
90 to 99	B+
100 to 105	A−
106 to 119	A
120 or more	A+

Source: A. P. Brief, R. S. Schuler, and M. V. Sell, *Managing Job Stress* (Boston: Little, Brown & Co., 1981), p. 87. Reprinted by permission of Arthur P. Brief.

Organizational and Work-Related Factors

We have discussed many organizational and work-related factors that may cause excessive stress. As shown in Exhibit 12-9, these range from having poorly defined job descriptions to having autocratic or permissive leadership. If these factors exist in an organization over a period of time, they will cause extensive damage in the form of dissatisfaction, high turnover, low productivity, incomplete goal accomplishment, and job burnout. As the following example shows, stress can even create an opportunity for union activity.

> A union organizer approached several employees from the home office of XYZ Life & Casualty Insurance Company. He was quickly told that they were not interested in joining a union, since they had excellent pay, good working conditions, and a high regard for their supervisors.

> Six months later, a supervisor retired from the claims department. The new supervisor, after being on the job a month, called two long-time employees into the office and gave them dismissal notices without a reason for doing so. That night, five employees drove 90 miles to a meeting in another city with the union organizer. Upon their return, they obtained enough employee signatures to force an election to determine whether the union would represent employees in the XYZ home office.

EXHIBIT 12-9

Organizational and Work-Related Factors that Cause Excessive Stress

- A highly centralized organization with decision making concentrated at the top.
- Many levels and narrow spans of control.
- Excessive and continuous pressure from higher levels.
- Conflicting demands on lower levels.
- Lack of clarity with respect to organizational and work objectives.
- Widespread autocratic leadership and close supervision.
- Little or no participation in decision making by supervisor and workers.
- Inconsistent application of company policies.
- Favoritism in decisions regarding layoffs, salary increases, promotions, and the like.
- Poor working conditions.
- Poor communication.
- Lack of structure and job descriptions.
- Widespread permissive leadership.
- Technical glitches with computer interfaces.

Burnout

burnout A malady caused by excessive stress in the setting where people invest most of their time and energy.

One of the most common results of excessive stress is burnout. **Burnout** is a stress-related malady that generally originates in the setting where people invest most of their time and energy. This setting is usually the work environment, but it could just as well be the home or the golf course.

The seriousness of the burnout problem has been highlighted by researchers Robert Golembiewski and Robert Munzenrider. Utilizing an adapted version of the *Maslach Burnout Inventory (MBI),* they discovered that 40 percent of more than 12,000 respondents in 33 organizations suffered from advanced phases of burnout.[8] Exhibit 12-10 explains the subscales used in the MBI and charts the eight phases of burnout. A person scoring in phase I would be highly energized and motivated by the positive aspects of stress. In Maslow's terms, such a person would be operating at the esteem and self-fulfillment level of the need hierarchy. To a lesser extent, the same would be true of a person in phases II, III, IV, and V. Difficulties occur when a person reaches phases VI, VII, and VIII, the advanced stages of burnout.

Candidates for job burnout have three distinguishing characteristics. First, they experience stress caused predominantly by job-related stressors. Second, they tend to be idealistic and/or self-motivated achievers. Third, they tend to seek unattainable goals.

Although over the long term the ideal way to deal with burnout is to address the factors that are causing it, in the short term burnout can be managed through use of any of a variety of strategies for coping with stress. Some of the ways companies are preventing or attacking burnout are through providing an on-site fitness center or a subsidy program. At Allied Signal, 74 percent of employees who use a fitness center or health club say working out raised their productivity and 62 percent say it improved stress coping abilities.[9] It is estimated that job stress and related problems cost companies an estimated $200 billion a year.[10]

EXHIBIT **12-10**

MBI Subclass and
Phases of Burnout

The adapted Maslach Burnout Inventory, or MBI, consists of 25 items, rated on a scale of 1 (very much *unlike* me) to 7 (very much *like* me). There are three subscales.

Depersonalization: Individuals with high scores on this subscale tend to view people as objects and to distance themselves from others. Example: "I worry that this job is hardening me emotionally."

Personal Accomplishment (reversed): Respondents with high scores on this subscale see themselves as not performing well on a task that they perceive as not being particularly worthwhile. Example: "I have accomplished few worthwhile things on this job."

Emotional Exhaustion: Individuals with high scores on this subscale see themselves as operating beyond comfortable coping limits and as approaching "the end of the rope" in psychological and emotional senses. Example: "I feel fatigued when I get up in the morning and have to face another day on the job."

Emotional exhaustion is considered most characteristic of advanced phases of burnout, and depersonalization is considered least virulent. Ratings of high or low on the three subscales determine the progressive phases of burnout, generating an eight-phase model of burnout:

	Progressive Phases of Burnout							
	I	II	III	IV	V	VI	VII	VIII
Depersonalization	Low	High	Low	High	Low	High	Low	High
Personal accomplishment	Low	Low	High	High	Low	Low	High	High
Emotional exhaustion	Low	Low	Low	Low	High	High	High	High

Adapted from Robert T. Golembiewski and Robert F. Munzenrider, *Phases of Burnout* Copyright © 1988, pp. 19–28. Reproduced with permission of Greenwood Publishing Group, Inc. Westport, CT.

Ways to Cope with Personal Stress

8 Elaborate on personal ways to cope with stress.

Four methods that have helped many supervisors to cope with stress are (1) engaging in physical exercise, (2) practicing relaxation techniques, (3) gaining a sense of control, and (4) developing and maintaining good interpersonal relationships.

Physical Exercise

People who exercise a minimum of two or three times a week are much less prone to the adverse symptoms of stress than those who do not. The exercise should be vigorous to the point of inducing perspiration. A person's muscles and circulatory system are not designed for a life of inactivity. People who revitalize their bodies are much less likely to worry and become upset over events and problems. The exercise can take many forms—tennis, handball, jogging, walking, swimming, gardening, or workouts at a health and exercise spa. Exhibit 12-11 highlights the special benefits of walking.

Earlier in the chapter, we highlighted the problems that Patrick Hogan was facing and saw how the stress of dealing with these problems had drastically changed his behavior. Patrick's manager noticed the change and counseled him regarding the situation. After Patrick had discussed his circumstances, the manager asked him if he engaged in

EXHIBIT 12-11

Walk, Don't Run

It's simple, it's cheap, and studies show that walking may be the best exercise for reducing the risk of heart disease, stroke and diabetes.

You want to get healthy. You know you need to exercise more. You may have even jump-started your New Year's resolutions by joining a gym. But if you're not ready to squeeze into shorts or a leotard and grunt through an hour of Spinning or Jazzercise or kickboxing, don't despair. There's growing agreement among exercise researchers that the intense physical activities offered by most health clubs is not the only—or even necessarily the best—path to better health. In fact, the best thing most of us can do, say the experts, may be to walk.

Yes, walk. Not run or jog or spring. Just walk, at a reasonably vigorous clip (3 m.p.h.–4 m.p.h.) for half an hour or so, maybe five or six times a week. You may not feel the benefits all at once, but the evidence suggests that over the long term, a regular walking routine can do a world of preventive good, from lowering your risk of stroke, diabetes and osteoporosis to treating arthritis, high blood pressure, and even depression.

Walking, in fact, may be the perfect exercise. For starters, it's one of the safest things you can do with your body. It's much easier on the knees than running and, beyond an occasional stitch in the side, doesn't trigger untoward side effects. "Regular physical activity is probably as close to a magic bullet as we will come in modern medicine," says Dr. JoAnn Manson, chief of preventive medicine at Harvard's Brigham and Women's Hospital. "If everyone in the U.S. were to walk briskly 30 minutes a day, we could cut the incidence of many chronic diseases 30% to 40%."

Source: Christine Gorman, "Walk, Don't Run," TIME, http://www.time.com/timecovers/1101020121/walking.html, accessed January 18, 2003. Copyright © 2003 TIME Inc. Reprinted by permission.

regular exercise. Patrick answered that he simply did not have the time as a result of having to moonlight at the restaurant.

Patrick's manager persuaded him to work out three times a week in the company exercise room. Within 2 weeks' time, Patrick's on-the-job behavior was back to normal, and he had begun developing a plan to cope with some of the problems outside of work.

Relaxation Techniques

Exhibit 12-12 summarizes several of the relaxation techniques that are easy to use and are effective. These techniques are particularly useful to supervisors/team leaders because they are neither time-consuming nor costly. Research shows that when practiced on a regular basis, these techniques enable one to deal more effectively with stress and may lower blood pressure and, in general, improve physical and emotional health.

A Sense of Control

Supervisors who have a sense of control over their own lives handle stress much better than those who feel they are manipulated by life's events or by other people. If they have other interests, supervisors are better able to look at work as only one aspect of life. Many of them also have a deep faith in religion, which allows them to cope with adversity. Some ways to gain control are as follows:

1. Plan. Look ahead, identifying both long- and short-term goals. Also, identify causes of stress and ways to alleviate them.

2. Get to know and like yourself. Identify your strengths and interests and pursue activities that capitalize on your strengths.

3. Perceive situations as challenges rather than as problems.

Physical exercise is one of the best ways to effectively manage stress.

© Tom & Dee Ann McCarthy/CORBIS

4. Take a long vacation rather than a series of short vacations.

5. Do things for others, either through a religious group or by becoming involved in some kind of volunteer work or youth activities such as Boy or Girl Scouts, Big Brother or Big Sister, or Junior Achievement.

6. Provide yourself with positive reinforcement when you do a task well. Treat yourself to a reward when you accomplish something worthwhile.

Developing and Maintaining Good Interpersonal Relationships

It is most important for one's mental health and happiness to give priority to close relationships—family and friends. These relationships provide a base of mutual support where one can discuss success, opportunities, issues, and problems.

According to psychologist Alex Michalos, good interpersonal relationships are much more important to one's happiness and well-being than either income or looks. When one is facing a major challenge or problem, it is helpful to be able to discuss it with a spouse or friend. It is also important to maintain relationships and confront problems between yourself and loved ones and friends through discussion rather than through avoidance. Exhibit 12-13 provides a summary of strategies that help make you feel great. The second strategy, "take control of your time," is discussed next.

EXHIBIT 12-12

Relaxation Techniques

Relaxation Response. One of the best studied stress-relievers is the relaxation response, first described by Harvard's Herbert Benson, M.D., more than 20 years ago. Its great advantage is that it requires no special posture or place. Say you're stuck in traffic when you're expected at a meeting. Or you're having trouble falling asleep because your mind keeps replaying some awkward situation.

- Sit or recline comfortably. Close your eyes if you can, and relax your muscles.
- Breathe deeply. To make sure that you are breathing deeply, place one hand on your abdomen, the other on your chest. Breathe in slowly through your nose, and as you do you should feel your abdomen (not your chest) rise.
- Slowly exhale. As you do, focus on your breathing. Some people do better if they silently repeat the word *one* as they exhale; it helps clear the mind.
- If thoughts intrude, do not dwell on them; allow them to pass on and return to focusing on your breathing.

Although you can turn to this exercise any time you feel stressed, doing it regularly for 10 to 20 minutes at least once a day can put you in a generally calm mode that can see you through otherwise stressful situations.

Cleansing Breath. Epstein, who has searched the world literature for techniques people have claimed valuable for coping, focuses on those that are simple and powerful. He calls them "gems," devices that work through differing means, can be learned in minutes, can be done any time, anywhere, and have a pronounced physiologic effect. At the top of his list is the quickest of all—a cleansing breath.

Take a huge breath in. Hold it for three to four seconds. Then let it out v-e-r-y s-l-o-w-l-y. As you blow out, blow out all the tension in your body.

Relaxing Postures. "The research literature demonstrates that sitting in certain positions, all by itself, has a pronounced effect," says Epstein. Sit anywhere. Relax your shoulders so that they are comfortably rounded. Allow your arms to drop by your sides. Rest your hands, palm side up, on top of your thighs. With your knees comfortably bent, extend your legs and allow your feet, supported on the heels, to fall gently outward. Let your jaw drop. Close your eyes and breathe deeply for a minute or two.

Passive Stretches. It's possible to relax muscles without effort; gravity can do it all. Start with your neck and let your head fall forward to the right. Breathe in and out normally. With every breath out, allow your head to fall more. Do the same for shoulders, arms, back.

Imagery. Find a comfortable posture and close your eyes. Imagine the most relaxed place you've ever been. We all have a place like this and can call it to mind anywhere, any time. For everyone it is different. It may be a lake. It may be a mountain. It may be a cottage at the beach. Are you there?

Five—Count 'Em, Five—Tricks. Since you can never have too many tricks in your little bag, here are some "proven stress-busters" from Paul Rosch, M.D., president of the American Institute of Stress:

- Curl your toes against the soles of your feet as hard as you can for 15 seconds, then relax them. Progressively tense and relax the muscles in your legs, stomach, back, shoulders, neck.
- Visualize lying on a beach, listening to waves coming in and feeling the warm sun and gentle breezes on your back. Or, if you prefer, imagine floating, with your eyes closed while waves gently rock you back and forth.
- Set aside 20 to 30 minutes a day to do anything you want—even nothing.
- Take a brisk walk.
- Keep an iPod handy and loaded with relaxing, enjoyable music.

"Beating stress is a matter of removing yourself from the situation and taking a few breaths," says Rosch. "If I find myself getting stressed I ask myself 'is this going to matter to me in five years?' Usually the answer is no. If so, why get worked up over it?"

Source: Adapted from John Carpi, "A Smorgasbord of Stress-Stoppers", Psychology Today 29(1), January/February 1996, p. 39. Reprinted with permission from Psychology Today Magazine, copyright © 1996 Sussex Publishers Inc.

EXHIBIT 12-13

Strategies that Make
You Feel Great

- Savor the moment. "Happiness," said Benjamin Franklin, "is produced not so much by great pieces of good fortune that seldom happen as by the little advantages that occur each day."
- Take control of your time. There is nevertheless a place for setting goals and managing time. Compared to those who've learned a sense of helplessness, those with an "internal locus of control" do better in school, cope better with stress, and live with greater well-being.
- Act happy. Study after study reveals three traits that mark happy people's lives: (1) They like themselves, (2) they are positive thinkers, and (3) they are outgoing. In experiments, people who feign high self-esteem begin feeling better about themselves.
- Seek work and leisure that engage your skills. Even if we make a lower but livable wage, it pays to seek work that we find interesting and challenging.
- Join the movement movement. A slew of recent studies reveal that aerobic exercise is an antidote for mild depression.
- Get rest. Happy people live active, vigorous lives, yet they reserve time for renewing sleep and solitude.
- Give priority to close relationships. People who can name several close, supportive friends—friends with whom they freely share their ups and downs—live with greater health and happiness.
- Take care of your soul. Actively religious people are much less likely than others to become delinquent, to abuse drugs and alcohol, to divorce, or to commit suicide. They're even physically healthier.

Source: Adapted from *The Pursuit of Happiness* by David G. Meyers. Copyright © 1982 by the David G. and Carol P. Meyers Charitable Foundation. Reprinted by permission of HarperCollins Publishers, Inc.

Managing Your Time

Organizations have three types of resources—human, physical, and financial resources. Some management experts would include *time* as a fourth resource. *Make no mistake about it, time is one of the greatest resources a supervisor has.* Therefore, effective time management is essential for effective supervision. **Time management** is the ability to use one's time to get things done *when* they should be done. Another definition, which reflects planning and prioritizing, is "arranging to accomplish the things you choose to get done within the time available." Without this ability, all of your other management skills are for naught. Even if you have excellent human relations skills, poor time management can leave you too easily distracted to effectively listen to an employee's problems. Or pressures can keep you from thinking clearly enough to use your conceptual skills fully. You may not even be able to take the time to display your technical skills by showing a new employee the ropes. To be effective as a supervisor, then, you must make effective use of your time.

time management Ability to use one's time to get things done when they should be done.

Time Management Matrix

Stephen Covey has shown that we spend our time in one of four ways. These ways can be diagrammed as shown in Exhibit 12-13. As you can see, two variables govern our usage: (1) the *importance* of what we do—or the results expected, and (2) the *urgency*—or whether the action requires immediate attention or not.

Exhibit 12-14 shows how our activities can be classified on this matrix. Quadrant I shows activities that are both "important" and "urgent." Activities that are important but lack urgency are shown in quadrant II. Urgent but unimportant activities fall into quadrant III. Finally, quadrant IV contains activities that are neither important nor urgent.

EXHIBIT 12-14

	Urgent	Not Urgent
Important	I ACTIVITIES: Crises Pressing problems Deadline-driven projects	II ACTIVITIES: Prevention, PC activities Relationship building Recognizing new opportunities Planning, recreation
Not Important	III ACTIVITIES: Interruptions, some calls Some mail, some reports Some meetings Proximate, pressing matters Popular activities	IV ACTIVITIES: Trivia, busy work Some mail Some phone calls Time wasters Pleasant activities

Source: Excerpted from *The 7 Habits of Highly Effective People*, © 1989 by Stephen R. Covey. The Time Management Matrix phrase and model are trademarks of Franklin Covey Co., www.franklincovey.com. Used with permission. All rights reserved.

While this matrix is helpful in managing our time, we need to see how the supervisor can use it in a practical manner. The following discussion should be useful to busy supervisors who want to improve their time management skills.

The Time Log: Where Your Time Goes

Time management experts say that the first step in making effective use of your time is to determine how your time is actually being spent. Conscientiously filling in a time log like the one shown in Exhibit 12-15 is an excellent way to get this information.

Setting Priorities: A "Must"

Once you know where your time is going, you can analyze whether it is going in the proper direction. Not everyone can do all that he or she wants to do. The secret, then, is to spend time on those activities that are most important and urgent and that contribute most significantly to your doing a top-notch job.

Hoi Mon Sol, whose time log is shown in Exhibit 12-15, said that he could not find enough time to do everything he wanted to do because he was so busy. Yet, when he got home, he looked back at his day and called his activities "wheel spinning." He didn't feel good about what he had accomplished. Sol, like many supervisors, typically spent his day handling many low-priority activities rather than the high-priority ones!

EXHIBIT 12-15

Daily Time Log

DAILY TIME LOG

Name _____

Date _____ *March 1, 2007* _____

On this log record each activity that you performed during the workday. Make sure that you include every activity performed such as telephone calls, conversations, rest breaks, reading, and so on. Do this for a period of time long enough to reflect normal "workdays." A week should normally be sufficient.

From – To	Minutes	Type of Activity	People Involved	Priority A	B	C
8:00 – 8:05	5	Talked in hall	Dan, Patsy			
8:05 – 8:15	10	Read status report on work progress				
8:15 – 8:20	5	Checked progress on slow job	Ronald			
8:20 – 8:30	10	Prepared for supt. meeting				
8:30 – 9:30	60	Attended supt. meeting	Dept. heads & Supt.			
9:30 – 9:45	15	Coffee	Al, Peter, Karen			
9:45 – 9:50	5	Tried to return two phone calls -- no luck				
9:50 – 10:02	12	Completed questionnaire from Personnel Dept				
10:02 – 10:06	4	Went for mail				
10:06 – 10:20	14	Opened & read mail				
10:20 – 10:23	3	Called Purchasing Dept. to check status of order	Kawahara			
10:23 – 10:50	27	Discussion with Supt. about objectives for Dept.	McWilliams			
10:50 – 11:00	10	Visited Personnel office to check status of applicants	Alice			
11:00 – 11:55	55	Met with United Way Committee	too many!			
11:55 – 12:10	15	Began work on dept. budget proposal				
12:10 – 12:50	40	Lunch	Dan, Patsy, Al			
—						
—						

To use a time log most effectively, one must establish a rating system for classifying the priority of activities to be performed in a given day, such as the following:

1. A activities are the most important—they are critical to your job.

2. B activities are of medium priority—important, but less so than A's.

3. C activities are of low priority—routine and/or relatively unimportant.

EXHIBIT 12-16

Eight Common Supervisory
Time Wasters

- Distractions and interruptions
- Failure to set priorities
- Procrastination
- Doing routine work that subordinates could handle
- Indecision
- Personal disorganization
- Failure to delegate
- Excessive or unnecessary paperwork

The more efficient supervisor will spend a greater percentage of his or her time performing A activities.

Many of the "brush fires" to which supervisors devote a large percentage of their time are B or perhaps even C priority items. In the next section, we hope to help you learn to spend more of your time on your A's!

✔ **SELF-CHECK**

Examine the list of activities shown in Exhibit 12-15. Identify an A activity and a C activity. On what types of activities did Sol spend most of his time?

9 Discuss some ways to effectively manage time.

Handling the Common Time Wasters

Many activities that you carry out during a typical day are time wasters—inefficient uses of your time (see Exhibit 12-16). These may include doing routine work that someone else could handle, socializing excessively, or fighting a losing battle against paperwork.

Supervisory jobs vary a great deal in terms of the demands on the supervisor's time. That's why maintaining a time log (Exhibit 12-15) is an important first step in diagnosing your time management habits. Exhibit 12-17 is a broad list of "do's," which may help you to use your time more effectively.

EXHIBIT 12-17

How to Use Your Time
More Effectively

1. *Set priorities.*
   a. Establish A, B, and C priorities.
   b. Determine daily priorities.
   c. Focus effort on high-priority items.
2. *Do not procrastinate.*
   a. Break big jobs into smaller parts.
   b. Get started, even if on a minor part of a job.
   c. Do the more unpleasant parts of a job first.
   d. Reward yourself for doing things on schedule.

EXHIBIT **12-17**

Continued

3. *Manage the telephone effectively.*
   a. Have someone else take your calls and handle them if possible.
   b. Handle all return calls at set times of the day.

4. *Make your meetings effective.*
   a. Prepare and announce an agenda before the meeting.
   b. Begin meetings on time.
   c. Stick to the topics on the agenda.
   d. Make decisions or come to conclusions.

5. *Learn to delegate.*
   a. Delegate details that are time consuming.
   b. Delegate jobs that will help employees to develop.
   c. Delegate jobs that employees can perform better than you.

6. *Handle people who drop in.*
   a. Close your door for periods of time.
   b. Stand up and remain standing until the visitor leaves.
   c. Meet long-winded persons at their work area, so that you can leave when you are ready.
   d. Train your boss and work group to respect your time.

7. *Be decisive.*
   a. Set a personal deadline for making a decision.
   b. Once you have the facts, make the decision.

8. *Get organized.*
   a. Use a daily time planner.
   b. Implement a filing system.
   c. See 1b above.

9. *Stay on top of paperwork.*
   a. Handle papers only once!
   b. Handwrite short notes directly on original documents and forward them to the persons concerned.
   c. Have someone classify papers according to importance and route them for you.

10. *Avoid distractions and interruptions.*
   a. Keep a neat desk; work and papers piled on a desk are distracting.
   b. Try to set aside uninterrupted blocks of time.
   c. Face your desk away from the view of others.

CHAPTER REVIEW

1 **Identify the causes of conflict.**

A key skill needed by supervisors is that of conflict management. Two of the causes of conflict are having unclear or different objectives and communication breakdowns.

2 **Discuss conflict management styles and identify when each would be appropriate.**

The five conflict management styles are avoiding, accommodating, forcing, compromising, and collaborating or joint problem solving. Two of the most widely used styles are forcing and collaborating. Collaborating seems to be most successful in dealing with conflicts caused by communication difficulties, whereas forcing is sometimes necessary when dealing with conflicts of personal values and personality.

IMPORTANT TERMS

burnout
integration process
life event
principled negotiation
stress
time management
Type A behavior
Type B behavior

3 Describe principled negotiation.

Principled negotiation holds promise in keeping personalities out of conflict by focusing on the problem rather than the person.

4 Explain why modern life makes us particularly vulnerable to stress.

Stress is any external stimulus that causes wear and tear on a person's psychological or physical well-being. Modern men and women react to stress as our primitive ancestors did, with a chemical reaction designed to ready the body for fight or flight. This chemical reaction is not helpful in normal situations today, so we need to develop ways to cope with and manage stress.

5 Describe both the costs and the benefits of stress.

When we are unsuccessful in coping with stress, the costs are enormous. Stress is a major cause of many illnesses, from the common cold to heart disease. It plays a role in absenteeism, accidents, and lost productivity. Not all stress is negative, however. Small and great achievements occur as a result of moderate amounts of stress.

6 Explain the major causes of stress.

Major causes of stress are life events, personal psychological makeup, and organizational and work-related factors. The death of a spouse or a divorce places tremendous stress on most individuals. Similarly, working in an extremely high-pressure environment under prolonged autocratic leadership can cause stress and job burnout.

7 Compare and contrast Type A behavior and Type B behavior.

A person's psychological makeup influences how that person handles stress. Type A people try to accomplish too many things in a short period of time and tend to lack patience when dealing with people. Type B people tend to be calmer and more realistic in their assessment of the length of time needed to complete an assignment.

8 Elaborate on personal ways to cope with stress.

Fortunately, many of us can do a better job of managing stress if we develop certain strategies and behaviors. On a personal level, we can (1) exercise, (2) practice relaxation techniques, (3) gain a sense of control over our lives, and (4) develop and maintain good interpersonal relationships. On the job, a supervisor can apply many of the concepts discussed throughout this book. Techniques particularly helpful in reducing stress in a work unit are to practice the concept of balance through participative management, when appropriate, and to delegate effectively without losing control, and to control our time.

9 Discuss some ways to effectively manage time.

One of a supervisor's greatest resources is time. But activities performed by supervisors vary in importance and urgency. The effective supervisor will concentrate on the more important and most urgent activities. Maintaining a time log is a necessary first step toward becoming a more efficient time manager. Such a log enables a supervisor to see exactly where his or her time is being spent. More effective supervisors spend a greater proportion of their time on A priorities—activities that are ranked number one in terms of importance to the effective performance of their jobs. The following time-saving tips can help you to make better use of your time: (1) Set priorities, (2) do not procrastinate, (3) manage the telephone effectively, (4) make meetings effective, (5) delegate to others, (6) handle people who drop in, (7) be decisive, (8) get organized, (9) stay on top of paperwork, and (10) avoid distractions and interruptions.

QUESTIONS FOR REVIEW AND DISCUSSION

1. Identify the five conflict management styles and describe when each one would be appropriate.

2. Discuss what is involved in principled negotiation. How does it differ from hard or soft negotiation?

3. Compare and contrast Type A behavior and Type B behavior.

4. What are the major causes of stress on the job? Off the job?

5. Explain why exercise and relaxation techniques are helpful for coping with stress.

6. What can a supervisor do to prevent stress in his or her unit?

7. Why and how can time management help with stress and the achievement of effective results?

Sam Hinton Construction

Skill Builder 12-1

Divide the class into teams of five to seven people. Each group is to assume the role of a consulting team that has been asked to help Sam Hinton in the preview of this chapter get control of his company and his life. Drawing from your own experience and from what you have learned in this class, develop objectives and an action plan for Sam to implement.

Have two members from each team present their recommendations to the rest of the class. Each class member will then vote for the team (excluding his or her own team) that he or she thinks had the best plan for SHC.

Up in Smoke—Are You Burned Out?

Skill Builder 12-2

Answer each question on a scale of 1 to 5 (1 = never; 2 = rarely; 3 = sometimes; 4 = often; 5 = always).

Do you

- Feel less competent or effective than you used to feel in your work?
- Consider yourself unappreciated or "used"?
- Dread going to work?
- Feel overwhelmed in your work?
- Feel your work is pointless or unimportant?
- Watch the clock?
- Avoid conversations with others (coworkers, customers, and supervisors in the work setting; family members in the home)?
- Rigidly apply rules without considering creative solutions?
- Get frustrated by your work?
- Miss work often?
- Feel unchallenged by your work?

Does your work

- Overload you?

- Deny you rest periods—breaks, lunch time, sick leave, or vacation?

- Pay too little?

- Depend on uncertain funding sources?

- Provide inadequate support to accomplish the job (budget, equipment, tools, people, etc.)?

- Lack clear guidelines?

- Entail so many different tasks that you feel fragmented?

- Require you to deal with major or rapid changes?

- Lack access to a social or professional support group?

- Demand coping with a negative job image or angry people?

- Depress you?

Add up your scores for the test and record your total:

Scores	Category
94–110	Burnout
76–93	Flame
58–75	Smoke
40–57	Sparks
22–39	No fire

The categories are interpreted as follows:

- **Burnout.** If your score is between 94 and 110, you are experiencing a very high level of stress in your work. Without some changes in yourself or your situation, your potential for stress-related illness is high. Consider seeking professional help for stress reduction and burnout prevention. Coping with stress at this level may also require help from others—supervisors, coworkers, and other associates at work and spouse and other family members at home.

- **Flame.** If you have a score between 76 and 93, you have a high amount of work-related stress and may have begun to burn out. Mark each question that you scored 4 or above, and rank them in order of their effect on you, beginning with the ones that bother you the most. For at least your top three, evaluate what you can do to reduce the stresses involved, and act to improve your attitude or situation. If your body is reflecting the stress, get a medical checkup.

- **Smoke.** Scores between 58 and 75 represent a certain amount of stress in your work and are a sign that you have a fair chance of burning out unless you take corrective measures. For each question that you scored 4 or above, consider ways you can reduce the stresses involved. As soon as possible, take action to improve your attitude or the situation surrounding those things that trouble you most.

- **Sparks.** If your score is between 40 and 57, you have a low amount of work-related stress and are unlikely to burn out. Look over those questions that you scored 3 or above, and think about what you can do to reduce the stresses involved.

- **No fire.** People with scores of 22 through 39 are mellow in their work, with almost no job-related stress. As long as they continue at this level, they are practically burnout-proof.

For many people, both the job and the home have the potential to produce high stress and burnout. For this reason, having at least one "port in a storm" is important. Ideally, if things are going badly on the job, rest and comfort can be found in the home. Similarly, if home conditions involve pressure, conflict, and frustration, having a satisfying work life helps. The person who faces problems on the job and problems in the home at the same time is fighting a war on two fronts and is a prime candidate for stress overload and burnout.

Source: From Stress Without Distress: Rx for Burnout 1st edition by Manning/Curtis. 1988. Reprinted with permission of South-Western, a part of Cengage Learning, www.cengage.com/permissions.

A Planning Strategy to Cope with Stress

Skill Builder 12-3

List the things that are causing stress in your life at the present time. Determine which factors are causing positive stress and which are potentially negative and harmful.

Develop an action plan that will enable you to cope with the negative factors more effectively. A good action plan looks ahead and deals with what, when, where, and how to solve the problem.

A Personal Time Survey

Skill Builder 12-4

To begin managing your time, you first need a clearer idea of how you use your time. The Personal Time Survey will help you to estimate how much time you currently spend in typical activities. To get a more accurate estimate, you might keep track of how you spend your time for a week. This will help you get a better idea of how much time you need to prepare for each subject. It will also help you identify your time wasters. But for now complete the Personal Time Survey to get an estimate.

The following survey shows the amount of time you spend on various activities. When taking the survey, estimate the amount of time spent on each item. Once you have this amount, multiply it by seven. This will give you the total time spent on the activity in one week. After each item's weekly time has been calculated, add all these times for the grand total. Subtract this from 168, the total possible hours per week. Here we go:

1. Number of hours of sleep each night $\times 7 =$

2. Number of grooming hours per day $\times 7 =$

3. Number of hours for meals/snacks per day $\times 7 =$ (include preparation time)

4a. Total travel time weekdays $\times 7 =$

4b. Total travel time weekends $\times 7 =$

5. Number of hours per week for regularly scheduled functions (clubs, church, get-togethers, etc.)

6. Number of hours per day for chores, errands, extra grooming, etc. $\times 7 =$

7. Number of hours of work per week

8. Number of hours in class per week

9. Number of average hours per week socializing, dates, etc. Be honest!

Now add up the totals:

Subtract the above number from 168. $168 - X =$

The remaining hours are the hours you have allowed yourself to study.

Study Hour Formula

To determine how many hours you need to study each week to get A's, use the following rule of thumb. Study 2 hours per hour in class for an easy class, three hours per hour in class for an average class, and four hours per hour in class for a difficult class. For example, basket weaving 101 is a relatively easy 3-hour course. Usually, a person would not do more than 6 hours of work outside of class per week. Advanced calculus is usually considered a difficult course, so it might be best to study the proposed 12 hours a week. If more hours are needed, take away some hours from easier courses, i.e., basket weaving. Figure out the time that you need to study by using the previous formula for each of your classes.

Easy class credit hours _____ × 2 = Average class credit hours _____ × 3 = _____
Difficult class credit hours _____ × 4 = _____
Total

Compare this number to your time left from the survey. Now is the time when many students might find themselves a bit stressed. Just a note to ease your anxieties: It is not only the quantity of study time but also its quality. This formula is a general guideline. Try it for a week, and make adjustments as needed.

Source: Prepared by the Self-Development Center, a service of the Counseling and Student Development Center, George Mason University. Reprinted with permission.

CASE

The Missed Promotion

Case 12-1

Susan Williamson was worried. For the past 6 months, her husband, Paul, had been a different person from the man she married. Up until that time, Paul had been a cheerful and caring husband and father. He took an interest in their children, was active in church, and had a zest for day-to-day living. In recent months he had been moody, abrupt, and withdrawn. He spent his time at home watching television and drinking beer. He never talked about his job as maintenance supervisor at the ABC Company as he once had. Recently Susan had asked if something at work was bothering him and, if so, whether he would discuss it with her. His reply was "No, there's nothing bothering me! You take care of the house and the children, and I'll take care of the job and making a living!"

Actually, the job had been bothering Paul for about a year. Before that, he was considered one of the outstanding maintenance supervisors. In those days, his two immediate supervisors, the maintenance superintendent and the maintenance manager, called on him frequently for advice and used him as a troubleshooter within the plant. Although Paul did not have a college degree in engineering, the maintenance manager had strongly hinted that when the maintenance superintendent retired, Paul would be promoted to his position. The maintenance manager had told Paul that, despite having three engineering graduates in the supervision group, he considered Paul the best in the department.

A year ago, the maintenance manager was transferred to another plant. A new maintenance manager came aboard who, from the start, favored college graduates. Gradually Paul was used less and less for troubleshooting assignments, and his advice was rarely sought. Then, 6 months later, the maintenance superintendent retired and a young engineering graduate named Bobbi, whom Paul had trained, was promoted to the superintendent's job. It was then that Paul's personality changed. He began sleeping longer each night, often falling asleep in front of the television set. He also developed a tightness in his stomach that was creating a burning sensation.

Bobbi, the engineer who had been promoted to maintenance superintendent, was worried. For the past several months she had been concerned about the performance and health of one of her maintenance supervisors, Paul Williamson. Paul had been Bobbi's boss at one time, and she had always admired his ability as a supervisor and his knowledge of the maintenance area.

Recently, while attending a regional meeting of maintenance managers from different plants of the ABC Company, Bobbi ran into the former maintenance manager at her plant, who was now at another plant. He asked how Paul was doing.

Bobbi, glad to share her concern with someone, said that she was really worried about him. "His performance has slipped, for one thing. Also, he used to have perfect attendance, but lately he's been calling in sick a lot."

The maintenance manager replied, "I wonder if disappointment over not being promoted to maintenance superintendent has affected his performance. No reflection on you, of course, but before I left, the plant manager and I had agreed that Paul would be promoted to maintenance superintendent. Then the home office changed its corporate policy so that only college graduates could be promoted to superintendent. This made Paul ineligible, and you got the job instead."

Bobbi hadn't realized that Paul had been the first choice for the position she now held. Upon reflection, she decided to have a coaching and counseling session with him when she returned to the plant, as she certainly didn't want to lose him.

Answer the following questions:

1. How should Bobbi approach Paul about the situation?

2. What do you think Paul's reaction(s) will be?

3. Do you agree with the company's policy of promoting only college graduates to the maintenance superintendent position? Why or why not?

Controlling

Stone/Getty Images

Chris Hamilton

13 Exercising Control

Stone/Getty Images

Mechanical failures represent just one example of work not going according to plan. However, these setbacks are often the result of poor controlling.

We tried to make some adjustments at halftime. They just didn't pan out.
   —PRO FOOTBALL COACH AFTER HIS TEAM WAS BEATEN IN THE PLAYOFFS

Changing Perceptions and Attitudes One Day at a Time

The health care industry is dramatically changing as costs continue to rise and the population gets older. Still, Beth Anderson, the administrator of a 406-bed acute care, urban hospital with over 900 employees believes that each day offers an opportunity to make a difference. Beth is aware of the daily challenges and her responsibility for ensuring quality care is provided and costs are managed so that the hospital remains viable long-term. To assist in accomplishing this goal, Beth hired outside consultants to conduct an employee opinion survey. The results were quite telling.

Overall, the employees enjoyed their jobs and felt committed to the hospital's mission. They really believed key services, such as the burn and trauma units, provided unique assistance to those in the community. However, they also perceived they were overworked, underpaid, and communications were inadequate. When asked whether their departments were adequately staffed, the employees' responses averaged a 2.2 on a 5-point scale. The perceived increased work demands were contributing to nonattendance issues. However, one of the more significant findings for Beth Anderson was that most of the respondents didn't believe that the hospital administration would act on the results. Beth and the assistant administrator, Elmer Sellers, were determined to initiate positive changes that would ultimately alter the employees' perceptions and attitudes.

The first step was to meet with department heads and staff to solicit input from these groups on the best ways to address the employees' concerns. A group of department heads actually initiated this effort when they approached Beth and shared their willingness to take on a leadership role as part of the organization's change effort. Over about a month, the group collected and tabulated 539 suggestions, of which many were implemented. For example, departments implemented flexible schedules for their employees to address concerns about work demand levels. Cross-training efforts were initiated for employees so that individuals could routinely be assigned to the highest work load areas during high-demand periods. The hospital also doubled the PRN pool over a 12-month period to alleviate concerns about staffing levels. In addition, the seventh-floor nurses station was converted to a fully equipped exercise facility for employees to burn off stress! To address pay concerns, the employees were provided with raises and adjustments twice during the following year!

Beth and Elmer had succeeded in changing the employees' perceptions and attitudes, but the challenge became maintaining the momentum. The Speak Easy, a one-on-one communication process, was utilized for this purpose. Speak Easy, as the name implies, is an informal means of interpersonal communication that enables administrators to gather employee input, while providing important information throughout the ranks. These informal departmental meetings were announced in advance and communicated to individuals in the hospital in a variety of ways, including the Intranet and screen-saver bulletin boards. Beth and Elmer chose this approach so that employees could prepare topics or questions in advance they wanted to share. The Speak Easys allowed Beth and Elmer to collect information "real time" so that appropriate actions could be taken without having to wait for the

Learning Objectives

After reading and studying this chapter, you should be able to:

1. Define control and explain how it relates to planning.

2. Discuss the characteristics of effective control systems.

3. Discuss the three types of control systems.

4. Discuss the four steps in the control process.

5. Identify the different types of standards.

6. Explain the importance of strategic control points.

7. Discuss management by exception.

8. Discuss the impact of technology on control.

annual employee opinion survey results. The benefits were improved communication and trust building.

Source: Consulting and conversations with Beth Anderson and Elmer Sellers with the USAMC.

When an organization's activities "go according to plan," it is often the result of good planning, but it is just as frequently the result of good control in implementing the plans! In this chapter we provide you with a broad overview of what is involved in the control function.

What is Control?

Have you ever been driving a car on a trip and had one of the dashboard warning lights come on? Perhaps it was the oil pressure or temperature light. Basically, the light indicates that something is wrong with the car. Without such a warning system, you would be caught by surprise when the car broke down, perhaps leaving you stranded far from home.

Managers and supervisors are often in a similar dilemma. They go along not knowing whether things are as they should be or not. Unfortunately, many of them find that things are not as they should be only when it is too late to do anything about it. They do not have the advantage of periodic feedback or warning lights to tell them whether or not they are on track. Thus, you might think of control as consisting of performance markers that tell you whether you and your unit's performance are moving in the right direction.

Controlling is defined as the management function that involves comparing actual performance with planned performance and taking corrective action, if needed, to ensure that objectives are achieved. Basically, control has three phases: (1) anticipating the things that could go wrong and taking preventive measures to see that they don't, (2) monitoring or measuring performance in some way to compare what is actually happening with what is supposed to be happening, and (3) correcting performance problems that occur. This last step is the therapeutic aspect of control.

Control's Close Links to Planning

Planning and controlling might be thought of as Siamese twins because they are so closely related. Planning "sets the ship's course," and controlling "keeps it on course." When a ship begins to veer off course, the navigator notices it and recommends a new heading designed to return the ship to its proper course. Essentially, supervisory control works the same way.

EXHIBIT **13-1**

Murphy's Laws

- Left to themselves, things always go from bad to worse.
- There's never time to do it right, but always time to do it over.
- If anything can go wrong, it will.
- Of the things that can go wrong, the one that will is capable of the most possible damage.
- If you think nothing can go wrong, you have obviously overlooked something.
- Of those things that "cannot" go wrong, the most unlikely one will.
- Inside every large problem are many small problems struggling to get out.
- Any object will fall so that it lands in the one spot where it is capable of doing the most damage.

EXHIBIT 13-2

Some Common Examples
of Supervisory Control

- At the end of the workday, a production supervisor spends 30 minutes examining a printout showing each employee's output, quality, and scrap. The supervisor notes those employees whose performance is below par and makes plans to discuss their performance with them the next day.
- A nursing supervisor studies a survey completed by all patients who were housed in her ward in the past 6 months. The survey lists items such as nurses' friendliness, professionalism, appearance, and a number of other factors related to job performance.
- A maintenance supervisor tours the building, examining the progress of each worker or work team.
- After a college football game, the head defensive coach views the game films several times, assigning performance grades to each defensive player. Grades below 60 reflect areas to which the coach must devote special attention during upcoming practices.

You set goals and seek information on whether they are being reached as planned. If not, you make the adjustments necessary to achieve your goals. Thus, controlling may be thought of as the process that supervisors use to help carry out their plans.

Importance of Controls

Perhaps you have heard the old saying: "Things never go as planned." That truth is a primary reason supervisors need to perform the control function effectively. Control is important in view of the many variables that can put things off track. Murphy's laws (some of which are listed in Exhibit 13-1) seem to operate everywhere. Because anything involving humans is imperfect, supervisors must use control to monitor progress and to make intelligent adjustments as required.

A nursing supervisor gathers information related to the nurses' friendliness, professionalism, appearance and a number of other factors related to job performance.

The Image Bank/Getty Images

Examples of Controls

 http://www.jci.com

We live in a world of controls. Circuit breakers in our homes and offices are examples of controls. When an electrical overload occurs, the system adjusts by shutting itself down. Security alarm systems send out signals when a protected area is violated. As mentioned earlier, the dashboard in your car contains numerous control signals to warn you when something is not the way it is supposed to be—low oil pressure, overheated engine, alternator malfunction, keys left in car, seat belt not on, and so on. Exhibit 13-2 illustrates a number of other common examples of control.

2 Discuss the characteristics of effective control systems.

Characteristics of Effective Control Systems

To be effective, a control system must have certain characteristics. Among them, the following are the most important:

1. Controls need to focus on appropriate activities. Effective controls must focus on critical factors that affect both the individual's and the organization's abilities to achieve objectives. These critical objectives should include the essential areas of production and personnel activities, as well as related costs.

2. Controls should be timely. Information needed for comparisons and control purposes needs to be in a supervisor's hands in order for him or her to take effective corrective action. Therefore, delays in generating, gathering, or disseminating information can prolong the occurrence—and extent—of deviations.

3. Controls must be cost-effective. The benefits of using appropriate controls should be worth their cost of installation and operation. Too much control can be worse than too little. The key is that controls should be appropriate for the situation and provide savings greater than the costs involved. An example of this need was pointed out by Senator William Cohen of Maine in the following statement:

   The U.S. Department of Defense could save millions of dollars annually if it revamped regulations covering employee travel vouchers. . . . The system the Pentagon has created to protect itself against travel waste and fraud is the equivalent of assigning an armored division to guard an ATM machine. . . . The precautions cost more than the potential loss.[1]

4. Controls should be accurate and concise. Controls must provide information about operations and people in sufficient quality and quantity to enable managers to make meaningful comparisons to operations standards. As with control, too much information can be as bad as too little.

5. Controls should be accepted by the people they affect. Controls and their applicability to specific situations should be communicated clearly to those responsible for implementing them and to those who will be governed by them.

   Although all of these characteristics are important, a given control system need not have all of them in order to do the job for which it is designed.

3 Discuss the three types of control systems.

feedforward controls
Preventive controls that try to anticipate problems and take corrective action before they occur.

Types of Control Systems

There are essentially three types of control systems. They are (1) feedforward controls, (2) concurrent controls, and (3) feedback controls.

Feedforward controls are preventive controls that try to anticipate problems and take corrective action before they occur. This type of control allows corrective action to be taken

EXHIBIT **13-3**

Tips for Establishing
Preventive Controls

1. Identify your department's major goals.
2. Identify those factors most crucial to accomplishing your department's major goals. These may be items such as properly running machinery and equipment, availability of raw materials, availability of key personnel, or a balanced demand for your department's services.
3. Determine the *most likely problems or circumstances* that could prevent the items in (2) from occurring. These could be factors such as machine breakdown or absence of key personnel.
4. Develop a plan for preventing the problems listed in (3). You might consider input from employees, staff personnel, your immediate supervisor, peers, and others in arriving at your preventive control plans.

before a real problem develops. For example, Hart Schaffner Marx, a leading producer of quality clothing, inspects every bolt of cloth it plans to use in its tailored men's clothing before starting to cut pieces.

See Exhibit 13-3 for some tips on establishing preventive controls. Notice that the first step is to focus on your goals or plans. Again, you can see how closely linked the planning and controlling processes are.

Concurrent controls (sometimes called screening controls) occur while an activity is taking place. Thus, an inspector or an inspection system can check items on the assembly line to see if they are meeting standards. Production systems today are capable of providing operators with a wealth of information.

> Carotek ECS offers a vision inspection system that can be used to trigger a shutdown of the production line if something looks amiss. First, "good" images are uploaded onto the system. Then, the cameras are trained on different points in the production line. The new images are automatically compared to the good images stored in the computer. If the images do not match, the system will either alert an operator or shut the system down entirely.[2]

Feedback controls measure activities that have already been completed. Thus, corrections can take place after performance is over. The following example of Occidental (Oxy) Permian Ltd.'s decision to install relays in its operations in New Mexico and the Permian basin of West Texas illustrates the benefit of employing feedback controls.

> [With] more than 6,400 producing wells in the greater Permian basin, Oxy Permian is the largest oil producer in Texas. Frequent storms (with lightning that wreaks damage to power systems) have plagued oil producers in the Permian basin since the 1920s when they first began drilling there.
>
> In an effort to avoid downtime caused by electrical storms, Oxy Permian installed Schweitzer electrical relays in order to learn more about the vulnerabilities of its power distribution system. . . Every ESP (electric submersible pump) shutdown compromises equipment and potentially reduces pumping life. Oxy Permian's power optimization resource team collected data hoping to determine what was happening with the power distribution system during and after electrical storms. Using Schweitzer relays, the team learned that lightning did not cause problems but actually amplified existing problems. Once Oxy understood this, it was able to take corrective action. Oxy Permian devised a strategy and design for a panel that would prevent motors from being damaged when the power system faltered during electrical storms.[3]

concurrent controls
Sometimes called screening controls these controls are used while an activity is taking place.

feedback controls Controls that measure completed activities and then take corrective action if needed.

✔ SELF-CHECK

What type(s) of control were used in the chapter preview? Explain.
....

http://www.nist.gov

Steps in the Control Process

The steps in the control process are illustrated in Exhibit 13-4. Note that step 4 may require going back to any of the previous three steps. It may consist of modifying the original standard, changing the frequency and manner of measuring performance, or achieving more insight into the possible cause of the problem. Let us examine the details of each of these steps.

Step 1: Establishing Performance Standards

The first step of the controlling process is really a part of the planning step. You set your sights on something you want to accomplish. As a supervisor, you exercise control by comparing performance to some standard or goal. A **standard** is a unit of measurement that can serve as a reference point for evaluating results. Properly communicated and accepted by employees, standards become the bases for the supervisor's control activities.

Types of Standards. Standards can be either tangible or intangible. **Tangible standards** are standards that are quite clear, concrete, specific, and generally measurable. For instance, when you say, "I want the machine online by 3 p.m.," the goal is very specific and concrete. Either the machine is online at 3 p.m. or it is not.

Tangible standards can be further categorized as numerical, monetary, physical, or time related. **Numerical standards** are expressed in numbers, such as number of items produced, number of absences, percentage of successful sales calls, or number of personnel who successfully complete training. **Monetary standards** are expressed in dollars and cents. Examples of monetary standards are predetermined profit margins, payroll costs, scrap costs, and maintenance costs. **Physical standards** refer to quality, durability, size, weight, and other factors related to physical composition. **Time standards** refer to the speed with which the job should be done. Examples of time standards include printing deadlines, scheduled project completion dates, and rates of production.

EXHIBIT 13-4

The Process of Control

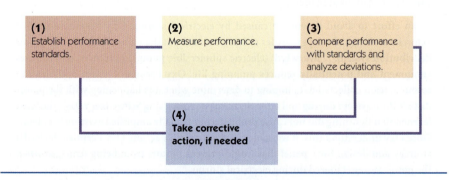

| (1) Establish performance standards. | (2) Measure performance. | (3) Compare performance with standards and analyze deviations. |

(4) **Take corrective action, if needed**

EXHIBIT 13-5

Controlling Intangible
Standards

Note that there may be some overlap among the types of tangible standards. For instance, when you say, "I want the machine online by 3 p.m.," you have obviously communicated a time standard, but the standard is expressed numerically. Monetary standards are also expressed numerically.

In contrast to tangible standards, **intangible standards** are not expressed in terms of numbers, money, physical qualities, or time, because they relate to human characteristics that are difficult to measure. Examples of intangible standards are a desirable attitude, high morale, ethics, and cooperation (see Exhibit 13-5). Intangible standards pose special challenges to the supervisor, as the following example illustrates.

intangible standards Relate to human characteristics and are not expressed in terms of numbers, money, physical qualities, or time.

> **Supervisor Maude Leyden of the State Employment Office overheard one of her newer employment counselors, David Hoffman, berating a job applicant. The tone of his voice was domineering, as though he were scolding a child, although the applicant was perhaps 30 years his senior. Maude heard David conclude the interview with the words, "Now don't come back here and bother us again until you've had someone fill this form out properly. That's not what I'm paid to do!"**
>
> **After the applicant left, Maude listened to David's explanation of what had just happened. He said he'd been under a lot of pressure that day and had grown very impatient, and he acknowledged his rudeness toward the applicant. Maude told him that he had not handled himself in a professional manner and discussed what he should have done differently. Later in the day, David was to call the applicant, apologize, and offer to be of further help.**
>
> **He did call and apologize.**

It is much more difficult to clearly explain an intangible standard, such as "interviewers must observe standards of professional conduct with clients," than to tell someone that the standard is "to service six malfunctioning computer systems each day." Just what is professional conduct? Is it patience, friendliness, courtesy, keeping a level head? Certainly it is less specific than "servicing six computers daily." As difficult as it may be, every supervisor has to establish, communicate, and control some types of intangible job standards.

✔ SELF-CHECK

Employee cooperation, desirable employee attitude, appropriate employee personal hygiene, and mature employee behavior are some intangible standards that organizations and supervisors typically must control. Can you think of others?

....

How Standards Are Set. Standards can be set in many ways. A supervisor will frequently set standards on the basis of familiarity with the jobs being performed by his or her employees. The supervisor is generally knowledgeable about the time required to perform tasks, the quality necessary, and the expected employee behavior. This is especially true of supervisors who have been promoted through the ranks. If you are not technically knowledgeable about the work performed in your department, there are a number of ways to become familiar with standards. You can gain insights from past records of performance, if available, and from fellow supervisors, employees, and your own boss. Exhibit 13-6 presents some types of standards for a variety of positions.

For many jobs, various staff departments will strongly influence the standards set. The industrial engineering department, for example, may utilize systematic studies of movements and speed of workers to set quantity and time standards. The quality control department may establish standards for finish, luster, or precision. Cost accounting may develop standards for material costs or scrap. Thus, many standards may already be established for the people you will supervise.

Staff departments may also have a hand in setting standards for supervisors. For example, the budget department may help determine standards regarding material and payroll costs. Personnel may establish standards regarding the quantity and quality of grievances and turnover in a department. The ability to meet your departmental standards, in turn, will determine the amount of control that your own boss will exercise over your activities.

EXHIBIT 13-6

Types of Standards
for Various Positions

Position	Type of Standard
Bank teller	Monetary (balance), time (speed of teller line), physical (orderliness of work area)
Postal letter carrier	Time (hours taken to complete run)
Server in a large restaurant	Physical (appearance), time (speed), intangible (courtesy and friendliness)
Real estate salesperson	Monetary (volume), numerical (number of listings and closings)
Offensive-line football coach	Numerical (yards per game rushing), intangible (leadership of players)
Upholsterer in a manufacturing plant	Numerical (number of units completed), physical (quality of units)
Third-grade teacher	Intangible (appearance, classroom behavior), physical (quality of lesson plans)

Step 2: Measuring Performance

Setting standards is an essential first step in control, but by itself it doesn't go far enough. A supervisor must monitor performance to ensure that it complies with the established standards. Two issues the supervisor must deal with are (1) how often to measure performance and (2) how to measure performance.

How Often to Measure Performance. Determining how often to measure performance is an important control decision supervisors must make. Sometimes this decision has already been made by the system, as shown in the following examples:

http://www.cargill
foods.com

> **Kay Davis, sales manager of City Motors, need only look at the sales chart prominently displayed on the sales floor outside her office to see how her sales personnel are doing. The chart lists the number of new and used cars sold by each salesperson for the week and the month, as well as total sales volume for the entire company.**

> **The production control room at DAVO Company provides a constant reading of activity on each of the production floor's operating machines. At any time, a production supervisor can visit the area and receive a printout of the work performed by any of the operators up to that time.**

6 Explain the importance of strategic control points.

Notice that in each of the preceding examples, performance is being constantly monitored. But this does not mean that supervisors should spend the entire day monitoring performance. Instead, they should establish strategic control points. As shown in Exhibit 13-7, a **strategic control point** is a performance measurement point located sufficiently early in an activity to allow any necessary corrective actions to be taken to accomplish the objective. For each job, ask yourself: Considering the importance of this job, at what point do I need to know the progress being made so that I can make any required adjustments and still complete the job as planned?

strategic control point
A performance measurement point located early in an activity to allow any corrective action to be taken.

Certain types of jobs, such as maintenance, personnel, and sales, don't lend themselves to frequent measurement of progress. Measurement takes time, unless an automated system is in place. On the other hand, effective monitoring is crucial for some jobs. For example, the work of an emergency room nurse requires more careful monitoring than does the work of a sales representative or a clerical worker.

EXHIBIT 13-7

Setting Strategic Control Points in the Control Process

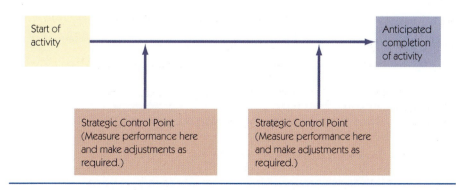

How to Measure. There are several basic ways for a supervisor to measure performance. These are as follows:

1. Personal observation.

2. Written or oral reports by or about employees.

3. Automatic methods.

4. Inspections, tests, or samples.

Exhibit 13-8 is an example of the second method, which could be used frequently, at very little cost. Notice how precisely the information requested is stated.

EXHIBIT **13-8**

Example of a Written
Report about an Employee

Management Encourages Your Comments

Date **5/19/2007**

Waiter or waitress **Phyllis**

Please circle meal   Breakfast   (Lunch)   Dinner

	Yes	No
1. Were you greeted by host or hostess promptly and courteously?	✓	___
2. Was your server prompt, courteous, and helpful?	✓	___
3. Was the quality of food to your expectations?	___	✓
4. Was the table setting and condition of overall restaurant appearance pleasing and in good taste?	✓	___
5. Will you return to our restaurant?	___	✓
6. Will you recommend our restaurant to your friends and associates?	___	✓

Comments

Food was overcooked. Potatoes were leftovers. Meat was tough. This

was my second visit and I brought a friend with me. We were

both very disappointed.

Name and address
(if you desire)

_____

_____

_____

Please drop this in our quality improvement box located near the exit.

Thank you and have a good day.

Can you suggest some instances or situations when each of these ways of measuring performance might be used?

In some jobs, supervisors and their employees work in the same area. The supervisor can easily move among the workers, observing their performance. In other departments, however, the supervisor may have workers spread out in various locations, which makes direct observation impractical. Consider a sanitation supervisor whose eight work crews collect garbage on various routes throughout the city. Such a supervisor must depend on written or oral reports or occasional inspections as the primary means of measurement. Here is what one sanitation supervisor said:

> **How do I know if my crews are doing the job properly? Mainly by the complaints I get from customers. Complaints range from garbage that isn't picked up on schedule to overturned trash cans, surrounded with litter. That's how I know what's going on in the field. Sometimes I will drive around and make a visual inspection. We also survey residents annually to see if our people are considered timely, friendly, and efficient.**

Sales supervisors may seldom see their employees if the sales work takes them outside the office. As a result, salespersons are required to complete reports about number of calls made, sales results, travel expenses, customer comments, and numerous other matters. These reports are received by supervisors or the home office staff. Many salespersons, in fact, complain that they are required to do too much paperwork!

Supervisors who are not in frequent contact with their employees must come up with some meaningful, valid ways to measure results. They need to find some means of making

Customer service representatives are monitored against time standards such as how quickly they answer the telephone and how long it takes them to help each customer.

© Sherwin Crasito/Reuters/Corbis

sure the measurements are reliable. Because of pressures to conform to standards, employees may attempt to falsify reports to make themselves appear better.

> Several years ago, a nationally respected youth organization set very high membership goals for its local offices. The results appeared spectacular until it was discovered that a number of local chapters had considerably inflated the number of new members enrolled to avoid looking bad.

In other words, you have to be careful about attempts to "beat" the control system. People may extort money, falsify documents, and distort oral reports in order to make themselves look good. For example, if you ask an employee to give you an oral report on a job's progress, he or she may tell you, "Everything's just fine, boss," when, in fact, it is not.

Step 3: Comparing Performance with Standards and Analyzing Deviations

Unfortunately, many supervisors receive information that demonstrates a serious departure from standards but make little effort to understand what caused the difference between planned and actual performance. Failure to meet standards may result from a variety of causes. A supervisor needs to understand the reasons for below-average performance. Many supervisors jump to conclusions about the causes of problems; as a result, the corrective action they take is ineffective.

> Suppose that the quality control standard for producing a certain part is 99/100. This means that there should be no more than one defective product per hundred units produced by a worker. You just received notice from the quality department that of the last 200 units produced by employee Kevin Rae, almost 13 percent were defective.
>
> What could have caused this problem? Could it have been poor materials? Might Rae's equipment be the cause? Is this like Rae's previous performance? What will you do about it? These are some questions you have to ask yourself. Simply giving Rae an oral or a written warning may be highly inappropriate and may not correct the problem!

It is also important to compare results that are substantially above standard in order to determine why they varied from standard. The supervisor should check to see if all operating procedures are being followed correctly, or if there is an improvement in operations that should be included in new standards.

It is important to find out the opinions of those close to a particular problem to determine why standards are not being met. For example, an employee's explanation or those of other employees or fellow supervisors might be obtained. Frequently, people in other departments can add insight. Here is what one supervisor said:

> I was all set to really chew Emily out. She had an important job to complete for me this morning and didn't show up as scheduled. Fortunately, before I made a fool of myself, I learned from one of her friends that she'd gotten here early and the plant manager had asked her to do an even more important job. I checked this out with the plant manager, and, sure enough, that was the case. She was supposed to notify me but had just forgotten.

Step 4: Taking Corrective Action if Necessary

The final step in the control process is to take corrective action if needed. You have undoubtedly seen many athletic contests turn completely around after halftime. This change is often due to corrective action taken by the coach—the modifications, adjustments, and fine-tuning done in response to problems encountered earlier.

When a quality control standard has not been met, a supervisor must investigate for possible causes.

The supervisor's job is much like that of a coach. Adjustments, fine-tuning, and perhaps even drastic actions may be necessary to pull off important tasks or to maintain standards. Examples of corrective actions a supervisor might take include the following:

1. Making a decision to retrain a new operator whose performance has not progressed as expected.

2. Shifting several employees from their normal jobs to help meet a deadline on another job.

3. Counseling an employee whose performance has recently been below standard.

4. Reprimanding an employee for failure to adhere to safety rules.

5. Shutting down a piece of equipment for maintenance after defective output is traced to it.

Management by Exception

Even under the best of circumstances, deviations from performance standards are bound to occur. Given the broad range of areas over which supervisors exert control, it is essential to distinguish between critical and less-critical deviations. The fact that many performance deviations are due to normal operating variances means that supervisors must exercise some discretion in distinguishing between variations that are relevant and those that are less so.

Under **management by exception,** a supervisor focuses on critical control needs and allows employees to handle most routine deviations from the standards. Exhibit 13-9 shows that the key issue is whether or not a deviation is exceptional.

The idea is to set priorities for activities, depending on their importance, and to focus your efforts on top-priority items. Management by exception works essentially the same way. Your attention should be focused on exceptional, rather than routine, problems.

7 Discuss management by exception.

management by exception A supervisor focuses on critical control needs and allows employees to handle most routine deviations from the standard.

EXHIBIT 13-9

Management
by Exception

✔ SELF-CHECK

Suppose you are a sales supervisor and your departmental sales goal is 800 units weekly (or 3,200 units monthly). Each of your eight sales representatives, then, has a goal of 100 units weekly (or 400 units monthly). At the end of the first week, your sales results are as follows:

Salesperson	Weekly Goal	Units Sold
A	100	105
B	100	95
C	100	90
D	100	102
E	100	102
F	100	88
G	100	98
H	100	115
Total = 800		795

What corrective action will you take?

UPS uses technology that allows the employee and supervisor to monitor and control desired results for their deliveries.

Managers who practice management by exception might do absolutely nothing about the previous situation. "But wait!" you say. "Look at Salesperson C, who performed 10 percent below standard, and Salesperson F, who was 12 percent below standard. Shouldn't a supervisor do something about these two employees?" Of course, a supervisor should be aware of these deviations. However, recall that only the first week has gone by. It is probably fairly normal to find such variances in a single week; the more pertinent information is how performance compares to the monthly benchmark of 3,200 units. With three weeks to go, the supervisor who gets too upset after week 1 may be overreacting. Naturally, the supervisor should keep an eye on sales data in the upcoming weeks to see whether Salespersons C and F improve their performances. In this situation, the assumption of management by exception is that Salespersons B, C, F, and G realize that they are below standard and will be working to improve.

✔ SELF-CHECK

Suppose that at the end of the second week, sales results are as shown:

Salesperson	Weekly Goal	Week 1	Week 2
A	100	105	107
B	100	95	101
C	100	90	97
D	100	102	101
E	100	102	101
F	100	88	84
G	100	98	99
H	100	115	126
Total = 800		795	816

What will you do now?

Sales have perked up, and, with the exception of Salesperson F, everyone is in reasonable shape. As supervisor, you'd be justified in entering the control process with Salesperson F, as the "red flag" is still up on this one. You may want to discuss this person's results, try to identify actions that produce below-standard results, and develop a plan of corrective action.

Note that Salesperson H has been setting the standards on fire, averaging more than 20 percent above standard the first 2 weeks. This performance is also an exceptional departure from standard. What is behind these results? Is Salesperson H using some techniques that will work for others? Is this person's territory so choice that it becomes easy to make the standard? Should you modify the standard for Salesperson H? Management by exception can be applied to both favorable and unfavorable deviations from standard.

The Impact of Technology on Control

8
Discuss the impact of technology on control.

As the world's economies—and their environments—continue to become more dynamic and complex, managers—including supervisors—must obtain, organize, and utilize huge amounts of information in order to make decisions and exercise control over them. Progressive managers are realizing that a high-speed information infrastructure is needed to cope with the rapid pace of operations in all types of economic activities.

One result of this "information revolution" is the redistribution of power in today's more advanced organizations. For example, decision making and control have now been shifted downward to lower levels of management, including the supervisory level. With practically unlimited types and sources of information at their fingertips, even operative employees no longer have to rely on others for facts and figures to make decisions. Thanks in part to networks and multimedia fusions, organizations such as Tiris are becoming more integrated. Tiris—a unit of Texas Instruments—is managed out of Bedford, England. Its line of low-frequency transponders is designed in Freising, Germany, and the units are produced in Kuala Lumpur, Malaysia, whence they are shipped to customers around the world.[4]

Organizations now have information and monitoring systems that permit supervisors to give instructions and control operations from a distance away from those activities.

> For example, at the start of his workday at 8:30 each morning, Washington R., a delivery person for United Parcel Service (UPS), picks up a bulky brown box resembling an oversize computer game. He carries the box with him all day as he makes his deliveries and returns to home base at night. His personal box has a window in which he can view all the day's tasks, each one timed to the minute.
>
> As he makes his deliveries, Washington keys the details into the box, which electronically transmits the data to his home depot. His supervisor can therefore determine at any time where he is and whether or not he is on schedule. At the end of the day, Washington hooks up his box to the UPS computer, and all the information he has accumulated during the day is automatically transferred to it.
>
> During the night, the computer downloads Washington's next day's itinerary and individual tasks into his box.[5]

click! http://www.ups.com

Today's information technology makes possible—for better or for worse—this form of digital monitoring and control.

CHAPTER REVIEW

1 **Define control and explain how it relates to planning.**
Controlling is the supervisory process of making plans and following through on them. Because of the many variables involved in executing and carrying out plans, supervisory control is an essential part of the management process.

2 **Discuss the characteristics of effective control systems.**
For control systems to be effective, they should (1) focus on appropriate activities, (2) be timely, (3) be cost-effective, (4) be accurate and concise, and (5) be accepted by people who will be controlled by them.

3 **Discuss the three types of control systems.**
The three types of control systems are (1) feedforward controls, which try to anticipate problems and take corrective action before they occur; (2) concurrent controls, which are used while an activity is taking place; and (3) feedback controls, which measure activities that are completed and then take corrective action if needed.

4 **Discuss the four steps in the control process.**
There are four steps in the control process: (1) Establish performance standards, (2) measure performance, (3) compare performance with standards and analyze deviations, and (4) take corrective action if needed.

5 **Identify the different types of standards.**
There are several types of standards. They can be tangible (numerical, monetary, physical, and time) or intangible (attitudes, ethics, morals). They can be set by supervisors or staff departments.

6 **Explain the importance of strategic control points.**
It is important that the supervisor establish strategic control points. These points measure performance early enough in the process to permit sufficient adjustments or corrective actions to be made in order to achieve the goal. Supervisors measure performance through direct observation, by written or oral reports by or about employees, through automatic methods, and by inspections, samples, or tests.

7 **Discuss management by exception.**
Management by exception focuses supervisory attention on exceptional departures from standard rather than on routine variances.

8 **Discuss the impact of technology on control.**
The growth of information technology has redistributed power in organizations, thus enhancing the position of supervisors.

IMPORTANT TERMS
concurrent controls
feedback controls
feedforward controls
intangible standards
management by exception
monetary standards
numerical standards
physical standards
standard
strategic control point
tangible standards
time standards

QUESTIONS FOR REVIEW AND DISCUSSION

1. In what ways are planning and controlling related?

2. Discuss the following statement made by a supervisor: "I don't have to worry much about controlling. My view is that, if you plan a job properly, things will go right; so you don't have to worry about control."

3. Name the primary characteristics of effective control systems.

4. Identify and explain each of the four steps in controlling.

5. Give an example of each type of standard:

    a. Numerical standard

    b. Monetary standard

    c. Physical standard

    d. Time standard

    e. Intangible standard

6. Name and explain the three types of control systems.

7. In management by exception, the supervisor focuses on exceptional deviations from the standard rather than on every deviation. Will employees grow lax when they realize that they can perform below standard as long as they are not too far below? Discuss.

8. Explain the impact technology has had on control.

Skill Builder 13-1

The Overcontrolling Supervisor

As a new operations supervisor, Clarise Rogers was very conscientious about wanting to do a good job and pleasing her boss. She spent a large part of the day watching her employees perform their jobs, moving from one workstation to another. She inquired how things were going and tried to engage in friendly small talk.

One day a senior operator asked to see Clarise in her office. The operator said, "We know you mean well, but there's no need for you to be constantly checking up on everybody. We had one of the best departments in this company under Morgan [the previous supervisor], and she stayed off our backs. We're professionals, and we don't need somebody constantly looking over our shoulders. We're going to do a good job for you. Just give us some breathing space."

Answer the following questions:

1. What should Clarise do?

2. Suppose Clarise had just taken over one of the poorest performing departments in the company. Would this make a difference in the control techniques she should use? How?

Skill Builder 13-2

Setting Standards and Measuring Performance

group activity

Instructions:

Form small groups to discuss each of the jobs listed below. Assume that each group member directly supervises that position. In each case, indicate the major type(s) of standard(s) that would be used (physical, monetary, time, or intangible) and the frequency and manner of measuring performance for each job.

Discuss with group members your ideas about how to handle each situation.

1. Bank teller

2. Postal letter carrier

3. Server in a large restaurant

4. Real estate salesperson

5. Offensive-line football coach

6. Upholsterer in a furniture manufacturing plant

7. Third-grade teacher in an elementary school

Skill Builder 13-3

Setting Course Standards

group activity

Assume that you are the instructor in a supervisory management course at the college of your choice. In the class are 25 students completing the course for college credit. You are required to assign grades based on students' performances in the class.

Instructions:

1. Identify at least one standard that you can establish for the course in each of the following areas:

   a. Physical standards

   b. Numerical standards

   c. Time standards

   d. Intangible standards

2. In small groups, compare and discuss your lists of standards. Were your standards in any of the areas similar? Which standards were most common? In which areas was there the most variety among standards?

3. Present your overall findings to the class.

CASE

Controlling Absenteeism

CASE 13-1

Anna McIntyre had been named head nurse of the university hospital pediatrics department the previous day. She would officially begin her new job in 1 week, when Carla Smith, the present head nurse, would be reassigned to a new department. Anna reflected on the conversation she'd had with Gail Sutherland, director of nursing, when Gail offered her the position. "Anna," Gail had said, "you'll be taking over a department that has 8 percent absenteeism compared to only 2 percent for other nursing units in the hospital. This has always been a problem, and Carla never could handle it—that's a major reason she was transferred. I want you to make it your number 1 priority."

Anna reflected on Carla's performance as head nurse. Carla had always been a skilled, competent nurse, but since being promoted to head nurse in pediatrics, she had just been too soft. Many nurses had taken advantage of her good nature—Carla had found it impossible to discipline—and the situation in pediatrics had begun to deteriorate. Anna knew from her own experience that absenteeism had been high in the department. This was especially true of weekend work. Carla never took action, even when it was obvious that personnel were making petty excuses.

Answer the following questions:

1. What additional information should Anna attempt to obtain regarding the absenteeism problem?

2. Advise Anna on the steps she should take to control absenteeism.

3. What types of standards should she use?

4. What strategic control points should she establish?

14 Controlling Productivity, Quality, and Safety

Women on the sales floor of Park Place Lexus help make it #1 in quality.

You can never inspect quality into products. You can only build it into them.

—AKIO MORITA, CHAIRMAN, SONY CORPORATION

Park Place Lexus: Committed to Excellence

On the outskirts of Dallas, Texas, in Plano, is one special auto dealer, Park Place Lexus (PPL). PPL differs from other dealerships in many ways, and not just because of the feminine touch supplied by six of its sales "members," who just happen to be females. The differences also go beyond its putting green, cafe, Internet access, and portable DVD players with movies loaned to clients who wait for their cars to be serviced, all ideas that were suggested by customer focus groups.

Dealer-owner Ken Schnitzer explains his motive in making the commitment in 1995 when he began putting the processes in place in 1995 to make PPL something special. "We wanted to distinguish ourselves among our competitors. We set out to prove that a 'car dealer,' can be run just as well, and can be just as great a place to work, as any other corporation in America." Jordan Case, Park Place dealership president and former quarterback of the Canadian Football League's Ottawa Rough Riders, states: "Buying a car doesn't rank up there with the top five things you like to do. So we try to make the experience different. We're always trying to raise the bar and think about how we can improve." For example, after attending a Lexus summit on best practices held at a Four Seasons Hotel, Case sent some of his own staffers to spend a weekend at a local Four Seasons. Hector Interiano, a lead PPL valet, was impressed when every Four Seasons staffer called him by name. Guess what? Now, when a car pulls up to PPL's service drive, valets can punch the vehicle ID number into a laptop that informs them of pertinent information, which allows the valets to call their clients by name.

Located in the Dallas suburbs, the company of more than 200 "members," as its personnel are called, has been very successful. Its 2004 sales approached 3,000-plus new vehicles and over 1,000 used. Starting with its vision—"To be the unparalleled retail automotive group in the U.S.,"—PPL sets lofty goals, is committed to reaching them, and can be counted on to set them higher the following year. Name an activity that involves a client and you can bet a performance standard and tracking system is in place, ranging from requiring phones to be answered within three rings to e-mail response within 24 hours. Continuously improving is its mantra. Here are but a few of PPL's performance achievements:

Learning Objectives

After reading and studying this chapter, you should be able to:

1. Explain the concept of productivity.

2. Identify and explain the ways in which management, government, unions, and employees affect productivity.

3. Describe some steps supervisors can take to increase productivity.

4. Differentiate between total quality and quality control.

5. Describe the role of variance in controlling quality.

6. Identify some important tools for controlling quality.

7. Explain what the Occupational Safety and Health Administration (OSHA) does.

8. Describe the supervisor's role in promoting safety.

- Customer satisfaction for new car clients approaches 100 percent; pre-owned vehicle clients' satisfaction has increased from 94 percent in 2000 to 96 percent in 2004.

- Customer satisfaction with service at the locations approaches 98 percent; 96 percent of service clients report their vehicle ready when promised.

- Customer problems/complaints have dramatically been reduced. Between 2002 and 2005 customer concerns that "promises were not met" dropped from 130 to 3; concerns about discourteous treatment from 28 to 1, and concerns about misinformation from 22 to 1.

- Seventy percent of customers say they will purchase their next vehicle from PPL.

To achieve these kinds of customer results, PPL is willing to commit resources. It has a human resources department, rare for an auto dealer. Its computer database includes all client interactions—needs and preferences, customer survey responses, follow-up interactions regarding sales and service, complaints, and special customer needs. Personnel in sales, service, parts, and accounting have this information available instantly from PPL's sophisticated information technology (IT) system. PPL's hiring process is stringent, including aptitude and personality testing, with special attention paid to integrity. New members follow a rigorous training plan that includes classroom, on the job training, coaching, and mentoring to help them succeed. Everyone received training in ethics, health, safety, wellness, quality improvement, documentation, reporting, and computer skills; English classes are offered to Hispanic employees with limited English skills. Member training has increased from 24 hours in 2001 to over 184 hours in 2006. Employee turnover runs at about 22 percent, which is half the typical large auto dealership.

To encourage member empowerment and motivation, a monthly "50-50 Meeting" is held, where half of the meeting focuses on ideas and concerns and half on solutions. A recent solution authorized employees to spend up to $250 on the spot to resolve a client's concern.

PPL has zero tolerance regarding unethical or illegal behavior, all managers receiving yearly ethics training in subjects ranging from sexual harassment to safety and health concerns. Leaders are expected to "walk the talk" as role models, with ethics commonly brought up at team meetings throughout the company. The company is active in the two communities its dealerships serve, one in Plano, the other in Grapevine, Texas, each generously donating funds to local charities throughout the year. It supports its members' volunteering time to support local programs.

PPL has been recognized not only by clients and competitors, but also by organizations that value excellence. General Mills, for one, has spent time benchmarking PPL's practices. The state of Texas awarded PPL its quality award for organizational excellence in 2002. And in 2005 the company achieved national recognition when it was named one of six U.S. organizations to receive the Malcolm Baldridge Award for Organizational Excellence. As owner Schnitzer says, "The typical car dealer wakes up in the morning and says, 'How can I sell more cars today?' We wake up and say, 'How can we run the company better today?'"

Source: Julia Chang, "At Your Service: for Park Place Lexus, Treating Customers and Employees Right Led to National Recognition and Increased Sales," *Sales and Marketing Management*, June 2006 v 158, pp. 42–3.

Control is the management function that ensures that organizational plans are executed properly and that objectives are met. This chapter addresses several key areas of control, some of which were directly reflected in the scenario that you just read and that concern managers and supervisors: productivity and costs, quality, and safety.

1 Explain the concept of productivity.

Improving Productivity and Cost Control

Productivity has been an "in" word in American business for the past two decades. Another name for it is efficiency. We hear about productivity at work, read about it in magazines and newspapers, and see it discussed on television. It has become the subject of business- and government-sponsored seminars. "Productivity centers" have sprung up around the country to research the subject.

High U.S. Productivity: Mid-1990s to Present

On a global level, a country's productivity indicates how efficiently its human resources are utilized in producing goods and services. The productivity of U.S. workers is higher than that of any other country's workers. Canadian workers, in fact, rank next to U.S. workers, producing about 95 percent of U.S. workers' output. Although the productivity of Japanese

Hanayoshi Yamaguchi/Bloomberg News/Landov

Japanese workers, while highly productive, still don't approach the U.S. level of production.

workers is much touted, actually the Japanese worker produces only about two thirds of the output of the U.S. worker.

During the 1980s, a major concern was the United States' productivity stagnation (Exhibit 14-1). As U.S. productivity suffered, Japanese and other foreign competitors stole market share with their high-quality products in autos, steel, electronics, earth-moving equipment, appliances, and many others. Plenty of blame was tossed at management, government,

EXHIBIT **14-1**

U.S. Productivity Growth in Manufacturing Output per Hour: 1960s–2006

Year	Annual Rate	Year	Annual Rate
1960s	2.2	1995	3.9
1970s	2.7	1996	4.1
1980s	1.4	1997	5.0
1990	2.5	1998	4.8
1991	2.3	1999	5.1
1992	5.1	2000	4.1
1993	2.2	2001	0.9
1994	3.1	2002	4.8
		2003	6.2
		2004	1.4
		2005	4.1
		2006 (1st Quarter)	3.7

Source: U.S. Bureau of Labor Statistics.

unions, and employees. The 1990s saw a dramatic turnaround as U.S. companies grabbed back the initiative and built new facilities, upgraded technology, transformed production processes and work methods, and invested heavily in employee training. Since the mid-1990s, U.S. productivity has remained strong, helping firms keep costs low and enabling them to weather the recent economic storms of financial crisis in Asia, recession throughout much of Europe, and a shaky U.S. economy.

Defining Productivity

productivity Measure of efficiency (inputs to outputs).

Productivity is a measure that compares outputs to inputs. It tells you how efficiently a system is performing. For example, your car's gas mileage is a productivity measure of energy performance. For a certain input, say 1 gallon of gas, your car achieves a certain output, say 22 miles of travel. The figure of 22 miles per gallon (MPG) is the productivity measure of your car's energy performance. How is this figure useful? You now have a basis for comparing (1) your car's performance to that of other cars and (2) your car's present performance to its previous performance. For example, if your MPG were to fall to 15, you would know that your car's performance had fallen, and you would try to determine the reasons—assuming, of course, that such an energy loss was important to you! Productivity is expressed as a ratio; that is, output is divided by input. In our example of the car's gas mileage, the ratio might look like this:

$$\frac{\text{Total miles (220)}}{\text{Number of gallons (10)}} = 22 \text{ MPG}$$

✔ STOP AND THINK

What would be some meaningful input–output relationships for the following service organizations: restaurants, community colleges, beauty salons, insurance companies, department stores?

The official productivity measure of the United States as shown in Exhibit 14-2 is based on labor output and input per hour. This is the productivity that is announced each quarter by the government and discussed in the media. Basically, it is the ratio of the total output of the nation's goods and services to the total hours of labor that went into producing those goods and services. Business organizations use numerous input–output performance measures, some of which are shown in Exhibit 14-2. Generally, when people in business discuss improved productivity, they are talking about total costs and total goods or services produced. Assume that a department has a mandate from upper management to increase productivity by 15 percent in the next year or it will be shut down. Upper management's goal, then, is that at the end of the next 12-month period, the department's productivity ratio would look like this:

$$\frac{\text{Total output of goods/services}}{\text{Total costs}} = 15 \text{ percent more than previously accomplished}$$

Basically, there are three ways to accomplish the 15 percent productivity increase:

1. *Increase* the total output without changing the total costs.

2. *Decrease* the total input costs without changing the total output.

3. *Increase* the output and *decrease* the input costs.

EXHIBIT 14-2

Examples of Productivity
Measurements

Input	Output
Salesperson labor hours	Sales volume per salesperson
Energy used, in BTUs	Number of pounds fabricated
Training hours for customer service personnel	Percent of error-free written orders
Number of hours of plantwide safety meetings	Number of accident-free days
Labor hours spent on preventive maintenance	Number of hours without a machine breakdown
Cost of raw materials	Quantity of finished goods produced
Total labor hours of service personnel	Total quantity of services produced
Total labor hours of production workforce	Total quantity of goods produced
Total costs	Total number (or value) of goods or services produced

BTU, British thermal unit.

Assume that the department produced 48,000 units (output) at a cost of $24,000 for raw materials, energy, and labor. The productivity ratio is as follows:

$$\frac{48,000 \text{ units (output)}}{\$24,000 \text{ (input)}} = 2.0 \text{ units/dollar}$$

To achieve a 15 percent increase in productivity, the department would need to raise the final ratio by 0.3 (that is, 2.0×15 percent). In other words, the department would need to produce 2.3 units per dollar to achieve a 15 percent productivity increase. There are three basic ways to achieve this, as discussed next.

Example 1: Increasing Output. One approach to attaining the productivity increase is to hold the line on costs while increasing output. How much additional output would be needed to reach the new productivity rate of 2.3? This can be calculated by the following steps:

(a) $\dfrac{\text{Total units}}{\$24,000} = 2.3$ units per dollar

(b) Total units $= 2.3$ units per dollar $\times \$24,000$

(c) Total units $= 55,200$

Since the department is presently producing 48,000 units, it would have to produce 7,200 additional units without increasing costs to attain the 15 percent productivity increase.

Example 2: Decreasing Input. Another approach is to maintain present output while reducing costs. By how much would the department need to reduce costs to attain the 15 percent increase? This can be calculated by the following steps:

(a) $\dfrac{48,000 \text{ units}}{\text{Costs}} = 2.3$ units per dollar

(b) Costs $= \dfrac{48,000 \text{ units}}{2.3 \text{ units per dollar}}$

(c) Costs $= \$20,870$

Producing the 48,000 units at a cost of $20,870 would provide the 15 percent productivity ratio improvement. The department would have to maintain production of 48,000 units while reducing costs by $3,130 (that is, $24,000 − $20,870).

Example 3: Increasing Output and Decreasing Input. Suppose that the department could reduce costs by only $1,000. By how much would the department have to increase output to achieve the 15 percent productivity increase?

(a) $\dfrac{\text{Total units}}{\$24,000 - \$1,000} = 2.3$ units per dollar

(b) $\dfrac{\text{Total units}}{\$23,000} = 2.3$ units per dollar

(c) Total units $= 2.3$ units per dollar $\times$ $23,000

(d) Total units $= 52,900$

Thus, reducing costs by $1,000 and increasing output by 4,900 units (52,900 − 48,000) would also provide the 15 percent productivity increase.

Why Productivity Is Important

Productivity is important for several reasons. From an individual company's standpoint, increased productivity translates into lower prices, larger market share, and greater profits. The firm's stronger financial position enables it to invest in research and development, to utilize new advanced technology, to increase wages and benefits, to improve working conditions, and so on.

The Harbour Report is the most widely recognized and quoted analysis of manufacturing productivity in the North American auto industry. Closely watched because of its link with vehicle cost and profitability, it measures manufacturing labor hours required to build a car or truck. As it has done for most of the past 10 years, Nissan led the pack, taking 28.46 labor hours to produce a vehicle. Toyota followed with 29.40 hours, followed by Honda at 32.51. General Motors (GM) was close by at 33.19, followed by the Chrysler Group at 33.71 and Ford at 35.79. Yet, there were some favorable results for the "Big Three" U.S. automakers. GM's car assembly plant in Oshawa, Ontario, where it builds the Impala sedan and Monte Carlo coupe, claimed title to the single most efficient vehicle assembly plant. Chrysler continued its improvement of the last 3 years, reducing its hours for vehicle production by 19 percent. To give you some idea of how manufacturing efficiency produces advantages, Nissan's leading labor hour per vehicle figure translated to $300 to $400 less cost for vehicle than less efficient competitors. Considering the millions of vehicles produced, a productivity edge is a major advantage.[1]

Productivity is important for smaller and service-oriented businesses as well. Let us examine the following example:

> Assume that you manage a steakhouse restaurant that uses seven waiters/waitresses. Their pay (including benefits but excluding tips) averages $10.00 hourly. The maximum number of tables that they can serve effectively is five per hour. Thus, the labor cost for serving each table is $10/5, or $2 per table. Assume that business has picked up recently. The kitchen can handle the extra business, and, by rearranging tables, five new tables could be added. Since the current waiter/waitress maximum of five tables served per hour has already been reached, a new waiter/waitress must be hired to handle the extra workload. Before hiring another waitress, though, you pose the problem to your waiters and they come up with a plan.

"We could each handle an extra table an hour if we didn't have to set each table," they say. "Couldn't the hostess who seats the party distribute the silverware and menus? Also, might we arrange each waiter's tables in a more compact area? This would reduce walking time among tables. The time saved with these two changes might allow us to effectively serve another table hourly (which, by the way, would mean an additional tip)."

So you try it out, and behold, it works. Your waiters/waitresses handle the extra table per hour effectively. Let's calculate the effect on productivity—it has increased by one fifth, or 20 percent. Moreover, your labor costs have decreased from $2.00 per table to $1.67 per table ($10.00 ÷ 6 tables = $1.67 per table). Since labor costs typically account for 30 to 60 percent of a company's expenses, increasing the efficiency of labor is very important to an organization's success.

On a larger scale, increased productivity greatly enhances the economic growth and health of the United States. In the international market, companies from the United States compete with firms from other nations. Increased productivity in the United States enhances the success of U.S. companies in international markets, keeps prices down, reduces inflation, and improves our standard of living.

Groups Influencing Productivity

As noted in Exhibit 14-1, the productivity growth rate of the United States picked up significant steam in the 1990s. But what caused the slowdown of U.S. companies' productivity in the 1980s? What is responsible for the impressive growth since the mid-1990s? Basically, four groups play important roles, as shown in Exhibit 14-3.

2 Identify and explain the ways in which management, government, unions, and employees affect productivity.

EXHIBIT **14-3**

Groups Influencing
Productivity

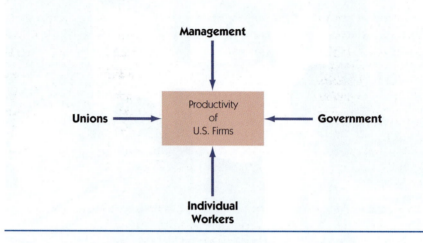

Management. A major force in determining productivity is management. Many experts placed major blame on complacent, conservative management for the United States' deteriorating performance of the 1980s when U.S. companies lost ground to highly productive foreign producers, especially the Japanese, in such industries as steel and autos (see Exhibit 14-4). Fortunately, a turnaround in the 1990s was fueled by management decisions to build more modern plants, upgrade equipment, improve processes, and train employees. However, some industries such as steel have never regained their dominant world market position.

EXHIBIT **14-4**

Toyota's Production
System

Toyota Production System
Toyota's philosophy and framework of organizing manufacturing facilities efficiently.

The global company with the strongest reputation for efficiency is unquestionably Toyota Motors. The "Toyota Production System" (TPS) has been admired, studied, and copied by most large manufacturers, including competitors. In fact in Erlanger, Ohio, Toyota has created a training center to teach outside firms its TPS. The "system" refers to Toyota's philosophy and framework of organizing manufacturing facilities and having them interact with suppliers and customers in the most efficient way. TPS's goal is the elimination of waste—be it through defective materials, overproduction, inefficient logistics, or inventory buildup. The TPS requires a strong top management commitment and what for many companies is a dramatic change from their current ways of doing things.

One of the best known aspects of Toyota's approach to efficiency is its effort to continuously improve, called "kaizen." Another is an "Andan," part of every Toyota plant, which is a cord that any employee can pull to stop the production line when a problem or defect is spotted. The story is told of an American supervisor in Toyota's Georgetown, Kentucky, plant who feared for his job after one of his crew pulled the Andan, shutting the line down for 4 hours to trace and remedy the problem. Afterward, he was called to the desk of the Japanese plant executive where he nervously explained the problem and the solution. Only then did he learn he was summoned not to explain the problem and shutdown, but to receive recognition for his team having done it.

Source: Jingshan Li and Dennis Blumenfield "Qualitative Analysis of a Transfer Production Line with Andan," *IIE Transactions* v 38 October 2006, pp 837–47. Dan Monk, "Productivity Machine," *Business Courier Serving Cincinnati-Northern Kentucky,* June 25, 1999 v 16, pp 1–2.

Government. Another important productivity player is government. For example, tax incentives can encourage business investment in new facilities and technology; government regulations also play an important role. During the 1980s businesses spent huge amounts on the costs of compliance to satisfy, for instance, pollution and environmental controls, consumer protection requirements, and employee safety and health, to mention some of the more costly areas. This not only diverted expenditures from more efficient labor-saving technology, equipment, and plants, but it also required many new positions—such as equal employment opportunity (EEO) specialists, record keepers, and clerks—to meet government requirements. These personnel do not contribute directly to output. While government regulation of business is necessary, the amount of regulation is a constant source of debate in this country as well as in others.

Individual Workers. Another important productivity player is the individual worker. Employees' ability, motivation, and commitment strongly affect individual and team performance. The age and education of employees impact their skill: During the 1980s the average age of workforce employees was much lower than in earlier years, which resulted in less-experienced, less-productive employees during that period. This situation has reversed itself and has fostered the United States' higher productivity during the 1990s to today.

Unions. Unions also play a role in productivity by their posture toward technology enhancements, new work methods, and displacement of inefficient jobs. We read about cases in which unions resist labor-saving devices and efficiencies and protect jobs that are considered nonproductive. Many people tried to make unions the scapegoat of the 1980s' productivity crisis; however, during this period, union membership was decreasing, as is the case today. Moreover, in the retail and wholesale industry, which had practically no union strength, the decline in productivity was similar to that which occurred in the more traditionally unionized industries.

> **A recent labor dispute between Daimler Chrysler and the Canadian Auto Workers (CAW) reflected productivity issues. While the pay contract offered by Chrysler was in line with that accepted by the CAW in negotiations with GM and Ford, the hangup was the union's opposition to other concessions. These included elimination of overtime pay for some weekend work, expanded use by the company of temporary part-time workers, and elimination of some break times. Also at issue was the CAW's desire to protect 1,100 CAW jobs at risk when Chrysler discontinued production of the Dodge Ram commercial van plant in Windsor, Ontario.[2]**

In summary, then, all of these groups play a role in productivity. However, management, which directly controls decisions about facilities, technology, research, and the company "productivity climate," is most responsible in that it strongly impacts relationships with its union and sets the stage in numerous ways for the productivity of individual employees.

The Supervisor's Role in Improving Productivity

Supervisors often have little control over spending for technology and equipment, but as the persons in direct contact with operating employees, they are very important players in the productivity issue. But how do you go about it? Suppose that you head a department of 20 employees who produced a total of 10,000 units last year. Under your plant manager's new mandate, you must increase production to 11,500 units. How would you do this? You could do some of the things listed in Exhibit 14-5.

The Supervisor's Role in Cost Control

As we pointed out earlier, the productivity of a department is based on its total outputs and total inputs. Upper management is cost conscious because costs represent major inputs.

3 Describe some steps supervisors can take to increase productivity.

EXHIBIT 14-5

- Train employees. Can their abilities be upgraded?
- Clearly communicate the need for high standards so that workers understand what is expected of them.
- Use motivation techniques to inspire workers to increase output. Pride, ego, and security are several important motivators available.
- Eliminate idleness, extended breaks, and early quitting time.
- Build in quality the first time work is done. Productivity is lost when items are scrapped or need to be reworked to be salvaged.
- Work on improving attendance and turnover in your work group.
- Reduce accidents. Accidents normally result in time lost to investigations, meetings, and reports—even if the employee does not suffer a lost–work-time injury.
- Seek to improve production measures. Will process or work-flow improvements help?
- Try to eliminate or reduce equipment or machinery breakdowns. Preventive maintenance is important.
- Exercise good control techniques. Follow up on performance and take corrective action promptly.
- Involve your employees in the process of improvement. Select their ideas and suggestions for improvement. Form special productivity improvement teams.

Supervisors direct the operating work of an organization; thus, they have a key role in controlling a firm's cost in labor hours and efficiency, maintenance of machinery and equipment, supplies, energy, and other matters.

Budgets are one aid that can help supervisors to control costs. Different budgets are normally prepared for sales, production, scrap, equipment, grievances, lost–work-time accidents, and the like. Moreover, they may be set for different time periods such as a week, a month, a quarter, or a year. Since a budget reflects expected performance, it becomes a basis for evaluating a department's actual performance (see Exhibit 14-6).

EXHIBIT 14-6

Name of department	Fabrication	Performance period	November 2006
Budgeted output	15,700 lbs.	Budgeted scrap	152 lbs.
Actual output	15,227 lbs.	Actual scrap	120 lbs.
Variance	−473 lbs.		+32 lbs.

Item	Actual	Budgeted	Variance
Direct labor	$32,000	$32,000	$ 0
Overtime	1,500	1,000	−500
Supplies	500	385	−115
Maintenance and repairs	4,250	3,000	−1,250
Utilities	1,300	1,200	−100
Scrapped material	1,200	1,520	+320
Total	$40,750	$39,105	−$1,645

Note in Exhibit 14-6 that the supervisor's department has performed well in some cost areas and not so well in others. Output is off by 473 pounds, overtime is 50 percent higher than budgeted, and maintenance and repairs are also over budget. On the plus side, the department has been efficient in using raw materials.

Budgets are not carved in stone; there will always be unusual occurrences that affect performance. An investigation of the unfavorable variances in Exhibit 14-6 may reveal that the supervisor or team member could have done little to avoid them. For example, perhaps a crucial piece of equipment had faulty parts, causing the high repair costs; or perhaps the high overtime resulted from an unexpected weekend job thrust upon the supervisor. A budget does, however, serve as an important supervisory tool by signaling areas that may need attention. Such attention might take the form of combining certain jobs, reducing scrap, achieving better quality production, or focusing on large-cost items rather than numerous smaller ones.

http://www.inventory management.com

Recently, advanced software technology has proved especially helpful to supervisors in achieving effective cost control. It is now possible for supervisors in some circumstances to have up-to-the-minute cost data on payroll, raw materials, utilities, and other costs as nearby as a computer monitor or printer.

Some Recent Productivity Improvement Methods

In an effort to improve productivity, three relatively recent productivity improvement measures have been introduced in manufacturing firms. These improvements, which have been due to advances in computer and machinery technology, are (1) robotics, (2) just-in-time (JIT) inventory control, and (3) computer-assisted manufacturing (CAM).

Robotics. A **robot** is a machine, controlled by a computer, that can be programmed to perform a number of repetitive manipulations of tools or materials. Japan makes the greatest use of robots in the world, having about one third of the 1,000,000 in use in the industrial world. The United States has fewer than half of Japan's number, about 162,000, with most in the automotive industry. However, they are also finding increased acceptance in the semiconductor, electronics, food and beverage, pharmaceutical, consumer goods, and appliance industries, and in other industries where precision materials handling and packing are required. It is estimated that these machines—often called "steel-collar workers"—operate for about $5 an hour, considerably less than the $15 to $20 per hour (including benefits) or higher wages paid to many employees.[3]

robot A machine that is controlled by a computer.

Just-in-Time Inventory Control. Pioneered by Toyota, under the **just-in-time (JIT) inventory control** system, needed materials arrive on the scene as close as is feasible to the time they are needed in the production process. Often, computers link the company with suppliers to keep them informed about the company's up-to-the-minute needs. With JIT, the proper components arrive in the right place at the right time. JIT allows an organization to minimize

just-in-time (JIT) inventory control Materials arrive when they are needed in the production process.

"Steel collar workers" operate at only $5 an hour, compared to their human counterparts at $15–$20 per hour.

inventory holding and storage costs and to utilize the space previously occupied by inventory waiting to be used.

> Toyota Motors has earned the reputation of being the best inventory manager around. Its Georgetown, Kentucky, plant operates with only 2.8 hours of inventory on hand at any one time, which saves millions. Parts from its suppliers, most located within 200 miles of the plant, are delivered some 16 times daily.[4]

> In 1994, Dana Corporation gambled and built a 110,000-square-foot truck frame plant in Stockton, California, hoping to get business from the joint venture Toyota/GM truck manufacturing plant. Since then, each of the 1 million truck frames built by Dana has gone on Toyota Tacoma trucks. As a preferred supplier, Dana's commitment to the "Toyota Production System" requires it to commit to the highest standards of efficiency and quality, including Toyota's JIT inventory requirements.[5]

The JIT approach has been used by many of the largest U.S. companies, such as Motorola, Chrysler, and other manufacturers. Retailers have also gotten into the act in a big way. Many large retail chains, such as Home Depot and Wal-Mart, practice JIT inventory from their hundreds of suppliers. A good example can also be found at Dillard's, a leading department store chain throughout the Southeast and Midwest. A computer-driven "direct response" program allows items such as Gant dress shirts and Christian Dior lingerie to be ordered directly from the vendor each week—by computer—based on the previous week's sales.

Computer-Assisted Manufacturing. In **computer-assisted manufacturing (CAM),** special computers assist automated equipment in performing the processes necessary for production. These computers can be reprogrammed to permit machinery to easily produce a product or part to different specifications. Whereas proper planning and coordination would normally take hours, CAM equipment can be programmed to make adjustments within seconds. CAM is especially useful when small orders of customized products must be filled. Once the computer has been programmed, the electronic signals control the machine processor, resulting in the correct sequence of steps to properly complete the task.

For example, at carpet manufacturers, computer software programs control patterns, weaves, and the size of carpets being produced. At apparel manufacturers, such as Hart Schaffner and Marx, computer software programs determine optimum cutting of patterns and sizes to minimize waste and ensure perfect cuts.

computer-assisted manufacturing (CAM)
Special computers assist equipment in performing processes.

Historical Insight

Evolution of the Quality Explosion in the United States

The background of today's surging quality movement in the United States can be traced to Japan. Following World War II, the words "Made in Japan" connoted cheap, inferior quality. As part of General MacArthur's program to help rebuild the country, 50-year-old W. Edwards Deming, a U.S. statistical quality control advocate, was brought to Japan to teach statistical quality control concepts. Deming addressed 21 top Japanese executives who were eager to learn and who represented the industrial leaders of the country. His theories formed the basis of **Deming's 85–15 rule.** This rule assumes that when things go wrong, 85 percent of the time the cause is attributed to elements controlled by management, such as machinery, materials, or processes, while only about 15 percent of the time are employees at fault. Thus, Deming believed that management rather than the employee is to blame for most poor quality. The Japanese embraced Deming's message and transformed their industries by using his techniques. His "14 points for quality," as shown in Exhibit 14-7, are the actions he believed necessary for an organization to successfully make the quality "transformation."

Deming's contributions were recognized early by the Japanese. In 1951, the Deming Application Prize was instituted by the Union of Japanese Scientists and Engineers, and Deming was awarded the nation's highest honor, the Royal Order of the Sacred Treasure, from the Emperor of Japan. By the mid-1970s the quality of Japan's products exceeded that of Western manufacturers, and Japanese companies made significant U.S. and global market penetration in areas such as autos, steel, computers, and electronics.

The United States' quality problem was first highlighted in a 1980 NBC program entitled "If Japan Can . . . Why Can't We?" The program introduced the then 80-year-old Deming who, although an American, was virtually unknown in this country. This program ignited a spark that awakened American executives and helped fuel a quality turnaround. Major companies, especially those that were threatened, embarked on extensive programs to improve quality. Ford Motors was among the first to invite Deming to help transform its operations. Within a few years, Ford's results improved dramatically; its profits became the highest for any company in automotive history. By 1992 its Ford Taurus unseated the Honda Accord as the best-selling domestic model.

In 1987, in an effort to encourage quality initiatives, the U.S. Congress established the Malcolm Baldrige National Quality Award (see Exhibit 14-8), which continues to generate remarkable interest in quality by American organizations.

The American quality story has been a successful one. Since the 1990s the quality of U.S. goods and services has achieved a stunning turnaround, making "Made in the USA" again a symbol of world-class quality.

Deming's 85–15 rule
Assumes that when things go wrong, 85 percent of the time the cause is from elements controlled by management.

http://www.quality.nist.gov

Deming's work has tremendous historical significance and his ideas are still relevant to current management practices.

Controlling Quality

In recent years, perhaps no other aspect of management has received the attention of organizations as the effort to improve quality. As you have learned from the previous section, quality of an organization's products and services and the organization's productivity are intricately linked. That is one reason why organizations are so "quality" oriented today. One quality expert, Dr. Philip Crosby, estimates that nonconformance—products and services that do not match up to requirements—cost the typical manufacturer about 20 percent of sales and the typical service firm 35 percent of sales. This includes the cost of scrapped materials, wasted time, costs of rework, and customers' exercise of warranties. So quality directly affects the bottom line.

A second reason for quality consciousness is global competition (see Historical Insight). Many U.S. firms such as Citigroup, 3M, Coca-Cola, Exxon, and others earn over half of their revenues from foreign markets. Moreover, high-quality foreign firms, such as Michelin, Toyota, Seiko, Nokia, Nestlé, and others, compete vigorously, which requires U.S. firms to keep up or lose market share. In another reflection of globalization, many organizations require all supplier firms to achieve ISO 9000 certification—an assurance that they meet international quality standards in such areas as product design, manufacturing processes, testing, inspection, and service.

A third reason for greater quality emphasis is the increased information available to the public regarding product and service quality. Media coverage quickly informs potential

EXHIBIT **14-7**

Deming's Fourteen Points
for Quality

1. Top management should establish and publish a statement of the organization's purpose and commitment to quality products and services and continuous improvement.
2. Everyone throughout the organization should learn the new philosophy.
3. Dependence on "inspecting" quality into products should be shifted to an attitude of "expecting" quality by having it built into the system.
4. There must be a systematic way to select quality suppliers, rather than simply on the basis of cost.
5. The organization must be devoted to continuous improvement.
6. All employees should be trained in the most modern quality and problem-solving techniques.
7. Leadership techniques consistent with getting the most commitment from employees should be practiced throughout the entire organization.
8. Fear should be eliminated from the work environment.
9. Teams and work groups must work smoothly together; barriers between functional departments must be eliminated.
10. Exhortations, posters, and slogans asking for new levels of workforce productivity must be backed by providing the methods to achieve these.
11. Numerical production quotas should be eliminated. Constant improvement should be sought instead.
12. Barriers that deprive employees from pride in their work must be removed.
13. A vigorous program of education, retraining, and self-improvement for all employees must be instituted.
14. A structure in top management that will push the thirteen points above to achieve the transformation must be created.

Source: From W. Edwards Deming, *Out of Crisis* (Cambridge, MA, MIT Press, 1986).

EXHIBIT **14-8**

The Malcolm Baldrige
National Quality Award

The prize is only a gold-plated medal encased in a crystal column 14 inches tall. But since 1987, when the U.S. Congress created the Malcolm Baldrige National Quality Award at the urging of business leaders, it has symbolized America's best in quality. Named for the much-admired former U.S. Secretary of Commerce, Malcolm Baldrige, who died in 1987, the award is administered by the National Institute of Standards and Technology, with endowments covering costs of administration and judging of applicants.

Applications are scored by examination teams drawn from senior ranks of business, consultants, and academics. The highest scoring applicants move on to stage two—a site visit by four to six examiners who verify the facts in the application and probe more deeply into organizational processes. They report back to a nine-judge panel, which recommends winners to the Secretary of Commerce. The White House makes the formal announcements.

Winning a Baldrige has proved tough. In 1988, the first year of eligibility, only three of 66 applicants were winners; in 1989, only two of 40. Organizations must observe eight essentials in order to win:

1. Establish a plan to seek improvement continuously in all phases of operations—not just manufacturing but purchasing, sales, human relations, and other areas.
2. Put in place a system that accurately tracks and measures performance in those areas.
3. Establish a long-term strategic plan based on performance targets that compare with the world's best in that particular industry.
4. Link closely in a partnership with suppliers and customers in a way that provides needed feedback for continuous improvement.
5. Demonstrate a deep understanding of customers in order to convert their wants into products.
6. Establish and maintain long-lasting customer relationships, going beyond product manufacture and delivery to include sales, service, and ease of maintenance.
7. Focus on preventing mistakes instead of developing efficient ways to correct them; that is, feedforward control is a must.
8. Perhaps most difficult, but imperative, is to make a commitment to quality improvement throughout all levels of the organization, including top, middle, and bottom.

Continued

EXHIBIT 14-8

Continued

Past winners since the award's inception in 1988 are given here:

2005	Manufacturing	Sunny Fresh Foods, Inc.			Boeing Airlift & Tanker Programs
	Service	DynMcDermott Petroleum Operations			Texas Nameplate Co.
	Small Business	Park Place Lexus	1997	Manufacturing	Solectron Corporation
	Education	Richland College			3M Dental Products Division
	Education	Jenks Public Schools		Service	Merrill Lynch Credit Corporation
	Health Care	Bronson Methodist Hospital			Xerox Business Services
2004	Manufacturing	The Bama Companies	1996	Manufacturing	ADAC Laboratories
	Small Business	Texas Nameplate Company, Inc.			Trident Precision Manufacturing, Inc.
	Education	Kenneth W. Monfort College of Business		Service	Dana Commercial Credit Corp.
				Small Business	Custom Research, Inc.
	Health Care	Robert Wood Johnson University Hospital Hamilton	1995	Manufacturing	Corning Telecommunications Products
2003	Manufacturing	Medrad, Inc.			Armstrong World Industries
	Service	Boeing Aerospace Support	1994	Service	AT&T Consumer Communication
	Service	Caterpillar Financial Services Corp.			GTE Directories
	Small Business	Stoner, Inc.		Small Business	Wainwright Industries
	Education	Community Consolidated School District 15	1993	Manufacturing	Eastern Chemical Co.
				Small Business	American Rubber Co.
	Health Care	Baptist Hospital, Inc.	1992	Manufacturing	AT&T Network Systems
	Health Care	Saint Luke's Hospital of Kansas City			Group/Transmission Systems
2002	Manufacturing	Motorola Commercial, Government, Industrial Solutions Division			Texas Instruments Defense Systems & Electronic Group
	Small Business	Branch-Smith Printing Division,	1992	Service	AT&T Universal Card Services
	Health Care	SSM Health Care			The Ritz-Carlton Hotel
2001	Manufacturing	Clarke American Checks		Small Business	Granite Rock Co.
	Small Business	Pal's Sudden Service	1991	Manufacturing	Solectron Corporation
	Education	Chugach, AK School District			Zytec Corp.
		University of Wisconsin–Stout		Small Business	Marlow Industries
		Pearl River, NY School District	1990	Manufacturing	Cadillac Motor Car Co.
2000	Manufacturing	Dana Corp., Spicer Driveshaft Division, KARLEE Co.			IBM Rochester
	Service	Operations Management Intl.		Service	Federal Express Corp.
	Small Business	Los Alamos National Bank		Small Business	Wallace Co.
1999	Manufacturing	STMicroelectronics, Inc.	1989	Manufacturing	Miliken & Co.
	Service	BI			Xerox Business Products & Systems
		The Ritz-Carlton Hotel	1988	Manufacturing	Motorola, Inc.
	Small Business	Sunny Fresh Foods			Westinghouse Commercial Nuclear Fuel Division
1998	Manufacturing	Caterpillar Inc., Solar Turbines Division		Small Business	Globe Metallurgical, Inc.

consumers about safety problems, such as the abrupt tilting of a Princess Cruise ship, which injured 240 passengers, contaminated beef by ConAgra Foods, or Dell and Apple Computers' recall of 6 million notebook computers which contained potentially hazardous Sony lithium batteries.[6] Additionally, independent quality ratings given by such organizations as JD Power and Associates (auto quality), AAA and Mobil (hotels and restaurants), and *Consumer Reports* (consumer products) significantly affect consumer behavior.

EXHIBIT 14-9

The Total Quality Chain

```
Improved              Increased              Increased
Products/Services  →  Market Share   →       Profitability
```

Total Quality and Quality Control

Sometimes the terms *total quality* and *quality control* are used interchangeably. However, they are not the same. **Total quality** refers to an organization's overall quality effort that strives to achieve customer satisfaction through continuous improvement of the organization's products, services, and processes. The term *total* indicates its comprehensiveness, involving all management levels, employees, suppliers, and customers. It is based on the quality chain shown in Exhibit 14-9: increased quality leads to more customers and increased market share, which enable greater profitability. It was this approach to quality that enabled Japanese firms to become so successful in the 1980s and such intense competitors today.

✔ STOP AND THINK

In the chapter preview, note how Park Place Lexus used a total quality approach.

Quality control, on the other hand, is a narrower process, consisting of the measurement and analysis of quality performance and actions taken to correct quality problems. It occurs during or after performance and may include inspection, testing, sampling, and statistical analysis.

Understanding Variance in Controlling Quality

Every product and service is the output or result of a process. You might consider a process to be a set of related activities designed to accomplish a goal.

The nature of processes is to exhibit variation; for example, items produced in a machining or manufacturing process are not all exactly alike. Some measurable dimensions, such as length, diameter, or weight, will vary. These variations may be quite small and imperceivable by the naked eye, but sophisticated gauges or test equipment will reveal these differences. Similarly, service processes are also subject to variation. Fast-food customers wait different periods of time before being served. Some luggage checked in on a commercial airline will not arrive with its owner. At a steak house, there is considerable variation among steaks prepared as "rare."

Two types of variation exist: common cause and special cause. Let's use a classic example to illustrate process variation: writing. Note the variations of handwritten letters below, though each one was carefully written by the same author.

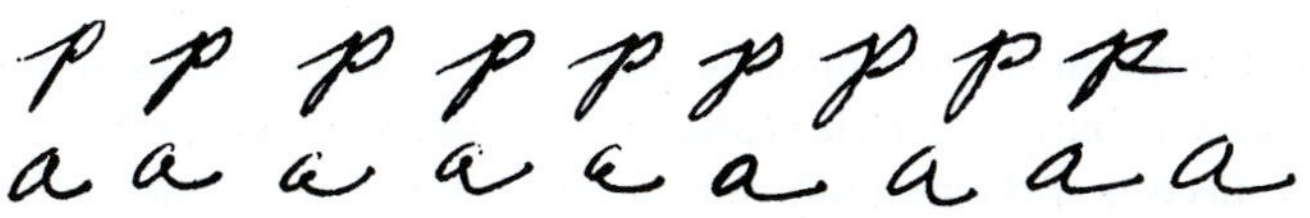

P P P P P P P P
a a a a a a a a

4 | Differentiate between total quality and quality control.

total quality Refers to an organization's overall effort to achieve customer satisfaction through continuous improvement of products or services.

quality control Defined measurements designed to check whether the desired quality standards are being met.

5 | Describe the role of variance in controlling quality.

You needn't use a magnifying glass to note that differences exist. The differences in each "p" are normal and to be expected. This we call *common cause variation.* Now look at the "a's." Note that the middle one is clearly different from the others. Perhaps the writer was bumped, or the paper quality in that one spot was different, or a different pen was used. (Actually, it was made by the same writer but using the other hand.) The variation is not routine or expected; clearly, there was excessive variation, or *special cause variation.* Common cause variation is a general, routine variation that is built into the system. Special cause variation occurs intermittently and is associated with a specific event.

Effective control of quality can have two focuses: (1) reducing common cause variation and (2) reducing special cause variation. As Deming and other quality experts note, special causes can sometimes be addressed by individual workers, but common causes can ordinarily only be corrected through management action to improve the process. This might include such things as upgrading raw materials, using more sophisticated equipment, providing additional training, and so on. Importantly, much of the effort by organizations to seek continuous quality improvement is aimed at reducing common cause variation by improving processes.

Reducing special cause variation entails identifying the problem, isolating it, examining the cause, and remedying it. This might mean, for instance, replacing an erratic piece of equipment, reassigning an employee who cannot keep pace with job demands, or reassigning personnel to handle peak customer demand periods. As a supervisor, it is important to understand variation and the extent to which different levels of quality performance can be attributed to normal or special cause variables. Statistical sampling is one useful tool for doing so, but is beyond our scope here. However, we will examine some other important tools.

6

Identify some important tools for controlling quality.

Some Tools for Controlling Quality

A number of tools are available to assist in effective control of quality. Often, these are used by individuals who are part of special problem-solving or quality-improvement teams. Among the tools discussed here are flowcharts, histograms, run charts, Pareto charts, control charts, and fishbone diagrams. Some, such as histograms, run charts, and control charts, represent displays of the actual performance data that must be addressed. Keep in mind that these tools apply not just to the quality of manufacturing processes (although this is perhaps the most common application), but to service processes as well.

flowchart Visual representation of the sequence of steps needed to complete a process.

Flowchart. A **flowchart** is a visual representation of the sequence of steps needed to complete a process. Its purpose is to help individuals understand the *process* they are attempting to control. Flowcharts are frequently used by problem-solving teams to address quality issues involving processes with a number of sequential steps to complete (see Exhibit 14-10). Often such processes cut across departmental lines. The visual representation of the process enables team members to examine the relevant steps and note where improvements can be made, as reflected in the following example:

> **Boise Cascade's Timber and Wood Products Division formed a team of 11 people from diverse backgrounds in administration, marketing, and operations to improve customer claims processing. The group first created a flowchart of the process and discovered over 70 steps needed to process each claim within each division; combined division steps for the same customer claim often took as many as hundreds of steps, taking months to resolve the claim. By studying systematically the steps involved in processing claims and addressing the concerns within each division, the team eliminated 70 percent of the steps in most claims.[7]**

histogram Graphical representation of the variation found in a set of data.

Histogram. A **histogram** is a graphical representation of the variation found in a set of performance data. It can provide clues about the population's characteristics. The visual presentation reflects how the process's output varies and what proportion of output falls

EXHIBIT 14-10

Flowchart of a Fast-Food
Drive-Through Process

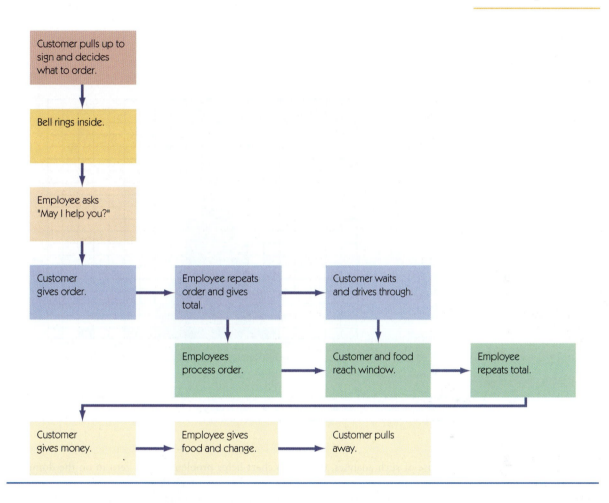

outside of the performance targets. The histogram in Exhibit 14-11 represents data on the length of time that it took a bank to process loan requests. Note how easy it is to see how the output of the process varies and what proportion falls outside of any specification limits.

Run Chart. A process sometimes performs differently over a period of time. A **run chart** is a data presentation that shows the results of a process plotted over a period of time. It might be used to show the number of hotel checkouts per hour, the number of employee absentees per day, or the percentage of customers waiting in excess of 1 minute to be seated. Note in Exhibit 14-12 how the run chart points out specific patterns of behavior in the process. The percentage of patrons who have to wait falls into a definite pattern. A much larger percentage waits early in the week, with the percentage decreasing throughout the week.

Pareto Chart. **Pareto charts** are problem-analysis charts that use a histogram to graphically illustrate the sources of problems. They typically list problem causes from left to right in descending order of seriousness. Named after Vilfredo Pareto, the economist who originated

run chart Data presentation showing results of a process plotted over time.

Pareto charts Problem-analysis charts that use a histogram to illustrate sources of problems.

EXHIBIT 14-11

Histogram Showing
Frequency and Length
of Time Taken by Home
Office to Process
Loan Request

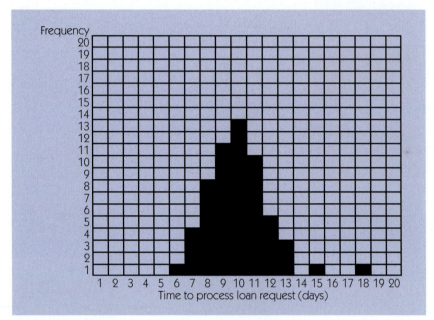

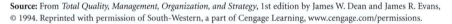

Source: From *Total Quality, Management, Organization, and Strategy*, 1st edition by James W. Dean and James R. Evans, © 1994. Reprinted with permission of South-Western, a part of Cengage Learning, www.cengage.com/permissions.

the use of such analyses, the Pareto chart helps problem solvers zero in on the dominant rather than trivial problem. For example, Exhibit 14-13 shows the results of an extensive survey of customer complaints in a restaurant over an extended period of time. The chart is a consistent reminder to the problem-solving team that its time would be best used by focusing on the complaints of customers waiting for seats and dealing with a poorly organized buffet table.

Cause-and-Effect Diagram. A very useful tool for understanding and identifying the causes of performance problems is the **cause-and-effect diagram.** This is also called a *fishbone* or *Ishikawa* diagram, named for the Japanese quality expert who popularized it. It represents a graphical display of a chain of causes and effects. The result, shown in Exhibit 14-14, resembles the skeletal system of a fish, with the horizontal line representing the problem being addressed and subsequent lines representing major causes and subcauses.

cause–and–effect diagram
A graphical display of a chain of causes and effects.

Control Chart. The **control chart** is the "backbone" of statistical process control (SPC) and displays the "state of control" of a process. If a process is free from special cause variation, the process is said to be under control. An example of a control chart is shown in Exhibit 14-15. In the exhibit, time is measured in terms of days on the horizontal axis; the value of a variable is on the vertical axis. The central horizontal line corresponds to the average value of the characteristic measured. In this case, as long as the values fall between

control chart Displays the "state of control" of a process.

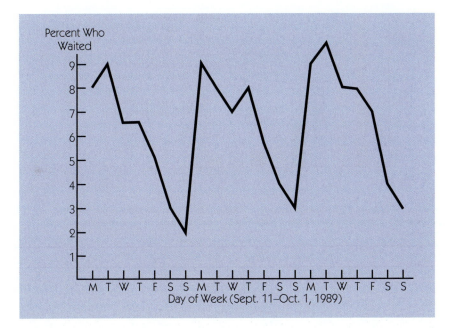

Source: From *Foundations of Total Quality Management: A Readings Book,* 1/e by Van Matre, p. 146. -0030078660. Copyright © 1995. Reprinted with permission of South-Western, a part of Cengage Learning, www.cengage.com/ permissions.

97 percent and 89 percent and no unusual pattern exists (such as a succession of decreasing values), it is likely that no special cause variation is present and that the process is "under control."

The Supervisor's Role in Achieving Quality

As you have noted throughout this chapter, upper management lays the foundation for achieving high quality by committing the organization's resources, communicating its values and norms, and creating rules and procedures. On a daily basis, though, lower-level managers and first-line supervisors have the critical role, as it is operating-level personnel who directly perform the activities of producing the goods or services that address customers' needs. One recent study confirmed the crucial role played by first-line supervisors. Written surveys of 3,500 employees in a food service company found that the quality of service that they felt they delivered was strongly impacted by the extent to which their first-line supervisor (1) emphasized the importance of high quality, (2) provided information and support to help employees achieve it, and (3) provided meaningful feedback.[8]

Motivating workers to perform high-quality work consistently is one of the most challenging jobs a supervisor faces. Two ways to do this are to (1) let employees know you expect quality performance and (2) involve workers in achieving quality.

EXHIBIT 14-13

Pareto Chart of
Customers' Complaints
about Restaurants

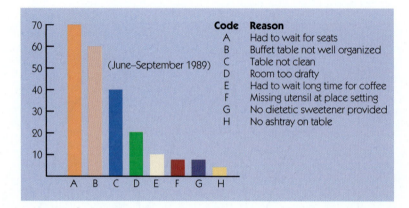

Code	Reason
A	Had to wait for seats
B	Buffet table not well organized
C	Table not clean
D	Room too drafty
E	Had to wait long time for coffee
F	Missing utensil at place setting
G	No dietetic sweetener provided
H	No ashtray on table

(June–September 1989)

Source: From *Foundations of Total Quality Management: A Readings Book*, 1/e by Van Matre, p. 146. -0030078660. Copyright © 1995. Reprinted with permission of South-Western, a part of Cengage Learning, www.cengage.com/permissions.

EXHIBIT 14-14

Cause-and-Effect Diagram
for "Why Tables Are Not
Cleared Quickly"

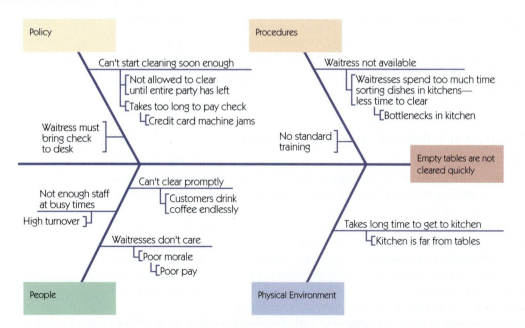

Source: From *Foundations of Total Quality Management: A Readings Book*, 1/e by Van Matre, p. 146. -0030078660. Copyright © 1995. Reprinted with permission of South-Western, a part of Cengage Learning, www.cengage.com/permissions.

EXHIBIT **14-15**

Example of a Control Chart

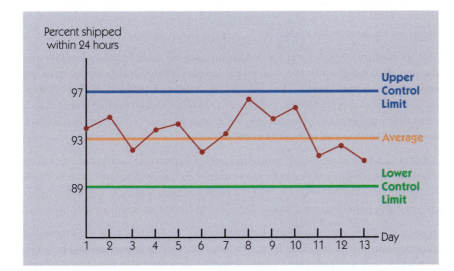

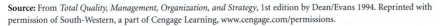

Source: From *Total Quality, Management, Organization, and Strategy*, 1st edition by Dean/Evans 1994. Reprinted with permission of South-Western, a part of Cengage Learning, www.cengage.com/permissions.

Let Employees Know You Expect Quality Performance. Many firms could be said to try to *inspect* quality into their product or service rather than *make it right* the first time. Fortunately, some companies and supervisors emphasize the right way from the start. They do this by stating their quality expectations for a job and including these expectations in their training of new personnel.

> **A large bank trains its new tellers not only in the technical aspects of the job, but also in how to interact with customers. In a number of trial runs, a "customer" walks up to the teller to complete a hypothetical transaction. The teller's actions are observed by a number of trainees and the trainer, and a critique is given of the way the customer was handled. Frequently, an experienced teller will demonstrate how the situation should have been handled. Included are such actions as smiling, looking directly at the customer, calling the customer by name, and efficiently handling the transaction. As a result, the bank's quality expectations are instilled in new tellers.**

The best place to make an impact regarding your quality expectations is with the new employee. Yet many current employees may have spotty quality records. What can you do about this? We can tell you one thing not to do! Ignoring poor-quality performance results in the following:

1. The employee concerned gets the message that you do not expect any better or that mediocre quality is acceptable to you.

2. Other employees will also assume that mediocre performance is acceptable.

Assuming that workers know the quality standards, you must exercise supervisory control over quality. Sometimes a quality control specialist will help a line supervisor determine the quality of workers' performance by presenting run charts, histograms, or other statistical units. In many departments, however, the supervisor must play the only role.

http://www.toyota
georgetown.com/
qualdex.asp

Involve Workers in Achieving and Controlling Quality. You noted in the chapter preview that operative-level associates at Park Place Lexus played a key role in helping the company continuously improve its quality. As Peter Coors, chief executive officer (CEO) of Coors Brewing, puts it, "We're moving from an environment where the supervisor says, 'This is the way it is going to be done,' to an environment where the supervisor can grow with the changes, get his [or her] group together and say 'Look, you guys are operating the equipment. What do you think we ought to do?'"[9]

> SSM Health Care (SSMHC), a St. Louis, Missouri, not-for-profit health system that won the first Baldrige given in the health care category (2002), makes extensive use of employee involvement teams. The company addresses such issues as developing standardized ways to care for SSMHC patients at its 24 hospitals and nursing homes in four states to improving outcomes of patients with congestive heart failure. In 2002, SSMHC employed 85 such teams, up from 14 in 1999.[10]

Quality teams are an important part of the quality scene. These may include special cross-functional teams, self-directed teams, or teams from within individual work groups. Problems (and opportunities) can be brought up by team members, team leaders, or higher management. Many companies allow these teams to call in staff experts for information or expertise as needed.

> At Pella Windows, a standard team *kaizen* session—the Japanese term for continuous improvement—meets anywhere from 1 to 5 days to address important quality issues. Over a thousand such yearly sessions have been the norm for Pella's kaizen teams. A typical 5-day schedule works like this: Get everyone thinking about the problem and how to attack it on Monday, come up with tentative solutions on Tuesday, and, if it's a production problem, move the machinery that night. Start working the new arrangement on Wednesday, tweaking as necessary. On Thursday, prove that it works, and on Friday show it off to everyone.[11]

Exhibit 14-16 presents the overall characteristics of effective employee involvement teams. The kinds of teams we have been discussing are implemented formally and require top management's approval and commitment. *Individual supervisors may, however, capture the spirit of employee involvement on their own.* The following comments, from the manager of a hotel convention center, show what can be achieved by encouraging employees to become involved:

EXHIBIT 14-16

Characteristics of
Effective Employee
Involvement Teams

- Managers at all levels, especially at the top, should be committed to the concept and give it their unqualified support.
- Projects undertaken should relate directly—or at least indirectly—to participants' work.
- Projects should be team efforts, not individual activities.
- Participants should be trained in quality-control, decision making, and problem-solving techniques.
- Team leaders also should be trained in group dynamics and leadership of a group.
- Teams should be given feedback—in the form of results—regarding their recommendations and solutions.

The best quality ideas come from the people who are directly involved in the work. Frequently, poor quality is not caused by something they directly control. We noted that many clients would show up for a meeting and say the room arrangement was not what they had requested. This often required hurriedly rearranging a stage, tables, and chairs for as many as 700 people. The clients would get flustered, as did our people.

The problem was that our meeting coordinator would talk with the client, usually by phone, and take instructions as to how the meeting room needed to be set up. There was much room for interpretation as to just what the client wanted and last-minute changes would drive everyone nuts.

We presented this problem to a team of four of our workers who met, studied the process used by our meeting coordinator, and learned that she usually took instructions by phone. This left much room for interpreting what the client wanted. They also learned that often the person who called in to make the booking wasn't the one who had responsibility for the event, but was perhaps a secretary or an assistant. This person's choice of room arrangement would then get overridden when the group arrived. Our team developed a form that graphically illustrates alternatives for arranging our rooms and audiovisual equipment we can provide. The client now selects the desired alternative, signs the form, and returns it to our coordinator. We now have something specific to go by, and our client is more committed to it. We'll still meet their last-minute needs or make adjustments if needed. But we've only had two such major cases all year.

The lesson here is to seek out workers' advice on how to improve the quality of their work. Since they are so directly involved in the work, they frequently have excellent suggestions.

Promoting Employee Safety

The final aspect of supervisory control that we will discuss in this chapter is employee safety. This subject has been in the business limelight since 1970, primarily as a result of the government's passage of the Occupational Safety and Health Act. But management has had an interest in employee safety for over a century because safety, efficiency, and productivity are closely related.

The results of poor safety are documented by the Bureau of Labor Statistics and the National Safety Council. In 2004, over 4.3 million reportable cases occurred, with over 5,700 fatalities (see Exhibit 14-17).[12] Even though safety performance in the United States has improved in recent years, the costs of poor safety have gone in the opposite direction. According to the most recent cost data released, organizations made an estimated $50 billion in wage and medical payments to U.S. workers injured on the job in 2003, an increase of $10 billion in 4 years (see Exhibit 14-18).

Assume that a company has a 10 percent profit margin. An accident costing $5,000 in direct and indirect costs would translate into a need to generate $50,000 in sales just to cover costs of the accident.[13]

✔ STOP AND THINK

Do such organizations as banks, supermarkets, and department stores really need to be concerned about occupational safety and health?

EXHIBIT 14-17

Top 15 Most
Dangerous Jobs

In recent years about four of every 100,000 workers suffered work-related fatalities. Which jobs are the deadliest? Below is a list of jobs that result in the most fatalities and their relative risk rates, according to the Bureau of Labor Statistics. (Relative risk rate is the fatality rate for a given group divided by the fatality rate for all workers. A rate of 2.0 means the worker is twice as likely as the average worker to die on the job.)

Occupation	Relative Risk	Leading Fatal Event
Fishers	21.3	Drowning
Timber cutters	20.6	Struck by Object
Airplane pilots	19.9	Airplane Crashes
Structural metal workers	13.1	Falls
Taxicab drivers	9.5	Homicide
Construction workers	8.1	Vehicular, Falls
Roofers	5.9	Falls
Electric power installers/ repairers	5.7	Electrocution
Truck drivers	5.3	Highway Crashes
Farm occupations	5.1	Vehicular
Police, detectives, supervisors	3.4	Homicide, Highway Crashes
Nonconstruction laborers	3.2	Vehicular
Electricians	3.2	Electrocution
Welders and cutters	2.4	Falls, Fires
Guards	2.3	Homicide

Source: *Careers and Colleges* 21(3), January–February 2002, p. 6(1).

What OSHA Does

7 Explain what the Occupational Safety and Health Administration (OSHA) does.

The **Occupational Safety and Health Administration (OSHA)** is a federal agency that was created by the Occupational Safety and Health Act in 1970 and went into operation in April 1971. Previously, different states had different emphases on occupational health and safety. So the federal government stepped into the picture to ensure uniformity and enforcement. Basically, OSHA ensures that state governments, labor, and management provide consistently safer and healthier working conditions for employees.

OSHA requires organizations to keep safety logs and records of illnesses and injuries incurred on the job (see Exhibit 14-19). OSHA also has the right to develop standards, to conduct inspections to see that standards are met, and to enforce compliance by issuing citations and penalties against organizations that fail to comply. In addition, OSHA provides help by performing pre-investigations upon invitation from the organization.

OSHA Created by the Occupational Safety and Health Act in 1970 to ensure safe working conditions for employees.

 http://www.osha.gov

Factors Influencing Safety

Several factors affect job safety. Among these are (1) the size of the organization, (2) the type of industry, and (3) the people.

EXHIBIT 14-18

Workplace Injuries
Cost Billions

Liberty Mutual released its annual Workplace Safety Index, revealing the ten leading causes of disabling workplace injuries that account for 80 percent of the estimated $51 billion in wage and medical payments made to U.S. workers injured on the job in 2003 (the most recent year for which data are available).

Rank	Injury Cause	Percentage of Total Direct Costs	Estimated Direct Cost Nationwide
1.	Overexertion	26.4	$13.4 billion
2.	Fall on same level	13.7	7.0 billion
3.	Bodily reaction	10.2	5.2 billion
4.	Fall to lower level	9.0	4.6 billion
5.	Struck by object	8.5	4.1 billion
6.	Repetitive motion	5.9	2.6 billion
7.	Highway accident	5.8	2.9 billion
8.	Struck by object	4.4	2.3 billion
9.	Caught in or compressed by equipment	3.9	2.0 billion
10.	Assaults & violent acts	0.8	4.1 billion
	Top 10 total	88.6	48.2 billion
	Total for all injuries	100	50.8 billion

Source: Liberty Mutual, Liberty Mutual Research Institute for Safety, 2005 annual report, p. 10.

Size of Organization. The safest places to work are the smallest and largest organizations. Companies with under 20 employees or over 1,000 employees have had better safety statistics than medium-sized organizations.

✔ STOP AND THINK

What do you think accounts for the fact that large companies of, say, 10,000 employees have better safety performance than those with 100 employees?

· ·

In a small firm, the owner or manager is more personally involved with employees and tends to take on the role of safety officer. Very large firms have more resources available, such as safety departments, whose sole mission is to improve employee safety. Medium-sized firms have neither the direct personal involvement of the top manager nor the resources to create full-fledged safety departments. Often, the person assigned to oversee the safety function has additional job responsibilities. The safety focus may therefore be diluted by other important assignments.

Type of Industry. Some types of industry are safer than others. Exhibit 14-20 shows rates of occupational injury and illness for various industries. Note that the rates are highest for iron foundries, mobile home manufacturers, ship builders/repairers, and automobile body manufacturers. But note also that safety issues affect a wide spectrum of service industries, such as hospitals, hotels, book stores, and even banks.

EXHIBIT 14-19

Record Keeping Required
by OSHA

U.S. Department of Labor
Occupational Safety and Health Administration

Form approved OMB no. 1218-0176

OSHA's Form 301
Injury and Illness Incident Report

This *Injury and Illness Incident Report* is one of the first forms you must fill out when a recordable work-related injury or illness has occurred. Together with the *Log of Work-Related Injuries and Illnesses* and the accompanying *Summary*, these forms help the employer and OSHA develop a picture of the extent and severity of work-related incidents.

Within 7 calendar days after you receive information that a recordable work-related injury or illness has occurred, you must fill out this form or an equivalent. Some state workers' compensation, insurance, or other reports may be acceptable substitutes. To be considered an equivalent form, any substitute must contain all the information asked for on this form.

According to Public Law 91-596 and 29 CFR 1904, OSHA's recordkeeping rule, you must keep this form on file for 5 years following the year to which it pertains.

If you need additional copies of this form, you may photocopy and use as many as you need.

Attention: This form contains information relating to employee health and must be used in a manner that protects the confidentiality of employees to the extent possible while the information is being used for occupational safety and health purposes.

Information about the employee

1) Full name *Robert L. Wikhelm*

2) Street *707 Eighth ST.*
   City *Sherman*   State *TX* ZIP *75059*

3) Date of birth *12 / 01 / 68*

4) Date hired *3 / 14 / 99*

5) ☑ Male
   ☐ Female

Information about the physician or other health care professional

6) Name of physician or other health care professional *Rita Sorenson, RN*

7) If treatment was given away from the worksite, where was it given?
   Facility *N/A*
   Street
   City   State   ZIP

8) Was employee treated in an emergency room?
   ☐ Yes
   ☐ No

9) Was employee hospitalized overnight as an in-patient?
   ☐ Yes
   ☑ No

Information about the case

10) Case number from the Log *31* *(Transfer the case number from the Log after you record the case.)*

11) Date of injury or illness *6 / 21 / 05*

12) Time employee began work *7:30* AM ☑ PM

13) Time of event *2:09* AM ☑ PM ☐ Check if time cannot be determined

14) **What was the employee doing just before the incident occurred?** Describe the activity, as well as the tools, equipment, or material the employee was using. Be specific. *Examples:* "climbing a ladder while carrying roofing material"; "spraying chlorine from hand sprayer"; "daily computer key-entry."
    CLEANING PIPES IN PREPERATION FOR PAINTING. WAS
    standing on stepladder.

15) **What happened?** Tell us how the injury occurred. *Examples:* "When ladder slipped on wet floor, worker fell 20 feet"; "Worker was sprayed with chlorine when gasket broke during replacement"; "Worker developed soreness in wrist over time."
    As he put stepladder down, sodium hypochlorite
    dripped inside face shield and entered right eye.

16) **What was the injury or illness?** Tell us the part of the body that was affected and how it was affected; be more specific than "hurt," "pain," or "sore." *Examples:* "strained back"; "chemical burn, hand"; "carpal tunnel syndrome."
    Chemical Burn in Right Eye

17) **What object or substance directly harmed the employee?** *Examples:* "concrete floor"; "chlorine"; "radial arm saw." *If this question does not apply to the incident, leave it blank.*
    Sodium hypochlorate

18) **If the employee died, when did death occur?** Date of death *N/A / /*

Completed by *Joseph Dixon*

Title *Supervisor*

Phone *903* *465* *1996*   Date *6 / 23/2005*

Public reporting burden for this collection of information is estimated to average 22 minutes per response, including time for reviewing instructions, searching existing data sources, gathering and maintaining the data needed, and completing and reviewing the collection of information. Persons are not required to respond to the collection of information unless it displays a current valid OMB control number. If you have any comments about this estimate or any other aspects of this data collection, including suggestions for reducing this burden, contact: US Department of Labor, OSHA Office of Statistical Analysis, Room N-3644, 200 Constitution Avenue, NW, Washington, DC 20210. Do not send the completed forms to this office.

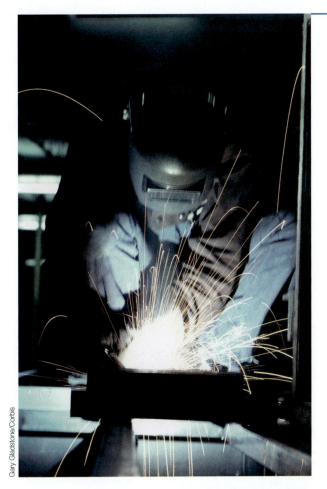

Gary Gladstone/Corbis

Despite increased safety emphasis, the fabricated metal products industry suffers from a high incidence of employee lost workdays due to job related injuries/illnesses.

Also important is the seriousness of cases of the industries listed. Air transportation and shipbuilding will have more serious accidents, resulting in a greater number of lost work days per incident.

People. The attitudes of managers and supervisors strongly influence the safety of work performance. Moreover, employees' attitudinal, emotional, and physical factors definitely impact their safety performance.

Causes of Accidents

What causes on-the-job accidents? Basically, job-related accidents are caused by three types of factors: human, technical, and environmental. *Human factors* include carelessness, horseplay, fighting, use of drugs, poor understanding of equipment or processes, the thrill of taking risks, poor attitudes, and fatigue. Human factors account for most work-related injuries. *Technical factors* include unsafe mechanical, chemical, and physical conditions, such as those caused by defective tools and equipment, poor mechanical construction or design, or improper personal protective equipment (safety shoes, glasses, or mechanical guards or shields). *Environmental factors* are factors that surround the job, such as poor housekeeping, inadequate lighting and ventilation, or management pressure to increase output.

EXHIBIT 14-20

Industry	Incidence Rate per 100 employees
Iron Foundries	15.3
Mobile Home Mfg.	15.0
Ship Building/Repair	12.3
Motor Vehicle Body Mfg.	11.3
Dairies	10.3
Soft Drink Producers	10.2
Airlines	10.0
Hospitals	7.6
Taxi Service	6.7
Grocery Stores	6.3
Hotels	5.7
Auto Dealerships	4.9
Full Service Restaurants	4.0
Book Stores	3.3
Real Estate Firms	3.2
Colleges and Universities	2.7
Women's Clothing Stores	2.4
Radio and TV Broadcasting	1.5
Banks	1.5
CPA Firms	0.3

Average incidence rate for all industries: 4.8

Source: U.S. Bureau of Labor Statistics.

The Supervisor's Role in Promoting Safety

8 Describe the supervisor's role in promoting safety.

Good safety practices among employees help the supervisor in many ways. For one thing, on-the-job injuries can take up much of a supervisor's time as he or she may have to fill out accident reports, attend meetings to investigate the injury, and make recommendations (see Exhibit 14-21). Furthermore, safety is linked to productivity. The work group's productivity suffers when an injured employee is being treated or is recovering from an accident. Temporary or full-time replacements must be recruited, selected, and trained, and an inexperienced worker is unlikely to be as productive as the more experienced employee being replaced.

Because human factors are the major cause of work-related injuries, the supervisor, as top management's link with operating employees, plays a crucial role in employee safety. He or she is accountable for safety, just as for output or quality. Good safety control by the supervisor begins with a positive attitude.

"Safety is very important at the company and especially in my work unit," said Vera Edwards, a machine tender for Supreme Manufacturing. "When you drive into the parking lot, a large sign shows our company's safety record for the week and the year.

EXHIBIT 14-21

Personal Injury
Investigation

Injured:	Fred Hanna
Position:	Lab Assistant
Presiding:	L. C. Smithson, Technical Supt.
Date of meeting:	4/15/2003
Time of meeting:	2:34 p.m.
Place of meeting:	Plant Conference Room
Present:	L. C. Smithson (Technical Supt.), Fred Hanna (injured), Jim Berry (Housekeeping), Tom Ahens (Safety Director), Kim Jernigan (Supervisor)
Nature of injury:	Fractured distal end of radius, right arm
Lost time:	42 days (estimated)
Accident time and date:	4/13/2003 at 7:15 a.m.
Cause of injury:	Floor was wet—appeared to be water. Investigation revealed that bags of Seperan (a synthetic polymer) had been rearranged during the 11 p.m.–7 a.m. shift. One bag was torn, and its contents had trickled onto the floor, causing it to be exceptionally slippery when washed at the end of the shift. Janitor noticed but did not flag it or attempt to remove hazard, as he noted at the end of his shift.

Corrective steps/recommendations:

1. Apply grit to slippery areas; mark with appropriate warning signs.
2. Remind incoming shift personnel of hazardous conditions.
3. Communicate to incoming shift personnel any job priorities.
4. Store Seperan in a more remote area of the plant.

Our supervisor is always talking safety, we have safety meetings monthly, and there are posters and signs throughout the work area. Our supervisor also makes us toe the line in following safety rules. He can really be tough on you when he catches you bending a rule such as not using your goggles or failing to put on your machine guard."

Exhibit 14-22 shows a number of steps that supervisors can take to improve safety performance in their departments. Even though supervisors play a critical role in controlling safety, they cannot do it alone. Top management must be committed to such factors as proper plant layout and design, safe machinery and equipment, and good physical working conditions. Note how recognition by management plays a major role in reinforcing safety for UPS, which has over 2,400 nonmanagement employee Comprehensive Health and Safety Committees at its locations throughout the United States.

At UPS, drivers travel a million miles yearly with less than one avoidable accident! This performance is no coincidence; UPS strongly emphasizes driver safety. At 5-year intervals, drivers with no avoidable accidents are feted with ceremonies at the local level. Drivers with a 25-year unblemished record are inducted into the company's Circle of Honor at a national celebration dinner where they receive a camel hair blazer and special plaque. Each year UPS publishes the names of its 2,700-plus Circle of Honor members in *The Wall Street Journal* and in *USA Today*.[14]

EXHIBIT **14-22**

What Supervisors Can Do
to Improve Safety

- Push for upgraded safety equipment and safer work methods.
- Establish and communicate safety goals for the department.
- Clearly communicate safety requirements to all employees.
- Listen to employee job complaints about safety-related matters, including noise, fatigue, and working conditions.
- Make sure new employees thoroughly understand equipment and safety rules.
- Prohibit use of unsafe or damaged equipment.
- Encourage safety suggestions from your workers.
- Post safety bulletins, slogans, and posters to reinforce the need for safety.
- Refuse to let rush jobs cause relaxed safety standards.
- Set a proper example. Don't bend safety rules yourself.
- Conduct periodic safety meetings, with demonstrations by employee safety specialists or insurance representatives.
- Refuse to tolerate horseplay.
- Compete with other departments in safety contests.
- Report to employees any accidents that occur elsewhere in the company.
- Review past accident records for trends and insights.
- Encourage reporting of unsafe conditions.
- Make regular safety inspections of all major equipment.
- Enforce the rules when they are broken—take appropriate disciplinary action to demonstrate your safety commitment.
- Look for signs of fatigue in employees, such as massaging shoulders, rubbing eyes, and stretching or shifting position to relieve pain or fatigue. In such a case, relief for the employee may be warranted.
- Thoroughly investigate all accidents and attempt to remedy the causes.
- Develop a system for rewarding or acknowledging excellent safety conduct.

CHAPTER REVIEW

1 **Explain the concept of productivity.**

This chapter examined three aspects of control that are important to supervisors. These are productivity, quality, and safety. Productivity is a measure of outputs compared to inputs. Company-wide, it refers to the total value of the units or services a company produced as compared to the total cost of producing them. Productivity can be increased by increasing output with the same input, decreasing input and maintaining the same output, or increasing output while decreasing input.

2 **Identify and explain the ways in which management, government, unions, and employees affect productivity.**

Four groups influence the productivity of U.S. firms. Management is considered by most experts to be the most influential group, since it controls spending for new or upgraded facilities and technology. Government also plays a role through its policies that require financial outlays by companies to meet federal laws for air and water pollution, energy, safety, and other regulatory requirements. Unions play a role in that, while management's job is to increase efficiency through new labor-saving technology and work methods, the role of unions is to protect the jobs of their members. Finally, employees play a role through their skill levels, motivation, and job commitment.

3 Describe some steps supervisors can take to increase productivity.

Actions that supervisors can take to increase productivity include upgrading workers' skills through training, improving worker motivation, using machinery and equipment better, improving quality, and preventing accidents.

Cost control is an important measure of a supervisor's productivity. One helpful device is a budget, which shows expected outcome for a given period expressed in numbers. Robotics, just-in-time (JIT) inventory systems, and computer-assisted manufacturing (CAM) are three recent productivity enhancement measures.

4 Differentiate between total quality and quality control.

A second major area discussed in this chapter was quality. Total quality is the entire system of policies, procedures, and guidelines an organization institutes to attain and maintain quality. Quality control, on the other hand, consists of after-the-fact measurements to see if quality standards are actually being met.

Quality control consists of actions taken during or after the fact to measure, analyze, and, if necessary, correct quality problems. It is a much narrower concept than total quality, which is an organization-wide commitment to quality and includes such factors as top management commitment, employee training, relationships with customers and suppliers, continuous quality improvement, and employee involvement in the quality process.

5 Describe the role of variance in controlling quality.

An understanding of variance is important in controlling quality. Common cause variance is built into organizational processes and is considered normal. Common causes can normally only be corrected through management action to improve a process through such things as upgrading raw materials, using more sophisticated equipment, or additional training. On the other hand, special cause variance is nonroutine and entails identifying the problem, isolating it, examining the cause, and remedying it. It might involve an erratic piece of equipment, damaged raw materials, or an employee who is not performing properly.

6 Identify some important tools for controlling quality.

A number of tools are available to help in controlling quality. Often these tools are used by individuals who are part of special problem-solving or quality-improvement teams. These include such tools as flowcharts, histograms, run charts, Pareto charts, cause-and-effect diagrams, and control charts. These tools are applicable to a broad range of manufacturing and service-related situations.

7 Explain what the Occupational Safety and Health Administration (OSHA) does.

Employee safety has become important to organizations in recent years, especially since the passage of the Occupational Safety and Health Act in 1970. The Occupational Safety and Health Administration, charged with enforcing compliance with the law, sets standards and regulations, requires organizations to maintain safety logs and records, conducts inspections, and has the authority to issue citations and penalties for violations found. Generally, the smallest and the largest organizations are the safest places to work. The nature of some industries makes them much more likely than others to have high injury incidence rates.

IMPORTANT TERMS

cause-and-effect diagram
computer-assisted
    manufacturing (CAM)
control chart
Deming's 85–15 rule
flowchart
histogram
just-in-time (JIT) inventory
Occupational Safety and
    Health Administration
    (OSHA)
Pareto charts
productivity
quality control
robot
run chart
total quality
Toyota Production System

8 **Describe the supervisor's role in promoting safety.**

Supervisors play an important role in promoting safety. Because supervisors are the primary management link with operating employees, supervisory behavior greatly impacts employee safety performance. Supervisors do this in many ways, such as in setting departmental safety goals, ensuring that employees understand safety requirements and procedures, conducting safety meetings, encouraging safety suggestions from employees, thoroughly investigating accidents, and enforcing rules when they are broken.

QUESTIONS FOR REVIEW AND DISCUSSION

1. Explain what happened to productivity of U.S. firms in the 1990s.

2. Do you believe that management and unions must always be on opposite sides of the productivity issue? Why or why not?

3. Identify some of the steps that supervisors can take to improve their department's productivity.

4. How does quality control differ from total quality? Explain.

5. Describe the role of variance in controlling quality.

6. Identify each of the following tools for controlling quality: Pareto chart, run chart, flowchart.

7. What does OSHA do?

8. Describe some ways in which supervisors impact safety performance.

Skill Builder 14-1

Determining Productivity Measurements

In this chapter, you learned that productivity is the ratio of inputs to outputs. Consider each of the following organizations:

a. Blockbuster Video store

b. community college

c. large laundry/dry cleaners

d. hospital

e. law firm

Instructions:

1. For each of the organizations shown, identify some important productivity measures that managers could use to measure the efficiency of their organization. (Hint: Think broadly, including measures that go beyond profitability or cost measures.)

2. Meet with groups of four to six other students and discuss your items.

3. Present your results to the whole class.

Quality Survey

Visit a local fast-food restaurant, such as McDonald's, Burger King, or Wendy's, and order a meal.

Instructions:

1. During your visit, perform a quality analysis of the store, including but not limited to:

   a. external store appearance, including shrubbery, cleanliness, and upkeep of outer building and parking lot

   b. drive-through, including ease, speed, and accuracy

   c. cleanliness of inner store, including tables, floors, and restrooms

   d. employee factors, including appearance, friendliness, and efficiency

   e. service factors, including speed and accuracy

   f. food quality, including taste, freshness, temperature, and portion size.

2. Assume that you are the store manager and want to improve the areas that you found to be weak. Outline the corrective actions that you would take.

3. Meet with other students in groups of five to six to discuss your findings.

Increasing Safety Performance

Assume the role of a newly appointed store manager of a regional food chain superstore. All stores in the chain have been pressured to turn a profit in this highly competitive industry. And, while the former store manager achieved his profit goal, he fell far short in another: the store's safety performance. You are expected to do much better.

Last year the store accident rate was twice that of other stores in the chain: 16 reportable incidents per 100 employees, nine of which involved lost workdays. These involved cuts, burns, slips, and falls. Many cuts occurred in the meat and deli areas; two burns occurred in the bakery area. One bagger sustained a fall in the parking lot while riding his empty grocery cart, a clear violation of policy. But the most serious fall resulted when a janitor left puddles of wax in an aisle and failed to put up warning cones when his work was interrupted to clean up a spill in another area. Another employee slipped on the wax and fell, injuring his left leg and head. This injury resulted in 9 months (and counting) of disability costs, nearly $200,000 of medical costs, and a reserve of about $150,000 for future rehabilitation payments. Analysis of the injury-causing incidents showed that all were caused by human error.

As the new store manager, you are expected to immediately address the safety issue with your employees.

Instructions:

1. Outline a plan for bringing your employees' safety performance next year up to the average of other stores in the chain. You may assume your boss has approved a one-time $1,000 safety budget allocation to spend as needed to help you achieve this goal.

2. Meet with a group of other students to share your ideas. Your instructor may ask you to select a spokesperson to summarize the ideas of your team members.

Using Quality Tools

Welz Business Machines sells and services a variety of copiers, computers, and other office equipment. The company receives many calls daily for service, sales, accounting, and other departments. All calls are handled centrally by customer service representatives and routed to other individuals as appropriate.

A number of customers had complained about long waits when calling for service. A market research study found that customers became irritated if the call was not answered within five rings. Scott Welz, the company president, authorized the customer service department manager, Tim Nagy, to study the problem and find a method to shorten the call-waiting time. Tim met with his service representatives, Robin Coder, Raul Venegas, LaMarr Jones, Mark Staley, and Nancy Shipe, who answered the calls, to attempt to determine the reasons for long waiting times. The following conversation ensued:

Nagy: This is a serious problem. How a customer phone inquiry is answered is the first impression the customer receives from us. As you know, this company was founded on efficient and friendly service to all our customers. It's obvious why customers have to wait: You're on the phone with another customer. Can you think of any reasons that might keep you on the phone for an unnecessarily long time?

Coder: I've noticed quite often that the person to whom I need to route the call is not present. It takes time to transfer the call and to see if it is answered. If the person is not there, I end up apologizing and transferring the call to another extension.

Nagy: You're right, Robin. Sales personnel often are out of the office on sales calls, away on trips to preview new products, or away from their desks for a variety of reasons. What else might cause this problem?

Venegas: I get irritated at customers who spend a great deal of time complaining about a problem that I cannot do anything about except refer to someone else. Of course, I listen and sympathize with them, but this eats up a lot of time.

Jones: Some customers call so often, they think we're long-lost friends and strike up a personal conversation.

Nagy: That's not always a bad thing, you realize.

Jones: Sure, but it delays my answering other calls.

Shipe: It's not always the customer's fault. During lunch, we're not all available to answer the phone.

Venegas: Right after we open at 9 a.m., we get a rush of calls. I think that many of the delays are caused by these peak periods.

Coder: I've noticed the same thing between 4 and 5 p.m.

Nagy: I've had a few comments from department managers who received calls that didn't fall in their areas of responsibility and had to be transferred again.

Staley: But that doesn't cause delays at our end.

Shipe: That's right, Mark, but I just realized that sometimes I simply don't understand what the customer's problem really is. I spend a lot of time trying to get him or her to explain it better. Often, I have to route it to someone because other calls are waiting.

Venegas: Perhaps we need to have more knowledge of our products.

Nagy: Well, I think we've covered most of the major reasons why many customers have to wait. It seems to me that we have four major reasons: the phones are short-staffed, the receiving party is not present, the customer dominates the conversation, and you may not understand the customer's problem. Next, we need to collect some information about these possible causes. Raul, can you and Mark set up a data collection sheet that we can use to track some of these things?

The next day, Venegas and Staley produced a sheet that enabled the staff to record the data. Over the next 2 weeks the staff collected data on the frequency of reasons why some callers had to wait. The results are summarized as follows:

Reason	Total Number
A Operators short-staffed	172
B Receiving party not present	73
C Customer dominates conversation	19
D Lack of operator understanding	61
E Other reasons	10

Instructions: Form groups of three to five students and, based on the conversation between Nagy and his staff,

1. Draw a cause-and-effect diagram.
2. Perform a Pareto analysis of the data collected.
3. Develop some possible actions that the company might take to improve the situation.

Source: Adapted from "The Quest for Higher Quality: The Deming Prize and Quality Control," by RICOH of America, Inc., and presented in James W. Dean and James R. Evans, *Total Quality* (Mason, Ohio: South-Western, 1994), pp. 96–98. Reprinted with permission of South-Western, a part of Cengage Learning, www.cengage.com/permissions.

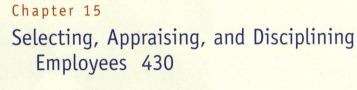

Part **6**

Managing Human Resources and Diversity

AP Photo/Douglas Healy

© VSTOCK/Alamy

15 Selecting, Appraising, and Disciplining Employees

Staffing problems affect all organizations with employees, including colleges and universities.

Here lies a man who knew how to enlist in his service better men than himself.
—ANDREW CARNEGIE'S EPITAPH

No one is free who cannot command himself.
—PYTHAGORAS

Ron Blount: Mentoring To Ensure the Next Generation is Prepared to Lead

Ron Blount, the Project Director of Construction for the Retirement Systems of Alabama for approximately $600 million of development, has worked in the construction business for over 30 years and sees the industry is in a state of "flux." Skilled leaders and laborers are not as plentiful as in years past, and Ron firmly believes effective mentoring can make a difference to ensure that a bright future exists for those who choose careers in this field. It made a difference for him, and it can make a difference for others.

Ron's first mentor, his father, helped him develop an appreciation for work. Ron's father worked two jobs to provide for his family and would typically awaken at 1:30 a.m. to deliver bundles of papers for distribution, getting a few additional hours of sleep prior to going to his regular job with the city of Atlanta, Georgia, where he managed several hundred employees. As a boy, Ron helped his dad with the early morning deliveries, but it wasn't until he was 15 that his dad gave him an opportunity to work for the city picking up leaves and rubbish on the side of the curbs. This was an attractive job for Ron because it paid adult wages. However, Ron's dad did not provide any preferential treatment to his son; rather he made sure that Ron got up and came down each Saturday morning at 5:30 a.m. to stand in line to be chosen for the day's work assignments. His dad believed it was important to instill a sense of responsibility, commitment, and pride in his son at an early age.

After graduating from high school, Ron worked for a development company. Even though he was only employed with the firm for 2 years, his relationship with one of the company's principles, Don Carl, had a tremendous long-term impact. Don encouraged Ron to "think big" and attempt to do great things in his career. Having a vision for one's future is extremely important, but it wasn't until Ron went to work for Jim Curnyn at George Hyman Construction Company that he truly developed the confidence necessary to actually achieve great things.

Jim Curnyn hired Ron as an estimator to work on the Atlanta Airport, a $95-million construction project during the 1970s. Within 2 years, Ron was project manager. His career trajectory was due in no small part to Jim's excellent mentoring. Not only did Jim encourage and support Ron, he actively managed his growth and development. Jim made Ron go beyond problem recognition and continually asked Ron his opinion on issues. He wanted Ron to feel comfortable analyzing situations and making recommendations regardless of the cost associated with the situation.

A turning point in Ron's career came when Jim was a no-show for an important meeting. It is still unclear whether Jim was delayed for the meeting due to other business or whether there was a method to his madness! History shows (e.g., Winston Churchill) that many times an individual's true abilities shine when he or she is thrust into a challenging situation. Ron was prepared for the meeting with the joint venture partner, and over the next several days, he successfully negotiated a multimillion dollar deal on the part of George Hyman Construction. Jim provided the opportunity for Ron to showcase his abilities, and once

Learning Objectives

After reading and studying this chapter, you should be able to:

1 Explain who is responsible for selecting, appraising, and disciplining employees.

2 Describe the steps in the employee selection procedure, including the proper orientation of new employees.

3 Explain what employee performance appraisal is and who performs it.

4 State why performance-appraisal interviews are difficult for both the employee and the supervisor.

5 Define discipline and explain why it is necessary.

6 Describe how discipline is imposed under due process.

7 Explain the supervisor's disciplinary role.

he proved to himself what he could accomplish, Ron began to negotiate $2–3 million contracts with major airlines on a regular basis. Ron states, "Jim was always there with a life preserver if I needed one, but ultimately he had confidence in me. Jim felt that I could handle challenges, solve problems, and basically, get it done."

Ron gained valuable insights from Don and Jim that have assisted in him becoming the great leader that he is today. When Ron was working for Avery Mays Construction in Dallas, Texas as a project manager, he got the opportunity to apply the leadership insights he gained from his mentors. Tim Cary was a Harvard graduate and a school teacher prior to being selected for Avery Mays' executive management program. Soon thereafter, he was paired with Ron to "learn the business." Ron saw some of himself in Tim and tried to provide the type of guidance needed for Tim to thrive in his new career. As Ron states, "The relationship grew, and Tim became part of our family. He would eat at our house and spend time during holidays with us." Tim really blossomed under Ron's tutelage, and the last Ron had heard Tim was executive vice president of a development company in Los Angeles, California.

Ron's second mentoring opportunity may be viewed by many as more challenging. Brent Clemens was the Chief Estimator at Avery Mays Construction. Not everyone got along with Brent, and it was believed he was about to be let go. Ron had always been gender neutral and color blind when it came to relationships. Therefore, he didn't hesitate when given the opportunity to accept the assignment of an African American as his project engineer. As Ron shares, "The job was a step down, but Brent has always approached every job he has had by giving 120 percent." In fact, Ron was so impressed with Brent's abilities and work ethic that when he was later managing a large project in Montgomery, Alabama, he hired Brent as his project manager. In the 92-year history of the Montgomery office of Algernon Blair, Inc., Brent was the first and only African American project manager. Ron showed the commitment and confidence in Brent that his mentors had shown him.

When the Montgomery job was winding down, Ron asked Brent "Have you ever thought about going into business as a major contractor?" Brent admitted that he had not, but with Ron's encouragement, Brent struck out and opened his own company. Fifteen years later, Brent is evidence of what a great mentor can provide to an individual with raw talent, ability, and drive. Brent now owns and operates a very successful Atlanta-based construction company.

Source: Interview with Ron Blount with RSA.

In this chapter, we will look at the processes of staffing, developing, appraising, and disciplining employees. When Art Linkletter, owner of over 75 companies, was asked the secret of his success, his answer was "I bet on people!" As the great industrialist Andrew Carnegie realized, an organization consists not merely of physical and financial resources but, most importantly, of people. Thus the supervisory challenge of the future will lie in properly selecting and developing people. Management must emphasize putting the right employees in the right jobs and then motivating them to perform well.

Candidates for a given job can be obtained from inside or outside the organization, but there must be some method of selection to find capable people. Then, the organization must improve employees' performance through training and developing their abilities adequately and then compensating them. Selecting, appraising, and disciplining employees are covered in this chapter.

We believe that supervisors need to "see the big picture" of the staffing process. Certainly not all supervisors are involved in the activities presented in this chapter, but, if they understand the total process of staffing, they will be in a better position to perform their part of this process.

Responsibility for Selecting, Appraising, and Disciplining Employees

1 Explain who is responsible for selecting, appraising, and disciplining employees.

An organization can be successful only if it has the right number and types of people to do the required work. Therefore, a primary duty of all supervisors is the proper selection, placement, training and development, compensation, and utilization of competent employees. How well—or poorly—supervisors perform these functions is a major factor in their success or failure.

A Shared Responsibility

Like almost all aspects of supervision, selecting, appraising, and disciplining employees are shared tasks, though the primary responsibility should be left to supervisors. In general, the responsibilities are divided as follows:

1. *Top managers* set human resources objectives, establish policies, and do long-range planning and organizing.

2. *Middle managers* control the operating procedures needed to achieve these objectives and carry out personnel policies.

3. *Supervisors* interpret policies for employees and carry out higher management's wishes as to selecting and training employees. Also, they interpret and transmit workers' interests to higher management.

With today's emphasis on *empowerment,* teams are often used at all three of these levels. It is especially important to have potential fellow employees involved in an advisory role, at least.

The Supervisor's Role

Operative employees usually have little contact with high-level managers. Therefore, they tend to think of their supervisor as being "management" or "the organization." Because employees interpret their supervisor's actions, attitudes, and methods as representing those of all managers, supervisors are probably the most important people in achieving an organization's human resources objectives. Supervisors usually have the final word in selecting, appraising and disciplining employees. Then they supervise and control the employees' daily activities.

✔ SELF-CHECK

In the Johnson Company, a large department store, sales positions are filled directly by the personnel office. When a selection decision is made, the sales department supervisor is notified, and the new employee reports to her or him for a job assignment. Typically, the new employee first meets his or her supervisor on the first day of work. What are the pros and cons of this system?

....

2 Describe the steps in the employee selection procedure, including the proper orientation of new employees.

Selecting Employees for Specific Jobs

A suggested procedure for selecting employees is shown in Exhibit 15-1. Individual employers may find it desirable to modify this procedure—or depart from it—under certain conditions. In this section, each of the steps listed in the exhibit is briefly explained.

EXHIBIT 15-1

Flowchart of a Suggested
Selection Procedure

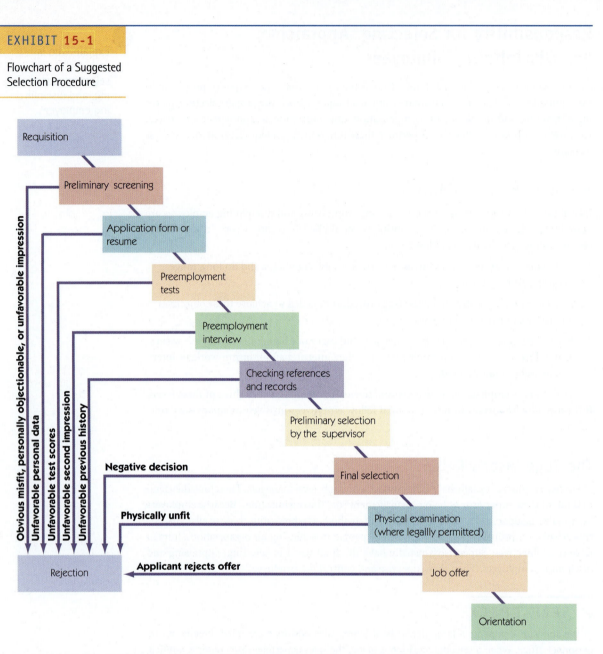

Source: Adapted from Figure 9-4, "Techniques for Gathering Information about Potential Employees," *Small Business Management: An Entrepreneur's Guidebook,* 4th ed., p. 228; Leon C. Megginson, Mary Jane Byrd, and William L. Megginson. Copyright © 2003. Reprinted by permission of The McGraw-Hill Companies.

Requisition

Selection really begins with a requisition from the supervisor to the human resource department. This requisition, which is based on the previously prepared job description and specification, is the authorization the department needs to recruit applicants for the position(s) available. In many small and medium-sized firms, the supervisor makes an informal visit or phone call to the senior officer who is authorized to make the final job offer.

A reminder is needed at this point! If you, as a supervisor, are involved in recruiting and selecting job applicants, all aspects of your procedures must conform to the EEOC's *Uniform*

Stone/Getty Images

Workers' emotional adjustment and attitude will have a strong impact on work performance, especially those requiring interpersonal skills.

Guidelines on Employee Selection Procedures. The guidelines cover *all selection procedures,* not just testing. Your procedures should also comply with your affirmative action program (AAP) for hiring people from various groups. The human resource officer, in particular, should be certain that the selection procedure conforms to national and local laws and customs.

When Bryan Seibt accepted the position of Human Resources Director for the City of Fairhope, Alabama, personal referral was the primary recruiting source used to match individuals with vacant jobs throughout the City's various departments. He has worked for several years with the department heads to proactively broaden the applicant pool. A multisource strategy using the City's web site, local and regional newspapers, the state's league of municipalities' network, and a variety of association groups have generated more diverse applicants. The result is more diversity within the City's departments.[1]

Preliminary Screening

Whether formal or informal, some form of preliminary screening helps weed out those persons who do not seem to meet the employer's needs—thus saving their time and yours. This step deals with such obvious factors as educational background, training, experience, physical appearance, grooming, and speech—if these are relevant to job performance. Also, the applicant should know something about the organization and the job being sought.

An early study found that 9 percent of college applicants were eliminated at this point for "personal reasons." Some of the reasons cited for not hiring were bad breath, dirty fingernails, and uncombed hair.[2]

> Mike, a bright, young college student, applied at a local hotel for employment while home on summer break. He was rejected at the preliminary interview because his hair was below his collar—even though it was neatly pulled back. He was told that even the groundskeepers and dry cleaning plant workers had to have their hair above their collars. The next year he was rejected by a grocery chain because he had a beard. Finally, he did find a lucrative job waiting tables at an English pub—with great tips and free meals.

Application Form or Résumé

After passing the preliminary screening, the job applicant usually completes an application form. (Some applications are submitted by e-mail, snail mail, or in person before preliminary screening.) The applicant usually lists such information as former employers, titles of jobs held, and length of employment with each one. Background, education, military status, and other useful data are listed. The form should be carefully designed to provide the information needed about the applicant's potential performance; it should not be a hodgepodge of irrelevant data. The completion of the form in longhand will provide you with a simple test of the applicant's neatness, thoroughness, ability to answer questions—and literacy, as the following example illustrates:

> **The manager of a tire store once told one of the authors that he requires all applicants to fill out an application in person on the premises. "When they ask to take it home," he said, "I can be almost sure they're illiterate and need help in reading it and filling it out."**

The EEOC and many states have restrictions concerning the kinds of questions that may be included on an application form. Therefore, you should check any laws that your state may have on such practices. See Exhibit 15-2 for a list of topics to avoid on application forms and during interviews.

Many recruiters are now tending to react negatively to what showed signs of becoming a popular method of submitting résumés to potential employees—via e-mail. The very success of the method led to its troubles. Some companies are getting thousands of résumés dumped into e-mail boxes each day. Not only is the volume overwhelming employers, but many of the résumés contain attachments that are difficult to open or decipher.[3]

EXHIBIT 15-2

Topics to Avoid When Interviewing Applicants

Here is a summary of ten of the most dangerous questions or topics you might raise during an interview.

1. *Children.* Do not ask applicants whether they have children, or plan to have children, or have child care.
2. *Age.* Do not ask an applicant's age.
3. *Disabilities.* Do not ask whether the candidate has a physical or mental disability that would interfere with doing the job.
4. *Physical Characteristics.* Do not ask for such identifying characteristics as height or weight on an application.
5. *Name.* Do not ask a female candidate for her maiden name.
6. *Citizenship.* Do not ask applicants about their citizenship. However, the Immigration Reform and Control Act does require business operators to determine that their employees have a legal right to work in the United States.
7. *Lawsuits.* Do not ask a job candidate whether he or she has ever filed a suit or a claim against a former employer.
8. *Arrest Records.* Do not ask applicants about their arrest records.
9. *Smoking.* Do not ask whether a candidate smokes. While smokers are not protected under the Americans with Disabilities Act (ADA), asking applicants whether they smoke might lead to legal difficulties if an applicant is turned down because of fear that smoking would drive up the employer's health care costs.
10. *AIDS and HIV.* Never ask job candidates whether they have AIDS or are HIV-positive, because these questions violate the ADA and could violate state and federal civil rights laws.

Source: Nation's Business, July 1992. Reprinted by permission, USChamber.com, 1992, Copyright © 1992, U.S. Chamber of Commerce.

Preemployment Testing

Various tests can be used to assess an applicant's intelligence quotient (IQ), skills, aptitudes, vocational interests, personality, and performance. Preemployment testing, especially "personality" or psychological testing, is growing in use by industry. These test(s) can minimize turnover, because companies are now trying to hire for "fit" between the workers and employees, and testing can help them ensure that "fit." However, the tests must be EEOC approved and be valid and reliable. Only the most popular are discussed here.

Types of Tests. **IQ tests** are designed to measure the applicant's capacity to learn, to solve problems, and to understand relationships. They are particularly useful in selecting employees for supervisory and managerial positions. **Aptitude tests** are used to predict how a person might perform on a given job and are most applicable to operative jobs. **Vocational interest tests** are designed to determine the applicant's areas of major work interest. While interest does not guarantee competence, it can result in the employee's working and trying harder. **Personality tests** are supposed to measure the applicant's emotional adjustment and attitude. These tests are often used to evaluate interpersonal relationships and to see how the person might fit into an organization.

Probably the most effective tests the supervisor can use in selecting operative employees are **achievement, proficiency,** or **skill tests.** These tests measure fairly accurately the applicant's knowledge of and ability to do a given job. They can also spot *trade bluffers*—people who claim job knowledge, skills, and experience that they don't really have. One type of proficiency test is a **work sampling** or **work preview,** in which the prospective employee is asked to do a task that is representative of the work usually done on the job. In addition to showing whether the person can actually do the job, the test gives the applicant more realistic expectations about the job.

Finally, some organizations now test for drug use, especially where the use of drugs by employees poses a serious safety risk, as in the case of machine operators or airplane pilots. While such tests are controversial, they are legal in most states.[4]

Validity of Tests. If tests are used in making the selection decision, employers must be prepared to demonstrate their validity. **Validity** is demonstrated by a high positive correlation between the applicant's test scores and some identifiable measure of performance on the job. Furthermore, the tests must be designed, administered, and interpreted by a professional (usually a licensed psychologist); be culturally neutral so that they don't discriminate against any ethnic group; and be in complete conformity with EEOC guidelines.[5] Tests must also have **reliability;** that is, the results will be the same if the test is given to the same person by different testers or by the same tester at different times. Care should be exercised in interpreting test results, as some persons are adept at faking answers. Because of these and other problems, many firms are dropping testing in favor of other selection techniques.

It should be reemphasized at this point that *all selection techniques are subject to scrutiny by the EEOC.* It should also be mentioned that the most frequently used selection criteria are supervisory ratings and job performance.

Preemployment Interviewing

In preparing for the employment interview, which is the only two-way part of the selection procedure, you should use the information on the application form and the test results to learn as much as you can about the applicant. A list of questions prepared before the interview can help you avoid missing information that might be significant in judging the applicant. Compare your list of questions with the job specification to ensure that you are matching the

---

IQ tests Measure the applicant's capacity to learn, solve problems, and understand relationships.

aptitude tests Predict how a person might perform on a given job.

vocational interest tests Determine the applicant's areas of major work interest.

personality tests Measure the applicant's emotional adjustment and attitude.

achievement, proficiency, or skill tests Measure the applicant's knowledge of and ability to do a given job.

work sampling or work preview A test in which the prospective employee must perform a task that is representative of the job.

validity A high positive correlation between the applicant's test scores and some objective measure of job performance.

reliability The probability that test results won't change if the test is given to the same person by different individuals.

---

individual's personal qualifications with the job requirements. Some specific questions you might ask are as follows:

1. What did you do on your last job?

2. How did you do it?

3. Why did you do it?

4. Of the jobs you have had, which did you like best? Which the least?

5. Why did you leave your last job?

6. What do you consider your strong and weak points?

7. Why do you want to work for us?

If you are observant and perceptive during the interview, you can obtain some impressions about the candidate's abilities, personality, appearance, speech, and attitudes toward work. You should also provide the applicant with information about the company and the job. Remember, the applicant needs facts to decide whether to accept or reject the job, just as you need information to decide whether or not to offer it.

The interview may be carried out individually by the supervisor or in cooperation with someone else—the human resource officer or some other senior manager. It may be structured or unstructured. **Structured interviews** are standardized and controlled with regard to questions asked, sequence of questions, interpretation of replies, and weight given to factors considered in making the value judgment as to whether or not to hire the person. In unstructured interviews, the pattern of questions asked, the conditions under which they are asked, and the basis for evaluating results are determined by the interviewer.

structured interviews
Standardized and controlled with regard to questions asked.

Not long ago, a former student started a new division within the family business. As part of the hiring process, she conducted numerous interviews to staff both clerical and production positions. At first, there wasn't a set structure to the interviews. She preferred for the interaction to naturally unfold. However, she quickly realized how difficult it was to make a decision by comparing the knowledge, skills, and abilities across applicants for a particular job using this approach. As a result, she structured her interviews, developing a list of questions to guide her actions. The structured interview setting helped her differentiate among applicants.

Checking References and Records

The importance of carefully checking applicants' references cannot be overemphasized.

Reference checks provide answers to questions concerning a candidate's performance on previous jobs. They are helpful in verifying information on the application form and other records, as well as statements made during the interviews. They are also useful in checking on possible omissions of information and in clarifying specific points. Yet, a Robert Half survey found that 68 percent of employers now find that former employers, fearing lawsuits, tend to say nothing—or only nice things—about past employees.[6] In fact, most former employers will only give dates of employment and position(s) held.

Reference checks made in person or by telephone are greatly preferable to written ones, as past employers are sometimes reluctant to commit to writing any uncomplimentary remarks about a former employee. Be sure to ask specific questions about the candidate's performance. The type of information you are allowed to seek is restricted by laws such as the Fair Credit Reporting Act and the Privacy Act. But you can check on dates and terms of employment, salary, whether termination was voluntary, and whether this employer would rehire the candidate. Many organizations are now using credit checks to obtain information about prospective employees. If this source is used and is the basis for rejecting a candidate, he or she has the right to see the report.

Preliminary Selection by the Supervisor

By this point in the selection process, you—the supervisor—have narrowed the number of candidates to one or a very few. If there is only one, the applicant can be hired on a trial basis. If you have more than one qualified candidate, a review of the information collected should reveal the best choice. Although your preliminary selection may be subject to approval by the human resource department or some higher authority, usually the person will be offered the job.

Final Selection

Human resource officers are usually brought in on the final hiring decision because of their expertise. They ensure that all laws and regulations, as well as company policies, are followed. Also, they have a voice in such questions as salary and employee benefits to be offered to the applicant.

Physical Examination

Formerly, the final step in the selection procedure was a physical examination to see if the applicant could do the job. However, the Americans with Disabilities Act (ADA) has limited this part of the process. *Employers may not now require an exam before a preliminary job offer is made.*[7] *Then, when an exam is allowed, the exam may only determine whether the worker can do the job being sought, and no medical history may be taken.*[8]

Job Offer

Job offers to applicants for nonmanagerial and nonprofessional positions are usually made by the human resource office. They are often in writing and contain the terms and conditions of employment. At this point, the offer is either accepted or rejected. If it is rejected, an offer may be made to the next most qualified applicant. If there are no other qualified candidates, the selection procedure must start all over again.

After a candidate has accepted the job offer, those not hired should still be kept in mind for any possible future openings. It is common courtesy to notify them that someone else has been selected, and a diplomatic rejection will maintain their goodwill.

✔ SELF-CHECK

Have you ever applied for a job and been told, "We'll let you know within a week if we want you"? Even when the week was up, were you still hoping you might get a call, if only to say definitely that you had not been hired? How did this uncertainty make you feel toward the employer?

··

Orientation

The first day on a new job is confusing for anyone. Therefore, a new employee should be given a proper **orientation.** A job description should be given to him or her and explained in detail. Proper instructions, training, and observation will start the employee off on the right foot. A tour of the facilities and a look at the firm's product or service will help the new employee understand where he or she fits into the scheme of things. The new employee

orientation Procedures of familiarizing a new employee with the company surroundings, policies, and job responsibilities.

Properly socializing employees who are new to an organization, through orientation and other means, can have a very positive impact on retaining good employees.

needs to know the firm's objectives, policies, rules, and performance expectations. Frequent discussions should be held with him or her during the orientation program to answer questions and to ensure proper progress.

A formal interview with the new employee may be appropriate at some point during the first week. Other interviews can be held during the probationary period, which is usually from three to six months. The purpose of these interviews should be to correct any mistaken ideas the employee may have about the job and to determine whether he or she feels that you and your people are fulfilling your commitments.

After orientation is completed, a checklist is usually gone over with the new employee. Then, the employee and a representative of the employer sign it, and it is placed in the employee's file as proof of knowledge of rules. If done properly by the supervisor, orientation should accelerate the building of a positive working relationship with the new employee.

A manufacturing company that one of the authors worked with was having employee retention problems. Even though turnover is relatively high in this particular industry, this firm seemed to have a higher-than-average rate of turnover. Examination of the problem identified a lack of proper socialization of new employees as one contributing factor. The company developed and implemented a detailed employee orientation program that includes an initial orientation day in which information about the company—policies, procedures, benefits, etc.—is communicated to all new employees. Each employee is given a "developmental book" during orientation to be used in conjunction with the supervisor to track the development of key task and performance objectives. The supervisor and the newly hired employee meet regularly each week during the first month to evaluate the employee's development and address any concerns. In addition, each person is informally paired with a more tenured employee within the work department who can be relied upon to answer questions and provide guidance. By implementing a multi-faceted socialization process, the manufacturer cut its turnover in half.

The Role of Performance Appraisals in Supervisory Management

3 Explain what employee performance appraisal is and who performs it.

Because performance appraisal is such an important part of the management process, enlightened managers are now trying to upgrade their appraisal programs. Most employers have already developed some kind of formal program for improving employee performance, growth and development.

It should be strongly emphasized that performance appraisals—when properly designed, conducted, and discussed with the person being appraised—are beneficial to the employee as well as the organization. In other words, reviews can be positive and motivational if they are conducted with an attitude designed to improve performance and help each employee move toward maximizing his or her potential. Regardless of the appraisal method used, however, *the appraisal should be constructive* and future oriented.

What Is a Performance Appraisal?

Performance appraisal is the process used to determine to what extent an employee is performing a job in the way it was intended to be done. Some other frequently used terms for this process are **merit rating, efficiency rating, service rating,** and **employee evaluation.** Regardless of the term used, the process always has the purpose of seeing how actual employee performance compares to the ideal or standard.[9]

performance appraisal *or* **merit rating** *or* **efficiency rating** *or* **service rating** *or* **employee evaluation** Determines to what extent an employee is performing a job the way it was intended.

How a Performance Appraisal Operates

If employees' output can be physically measured, then their rewards can be based on their actual output and there would be little need to formally appraise them. However, many jobs today do not lend themselves to physical measurement. Therefore, the supervisor tries to determine what personal characteristics an employee has that lead him or her to have satisfactory performance. As you can see from Exhibit 15-3, the process works as follows: An employee's personal qualities (1) lead to job behaviors (2) that result in work performance (3), which the manager appraises (4) and that appraisal results in some kind of personnel action (5).

EXHIBIT 15-3

How Performance Appraisals Operate

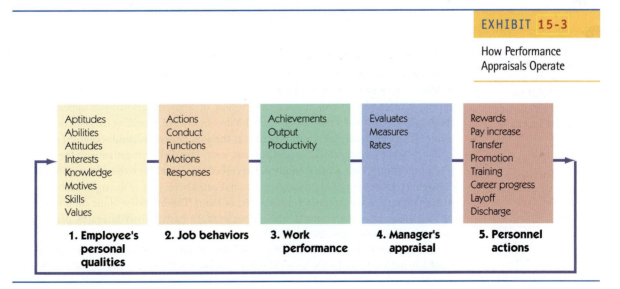

Aptitudes Abilities Attitudes Interests Knowledge Motives Skills Values	Actions Conduct Functions Motions Responses	Achievements Output Productivity	Evaluates Measures Rates	Rewards Pay increase Transfer Promotion Training Career progress Layoff Discharge
1. Employee's personal qualities	**2. Job behaviors**	**3. Work performance**	**4. Manager's appraisal**	**5. Personnel actions**

An *employee's qualities* are abilities, attitudes, interests, skills, knowledge, and values. These qualities lead the employee to take certain actions that result in output or productivity. The manager appraises the employee's performance and then may reward the employee through a pay increase, transfer, promotion, training and development, or career progress.

Most human resource departments now have computerized files on all employees. *These management staffing and development programs* should include appraisal criteria and ratings along with consistent definitions of skills, level of experience, and development activity.[10]

Purposes of the Performance Appraisal

Some specific reasons for appraising employee performance are (1) to recognize "good" performance, (2) to point out areas that need improvement, especially if the employee hopes to progress in the organization, (3) to validate selection techniques in order to meet Equal Employment Opportunity Commission (EEOC)/Affirmative Action Program (AAP) requirements, and (4) to provide a basis for administrative actions such as wage increases, promotions, transfers, layoffs, and/or discharges. Appraisal for these purposes is usually done by comparing the performance of one employee to that of others.

Administrative action sometimes takes the form of dealing with managers who are having problems, as well. A well-developed appraisal system can help detect "problem managers" in time to take appropriate action.[11]

click! http://www.eeoc.gov/

✔ SELF-CHECK

Notice in Case 15-1 how Robert Trent manipulates the appraisal of Jane Smith to get her transferred. Although we do not condone the method he used, the case does show how a performance appraisal can be used as a basis for administrative action.

• •

Performance appraisals can also be used for communications and motivational purposes, such as to provide a basis for giving advice, coaching, or counseling so that employees will have better expectations on the job, or as a basis for career planning and development. When used for these purposes, performance appraisal is usually done by comparing employees' actual performance to some previously determined work standard(s). In such cases, the role of the supervisor is that of a counselor, a mentor, or an instructor, and the appraisal should serve to motivate employees by giving them a better understanding of their job responsibilities, of what is expected of them, and of their training needs.

The Role of the Appraisal Interview

4 State why performance-appraisal interviews are difficult for both the employee and the supervisor.

Most organizations cannot afford poor performance, and workers cannot afford poor reviews. One way to satisfy both these requirements is for the supervisor to conduct an **appraisal interview** to communicate the results of a given performance appraisal to an employee. This method seems compatible with the objective of providing feedback on workers' progress and encouraging improvement on the job. However, conducting the appraisal interview is the job aspect that supervisors like least. This dislike, together with the poor way the appraisal interview is often handled, has caused this interview to be criticized heavily for damaging relationships between supervisors and employees. One of the main problems with such interviews is that too much is expected of them. The interview alone cannot improve performance, uncover training needs, and serve as the basis for pay increases, promotions, and so forth—but it can certainly help!

appraisal interview
Supervisor communicates the results of a performance appraisal to an employee.

The appraisal interview is one of the most difficult duties required of a supervisor. Such an interview used to be along the lines of "Call Joe in and tell him what needs to be straightened out and what's expected of him." Today, however, interviewers are expected to aim at cooperation, constructiveness, and greater understanding.[12] Let us look at what tends to happen during the typical interview, even though it is conducted according to the rules of good performance-appraisal interviewing.

> Once a year Gloria Rogers calls her employees in one at a time for the appraisal interview. Both parties tend to "psych up" for this event. Rogers plans what she's going to say, and the employee tends to be apprehensive about what he or she is going to hear. At the beginning, Rogers tries to put the employee at ease by talking about the weather, the latest major league baseball game, or the employee's family. The employee knows that this is just the prelude to getting down to serious business—and tends to resent the delay.
>
> Then Rogers explains her overall appraisal in broad terms. Initially, she'll mention some good aspects of the employee's performance and give the employee a chance to express his or her views. Next, she enumerates the employee's weaknesses and past failures. She allows the employee to explain these. Then, she explains what steps are needed to improve the employee's performance. At this point, she may ask for the employee's ideas on improvement. One variation of the procedure allows the employee to give his or her own self-evaluation and compare it with Rogers' evaluation after it is given.

The conventional approach to the appraisal interview is emotionally upsetting for both the supervisor and the employee. There is no doubt in the employee's mind that he or she is in the hot seat and that there's little point in disagreeing with the supervisor about her judgments. It's best simply to remain submissive and accept the criticism, even if the employee disagrees with it. Supervisors likewise tend to feel anxiety over performance appraisal, for, as management theorist Douglas McGregor points out,

> Managers are uncomfortable when they are put in the position of "playing God." . . . [We become] distressed when we must take responsibility for judging the personal worth of a fellow man. Yet the conventional approach to performance appraisal forces us not only to make such judgments and to see them acted upon, but also to communicate them to those we have judged. Small wonder we resist.[13]

It is fairly common practice for employers to require managers to discuss their appraisals with employees. The authors of this textbook have talked with numerous supervisors who suffer the double-barreled discomforts of performance appraisal. These supervisors dislike being appraised by their own bosses, and they dislike appraising their employees—or at least telling them the results. All this may lead to appraisal inflation. For example, in one company, when a policy was adopted requiring supervisors to give their appraisals to their employees, their appraisals of their employees suddenly jumped remarkably.[14] Another important aspect of performance appraisals is that they should contain aspects of career planning for the employee. In other words, the appraisal should help the employee plan for the future.

In summary, the appraisal interview presents both an opportunity and a potential danger for the supervisor, as both praise and constructive criticism must be communicated. A major effort should be made to emphasize the positive aspects of the employee's performance while also discussing ways to make needed improvements. One classic study showed that one group of employees, who took some form of constructive action as a result of performance appraisals, did so because of the way their supervisor had conducted the appraisal interview and discussion.[15] Exhibit 15-4 provides some helpful hints for conducting a more effective interview.

Do

- Prepare in advance.
- Focus on performance and development.
- Be specific about reasons for ratings.
- Decide about specific steps to be taken for improvement.
- Consider your role in the employee's performance.
- Reinforce the behavior you want.
- Focus on future performance.

Don't

- Lecture the employee.
- Mix performance appraisal and salary or promotion issues.
- Concentrate only on the negative.
- Do all the talking.
- Be overcritical or "harp on" a failing.
- Feel it is necessary that both of you agree on all areas.
- Compare the employee with others.

Source: Robert L. Mathis and John H. Jackson, *Personnel/Human Resources Management,* 7th ed. (Mason, Ohio: South-Western, 1994), p. 318. Reprinted with permission of South-Western, a part of Cengage Learning, www.cengage.com/permissions.

The Need for Discipline

⑤ Define discipline and explain why it is necessary.

Effective job performance requires that both managerial and nonmanagerial employees maintain discipline. Most employees would rather work with a group that is well organized, well trained, and well disciplined than with one that is not. Employees benefit from discipline and suffer from disorder. An early study found that, although workers do not necessarily want to be personally punished, they do want to be supervised "not too much—but also not too little."[16] Successful supervisors know how to find the "middle road" that allows their employees to know exactly what they may and may not do. These generalizations may lead to confusion unless the question, "what is discipline?" is answered.

What Is Discipline?

To start out, let us emphasize that good discipline is based on good leadership. On that assumption, the term *discipline* will be used in this chapter to refer to any of three concepts: (1) self-control, (2) conditions leading to orderly behavior in a work environment, or (3) punishment for improper behavior. Many companies say in their discipline policy that **discipline** is training that corrects, molds, or perfects knowledge, attitudes, behavior, or conduct. We agree with this overall definition.

discipline Training that corrects and molds knowledge, attitudes, and behavior.

Discipline as Due Process

The Fourteenth Amendment to the U.S. Constitution guarantees every citizen due process under the law. Essentially, the following conditions ensure that an individual receives justice in the form of **due process:**

due process Guarantees the individual accused of violating an established rule a hearing to determine the extent of guilt.

1. Rules or laws exist.

2. There are specific, fixed penalties for violating those rules, with progressive degrees in the severity of penalties.

3. Penalties are imposed only after a hearing has been conducted for the accused, at which time the extent of guilt is determined after considering the circumstances of the situation.

Unions have insisted that this same process be used within organizations in disciplining employees; even nonunion employers now use it. Today, most arbitrators will uphold a disciplinary action if it can be shown that (1) the rules are reasonable, (2) the penalty is related to the severity of the offense, and (3) the worker was given a fair hearing. Underlying the due process concept is the assumption that the employer has the right to maintain a well-disciplined work environment and the right to administer discipline when rules are violated. Of course, where there's a union, its representative wants to be present when a member is disciplined. At this point, we would like to emphasize that employers can avoid employee grievance proceedings by developing equitable and objective disciplinary procedures.[17]

How Disciplinary Due Process Operates

6 Describe how discipline is imposed under due process.

As indicated earlier, disciplinary due process involves three steps. First, rules are established. Second, fixed penalties are set for each infraction of a rule (the penalties usually vary according to the degree of severity of the offense and how many times the rule is broken). Third, the penalty is imposed only after the employee has been given a fair hearing.

Establishing Rules of Conduct. If employees are to maintain self-discipline, they must know what they can and cannot do, and they must know it in advance. Therefore, most progressive organizations publish rules, usually in their employees' handbook.

Determining Penalties. The types of penalties, as well as the ways they are used, generally are determined in consultation with the union. What usually results is termed **progressive discipline,** because it involves a graduated scale of penalties. If there is no union, the penalties stem from management's philosophy of how to treat employees, as well as from its fear of the entry of a union or government action.

progressive discipline Discipline that uses a graduated scale of penalties.

The normal steps in a progressive-discipline policy are as follows:

1. *Oral warning* that does not go into the employee's record.
2. *Oral warning* that goes into the employee's record.
3. *Written reprimand,* which usually comes from some level above the supervisor.
4. *Suspensions,* which usually consists of a layoff lasting from a day to a number of months.
5. *Discharge,* the ultimate penalty, which constitutes a break in service and wipes out the employee's seniority. Most supervisors are reluctant to use it because it is the economic equivalent of the death penalty and it affects the worker's family as well as the worker. Justification must be strictly established because discharge is almost always subject to the grievance procedure and arbitration.

Some other infrequently used penalties are demotions, transfers, and the withholding of benefits such as promotions, raises, or bonuses.

Unions, personnel managers, and most supervisors favor using a **graduated scale of penalties,** under which punishment for a given violation becomes progressively more severe each time the violation is repeated. The penalty may be, first, an oral warning; second, a written warning; third, suspension; and fourth, discharge. However, when the disciplinary problems are of such a drastic, dangerous, or illegal nature that they severely strain or endanger employment relationships, they are called **intolerable offenses,** and the first time one is committed, the employee is discharged.

graduated scale of penalties Penalties become progressively more severe each time the violation is repeated.

intolerable offenses Disciplinary problems of a drastic, dangerous, or illegal nature.

Imposing the Penalty Only After a Fair Hearing. Supervisors must follow the correct procedure in taking any action against an employee. In other words, discipline must be properly administered in accordance with previously established and announced rules and procedures. Penalties should be based on specific charges, with notice given to the employee and the union, if there is one, usually in advance of management's attempt to take corrective action. The charges and their underlying reasons should be definite and provable. There should be provisions for a prompt hearing, witnesses, protests, and appeals. Finally, adequate remedies should be available to employees whose punishment has failed to meet the requirement of "fair play."

In summary, the main requirements for a proper disciplinary procedure are (1) to make definite charges; (2) to notify the employee (and union), in writing, of the offense; and (3) to have some provision for the employee to answer the charges either by protest or by appeal.

7 Explain the supervisor's disciplinary role.

The Supervisor and Discipline

Regardless of whether supervisors work in unionized firms, they must exercise discretion when recommending or imposing penalties on employees. In dealing with mistakes, supervisors must consider what the mistakes were and under what circumstances they were made. Mistakes resulting from continued carelessness call for disciplinary action. Honest mistakes should be corrected by counseling and positive discipline, not by punishment. These should be corrected in a way that will help the employee learn from the mistakes and become a more proficient and valuable worker.

In light of recent incidences of violence in the workplace, supervisors need to be proactive in establishing boundaries, identifying problems, counseling employees, and taking corrective actions. Violent behaviors at work are not random acts. These types of behaviors are caused by a series of events that occur over time and that come to a head. In most cases, coworkers

Employees who understand exactly what is and what is not expected of them are better equipped to avoid unpleasant disciplinary measures.

© Kaluzny-Thatcher/Stone/Getty Images

and supervisors were aware that it was just a matter of time before the person "snapped." First-line supervisors are the key to preventing workplace violence. How they choose to deal with issues and handle employees can have an impact.[18]

The Supervisor's Disciplinary Role

One of the primary duties of present-day supervisors is to maintain discipline. Top managers expect—and depend on—their supervisors not only to set disciplinary limits but also to enforce them. Only then does an organization operate effectively.

In order to achieve this goal, supervisors must instill a desire for self-discipline in employees. If employees are not required to face up to the realities of their jobs, their goals, their resources, and their potential, they are in a poor position to function properly and make their best contribution to the organization. It's surprising how quickly organizational problems melt away when interpersonal forthrightness is applied.

When applying discipline, a supervisor must consider these points:

1. Every job should carry with it a certain margin for error.

2. Being overly concerned with avoiding errors stifles initiative and encourages employees to postpone decisions or avoid making them altogether.

3. A different way of doing something should not be mistaken for the wrong way of doing it.

Supervisors are more likely than higher-level managers to avoid administering severe disciplinary action because of the likelihood of generating undesirable effects. Other managers, including some personnel managers, take a stronger—perhaps more punitive—position on matters of discipline. A possible explanation is that supervisory managers are inclined to give stronger consideration to individual circumstances and behavior than are top managers. Also, supervisors are somewhat reluctant to follow rules strictly for fear they'll lose the cooperation of their employees if they're too severe.

Principles of Effective Discipline: The Hot-Stove Rule

Four important principles of effective discipline are discussed in this section. These principles are often referred to as the **hot-stove rule,** because they draw a comparison between touching a hot stove and experiencing discipline. Here are the four principles, as illustrated in Exhibit 15-5:

hot-stove rule Compares a good disciplinary system to a hot stove.

1. You know what will happen if you touch a hot stove (it carries a clear warning).

2. If you touch a hot stove, it burns you right away (it is immediate).

3. A hot stove always burns you if you touch it (it is consistent).

4. A hot stove doesn't care whom it burns (it is impersonal).

Discipline Carries a Clear Advance Warning. Employees should know what is and what is not expected of them. This means that there must be clear warning that a given offense will lead to discipline, and there must be clear warning of the amount of discipline that will be imposed for an offense.

> Supervisor C. D. Yates* had long ignored a safety rule that the employees wear short-sleeved shirts while operating their machines. In fact, for over a year, several employees had routinely worn long-sleeved shirts in the department. After learning of an injury in another department when an employee's long-sleeved shirt got caught in a conveyor belt, Yates immediately wrote up warnings to five employees in his department who were wearing long-sleeved shirts that day.

*The name has been changed.

EXHIBIT 15-5

The Hot-Stove Rule

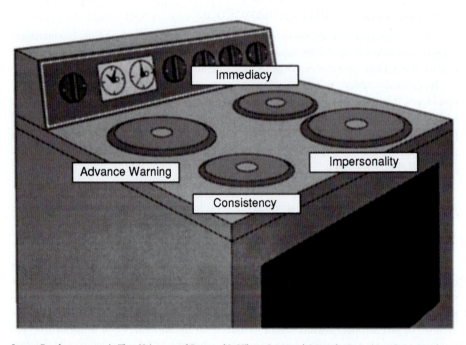

Source: Based on concepts in Theo Haimann and Raymond L. Hilgert, *Instructor's Manual—Supervision: Concepts and Practices of Management,* 6th ed. (Mason, Ohio: South-Western, 1995). Reproduced with permission of South-Western, a part of Cengage Learning, www.cengage.com/permissions.

✔ **SELF-CHECK**

If you were one of the five employees, would you consider Yates' action fair? Probably not. Since the safety rule was so openly ignored, it was the equivalent of no rule at all. For adequate warning to take place, Yates needed to communicate to his employees that, although the rule had been ignored in the past, it would now be enforced in the department. If you were an outside arbitrator, how would you rule? Why?

Discipline Is Immediate. The supervisor should begin the disciplinary process as soon as possible after he or she notices a violation. This is important for the following reasons:

1. An employee may feel that he or she is "putting one over" on the supervisor and may try to violate other rules.

2. An employee may assume that the supervisor is too weak to enforce the rules.

3. An employee may believe that the supervisor doesn't consider the rule important enough to be enforced. Thus, all the other employees may be encouraged to break or stretch the rule as well. It is not surprising to find an employee responding, "Well, I've been doing this for several days (or weeks) and nobody said anything about it to me before."

Discipline Is Consistent. This principle means that for similar circumstances, similar discipline should be administered. If two people commit the same offense under the same circumstances, they should receive the same punishment.

> Helen* had a very high absenteeism record. Recently she missed work for 2 days without a legitimate excuse. Considering her past record, this offense would justify an immediate 1-week suspension. However, her skills were badly needed by the supervisor, since the department was snowed under by a tremendous backlog of work. Helen was given only an oral warning.

What will Helen's supervisor do when another worker misses work for 2 days without a legitimate excuse? If the supervisor is inconsistent, he or she will develop a reputation for playing favorites and losing credibility with employees. Does this mean a supervisor always has to dish out identical penalties for similar offenses? Note that we said the supervisor must be consistent as long as circumstances are similar. An employee's past record is a major factor to consider.

> Two employees were caught drinking an alcoholic beverage on the job. The rules clearly prohibited this. For one employee, it was the first such offense; for the second worker, it was his third in the past year. Would the supervisor be justified in giving the second employee a more serious penalty than the first? You better believe it!

✔ SELF-CHECK

What are the pros and cons of giving an employee a "break" regarding discipline?

....

Discipline Is Impersonal. As a supervisor, you shouldn't get into personalities when administering discipline. You need to be as objective as possible. Moreover, after administering discipline to an employee, try to retain a normal relationship with that person. Two common mistakes supervisors make in imposing discipline are apologizing to employees and bawling out employees. Discipline the act, not the person. Your focus should be *on getting the employee's work behavior consistent with the rules.*

Applying Discipline

Two of the more unpleasant aspects of the supervisor's job are (1) laying off a worker for disciplinary reasons and (2) discharging an unsatisfactory employee.

Disciplinary Layoff. If an employee has repeatedly committed major offenses and previous warnings have been ineffective, a **disciplinary layoff,** or **suspension,** is probably inevitable. Such a layoff involves a loss of time—and pay—for several days. This form of discipline usually comes as a rude shock to workers. It gets their attention! And generally it impresses on them the need to comply with the organization's rules.

disciplinary layoff *or* **suspension** Time off without pay.

Because this form of discipline is quite serious and involves a substantial penalty—loss of pay—most organizations limit the power to use it to managers who have attained at least the second level of management; often the human resources manager is involved as well. Yet supervisors have the right to recommend such action.

Not all managers believe the layoff is effective, and some seldom apply it as a disciplinary measure. First, they may need the worker to continue production. Second, they may feel that the worker will return with an even more negative attitude. Still, when properly used, it is an effective disciplinary tool.

*The name has been changed.

A supervisor may find it necessary to utilize a disciplinary layoff or suspension as means of redirecting an employee's behavior.

Photodisc/Getty Images

termination-at-will rule
An employer can dismiss an employee for any reason.

Discharge. In 1884, a Tennessee court established the **termination-at-will rule,** whereby an employer could dismiss an employee for any reason—or even for no reason at all—unless there was an explicit contractual provision preventing such action.[19] The reasoning behind this decision was that if an employee can quit work for any reason, then the employer should be able to discharge for any reason.

Subsequent legislative enactments and court decisions, as well as union rules and public policy, have swung the pendulum of protection away from the employer and toward the employee by limiting the termination-at-will rule.[20] Most union agreements have a clause requiring "just cause" for disciplinary discharge and detailing the order in which employees can be laid off. EEO/AA regulations do essentially the same.

In general, court decisions suggest that the safest (legal) grounds for discharge include incompetent performance that does not respond to training or accommodation, gross or repeated insubordination, excessive unexcused absences, repeated and unexcused tardiness, verbal abuse of others, physical violence, falsification of records, drunkenness or drug abuse on the job, and theft.

Since discharge is so severe, supervisors can only recommend it. The discharge must be carried out by top management—usually with the advice and consent of the human resources manager.

Unions are quite involved in discipline when they represent the employees. Even many nonunionized organizations now follow the union's disciplinary procedure.

Supervisors' Personal Liability for Disciplining Employees

Recent court decisions holding supervisors personally liable for discharging disabled employees are making some supervisors reluctant to exercise their judgment in hiring, promoting, and firing employees. They are unwilling to take the punitive action indicated for unsatisfactory actions of employees if their personal assets, such as their houses or cars, can become subject to steep jury awards.

Supervisors have been held individually liable in some blatant and serious sex and race harassment cases.

click!
http://www.usdoj.gov/
crt/ada/adahoml.htm

CHAPTER REVIEW

1 **Explain who is responsible for selecting, appraising, and disciplining employees.**

This chapter has presented ways to select, appraise, and discipline employees. In general, the human resource department is responsible for overall planning, recruiting, and handling the details of staffing. The role of supervisors is to requisition needed workers, interview applicants, orient new employees, and appraise and discipline current employees.

2 **Describe the steps in the employee selection procedure, including the proper orientation of new employees.**

The procedure for selecting employees for specific jobs includes (1) a requisition from the supervisor, (2) a preliminary screening-out of the obvious misfits, (3) the applicant's completion of an application form, (4) preemployment tests, (5) various interviews by the supervisor and human resource officer, (6) checking records and references, (7) a preliminary selection made by the supervisor, (8) physical exam, if legal, and (9) a job offer. If the offer is accepted, the new employee is given a job orientation by the supervisor.

3 **Explain what employee performance appraisal is and who performs it.**

An employee's performance is always being appraised, either formally or informally. The purpose of formal performance appraisals, however, is to compare employee performance to a standard or ideal—a sort of personnel quality control. Appraisal is more critical for employees whose output cannot be easily measured. Specific reasons for appraising employee performance are to provide a basis for some administrative action (such as a pay increase, promotion, transfer, layoff, discharge, or recommendation for training or development), to justify these actions for EEO/AA purposes, and to improve supervisor-employee relationships. Performance appraisals can be done by employees rating themselves, by employees rating supervisors, or by employees rating one another, but the immediate supervisors should be ultimately responsible, since they are most familiar with their employees' work.

4 **State why performance-appraisal interviews are difficult for both the employee and the supervisor.**

One of the jobs supervisors like least is conducting the appraisal interview, which is used to communicate the results of the appraisal to the concerned employee. A supervisor's reluctance to criticize employees may lead to appraisal inflation.

5 **Define discipline and explain why it is necessary.**

Another important supervisory activity is applying discipline. Because discipline is necessary for supervisory success, higher-level managers expect supervisors to set and enforce disciplinary limits. There are three types of discipline: (1) self-control, (2) conditions for orderly behavior, and (3) punishment. Employee discipline is a process of control, either internally or externally imposed. As such it is a method of maintaining management's authority—authority that is necessary to keep an organization operating effectively.

6 **Describe how discipline is imposed under due process.**

Although the right to discipline is still management's responsibility, today supervisors must be sure they follow due process, which requires (1) stated rules, (2) specific penalties, and (3) an orderly procedure for assessing guilt and punishment. The rules

IMPORTANT TERMS

achievement, proficiency, *or* skill tests
appraisal interview
aptitude tests
disciplinary layoff *or* suspension
discipline
due process
graduated scale of penalties
hot-stove rule
intolerable offenses
IQ tests
orientation
performance appraisal *or* merit rating *or* efficiency rating *or* service rating *or* employee evaluation
personality tests
progressive discipline
reliability
structured interviews
termination-at-will rule
validity
vocational interest tests
work sampling *or* work preview

usually classify offenses as (1) minor infractions, (2) major violations, or (3) intolerable offenses. Penalties can include (1) oral warnings, (2) oral warnings with a written record, (3) written reprimands, (4) suspension, and (5) discharge. Usually a graduated scale of penalties is imposed, in which the penalty increases with the frequency and severity of violations.

7 Explain the supervisor's disciplinary role.

To be effective, discipline must be enforced. The manner of enforcement, in turn, affects the morale of the organization. One of the most difficult supervisory tasks is to strike an acceptable balance between severity and leniency in administering discipline. Four principles of effective discipline, collectively referred to as the "hot-stove rule," are that discipline should (1) carry a clear warning, (2) be immediate, (3) be consistent, and (4) be impersonal.

When lesser forms of discipline imposed by the supervisor are ineffective, it may be necessary to resort to layoff or discharge of the employee. Usually such action is carried out only by higher levels of management. In any case, it is important to be sure that due process has been observed and that there is just cause for such action.

QUESTIONS FOR REVIEW AND DISCUSSION

1. Explain why performance appraisal is such an important part of the management process.

2. What is performance appraisal, and what are some of the other names for it?

3. What are some of the purposes of performance appraisal? Explain.

4. Name and explain the steps in the suggested procedure for selecting workers for specific jobs.

5. What is discipline?

6. Why is discipline so very important in organizations?

7. What is the due process of discipline, and why is it so important?

8. What is the union's role in the disciplinary process?

9. Why should disciplinary layoff and discharge decisions be restricted to higher levels of management?

Skill Builder 15-1

What Would You Do?

Three people have applied to you for an opening as a lathe operator. One is totally unqualified. One is experienced, but has a very poor attitude. The third lacks experience, but seems especially eager for the job; you think she would be a good worker if she had more experience, but you're not sure.

You have some rush work that you need to get out. Which of the following courses would you choose?

1. If the eager applicant has good references, hire her for a probationary period. But keep looking for a more qualified person in case she doesn't work out.

2. Pass up the three applicants. Keep looking.

3. Hire the experienced person, ignoring his attitude—you've got work to get out!

What Do You Want from Your Job?

Skill Builder 15-2

Rank the employment factors in the following chart in order of their importance to you at three points in your career. In the first column, assume that you are about to graduate and are looking for your first full-time job. In the second column, assume that you have been gainfully employed for 5 to 10 years and are presently working for a reputable firm at the prevailing salary for the type of job and industry in which you work. In the third column, try to assume that 25 to 30 years from now you have found your niche in life and have been working for a reputable employer for several years. (Rank your first choice as "1," second as "2," and so forth, through "9.")

Employment Factor	Your Ranking		
	As You Seek Your First Full-Time Job	5–10 Years Later	15–20 Years Later
Employee benefits	_____	_____	_____
Fair adjustment of grievances	_____	_____	_____
Good job instruction and training	_____	_____	_____
Effective job supervision by your supervisor	_____	_____	_____
Promotion possibilities	_____	_____	_____
Job safety	_____	_____	_____
Job security (no threat of being dismissed or laid off)	_____	_____	_____
Good salary	_____	_____	_____
Good working conditions (nice office surroundings, good hours, and so on)	_____	_____	_____

Answer the following questions:

1. What does your ranking tell you about your motivation now?

2. Is there any change in the second and third periods?

3. What changes are there, and why did you make them?

Source: Donald C. Mosley, Paul H. Pietri, and Leon C. Megginson, *Management: Leadership in Action.* Copyright 1996, Addison Wesley Longman, Inc. Reprinted by permission of Addison Wesley Longman.

Gloria Rogers Appraises Her Employees

Review the example of how Gloria Rogers conducts her performance appraisal interviews. Notice that they are "conducted according to the rules of good performance appraisal interviewing."

Instructions:

Assume that you are Gloria's supervisor (manager). How would you advise her to improve her performance appraisals?

CASE

When the Transfer Backfires

Case 15-1

Jane Smith abruptly rose and stormed out of the office of Robert Trent, the director of purchasing at a major eastern university. As she made her hasty exit, Trent began to wonder what had gone wrong with a seemingly perfect play—one that would have rid his department of a "problem" employee. How could his well-constructed plan, using the university's formal transfer system, have failed so miserably, leaving him with an even more unmanageable situation?

It had all begun in January, when Trent decided that something must be done about Smith's performance and attitude. The process was made a little more awkward by the university's not having a formal employee performance-appraisal policy and program. Each department was left with the right to develop and conduct its own employee appraisals. This meant that each department could choose whether or not to appraise an employee, as well as choose the format and procedure to be used.

In January, Trent decided to conduct an appraisal of Smith. After writing down some weaknesses in her performance and attitude, he called her in to discuss them. He cited the various weaknesses to her, but, admittedly, most were highly subjective in nature. In only a few instances did he give specific and objective references, and he did not give Smith a copy of his findings. During the appraisal interview, he even hinted that possibly she didn't "fit in" and that she "probably would be much happier in some other place." In any event, he was satisfied that he had begun the process for eventually ridding the department of her. He reasoned that, if all else failed, this pressure would ultimately force her to quit. At the time, he hardly noticed that she was strangely quiet through the whole meeting.

As time went by, Smith's attitude and performance did not improve. In March, Trent was elated to learn that an opening existed in another department and that Smith was most interested in transferring. The university's formal transfer policy required that Trent complete the Employee Transfer Evaluation Form—which he gladly did. As a matter of fact, he rated Smith mostly "outstanding" on the performance and attitude factors. He was so pleased at having the opportunity to use the transfer system that he called the other department manager and spoke glowingly of Smith's abilities and performance. Although he had been the purchasing director for only eight months, having been recruited from another college, he even pointed with pride to Smith's five years' experience.

In April, much to Trent's dismay, it was announced that Smith had lost the transfer opportunity to a better qualified candidate. Robert Trent was shocked when Smith's transfer was turned down. To further complicate matters, Trent realized that he would have to face Smith in May when it would be time to discuss annual pay raises, which would include both merit pay considerations and a cost-of-living adjustment. This would be even more difficult because Smith's performance and attitude had not improved since the January appraisal. If anything, they were worse.

Trent had just finished the May meeting with Smith by telling her the bad news: On the basis of both performance and attitude, she should not be recommended for a cost-of-living or merit-pay increase for the new year beginning July 1. Smith, armed with the transfer evaluation forms (completed and given to her in March), threatened to use all internal and external systems for organizational justice due her.

As Trent pondered this dilemma, he fully recognized Smith's unique status within the university community. She was the wife of a distinguished, tenured professor of business, and this situation provided additional pressure. As if this were not enough, he had to contend with the office social process pivoting around a weekly coffee group that was greatly influenced by Smith. It was not unusual for the former director of purchasing (who had retired after 25 years of service) to attend these gatherings. Of course, Smith had kept this group fully apprised of her continuing troubles with "this new, young purchasing director who is hardly dry behind the ears."

Answer the following questions:

1. What are the facts Trent must consider now?

2. What avenues are now open to Trent? What does this case say to you about the need for supervisors to act morally?

3. Do you believe that some supervisors are untruthful where recommendations are concerned? Explain.

4. What three functions are salaries meant to perform?

5. To what extent should employee appraisals be used in salary adjustments? Explain.

Source: Prepared by M. T. Bledsoe, Associate Professor of Business, Meredith College, Raleigh, North Carolina.

16 The Supervisor, Labor Relations, and Legal Issues

AP Photo/Douglas Healy

An employer has far greater resources than employees have as individuals. For this reason, labor unions unite workers so that they can effectively petition for better benefits and working conditions.

All your strength is in your union,
All your danger is in discord;
Therefore be at peace henceforward,
And as brothers live together.
—HENRY WADSWORTH LONGFELLOW

Long ago we stated the reason for labor organizations. We said that union was essential to give laborers opportunity to deal on an equality with their employer.
—U.S. SUPREME COURT

Preview

The Union Organizer

Bobby Sutton managed Quality Service, a small hauling and delivery firm in California.* His father had just bought it from an aging proprietor who had let the business slide. The elder Sutton had retained the employees—a secretary, a clerk, two warehouse workers, and three drivers. A month had passed when Marvin Wiley, an organizer for the Teamsters Union, came in and demanded that Bobby recognize the union as the bargaining agent for the firm's warehouse workers and drivers. Marvin said that most of them had joined the union and wanted it to represent them. Also, the firm owed each of them $800 in back wages in order to bring them up to the union scale. Bobby indicated that he had no evidence that the workers either belonged to or wanted to belong to a union. When Marvin threatened to take the workers out on strike, Bobby said he'd consider them absent without permission and fire them if they walked off the job. Marvin said, "You'd better not do that," and left.

Bobby was quite upset and shaken by the incident. While he was trying to figure out what to do, Joe, a driver, came in to talk about the situation. Joe said he and the two warehouse workers did not want to join but that they were being pressured by Marvin and Bill, another driver. Bill was quite dissatisfied and was actively pushing the others to sign up. The third driver, Tony, was neutral and would do what the majority wanted to do. Going back to his office, Bobby felt betrayed by Bill and Tony.

About a week after the incident at Quality Service took place, Marvin Wiley walked in, slapped a contract on Bobby Sutton's desk, and said, "Sign it!" After reading it, Bobby refused, explaining that he would go broke if he signed it. He said he was already paying near the union scale; he would pay the workers more when he could afford it and if they deserved it. Marvin said, "We'll see about that!" and angrily stalked out with the unsigned contract in his hand.

Although he could not do it legally, Bobby decided that if he was to keep the union out, he'd have to get rid of Bill. As business was slow during the winter months, Bobby laid Bill off, telling him he would rehire him when things picked up. Bobby would drive the third truck if this became necessary.

Things went well for Bobby during the next 4 years. Business grew and he had to add personnel. Each time he interviewed an applicant, he'd inquire as to the applicant's attitude toward various organizations, including unions. If the applicant showed a favorable attitude toward unions, Bobby would find a reason for not hiring him or her.

During its fifth year of operation, business was booming for Quality Service. Bobby Sutton had 22 employees, including 3 office employees, 7 warehouse workers, and 12 truck drivers. His father had bought another firm in a nearby city, and Bobby was running both businesses, with a supervisor at each location. Bobby had contracted to buy five new trucks and was trying to hire new drivers for them, but the number of capable drivers available for employment was quite limited.

*The names have been changed at the company's request.

Learning Objectives

After reading and studying this chapter, you should be able to:

1. Explain what is meant by labor relations.

2. Trace the development of unions in the United States.

3. Explain why union membership is declining.

4. Name and explain some of the basic laws governing labor relations.

5. Describe union principles and objectives and discuss the methods used to achieve those objectives.

6. Name three things that a supervisor must know in order to live with the union agreement.

7. State the laws providing equal employment opportunity for protected groups of employees.

8. Describe the most commonly provided employee benefits.

After hearing nothing from the union for 4 years, Bobby was surprised when Marvin Wiley walked in and laid down authorization cards from five warehouse workers and two drivers. Marvin said, "Bobby, the last time I was here, you said you couldn't afford to unionize. But now you're the largest delivery firm in town. I think your people had better be working under a contract."

Again, Bobby refused to accept the union as the representative of his employees. The seven employees subsequently petitioned for an National Labor Relations Board (NLRB) election, but lost it by a vote of six for the union and 13 against it. From then on, Bobby and his supervisors became more concerned about employee relations.

The opening quotations illustrate one of the most basic reasons why labor unions are needed. That is, individual employees cannot compete with the employer's resources by themselves. But when united, employees as a group can successfully contend with management.

A **labor union** is an organization of workers banded together to achieve economic goals, especially increased wages and benefits, shorter working hours, improved working conditions, and both personal and job security. The individual employee has very little bargaining strength when negotiating with the employer. But when employees band together to form a labor union, they are better able to protect their interests and to obtain economic benefits.

It is impossible to cover everything about dealing with unions in one chapter, but we will include the most important ideas to help you understand the supervisor's role in labor relations. Even if you are—or expect to be—a supervisor in a nonunion firm, you need to understand how labor relations affect supervisory activities and relationships, for they affect nonunion employers as well as unionized ones.

> **labor union** An organization of workers banded together to achieve economic goals.

✔ SELF-CHECK

Even in nonunion firms, supervisors use due process in applying discipline. Do you think this approach by enlightened supervisors improves labor–management relations? Why or why not?

1 Explain what is meant by labor relations.

What Are Labor Relations?

Terms such as **labor relations, union–management relations,** and **industrial relations** are often used to refer to the relationships between employers and their unionized employees. In this text, these terms will be used interchangeably.

The growth of unionism has forced managers—especially supervisors—to change many of their ways of dealing with employees, especially in matters concerning wages, hours, working conditions, and other terms and conditions of employment. Managers in unionized companies are constantly being challenged by union leaders in these areas. These challenges force supervisors to consciously or unconsciously consider the rights of workers when developing and applying policies and procedures. Thus, management's freedom of choice has been greatly limited by the emergence of unions. For example, managers can no longer reward an employee on the basis of favoritism or punish one without just cause.

Labor relations are more than a power struggle between management and labor over economic matters that concern only themselves. Instead, hurt feelings, bruised egos, disappointments, and the hopes and ambitions of workers, managers, and labor leaders are involved. Also, these relationships affect and are affected by the total physical, economic, social, technological, legal, political, and cultural environment in which they occur.

> **labor relations or union–management relations or industrial relations** The relationship between an employer and unionized employees.

Think about the last serious strike you can remember. Did it affect you in any way, either directly or indirectly? Even if it didn't affect you, what were the economic, social, political, and cultural effects on your community? On the nation? Did any workers in affected organizations lose jobs or wages? Did any companies lose output or go out of business? Were the sales at retail stores hurt? Were tax receipts reduced? Was there any violence? Did it affect any social or cultural events?

How Unions Developed in the United States

2 Trace the development of unions in the United States.

In general, employees were treated well in the early colonies because of the severe shortage of workers. By the end of the 19th century, however, the situation had changed. The high birthrate, rapid and uncontrolled immigration, the concentration of wealth and industry in the hands of a few businessmen, political abuses by some employers, and the large numbers of workers in crowded industrial areas led to many abuses against workers.

http://www.aflcio.org

Early Union Activities

Labor unions existed in the United States as early as 1789, but they were small, isolated, and ineffective **craft unions** of skilled, experienced workers in specific skills, crafts, or trades. As more concerted action and stronger efforts were needed to improve the workers' plight, several of the craft unions joined together in 1869 to form the Knights of Labor. As the organization was only moderately successful, a more conservative national union was formed in 1881. It was named the American Federation of Labor (AFL) in 1886. Under the leadership of Samuel Gompers, the AFL grew and had great impact, especially during World War I and World War II. The basic concepts of a labor union were developed under his leadership. When asked what unions wanted for their members, Gompers invariably replied, "More!"

craft unions Workers in a specific skill, craft, or trade.

Period of Rapid Union Growth

During the 1920s and early 1930s, business became so powerful that workers again felt they were being exploited. They were hired, rewarded, punished, and fired at the whim of first-line supervisors, many of whom acted unfeelingly. Therefore, several laws were passed in the 1930s that forced management to recognize unions and protected workers from exploitation.

Until that time, the AFL and its affiliates had been organized on a craft basis. Union growth was thus limited, because there were few craft workers left to organize. But some workers had started organizing **industrial unions,** in which all the workers in a given industry—such as those in iron, coal, and autos—belonged to the same union, whether they were craftsmen, unskilled workers, or clerical employees. These unions broke away from the AFL in 1936 to form the Congress of Industrial Organizations (CIO).

industrial unions Unions composed of all the workers in an industry.

Because of laws and government actions favorable to workers, and the demand for workers resulting from World War II, union membership grew rapidly until 1945, when 35.5 percent of the workforce was unionized. Then, as Exhibit 16-1 shows, membership increased more slowly through the mid-1950s and afterward. By the year 2003, only 13.5 percent of all nonagricultural wage and salary workers were members of unions. So, out of the total workforce, only 16.3 million were union members, and that number has held almost constant during the last decade.

EXHIBIT 16-1

Membership of National
Unions as a Percentage
of the Total Labor Force

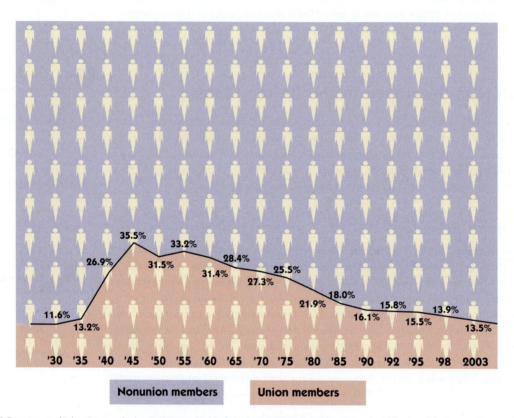

Nonunion members   Union members

Source: U.S. Department of Labor, Bureau of Labor Statistics; and "Union Membership," *Bulletin to Management* (a publication of the Bureau of National Affairs), March 4, 1993, pp. 68–70. Adapted from Leon C. Megginson, Geralyn M. Franklin, and M. Jane Byrd, *Human Resource Management* (Houston: Dame Publications, 1995), p. 480. Updated from Leigh Strope, "Democratic Candidates Start Wooing Labor," *Mobile (Ala.) Register*, February 16, 2003, p. 9A.

Recent Limited Union Growth

After peaking at 35.5 percent of the total workforce in 1945, union membership declined until 1955, when it reached 33.2 percent of the workforce. That was the highest point reached in the post–World War II period. Because of this leveling off of union participation by American workers, and in hopes of reversing this trend, the AFL and CIO in 1955 merged into the AFL-CIO. But this move—and other concerted activities—did not stop the decline.

Total union membership did increase during the 1960s and 1970s when new types of unions, namely **employee associations,** emerged. For example, after President Kennedy issued Executive Order 10988 in 1962, the unionization of government workers escalated until 37.4 percent of all government employees were unionized in 2001. At the same time, only 6.2 percent of all workers in private, nonagricultural industries were members of unions, as shown in Exhibit 16-2.

employee associations
Organizations that function as labor unions.

EXHIBIT **16-2**

Unionization Rates High
in Government

Government workers
made up about two-
fifths of the 16.3 million
unionized workers in
2001. Yet the rate of
unionization for all
government workers
was much higher than
in the private sector.

**Unionization rates
broken down by industry**

☐ Government workers

☐ Private, nonagricultural
industries

37.4%

9.0%

Source: U.S. Department of Labor, Bureau of Labor Statistics.

✔ **SELF-CHECK**

Around seven out of eight employed workers *do not* belong to a union. Why do you think this is so?

http://stats.bls.gov/news.
release/union2.toc.htm

click!

Some Reasons for Declining Union Membership

③ Explain why union membership is declining.

There are many reasons for this declining union membership. First, there has been a major shift in the economy from manufacturing jobs, which are relatively easy to unionize, to service work, which is more difficult to organize. For example, there has been nearly a 40 percent drop in union membership in the auto, machine-working, and steel industries in just the last two decades.

Second, there is a new kind of service worker—more educated and technologically oriented. These mobile employees are less interested in long-term union contracts, with payments in the distant future, than in such things as portable pensions and employer contributions to retirement plans. They also enjoy "employee involvement" schemes such as quality circles and self-managing teams, which traditional unions tend to oppose but which employees enjoy.

Another problem for U.S. unions is the growing global economy. U.S. firms are under pressure to cut costs in order to compete, so many employers have become more aggressive in opposing union organizing drives.[1] Also, they feel that they cannot compete with foreign competitors if they are bound by the industrywide bargaining required by U.S. unions.

For example, several years ago, Caterpillar, a leading producer of earth-moving equipment, accepted a prolonged strike from the United Auto Workers union rather than sign an agreement that its U.S. competitors had already accepted. Its management believed that the company would lose sales to "competitors with more flexible labor deals abroad."[2]

Caterpillar represents a current trend in taking a hard stance against unions, given changing global markets that are very competitive.

© Tom Wagner/CORBIS SABA

http://www.cat.com

http://www.uaw.org

Fourth, the growing emphasis on employing part-time and temporary workers has also contributed to the decline in union membership. Also, the telecommuting "explosion" makes it difficult to organize workers. According to one recent estimate, 24 million Americans telecommuted during one recent year.[3]

Next, the growing "small is beautiful" world of business is working to discourage union membership. U.S. small businesses provide most of the new jobs in the United States. As an indication of the problem this trend poses for unions, there are now many more small business *owners* (over 23 million) than there are union members, and small firms are very difficult for unions to organize.[4]

④ Name and explain some of the basic laws governing labor relations.

Some Basic Laws Governing Labor Relations

The legal basis of union–management relations is provided by the National Labor Relations Act of 1935 (also called the *Wagner Act*), as amended by the Labor Management Relations Act of 1947 (the Taft-Hartley Act), the Labor Management Reporting and Disclosure Act of 1959 (the Landrum-Griffin Act), and others. This complex set of laws establishes public policy and controls labor relations. Exhibit 16-3 shows the coverage, basic provisions, and agencies administering these laws. We'll provide only a few more details about them in the text.

The Most Important Labor Laws

In this section we examine why the basic labor laws were passed. We also point out the important features of these laws and explain how they are administered.

unfair labor practices
Specific acts that management may not commit against the workers and the union.

Wagner Act. The National Labor Relations Act (Wagner Act) was passed to protect employees and unions by limiting management's rights. It gave workers the right to form and join unions of their own choosing and made collective bargaining mandatory. It also set up the NLRB to enforce the law. The act defined specific **unfair labor practices** that management could not commit against the workers and the union, but it had no provision for unfair

EXHIBIT 16-3

Basic Laws Governing
Labor Relations

Laws	Coverage	Basic Provisions	Agencies Involved
National Labor Relations Act (NLRA) as amended (Wagner Act)	Nonmanagerial employees in nonagricultural private firms not covered by the Railway Labor Act; postal employees	Asserts the right of employees to form or join labor organizations (or to refuse to), to bargain collectively through their representatives, and to engage in other concerted activities such as strikes, picketing, and boycotts; establishes unfair labor practices that the employer cannot engage in.	National Labor Relations Board (NLRB)
Labor–Management Relations Act (LMRA) as amended (Taft-Hartley Act)	Same as above	Amended NLRA; permits states to pass laws prohibiting compulsory union membership; sets up methods to deal with strikes affecting national health and safety.	Federal Mediation and Conciliation Service
Labor–Management Reporting and Disclosure Act (Landrum-Griffin Act)	Same as above	Amended NLRA and LMRA; guarantees individual rights of union members in dealing with their union; requires financial disclosures by unions.	U.S. Department of Labor

Source: U.S. Department of Labor publications and the basic laws themselves, as amended.

practices that unions might commit against workers and management. As a result, many union abuses arose. One major abuse was that unions could impose requirements as to how employees could get or keep a job. On the other hand, many managers, as well as employees, assumed that the right to join a union carried with it the right *not* to do so. This assumption was changed during World War II, when agreements such as the union shop, the closed shop, and the agency shop became legal.

Under a **union shop** agreement, all employees must join the union within a specified period—usually 30 days after being hired—or be fired. Under a **closed shop** agreement, all prospective employees must be members of the recognized union before they can be employed, and all current employees must join within a specified time in order to retain their jobs. In an **agency shop,** all employees must pay the union dues even if they choose not to join the union. The **maintenance-of-membership clause** says that once an employee joins the union, he or she must maintain that membership as a condition of employment.

union shop All employees must join the union within a specified period.

closed shop All prospective employees must be members of the recognized union before they can be employed.

agency shop All employees must pay union dues even if they choose not to join the union.

maintenance-of-membership clause An employee who has joined the union must maintain that membership as a condition of employment.

✔ SELF-CHECK

Do you have trouble seeing the difference between a union shop and a closed shop? In a union shop, management can employ the people it chooses and then these people must become members of the union. In a closed shop, management must hire the workers sent by the union according to each worker's seniority as a member of the union.

Taft-Hartley Act. Following World War II, with evidence of abuse of power by some union leaders, Congress passed the Labor–Management Relations Act (Taft-Hartley Act). Enacted in 1947, this act greatly changed the Wagner Act, making it more evenhanded, so that unions as well as management could be charged with unfair labor practices.

EXHIBIT 16-4

States with Right-to-Work Laws

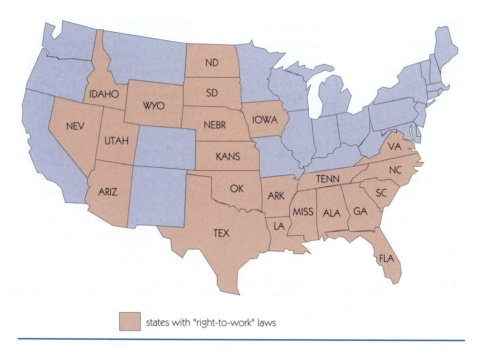

states with "right-to-work" laws

The Taft-Hartley Act prohibited the closed-shop agreement, except in the construction and shipping industries. Also, Section 14(b) of this act gave states the right to pass laws prohibiting the union shop. By 1996, 21 states had used Section 14(b) to pass **right-to-work laws,** which give workers the right to join or refuse to join a union without being fired. The states with right-to-work laws are highlighted in Exhibit 16-4.

right-to-work laws The right of employees to join or refuse to join a union without being fired.

Landrum–Griffin Act. In 1959, Congress passed the Labor–Management Reporting and Disclosure Act (Landrum-Griffin Act) in an effort to prevent corruption and abuse of employees by some union leaders and managers. It provided an **employees' bill of rights,** which protects employees from possible abuse by unscrupulous managers and union leaders.

employees' bill of rights Protects employees from possible abuse by unscrupulous managers and union leaders.

Employees, unions, and employers all have certain specified and implied rights and privileges under the basic labor laws. Exhibit 16-5 contains the rights of employees. Exhibit 16-6 shows what unions may not do, and Exhibit 16-7 lists what employers may not do under these laws.

Administration of Labor Laws

The five-person NLRB has the power to enforce the basic labor laws. The functions of the NLRB are (1) to certify unions as the exclusive bargaining agent for employees and (2) to see that unfair labor practices either are not committed or are punished. Its specific duties are as follows:

- To hold an election to establish the bargaining agent for employees of a given firm.

- To investigate charges of unfair labor practices against the employer or the union.

- To issue complaints against either management or labor.

EXHIBIT **16-5**

Rights of Employees

- To organize.
- To bargain collectively.
- To expect no discrimination against them by management because they are union members.
- To expect no discrimination against them by management if they bring charges of unfair labor practices against the employer.
- To get a job without first being a member of a union.
- Not to have to join a union unless the union and the employer have signed a valid union-shop agreement in one of the states that do not have right-to-work laws.
- Not to be charged exorbitant initiation fees and dues by a union with a valid union-shop agreement.
- To receive financial reports from the union.

EXHIBIT **16-6**

Unfair Labor Practices of Unions

- To coerce employees into or restrain them from engaging in union activities.
- To force management to discriminate against employees in violation of the law.
- To refuse to bargain in good faith.
- To require managers to pay money for work not done.
- To engage in a strike or boycott to force management to commit illegal acts.
- To charge excessive initiation fees and dues where there is a union shop.

■ To prosecute unfair labor practices and determine guilt.

■ To assess fines and prison sentences.

■ To ask federal courts to control activities of both management and labor by citing them for contempt.

Union Principles, Objectives, and Methods of Attaining Objectives

5 Describe union principles and objectives and discuss the methods used to achieve those objectives.

A wise man had seven sons who were intelligent, personable, and otherwise attractive, but they had one common fault—they were constantly fighting and squabbling with one another, even when being attacked by others outside the family. One day, the father decided to teach them a lesson. He called them together, gave each one of them a long wooden stick, and said to each one, in turn, "Break this stick over your knee." Each one of the sons broke his stick with very little effort.

Again, the wise man handed each son a stick, but this time said to them, "Bind the seven sticks together in a bundle." They did as he asked. "Now try to break the sticks," he said to each son as he handed him the bundle. None of them could break the bundle of sticks. "Remember," he said, "in union there is strength."

EXHIBIT **16-7**

Unfair Labor Practices
of Employers

- To interfere with, restrain, or coerce employees who are exercising their rights under the law.
- To dominate or interfere with the forming or administering of unions, or to contribute support to them.
- To discriminate in hiring or in any other terms of employment in such a way as to encourage or discourage membership in a union.
- To discharge or otherwise discriminate against employees for filing charges against the employer or testifying under the law.
- To refuse to bargain with the union representative.

This fable illustrates the truth that the main reason unions exist is to protect individual workers from the economic power of an employer or employer groups. Unions try to achieve certain objectives for their members and follow certain principles to do so.

Samuel Gompers, the AFL's first president, identified the following principles on which unionism is based: (1) strength through unity, (2) equal pay for the same job, and (3) employment practices based on seniority. If any one of these principles is threatened, the union and its members will fight back, as these are cardinal, nonnegotiable beliefs.

These principles of unionism lead to the practical objectives unions have for their members. These goals are (1) higher pay; (2) shorter hours of work on a daily, weekly, or annual basis; (3) improved working conditions, both physical and psychological; and (4) improved security, both of the person and of the job.

How do unions achieve their objectives? The usual methods they use are (1) to organize a firm's employees, (2) to become recognized as the employees' exclusive bargaining agent, (3) to engage in collective bargaining, (4) to go on strike or threaten to strike, and (5) to process grievances. Let us look at each of these methods.

Organizing Employees

union authorization card
Authorizes a particular union to be an employee's collective bargaining representative.

First, the union leader must persuade the employees of a firm to organize and join the union. The union organizer tries to get the employees to sign a **union authorization card,** which states that the employee wants the specified union to be his or her bargaining representative. An example of such a card is shown in Exhibit 16-8.

Things to Do Before the Union Calls. There are many things supervisors and other managers can do to minimize the chances of employees' joining a union—if that's their wish. The most important ones are these:

1. The company and its higher-level managers must pay close attention to supervisors, for they are the key to successful labor relations. Supervisors should receive substantially more pay than their employees. They should also get support from their boss for the orders they give and the decisions they make, because unhappy supervisors can do tremendous harm to an employer's labor relations. Treat supervisors right, keep them well informed, and make them an integral part of the management team.

2. Make sure that no item in the wage–benefit package lags far behind the norm for the area and industry.

3. Improve employee benefits as quickly and as extensively as is feasible.

Samuel Gompers identified the importance of strength through unity, equal pay for equal work, and seniority in relationship to labor unions.

4. Review jobs frequently to see if they need to be upgraded because responsibilities or working conditions have changed.

5. Make sure employee facilities are adequate, safe, well lighted, well ventilated, and reasonably clean.

6. Keep records of good—and bad—performance by employees and have programs for boosting employee performance, loyalty, and morale.

7. Be firm but fair when imposing discipline.

8. Provide a practical release valve, such as a grievance committee, for employee frustrations and complaints.

9. Be alert for any complaints of abuse or favoritism by employees or supervisors.

10. Establish clear-cut lines for two-way communications with all employees.

11. Have clear, definite, and well-communicated work rules, making sure that their wording doesn't violate NLRB or Equal Employment Opportunity (EEO)/Affirmative Action (AA) rules.

12. Use discretion in hiring new employees.

Notice throughout the above list the importance of good supervisory practices. It cannot be said too strongly that first-line supervisors play an integral role in making unions unnecessary!

A classic research study found some marked differences in attitude between pro-union and pro-employer workers. In general, pro-employer workers showed a greater need for achievement, perfection, and success; a higher level of independence; and an identification with management. Pro-union workers showed a greater need for and dependence on attention, sympathy, and support from someone other than themselves. Their achievement level was low, as was their endurance.[5]

EXHIBIT 16-8

Example of a
Representation
Authorization Card

click!
http://www.cwa-union.org

COMMUNICATIONS WORKERS of AMERICA, A.F.L.-C.I.O.

Name _____
(Please Print)   First   Middle   Last

Address _____
                     Street

_____
          City   State   Zip Code

Tel. No. _____ Job Title _____

I am an Employee of _____,

Department _____, Section _____, Shift _____
and I hereby designate the Communications Workers of America, as my
collective bargaining representative.

Date _____ Signature _____

FORM O-100   **REPRESENTATION AUTHORIZATION**
1-77

What the Supervisor Should Do—and Not Do—When the Union Enters. A tactic frequently used to gain recognition is for the union organizer to meet with the supervisor and hand over some signed authorization cards. Then, as illustrated in the chapter preview about the Quality Service firm, the union representative says that he or she represents the workers and asks to be recognized as the workers' exclusive bargaining agent to sign or negotiate a contract.

Most labor-relations specialists suggest that supervisors not touch or examine the cards, for if they do, this action can be construed as acceptance of the union as the workers' agent. Nor should supervisors make any comments to the union representative. If the representative asks, "Are you refusing to recognize the union?" the supervisor should reply, "Any comment concerning the company's position must await full consideration of the matter by higher levels of management." If the representative asks, the supervisor should give the name, address, and telephone number of the company's labor relations manager. Of course, as soon as the representative leaves, the supervisor should inform his or her boss about the visit. Exhibit 16-9 contains some suggestions as to what you *may* legally do when a union tries to organize your employees. Some things you should *not* do are listed in Exhibit 16-10.

Becoming Recognized as the Employees' Exclusive Bargaining Agent

exclusive bargaining agent
Deals exclusively with management over questions of wages, hours, and other terms and conditions of employment.

Once the cards have been signed, the union tries to become recognized as the employees' exclusive bargaining agent. An **exclusive bargaining agent** is the employees' representative who has the exclusive right to deal with management over questions of wages, hours, and other terms and conditions of employment. A certified union has the sole right and legal responsibility to represent all of the employees—nonunion members as well as union members—in their dealings with management.

- Keep outside organizers off premises.
- Inform employees from time to time of the benefits they presently enjoy. (Avoid veiled promises or threats.)
- Inform employees that signing a union authorization card does not mean they must vote for the union if there is an election.
- Inform employees of the disadvantages of belonging to the union, such as the possibility of strikes, serving on a picket line, dues, fines, assessments, and rule by cliques or one individual.
- Inform employees that you prefer to deal with them rather than have the union or any other outsider settle grievances.
- Tell employees what you think about unions and about union policies.
- Inform employees about any prior experience you have had with unions and whatever you know about the union officials trying to organize them.
- Inform employees that the law permits you to hire a new employee to replace any employee who goes on strike for economic reasons.
- Inform employees that no union can obtain more than you as an employer are able to give.
- Inform employees how their wages and benefits compare with those in unionized or nonunionized concerns where wages are lower and benefits are less desirable.
- Inform employees that the local union probably will be dominated by the international union, and that they, the members, will have little say in its operations.
- Inform employees of any untrue or misleading statements made by the organizer. You may give employees corrections of these statements.
- Inform employees of any known racketeering or other undesirable elements that may be active in the union.
- Give opinions on the unions and union leaders, even in derogatory terms.
- Distribute information about unions such as disclosures of congressional committees.
- Reply to union attacks on company policies or practices.
- Give the legal position on labor–management matters.
- Advise employees of their legal rights, provided you do not engage in or finance an employee suit or proceeding.
- Declare a fixed policy in opposition to compulsory union membership contracts.
- Campaign against a union seeking to represent the employees.
- Insist that no solicitation of membership or discussion of union affairs be conducted during working time.
- Administer discipline, layoff, and grievance procedures without regard to union membership or nonmembership of the employees involved.
- Treat both union and nonunion employees alike in making assignments of preferred work or desired overtime.
- Enforce plant rules impartially, regardless of the employee's membership activity in a union.
- Tell employees, if they ask, that they are free to join or not to join any organization, so far as their status with the company is concerned.
- Tell employees that their personal and job security will be determined by the economic prosperity of the company.

Source: Leon C. Megginson et al., *Successful Small Business Management,* 6th ed. (Homewood, IL: Richard D. Irwin, 1991). pp. 821–822. Reprinted by permission of The McGraw-Hill Companies.

Management may voluntarily recognize the union or may be forced to accept it because of the union's superior bargaining strength. Ordinarily, a secret-ballot election is conducted by the NLRB when requested by the union or the company. If 30 percent or more of the eligible employees sign authorization cards or a petition requesting a representation election, the NLRB will conduct one. If a majority of the voting employees vote for the union, it is named the exclusive representative of the employees in their dealings with management.

Appeals Used by Union Organizers. The technique most commonly employed by union organizers to obtain union recognition is to compare the target company's practices to items in contracts that the union has with other companies, perhaps in an entirely different industry. If the terms of employment in the target company lag far behind, the union has a ready-made argument. Of course, the organizer will focus on those parts of the wage–benefit package that will make the employer look bad.

EXHIBIT 16-10

Things Supervisors May Not Do When a Union Tries to Organize Their Company

- Engage in surveillance of employees to determine who is and who is not participating in the union program; attend union meetings or engage in any undercover activities for this purpose.
- Threaten, intimidate, or punish employees who engage in union activity.
- Request information from employees about union matters, meetings, etc. Employees may, of their own volition, give such information without prompting. You may listen but not ask questions.
- Prevent employee union representatives from soliciting memberships during nonworking time.
- Grant wage increases, special concessions, or promises of any kind to keep the union out.
- Question a prospective employee about his or her affiliation with a labor organization.
- Threaten to close up or move the plant, curtail operations, or reduce employee benefits.
- Engage in any discriminatory practices, such as work assignments, overtime, layoffs, promotions, wage increases, or any other actions that could be regarded as preferential treatment for certain employees.
- Discriminate against union people when disciplining employees for a specific action, while permitting nonunion employees to go unpunished for the same action.
- Transfer workers on the basis of teaming up nonunion employees to separate them from union employees.
- Deviate in any way from company policies for the primary purpose of eliminating a union employee.
- Intimate, advise, or indicate in any way that unionization will force the company to lay off employees, take away company benefits or privileges enjoyed, or make any other changes that could be regarded as a curtailment of privileges.
- Make statements to the effect that you will not deal with a union.
- Give any financial support or other assistance to employees who support or oppose the union.
- Visit the homes of employees to urge them to oppose or reject the union in its campaign.
- Be a party to any petition or circular against the union or encourage employees to circulate such a petition.
- Make any promises of promotions, benefits, wage increases, or any other items that would induce employees to oppose the union.
- Engage in discussions or arguments that may lead to physical encounters with employees over the union question.
- Use a third party to threaten or coerce a union member, or attempt to influence any employee's vote through this medium.
- Question employees on whether or not they have been affiliated or signed with the union.
- Use the word *never* in any predictions or attitudes about unions or their promises or demands.
- Talk about tomorrow. When you give examples or reasons, you can talk about yesterday or today instead of tomorrow, to avoid making a prediction or conviction which may be interpreted as a threat or promise by the union or the NLRB.

Source: Leon C. Megginson et al., *Successful Small Business Management,* 6th ed. (Homewood, IL: Richard D. Irwin, 1991). pp. 823–824. Reprinted by permission of The McGraw-Hill Companies.

Union organizers appeal to five main desires of employees:

1. *Job protection.* Unions stress that they continually try to ensure that employees have a job—or at least an income—for a lifetime. With most employees already enjoying generous benefits, many seem more interested in job security than in higher pay rates. But there are exceptions to this generalization.

   Unionized employees at an Alcoa plant in Mobile, Alabama, voted to permit the plant to close rather than take cuts in income and benefits. They received quite high unemployment compensation, as well as supplemental payments from the company, for 3 years.

2. *Interference running.* Unions assure employees that they will act as their agents in grievances and disputes. They will go to bat for employees, and they claim to have the know-how to protect employees' interests.

AP Photo/Peter Cosgrove

Union activity in this country has varied considerably, ranging from peaceful negotiations that resolve quickly to strident, impassioned disagreements that take place over a long period of time.

3. *Participation in management.* Unions insist that they can and will give employees a greater voice in deciding the policies, procedures, and rules that affect them and the work they do.

4. *Economic gains.* Higher wages, reduced hours, and better benefits are still at the top of an organizer's checklist.

5. *Recognition and participation.* Knowing that pro-union workers need and are dependent on attention, sympathy, and support, union organizers promise employees that they'll have greater recognition and participation through union activities.

Additional Precautions for Supervisors. Besides observing the "do's" and "don'ts" given in Exhibits 16-9 and 16-10, management should make sure there is nothing in personnel policies and work rules that the NLRB can construe as being anti-union. For example, suppose a company has the following sign displayed: "No solicitation at this company." *This prohibition can actually be ruled an unfair labor practice unless it is enforced against all types of solicitation—even by charitable groups—not just union organizing.* A company is obliged to permit solicitation and distribution of literature by union organizers in nonwork areas such as locker rooms and parking lots. Of course, managers can prohibit nonemployees from being on company property at any time.

Next, supervisors and anyone else in a position to reward or punish voting employees should stay away from the voting area during a representation election.

Finally, neither threat of reprisal nor any promise of reward should be given before the election, although it is permissible to tell employees what has happened at other plants where workers unionized—if it is factual.

Engaging in Collective Bargaining

Once the union has been recognized as the employees' bargaining agent, it starts negotiating with management to try to reach an agreement (which in effect is a contract between the company and the union). Legally, **collective bargaining** is the process by which (1) representatives of the employer and the employees (2) meet at reasonable times and places (3) to confer in good faith (4) over wages, hours, and other terms and conditions of employment. Note that the representatives of the two parties are only required to meet in a "reasonable place," usually a conference room at a hotel or motel, and at a "reasonable time," usually the firm's normal daily working hours. They must negotiate "in good faith" by making valid offers and counteroffers about any question involving wages, hours, and other "terms and conditions of employment." Once an agreement has been reached, both parties must have the opportunity to sign it if they want to—which they usually do.

It's a "must" that supervisors be consulted at each step of this bargaining procedure. They should carefully examine every union proposal—and management counterproposal—to see how they would affect the supervisors' relationships with the employees. Also, supervisors should be consulted about concessions to be asked of the union negotiators.

If no agreement is reached, an impasse develops. At this point there are three alternatives: (1) to call in an outside **mediator,** provided by the Federal Mediation and Conciliation Service, who will bring the parties together and try to help them reach an agreement; (2) to agree to bring the issue to an outside **arbitrator,** who will make a decision that will be binding on both parties; or (3) for the union to go on strike or for management to stage a lockout.

Conducting a Strike or Lockout

The ultimate strategy used by unions to achieve their objectives is the strike. A **strike** occurs when employees withhold their services from an employer in order to achieve a goal. The employees tell the public why they are striking by means of **picketing**—walking back and forth outside the place of employment, usually carrying signs.

It cannot be emphasized too strongly that most union leaders *do not like to use the strike.* It is costly, it carries a certain stigma for those walking the picket line, and it is potentially dangerous to the union because of the possible loss of membership and power if the strike fails. In fact, only a very small percentage of the thousands of contract negotiations conducted annually result in strikes. Although the strike itself is the ultimate device in collective bargaining and is the technique resorted to when all other methods of resolving differences fail, the *threat of a strike* is a continuing factor in almost all negotiations. Both the union and the employer frequently act as if one could occur.

Just as the union can call a strike if it isn't satisfied with the progress of negotiations, so can management stage a lockout. A **lockout** is closing company premises to the employees and refusing to let them enter in order to resume work.

Reaching an Agreement

When an accord has been reached, a document is prepared that becomes the **agreement** or **contract** among the company, the union, and the workers. It usually contains clauses covering at least the following areas:

1. Union recognition
2. Wages
3. Vacation and holidays
4. Working conditions
5. Layoffs and rehiring
6. Management prerogatives
7. Hours of work

8. Seniority

9. Arbitration

10. Renewal clause

Specifics are set forth in each of these areas, and rules are established that should be obeyed by management and the union. The management prerogatives clause defines the areas in which supervisors have the right to act, free from questioning or joint action by the union.

Living with the Agreement

6 Name three things that a supervisor must know in order to live with the union agreement.

Once the agreement has been signed, managers and supervisors have to live with the contract until it is time to negotiate a new one. Therefore, all management personnel—especially first-level supervisors—should be thoroughly briefed on its contents. The meaning and interpretation of each clause should be reviewed, and the wording of the contract should be clearly understood. Supervisors' questions should be answered to better prepare them to deal with labor-relations matters. Also, it should be impressed on supervisors that their counterpart—the union steward—will probably be better trained, know the contract provisions in greater detail, and be better equipped in the practice of contract administration.

Supervisors' Rights under the Agreement

Supervisors should view the agreement as the rules of the game, for it spells out what they may and may not do. They should take a positive view of what they *may do* rather than a negative one of what they *may not do*. Although agreements differ in detail, most give supervisors the following rights:

1. To decide what work is to be done.

2. To decide how, when, and where it will be done.

3. To determine how many workers are needed to do the work safely.

4. To decide who will do each job, as long as the skill classifications and seniority provisions are observed.

5. To instruct, supervise, correct, and commend employees in the performance of their work.

6. To require that work performance and on-the-job personal behavior meet minimum standards.

7. To recommend promotions and pay increases, as long as they do not violate the union agreement.

8. To administer discipline according to the agreed-upon procedure.

See Exhibits 16-9 and 16-10 for a more definitive list of "do's" and "don'ts" for supervisors.

If uncertain as to their authority, supervisors should check with the firm's human resources or labor relations experts. Supervisors need to have a working knowledge of the agreement's details because the employees and their advocate, the union steward, will be aware of these details.

✔ **SELF-CHECK**

Would you rather be a supervisor in a unionized or a nonunionized company? Why?

The Supervisor and the Union Steward

The **union steward,** a union member who has been elected by other members to represent their interests in relations with management, is the supervisor's counterpart. He or she is the link between the workers and their union and between the union and the company, especially in case of controversy. The supervisor represents the company and its interests to workers, who play the dual roles of employees of the company and members of the union. The steward represents the union's position to the workers and to the company. The steward is at the same level in the union hierarchy as the supervisor is in the company hierarchy.

As equals, the steward and the supervisor must maintain production operations within the framework of the agreement. Frequently, the goals of the steward and the supervisor conflict, for the supervisor's job is to obtain maximum productivity, whereas the steward's aim is to protect the workers' interests—including not working too hard and not working themselves out of a job.

The Role of Seniority

One of the most basic union principles is **seniority,** which means that workers who have been on the job the longest get preferred treatment and better benefits. One of the supervisor's greatest challenges is to maintain high productivity while assigning work, especially preferred jobs and overtime, to the most senior employee, who is not necessarily the most capable worker. Also, whom does the supervisor recommend for promotion—the most capable worker or the most senior employee? These issues, plus discipline, lead to most grievances against supervisors.

Handling Employee Complaints

In unionized companies, employees' complaints take the form of grievances. The **grievance procedure** is a formal way of handling these complaints. In nonunionized companies, employees may present their complaints to their supervisors for proper disposition.

Grievance Procedures. Exhibit 16-11 shows a typical grievance procedure, such as is usually found in unionized organizations. The form and substance of the grievance procedure depend on several factors:

1. The type of industry (the old-line, "smokestack" industries, such as steel, auto, and transportation, have the most formal and rigid procedures).

2. The size and structure of the organization (the larger, more highly structured organizations have the most formal and inflexible procedures).

3. The type of union (the older, craft-oriented unions tend to have a highly structured procedure).

There are usually five steps in a formal grievance procedure in a unionized organization. However, the *actual* number of steps taken will depend on the number of managerial levels in the organization and whether or not the grievance is submitted to arbitration.

1. Step 1 begins when an employee complains to the supervisor about a presumed wrong. From the employee's viewpoint, the supervisor may be violating the labor agreement or doing something that dissatisfies the employee. If the supervisor straightens out the matter satisfactorily, that's the end of the grievance.

2. Frequently, though, the issue is not resolved, so the employee goes to the union steward to present a grievance. The steward then tries to obtain satisfaction from the supervisor. This is step 2. The vast majority of grievances are settled at this stage.

3. In step 3, the union committee person or business agent tries to resolve the complaint with middle management, such as a department head.

EXHIBIT **16-11**

Typical Grievance
Procedure in a Unionized
Organization

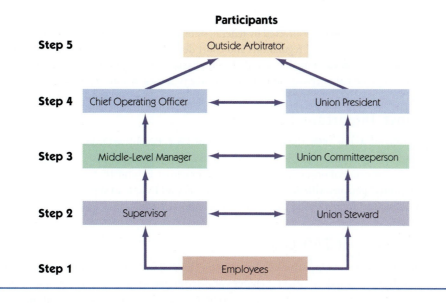

Participants

	Participants

4. In step 4, the union president and the chief operating officer try to resolve the difference. If they succeed, that ends the grievance.

5. If the chief operating officer and the union president cannot resolve the grievance, it is submitted to outside arbitration. A mutually agreed upon arbitrator makes the decision. This is Step 5.

Complaint Procedures in Nonunionized Organizations. Many nonunion organizations have formal complaint procedures that are comparable in many ways to the formal union grievance procedures. These procedures permit complaints to go beyond the supervisor to committees composed of higher-level executives, including the personnel officer and sometimes even top executives. However, they do not provide for arbitration, since the primary purpose of these procedures is to ensure fairness in employee relations and to improve employee attitudes, rather than to interpret human resources policies and practices. Such procedures are frequently found in public organizations such as government agencies.

Supervisors can improve employee–employer relationships if they understand the types of employees who are prone to file complaints or grievances. For example, an early study found that the more sensitive people are, the more apt they are to file. Young employees who are well educated but not well paid tend to file grievances, as do employees who have not been with the company long but are military veterans.[6] Supervisors have two alternatives for dealing with employees of these types. In some cases they may try to avoid hiring them; alternatively, they can try to find ways to accommodate them.

Caution Needed in Terminations

Supervisors at one time had the right to terminate, or "fire," an employee in a nonunionized company "at will," that is, without having to show cause or even give a reason.

However, subsequent legislation, union bargaining, and court decisions have largely eliminated that practice. Now an employer must offer a valid, documented reason for such action.

7
State the laws providing equal employment opportunity for protected groups of employees.

Complying with Equal Employment Opportunity (EEO) Laws

All aspects of employment are affected by federal, state, and local laws, regulations, and court decisions. Some of the federal regulations and court decisions, and their effects on recruiting and selection, are now explained. It should be emphasized at this point, however, that EEO laws build on—and enhance—good human resource practices by most employers.

The Most Important EEO Laws

The Civil Rights Act of 1866, the Civil Rights Act of 1964, Executive Order 11246, the Civil Rights Act of 1991, and other legislation prohibit discrimination based on race, color, religion, sex, or national origin in all employment practices. Exhibit 16-12 shows additional laws that protect persons with disabilities, older workers, and Vietnam veterans. It also shows the laws' basic requirements and the agencies that enforce them.

Enforcement of EEO Laws

affirmative action programs (AAPs) Programs to put the principle of equal employment opportunity into practice.

The Equal Employment Opportunity Commission (EEOC) is the primary agency enforcing EEO laws. It receives and investigates charges of discrimination, issues orders to stop violations, and may even go to a U.S. District Court to enforce its decrees. The commission encourages **affirmative action programs (AAPs),** which are plans to put the principle of equal employment opportunity into practice. These programs are required by the Office of Federal Contract Compliance Programs (OFCCP) in the Labor Department, which enforces Executive Order 11246; by the Vocational Rehabilitation Act; and by the Vietnam Era Veterans' Assistance Act.

In essence, an organization, through an AAP, promises to do the following:

1. Make good-faith efforts to recruit from diverse groups (which include women, African-Americans, Hispanics, Vietnam-era veterans, native Americans, people with disabilities, and older workers) through state employment services.

2. Limit the questions that are asked of applicants on their application forms or during interviews (see Exhibit 15-2).

3. Set goals and timetables for hiring the protected groups.

4. Avoid testing applicants unless the tests meet established guidelines.

Workplace Harassment

From 1993 to 1999, each year an average of 1.7 million U.S. workers were victims of violent crime based on a Bureau of Justice Statistics (BJS) report. Nineteen percent of these incidents were aggravated assaults; 75 percent were simple assaults. For the same time period, over 800 workplace homicides occurred yearly according to the Bureau of Labor Statistics' Census of Fatal Occupational Injuries.[7] Violence at work may occur for a variety of reasons, including prejudice and discrimination, work-related stress, personality differences, as well as non–work-related,

Laws	Basic Requirements	Coverage	Enforcement Agencies
Section 1981 of Civil Rights Act of 1866	Prohibits racial discrimination in employment.	All private employers, labor unions, and employment agencies	Judicial system
Title VII of Civil Rights Act of 1964	Prohibits employment discrimination based on race, color, religion, sex, or national origin.	Private employers engaged in interstate commerce with 15 or more employees, labor unions, employment agencies, federal government workers, and state and local government workers	Equal Employment Opportunity Commission (EEOC)
Executive Order 11246 of 1965, as amended	Prohibits employment discrimination based on race, sex, color, religion,or national origin, and requires contractors employing 50 or more workers to develop affirmative action plans (AAPs) when contracts exceed $50,000 a year.	Federal contractors and subcontractors holding contracts of $10,000 or more	U.S. Department of Labor's Office of Federal Contract Compliance Programs (OFCCP)
Age Discrimination in Employment Act of 1967, as amended	Prohibits employment discrimination against persons over age 40.	Same as those under Title VII, except that private employers with 20 or more employees are covered	EEOC
Vocational Rehabilitation Act of 1973	Prohibits employment discrimination against otherwise qualified handicapped persons, requires reasonable accommodation, and requires development of AAPs.	Federal contractors and subcontractors holding contracts in excess of $2,500, organizations that receive federal assistance, and federal agencies	OFCCP
Vietnam Era Veterans' Assistance Act of 1974	Requires contractors to develop AAPs to recruit and employ qualified disabled veterans and veterans of the Vietnam War.	Federal contractors and subcontractors holding contracts in excess of $10,000	OFCCP
Immigration Reform and Control Act of 1986	Prohibits recruiting, hiring, or referring aliens who are not eligible to work in the United States; prohibits employment discrimination based on national origin or citizenship.	Private employers, labor unions, and employment agencies	U.S. Department of Justice's Special Counsel for Unfair Immigration-Related Employment
Americans with Disabilities Act of 1990	Prohibits employment discrimination against qualified individuals with a disability and requires reasonable accommodation.	Same as Title VII	EEOC
Civil Rights Act of 1991	Amends Title VII and the Americans with Disabilities Act to allow for punitive and compensatory damages in cases of intentional discrimination and more extensive use of jury trials.	Same as Title VII	EEOC

Source: Various government and private publications.

personal problems. The end-of-the-chapter case (Case 16-2) explores the causes and ramifications of workplace harassment and the need for managers to be proactive in addressing issues at work.

Sexual Harassment

A particularly perplexing area of concern for supervisors and their managers is how to handle the problem of fair and equal treatment of women. At one time sexually oriented "kidding" between supervisors and their employees was of no concern to management. Needless to say, this is no longer true! Instead, such verbal activities would now probably be considered sexual harassment.

On June 22, 1999, the U.S. Supreme Court ruled that "victims of workplace sex discrimination can win punitive damages from employers even if the boss's behavior was not 'egregious.'"[8] Federal law now permits victims of such workplace bias to recover punitive damages of up to $300,000 from the employer, in addition to any actual losses—such as lost wages. In the 1999 discussion, the Court said that "employers can defend themselves against such damages if they can show they made a sincere effort to prevent sex discrimination."

sexual harassment
Unwelcome sexual advances that create a hostile, offensive, or intimidating work environment.

The EEOC's *Guidelines on Discrimination Because of Sex* defines **sexual harassment** as unwelcome sexual advances, requests for sexual favors, and other physical *or* verbal conduct, by a member of either sex, when such actions result in one of several consequences. Those consequences are (1) submission to the conduct is made, either implicitly or explicitly, a condition of employment; (2) submission to, or rejection of, the request(s) is used in making employment decisions involving the employee; or (3) the purpose or effect of such conduct is to unreasonably interfere with the employee's work performance or create a hostile, offensive, or intimidating work environment.[9]

Supervisors and their managers should take strong, quick, and positive measures to discourage sexual harassment, because *employers are responsible for such harassment by, or of, their employees.* Such measures should include express declarations against sexual harassment that are regularly—and clearly—communicated to all employees, and those statements should be quickly and effectively implemented. Also, internal procedures for conducting immediate, thorough, and impartial investigations should be well established and publicized. One way to ensure that such investigations are impartial is to have someone—a lawyer or an

Companies must take measures against sexual harassment and regularly communicate their policies about it.

Digital Vision/Getty Images

employment specialist—from outside the organization to conduct them.[10] Today, sexual harassment litigation is a big business with thousands of cases a year filed at the EEOC. Since 1995, dollars paid in EEOC settlements have more than doubled, reaching $53 million in 2001.[11] The EEOC rigorously explores these sexual harassment charges, and, when guilt is determined, the penalties are steep, as the following example illustrates.

> On June 23, 2003, the Equal Employment Opportunity Commission (EEOC) announced that a jury in Federal District Court in Tampa, Florida, had returned a $1,550,000 verdict in a major sexual harassment lawsuit brought by the EEOC and the private law firm of Florin, Roebig & Walker, P.A. The lawsuit was originally brought against Applebee's International, Inc., Rio Bravo International, Inc., and Innovative Restaurant Concepts, Inc., for sexual harassment (of five former waitresses and hostesses) occurring from approximately 1994 until early 1998 at their formerly owned Rio Bravo Cantina Restaurant in Clearwater, Florida.[12]

Other Legal Issues

Up to this point we have discussed several legal issues dealing with labor–management relations, as well as equal opportunity laws. Now, we need to explain some other important supervisory responsibilities, including employee benefits, the comparable worth issue, and other factors affecting wage rates.

Legally Required Benefits

Employers are required by law to provide all employees with Social Security and Medicare, workers' compensation, and unemployment insurance. Also, some employers must provide certain employees with family and medical leave. Each of these types of legally required benefits is explained in the following paragraphs.

Social Security and Medicare. The Social Security system is in reality two separate systems. One provides retirement benefits for workers, and the other provides disability, survivors', and Medicare benefits. To be eligible for the program, a worker must have contributed taxes into the system for 10 years (or 40 quarters).

Benefits are financed by a payroll tax paid by both employer and employee. The tax rate, the earnings base on which it is paid, and the benefits are subject to frequent congressional changes. The Social Security tax rate for 2003 was 6.2 percent of the first $87,000 of an employee's earnings, with both the employer and the employee paying that amount. In addition, there is a Medicare tax of 1.45 percent on *all earnings*.

Workers' Compensation. All states have passed laws requiring workers' compensation. These laws protect employees and their families from permanent loss of income and high medical payments as a consequence of accidental injury, illness, or death resulting from the job. The amount to be paid for a given condition, such as loss of a hand or an arm, is stipulated in the law.

Workers' compensation funds are provided primarily through employer contributions to a statewide fund. Employers may purchase insurance from private insurance companies to supplement these state funds. In general, employees are able to recover all medical expenses and up to two-thirds of the income loss due to disability or missed work.

Unemployment Insurance. In most states, unemployment insurance laws require that the government provide unemployed workers with benefits from a fund of payroll taxes imposed on employers. The amount paid into the fund by employers varies according to the unemployment rate within the state and the employer's record of unemployment or **experience rating.** To receive benefits under the law, the unemployed worker is required to register for employment

8

Describe the most commonly provided employee benefits.

experience rating
Determining, from the record of unemployed workers, the amount the employer must pay into the state's unemployment insurance fund.

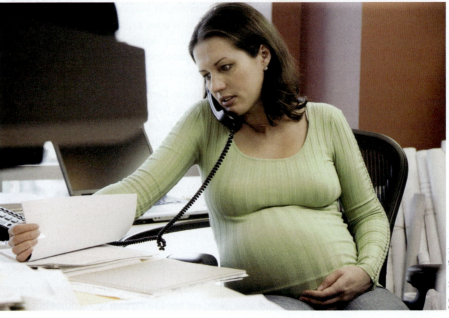

The Family and Medical Leave Act requires an employer to provide up to 12 weeks of unpaid leave for the birth of a child.

© Don Mason/Corbis

at the state employment office and usually must have worked for a certain length of time before becoming unemployed.

Family and Medical Leave. The Family and Medical Leave Act of 1993 required employers with 50 or more employees within a 75-mile radius of the home office to offer employees—except *key* employees—up to 12 weeks of unpaid leave during a 12-month period for (1) the birth of a child; (2) placement of a child for adoption or foster care; (3) caring for a spouse, child, or parent with a serious health condition; or (4) the employee's serious health condition. The employer must continue providing health care coverage during the absence and place the employee in the same or a comparable position upon return.

The Comparable Worth Issue

In spite of the Equal Pay Act of 1963, which prohibits unequal pay for men and women doing the same job, women are often still paid substantially less than men for *similar* jobs. There is much controversy as to the cause of this disparity. The problem, according to advocates of "pay equity," goes far beyond equal pay for the same job. The real issue is this: *Are women being systematically underpaid for work that requires the same skills, knowledge, and responsibility as similar jobs performed by men?*

comparable worth or pay equity Jobs with equal points for the amount of education, effort, skills, and responsibility have equal pay.

Advocates say the solution lies in a system of **comparable worth,** or **pay equity,** in which a formula is used to assign points for the amount of education, effort, skills, and responsibility required for an individual job.[13] These points are then used, along with job evaluation, to set salary rates. Critics say such wage adjustments would destroy the market forces of supply and demand. The arguments of advocates and critics of comparable worth are shown in Exhibit 16-13.

✔ SELF-CHECK

Do you think jobs of comparable worth should receive comparable pay? Which arguments in Exhibit 16-14 do you accept and why?

EXHIBIT **16-13**

Should Jobs of
"Comparable Worth"
Receive Comparable Pay?

Some women's groups believe that the principle of equal pay for work of equal value has been violated in that whole classes of jobs—such as those in the clerical area—are undervalued because they have traditionally been held by women. They want this practice changed so that pay for all jobs will be based on their value to the business or community, rather than on who holds the jobs.

The arguments *for* comparable pay for comparable work are as follows:

1. If one employee contributes as much to the firm as another, the two should be paid the same.
2. It is needed to raise women's pay, which is now only about 65 percent of men's.
3. It will give women greater internal job mobility.
4. This is one way to further women's career ambitions.
5. It would motivate women to be more productive.

The arguments *against* comparable pay are:

1. Federal law only requires equal pay for equal jobs.
2. It violates a firm's structured job evaluation system.
3. Employers must pay salaries competitive with those of other employers, which are based on what employees produce and on the economic value of the work performed.
4. Women receive less than men because two-thirds of new employees are women, and they always receive less than more senior employees.
5. It is practically impossible to determine accurately the real value of a job.

Source: Leon C. Megginson, Geralyn M. Franklin, and M. Jane Byrd, *Human Resource Management* (Houston: Dame Publications, 1995), p. 404.

Factors Affecting Wage Rates

What most employers think they *should* pay is "competitive wages," but some specific factors affect what they actually pay. Most of these factors relate to what employers *have* to pay, but a final factor is what they are *able* to pay. The most important of these factors are government factors and collective bargaining.

Governmental Factors. Governmental laws, rules, and regulations largely determine what an employer *has to pay* workers. Some of these laws are the Fair Labor Standards Act, commonly called the Wage and Hour Law; the Walsh-Healey Act; the Davis-Bacon Act; the Equal Pay Act; and various EEO/AA laws, such as the Civil Rights Act, the Vocational Rehabilitation Act, the Americans with Disabilities Act, and the Vietnam Era Veterans' Assistance Act.

The Fair Labor Standards Act covers all employees working in interstate commerce, all federal employees, and some state employees. Some employees, referred to as **exempt employees,** including executives, administrative and professional employees, outside sales personnel, and other selected groups, are not covered by the provisions of this law. All other employees, called **nonexempt employees,** are covered and must be paid at least the basic minimum wage. If employees work over 40 hours in a given workweek, they must be paid one and a half times their regular rate of pay for each hour worked over 40 hours. However, there are provisions for employing full-time students at rates lower than the minimum wage. This law also prevents child labor. Age 14 is the minimum working age for most nonfarm jobs. On nonhazardous jobs, persons of age 14 and 15 can work no more than 3 hours on a school day, 8 hours on any other day, or 40 hours per week. Those who are 16 and 17 years old can work in nonhazardous jobs for unlimited hours.

exempt employees Not covered by the provisions of the Fair Labor Standards Act.

nonexempt employees Covered by the provisions of the Fair Labor Standards Act.

The Davis-Bacon Act and the Walsh-Healey Act have different provisions. Construction firms with government contracts or subcontracts in excess of $2,000 are covered by the Davis-Bacon Act; other employers with government contracts exceeding $10,000 are covered by the Walsh-Healey Act. These acts differ from the Fair Labor Standards Act in two aspects. First, the actual rate of pay is set by the Secretary of Labor. This rate of pay is called the **prevailing wage rate** in the area and approximates the union wage scale for the area in the given type of work. A second difference is that overtime is paid at "time and a half" for all hours worked over 8 hours in a given day as well as over 40 hours in a given week.

Public policy now prohibits discrimination in pay unless it is based on performance. For example, the Equal Pay Act prohibits different rates of pay for men and women doing the same type of work. Title VII of the Civil Rights Act prevents discrimination based on race, color, religion, sex, or national origin. The Age Discrimination in Employment Act prohibits discrimination against persons 40 years of age and older. Finally, the Vocational Rehabilitation Act and Americans with Disabilities Act prohibit discrimination against persons with handicaps.

Collective Bargaining. When unions are involved, basic wages, job differentials, individual rates of pay, and employee benefits tend to be determined through the collective bargaining process. The actual amount of compensation is determined by the relative strength of the union and the employer. However, even nonunionized employers are affected by the wage rates and the amounts of benefits paid by unionized firms.

prevailing wage rate
Approximates the union wage scale for the area in the given type of work.

CHAPTER REVIEW

1 Explain what is meant by labor relations.
Labor relations, which are the relationships between employers and their unionized employees, are particularly important to supervisors, for they are the managers who must deal with operative employees on a day-to-day basis. An employer usually has good labor relations if the supervisors have good relationships with employees.

2 Trace the development of unions in the United States.
Union activities grew slowly in the United States until the formation of the AFL. Then membership increased steadily until after World War I, when it leveled off. Membership mushroomed during the period from 1935 to 1950, when favorable laws were passed and industrial unions became popular. Since then, union membership has grown more slowly so that now only 13.9 percent of all employees, and only 9.5 percent of private employees, are members of a union.

3 Explain why union membership is declining.
Some of the reasons for declining interest in unions among U.S. employees are (1) the economy has shifted from manufacturing jobs, which are relatively easy to unionize, to service work, which is more difficult to organize; (2) today's more educated and technologically oriented service workers are more interested in empowerment-type activities; (3) the global economy is forcing U.S. companies to cut costs by resisting organizing drives; (4) the influx of part-time workers resists unionization; and (5) the proliferation of small businesses makes organizing more difficult.

4 Name and explain some of the basic laws governing labor relations.
The basic law governing labor relations is the Wagner Act, which gives workers the right to freely join unions of their choosing and to engage in concerted actions to achieve

their goals. The Taft-Hartley Act prohibits the closed shop and provides for states to pass right-to-work laws prohibiting the union shop. The Landrum-Griffin Act provides employees with a bill of rights that protects them from exploitation by unscrupulous management and union leaders. These laws are administered by the NLRB, the Federal Mediation and Conciliation Service (FMCS), and the U.S. Department of Labor. The NLRB tries to prevent both unions and management from engaging in unfair labor practices.

5 **Describe union principles and objectives and discuss the methods used to achieve those objectives.**

Union objectives are higher pay, shorter hours of work, improved working conditions, and improved personal and job security. To achieve those objectives, unions organize (or recruit) an employer's workers into a union, then try to become recognized as their exclusive bargaining agent in dealing with management, usually through an NLRB-conducted, secret-ballot election. Unions have greater difficulty organizing employees in firms that have effective supervisors and good employee relations. Management can try to keep the union out as long as its policies and actions stay within the law. When the union becomes the bargaining agent, it bargains collectively with representatives of management over wages, hours, and the other terms and conditions of employment. Supervisors are critical to success at this point, so they should help formulate demands to be made of the union, evaluate proposals made by the union bargaining team, and be kept informed of progress made in the negotiations.

If the two parties cannot agree and reach an impasse, there are several options: (1) they can call in an outside mediator, (2) they can agree to send the issue to an arbitrator, who will make a binding decision, or (3) the union can conduct a strike, or management can stage a lockout. Most negotiations end with an agreement, which becomes the contract between management and the employees.

6 **Name three things that a supervisor must know in order to live with the union agreement.**

It is then up to the supervisor to live with the contract. Disagreements over interpretation of the agreement are settled through the grievance procedure. If agreement is not reached within the company, the issue goes to an arbitrator for resolution. Supervisors by and large can no longer terminate an employee without a valid, documented reason.

7 **State the laws providing equal employment opportunity for protected groups of employees.**

Minorities, women, older workers, persons with disabilities, and Vietnam veterans are protected by various laws and regulations. The EEOC is the primary agency for enforcing these laws.

8 **Describe the most commonly provided employee benefits.**

Employee benefits are noncash forms of compensation. Those that employers are legally required to provide are (1) Social Security and Medicare, (2) workers' compensation, (3) unemployment insurance, and (4) family and medical leave.

IMPORTANT TERMS

affirmative action programs (AAPs)
agency shop
agreement or contract
arbitrator
closed shop
collective bargaining
comparable worth
or pay equity
craft unions
employee associations
employees' bill of rights
exclusive bargaining agent
exempt employees
experience rating
grievance procedure
industrial unions
labor relations or union–
management relations
or industrial relations
labor union
lockout
maintenance-of-
membership clause
mediator
nonexempt employees
picketing
prevailing wage rate
right-to-work laws
seniority
sexual harassment
strike
unfair labor practices
union authorization card
union shop
union steward

QUESTIONS FOR REVIEW AND DISCUSSION

1. Define labor relations.

2. When did unions grow the fastest? Why?

3. Why has union growth slowed?

4. How do you interpret the union membership trends shown in Exhibits 16-1 and 16-2?

5. Do you believe that union power will increase or decrease in the future? Why?

6. Name the laws that form the legal basis for labor relations, and explain their general provisions.

7. What are the differences among the union shop, the closed shop, and the agency shop? Are these differences really significant? Explain.

8. What are "unfair labor practices," and what are some unfair labor practices that management sometimes commits?

9. What are some unfair labor practices that unions sometimes commit?

10. What are the primary objectives of unions?

11. What are the methods used by unions to achieve their objectives?

12. What provisions are usually included in a labor agreement?

13. Describe the typical grievance procedure.

14. Why has "termination at will" declined as a management tool?

15. How do EEO laws affect recruiting and selecting of employees?

16. Name and describe the four legally required employee benefits.

Skill Builder 16-1

The Union Organizer

Refer to the chapter preview and assume that you are Marvin Wiley and are trying to get the employees of Quality Service to organize and vote for your union. What would you do? How would you go about getting the 13 employees who voted against the union (and any new ones) to sign authorization cards and vote for the union?

Skill Builder 16-2

Would You Sign a Union Authorization Card?

Assume that you encounter the following independent situations.

Situation A: You are 30 years old and have a job paying $8.50 per hour. Because of your personal situation, this is a fairly good job for you and will probably be the best job you can hold. Your spouse also does similar work at the company, so your combined income is about $34,000 per year (2,000 hours per person per year $\times$ $8.50/hour $\times$ 2 persons). Some of the workers are talking about joining a union.

Situation B: You hear that some layoffs have recently been made to improve company profits. You also know that about once a month someone is injured.

Answer the following questions:

1. Would you sign a union authorization card in Situation A? Why or why not?

2. Would you sign a union authorization card in Situation B? Why or why not?

Source: H. Giles Schmid, Winona State University. Reprinted by permission of Giles Schmid, PhD., Professor of Management.

Major League Baseball Umpires Foul Out

Case 16-1

When future college textbooks are written on labor–management relations, the 1999 saga of baseball and its umpires may well be included as a case study in how not to do it—not only for unions but for employers as well.

On Thursday, September 2, 1999, 25 replacement umpires worked American and National League games, filling holes left by mass resignations of regular umpires, an ill-conceived strategy that backfired.

The leaders of the umpires union made a fatal mistake: They wrongly believed they had the power to shut down the business of baseball with a threat to withhold their services. As other unions have learned the hard way, a strike—by any name—is lost the moment the employer can keep going without them.

The tactic was almost certainly doomed from the start. An alternative, if not equally experienced, supply of qualified workers was readily available in the top minor leagues. And managers had not concealed their willingness to use that source.

While thinking they were cleverly getting around a no-strike agreement by resigning, the umpires foolishly placed themselves outside the coverage of the labor laws designed to protect the rights of bona fide strikers.

But management had no reason to rejoice, either, for the real roots of the confrontation lay in the fact that baseball's owners hadn't been "tending to business" in the matter of umpiring. Over time, the owners had delegated to the umpires their own prerogatives over everything from performance reviews to the location of the strike zone. The umpires had gradually gained veto power over who could supervise them, whether they could be required to stay in physical shape, and even whether they could be told to dust off home plate.

Thus, when the baseball commissioner's office, in the spring of 1999, tried to tell the umpires to call balls and strikes with some uniformity—and with at least a nod in the direction of the rule book—the umpires took it as an affront.

Such a posture would be laughable in most other workplaces, but it's hardly unique. Other employers have awoken too late to realize they have similarly given away control of their businesses. And restoring a proper balance is nearly always painful. But for both management stupidity and union arrogance, the umpires are hard to top.

Answer the following questions:

1. What does this case illustrate about the need for management to prepare for dealing with a union?

2. What should management have done differently?

3. What should the umpires have done differently?

Source: Adapted from "Umps Foul Out," *USA Today*, September 3, 1999, p. 16A. Reprinted with permission.

United States Freight Group

Case 16-2

Company Background

United States Freight Group (USFG) was founded in the mid 1960s as a small bulk carrier in the transportation industry. Through internal growth, acquisitions, and partnerships, the organization has grown into a diversified transportation company employing over 800 people, 500 of whom are drivers. The company operates internationally in the United States, Canada, and Mexico and is either number one or in the top five of most markets that it currently serves. The company is "quality driven" and committed to meeting customer needs 100 percent of the time—providing on-time, contaminate-free deliveries, and efficient and accurate billing. The company offers a variety of services ranging from dry bulk transportation to remote silo inventory management. Since 1990, it has been the recipient of 8 quality service awards and recently was designated as "supplier of the year." With such a wide range of services and equipment and a focus on quality, USFG has proven it can handle most client needs.

The following situation takes place at one of USFG's remote transloading facilities in the southeastern United States. Operations at this facility entail unloading materials from railcars into trucks and transporting these goods to customers in the surrounding area 24 hours a day, 7 days a week. Since the customer base is "local," the drivers typically travel in a 200–square-mile radius of the transloading facility. While this remote location is managed by the regional manager who is physically located in a different state, a human resources representative (HRR) is on-site from 8:00 a.m. to 5:00 p.m., Monday through Friday, to handle the daily duties, such as scheduling, paperwork, and employee relations. Thus, the HRR provides staff support without direct line authority. Two shifts (6 a.m. to 6 p.m. and 6 p.m. to 6 a.m.) are utilized at the facility with employees working 12-hour schedules. The HRR sets the schedules on a rotation basis, so that the process is considered fair by the employees.

The Model Employee

James Redmond enjoyed working at USFG. In fact, he liked it so much that he had stayed with the company for over 8 years—twice as long as the next senior employee. James liked the company for many reasons. Initially, the pay and benefits attracted him. The benefits included medical, dental, and life insurance, as well as a matching 401K plan. The safety incentive programs, number of holidays, and paid vacations after time in service also made employment at USFG attractive to James. Another plus was that USFG paid its employees on a multitiered commission basis tied to the number of loads delivered during an employee's schedule. Drivers made $35 per delivery, while loaders made $30. If an employee had the ability, training, and experience to be a loader and a driver, he could earn up to $65 per delivery by doing both jobs. Approximately four to five deliveries could be made during a normal 12-hour shift. Usually, the more senior employees were given the dual designation of "loaders/drivers." Thus, James was motivated early on to obtain additional job and safety training to gain the dual designation and earn the maximum amount possible.

James had been the facility's number one loader/driver in terms of performance, efficiency, and safety for over 6 years. He was a model employee whose recent injury had a big impact on the facility's overall performance. James was injured on the job when the hose used to transfer the material from the container to the truck "broke loose" during loading. The end of the hose hit James in the arm, breaking his arm and causing major nerve damage. The injury was so severe that even after the break had healed and he had been through physical therapy, he continued to experience "deadness" in his arm due to the nerve damage. As a result, he could no longer load the trucks. He could only drive.

Given that James was such a model employee, USFG welcomed him back in whatever capacity he could perform.

James felt equally as blessed to be back even if it meant only performing part of his old job. It was less money, but he still enjoyed working at USFG. The individual-based work was well suited for his personality. It provided him opportunity to have time alone, which with a family of five was a precious commodity. Plus, his previous employer, a local shipbuilder, had switched to a team-based culture, which James never really felt comfortable with. It was supposed to be a more positive environment with everyone pulling together, but he found it to be just the opposite. The employees tried ways to outshine everyone else to gain favorable recognition, so James found himself always having to watch his back. That was the great thing about USFG, you didn't have to play politics or worry about dealing with complainers, slackers, or brown nosers. Just do your job, perform it well, and get paid, or so James thought.

The Management Problem

Shortly after James returned to work, USFG lost a local contract that represented a significant amount of work for the transloading facility. Kathy Prunel, the regional manager, was confronted with the challenge of how to keep the employees working when her facility had just lost over 25 percent of its business. This remote location was not a top priority for upper management, as evidenced by the lack of marketing efforts for the facility. Without the proper marketing, the facility's client base and production capacity was limited. In the short-term while Kathy explored marketing opportunities with upper management, she decided to change the schedule from 12- to 8-hour shifts (7 a.m. to 2 p.m., 2 p.m. to 10 p.m., 10 p.m. to 7 a.m.) and increase the amount of "standing time" for each employee on each shift. "Standing time" was time spent in the yard at the facility performing activities such as prepping, cleaning, or maintaining the equipment. While a certain amount of "standing time" was necessary during every employee's schedule, 3 to 4 hours became mandatory. This policy change led to lots of discussion and discord around the yard, because "standing time" paid $16 an hour, considerably less than one could make loading or driving.

The workers were told the situation was temporary. "Just get through the next several weeks and things will get back to normal," Kathy told them. After 2 weeks, all of the equipment was spotless and running smoothly, forcing the workers to spend more time together in the yard. Not everyone was happy about the increased interaction. James felt like the company was doing what it could to avoid layoffs, but some of the newer employees, A. J. Johnson in particular, couldn't seem to see anything but the negative in the situation. James had known others like A. J., always complaining about their situation and what they were going to do if the company didn't do right by them.

After several weeks of hearing A. J. spout off, James finally had had enough. "If you hate it here so much, why don't you quit," asked James. "I never quit nothin' in my life, and I ain't startin' now!" replied A. J. "That manager better get her act together and start doing something or she's gonna be hearin' from me! And, what's it to you anyway old man!" barked A. J. The conversation escalated to such a point that James and A. J. had to be restrained by their co-workers. On his way to his car, James could hear A. J. screaming behind him, "You're lucky your buddies were here! You better watch out! Don't let me catch you alone!"

The next day, Cindy Smith, the HRR, was informed of what transpired between James and A. J. the previous night. She was very concerned. She suspected that A. J. was the one stealing from the office—supplies, coffee, sugar, etc. She knew A. J. was trouble, but as long as the facility was operating at full capacity, he didn't have an opportunity to interact much with the other workers. Now, things were different! Cindy immediately contacted Kathy Prunel who flew down the next day with Mike Ebersol, the safety manager, to meet with Cindy, James, and A. J.

The meeting went as well as could be expected. The regional manager hated to involve Mike, but she saw no other way. Mike was a big man, and he had a way of presenting a situation such that all parties agreed to act responsibly. Basically, Mike threatened James and A. J. such that if they couldn't resolve their differences amicably and Kathy had to be brought in again, they would be real sorry! James left the meeting with an uneasy feeling. He didn't think that Mike's message had much of an impact on A. J. What was he going to do when A. J. pushed the envelope? How was he going to react? He went to Cindy and asked her not to schedule he and A. J. on the same shift. Cindy knew James was a good person, and she was just as concerned as he was. She agreed.

The next several weeks passed without incident, well sort of. While James and A. J. had no direct contact with each other, thanks to Cindy's scheduling, A. J. attempted to indirectly agitate James. At the end of his schedule, A. J. would "accidentally" spill coffee on the seat of the front-end loader, so that when James came on he would sit in it. He tried soiling the equipment (spitting on the steering wheel), because he knew how much pride James took in keeping his machinery clean. A. J. even went as far as to break the front-end loader so James would get blamed. Cindy was well aware of his deliberate antics, and she feared that James might eventually be pushed to the breaking point and retaliate. After much deliberation, she called Kathy.

Kathy had not been sure that Mike's approach was going to work, so she was not completely caught off guard by Cindy's call. She thanked Cindy for contacting her and began to develop a plan of action. Kathy realized that she didn't have any substantial evidence against A. J. And, if he and James got into another altercation, then both had to be let go for fighting. She decided to do two things. First, Cindy should continue scheduling the work so James and A. J. didn't come into direct contact. Second, Cindy would begin implementing a "checklist." The "checklist" was a list of safety, maintenance, and cleaning items that had to be performed by each worker on his equipment prior to the end of each scheduled shift. Kathy believed this to be the perfect means of documenting any inappropriate behavior that might be grounds for dismissal. Cindy immediately created and distributed the lists noting the change in policy with the employees on the next shift.

When Mike Ebersol heard about the checklist being used at the remote transloading facility, he thought to himself, "How is Kathy ever going to learn to be a good manager without confronting these problems head on? She always sidesteps issues. Now is the time to force her to deal with this problem directly." He called Cindy and told her to schedule James and A. J. for the same shift for the upcoming Saturday night. "This will force things to a head! They'll solve their differences one way or the other, and then Kathy can take action," Mike thought to himself.

Cindy was panic stricken! She just knew someone was going to get hurt. A. J. was going to cause trouble for sure, but how was James going to be able to defend himself with his injured arm. She was unable to contact Kathy who was on vacation for 7 days. Without being able to speak with Kathy, she had no choice but to follow Mike's instructions. She scheduled the two for Saturday's night shift.

The Showdown

James couldn't believe his eyes when he saw Saturday's schedule. It must be a mistake. He went to talk with Cindy. Cindy was visibly upset and told him what had happened. James went into the yard to begin working and planning how he was going to handle the situation. He was adjusting a piece of equipment on the front-end loader when a co-worker approached him and said, "James, what you gonna do man? I saw Saturday's schedule, and it ain't good. I heard A. J. flappin' his gums day before yesterday about how he was gonna be packin' some heat. Said if you wuz to get out of line, he'd have to pop you one! You better be real careful James, A. J. is one bad dude!"

Epilogue

Trouble began shortly after A. J. and James started their Saturday night shift. A. J. started talking "smack," and James couldn't contain himself. James verbally defended himself and even went as far as telling A. J. that he thought A. J. was responsible for most, if not all, of the problems at the yard. This bantering back and forth did not end until

A. J. went to his car and returned with a .357 magnum which he preceded to fire at James. Fortunately, A. J. missed his intended target—he wasn't as great a marksman as he proclaimed to be! A. J. was immediately fired for leaving his work area and carrying a weapon. USFG is currently trying to replace its lost client (and revenues) but has not been able to find another. A. J.'s position has not been filled. Recently, the employees have been able to return to longer shifts with less "standing time."

Questions

1. From a management perspective, why did the company allow the initial childish behavior (coffee on the seat, spit on the steering wheel, etc.) to escalate into employee confrontation?

2. When does childish behavior become a harassment issue? At what point does one's practical jokes or intimidating actions toward one employee impact all employees?

3. Visit the Occupational Safety & Health Administration's Website and review the agency's "Fact Sheet" on workplace violence: (http://www.osha.gov/OshDoc/data_General_Facts/factsheet-workplace-violence.pdf). What kind of policy statement and/or plan should the company include in its overall policy and procedures manual to avoid violence in the workplace? What type of training should the company provide all employees on this issue?

4. What additional legal issues does this case problem raise for USFG?

5. Would USFG face potential liability if it fired A.J. based on the rumored threats of violence?

6. The National Rifle Association is lobbying for states to pass laws that would prohibit employers from stopping an employee from bringing a gun to work in the employee's car. Such a law has been enacted in Oklahoma. The Oklahoma statute gives employees the right to keep guns locked in their cars. Other bills are being modeled after the Oklahoma statute. Many employers and business groups oppose the law. Discuss.

Source: Prepared by Don C. Mosley, Jr., John S. Bishop, Jr., and Kelly Collins Woodford, Mitchell College of Business, University of South Alabama, Mobile, Alabama. The company and individual names are fictitious.

Chapter 1

1 Andreas Priestland and Robert Hanig, "Developing First-Level Leaders, Harvard Business Review 83 June, 2005, p. 112.

2 Henry Mintzberg, "The Manager's Job: Folklore and Fact," Harvard Business Review, July-August 1975, pp. 489-561.

3 See Rene Cordero, George F. Farris, and Nancy DiThomasco, IEEE Transactions on Engineering Management(51), Feb. 2004, pp. 19-30. The authors studied over 2,000 technical professionals and found that for them to have a "stimulating" work environment, it was more important for their supervisors to possess people and administrative skills rather than technical skills. As the authors stated, "This appears a reversal from the traditional assumption that technical skills are the most important qualifications for promoting technical professionals into supervision."

4 Tiziano Casciaro, Migues Sousa, and Mark Lobo, "Competent Jerks, Lovable Fools, and the Formation of Social Networks, Harvard Business Review (83), June 2005, pp. 92-100.

5 A Janice Klein and Pamela Posey, "Good Supervisors Are Good Supervisors—Anywhere," Harvard Business Review 64, November-December 1986, pp. 125-128.

6 http:/ftp//ftp.bls.gov/pub/special.requests/ep/labor.force/clfa0414txt

7 Ibid.

8 http://www.bls.gov/emp/empmost-growth.htm.

9 James W. Dean and James R. Evans, Total Quality, 2nd ed. (Cincinnati:South-Western College Publishing, 2000), p. 13.

10 Simon Zadek, "The Path to Corporate Responsibility," Harvard Business Review (82) December 2004, pp. 125-133.

11 Bruce Drake, Mark Meckler, and Debra Stevens, "Traditional Ethics: Responsibilities of Supervisors for Supporting Employee Development," Journal of Business Ethics, June 2, 2002, pp. 141-155.

12 Nancy Hatch Woodward, "Lessons Learned from the Gulf Coast Can Help You Manage Employee Communication in the Aftermath of the Unthinkable," HRMagazine (50) December 2005, pp. 52-57.

Chapter 2

1 Interviews with Chris Browning, Jennifer Fidler, James Gillespie, Dan McCrory, and Steve Seay by Don Mosley, Jr., May 2006.

2 Gene Marino, "Contingency Planning Essentials," Industrial Engineer, July 2003, p. 24.

3 Interviews with Chris Browning, Jennifer Fidler, James Gillespie, Dan McCrory, and Steve Seay by Don Mosley, Jr., May 2006.

4 William L. Megginson, M. Jane Byrd, and Leon C. Megginson, Small Business Management, 4th ed. (New York: McGraw-Hill/Irwin, 2003), p. 203.

Chapter 3

1 William L. Megginson, Mary Jane Byrd, and Leon C. Megginson, Small Business Management, 4th ed. (New York: McGraw-Hill/Irwin, 2003), p. 257.

2 "Do Many Chief Executives Lose Their Drive as They Advance in Age?" The Wall Street Journal, November 18, 1997, p. 1A.

3 See Anne Fisher, "How Sharp Is Your Intuition?" Fortune, February 10, 2003, www.fortune.com.

4 See Mortimer R. Feinberg and Aaron L. Wenstein, "How Do You Know When to Rely on Your Intuition?" The Wall Street Journal, June 21, 1982, p. 16.

5 Prepared by Julia Allen, University of South Alabama, from various sources, including "Persons of the Year," Time, December 30, 2002/January 6, 2003, pp. 30-31.

6 Andrew Caffrey, "FBI Takes Up Heavy Load of Corporate Fraud Probes," Boston Globe, May 6, 2003, p. Al.

7 For further details, see A Matter of Judgment and Ethics at Work, videos produced by the Ethics Resource Center.

8 Patricia Haddock and Marilyn Manning, "Ethically Speaking," Sky, March 1990, p. 128.

Chapter 4

1 Martin Peers and Matthew Rose, "AOL Shake-Up May Give Important Roles to Logan, Bewkes," The Wall Street Journal, July 18, 2002, p. B1.

2 Peter Drucker, "The Coming of the New Organization," Harvard Business Review 76, January-February 1988, pp. 45-53.

3 Richard L. Bunning, "The Dynamics of Downsizing," Personnel Journal 69, September 1990, p. 69.

4 Phillip R. Nienstedt, "Effective Downsizing Management Structures," Human Resources Planning 12, 1989, p. 156.

5 Bunning, "The Dynamics of Downsizing," p. 70.

6 Ronald Henkoff, "Getting Beyond Downsizing," Fortune, January 10, 1994, p. 58.

7 Wayne F. Cascio, "Downsizing: What Do We Know? What Have We Learned?" Academy of Management Executive 2(1), February 1993, p. 95.

8 This section is adapted from Michael Hammer and James Champy, Reengineering the Corporation (New York: Harper Business, 1993).

9 Ibid., p. 31.

10. Ibid., p. 32.

11 Rensis Likert, New Patterns of Management (New York: McGraw-Hill, 1961); Rensis Likert, The Human Organization (New York: McGraw-Hill, 1967).

12 Frank Ostroff, The Horizontal Organization (New York: Oxford University Press, 1999), pp. 22-24,

13 Nancy K. Austin, "Reorganizing the Organization Chart," Working Woman, September 1993, p. 24.

Chapter 5

1 Peter M. Senge The Fifth Discipline: The Art and Practice of the Learning Organization, Doubleday, New York, January 1990, p. 4.

2 With Carl Moore, currently Dean of the Mitchell College of Business, the University of South Alabama.

3 Interview with Dan Burns by Don Mosley, Sr., Summer, 1988.

4 Interview with Larry Bonine, Partnering News, Arizona Department of Transportation, Summer, 1993.

5 Don Mosley interview with Larry Bonine, June 2003.

6 Chester Barnard, The Functions of the Executive, Harvard University Press (Cambridge, MA), 1938.

7 Personal experience as related to one of the authors.

8 Personal experience as related to one of the authors.

9 J.R.P. French, Jr., and Bertram Raven, "The Bases of Social Power," Studies in Social Power, ed. D. Cartwright (Ann Arbor, MI, Institute for Social Research), 1959.

10 Excerpts from Polly Labarre, "The Agenda—Grassroots Leadership," Fast Company Magazine, 23 (April 1999), p. 114.

11 Jeffrey Pfeffer, Robert B. Cialdini, Benjamin Hanna and Kathleen Knopoff, Faith in Supervision and the Self-Enhancement Bias: Two Psychological Reasons Why Managers Don't Empower Workers, Basic and Applied Social Psychology, 20(4), pp. 313-321.

12 Gary Yuki and Ping Ping Fu, "Determinants of Delegation and Consultation by Managers, Journal of Organizational Behavior,20, 1999, pp. 219-212.

13 J. Richard Hackman and Greg Oldham, "Development of the Job Diagnostic Survey," Journal of Applied Psychology, Vol. 60 (1975), pp. 159-170.

14 Ronald A. Heifetz, Leadership Without East Answers, the Belknap Press of Harvard University Press, Cambridge, MA, 1994.

15 Ronald A. Heifetz and Donald L. Laurie, Harvard Business Review (January-February 1997) p. 124.

16 Partnering: The Central Artery/Tunnel Manuaal (Boston: MA, Massachusetts Highway Department, 1993), p. 2.

17 Stephen E. Amrose, Eisenhower, Soldier and President (A touchstone Book, Published by Simon and Schuster, New York, 1990) pp. 39-40

18 Stephen E. Ambrose, Soldier, General of the Army, President-Elect, 1890-1952, (Simon and Schuster, New York, 1983), p. 77.

19 Ibid, p. 78.

20 Ibid, p. 79.

21 Le G. Bolman and Terrence F. Deal, Reframing Organizations, (Jossey-Bass Publishers, San Francisco, 2e, 1994) p. 280.

22 Comments about the autobiography by Jack Welch, Jack—Straight from the Gut (Warner Books, Inc., New York, NY, 2001) appearing on the back cover.

23 Sidney Finkelstein, "7 Habits of Spectacularly Unsuccessful Executives," Fast Company, July 2003, pp. 86-89.

24 Ibid, p. 86.

Chapter 6

1 Richard L. Daft, Management, 7th ed. (Mason, OH: Thomson/South-Western, 2004) pp. 328-329.

2 Personal interview by one of the authors with Amanda Phillips, May 18, 2006.

3 Albert Mehrabian, "Communication Without Words, "Psychology Today 2, September 1968, pp. 53-55; also cited in Ricky W. Griffin, Management, 7th ed. (New York:Houghton Mifflin Co., 2002) p. 570.

4 "Ten Killer Job Search Mistakes", National Business Employment Weekly Winter/Spring 1995, p. 5.

5 "Why Am I Here? Cosmic Question Gets Frequently Asked at Work," Training 43, April, 2006, p. 13.

6 One recent study showed when high disclosing supervisors are especially valued by team members. Employees whose jobs involve working with people outside the organization in unstructured, often ambiguous circumstances and were physically remotely located from their supervisor (such as sales, customer service work) rated as "most supportive" supervisors considered to be high disclosers. See Mark C. Johite and Dale F. Dohan "Supervisory communication practice and Boundary Spanner Role Ambiguity," Journal of Managerial Issues 13, Spring 200l, pp. 87-103.

7 Patricia Karathanos and Anthony Averiemmo, "Care and Feeding of the Organizational Grapevine," Industrial Management 41 (2), March-April 1999, pp. 26-30.

8 Elizabeth A Tuleja, Intercultural Communication for Business (Mason, OH: Thomson/South-Western, 2005) p. 4.

9 "Language Barriers in Firefighting: Rising Number of Hispanics Fight Western Wildfires," The South Bend Tribune, August 21, 2003, A6.

10 Mark Hinrichs, "Como Se Dice? Break Down the Language Barrier Between You and Your Employees," Entrepreneur 33, December 2005, pp. 113-114.

11 Donald Fishman, "ValuJet Flt 592: Crisis Communication Theory Blended and Extended," Communication Quarterly 47 (4) Fall, 1999, pp. 345-356.

12 Deborah Tannen, "Language, Sex, and Power: Women and Men in the Workplace," Training and Development, September 1997, pp. 34-40.

13 Edward Wong, "A Stinging Office Memo Boomerangs," New York Times April 5, 2001, p. C1.

14 Stephen R. Covey, The Sever Habits of Highly Effective People (New York: Simon & Shuster, 1990), pp. 234-260.

15 J. Hart Seibert, "Listening in the Organizational Context," in Listening Behavior: Measurement and Application,ed. Robert Bostrom (New York: The Guilford Press, 1990), pp. 119-127.

Chapter 7

1 Holly Dolezeak, "Sick Day or Just Sick and Tired?" Training 42, December 2005, p. 8.

2 Gerald H. Siejts and Dan Crim, "What Engages Workers the Most, or the Ten Cs of Employee Engagement," Ivey Business Journal (online) March-April, 2006, pp. 1-5.

3 Saul W Gellerman, Motivation and Productivity (New York: American Management Association. 1963), pp. 20-22; Daniel A. Wren, The Evolution of Management Thought (New York: The Ronald Press Co. 1972, pp. 275-281.

4 Jennifer M. George and Gareth R. Jones, Organizational Behavior, 3rd ed. (Upper Saddle River, N.J.: Prentice-Hall, 2002), p. 182.

5 Reported in Thomas J. Peters and Robert Waterman, In Search of Excellence: Lessons from America's Best Run Companies (New York: Harper and Row, 1982), p. xxi.

6 Gareth R. Jones and Jennifer M. George, Contemporary Management, 3rd ed. (New York: McGraw-Hill, 2003), p. 411.

7 William A. Cohen, The Art of the Leader (Englewood Cliffs, N.J.: Prentice-Hall, 1990), pp. 18-19.

8 Robert Levering and Milton Moskowitz, "The 100 Best Companies to work for," Fortune, January 12, 1998, p. 84.

9 See Frederick Herzberg, "One More Time: How Do You Motivate Employees?" Harvard Business Review 81(1), January 2003, pp. 41-47.

10 "Enjoyment Is the Top Motivator," Personnel Today, April 8, 2003, p. 55.

11 See Michael Byrne, "The Implications of Herzberg's Motivation-Hygiene Theory for Management in the Irish Health Sector," The Health Care Manager, 25. (January-March, 2006) pp. 4-12.

12 Stephanie Armour, "Cash or Critiques: Which is Best?" USA Today, December 16, 1998, p. 6B.

13 Fred Luthans, Organizational Behavior, 7th ed. (New York:Mcgraw-Hill, 1995), p. 156.

14 Bob Nelson, "Making the Job Meaningful down the Line," Business Week, May 1, 2006, p. 60.

15 Samantha Oller, American Printer, October 1, 2002.

16 H. Klean and J. Kim, "A Field Study of the Influence of Situational Constraints, Leader-Member Exchange, and Goal Commitment on Performance," Academy of Management Journal 41(1), February 1998, pp. 88-96.

17 L.M. Sixel, "Driven by Boss's Challenge," Houston Chronicle, May 20, 2006, p. (na).

18 Condensed from Peters and Waterman, In Search of Excellence, p. 68.

19 Kevin McManus, "A Simple Thank You," Industrial Engineer 37, February, 2005, p. 19.

20 As cited in Alan Zaremba, Organizational Communication (Mason, Ohio: South-Western, 2003), p. 34.

21 Susan Eisner, "Managing Generation Y," SAM Advanced Management Journal, 70, August 2005, p. 4. An excellent discussion of the four generations is contained in this article.

22 Lynne Curry, "Managing the GenX/Y Employee, Alaska Business Monthly 19, November 2003, p. 31.

23 Glenn Bakers, "The Young Ones: So You Want to Attract More Young Talent to Your business, But Don't Know How? You Need to Understand a Generation Before You Can Successfully Recruit and Manage It," NZ Business 20, April, 2006, pp. 24-30.

24 Dave Hotler, "21st Century Management and the Quest for Excellence," Supervision 63(10), October 2002, pp. 3-7.

Chapter 8

1 Douglas McGregor, The Human Side of Enterprise (New York: McGraw-Hill Book Co., 1960), pp. 33-42.

2 Notes from Workshop on Process Consultation conducted by Edgar Schein, Albert Einstein Institute, Cape Cod, August 1991.

3 Interview with Dr. Paul Hersey, Trainer's Bookshelf (San Diego, CA: Learning Resources Corporation, 1982).

4 Robert R. Blake and Jane S. Mouton, The Managerial Grid III: The Key to Leadership Excellence (Houston, TX: Gulf Publishing, 1985).

5 Paul Hersey and Kenneth H. Blanchard, Management of Organizational Behavior: Utilizing Human Resources, 3rd ed. (Englewood Cliffs, N.J.; Prentice-Hall, 1977), pp. 161-162.

6 Hersey and Blanchard acknowledge that they were strongly influenced by William J. Reddins, "3-D Management Style Theory," found in William J. Reddins, Management Effectiveness (New York: McGraw-Hill, 1970). We use Hersey and Blanchard's model because it is better known.

7 Robert Tannenbaum and Warren Schmidt, "How to Choose a Leadership Pattern," Harvard Business Review 51, May-June 1973, pp. 162-180.

8 Leonard M. Apcar, "Middle Managers and Supervisors Resist Moves to More Participatory Management," The Wall Street Journal,I September 16, 1985, p. 25.

9 David L. Bradford and Allen R. Cohen, Managing for Excellence (New York: John Wiley and Sons, 1984), pp. 71-98.

10 John MacGregor Burns, Leadership (New York: Harper and Row, 1978).

11 Bernard Bass, Leadership and Performance Beyond Expectations (New York: The Free Press, 1985).

12 B. M. Bass, B. J. Avolio, and L. Goodheim, "Biography and the Assessment of Transformational Leadership at the World Class Level," Journal of Management 13, Spring 1987, p. 7.

13 Ibid., p. 16.

14 George R. McAleer, "Leadership in the Military Environment," Association for Psychological Type, Special Topic Symposium, Type and Leadership, Crystal City, VA, March 5-7, 1993.

15 Bennett J. Sims, Servanthood—Leadership for the Third Millennium (Boston: Cowley Publications, 1997).

16 Operation Sagebrush, Fall 1955, experienced by Donald C. Mosley.

17 Robert K. Greenleaf, Servant Leadership (Mahwah, N.J.: Paulist Press, 1991), p. 3. Copyright by the Robert K. Greenleaf Center.

18 Ibid., p. 21.

19 William D. Hitt, "The Model Leader: A Fully Functioning Person," Leadership and Organization Development Journal 14(7), December 1993, p. 10.

20 Bill Donaldson, hospital middle-level manager, interview by author, Cape Cod Institute's Leadership Course, July 1-4, 2003.

21 Kenneth Cloke and Joan Goldsmith, The End of Management and the Rise of Organizational Democracy (San Francisco: Jossey-Bass/John Wiley & Sons, 2002), p. 179.

22 Ibid., p. 179.

23 Maureen McNamara, interview by Author, Cape Cod Institute's Leadership Course, July 1-4, 2003.

24 Daniel Goleman, "What Makes a Leader?" Harvard Business Review, November-December 1998, pp. 93, 94.

25 A. J. Rathje, interview by author, Mobile, AL, June 2002.

26 Mel Johnson, service manager, and Jeff Matherne, finance and sales manager, Lexus dealership, interview by author, Mobile, AL, October 9, 2002. The awards were given for self-regulation—trustworthiness and integrity, and empathy—service to clients and customers.

27 Doris Kearns Goodwin, "The Master of the Game, Time, July 4, 2005, pp. 48-54.

28 Doris Kearns Goodwin, Team of Rivals; the Political Genius of Abraham Lincoln (New York, Simon and Schuster, Date?) Winner of the Pulitzer Prize.

29 Richard E. Boyatzis, Ellen van Oosten, "A Leadership Imperative: Building the Emotionally Intelligent Organization, Ivey Business Journal, January/February 2003, pp. 1-5.

30 Ibid., p. 2.

31 Ibid., p. 5.

Chapter 9

1 Excerpts from handout from the Ritz-Carlton, Island of Maui, Hawaii; Edwin McDowell, "Ritz-Carlton Keys to Good Service," New York Times, March 31, 1993, pp. C1-C3; Portrait: The Ritz-Carlton Hotel Company; interviews and discussions with Lenny Litz, General Manager, and staff of Ritz-Carlton, Maui; discussion with Sue Musselman, assistant to the Vice-president of quality, Ritz-Carlton Hotel Company, Atlanta, GA; and Mark Memmot, "The Quality Quest," USA Today, June 28, 1993, p. 2B.

2 George Benson "Why the Ritz Is the Ritz," Georgia Trend 15, August 2000, p. 99.

3 Robyn Lamb, "Ritz-Carlton Moving Headquarters to Chevy Chase," Baltimore Md Daily Record, March 6, 2003.

4 Terrence R. Mitchell and William B. Scott, "America's Problems and Needed Reforms: Confronting the Ethic of Personal Advantage," Academy of Management Executive 4, August 1990, pp. 23-25.

5 B. W. Tuckman, "Developmental Sequence in Small Groups," Psychological Bulletin, May 1965, pp. 384-399.

6 See, for example, F. Steven Heinen and Eugene Jacobson, "A Model of Task Group Development in Complex Organizations and Strategy of Implementation," Academy of Management Review 1, October 1976, pp. 98-111.

7 Don Hellriegel, John W. Slocum, Jr., and Richard Woodman, Organizational Behavior, 5th ed. (Mason, Ohio: South-Western Publishing, 1989), p. 210.

8 R. Bruce McAfee and Paul J. Champage, Organizational Behavior: A Manager's View (Mason, Ohio: South-Western Publishing, 1987), p. 250.

9 Don Hellreigel and John W. Slocum, Jr., Management (Reading, Mass: Addison-Wesley, 1986), pp. 539-542.

10 W. Allen Randolph, Understanding and Managing Organizational Behavior (Homewood, IL: Richard D. Irwin, 1985), p. 399.

11 William C. Dyer, Team Building: Issues and Alternatives (Reading, Mass.: Addison-Wesley, 1977), p. 4.

12 Don Hellriegel and John W. Slocum, Jr., Management, 7th ed. (Mason, Ohio: South-Western, 1995), p. 52.

13 Donald C. Mosley, Carl Moore, Michelle Slagle, and Daniel Burns, "The Role of the O.D. Consultant in Partnering," Organizational Development Journal 8(3), Fall 1990, pp. 43-49.

14 Partnering: The Central Artery/Tunnel Manual (Boston, Mass.: Massachusetts Highway Department, 1993), p. 2.

15 Roger Daniels, "WINS and Partnering Working Together to Improve the Way We Do Business on the CA/T," unpublished paper, December 1993.

16 Observation of team meeting by Donald D. Mosley, Sr. and discussion with Matt Callan after the meeting on October 27, 2005.

17 Anthony J. Mayo and Nitis Nohrid, "In Their Time: The Greatest Business Leaders of the Twentieth Century,

Harvard Business School Press, 2005, p. xxviii.

18 Ibid.

19 Jennifer Raingold, "Bob Nordelli Is Watching. Why Does a 21st Century Leader Look Like?" Fast Company, December 2005, pp. 78-80.

20 James W. Robinson, Jack Welch and Leadership (Roseville, CA:PPrima Publishing Co., 2001), pp. 129-130.

21 Del Jones, "GE Enters New Era As a Legend Leaves." USA Today, September 7, 2001.

22 Ibid.

23 Jack Welch with John A. Byrne, Jack, Straight from the Gut (New York: Warner Books, 2001), p. 158.

24 Penelope McClenny, "Cancer Fighters Join Hands," Mobile Press-Register, Mobile, Alabama, July 27, 2006, pp. 1A, 4A.

25 Charles C. Manz and Henry P. Sims, Jr., "Superleadership: Leading Others to Lead Themselves to Excellence," in The Manager's Bookshelf, ed. Jan L. Pierce and John W. Newstrom (New York: Harper & Row, 1988), p. 328.

26 Mike Odom, Kay Montgomery, and others, interviews by Don Mosley, Sr., November 2002.

Chapter 10

1 Kitty Locker and Stephen Kyo Kaczamarek, Business Communication, Third Edition (New York: McGraw-Hill/Irwin), 2007, p. 323.

2 Daniel L. Plung and Tracy Montgomery, Professional Communication: The Corporate Insider's Approach (Mason, OH: South-Western , 2004), p. 237

3 Ibid.

4 Daniel McGinn, "Mired in Meetings," Newsweek, October 16, 2000, p. 152.

5 Ibid.

6 Heera Singh "Ensuring Effective Meetings," Asia African Intelligence Wire, November 12, 2005 (pna).

7 Alan Zaremba, Organizational Communication (Mason, OH: South-Western, 2003), p. 142.

8 Zaremba, Organizational Communication, p. 199.

9 McGinn, "Mired in Meetings."

10 McGinn, "Mired in Meetings."

11 Cited in Robyn D. Clarke, "Whipping Up a Great Meeting," Black Enterprise 31, December 2000, p. 82.

12 John V. Thill and Courtland I. Bovee, Excellence in Business Communication, Chapter 2: "Communicating in Teams;

Collaboration, Listening, Nonverbal, and Meeting Skills," 5th ed. (Upper Saddle River, N.J.: Prentice-Hall, 2002), p. 29.

13 Edgar H. Schein, Process Consultation, vol. 1, 2nd ed. (Reading, Mass.: Addison-Wesley, 1988), p. 6.

14 Ibid., p. 9.

15 Client evaluation feedback to the Synergistic Group, Mobile, Alabama.

16 Joe Howell, Anna Raley, and Michael Wilkinson, interviews by Don Mosley, December 2002, January 2003.

Chapter 11

1 JoAnn Greco, "Hey Coach," Journal of Business Strategy 22(2), March 2001, p. 28.

2 Kathleen Kingsbury, "New Shrink Gig: Executive Coach," Time, February 13, 2006 (Bonus Section, p. A17.

3 D.T. Hall, K. L. Otazo, and G. P. Hellenbeck, "Behind Closed Doors: What Really Happens in Executive Coaching," Organizational Dynamics 27(3), 1999.

4 Dennis C. Kinlaw, Coaching for Commitment (San Diego: Pfeiffer & Co., 1993), p. 19.

5 "Use these 10 Tips to Brush Up Your Coaching Skills," Pay for Performance Report, January 2002, p. 10.

6 Julie Barker, "Too Good to Ignore: Getting More Out of Top Producers: That's Right, "A" Players Need Coaching Too," Sales and Marketing Management 157, March 2005, pp. 38-41.

7 K.R. Phillips, "The Achilles' Heel of Coaching, Training and Development 52(3), March 1998, pp. 41-46; C. Hymowitz, "How to Tell Employees All the Things They Don't Want to Hear," The Wall Street Journal, August 22, 2000, p. B1.

8 Dennis C. Kinlaw, Coaching Skills for Inventory (San Diego: Pheiffer & Co., 1993), pp. 1-13.

9 David Bicknell, "Keep It Personal and Keep Your Staff," Computer Weekly, July 8, 1999, p. 22.

10 See Marcus Buckingham, "What Great Managers Do," Harvard Business Review 83, March 2005, pp. 70-79.

11 Thomas Gordon, Leader Effectiveness Training (New York: Wyden Books, 1977), pp. 92-107.

12 George Bolander, Scott Snell and Arthur Sherman, Managing Human Resources, 12th ed. (Mason, OH: South-Western, 2001) p. 463.

13 Leah Carlson, "EAP Use Increasingly Centers Around Stress, Family Issues," Employee Benefit News 19, December 2005, pp. 35-37.

14 Steve Davolt, "Comcast Employees Tune into Employee Assistance Programs," Employee Benefit News 20. April 2006, pp. 57-59.

15 "It's Your Problem Too," Business Week 3670, February 29, 2000, p. 26.

16 Chelle Daivas and Dave Marks, "Evidence of an EAP Cost Offset," Behavioral Health Management 20(4), July 2000, p. 34; Deanna Thompson, "EAPs Help Companies by Helping Workers," Business Courier Service Cincinnati-Northern Kentucky 27(26), October 13, 2000, p. 11b.

Chapter 12

1 Roger Fisher and William Ury, Getting to Yes (New York: Penquin, 1993), pp. 3-4.

2 Kathryn Tyler, "Extending the Olive Branch: Conflict Resolution Training Helps Employees and Managers Defuse Skirmishes," HRMagazine, November 2002, p. 47

3 Ibid.

4 A. P. Brief, R. S. Schuler, and M. W. Sell, Managing Job Stress (Boston: Little, Brown, & Co., 1981), p. 2.

5 "The Road to Happiness," Psychology Today 27(4), July-August 1994, p. 34.

6 Claudia Wallis, "Stress: Can We Cope?" Time, June 6, 1983, p. 52.

7 W. W. Suoganen and Donald R. Hudson, "Coping with Stress and Addictive Work Behavior," Business (College of Business Administration, Georgia State University) 31, January-February 1980, p. 11.

8 Robert T. Golembiewski and Robert F. Munzenrider, Phases of Burnout (New York: Praeger, 1988), p. 220.

9 "Fitness Programs Are Working Out," USA Today, Wednesday, June 17, 1998, p. 5B.

10 Stephanie Armourn, "Workplace Hazard Gets Attention," USA Today, May 5, 1998, p. 1B.

Chapter 13

1 "Pentagon Travel Costs," USA Today, March 28, 1995, p. 4A.

2 Andres Kaplan, "Mission Control: Systems for Monitoring Beverage Production Can Keep Lines Running as Smoothly as Possible, While Trimming Excess Costs at the Same Time," Beverage World 122, July 15, 2003.

3 "Relays Help Prevent Storm-Generated Power Failures," Oil & Gas Journal 101, January 13, 2003.

4 Myron Magnet, "Who's Winning the Information Revolution," Fortune, November 30, 1992, pp. 110-111.

5 Simon Head, "Big Brother in a Black Box," Civilization, August/September 1999, pp. 52-55.

Chapter 14

1 Jason Roberson, "G.M. Closing Productivity Gap: Harbour Report Puts It 4th After Japanese Carmakers," Detroit Free Press, June 2, 2006, p.na.

2 John Gallagher, "Deadline Looms for Chrysler, Canadian Auto Workers," Knight Ridder News Service, October 14, 2002, p. K4145.

3 Tim Kelly, "The Robots Are Coming," Forbes Global, Sept. 4, 2006, vol. 2, p. 120; John Teresko, "Robots Revolution," Industry Week, 251, Sept. 2002, pp. 24-28.

4 N. Shirouzi, "Why Toyota Wins Such High Marks on Quality Surveys," The Wall Street Journal, March 15, 2001, p. A1.

5 Doug Bartholomew, "One Product, One Customer: TPS, Teamwork and Kaizen Pay Off for Auto Frame Plant," Industry Week 251(8), October 2002, pp. 50-55.

6 Machingo Nakamoto, "Battery Trouble Hinders Sony Bid for Global Brand Supremacy," The Financial Times August 26, 2006, p. 19.

7 James R. Evans and William Lindsay, The Management and Control of Quality, 5th ed. (Mason, Ohio: South-Western, 2002), pp. 604-605.

8 Deanne N. Den Hartog and Robert M. Verburg, "Service Excellence from the Employees' Point of View: The Role of First Line Supervisors," Managing Service Quality (3), 2000, pp. 159-164.

9 Quoted in Evans and Lindsay, The Management and Control of Quality, p. 301.

10 Malcolm Baldrige National Quality Award Profile, http://www.nist.gov/public_affairs/releases/ssmhealth.htm, accessed November 22, 2002.

11 Philip Seikman, "Glass Act: How a Window Maker Rebuilt Itself; Not Waiting for Perfect Answers, Pella Conducted Thousands of Kaisen or Continuous Improvement Sessions," Fortune 142(11), November 13, 2000, p. 384.

12 Bureau of Labor Statistics, Industries with at Least 100,000 Non-Fatal Occupational Injuries and Illnesses, 2004.

13 Deane Seals and Jack Hale, "Safety in Numbers: Focus on Safety Programs for Cost Saving Opportunities," Management Accounting 73(11), May 2002, p. 45.

14 "National Safety Council Lauds UPS Safety Program," U.S. Newswire, June 24, 2002, p. 1008175.

Chapter 15

1 Interview with Bryan Seibt in October, 2006.

2 "Taking Advantage," WGN TV station (Chicago, I11.) February 19, 1984.

3 Stephanie Armour, "Employers: Enough Already with the e-Résumés," USA Today, July 15, 1999, p. IB.

4 "Drug Testing: The Things People Will Say," American Salesman, March 2001, pp. 20-24.

5 See "Adoption by Four Agencies of Uniform Guidelines on Employee Selection Procedures (1978)," Federal Register 43, August 1978, pp. 290-315.

6 "Labor Report," The Wall Street Journal, February 23, 1993, p. Al.

7 Julia Lawlor, "Disabilities No Longer a Job Barrier," USA Today, June 22, 1993, pp. 1A and IB.

8 Michael A. Verespej, "How Will You Know Whom To Hire? No More Questions About Medical History," Industry Week, September 17, 1990, p. 70.

9 Robert Cyr, "Seven Steps to Better Performance Appraisals," Training and Development 47, January 1993, pp. 18-19.

10 Ren Nardoni, "Corporatewide Management Staffing," Personnel Journal 69, April 1990, pp. 52-58,

11 Kenneth M. Golden, "Dealing with the Problem Managers," Personnel 66, August 1989, pp. 54-59.

12 Mary Mavis, "Painless Performance Evaluations," Training and Development 48, October 1994, pp. 40-44.

13 Douglas McGregor, "An Uneasy Look at Performance Appraisals," Harvard Business Review 35, May-June 1957, p. 90.

14 L. Stockford and W. H. Bissell, "Factors Involved in Establishing a Merit Rating Scale," Personnel 26, September 1949, p. 97.

15 H. H. Meyer and W. B. Walker, "A Study of Factors Relating to the Effectiveness of a Performance Appraisal Program," Personnel Psychology 14, August 1961, pp. 291-298.

16 For further details, see Irwin H. McMaster, "Universal Aspects of Discipline," Supervision 36, April 1974, p. 19.

17 M. Michael Markowich, "A Positive Approach to Discipline," Personnel 66, August 1989, pp. 60-65.

18 Jennifer Gatewood, "Attacking Violence: Former Hostage Negotiator Warns Workplace Violence Won't Go Away until Managers Take an Aggressive Approach," Risk & Insurance, March 14, 2003, http://infotraccollege. thornsonlearning.com/itw/infomark/ 366/90.../32!xrn_52_0_A9888033.

19 Payne v. Western &A.R.P. Co., 81 Term. 507 (1884).

20 S. A. Youngblood and G. L. Tidwel, "Termination-at-Will: Some Changes in the Wind," Personnel 58, May-June 1981, p. 24.

Chapter 16

1 "Are Unions Striking Out?" U.S. News and World Report, June 12, 1995, p. 26.

2 "Unions on the Ropes," USA Today, June 14, 1995, p. 12A.

3 Leon C. Megginson, Mary Jane Byrd, and William L. Megginson, Small Business Management: An Entrepreneur's Guidebook. (New York: McGraw Hill/Irwin, 2003), p. 290.

4 Ibid.

5 Joseph P. Cangemi et al., "Differences between Pro-Union and Pro-Company Employees," Personnel Journal 55, September 1976, pp. 451-453.

6 Philip Ash, "The Parties to the Grievance," Personnel Psychology 23, Spring 1970, pp. 13-37.

7 NIOSH Safety and Health Topic: Traumatic Occupational Injuries. (n.d.) Retrieved October 18, 2006, from http://www.cdc.gov/niosh/ injury/traumaviolence.html

8 Tony Mauro, "Sex Bias Ruling Is 'Mixed,'" USA Today, June 23, 1999, p. 3A.

9 Equal Employment Opportunity Commission, Guidelines on Discrimination Because of Sex, 29 C.F.R., Section 1064.11, July 1, 1992.

10 Constance Johnson, "Court Cases Give Firms Guidance on Sexual Harassment," The Wall Street Journal, May 17, 1995, p. B2.

11 Daniel Lyons and Lea Goldman, "Accusing the Boss," Forbes 170, July 22, 2002, p. 100.

12 The U.S. Equal Employment Opportunity Commission, "EEOC Wins $1.55 Million Jury Verdict in Sexual Harassment Suit Against Florida Restaurant," June 23, 2003.

13 George Ming, "All the Points of Comparable Worth," Personnel Journal 69, November 1990, p. 99.

accountability The obligation created when a person accepts duties and responsibilities from higher management.

achievement, proficiency, or skill tests Measure the applicant's knowledge of and ability to do a given job.

acknowledging Showing by nonevaluative verbal responses that you have listened to what the employee has stated.

active listening The listener makes a response so as to encourage feedback.

adaptive challenges Changes in societies, competition, and technology that force organizations to clarify values, develop new strategies, and learn new techniques.

administrative skills Establishing and following procedures to process paperwork in an orderly manner.

advisory authority Authority of most staff departments to serve and advise line departments.

affirmative action programs (AAPs) Programs to put the principle of equal employment opportunity into practice.

affirming Communicating to an employee his or her value, strengths, and contributions.

agency shop All employees must pay union dues even if they choose not to join the union.

agreement or contract Prepared when an accord has been reached to bind the company, union, and workers to specific clauses in it.

alternatives Possible courses of action that can satisfy a need or solve a problem.

appraisal interview Supervisor communicates the results of a performance appraisal to an employee.

aptitude tests Predict how a person might perform on a given job.

arbitrator Will make a binding decision when collective bargaining reaches an impasse.

attending Showing through nonverbal behavior that you are listening in an open, nonjudgmental manner.

authority The right to tell others how to act to reach objectives.

authority compliance The leader's having a high concern for production results and using a directive approach.

body signals Nonverbal signals communicated by body action.

budget A forecast of expected financial performance over time.

burnout A malady caused by excessive stress in the setting where people invest most of their time and energy.

cause-and-effect diagram A graphical display of a chain of causes and effects.

channel The means used to pass a message.

closed shop All prospective employees must be members of the recognized union before they can be employed.

closure Successfully accomplishing the objective for a given item on the agenda.

coaching Supervisors helping individuals to reach their highest levels of performance.

coaching and selling style Used with individuals or groups that have potential but haven't realized it fully.

collective bargaining Conferring in good faith over wages, hours, and other terms and conditions of employment.

communication process model Model of the five components of communication and their relationships.

comparable worth or pay equity Jobs with equal points for the amount of education, effort, skills, and responsibility have equal pay.

computer-assisted manufacturing (CAM) Special computers assist equipment in performing processes.

conceptual skills Mental ability to become aware of and identifying relationships among different pieces of information.

concurrent controls Sometimes called *screening controls* these controls are used while an activity is taking place.

confirming Making sure an employee understands what has been said or agreed upon.

confronting/challenging Establishes clear performance standards, compares actual performance against them, and addresses performance that doesn't meet those standards.

consensus The acceptance by all members of the decision reached.

contingency planning Thinking in advance about possible problems or changes that might arise and having anticipated solutions available.

continuum of leadership behavior The full range of leadership behaviors in terms of the relationship between a supervisor's use of authority and employees' freedom.

control chart Displays the "state of control" of a process.

controlling Comparing actual performance with planned action and taking corrective action if needed.

cost/benefit analysis Estimating and comparing the costs and benefits of alternatives.

counseling Supervisors helping an individual recognize, talk about, and solve either real or perceived problems that affect performance.

country club management High concern for people.

craft unions Workers in a specific skill, craft, or trade.

critical path The series of activities in a PERT network that comprise the longest route, in terms of time, to complete the job.

decentralization The extent to which authority is delegated from one unit of the organization to another.

decision making Considering and selecting a course of action from among alternatives.

delegating style Used with exceptionally ready and capable individuals and groups.

delegation of authority Managers grant authority to the people who report of them.

Deming's 85–15 rule Assumes that when things go wrong, 85 percent of the time the cause is from elements controlled by management.

departmentalization The organizational process of determining how activities are to be grouped.

developmental leadership An approach that helps groups to evolve effectively and to achieve highly supportive, open, creative, committed, high-performing membership.

disciplinary layoff or suspension Time off without pay.

discipline Training that corrects and molds knowledge, attitudes, and behavior.

dissatisfier factors Factors that employees said most affected them negatively, or dissatisfied them about their job, including low pay, low benefits, and unfavorable working conditions.

diversity Refers to the wide range of distinguishing employee characteristics, such as sex, age, race, ethnic origin, and other factors.

downsizing Striving to become leaner and more efficient by reducing the workforce and consolidating departments and work groups.; Eliminating unnecessary levels of management.

downward communication Flows that originate with supervisors and are passed down to employees.

due process Guarantees the individual accused of violating an established rule a hearing to determine the extent of guilt.

ego need The need for self-confidence, independence, appreciation, and status.

e-mail Documents created, transmitted, and read entirely on computer.

emotional intelligence An assortment of skills and characteristics that influence a person's ability to succeed as a leader.

Employee Assistance Programs (EAPs) Professional counseling and medical services for employees with unresolved personal or work-related problems.

employee associations Organizations that function as labor unions.

employees' bill of rights Protects employees from possible abuse by unscrupulous managers and union leaders.

empowerment Granting employees authority to make key decisions within their area of responsibility.

ethical dilemmas Situations in which the supervisor is not certain what the correct behavior is.

ethics Standards used to judge "rightness" or "wrongness" of one person's behavior toward others.

exclusive bargaining agent Deals exclusively with management over questions of wages, hours, and other terms and conditions of employment.

exempt employees Not covered by the provisions of the Fair Labor Standards Act.

expectancy theory Views an individual's motivation as a conscious effort involving the expectancy that a reward will be given for a good result.

experience rating Determining, from the record of unemployed workers, the amount the employer must pay into the state's unemployment insurance fund.

experiential learning Learning by doing and using mistakes as an opportunity to figure out how to avoid them in the future.

external change forces Forces outside the organization that have a great impact on organizational change. Management has little control over these numerous external forces.

extrinsic motivation Behavior performed not for its own sake, but for the consequences associated with it. The consequences can include pay, benefits, job security, and working conditions.

facial signals Nonverbal messages sent by facial expression.

fact-finding meeting Held to seek out relevant facts about a problem or situation.

feedback The response that a communicator receives.

feedback controls Controls that measure completed activities and then take corrective action if needed.

feedforward controls Preventive controls that try to anticipate problems and take corrective action before they occur.

feeling decision process Giving great weight to the "people" side of a decision.

financial resources The money, capital, and credit an organization requires for operations.

financing Providing or using funds to produce and distribute an organization's product or service.

flowchart Visual representation of the sequence of steps needed to complete a process.

formal group A group prescribed and/or established by the organization.

functional authority A staff person's limited line authority over a given function.

functional departmentalization A form of departmentalization that groups together common functions or similar activities to form an organizational unit.

Gantt chart Identifies work stages and scheduled completion dates.

glass ceiling Invisible barrier that limits women from advancing in an organization.

goal-setting theory The theory that task goals, properly set and managed, can be an important employee motivator.

graduated scale of penalties Penalties become progressively more severe each time the violation is repeated.

grapevine The "rumor mill."

grievance procedure A formal way of handling employees' complaints.

group Two or more people who communicate and work together regularly in pursuit of one or more common objectives.

group cohesiveness The mutual liking and team feeling in a group.

group facilitation The process of intervening to help a group improve in goal setting, action planning, problem solving, conflict management, and decision making in order to increase the group's effectiveness.

group-centered approach Used at meetings in which group members interact freely and address and question one another.

heroic managers Those managers who have a great need for control or influence and want to run things.

hierarchy of needs Arrangement of people's needs in a hierarchy, or ranking, of importance.

hierarchy of objectives A network with broad goals at the top level of the organization and narrower goals for individual divisions, departments, or employees.

histogram Graphical representation of the variation found in a set of data.

hot-stove rule Compares a good disciplinary system to a hot stove.

human relations skills Understanding other people and interacting effectively.

human resources The people an organization requires for operations.

"I" message An appeal, rather than a demand, that the other person change.

impoverished management Little concern for people or production.

industrial unions Unions composed of all the workers in an industry.

informal communication Separate from a formal, established communication system.

informal group A group that evolves out of the formal organization but is not formed by management or shown in the organization's structure.

information exchange meeting Held to obtain information from group members.

information richness The sheer amount of information that a communication channel carries.

information-giving meeting Held to announce new programs and policies or to update present ones.

intangible standards Relate to human characteristics and are not expressed in terms of numbers, money, physical qualities, or time.

integration process A conflict resolution strategy in which everyone wins.

internal change forces Pressures for change within the organization such as cultures and objectives.

intolerable offenses Disciplinary problems of a drastic, dangerous, or illegal nature.

intrinsic motivation Behavior that an individual produces because of the pleasant experiences associated with the behavior itself.

intuition Unconscious influence of a person's cultural background, education, and training, as well as knowledge of the situation.

inverted pyramid A structure widest at the top and narrowing as it funnels down.

IQ tests Measure the applicant's capacity to learn, solve problems, and understand relationships.

job descriptions Written statements of the primary duties of specific jobs.

just-in-time (JIT) inventory control Materials arrive when they are needed in the production process.

labor relations or union–management relations or industrial relations The relationship between an employer and unionized employees.

labor union An organization of workers banded together to achieve economic goals.

lateral-diagonal communication Flows between individuals in the same department or different departments.

leader-controlled approach Used at meetings of large groups in which the leader clearly runs the show and the open flow of information is impeded.

leadership Influencing individual and group activities toward goal achievement.

Leadership Grid® Categorizes leadership styles according to concern for people and concern for production results.

leading Conducting, guiding, influencing, and motivating employees in the performance of their duties and responsibilities.

life event Anything that causes a person to deviate from normal functioning.

life-cycle theory of leadership Leadership behaviors should be based on the readiness level of employees.

line authority Power to directly command or exact performance from others.

line organization An organization concerned with the primary functions of the firm—in this case, production, sales, and finance.

line personnel Carry out the primary activities of a business.

line-and-staff organization An organization structure in which staff positions are added to serve the basic line departments and help them accomplish the organization objectives more effectively.

lockout A closing of a company's premises to the employees and refusing to let them work.

maintenance-of-membership clause An employee who has joined the union must maintain that membership as a condition of employment.

management Working with people to achieve objectives by effective decision making and coordinating available resources.

management by exception A supervisor focuses on critical control needs and allows employees to handle most routine deviations from the standard.

managerial functions Broad classification of activities that all managers perform.

marketing Selling and distributing an organization's product or service.

matrix departmentalization A hybrid type of departmentalization in which personnel from several specialties are brought together to complete limited-life tasks.

mediator Tries to bring the parties together when collective bargaining has reached an impasse.

mentoring Helps develop careers in others.

message Words and/or nonverbal expressions that transmit meaning.

middle management Responsible for a substantial part of the organization.

middle of the road management Places equal emphasis on people and production.

minutes A written record of the important points discussed and agreed on at a meeting.

mission Defines the purpose the organization serves and identifies its services, products, and customers.

monetary standards Expressed in dollars and cents.

motivation Willingness to work to achieve the organization's objectives.

nonexempt employees Covered by the provisions of the Fair Labor Standards Act.

norms Rules of behavior developed by group members to provide guidance for group activities.

numerical standards Expressed in numbers.

object signals Nonverbal messages sent by physical objects.

objectives The purposes, goals, and desired results for the organization and its parts.

operational planning Consists of intermediate and short-term planning.

operations Producing an organization's product or service.

opportunity A chance for development or advancement.

organization A group of people working together in a structured situation for a common objective.

organizational effectiveness The result of activities that improve the organization's structure, technology, and people.

organizing Deciding what activities are needed to reach goals and dividing human resources into work groups to achieve them.

orientation Procedures of familiarizing a new employee with the company surroundings, policies, and job responsibilities.

OSHA Created by the Occupational Safety and Health Act in 1970 to ensure safe working conditions for employees.

Pareto charts Problem-analysis charts that use a histogram to illustrate sources of problems.

parity principle When duties are assigned, adequate authority is delegated to those who must carry out the assignments.

participating and supporting style Best used with ready individuals or groups.

partnering A variation of team building and strategic planning, initially designed to improve efficiency and effectiveness in large construction projects.

perception How one selects, organizes, and gives meaning to his or her world.

performance appraisal or merit rating or efficiency rating or service rating or employee evaluation Determines to what extent an employee is performing a job the way it was intended.

personality tests Measure the applicant's emotional adjustment and attitude.

Peter principle States that in a hierarchy, every employee rises to his or her level of incompetence.

physical resources Items an organization requires for operations.

physical standards Refer to quality, durability, size, and weight.

physiological need The need for food, water, air, and other physical necessities.

picketing Walking back and forth outside the place of employment, usually carrying a sign.

pinpointing Providing specific, tangible information about performance to an employee.

planning Selecting future courses of action and deciding how to achieve the desired results.

policy Provides consistency among decision makers.

power The ability to influence people, events, and decisions.

prevailing wage rate Approximates the union wage scale for the area in the given type of work.

principled negotiation Negotiation on the merits.

proactive (planned) process of change Management tries to change things by setting a new course rather than by correcting the current one.

probe Directs attention to a particular aspect of the speaker's message.

probing Asking questions to obtain additional information.

problem An existing unsatisfactory situation causing anxiety or distress.

problem-solving meeting Held to identify the problem, to discuss alternative solutions, and to decide on the proper action to take.

procedure Steps to be performed when a particular course of action is taken.

process consultation A consultation model that involves others in making a joint diagnosis of the problem and eventually provides others with the skills and tools to make their own diagnoses.

product departmentalization A form of departmentalization that groups together all the functions associated with a single product line.

productivity Measure of efficiency (inputs to outputs).

program A large-scale plan composed of a mix of objectives, policies, rules, and projects.

Program Evaluation and Review Technique Shows relationships among a network of activities to determine the completion time of a project.

programmed decisions Routine and repetitive decisions.

progressive discipline Discipline that uses a graduated scale of penalties.

project A distinct part of a program.

quality control Defined measurements designed to check whether the desired quality standards are being met.

reactive process of change Management tries to keep the organization on a steady course by solving problems as they come up.

readiness level The state of a person's drive or need for achievement.

receiver The ultimate destination of the sender's message.

reengineering Rethinking and redesigning processes to dramatically improve cost, quality, service, and speed.; "It means starting over. . . . it means asking and answering this question: If I were creating this company today, given what I know and given current technology, what would it look like?"

reflecting Stating your interpretation of what the employee has said.

reflective statement The listener repeats, in a summarizing way, what the speaker has just said.

reframing Emphasizing management training and development programs.

reinforcement theory Based on the law of effect, holds that behaviors that meet with pleasant consequences tend to be repeated, whereas behaviors that meet with unpleasant consequences tend not to be repeated, and rewards and punishments are used as a way to shape the individual's behavior.

reinvention Organizations dramatically changing such elements as their size, organizational structure, and markets.

relationship behaviors Providing people with support and asking for their opinions.

reliability The probability that test results won't change if the test is given to the same person by different individuals.

resourcing Providing information, assistance, and advice to employees.

responsibility The obligation of an employee to accept a manager's delegated authority.

reviewing Reinforcing key points at the end of a coaching session to ensure common understanding.

right-to-work laws The right of employees to join or refuse to join a union without being fired.

risk The possibility of defeat, disadvantage, injury, or loss.

robot A machine that is controlled by a computer.

roles Parts played by managers in the performance of their functions.

rule A policy that is invariably enforced.

run chart Data presentation showing results of a process plotted over time.

safety need The need for protection from danger, threat, or deprivation.

satisfier factors Factors that employees said turned them on, such as recognition, advancement, achievement, challenging work, and being one's own boss.

scenario planning Anticipating alternative future situations and developing courses of action for each alternative.

schedule A plan of activities to be performed and their timing.

self-fulfillment needs Needs concerned with realizing one's potential, self-development, and creativity.

self-managing work teams Groups that tend to operate by member consensus rather than management direction.

sender Originates and sends a message.

seniority An employee's length of service in a company; provides the basis for promotion and other benefits.

servant leadership Defines success as giving and measures achievement by devotion to serving and leading. Winning becomes the creation of community through collaboration and team building.

sexual harassment Unwelcome sexual advances that create a hostile, offensive, or intimidating work environment.

"Siamese twins" of management Planning and controlling.

single-use plans Developed to accomplish a specific purpose and then discarded after use.

Situational Leadership® Model Shows the relationship between the readiness of followers and the leadership style.

social need The need for belonging, acceptance by colleagues, friendship, and love.

space signals Nonverbal messages sent based on physical distance from one another.

span of control principle States that there is a limit to the number of people a person can supervise effectively.

span of management The number of immediate employees a manager can supervise effectively.

staff personnel Have the expertise to assist line people and aid top management.

staffing Recruiting, training, promoting, and rewarding people to do the organization's work.

standard A unit of measurement that can serve as a reference point for evaluating results.

standing plans or repeat-use plans Plans that are used repeatedly over a period of time.

stereotyping The tendency to put similar things in the same categories to make them easier to deal with.

strategic control point A performance measurement point located early in an activity to allow any corrective action to be taken.

strategic planning Has longer time horizons, affects the entire organization, and deals with its interface to its external environment.

strategies The activities by which the organization adapts to its environment in order to achieve its objectives.

stress Any external stimulus that causes wear and tear on one's psychological or physical wellbeing.

strike When employees withhold their services from an employer.

structured interviews Standardized and controlled with regard to questions asked.

structuring and telling style Used with individuals or groups relatively less ready for a given task.

summarizing Pausing in the coaching conversation to summarize key points.

supervisory management Controls operations of smaller organizational units.

synergy The concept that two or more people working together in a cooperative, coordinated way can accomplish more than the sum of their independent efforts.

tangible standards Clear, concrete, specific, and generally measurable.

task behaviors Clarifying a job, telling people what to do and how and when to do it, providing follow-up, and taking corrective action.

team A collection of people who must rely on group cooperation.

team advisors Share responsibility with team for cost, quality, and prompt delivery of products.

team management High concern for both people and production.

technical skills Understanding and being able to supervise effectively specific processes required.

termination-at-will rule An employer can dismiss an employee for any reason.

Theory X The average person has an inherent dislike of work and wishes to avoid responsibility.

Theory Y Work is as natural as play or rest.

thinking decision process Focusing predominantly on analysis, logic, and objectivity to solve problems.

time management Ability to use one's time to get things done *when* they should be done.

time signals Nonverbal messages sent by time actions.

time standards Expressed in terms of time.

top management Responsible for the entire or a major segment of the organization.

total quality Refers to an organization's overall effort to achieve customer satisfaction through continuous improvement of products or services.

touching signals Nonverbal messages sent by body contact.

transactional leadership Leaders identify desired performance standards and recognize what types of rewards employees want from their work.

transformational leadership Converts followers into leaders and may convert leaders into moral agents.

tutoring Helps a team member gain knowledge, skill, and competency.

Type A behavior A behavior pattern characterized by (a) trying to accomplish too much in a short time and (b) lacking patience and struggling against time and other people to accomplish one's ends.

Type B behavior A behavior pattern characterized by (a) tending to be calmer than someone with Type A behavior, (b) devoting more time to exercise, and (c) being more realistic in estimating the time it takes to complete an assignment.

unfair labor practices Specific acts that management may not commit against the workers and the union.

unified planning Coordinating departments to ensure harmony rather than conflict or competition.

union authorization card Authorizes a particular union to be an employee's collective bargaining representative.

union shop All employees must join the union within a specified period.

union steward A union member elected by other members to represent their interests to management.

unity of command principle States that everyone should report to and be accountable to only one boss.

unprogrammed decisions Decisions that occur infrequently and require a different response each time.

upward communication Flows from lower to upper organizational levels.

validity A high positive correlation between the applicant's test scores and some objective measure of job performance.

vocational interest tests Determine the applicant's areas of major work interest.

voice signals Signals sent by placing emphasis on certain words, pauses, or the tone of voice used.

wagon wheel An organization form with a hub, a series of spokes radiating from the hub, and the outer rim.

work sampling or work preview A test in which the prospective employee must perform a task that is representative of the job.